CODE RED:

Computerized Elections

and

The War

on

American Democracy

Election 2020 Edition

D1265248

Jonathan D. Simon

www.CodeRed2020.com

Praise for *CODE RED*:

Jonathan Simon's *CODE RED* is unique, timely, easy-to-understand, and vastly important. The book uses an innovative Q&A format to enable readers to comprehend why computerized elections fraud represents an unprecedented challenge to democracy. The author has been a pioneering expert in this research, which has been widely ignored by traditional watchdog institutions and the political media. His book provides a convenient news-peg for them to start doing their jobs instead of continuing the go-along, get-along game.

Andrew Kreig, Justice Integrity Project director and author of
Presidential Puppetry: Obama, Romney and Their Masters

Jonathan Simon has been alerting us to the dangers of our insecure, computerized election system long before anyone had even considered the likelihood of malign foreign actors exploiting its weaknesses. The 2016 presidential election was a watershed moment for public awareness, but as Simon showed in 2018, and now again in 2020, the vulnerabilities still exist, and, more than ever, imperil our democracy.

CODE RED is both a prescient history and a clarion call to fix the way we vote before government by the people is a fading memory.

Sue Halpern; Staff Writer, **The New Yorker**

Jonathan Simon's new edition of *CODE RED* is a modern-day clarion call to action for all Americans concerned about the efficacy and integrity of our voting process.

Poorly built voting machines, lacking in critical security protections, operating in local election offices without public transparency, and without the most basic of protections—robust audits to verify our votes are accurately tabulated—are bad enough, but when combined with the larger picture of our hyper-partisanship, the willingness to suppress legal voters, and even break laws, we are left with no other conclusion but that our approach to our elections must immediately be changed if our democratic republic is going to survive.

Kudos to the author for looking at the forest, and not just the trees, in this high-level examination of America's voting crisis.

Ion V. Sancho, Supervisor of Elections of Leon County, Florida, 1989 - 2016

CODE RED lays out the case that election fraud has been occurring via the targeting and manipulation of computerized voting equipment across America.

Dr. Simon supports his conclusions with detailed and extensive data-gathering and analysis. He asks why we continue to entrust our voting process to this inherently non-transparent and vulnerable equipment. And he shows us how we can restore an observable process and reclaim ownership of our democracy.

As a professional statistician, I found *CODE RED*'s data, analyses, and conclusions compelling.

Dr. Elizabeth Clarkson; Chief Statistician, National Institute for Aviation Research, Wichita State University

What is more important in a democracy than an accurately counted secret ballot? And the means of counting it, in public so everyone can know it was accurate? That's the machinery of democracy, and if the people can't tell if that machinery is working, then just how should we expect them to feel about their democracy?

I first heard Jonathan Simon speak when I heard his 2014 *Guns and Butter* interview. That was four years after I, with my co-commissioner, had implemented near-100% public hand counts of paper ballots that had been tabulated by computer. That computerized tabulation was a New York State mandate, and a black-box count suited neither of us—he a Republican, I a Democrat. So, within months of hearing *Guns and Butter*, Jonathan and I had connected, and ever since, thanks in large part to his efforts, I've traveled hither and yon to tout my county's unique hand count. The truth is that it's not that hard, it doesn't take that long, and it doesn't cost that much. It's a wonderful exercise in participatory democracy. But it's been a hard sell out in election land.

Jonathan's proposal is better. In fact, it borders on genius. I salute Jonathan's tireless efforts and enthusiastically endorse his Split The Difference Audit. It just might Save This Democracy for America.

Virginia Martin, PhD; former Election Commissioner, Columbia County, NY

CODE RED is a chilling, thrilling, and fascinating account of the role that computerized elections may have played in bringing American democracy to its knees. It's a risky book. Reading it helped inspire (compel, really) my own interest in and work for election integrity. One of my favorite books on this subject!

Jennifer Cohn, Election Transparency Advocate and Writer

CODE RED is a spirited, data-driven argument that our computerized voting system is frighteningly vulnerable to corruption. ... Simon—the executive director of Election Defense Alliance, a nonprofit voting-rights watchdog— argues that what at first appears to be a triumph of progress, the widespread application of new voting technology, actually generates myriad opportunities for partisan sabotage. ...[T]he allure of greater convenience comes at the price of transparency: newly secretive elections ... take place in the "impenetrable darkness of cyberspace." ... The scope of the book is broad, covering related topics like campaign finance and gerrymandering, and includes an instructive discussion of exit polls and Internet voting... Much of the work is written in a "Q&A format," which makes for highly readable prose, ... an often-rigorous account of an important issue.

Kirkus Reviews

CODE RED by Jonathan Simon, co-founder of Election Defense Alliance, is not a fun read. Nor was it fun to write, Simon admits. But that doesn't make it any less important. Simon sees our nation heading over a cliff, democratically speaking; hence, his sense of urgency. He is desperate for us to get active and do something, but without the facts we are powerless. And without familiarity with computerized election history, there is no context in which to comprehend what has happened in recent electoral contests.

As Simon says, in his Foreword, "The Big Picture of American politics has become an ugly one and one that will only get uglier with time and inaction. So let's take an unblinking look at what the hell is happening to America and what we still just might be able to do about it." He dives in with a question-and-answer section that puts the major facts out there for people to examine and evaluate for themselves. We owe it to ourselves and the tattered system we hold dear to do that. The sooner the better.

Joan Brunwasser, OpEd-News

Jonathan Simon has been reading tea leaves and sounding the alarm about the invisible vulnerabilities of our fragile electoral system since the dawn of the electronic voting and tabulation age. In *CODE RED* he not only reads those leaves but explains why they matter and what we, the American public, can and must do to insist on publicly overseeable elections in the U.S.

While I may not always concur with every point of his analyses, they are each well-researched and worth checking and double-checking one's own biases to make certain which of us may have it right. Jonathan's batting average, on that score, is well above that of the mainstream corporate media—and many in the academia set—who have yet to even understand the importance of elections in which every voted is counted, counted accurately, *and in a way that the public can KNOW they have been counted accurately.*

While disagreement and fact-based conflict are at the very heart of democracy, that beating heart disappears as easily a vote tally inside a computer tabulator once the public—and its oversight—are removed from the most critical core of our representative republic: a 100 percent verifiable public election system.

CODE RED helps us all to understand what is at stake and how easily it can vanish inside the bits and bytes of a bastardized, computerized "democracy."

Brad Friedman, BradBlog

On one level, *CODE RED* is straightforward and refreshingly direct. No punches are pulled. But that doesn't make it easy to absorb. So many things I used to believe must be re-thought. Amid the upheaval, I remind myself of a profoundly optimistic consequence of all this gut-wrenching shift in perspective.

I had thought democracy had just failed. People are too stupid, too easily manipulated. The power of money to corrupt politicians and to buy propaganda has just overwhelmed our democratic machinery.

But now I see we may not have given democracy a chance. Before we give up on majority rule, let's try counting the votes in an open and verifiable process. Before we talk about a revolution or a new Constitutional Convention, let's dust off the Constitution we've got, exercise the rights it gives us, and see how far it can take us.

Josh Mitteldorf, PhD
Co-author (with Dorion Sagan) of Cracking the Aging Code

Stalin is rumored to have said it best: "It's not who votes that counts, it's who counts the votes." American exceptionalism notwithstanding, such thoughts have a way of crossing borders. Games are games, wherever played. What *CODE RED* refuses to do is give America a pass *because it is America.*

Jonathan Simon, whose experience in election forensics dates to the very beginning of America's computerized voting era, doesn't blanch at the evidence and turn politely away. Where he comes out is pretty simple: until we return to counting votes in public, we will be putting everything we value at risk. If we don't want the rapid decline of personal freedom, democracy, and moral integrity to continue, the first thing we need to do is secure our electoral and vote-counting processes against manipulation—by anyone.

Confronting the truth may depress you, but it will also give you the knowledge and the tools to take back the country. I hope we have the individual and collective fortitude to face how negligent we've been and see that there is a way out, if not an easy one.

James Fadiman, PhD; author of **Personality and Personal Growth**

For nearly two decades, virtually all of our elections have been conducted on privately owned and programmed computers with unexaminable proprietary code. From its very beginning, Jonathan Simon has been investigating, explaining, and trying to beat back this assault on our democracy.

In the era of computerized voting, a statistically all-but-impossible serial "red" shift of victories to Republican candidates remains beneath the national consciousness even while disinformation, ruthless gerrymandering, and voter suppression in Republican-controlled states are acknowledged. These depredations feel more possible to identify, oppose, and potentially correct.

As a psychiatrist I can only conclude that recognizing, much less correcting, computerized election fraud evokes a sense of helplessness and is a horror that most Americans cannot bear to contemplate. In these extraordinarily perilous times, however, we have no choice but to confront this reality and to take swift, drastic, and corrective action.

CODE RED points the way to recovery of our democracy.

Susan G. Lazar, M.D.; Clinical Professor of Psychiatry, George Washington University School of Medicine and Uniformed Services University of the Health Sciences; Supervising and Training Analyst, Washington Baltimore Psychoanalytic Institute

Whenever a U.S. election ends with an astounding "upset victory" (of late a weirdly normal "fluke" in the United States), the watchdogs of our Free Press quickly tell us *why* the likely winner didn't win—confidently noting the fatuity of the exit polls and all the previous opinion polls; the losing campaign's glaring tactical and/or strategic errors; how this or that key bloc of voters inexplicably did not turn out, while this or that one *did*, in record numbers; these social, cultural and/or economic trends, and/or those technological advances; this or that Big Story in the news, the weeks or last few days before Election Day; and/or whatever else might help explain that inexplicable "defeat" away.

From that flash-flood of journalistic speculation, partisans on either side absorb whichever notions suit their own world-view. Thus Trump's folk ferociously repeat the media's repentant mantra that "the media got it wrong" before Election Day, blind to Trump's "deplorable" majority support in Michigan, Wisconsin, and Pennsylvania. Thus Hillary's troopers tell each other what both Hillary and the media have all bitterly asserted since Election Day: that Hillary lost because of Putin and the FBI, Jill Stein and misogyny. Meanwhile, those who voted (or tried to vote) for Sanders and/or Stein have *their* self-serving take on Trump's outrageous victory, arguing that he prevailed because a (bare) majority (in certain states) detested Hillary as much as they do, and for the same reasons.

All that tribal yammering about the *how* and *why* of Trump's election is as credulous as it is uninformed; for there is, in fact, no solid evidence that Trump *did* win—any more than Clinton had really won her party's nomination.

As Jonathan Simon masterfully explains in this essential new edition of *CODE RED*, there *is* compelling evidence that both of those unlikely "victories" were likely products of rampant vote suppression and computerized election fraud. Those anti-democratic means seem to have been increasingly deployed throughout this century to thwart the will of the American electorate—as Simon has been warning expertly, and tirelessly, in countless articles and interviews, and in successive editions of this essential book, which *all* of us must read, so we can finally grasp what's really happened here, and know what we must do to make things right, before it really is too late.

Mark Crispin Miller, Professor of Media, Culture, and Communication, New York University; Guggenheim Fellow (2011); author of **Fooled Again: The Real Case for Electoral Reform** *and* **Cruel and Unusual,** *and editor of* **Loser Take All: Election Fraud and the Subversion of Democracy, 2000-2008**

Jonathan Simon has provided an important public service. *CODE RED* must not only be widely read and distributed among people who care about the integrity of our elections but should provide enough fodder for a comprehensive investigation of ballot counting procedures. Such an investigation needs to happen soon, and it cannot be conducted by congressional or other political leadership. Simon's research is thorough and his case is more than compelling.

John Zogby, Founder of the Zogby Poll

CRPublishing
P.O. Box 66812
Scotts Valley, CA 95067

To the memory of my parents, Ruth and Saul, who taught me to look into things; and to my daughter Emily, to whom it seems to come naturally.

Holly says tell folks the truth and they will sooner or later come to believe it, and Aaron says the same.

— Mark Harris, **The Southpaw**

TABLE OF CONTENTS

How would you go about altering the outcome of an election?

00010100   (20)

What does a rigged election *look* like?

00011000   (24)

How did America come to accept such a dangerous system?

00011001   (25)

Have elections actually been corrupted and stolen?

00011011   (27)

Is there a "smoking gun" for non-statisticians?

00011110   (30)

What about whistleblowers?

00100001   (33)

What response from the "immune system?"

00100100   (36)

Are elections are being stolen right under officials' noses?

00100101   (37)

What about the Democrats? Why would they play ostrich?

00100110   (38)

Where's the media? Wouldn't this be their biggest story ever?

00101010   (42)

Is it really possible to "count every vote as cast?"

00110000   (48)

How do U.S. elections compare to those of other democracies?

00110010   (50)

Do the corporations counting our votes really care who wins?

00110011   (51)

Why "rig to lose" in 2006, 2008, 2012?

00110101   (53)

Would you work as hard if the evidence were for a "blue shift?"

00111000   (56)

What do you say to one who believes it's the *left* that's rigging?

00111010   (58)

How do you deal with the "conspiracy theory" label?

How do we know how red or blue America actually is?

Is election theft related to the GOP's veering so far to the right?

What is the significance of the year 2010?

What does it mean when polls are *accurate*?

What about exit polls?

Don't *Citizens United* and Big Money explain the Right's success?

Are Big Money, voter suppression, etc. just red herrings?

What does it take to know that an election has been honest?

What about audits?

Is Internet Voting a step in the right direction?

Can Digital Ballot Images help?

What about a "deal": Photo-ID for HCPB?

Given other signs of breakdown, does vote counting even matter?

Has Election Integrity made any real progress?

Is there a real prospect for honest elections in the United States?

VI. TRUTH AND ELECTIONS IN THE AGE OF TRUMP

10101101 (173)

VII. THE WAY FORWARD
11011001   (217)

GLOSSARY OF TERMS

FOR FURTHER REFERENCE

ACKNOWLEDGEMENTS

FOREWORD to ELECTION 2020 EDITION

During [Donald] Trump's impeachment trial, the House managers repeated a quotation attributed to Ben Franklin over and over again: "A republic, if you can keep it." We haven't kept it. The question now is whether we ever get it back.

-- **Michelle Goldberg,** The New York Times, *February 16, 2020*

Mein Gott.

-- *Capt.-Lt. Henrich Lehmann-Willenbrock, "Das Boot"*

Maybe it's too late.

In the film *Das Boot*, the German submarine, hit with depth charges, has dropped to the ocean floor. *Everything* has been damaged, virtually *nothing* works, leaks abound, and the hull is being squeezed by the immense external pressure to the point of implosion. The crew can't get the engines started, can't get the sub to lift off the deadly bottom, and oxygen is running out. In the midst of this subterranean hell, the young and thoroughly Nazified first officer approaches the old and thoroughly unNazified captain to formally report something about the state of repair of a certain component of the navigation system. It matters *but*—and here the captain's look tells us everything—only if the hull doesn't implode and they can somehow get the engines started and get the flooded boat to rise, and if they don't wind up asphyxiated first.

Is that where we are now? Or *were*. Because I mean *pre*-pandemic. So much damaged, so much broken down, so much we once thought unthinkable normalized, that one may well ask whether restoring public, observable vote counting to our elections—even if it could be accomplished in time for November 2020—would save the ship.

"We haven't kept it. The question now is whether we ever get it back."

Michelle Goldberg is not alone in seeing our republic as *already* lost. Some believe Donald Trump will not leave office if defeated in November; pretexts will be found to cancel or nullify the election, as they have been found for countless other lesser assaults upon the rule of law. Many others believe that Trump and the GOP phalanx that has formed around him will manage to put enough thumbs on the electoral scales to avoid that defeat and hold onto power without having to resort to overtly authoritarian tactics. And still others believe that what was the "great economy," his "presidential" response to COVID-19, the Electoral College, and/or a barrage of lies-become-truth-by-repetition will see Trump through "fair and square" and with coattails to boot.

In this general maelstrom of anxiety, amidst all its ghastly pathologies and contingencies, concern about the particular process we rely on to tabulate votes can seem somehow quaint, as if it were just another damaged navigation system component needing repair on a ship that is doomed.

It is not.

It is largely responsible for how we wound up here, on the ocean floor, in the first place. It's our democracy's very core, and repairing it offers us our best, if not only, chance of rising again and getting back the republic we have failed to keep.

This book has grown in weight as it has grown in size. If elections didn't seem to matter all that much *before*, they sure as hell matter *now*. I am hardly alone in wondering whether, social distancing-limited as we may be in our menu of feasible reforms, we are looking at our last peaceful opportunity to change our nation's course and fate. *I think what it comes down to is that we must act as if we are and hope to hell we are not.*

I have chosen to retain the forewords from the previous three editions of *CODE RED*, presented in chronological order following this one. Their value is in charting—edition by edition, beginning well before the advent of Trump—the intensifying crisis of computerized vote counting and its powerfully corrosive impact on our political process and our democracy. In the brief excerpts from each, below, the warnings keep sharpening:

> America's electoral system has been corrupted in the most direct and fundamental of ways: the computers that now count virtually all our votes in secret can be—and, the evidence indicates, *have been*—programmed to cheat... The Big Picture of American politics has become an ugly one and one that will only get uglier with time and inaction.
> ***December 21, 2014***

Our electoral system has failed badly in the translation of public will into electoral outcomes and representative government, and the result has been a rapidly metastasizing politics of disgust and distrust.
August 19, 2016

There's an old joke about a guy who jumps off the top of the Empire State Building. Someone with an office on the 42nd floor sticks her head out the window and asks how he's doing. "OK, so far!" comes the answer. If this once applied to America in the computerized voting era, that time is past.
May 9, 2018

Whatever grim satisfaction I might take in the essential accuracy of these increasingly urgent assessments and predictions is gutted by the frustration that they fell on deaf national ears. We continued merrily on our way, election to computerized election, sending our votes into the partisan pitch-dark of cyberspace with nothing much besides our thoughts and prayers to protect them. The Age of Trump came, the depth charges hit home, a cottage industry of where-did-we-go-wrong books sprang into being, we soldiered on in shock and awe, and we're *still* planning this year once again to send our votes off into cyberspace with our thoughts and prayers.

Can we agree it's time to rethink this? Maybe it is too late.

Maybe it's not.

Jonathan D. Simon
April 9, 2020 – Felton, California

FOREWORD to ELECTION 2014 EDITION

It was the best of times, it was the worst of times, it was the age of wisdom, it was the age of foolishness, it was the epoch of belief, it was the epoch of incredulity, it was the season of Light, it was the season of Darkness, it was the spring of hope, it was the winter of despair.

— Charles Dickens, A Tale of Two Cities

THIS is a book for everyone who has been wondering just what the *hell* is happening in America and why American politics have become so increasingly warped as this new century has unfolded.

It is a book for everyone who has wondered what is behind the gridlock in Washington, and the political hyperpolarization everywhere in America.

It is a book for everyone who has been scratching his or her head as election results show voters seeming to be voting against their own interests and contrary to virtually all measurements of their opinions, in the process transforming America into a harsh, mean, and baffling land.

And it is a book for those who cannot quite believe this is the real America they are seeing—who say to themselves, and increasingly to each other, "There's something wrong with this picture."

This is also a book I'd rather not write, and it is one that I believe most Americans would rather not read. The story it tells is grim and a 'happy ending' will depend on an exercise of public will not seen in America within living memory. Yet, if America is to be rescued from the slow-rolling coup that is turning our nation into an unrecognizable place, this book *must* be written and *must* be read, and such an epochal exercise of will *must* rapidly become a reality.

The grim truth that is so hard to tell and so hard to swallow is that America's electoral system has been corrupted in the most direct and fundamental of ways: the computers that now count virtually all our votes in secret can be—

and, the evidence indicates, *have been*—programmed to cheat. To override the will of the voters and change the outcome of elections. To steal and hold power that could not be gained and held legitimately. Ultimately to reshape America more effectively than could a junta rolling tanks down Pennsylvania Avenue. The junta would, by its very visibility, at least provoke resistance.

I can only wish it were a fantasy, a fiction, the fevered invention of easy-to-dismiss, get-a-life "conspiracy theorists." I can't blame anyone for reflexively wanting to write it off as such, for asking, reasonably, "If this is happening, why aren't election administrators all over it? If this is happening, why aren't the losing candidates and/or their party all over it? If this is happening, why isn't the media all over it?" And I can't blame some for saying, with great indignation, "America is the world's Beacon of Democracy—*this is the one thing that could never happen here!*"

To which I can respond only by asking you to set that cherished, comforting, and dangerous vision of Exceptional America aside as we take a hard look at the core danger of computerized vote counting and the evidence that its vulnerability to wholesale fraud is being exploited to alter the very nature and direction of our country against the will of the majority of its people. Yes, it will most likely ruin your day. It will, if you're anything like me, leave you angry. Beyond angry. And I hope therefore ready to act, and determined to keep acting, until we Americans have our democracy back.

I've chosen to present a good part of this book in a Q&A format. I believe it makes things clearer and gets down to brass tacks quicker. There is so much about elections, vote counting, computerization, polling, and media coverage of each of these that is generally unknown or not well understood. Once the questioning process is begun, each question tends to lead to another, until the whole picture seems to take shape. The Q&A precedes an examination of the current state of affairs and an appendix presenting forensic evidence and analyses, and finally an ample bibliography for readers who feel the need to explore further before swinging into action mode.

I am well aware that, much as in the aftermath of the 2008 election ("E2008"), the Obama/Democratic victory in E2012 left the vast majority of potentially skeptical observers believing that *nothing* is rotten in Denmark (If the Right *could* rig, why *wouldn't* it? And if it *did* rig, why would it *lose*?) and that it's perfectly safe to go back in the water. We address this tragically misguided belief and answer those perfectly logical questions. We will see that there is nothing safe about the water and that the Denmark of American vote counting is rotten to its unobservable core.

The Big Picture of American politics has become an ugly one and one that will only get uglier with time and inaction. So let's take an unblinking look at what the hell is happening to America and what we still just might be able to do about it.

Jonathan D. Simon
December 21, 2014 – Arlington, Massachusetts

FOREWORD to ELECTION 2016 EDITION

The saddest aspect of life right now is that science gathers knowledge faster than society gathers wisdom.

-- Isaac Asimov

THIS is still, as it was two years ago, a book for everyone who has been wondering what the hell is happening in America and in American politics.

And it still tells the story of how America's electoral system has been corrupted in the most direct and fundamental of ways: vote counting, the bedrock protocol of our democracy, has been computerized, outsourced, and made unobservable. In the darkness of cyberspace, common sense and the experts tell us, the vote count is vulnerable to manipulation—hacking by outsiders, rigging by insiders. And the forensic evidence indicates that the vulnerability has been exploited.

None of this is new. So why a new edition for *CODE RED*?

Election integrity and security is, as news anchors put it, a *developing story*. The "R-word" is being thrown about by, among others, a major-party presidential nominee. Serious articles in our "newspaper of record" warn of potential foreign interference with the vote counts of American elections. Things are moving, and moving fast.

Whatever one's opinion of Donald Trump as an avatar of electoral integrity, it was only a matter of time before *someone*, whether from a place of fairness or from one of self-interest, called into question a vote counting system that cannot be seen. This emperor has been walking around naked for 15 years now and the real mystery is why it has taken that long for *anyone* to mention the obvious. Nor is Trump the only one speaking publicly of rigging and hacking: the forensically bizarre 2016 primaries triggered such allegations, lawsuits, and a wave of distrust from millions of supporters of the Sanders candidacy.

However you feel about such stirrings, you can sense that the political and electoral environments have undergone a sea change. Our electoral system has failed badly in the translation of public will into electoral outcomes and representative government, and the result has been a rapidly metastasizing politics of disgust and distrust.

Whether and how this may come to a head in November and beyond remains to be seen, but it is hard to imagine a restoration of trust in our elections and our political system without the restoration of an observable vote counting process. The new chapters **"E2014: What Democracy Doesn't Look Like"** and **"E2016: The Chickens Come Home"** address our recent rapid descent into this hole; **"The Way Forward"** crucially offers a plan of action for digging ourselves out.

We are in a strange and difficult but not entirely a hopeless place. We will have to work to restore our democracy and reclaim our sovereignty—work together with grit and tenacity. It begins with becoming informed, then trusting our common sense, calling out the holes in narratives of comfort and convenience, communicating, organizing, moving mountains. The inertias are great but so is the strength of a people acting together to overcome them. We possess that strength and we owe it to ourselves and to the future to find it and use it.

Jonathan D. Simon
August 19, 2016 – Felton, California

FOREWORD to ELECTION 2018 EDITION

Voting is a profound act of faith, a belief that even if your voice can't change policy on its own, it makes a difference.

-- The New York Times Editorial Board, March 11, 2018

So here we are. Welcome to the Age of Trump. If your 'faith' is a bit shaken, if you are still wondering just how we got here, there are hundreds, perhaps thousands, of published accounts to map it all out for you. You know: the Clinton campaign this, the economy that, the white suburban voters without college the other thing . . .

As varied as they may be, what all these accounts have in common is the assumption that, one way or another, *we voted our way here*. That is to say, Americans collectively cast the billions of ballots that over the years of this New American Century added up to where we are now. As if we all got behind the wheel of the national car and somehow steered it to this destination, two wheels spinning over the edge of the cliff.

That is not the account offered by this book.

CODE RED **challenges the fundamental assumption that we voted our way over the cliff.** It challenges the fundamental assumption that votes have been counted as cast; that American voters have in fact been, at all points, steering the car; that we're really such awful drivers.

It instead explores the possibility that, since the dawn of the computerized vote-counting era and through a series of faith-based elections, the national car has behaved more like a self-driving car, programmer unknown. It examines those elections and the veer in American politics, culminating in the Age of Trump, that they have produced—reaching conclusions about who or what has been driving the car that are both more chilling (it's not us) and more encouraging (it's not us) than anything else you are likely to read.

Most important, it's a book to read if you're asking how we can re-take the wheel. Because, while it may be of some comfort to realize that we did not vote our way to this scary place, the correlate is that there is some serious and urgent work to be done if we are to be able to vote our way *out* of it.

It is the thesis of this book that, in this new age of easy lies, the electoral system of the United States—and particularly its vote counting component—has itself become a lie, in a sense the worst and most dangerous of all the lies. If this blunt statement is too much for you, a more agnostic framing would be that the truth of our elections, whatever it may be, is incapable of verification. Our elections—and the leadership, policy, and national direction that depend on their results—are, at best, faith-based; at worst, catastrophically corrupted at their computerized core.

If even *that* is a message you don't want to hear, let alone act on, you are hardly alone. The resistance to it—political, journalistic, psychological, personal—is very strong indeed. All evidence indicates that our current predicament has been nearly two decades in the making, and that the Big Lie long pre-dated the advent of the Big Liar. Yet even *now*, as we flirt with depravity and fascism, who has been willing to look in the cupboard marked "Alternative Facts" and open the box marked "Alternative Votes"? Certainly neither government nor media. They both blanch at the mere thought of "undermining voter confidence in our elections." It *is* a serious concern, especially when it is likely to be part of the game plan of a defeated Donald Trump. But we must note that that is precisely what has given computerized election theft such a big leg up. To pull that leg down will likely *require* some undermining of voter confidence in our elections—but is any confidence based on a blind-faith refusal to examine the evidence really worth protecting?

Because that voter confidence has been so diligently, indeed desperately protected, Americans—who no longer trust their leaders, no longer trust the media, and no longer trust each other—paradoxically remain the picture of trust when it comes to one thing: when push comes to shove, somehow we manage to wind up trusting our elections. We are about to head into the most critical set of elections in living memory *continuing* to permit our votes to be counted unobservably and without verification in the partisan, proprietary, pitch-dark of cyberspace and trusting that manifestly corruptible process to deliver the truth—an honest and accurate counting of our votes. What a strange faith to cling to in this Age of Lies and Mistrust!

If we are to survive the Age of Trump and find our way back from the brink of the cliff, it will have to start with replacing that easy faith with serious inquiry—building upon facts and not shrinking, either out of tact or on the sage advice of the marketing department, from calling a spade anything but a spade.

———

Democracy begins to end when its beneficiaries go lazy and passive, when they are seduced by speed, ease, convenience, entertainment. And that happened Before Trump, and it happened before the "Russians" took an interest in influencing who won our elections. It happened when the U.S. began counting votes in the dark, entrusting that critical process to a handful of private, partisan, secretive outfits, and expecting—in fact with unshakable faith—that it would proceed honestly and accurately.

After all, we figured, we can see why someone would shoot up with PEDs to win a pennant or the *Tour de France*, but who would *ever* want to steal a U.S. election?

The evidence is plentiful that the Republican (and not just Republican, but increasingly far-right Republican) dominance at both national and state levels owes its existence—with but-for causality—to the corruption of the electoral process in the computerized vote counting era. And it is that dominance that is enabling Trump's romp over the rule of law and into autocracy, though it is not clear from their behavior that the Democrats have much greater interest than do their right-wing counterparts in restoring public sovereignty.

And the media? Well, aren't they having the time of their lives! Nothing like a horny dragon to slay! But public, observable vote counting, the desperate need for *serious* electoral reform? *No, we don't go there, at least not with the urgency this crisis demands*—because that urgency would derive from consideration of the possibility that the problem is not merely one of *hypothetical* vulnerability. That remains a bridge too far.

The price for not crossing that bridge is nothing less than all we value. And while I enjoy, in a grim sort of way, the torrents of Trump-disparaging adjectives and adverbs, I really don't see much hope in them. On this, at least, *The New York Times* agrees. Their editorial, from which I quoted at top, is titled "Angry? Go Vote." And it continues:

> "This is a fragile moment for the nation. The integrity of democratic institutions is under assault from without and within, and basic standards

of honesty and decency in public life are corroding. If you are horrified at what is happening in Washington and in many states, you can march in the streets, you can go to town halls and demand more from your representatives, you can share the latest outrageous news on your social media feed—all worthwhile activities. *But none of it matters if you don't go out and vote.*" [emphasis added]

The *Times*, of course, is right. There is *one* official scoreboard and it is known as an *election*. But an election comes down to *vote counting*. And if that remains computerized, privatized, and secret, is there any reason to expect reason to prevail over derangement on the official scoreboards of 2018 and 2020?

We have watched the situation go from perilous to critical to surrealistic (you can follow the progression in my Forewords to the 2014 and 2016 editions). Let's hope it has not gone beyond rescue.

This edition of *CODE RED* updates the latest developments, including of course the 2016 elections and what they have bestowed on America, but also the rise and potential impact on both politics and election integrity of the Parkland students and other sprouts of genuine resistance. It considers the (dim) prospect of effective electoral reform emerging from our conventional political processes. It proposes fresh and outside-the-box solutions, both technical and political, befitting the urgency we confront. And, like the *Bulletin of the Atomic Scientists*, it sets a Doomsday Clock.

The good news is that it's not *quite* midnight. We can turn this country around, but only if we first restore public, observable vote counting to our elections. How does the old adage go? "For want of a nail . . ." It is a simple, basic thing: but until we do it, we will continue putting everything we value at risk.

———

It would be highly disingenuous were I to pretend to be free of strong convictions about both the policies and the personal ethics and behavior of Donald Trump. For better or for worse, the divisions of these years are as passionate as they are polarized, and if credibility is to be gained by masking them, then it is a deceptive credibility. So forgive me if at times I wear my anger on my sleeve.

I can attest, however, that such feelings have not played a part in my presentation of data, analysis, or arguments on behalf of an honest electoral system and a public, observable vote-counting process. The data are the data (the sources are all official postings and/or archives), the analyses are objective (with an open invitation to replicate), and the changes argued for speak to the foundations and hallmarks of democracy itself and are goals I should think we, as citizens and voters, would all share—however we feel about guns, God, gays, global warming, healthcare, corporations, regulations, immigration, trade, or Trump.

There's an old joke about a guy who jumps off the top of the Empire State Building. Someone with an office on the 42nd floor sticks her head out the window and asks how he's doing. "OK, so far!" comes the answer.

If this once applied to America in the computerized voting era, that time is past.

Jonathan D. Simon
May 9, 2018 – Felton, California

— I —

INTRODUCTION

There's something happening here and you don't know what it is,
do you, Mr. Jones?

— Bob Dylan

Who among us would trust an election where the ballots were handed to a man, dressed in a magician's costume, who took them behind a curtain and emerged sometime later, claiming he had counted and then shredded them, to tell us who won? What if the man were wearing a "So-And-So For President" button or some other partisan signifier? And what if the results of key and close elections—elections that shaped American politics by determining the balance of power in the federal government and statehouses—kept going *that same way*? How many, and what overall pattern of, strange results would it take before we insisted on going behind the curtain with him, or at least sending a trusted representative of our interests, to observe the count?

Nothing should be more self-evident than the simple statement that for an election to have *legitimacy,* the counting process must be *observable*. If the votes are counted in secret "behind a curtain," it does not matter how or by whom, no one other than the counter can really know who won and the results therefore are *automatically* subject to question. The outcome is not evidence-based. It is faith-based. There is simply no adequate basis for trust.

If you do not accept this basic statement, you may as well save yourself the time and put this book down now, because nothing else I have to say will make much of an impression. Please take a moment, indeed as much time as you need, to think it through and decide for yourself. Would you shrug, say "Ah, what the hell," and simply trust the man behind the curtain with the fate of our nation and, given our nation's position in it, much of the world? Or would you take democracy seriously enough to demand a vote count that could be observed? If so, read on and get ready to roll up your sleeves.

We began with an imaginary, hypothetical election counted in secret. Now let's look at our real elections, the ones that determine the leadership and direction of our towns, states, and country. The ones where we rely upon the media to tell us who won (and why). We have long employed the secret ballot process, and for most of our nation's history an open, public counting process was the norm. Votes cast in private, counted in public. Makes sense.

But that is no longer the case. In 21st-century America, aside from a few tiny pockets where ballots are still counted observably in public by humans, vote counting is an entirely secret enterprise, taking place on chips and memory cards concealed inside computers or, worse yet, in servers arrayed along a network, often far distant from where the votes are cast, in the full, impenetrable darkness of cyberspace. The fog of war has *nothing* on the fog of American elections.

The first alarm sounded by this book is that these elections are in practice no different from the charade of the man in the magician's costume "counting" behind the curtain. Because they are all counted in secret, not one of these elections—from presidential to congressional to dog-catcher to ballot measure—warrants the trust necessary to claim legitimacy and provide the foundation for the democratic process in which we take such reflexive pride. We hold ourselves out as the Beacon of Democracy but—in this core, determinative function—much even of the Third World is well out in front of us.

Why would a nation install, and why would its people acquiesce in, such a patently untrustworthy process for making its most critical decisions and for transforming the public will into leadership, policy, and direction?

We will return to this question often in the course of this book; it has several disturbing answers. But for the moment we think it fair to observe that we live in a time and a place where *convenience is king*. Every improvement in speed, each yet slicker technological "advance," has been embraced with reflexive zeal. Our cultural impatience (Faster connection time! Faster downloads! Tweet! Swipe Right!) seems to know no bounds.[1]

---

[1] Perhaps the only real exception to our pan-cultural haste is our embrace of video review in our various sports (now trickling down even to the high school level). We accept these delays because of the importance we have come to place on accurate athletic outcomes and sports justice—i.e., because "football matters."

After all, isn't it obvious that, as the too-cute kids seated at the table with the friendly corporate suit kept reminding us in that brilliant and ubiquitous (and already ancient) TV ad for the latest happiness-bestowing smartphone, *"faster is better?"* Moreover, we seem to have a collective affinity for that which *looks* sophisticated—sleek, digital, graphic, multi-layered, multi-colored, rapid and impeccable. Isn't a glistening iPad, quite apart from its utility, also a comforting symbol to us of how far removed and safe we are from the raw, naked dangers of the pioneer's cabin, the medieval hut, the prehistoric night?

This hi-tech, hi-speed ethos is, of course, not entirely new, but the grip that speed, convenience, and sit-back-and-enjoy-the-show choreographed entertainment now hold on our culture is tight and getting tighter every minute. "Progress," so defined, has become a *habit* and seems inexorable. Thus when it comes to elections, there is, in effect, a mandate that virtually every one be decided within hours, if not minutes, of poll closing, and that, in our major biennial elections, the direction that America will be taking be brilliantly and artistically laid out in a mélange of pie-charts, blue and red blinking states, and punditory consensus, all before it is time for bed. This is such a *fait accompli,* such a *ritual,* that it is hard to remember that it wasn't *always* this way and, when it comes right down to it, isn't necessary—much less to contemplate the price paid for our convenient and entertaining experience.

The price is simply that we as citizens have no basis for trusting it.

Behind this festive TV extravaganza—reassuringly presented as "DECISION 20XX"—are those vote-counting computers and computer networks, *not one of which is one iota different from the magician behind the curtain,* a faith-based enterprise where votes are counted in secret and results announced (and accepted) with the straightest of straight faces. In fact, it is as a prop to this media production and its programmed primetime-slot narrative that the vote-counting computers are deemed indispensable.

How long this irrational situation has been going on is open to question. Computers in one form or another (initially mainframes using punch cards) have been employed in vote counting since as early as the 1960s, and there is some evidence that they were sporadically being used to manipulate electoral results almost from their first deployment. So even in the "good old days" when the nation watched the votecount numbers rolling up behind such trusted icons as Walter Cronkite or David Brinkley, it did so without any real assurance that there wasn't a thumb (or two or ten) on a scale somewhere in the pipeline where computers could be programmed to add, delete and shift votes.[2]

What has happened since then, however, is that with rapidly advancing technology it has become *infinitely easier* to alter far more election results, with far greater effect, efficiency and precision, and far less risk of exposure. What was once highly labor-intensive—requiring a good-sized crew to hack punch cards or cover up falsified lever machine check-sheets machine by machine in a single contest—can now easily be accomplished by a single insider or hacker, even one working from outside our borders anywhere in the world. A single individual—especially one with insider access—can change the results of dozens, indeed hundreds of elections, with virtually no risk of detection. With the help of a few cohorts, such an individual can essentially stage an undetectable rolling coup. The system is *that* vulnerable, a hunk of red meat lying on the ground of an unfenced yard in a neighborhood full of salivating dogs.

Too dramatic? Too purple? Study after study, by the most prestigious researchers and institutions, tells us that we can be sure about the red meat, the vulnerability.[3] But is it paranoid to imagine the *dogs*, hungry and willing to exploit it? In other words, given the opportunity, who would *want* or *dare* to steal an election, or a nation, that was lying unguarded in the yard? Who would set their sights so high and sink so low?

To answer this, we need first to make a quick sketch of our era, and the ethics of our time. Author David Callahan has done some of this work for us. In his 2004 best-seller *The Cheating Culture: Why More Americans Are Doing Wrong to Get Ahead*,[4] Callahan is hard-pressed to find a single nook of competitive

---

[2] See Collier J, Collier K: *Votescam: The Stealing of America,* Victoria House Press 1992, at http://www.amazon.com/dp/0963416308, for the history of electoral manipulation and its cover-up in the early computer age, before the passage of the Help America Vote Act opened the floodgates in 2002.

[3] See, e.g., http://brennancenter.org/dynamic/subpages/download_file_39288.pdf, https://www.princeton.edu/news/2006/09/13/researchers-reveal-extremely-serious-vulnerabilities-e-voting-machines-0, http://www.blackboxvoting.org/BBVtsxstudy.pdf, http://www.blackboxvoting.org/BBVreport.pdf, https://oversight.house.gov/wp-content/uploads/2017/11/Blaze-UPenn-Statement-Voting-Machines-11-29.pdf, http://www.gao.gov/new.items/d05956.pdf. It is of interest that the comprehensive reviews undertaken by the states of California and Ohio have been removed from the official websites and are no longer available to the public.

[4] See https://www.amazon.com/dp/0156030055; see also, Michael Lewis, "Extreme Wealth Is Bad for Everyone—Especially The Wealthy," *The New Republic*, 11/12/2014 (reviewing West D: *Billionaires: Reflections On the Upper Crust.* Brookings, 2014), in

endeavor where cheating or rigging to achieve some goal has not become commonplace. From students, to job applicants, to athletes at every level, to financiers, to corporations, to public officials—Callahan takes us on a grand tour of what has been happening where and when no one is looking in today's 'just win, baby' America. And that was *before* Donald Trump "drained the swamp."

It is not pretty.

And at every turn the vast majority of us have been, at least initially, very reluctant to believe the extent of the rot, the malignancy of the tumor. It would seem that a painful cognitive dissonance with ingrained beliefs in human perfectibility, historical semper-improvement, and American exceptionalism has contributed to our collective naivety.

When 500-foot home runs were flying off the bats of Mark McGwire and Sammy Sosa, we desperately wanted to believe that healthier diets and better workout regimens could account for it. Few were willing to give any credence to former major-leaguer Jose Canseco's claim that these new supermen were juiced.[5] Something did seem wrong with that picture[6]—as something seemed wrong with Bernie Madoff's Ponzi scheme, with credit default swaps, with the anthrax in the vial at the U.N. and the supposed WMD's in Iraq, and now seems wrong with a host of Trump administration official stories—but it was not something that as a culture we were willing to acknowledge. All that taint was just too much to face, *until we were forced to*. Until we were *made* to look hard at how our high stakes "games"—from Wrigley Field to Wall Street to the White House—were actually being played.

The question we are compelled to ask—by all that once was holy; by the Houston Astros;[7] by the state-doped stable of Russian athletes now banned

---

which copious research is presented showing the propensity to cheat to be correlated with increasing wealth.

[5] Canseco J: *Juiced: Wild Times, Rampant 'Roids, Smash Hits, and How Baseball Got Big.* New York: William Morrow & Co., 2005. *Publishers Weekly*, in describing *Juiced* as "poorly written, controversial," was typical in doubting whether Canseco "really knows anything about the problem beyond his own use." Canseco's next book, written three years later when events and investigations had borne him out, was entitled *Vindicated: Big Names, Big Liars, and The Battle to Save Baseball.*

[6] Though we must note that at least as often *nothing* seems wrong with the picture: what, for example, seemed wrong with the Houston Astros' 2018 championship season? What seems wrong with the numbers that tell us who won a typical election?

[7] The 2018 Major League Baseball season and the Astros' tainted World Series championship present a fascinating case of cheating by a combination of hi-tech (video

from the 2020 Olympics; by Bernie Madoff and Lance Armstrong and A-Rod; by the signaling cheaters exposed at the top of the impeccably-mannered *contract bridge* world;[8] by the ring of computer hackers charged with the theft and use of 160 million credit card numbers from the likes of Citibank and NASDAQ;[9] by the fraudsters at Volkswagen who programmed the computers in their cars to cheat on emissions tests, got turned in by a whistleblower, and agreed to pay $14.7 billion in settlement to U.S. consumers alone;[10] by the apparent foreign-state cyber-incursion manifest in the "Sony" hack and of course the "DNC" hack of 2016;[11] by the Equifax hack and the plethora of hacking and rigging schemes that are now barely even newsworthy—is how a computerized U.S. election, supremely vital and supremely vulnerable as it is, could *not* be a target for skullduggery?

Are the stakes anywhere in any endeavor in the entire world ever higher than in a biennial American election? We know of no pot of gold—home runs, capital, fame, power, policy—that can compare to that at stake in American elections.[12] Winning elections confers the power to reward friends and punish

---

recording and computer analysis of opponents' signs) and lo-tech (relaying that information to Astros' batters by banging on garbage cans in the dugout). It's amazing how much easier hitting gets when you know what pitch is coming, and amazing how much easier winning elections gets when someone is doing the equivalent of sign-stealing on your behalf. It's surprising that other teams didn't pick up on the garbage-can signals and deviously switch pitches accordingly, an option of course not available to candidates whose votes are being flipped in cyberspace. Computerized election riggers have found no real use for garbage cans, though they may have a role in vote *suppression* as a repository for valid but undesirable provisional and mail-in ballots.

[8] See http://www.newsweek.com/big-rich-cheaters-bridge-world-rocked-top-players-busted-375414.

[9] See http://www.bbc.com/news/technology-23448639. One of the ring's members, Mikhail Rytikov, was charged with having the sole role of covering up the ring's tracks. By 2018 such massive cybercrimes have become rather ho-hum, barely generating headlines. Among them the Equifax breach, the Uber breach, and the attempted hacking of what appears to be a good part of the U.S. national voter database.

[10] See http://www.nytimes.com/2016/06/28/business/volkswagen-settlement-diesel-scandal.html.

[11] As Ajay Arora, CEO of cybersecurity firm Vera, put it in warning that the DNC hack might be the new normal: "This is a bellwether of things to come. The techniques are advancing. There are strategic attacks, and then there is tactical warfare. There are parties out there now thinking, 'hey, let's affect outcome of whole election.'" (http://www.aol.com/article/2016/07/26/the-worst-might-be-yet-to-come-with-the-dnc-email-hack/21439542/). Presumably, those "parties out there" have grasped that "whole election" includes the part where the votes are counted.

[12] Although it is hardly possible to quantify the "net worth" of an election, it bears mention that more than $7 billion was spent to win federal office alone in E2012 [a shorthand I use throughout this book] (http://www.politico.com/story/2013/01/7-

enemies, along with the opportunity to set policies that can engender enormous profits. But, just as dogs of many different breeds might find the unguarded hunk of beef irresistible, so those moved to rig elections may be of different breeds and driven by different hungers. Besides the obvious yearning for practical power and profit, there is the "true belief" of the political extremist and, at the other end of the spectrum entirely, the climb-Everest-because-it's-there lure for the conscienceless "pure player"—one who, not necessarily in the service of any heart-felt conviction but just for the "rush" (though such operatives are unlikely to go unpaid), would be the human god, the Master of the Dance who from an unseen perch alters politics on the grandest scale, and with it the course of history.[13]

Some true-believers—who now abound in American politics, have made a successful bid for control of the Republican Party, and (as we shall see) were chief among the founders of the voting computer industry—are so strongly motivated and inspired by an outcome vision (whether fundamentally religious or secular in nature) that they can thoroughly rationalize an ends-justify-the-means approach to their activities. From the standpoint of such a true-believer, there *are* no ethics as compelling as that true belief.[14] And from the standpoint

---

billion-spent-on-2012-campaign-fec-says-87051.html). The amount was comparable in E2016, a good part of it post-*Citizens United* "dark money." E2018 was worth a record (for a midterm) $5.7 billion. With lobbyists enjoying an ROI of better than 100-to-1, it is not hard to see that, even calculated in cold monetary terms, the value of an election—which of course is concentrated in the relatively few key contests that determine control of the governmental apparatus at various levels—is astronomical.

And of course when an athlete or team is found to have cheated to win, we can put an asterisk in the record books and go on our way; with the theft of elections and public office an asterisk is small consolation to a nation and planet permanently altered by such an outcome and the resulting political and historical veer.

[13] To the long-list of actors with a vital gaming interest in the outcome of a given U.S. national election, we can add macro traders. Macro traders make (and lose) fortunes by keeping their fingers on global, regional, or national economic and political pulses. The fate of a macro trader's billion-dollar bet to go long or short on a currency or commodity has been known to come down to who wins a single election (see, e.g., the ruinous impact of a Brazilian presidential election result on one such trader: https://www.newyorker.com/magazine/2018/04/16/a-sidelined-wall-street-legend-bets-on-bitcoin). With literally billions immediately at stake for such a trader, his or her firm and clients, the ROI for the services of an election hacker or insider would be, to say the least, dangerously lucrative—and the loss of such a bet dangerously catastrophic.

[14] Harvard-based political scientists Steven Levitsky and Daniel Ziblatt, in their 2018 best-seller *How Democracies Die* and in subsequent articles, have characterized the "any means necessary" approach to political battle adopted by the contemporary GOP as spurred by an existential panic brought on by ominous demographic trends and an expanding franchise in the wake of the Voting Rights Act and the end it and other legislation brought to *de jure* restrictions of the voting rights of citizens of color. They

of a pure player, there are no ethics, period: *if you ain't cheatin', you ain't tryin'.*

And then we have still another breed of dog, the true believer not in some righteous cause but in *himself*. It took, of all people, retired Harvard Law Professor Alan Dershowitz, speaking on the U.S. Senate floor in Donald Trump's impeachment trial defense, to lay out the case for *election rigging in the public interest*.[15] Suborning election interference from Ukraine was not, according to Dershowitz, an impeachable offense, because President Trump sincerely believed, *as do most leaders*, that his own reelection was "in the public interest" and therefore could innocently be advanced by such means as extorting a foreign nation to gin up dirt on his prospective opponent. It was not clear where the line might be drawn on the spectrum of such questing: would it be OK, one might have asked, to simply shoot one's opponent to facilitate one's election in the public interest? While Dershowitz was roundly and rightly pilloried for his novel and, it seemed to many, equal parts dangerous and idiotic *l'etat c'est moi* argument, it perfectly captured the mindset of officeholders who have conveniently come to conflate their own political fate with the general welfare.

We've seen that ethical barriers can all too easily be surmounted with everything ranging from such sophistries to a simple shrug. Thus an individual or group might feel *justified* in, say, sending "Vote Wednesday" informational flyers or making "Vote Wednesday" robocalls to the homes of opposing voters when the election is Tuesday. In fact they *have*, repeatedly.[16] Is there a bright line then, we must ask, between behavior so blatantly unethical and, say, a more *efficient* gambit—simply offsetting the zero-counters on the memory cards of voting computers to +X for the candidate you favor and –X for the candidate you oppose, so that at the end of the day (as explained in the next chapter) the vote totals will reconcile with the poll tapes recording the number

---

compare the GOP's behavior with that of the Democrats of the South following the end of Reconstruction in 1876, when all means, fair and foul, were called upon to rig the electoral game by preventing all but an insignificant portion of Southern black citizens from voting, thus keeping control in the hands of whites for the next century.

I would add only that both existential fears and a yearning for political hegemony (Karl Rove's "perpetual rule") would seem to have driven the new no-holds-barred, total-war politics that Levitsky and Ziblatt cite as a mortal danger to a democracy.

[15] See https://www.realclearpolitics.com/video/2020/01/29/dershowitz_not_impeachable_if_president_does_something_he_believes_will_help_him_get_elected_in_the_public_interest.html.

[16] See http://www.motherjones.com/politics/2012/11/election-dirty-tricks for a record of this and other dirty tricks recently relied upon to gain electoral advantage.

of voters, the election administrator will see and certify a "clean" election, and you will have stolen a net of 2X votes per machine so rigged? Indeed, it would be hard to resist if you were a "Vote Wednesday" kind of true-believer (in cause *or* self) who had a pipeline to those memory cards, or to the cyber-networks on which millions of votes are now "processed." And just another day on Mt. Everest for a pure player.

Consider democracy schematically as a combination of process, method, and outcome. The core *process* is the casting and counting of votes—whether by the thousands or tens of millions. The *method* consists of all the various means to influence the casting of those votes—campaigning, broadly understood: strategizing, raising and spending money, telling truths and lies in the rough and tumble of the eternal political battle. The *outcome* is victory or defeat in each contest and ultimately, when those contests are summed, *power*. In theory the process is sacrosanct, the method roughly bounded, the outcomes legitimate and accepted.

But imagine an actor—and world and U.S. history have seen many such—for whom the outcome takes on a compelling priority over all respect for process.[17] Might not such an operative address his method not just to influencing the *casting* of votes but to influencing the *counting* of those votes? In such a compulsively outcome-driven view, what cannot be achieved by campaigning might well be achieved—more directly, in fact—by manipulating the counting process where the opportunity presented itself. The more so once politics itself evolves, or degenerates, into the equivalent of total war—the ethos that characterizes the Age of Trump[18] but that has been building throughout the computerized voting era.

Considering this, we must ask a hard question: Lip-service aside, just how sacred *are* elections and just how sacrosanct *is* the counting of the votes?[19]

---

[17] For a fascinating inquiry into the mindset and behavior of such actors, see https://www.wnycstudios.org/podcasts/otm/episodes/on-the-media-dead-consensus?tab=summary, a December 2019 *On The Media* interview with Matthew Sitman.

[18] Perhaps inevitably, as one characterized by many psychologists as a malignant narcissist, Trump has striven relentlessly to make *everything* about himself. Thus, to take one recent example, when Democrats or the media express concern over the spread and handling of coronavirus, it is a "another Democratic hoax," the only purpose of which is to bring the president down. Trump has made himself the peg in the ground over which a kind of vicious, total war is to be fought to the finish, a war in which if not *all* then certainly *more* is fair than has previously been imaginable in our politics.

[19] Because a major election is virtually *never* decided by a single vote, the value we place upon a single vote *in actuality* tends to be a good deal lower than our exalted

And a follow-up: How does the democratic process *per se* stack up against a burning true belief, a craving for power, or a boatload of money? Is it possible that, for some, "democracy"—no longer a majestic and awe-inspiring novelty—is just another *impediment* to be dealt with, something old and in the way on the path to power or reward? Just how deep and abiding a respect for democracy itself, how much pure *principle*, would it take to overcome the tremendous temptation to palm a card or two and *have things your way*, alter the course of history, and create (as George W. Bush was once praised for doing) your own reality?[20]

In the Age of Trump, the "reality creation" that once seemed novel has become—in the hands of such practitioners as *Breitbart News*, Kellyanne Conway, Sarah Huckabee Sanders, Rush Limbaugh, Rudy Giuliani and, leading the way, the president himself—standard operating procedure.

Having made a realistic appraisal of the behavior, mindset, and character of some of the political actors and operatives now on the scene,[21] do we really believe that a deep and abiding respect vests in every player in the game of "democracy" as it is currently being played in The New American Century?

Even before Trump arrived on the scene, and before any documented Russian "meddling," many observers had begun to question, and often deplore, the

---

rhetoric would have it. It may be that this low pragmatic value assigned the individual vote in turn colors our laissez-faire attitude toward the voting and vote-counting process as a whole.

[20] There is a chilling and revealing testament to none other than Karl Rove's fervent embrace of this approach to political action, as captured in an October 17, 2004 article written by Ron Suskind for *The New York Times Magazine*, as part of which Suskind interviews the at-the-time anonymous Rove:

> The aide [subsequently identified as Rove] said that guys like me were "in what we call the reality-based community," which he defined as people who "believe that solutions emerge from your judicious study of discernible reality. . . . *That's not the way the world really works anymore*," he continued. "We're an empire now, and *when we act, we create our own reality.* And while you're studying that reality— judiciously, as you will—we'll act again, creating other new realities, which you can study too, and that's how things will sort out. *We're history's actors ... and you, all of you, will be left to just study what we do.*" [emphases added]

[21] Beginning with the president and adding, with a nod to the likely perpetrators of the 2016 DNC and voting system hacks, states and political actors and operatives anywhere in the world who have a rooting interest in American electoral outcomes.

"new madness" of American politics.[22] Taking in the hyperpolarization, the intransigent hyper-radicalism of the Right and what seems to be its poll- and explanation-defying endorsement at the ballot box by a traditionally moderate electorate, many wondered what was happening in and to America. Witness Thomas Mann's and Norman Ornstein's mid-Obama-era 2012 bestseller, *It's Even Worse Than It Looks*.[23] Many explanations were offered up, from clever messaging to voter suppression and gerrymandering to the role of dark money. Pundits, after all, are not paid to be stumped. But there remained a nagging disquiet, a sense that all these explanations didn't quite explain enough.

Now in the Age of Trump, these same pundits are tying themselves in knots trying to explain the inexplicable, fathom the unimaginable, while millions of Americans seem to be walking around in a state of it-does-not-compute bewilderment. Something is happening that defies not only conventional political wisdom but plain old common sense, as if the Political Universe had been taken over by some new asymmetrical non-Euclidean geometry.[24] There seems to be a missing force, an X-factor analogous to cosmic dark energy, that is needed to explain what is happening to America.

We will present compelling evidence that the X-factor has been the electronic manipulation of votecounts and that, all other factors notwithstanding, what is happening here in America would *not* be happening in its absence.

For anyone persuaded by the evidence, presented in the chapters that follow,[25] that the electoral process in America has been subverted, or even that it is

---

[22] See, e.g., *New York Review of Books*, 9/27/2012, cover headline: "OUR WEIRD POLITICS NOW," featuring separate pieces on the theme by Andrew Hacker, Ezra Klein, Jacob Hacker, and Paul Pierson.

[23] Mann TE, Ornstein NJ: *It's Even Worse Than It Looks: How The American Constitutional System Collided with The New Politics of Extremism*. New York: Basic Books, 2012, https://www.amazon.com/dp/0465096204/ref.

[24] It must be acknowledged that this political veer has not been confined to America. A hard-right populism has sprung up in a number of promising democracies in both hemispheres. A comprehensive comparative study of vote-counting processes and security protocols is beyond the scope of this book, but we have observed at least a rough correlation between public, observable vote counting and resistance to such sharp right turns toward autocracy. Notably, countries such as Norway and the Netherlands—which restored hand counting to their elections in 2017, have not followed countries such as Hungary and Brazil in their veer to the far-right.

[25] Election forensics is not, for better or worse, the stuff of soundbites; but neither does it have to be eye-glazingly abstruse and obscure. I have sought to balance comprehensiveness with clarity and have provided links and references for additional exploration as appropriate.

merely vulnerable to and perhaps teetering on the brink of such subversion,[26] our predicament takes on a nightmarish quality—one of those dreadful dreams where you are running without moving while the locomotive speeds on to its inexorable impact with the child who has wandered onto the tracks.

Virtually everything about the situation is surrealistic and absurd. Election integrity activists are told to produce "a smoking gun," when all such "hard evidence" materials are strictly off-limits to investigation; statistical evidence, no matter how copious and consistent, is dismissed with a shrug; reform proposals such as hand-counted paper ballots for federal and statewide elections are shot down as ludicrous Luddite nonstarters; "rogue" journalists and whistleblowers are cowed, exiled, silenced, or ignored. America seems hell-bent on sticking with its faith-based election system, no matter how vulnerable it is shown to be and no matter how weirdly distorted our politics become.

And yet . . . and yet, America is one examined memory card (however obtained), one white-hat real-time election hack ("Mickey Mouse gets 4 billion votes!"), one open and honest recount, one "Opscan Party" (where citizens form a ring around an optical scanner and call for a public, observable count of the voter-marked ballots within), or even one serious article in *The New York Times* or *The Washington Post* away from *critical mass*, from the sudden explosive recognition that something thought too ghastly to imagine (even *worse* than the idea that *baseball* was not the wholesome Norman Rockwell game it seemed) will *have* to be imagined and then dealt with.

Given how unimposing the civic duty of public, observable vote counting is in actuality,[27] the problem can be *dealt with* easily enough. The real challenge is not in the dealing with, but in the collective imagining—and the willingness to think seriously and rationally about the situation.

There are some indications that the American *people* at least—after a more than generation-long embrace of the private, and rejection of the public,

---

[26] This is a concern shared, according to a NORC poll conducted in February 2020, by two-thirds of Americans (see https://www.nytimes.com/aponline/2020/02/27/us/politics/ap-us-ap-poll-election-security.html).

[27] It has been calculated that hand counting the federal and statewide races would require a *maximum of four hours per lifetime from each American voter*, a civic burden far less onerous than jury duty and one that Americans of previous generations assumed and Canadians, Germans, and Australians, among others, perform today. A uniform, public, observable, Election Night audit process—as proposed in Chapter VIII, Study VII—for *all* contests would make about the same modest demand.

sphere—are ready once again to invest in the common good, and perhaps even to part with a few of the expedients and conveniences that are now being seen to do us both individual and collective ill.[28] There is an emerging, priority-reordering, "anti-seduction" culture that could come to support a demand for reform of our voting system and could be mobilized to let our representatives know that we are both ready to serve and determined to defend our democracy. And of course, courtesy of Donald Trump, there's a renewed sense among millions that politics and elections *really matter*—a great awakening to what is at stake.

Yet there continues to be a great reluctance to connect what is happening to our nation politically with the vagaries and vulnerabilities of our computerized vote counting processes. Realistically, *absent a galvanizing catastrophe or a complete media about-face*, there have been few signs that such reforms as hand counting or even effective auditing are in the offing.

It is one thing to bewail a shocking political reality, or even to question a particular president's legitimacy, and another thing entirely to insist upon the concrete reforms necessary to prevent the serial recurrence of fraudulent elections. In this appalling lack of traction, vote counting reform is not alone: think gun safety, climate change. *At least as now represented by our elected leaders*, we are a conservative nation, reactive rather than pro-active, simultaneously smug and insecure, paradoxically hubristic yet with a fragile self-esteem giving rise to much denial.

It does not have to be this way. The Dutch took one whiff of *our* 2016 elections and promptly decided to count *their* critical 2017 national election by hand. So did the Norwegians. Here in the Beacon of Democracy—as we rest on our wilting laurels, on guard as always against *external* enemies—it is now at least permitted to talk of "Russian meddling." We are assured, though, by such watchdogs as our Department of Homeland Security that—after deciding *not* to examine a single memory card, string of code, or voter-marked paper ballot—they have determined that "no actual votes were affected" by such "meddling."[29] What cannot enter our national discourse, cannot even now be

---

[28] Apart from the bevy of books and blogs blasting Walmart culture and its corporate-serving anomies, we can look around us and see the regrowth of participatory communal foci such as farmers' markets and food co-ops. While alienation, speed, convenience, and self-interest clearly remain the dominant cultural modes, it appears that a turning point may finally be in sight. When Greta Thunberg asked world leaders "How dare you?" it seems no one could even venture an answer.

[29] See http://talkingpointsmemo.com/muckraker/dhs-doesnt-want-to-know-about-vote-hacks.

seriously debated or explored, is the possibility that, as Pogo once said, "we have met the enemy and he is us." Meaning simply that the "meddling" is at least as likely to be undertaken by *domestic* actors with ties to the vendors and programmers—insiders with keys to the front door—as by foreign hackers who have to break in through a window.[30]

If, in one way or another, a massive electoral theft *were* exposed beyond all cover-up and forced upon the public consciousness, it would of course be technically and pragmatically possible to quickly restore hand counting or at least a comprehensive and effective auditing protocol. Neither is beyond our capacities—hell, did we or did we not put a man on the Moon?—and both cost not only much less than the computerized equipment (and service contracts) now being purchased,[31] but a tiny speck of what we have recently spent bringing "democracy" to foreign soils.[32]

---

[30] Consider this extraordinary 2016 revelation by the inimitable Roger Stone—the insider's insider, long-time Trump advisor (sentenced to 40 months for lying to Congress to protect his boss), veteran of Republican campaigns dating to the Nixon years, and *New York Times* best-selling author—at http://thehill.com/blogs/pundits-blog/presidential-campaign/291534-can-the-2016-election-be-rigged-you-bet:

> "Both parties have engaged in voting machine manipulation. Nowhere in the country has this been more true than Wisconsin, where there are strong indications that Scott Walker and the Reince Priebus machine rigged as many as five elections including the defeat of a Walker recall election. . . The computerized voting machines can be hacked and rigged and . . . there is no reason to believe they won't be."

Out of the mouths of babes and operatives.

[31] Recent "upgrades" to computerized voting and vote-counting equipment cost the states of South Carolina and Georgia $51 million and $107 million respectively. Mecklenburg *County* in North Carolina is expected to pony up $15 million for its new equipment this year; Los Angeles County spent $400 million for its new, already troubled, system.

[32] It is perhaps worth recalling here that our wars in Iraq, Syria, and Afghanistan will end up costing the United States a total of over $6 trillion (see https://www.cnbc.com/2019/11/20/us-spent-6point4-trillion-on-middle-east-wars-since-2001-study.html), an *average* of more than $5 billion *every week* (www.costofwar.com) since their inception. A *single month* worth of those wars would pay (at $20/hour per counter) for hand counting our *American* ballots for a minimum of 40 biennial election cycles, or fully *three generations*.

Why, it must be asked, can't we do this? Why, for that matter, is our computerized voting equipment, in addition to being so corruptible, also aged into obsolescence and dysfunction? Why are we so lavish with our *global* democracy-promotion follies and so ridiculously, and it would appear intentionally, cheap with our *own* democracy?

Whether it would be *politically* possible would remain to be seen. When majority control at critical levels[33] is held by those who have achieved that control as the beneficiaries of years of systemic fraud, can they be expected to willingly institute honest elections and so inevitably surrender power and go gentle into that good political night? And, apart from that particular Catch-22, what would motivate a majority of elected officeholders, independent of party affiliation, who asked themselves quite reasonably, "Why mess with a system that has worked for *me* by putting me in office?"

What form and intensity of public pressure would it take to move our successfully elected lawmakers and officeholders? Would marches and sit-ins and massive demonstrations persuade our leaders to restore our sovereignty or would these—when push came to shove—rather be ruthlessly suppressed in the name of security and domestic tranquility? Would it come down to voting boycotts, mass civil actions, or general strikes? Would the simmering subliminal battle between the newly awakened public and its newly exposed oppressors come shockingly to a turbulent and violent head?

It is grim to speculate on these scenarios. *But I think it is fair to say that the later in the game this critical mass of public awareness and outrage is reached, the less likely that an ordinary political remedy will be possible.* So the first thing to be done is to engender awareness, and that right soon. Thus the urgency of this writing. It is a CODE RED.

I'd like to think this story will have a happy ending, that history will review in appreciative terms the struggle of a few activists—Cassandras really—to prod leaders and public alike to scale the towering Never-Happen-Here Wall Of Denial so that they can then act together to restore the essential process of public, observable vote counting to our nation. Most truths eventually come out. All we can do is keep trying in every way possible to help this one find its way into the light.

We will, in the series of questions and answers to follow, examine computerized election theft from many angles. We will explore motive, means, opportunity, and, of course, the evidence for such a ghastly criminal enterprise. We will also explore why it continues to remain hidden, the quintessential Big Lie quietly corrupting our nation and its democracy. We will look unblinkingly

---

[33] The Senate blockade of all election security legislation worth the name will be discussed in more detail in chapters II and VI. It is worth noting that the electoral process has "worked" on an individual basis for *all* our elected office-holders regardless of party or majority-minority status.

at democracy down and ask realistically whether there is any chance that it can get back up. We will ask you to override the powerful "naaaah" reflex and be among the first to scale with us that towering Never-Happen-Here Wall of Denial.

It will be a rough ride we are taking. For ourselves, our children, and the life that shares the planet with us, it will be a lot rougher if we choose not to take it.

— II —

QUESTIONS AND ANSWERS

In searching out the truth, be ready for the unexpected,
for it is difficult to find and puzzling when you find it.

— Heraclitus

Q: In 100 words or so, tell me what you believe is happening with American elections.

A: Computerized vote counting has opened the door wide, over the past two decades, to the prospect of systemic fraud and election theft. Virtually all the vote counting equipment is produced and programmed by a few corporations with partisan ties. It is secure neither against outside hacking nor against malicious insider programming. There is persistent forensic evidence that votecounts are being shifted, altering key election outcomes. Mystifyingly, political intransigence and seemingly gross miscalculation are often electorally rewarded rather than punished. As a result, even as the pendulum *appears* to swing, American politics has veered inexorably and inexplicably to the right. This amounts to a rolling coup that is transforming America while disenfranchising an unsuspecting public.

Q. Haven't there always been attempts to steal elections? Why is now any different?

A: Yes, political history is full of skullduggery. But, as IT expert Chuck Herrin memorably put it, "It takes a long time to change 10,000 votes by hand. It takes three seconds to change them in a computer."[1] What computerized elections

---

[1] Herrin, a Republican, was interviewed in Dorothy Fadiman's 2008 documentary *Stealing America: Vote by Vote*, http://www.stealingamericathemovie.org/. He concluded, "I think the most appropriate technology is what we should be going for, instead of the latest and greatest."

have brought us, along with speed and convenience of counting,[2] is the opportunity to alter electoral outcomes strategically, surgically, systemically, and covertly. And, because of selective access stemming from partisan control over the equipment itself, it has not been equal-opportunity rigging—the evidence has shown that it virtually always goes in the same direction.

The "retail" fraud of the past—schemes like stuffing the ballot box in local fiefdoms—tended to wind up a net wash overall and over time, as it was a game open to both sides in their respective strongholds. The "wholesale" fraud of computerized rigging is a far more potent and incomparably more dangerous phenomenon; you might call it the Jaws of the Electoral Ocean, a Great White submerged among the minnows.[3]

Q: How do you *know* the computers on which we vote are so susceptible to fraud?

A: There is virtual unanimity among the experts who have studied electronic voting that insiders or hackers can change the results of elections without leaving a trace—at least not the kind of trace that any election administrator is likely to find. These studies have come from institutions such as Johns Hopkins, Princeton, the University of Michigan, The Brennan Center for Social Justice at NYU, the states of California and Ohio, and even the U.S. Government Accountability Office.[4] White-hat hackers such as Harri Hursti and Alex

---

[2] I specify "counting" because computerized voting, whether by touchscreen DREs (Direct Recording Electronic) or the new wave of BMDs (Ballot Marking Devices), can dramatically *slow* the vote *casting* process, creating bottlenecks not found with hand-marked paper ballots and often resulting in hours-long voting lines, especially in precincts targeted for vote suppression by partisan administrators.

[3] Its only non-computerized precursor might be the post-Reconstruction Jim Crow laws, regulations, and extra-legal intimidation that disenfranchised virtually the entire non-white electorate across the South (and also reared its ugly head in pockets of the rest of the country), thereby entrenching the power of what was often a minority-white constituency, which during that era was aligned with the Democratic Party but was by nature reactionary in its politics.

The civil rights movement having largely succeeded in removing those particular thumbs from the electoral scales—or at least lightening their weight—a replacement was sought and found in computerization. Its reach was national rather than regional, and it happens that the reactionary forces seeking such advantage in modern times are generally Republican in their allegiance.

[4] See, e.g., California Secretary of State: *Top to Bottom Review (TTBR) of Voting Systems*, http://www.sos.ca.gov/elections/voting-systems/oversight/top-bottom-review/; Feldman A J, Halderman J A, Felten E W: *Security Analysis of the Diebold AccuVote-TS Voting Machine*; Princeton University, Center for Information Technology Policy

Halderman have demonstrated how quick and easy it is to swap or reprogram memory cards in voting machines (inserting cards with malicious code) or break into the networked vote-counting computers increasingly in use.[5]

Indeed, it doesn't take hackers or IT pros with the chops of Halderman or Hursti—a couple of 11-year-olds turned the trick easily enough.[6]

---

and Dept. of Computer Science, Woodrow Wilson School of Public and International Affairs, September 13, 2006, https://www.acm.org/binaries/content/assets/public-policy/usacm/e-voting/reports-and-white-papers/ts06_evt.pdf; Ohio Secretary of State: *Project EVEREST (Evaluation and Validation of Election Related Equipment, Standards and Testing)*, https://votingmachines.procon.org/sourcefiles/Everest.pdf ; Hursti H: *Security Alert: Critical Security Issues with Diebold Optical Scan Design*, Black Box Voting, July 4, 2005, http://blackboxvoting.org/BBVreport.pdf.

For two more recent overviews, see Sue Halpern, "America Continues to Ignore the Risks of Election Hacking"; *The New Yorker*, 4/18/2018, at https://www.newyorker.com/news/news-desk/america-continues-to-ignore-the-risks-of-election-hacking; and Kim Zetter, "The Crisis of Election Security," *The New York Times Magazine*, 9/26/2018, at https://www.nytimes.com/2018/09/26/magazine/election-security-crisis-midterms.html.

[5] The "Hursti Hack" was demonstrated in the 2006 film *Hacking Democracy*, Simon Ardizzone director, http://www.hackingdemocracy.com. The topic is revisited, to devastating effect, in the same group's 2020 HBO documentary *Kill Chain: The Cyber War on America's Elections* (see https://www.hbo.com/documentaries/kill-chain-the-cyber-war-on-americas-elections and https://www.youtube.com/watch?v=3c8LMZ8UGd8).

Halderman, a professor of engineering and computer science at the University of Michigan, was invited, on three days' notice, to attempt to penetrate the security of the then-new Washington D.C. internet-based voting system; within 36 hours of the D.C. system's launch, Halderman and a group of three student assistants had not only penetrated the system's security, but had gained "almost total control of the server software, including the ability to change votes and reveal voters' secret ballots;" they also found evidence of other attempts to breach the system's security originating from IP addresses in China, India, and Iran. See https://jhalderm.com/pub/papers/dcvoting-fc12.pdf.

[6] This was demonstrated dramatically in the summer of 2017 at the annual DefCon hacking convention in Las Vegas, and again at DefCons 2018 and 2019. The organizers set up what they called a "Voting Village" supplied with election equipment, and let the hackers have at it. Not a single voting machine was able to prevent its hacker(s), including a bunch of youngsters, from getting in (some physically, some remotely), and accessing and altering its code—some within minutes.

The stunning (to everyone except election transparency advocates) results made national news and had immediate influence in some quarters, with Virginia most notably citing the DefCon revelations as its main reason for quickly scrapping its paperless touchscreen voting in time for its November 2017 statewide election—a move we will revisit later in this book.

See https://www.forbes.com/sites/thomasbrewster/2017/07/29/def-con-hacking-election-voting-machines/#5a12bc321d55, https://www.pbs.org/newshour/nation/an-11-year-old-changed-election-results-on-a-replica-florida-state-website-in-under-10-

The level of security of all this equipment is orders of magnitude *below* that found at major banks, corporations, and governmental institutions, and yet all those *high-security* enterprises have been hacked and compromised repeatedly over the past several years, with increasing frequency.[7] And it only gets *easier* when the "hacker" is working from the *inside* or has been let in the door by someone with keys to the house.

Why, on what basis; *why*, by what logic; *why*, according to what understanding of human nature; *why*, from what view of history, politics, and the way high-stakes games are played by those high-rollers for whom, in Vince Lombardi's words, winning is the *only* thing; *why, why, why, why, why* do we so blithely *assume* that hundreds of millions of votes counted in secret, on partisan-produced and -controlled equipment, will be counted honestly and that the *public* trust will be honored to the exclusion of any *private* agenda, however compelling?!

Why and how, in the face of this level of *risk*, do we just rest easy that all is going well and fairly in the depths of cyberspace where our choices have become 1s and 0s dancing by the trillions in the dark? That dance is the embodiment of our sovereignty. It is from that dance that our future emerges and whoever programs the computers can, if so inclined, call the dance. *Setting aside for a moment all evidence of fraud*, how can we possibly be OK with *that*?

Q: If you wanted to alter the outcome of an election, give me an example of how you might do it?

A: It depends upon the type of computer, but there are many ways to manipulate votes. One very basic scheme, where optical scanning voting computers ("opscans") are in use,[8] would be to set the "zero counters" on the

---

minutes, and https://www.washingtonpost.com/business/2019/08/12/def-con-hackers-lawmakers-came-together-tackle-holes-election-security/.

[7] See, e.g., http://www.wired.com/threatlevel/2012/02/anonymous-friday-attacks/; also http://about.bloomberglaw.com/legal-news/5-hackers-charged-in-largest-data-breach-scheme-in-u-s/; and http://www.informationisbeautiful.net/visualizations/worlds-biggest-data-breaches-hacks/.

[8] Opscans—which use spatial programming to scan, and record as votes, marks made by voters on paper ballots—counted approximately 56% of the ballots nationwide in 2012, a percentage that had risen to above 60% by 2016 and continues to rise as election administrators turn away from touchscreen voting; see

memory card in each machine to, say, +100 for the candidate you want to win and -100 for the one marked for defeat.[9] At the end of the day the positive and negative offsets are a wash, summing to zero, so the total of votes (for that contest) recorded by the opscan closely matches the total of voters signing the log books, the election officials are satisfied that the election was "clean," *and you have shifted a net of 200 votes on each machine so rigged*, PDQ.

This takes just a few lines of programming out of the hundreds of thousands of lines of code on the memory card.[10] It would be detectable only by a very painstaking examination of the card and its code, but the cards are regarded as *strictly corporate property*, completely off-limits to public inspection; in fact, not even election administrators are allowed to look. The command to alter the zero counters can of course be written not to take effect until actual vote counting begins on Election Day so that the opscans pass any pre-testing that election administrators might perform,[11] and it can also be written in self-deleting code so that literally no post-election trace remains.

None of this is difficult or beyond the skills of even a high school-level programmer. Nor, for that matter, are rigs that instead work by shifting every n[th] vote or simply capping one candidate's vote total and assigning all subsequent votes to her opponent. And, since opscans are programmed to "read" the marks voters make on ballots spatially, it is easy enough to alter the

---

http://www.pewresearch.org/fact-tank/2016/11/08/on-election-day-most-voters-use-electronic-or-optical-scan-ballots/

[9] The "zero counter" refers to the number assigned to the first vote recorded for a given candidate or proposition; i.e., where the count begins. Logically that number is "1" and if you were counting ballots by hand "zero" would be the bare table. But in a computer there *is* no fixed starting point known as "zero." A single line of code can be inserted into the 500,000+ lines already on the memory card to start a candidate's count at *any* number, positive or negative.

[10] The memory card—a programmable module smaller in size than a credit card, which both controls how the computer "reads" the ballots and tallies the votes cast—is produced in such a way that code containing the rig can easily be replicated onto however many cards needed to shift the total number of votes projected as required to alter a targeted contest's outcome. It is worth noting that the "factory" computers used to program these memory cards are themselves generally connected to the internet.

[11] Perhaps the best known illustration of the potential futility of pre-testing of computer function was the VW emissions scandal in which the cars were programmed to generate one set of (sham) "clean" results when being tested "in the lab" and then belch banned levels of emissions once on the road. See, e.g., https://www.nytimes.com/2019/07/26/business/audi-vw-emissions-scandal.html. Two takeaways from the VW mess: 1) computers can "know" when they're being tested and need to be on best behavior; and 2) not every conspiracy is a theory.

code in the ballot definition files to flip votes by reading the area for Candidate A as a Candidate B vote, and vice versa,[12] or to be more or less sensitive to inevitable stray marks on the ballot, so as to selectively void more ballots in precincts known to be strongholds of the candidate(s) targeted for defeat.[13]

Where "touchscreen" (also known as Direct Recording Electronic or "DRE") computers are in use, their programming can be altered to cause the screen button pushed for "A" to record instead a vote for "B." DREs that print out a "receipt" for the voter to "verify" (the vaunted "paper trail") are of little help, as it is a trivial step to program the DRE to print a vote for "A" on the receipt while recording a vote for "B" in its cumulative count. While such a rig would lead to a disparity between the paper trail and the machine count, uncovering that mismatch would require a hand count of the paper-trail and the reality is that both the voter-marked ballots deposited into opscans and the "receipts" generated by paper-trail DREs are off-limits to public inspection and virtually never see the light of day, no matter how suspect an election's results.[14]

Ballot Marking Devices (BMDs) provide still another vector for fraud. Originally designed and intended to facilitate the voting process for the discrete group of voters not capable of marking a ballot as the result of a disability, BMDs have suddenly swung into vogue for general usage by all voters—though an able voter needs a BMD like a fish needs a bicycle. The problem with BMDs currently being marketed and purchased by many states to replace their aging equipment is that they do not simply mark a ballot with a check in a box for the candidate selected by the voter on a touchscreen, but rather create a *barcode* (or QR code) impounding, we are obliged to believe, the voter's choices.

Needless to say, the voter cannot read or verify the code (indeed, most often the code is proprietary and cannot even be read by an ordinary bar code

---

[12] It is also possible to expand or contract the area in which the memory card directs the scanner to "look" for the voter's mark. This more sophisticated rig can subtly but, in the aggregate, fairly predictably alter vote totals by "seeing" imperfect and off-center marks for Candidate A, while missing them for Candidate B.

[13] Because memory cards must be precisely tailored for the particular ballot, down to the local level, each card is specifically earmarked for use in a given precinct (in other words, they are not generic). The destination of a memory card must therefore be known to its programmer, generally a corporate entity. Knowing the card's destination permits manipulations that are dependent on the political or demographic nature of such destinations.

[14] An additional impediment in the case of "paper trail" DREs is the propensity of the paper rolls to jam, smear, and run out, such that a full trail is rarely if ever available for post-election verification of the computer count.

scanner). But that unverifiable barcode is what gets read by the precinct (or central) scanner and constitutes the official vote. Under pressure from election transparency advocates, vendors have grudgingly modified some of their designs to include voter "summary sheets," of varying degrees of clarity and readability, for the voters to verify their votes. Apart from the fact that many voters don't bother with that step, or find the summary sheet format illegible or confusing, there is no reason the printed (in letters) summaries of the votes have to match what is embedded in the barcode (essentially the same problem as with "paper trail" DREs).

Even more troubling, one popular model of BMD, known as a Hybrid, sends the ballot under the print head *after* the voter has chosen whether or not to waive her option to verify. This, in effect, makes the voter "play first," so that the computer "knows" when the ballot will not be verified, allowing it to alter— with *zero* risk of detection—voter choices embedded in the barcode that is the official vote. You'd think that no election administrator in their right mind would purchase such equipment, dubbed "permission to cheat" by cyber-security experts. But you would be wrong.[15] The battle over barcode BMDs is currently playing out in state-by-state, and indeed often county-by-county, trench warfare—involving vendors, administrators, legislators, the disabilities lobby, and of course election transparency advocates.

Where the voting equipment is networkable (that is, as is often the case, equipped with a modem[16]), votes can be added, deleted, and shifted *at will, as needed, in real time* on Election Night. Millions of votes are sent through IP networks off-site and often out-of-state for "processing." This saves manipulators from having to guess in advance how many votes they will need to shift, and so permits real-time-calibrated, "tidier" rigs—contests successfully stolen with a smaller numerical footprint. Unexpected veers in the running vote totals, especially late in the evening after most of the votes have been tabulated, may, in the absence of plausible benign explanations, indicate such a "real-time" rig at work.[17]

---

[15] See https://www.theguardian.com/us-news/2019/apr/22/us-voting-machines-paper-ballots-2020-hacking.

[16] Vendors and election administrators alike have been loath to acknowledge the existence of modems in their equipment, issuing denial after denials until forced to admit the truth. See, e.g., https://www.nbcnews.com/politics/elections/online-vulnerable-experts-find-nearly-three-dozen-u-s-voting-n1112436.

[17] Confronted with such a veer late on Election Night 2004, *CNN's* Judy Woodruff famously shrugged and said, "What I'm telling you is that the numbers changed and sometimes these things happen."

It has recently come to light, through the investigative and analytic work of election integrity advocate Bev Harris and programmer Bennie Smith,[18] that in the voting equipment that uses the GEMS operating system, a "fractional vote feature" is embedded, such that votes may be recorded not as integers (1, 2, 3 . . .) but as decimal fractions (0.75, 0.47, 1.29 . . .).

According to Harris and Smith, this strange feature can be used to "invisibly, yet radically, alter election outcomes by pre-setting desired vote percentages to redistribute votes. This tampering is not visible to election observers, even if they are standing in the room and watching the computer. Use of the decimalized vote feature is unlikely to be detected by auditing or canvass procedures and can be applied across large jurisdictions in less than 60 seconds." Fractionalized voting—or "fraction magic," as Harris and Smith dubbed it—has very little legitimate use (e.g., extremely rare land use-related elections in which voting power might be proportional to land owned) but great potential as a tool for manipulating votecounts.[19]

Q: Do a rigged or hacked election's votecounts look any different from a valid election's votecounts?

A: No, not in the slightest. This may seem so obvious to some that you may wonder why I bothered including such a silly question. It is included because I suspect that somewhere, deep down, many of us just *feel* that we'd know a rigged election if we saw one, that something "not quite right" about the vote totals would give it away. That's a feeling we'd do well to get over. Because when a hacker or rigger attacks a computer-counted election, the vote totals *look just like normal vote totals*: e.g., 2,387,901 to 2,159,226. Not 5,000,000 to 152.

The outcome may be surprising, even shocking; the margin of victory not what tracking or exit polls or pundits predicted (though explanations will be found

---

See http://transcripts.cnn.com/TRANSCRIPTS/0411/03/se.05.html and, for the full effect, www.StealingAmericaTheMovie.com.

[18] Smith was appointed to the Shelby County (Nashville), Tennessee Board of Election Commission in April 2019. See https://shelbycountytn.gov/127/Election-Commission.

[19] A detailed and chilling six-part walk-through of decimalized vote counting and its implications for votecount manipulation may be found at http://blackboxvoting.org/fraction-magic-1, an even chillier video at http://blackboxvoting.org/fraction-magic-video.

somewhere and the election virtually always manages to pass the stuffed-nose smell test the media applies). But there will be *nothing in the numbers themselves*, the collection of numerals that make up the votecounts, to give us so much as a clue. There's no visible "calling card." It doesn't *look* rigged.

Q: How did we ever come to approve and accept such a dangerous system?

A: That is a difficult and complex question with answers rooted deep in our political culture and in our attitudes toward democracy, technology, public responsibility, the value of the vote, and time itself. But the short answer is that the highly publicized debacle of "hanging chads" in the presidential election of 2000 engendered a panic situation that was shrewdly exploited (if not in fact engineered) by those whose *a priori* agenda was to computerize American elections. The needs of disabled voters, which could have been effectively addressed without the introduction of computers,[20] were also cynically exploited by computerization's proponents. The Help America Vote Act (HAVA) was passed in 2002, creating a powerful mixture of incentives ($3.9 billion in federal money) and mandates for states to rapidly computerize their elections—with virtually no serious requirements for security or transparency.[21]

HAVA's Republican architects[22] secured Democratic cooperation by emphasizing that its passage would lead to increased voter turnout. This

---

[20] Non-computerized devices, such as the VotePad, had already been developed to allow blind and mechanically disabled voters to mark ordinary paper ballots with their votes; see http://www.bradblog.com/?p=2330. The needs of disabled voters have come into play once again with the current wag-the-dog attempt in some states to force *all* voters to use BMDs—one argument being that it is "unfair" to not mandate a uniform method of voting (ignoring the fact that mail-in voting perforce uses hand-marked ballots), another being that limiting BMD use to the disabled may undercut their ballot secrecy (ignoring all less drastic ways to safeguard ballot anonymity).

[21] For a superb overview of both the genesis and the consequences of America's casual turn to computerized voting by one with deep experience questioning and challenging it, see Teresa Hommel's "Democracy or Trump: Our Choices Now," reprinted at https://codered2014.com/democracy-or-trump/.

[22] HAVA's chief congressional sponsor was Bob Ney. A senior Republican representing Ohio's 18th Congressional District, Ney was convicted in 2007 on federal corruption charges (pleading guilty to conspiracy and making false statements to federal investigators) and served a 30-month term in federal prison. HAVA is widely regarded as Ney's signature legislative accomplishment.

The two other most notable HAVA principals were Senators Roy Blunt (R-MO) and Mitch McConnell (R-KY), both still serving and the latter very much involved in keeping vote-counting concealed by blocking in the Senate all bills to alter that status.

should have thrown up a glaring red flag since for the better part of a century the GOP had done (and continues to do) everything in its power to *decrease* overall voter turnout.[23] Given that they recognized that computerizing the voting process would likely promote ease of voting and increase turnout among marginal (i.e., predominantly Democratic) voters, and given that this goal was just about the *last* thing that they wished to see accomplished, we must ask just what HAVA's GOP promoters expected in the way of partisan *advantage* from computerization that would be alluring enough to outweigh that hefty partisan disadvantage.

In the climate of post-debacle panic, few thought to question the appropriateness and safety of computers, so much a part of our modern world, for the particular task of vote counting. And those who did were drowned out by a chorus of derision from well-financed promoters. The rush was on. Once the computers were paid for and deployed, it became a powerful *fait accompli* and any return to noncomputerized counting was written off as a ridiculous Luddite retreat.

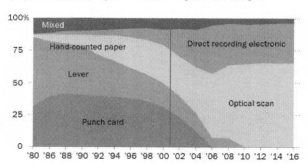

Estimated share of registered voters in precincts using ...

Notes: Excludes precincts that are entirely vote-by-mail. The estimated share of registered voters in precincts using hand-counted paper ballots is 0.1% in 2016. Source: Election Data Services.

PEW RESEARCH CENTER

Other HAVA-promoting notables included Republicans Mike Pence (IN-6), Tom Price (GA-6), Paul Ryan (WI-1), Kevin McCarthy (CA-22), Steve King (IA-5), Jim Jordan (OH-4), Louis Gohmert (TX-1), and Tom Feeney (FL-24). Eighteen years later, the preponderance, in this honor roll, of politically surviving, highly visible far-right Republicans is rather striking.

[23] With the end of Reconstruction (1876), it was the southern *Democrats* who pulled out all the Jim Crow stops to suppress turnout (to near zero) among newly enfranchised African-American voters. But voter suppression is an old tool eternally ready to the hand of endangered ruling minorities. Since the mid-20th century, it has served the GOP's political craftsmen.

Q: You say that the system is indisputably vulnerable and dangerous but what makes you think that it has *actually* been corrupted and elections have *actually* been stolen?

A: Introducing the Red Shift. When official votecounts come out to the right of other measures of voters' intent—such as exit polls, pre-election polls, post-election polls, and handcounts—forensic analysts refer to it as a "red shift."[24] Since 2002, when the computers took over the counting, the red shift has been *pervasive*: election after election and with few exceptions, in competitive contests bearing national significance[25] the official votecount has been to the right of *every* baseline measure. We very rarely see the reverse, which we would call a "blue shift."[26] There is a tremendous amount of data and it all points in the same direction.[27]

---

[24] The term "red shift" was in fact coined by this author (with apologies to Herr Doppler) in reference to the exit poll-votecount disparities favoring Bush in E2004; it has been adopted into general usage when describing such disparities.

[25] Contests bearing national significance include, obviously, the federal elections for president, Senate, and House (where majority or super-majority control is at stake), but also key governorships, state administrative posts, and state legislative control. On rare occasions a contest without *direct* bearing on national politics—an example being the 2011 Wisconsin Supreme Court election—will take on national significance as a proxy or bellwether test of political strength. A more recent contest with great proxy significance—the special election for Georgia's Sixth Congressional District in June 2017—will be examined in Chapter VI.

[26] One fascinating example of such a blue shift was the 2017 Alabama Special Election for U.S. Senate between Republican Roy Moore and Democrat Doug Jones; it will be examined in Chapter VI.

[27] See Chapter VIII for several evidentiary studies, including: *The 2004 Presidential Election: Who Won the Popular Vote? An Examination of the Comparative Validity of Exit Poll and Vote Count Data* (2004); *Landslide Denied: Exit Polls vs. Vote Count 2006, Demographic Validity of the National Exit Poll and the Corruption of the Official Vote Count* (2007); *Fingerprints of Election Theft: Were Competitive Contests Targeted?* (2007); see also Freeman, S; Bleifuss, J: *Was the 2004 Presidential Election Stolen? Exit Polls, Election Fraud, and the Official Count*, Seven Stories Press 2006; and Miller, MC (ed): *Loser Take All; Election Fraud and the Subversion of Democracy, 2000-2008*, Ig Publishing 2008.

If, in noting the "ancient" dates of these studies, you encounter any temptation to comfort yourself with a "that was then, this is now" qualification, note as well that nothing of significance has been done at any point along the way to give current elections any more protection than the ones subject to these early forensic examinations. And indeed E2016, examined in Chapter V, was forensically the most egregious red-flag election to date. Evidence of a vulnerability and its exploitation gathered from 2004 applies with equal force to 2020, and indeed indefinitely until such time as the counting process is made public and observable.

From a forensic standpoint, much of our work goes into determining whether those baselines from which the official votecounts keep diverging are themselves valid. Naturally, *if you simply assume all votecounts are valid,* you will then look for reasons to dismiss any data that disagrees with them. You could, for example, disparage all the incongruent exit polls as "off again" because they "oversampled Democrats." However, we have examined specific exit poll samples and other baselines closely and found that such is not the case—the problem is definitely *not* that all these other measures of voter intent are chronically incompetent or corrupted.

In 2006, for instance, we examined the national exit poll sample and found that it was to the *right* of every other measure of the national electorate. We knew, therefore, that the massive red shift we found in the 2006 election could not have been a function of a faulty (i.e., left-skewed) exit poll baseline, leaving mistabulation of the votes as the only explanation for the shift that could not be discounted.[28] We went further in 2006 (and again in 2008) and, recognizing that competitive races are natural targets for rigging (the winner can be changed with a modest manipulation, yielding a high reward/risk ratio) while noncompetitive races are not (much higher risk factor: to change the winner you have to shift too high a percentage of votes to pass the smell test), we compared competitive with noncompetitive races relative to an identical baseline. We found that the more competitive a race the more likely it was to be red shifted—the correlation was dramatic.[29]

In 2010[30] we were able to compare hand-counted to computer-counted ballots in a critical U.S. Senate race and again found an outcome-altering red shift of the computer-counted votes, one that we were unable to explain by any factor other than strategically mistabulated votecounts.

More recently, in 2016, our analysis of the respective party primaries found that, while the exit poll results were consistently accurate throughout nearly all the Republican primaries, they were wildly and broadly inaccurate in the

---

[28] Simon J, O'Dell B: *Landslide Denied: Exit Polls vs. Vote Count 2006, Demographic Validity of the National Exit Poll and the Corruption of the Official Vote Count* (2007), https://codered2014.com/wp-content/uploads/2020/04/landslideDenied_v.9_071507.pdf.

[29] Simon J, et al: *Fingerprints of Election Theft: Were Competitive Contests Targeted?* (2007), https://codered2014.com/wp-content/uploads/2020/04/fingerprintsOfElectionTheft_2011rev_.pdf.

[30] Simon J: *Believe it (Or Not): The Massachusetts Special Election for U.S. Senate* (2010), https://codered2014.com/wp-content/uploads/2020/04/believeIt_OrNot_100904_2011rev_.pdf.

Democratic primaries, exhibiting a pervasive intra-party "red shift" to the detriment of Bernie Sanders. It seems very unlikely that the same pollsters, employing the same methodological techniques and interviewing voters at the same precincts on the same days, would be competent and consistently successful with Republicans but somehow incompetent and consistently unsuccessful with Democrats.[31]

In the 2016 general election, while the *national* exit poll was within the error margin for its sample size (i.e., accurate), the critical "swing" states that provided Trump's electoral college majority—including Wisconsin, Pennsylvania, Ohio, and North Carolina—were egregiously red-shifted, with poll-votecount disparities far outside the error margins. Florida and Michigan, which completed Trump's improbable table-run of must-win states, fell out of this dramatic-red-shift group only because of a geographical oddity: a tiny piece of each state crosses from the Eastern to the Central time-zone. This means the polls at the extreme western tips of the Florida panhandle and the Michigan upper peninsula close an hour later than those in the rest of the state—and exit polls were not posted until that time, an hour after the polls had closed in 99 percent of each state. This in turn permitted the "adjustment" of those polls almost all the way to congruence with the votecounts *prior* to public posting, effectively eliminating the tell-tale red shift.[32]

The pattern of an outcome-determinative red shift cluster *so concentrated in states where it mattered* defies both the laws of probability and attempts at benign explanation. There is hardly a democracy on earth where it would have passed muster.[33]

Exit poll-votecount and similar comparisons constitute an *extrinsic* analysis, comparing the votecounts with alternate measures of voter intent. Analysts have also, more recently, begun to employ a powerful tool of *intrinsic* measurement known as Cumulative Vote Share ("CVS") analysis—"intrinsic" because it measures and analyzes only the votecount itself.[34] A peculiar and

---

[31] This pattern in the 2016 primaries will be explored in greater detail in Chapter V. See also the work of Theodore de Macedo Soares at www.tdmsresearch.com.

[32] See Chapter V for a full analysis of the Election 2016 forensic data.

[33] See discussion of exit polls as verifiers in USAID's "Assessing and Verifying Election Results: A Decision-Maker's Guide to Parallel Vote Tabulation and Other Tools" at https://www.usaid.gov/what-we-do/democracy-human-rights-and-governance/technical-publications.

[34] See, e.g., the work of Wichita State University statistician Elizabeth Clarkson, at www.bethclarkson.com. See also "An Electoral System in Crisis," a 2016 paper by

consistent pattern has emerged from analysis of precinct-level votecount data from suspect elections: the cumulative vote share of the candidate who is the suspected beneficiary of votecount manipulation unexpectedly increases with increasing precinct size. This "CVS Upslope" does not appear to reflect either demographic or partisanship tendencies of the precincts. It does, however, fit perfectly with what would be a highly rational tactical decision to shift votes in larger rather than smaller precincts: the "splash" made by a vote theft of equal size is correspondingly smaller and less noticeable the larger the pool from which the votes are taken.

I hope that you will take the time to examine the studies included in the "Evidence and Analysis" chapter (Chapter VIII), all of which are fully accessible to the non-statistician. For now, the key point is that it is not just a few instances or an equivocal pattern—it is pervasive. It is well-nigh impossible to look at all this data gathered together and *not* emerge gravely concerned that elections have been systematically manipulated.

Q: What about for those of us who don't "get" statistics and numbers? Are there any other signs of foul play? What about a "smoking gun?"

A: It is not something that has been thought about or talked about much, but the vote counting process in the United States is *designed for concealment*. Most absurdly, the code that counts or miscounts votes has been ruled a corporate trade secret that cannot be divulged or examined under any circumstances. Take a moment to give that elevation of corporate over public rights—the utter concealment of a process that should by its very nature be a public trust—a chance to sink in.

Nor does the concealment stop with the code. *All* the "hard" evidence— memory cards, programming code, server logs, and actual cast ballots—is strictly off-limits to the public and, in most cases, to election administrators as well. It is precisely because of the secretive nature of the American vote counting process, and because all the hard evidence is inaccessible, that the forensic investigation of election authenticity perforce has come down primarily to numerical, statistical, and pattern analysis. Following along after the election circus with a forensic pooper-scooper (only, as you will see, to have all such evidence ignored or dismissed by the media and the powers-that-

---

Lulu Friesdat and Anselmo Sampietro, in collaboration with Fritz Scheuren, former president of the American Statistical Association, currently accessible at http://www.hollerbackfilm.com/electoral-system-in-crisis/.

be) is a rather ridiculous way to try to insure democracy. But until the public reclaims its right of access to voted-on ballots and the counting process, *it just happens to be the only way we've got.*

That said, such numerical, statistical, and pattern analysis is relied upon routinely in fields ranging from aerospace to economics, climate study, epidemiology and disease control. It is also routinely applied, often with the sanction of the government of the United States, to elections pretty much everywhere on Earth *other* than in the United States, periodically contributing to official calls for electoral investigations and indeed electoral re-dos.[35] Exit poll disparities—i.e., foreign correlates of the red shift—have factored in the overturning of elections from the Ukraine to Peru and are relied upon for validation of votecounts in Western democracies such as Germany.[36]

---

[35] See, e.g., Kharchenko N, Paniotto V: "Exit Polling in an Emergent Democracy;" *Survey Research Methods* (2010), Vol.4, No.1, pp. 31-42.

Although certain critics of reliance on exit polls in U.S. elections have argued that they are fundamentally different from exit polls elsewhere in the world—which are somehow designed, they say, to ferret out fraud while ours are not—no one has, to my knowledge, backed up that assertion with concrete comparisons.

The claim that foreign exit polls use larger samples, even if true, would, in and of itself, be a red herring, since error margins (whether purely mathematical "Margin of Error" [MOE] or the more encompassing "Total Survey Error" [TSE]) are correlates of sample size: a smaller sample has a larger MOE/TSE, and results that fall outside that margin are just as improbable as results that fall outside the smaller MOEs/TSEs said to be found abroad. The sample size, *whatever it may be*, yields an MOE/TSE and *that MOE/TSE* becomes the scale that we use to evaluate disparities. MOE/TSE-exceeding statistical red flags have exactly the same fraud-indicating probative value *here* as do MOE/TSE-exceeding statistical red flags abroad.

It must be acknowledged, however, that exit polls in the U.S. are to a significant extent dependent on a demographic weighting process that rests in turn on informed advance *estimations* of the particular electorate that will turn out for any given election. For various reasons, such estimates tend to be more precise in some situations (e.g., general elections with stable pre-election dynamics) and more susceptible to error in others (e.g., primary elections with high volatility and late movement).

Thus the practice of exit poll-based forensics requires an in-depth understanding of a variety of factors that may strengthen or weaken the probative value of any given exit poll or set of exit polls. This challenge will be revisited throughout this book.

[36] On the other side of the fence, repressive regimes such as Uzbekistan have seen fit to ban exit polls entirely, a nod to their utility as indicators of election theft. In 2016 the United States seemed to take a page from the Uzbekistani playbook, canceling all exit polling for the remaining states, including critical California, after a long string of unidirectional embarrassments in the first two dozen Democratic state primaries (see http://www.democraticunderground.com/12512018534; a search of the *New York Times* and *Washington Post* databases revealed no coverage of the cancellations).

There are also other, non-statistical signs of manipulation. In 2004, for example, in several battleground states touchscreen voters who attempted to vote for John Kerry found that the computers switched and recorded their vote for George Bush. The pattern of reports of vote flipping was over 10-to-1 in that direction.[37] You don't need a graduate course in statistics to recognize that unintentional "glitches" would *go both ways* and eventually (as the number of them increased) even out, fifty-fifty not ten-to-one.

In 2010 in a Democratic primary for U.S. Senate in South Carolina, run on paperless touchscreen voting computers (a.k.a. "DREs"), a "phantom" candidate, who had never campaigned and didn't even have a website, *received 59 percent of the statewide vote*, beating a well-known opponent, a state judge who after campaigning vigorously had pulled within seven percentage points of the far-right Republican incumbent in the tracking polls anticipating their November general election match-up. This showing in tracking polls attested to judge's high standing among Democratic voters in a solidly Republican state, a popularity that mysteriously disappeared at the counting of the votes. The shockingly defeated candidate brought his case— including the evidence that, where early and absentee votes were tallied on optical scanners (where, at least in theory, a paper ballot would be available for recounting), he had won handily—to the Democratic Party State Committee, which went into closed session and then voted overwhelmingly to shut down the investigation.[38]

More recently, in the 2017 Special Election Runoff for Georgia's 6th CD— another election counted primarily on paperless DREs, and the most expensive U.S. House race in history—the disparity between theoretically verifiable votes counted on optical scanners and those counted on unverifiable DREs was an eye-popping 44 percent. The Democratic candidate, Jon Ossoff, won the verifiable vote by a landslide 64 percent to 36 percent, only to lose the election to Republican Karen Handel when she shockingly won the unverifiable DRE-counted vote 58 percent to 42 percent. It was revealed that the entity

---

[37] See "Reports of vote switching from the 2004 national Election Incident Reporting System (EIRS)," at http://www.openvotingconsortium.org/files/project_evoting_vvf.pdf. The same phenomenon was more recently reported by Texas voters attempting to vote for Democrat Beto O'Rourke in E2018's U.S. Senate race and seeing their vote flip on-screen to Republican incumbent Ted Cruz.

[38] The story of this bizarre election, presented in greater detail at pp. 69-70, is the subject of the 2016 documentary feature film *I Voted?*, directed by Jason Grant Smith and co-produced by Katie Couric (see https://ivotedmovie.com). The lack of an official investigation ensured that benign and malignant explanations were never sorted out.

responsible for programming the vote-counting computers, the Election Center at Kennesaw State University, had known about and failed to correct major security breaches during the months preceding the election. When an advocacy group sought access to the Center's records as part of its suit to decertify the unverifiable, paperless DREs, it was further revealed that the Center had permanently erased all data and code pertaining to the programming of the election—four days after the filing of the suit.[39]

The past two decades, inaugurating the New American Century of computerized elections, are strewn with such bizarre, shocking, and anomalous results, virtually all of them favoring the more right-wing candidate or proposition.[40] Election integrity advocates have routinely been told to produce a "smoking gun" as a *prerequisite* to the launching of any governmental or journalistic investigation. Since memory cards, software, code, servers, voted-on ballots, and of course corporate correspondence are all regarded as strictly proprietary and off-limits to citizen investigation (and have an uncanny talent for getting shredded, wiped clean, or otherwise destroyed in those extremely rare instances in which that protective wall seems about to be scaled), this demand is an absurd Catch-22.

It really comes down to an inverted burden of proof. There is essentially an irrebuttable "presumption of innocence" when it comes to the secret process of vote counting in America. You would think that at *some* point and in *some* way the process itself, and those who control it and conceal its workings, would be called upon to produce *some* solid evidence that it is functioning honestly and accurately—and all of the time, not just some of the time—to translate collective voter intent into electoral results. You would be wrong.

Q: What about whistleblowers? Wouldn't at least a few who were involved in such an enterprise come forward?

A: They have. With a couple of chilling exceptions, they have been ignored. Clint Curtis testified under oath in a congressional hearing that, as a programmer, he was commissioned by the Republican speaker of the House of

---

[39] See http://thehill.com/policy/cybersecurity/357323-georgia-election-server-wiped-days-after-lawsuit and https://www.apnews.com/877ee1015f1c43f1965f63538b035d3f. The GA-6 election and its red flags will be examined in greater detail in Chapter VI.

[40] See Chapter VIII, Study VIII, for a timeline of "anomalies."

Florida to write a program designed to "flip the vote" in south Florida.[41] Having twice passed a lie-detector test administered by the retired chief polygraph officer for the state, Curtis was ignored. Apparently not ignored, however, was Raymond Lemme, the reporter actively investigating Curtis's allegations, who was found to have committed suicide—evidently, according to forensic photographs, by the always-popular method of stabbing and beating himself to death.[42]

Mike Connell, known as Karl Rove's "IT guru," who had set up the off-site SmarTech servers (in Chattanooga, Tennessee) that processed the decisive Ohio presidential vote in 2004, was compelled to testify in a lawsuit challenging the improprieties in that election.[43] After giving a sealed deposition (under the watchful eye of Rove's legal team) and being informed that he would likely be compelled to return the following month to provide further testimony, Connell was killed when the plane he was piloting crashed.

The attorneys for the plaintiffs in the case, who took seriously threats made by Rove against a wavering Connell, had requested but been denied FBI protection for their star witness. The official investigation of the crash was cursory at best, breaching standard protocol on several key fronts. It was left to Connell's *widow*, combing the crash site, to find the *earpiece* to Connell's notorious Blackberry, known to contain on its drive thousands of emails between Connell and Rove. The Blackberry itself vanished.[44] *It is not difficult to imagine other prospective witnesses and whistleblowers getting the message.*

Another factor to bear in mind is that, although the election-theft enterprise can have a massive, balance-of-power-altering effect, its execution requires

---

[41] See http://www.bradblog.com/?page_id=9437 and https://www.youtube.com/watch?v=kelVrADzPYU.

[42] See http://journals.democraticunderground.com/Time%20for%20change/402 and http://www.bradblog.com/?page_id=5479.

[43] *King Lincoln-Bronzeville Neighborhood Association et al v. J. Kenneth Blackwell et al,* filed 8/31/2006 in U.S. District Court, Southern District of Ohio. Reverend William Moss, the lead plaintiff in *Moss v. Bush,* an earlier legal challenge to Bush's 2004 election, died on August 2, 2005, following a stroke. While the death of Reverend Moss may best be filed in the "sometimes a cigar" drawer, the deaths of Lemme and, particularly, Connell have both the uncanny timing and the evidentiary hallmarks of something more troubling.

[44] See Worrall S: *Cybergate: Was The White House Stolen by Cyberfraud?* Amazon Digital Services, 2012 at https://www.amazon.com/dp/B0074NQ5UK/ref.

the participation of no more than a tiny cast of characters. This minimalism keeps the potential ranks of whistleblowers and leakers tiny as well.

And finally—as the cases of Chelsea Manning, Edward Snowden, Harold Martin, Reality Winner, *et al* illustrate—whistleblowers whose revelations tarnish the revered patina of American democracy are apt to be treated, by officialdom at least, not as heroes but as criminals.[45]

Former NSA contractor Reality Winner in particular deserves to be singled out, as her "crime" consisted of making public a single document exposing Russian penetration of a Florida-based voting equipment vendor prior to the 2016 election. Without Winner's action, it is highly doubtful whether the Russian efforts to directly target the voting and counting components of our elections would ever have come to light. Following on Winner's revelations, we now know that all 50 states and a variety of equipment were subject to Russian meddling, of great significance to historians if not to the Trump administration. Winner, meanwhile, sits in a jail cell serving a five-year sentence (Trump's prosecutors threatened her with 10 years and a quarter-million dollar fine, leveraging her into a plea deal), including time in solitary, in return for her vital service to our country. The unprecedently harsh punishment for Winner, a one-time offender (if we can call her an "offender" with a straight face), was celebrated by Trump's assistant attorney general for national security, John C. Demers, who said "I hope [the prosecutors'] success will deter others from similar unlawful action in the future."[46] When it comes to keeping threats to the security, integrity, and transparency of the electoral process under wraps, deterrence of those who might come forward is openly the name of the game.

---

[45] The Obama Administration was especially and unexpectedly harsh in its treatment of whistleblowers, exceeding all prior administrations in its prosecutorial zeal. See http://www.counterpunch.org/2015/10/09/mouths-wide-shut-obamas-war-on-whistleblowers/ and http://www.washingtonsblog.com/2015/05/obama-has-sentenced-whistleblowers-to-31-times-the-jail-time-of-all-prior-u-s-presidents-combined.html.

Although he did sign the 2012 Whistleblower Protection Enhancement Act, Obama's hard line with whistleblowers set the table for Trump, who most notably has recommended the identification, investigation and *execution* of the Ukraine phone call whistleblower (specifically accusing him of "treason" and suggesting that he be treated the way traitors were "in the old days") and, in an aside that would provide fodder for late-night comedians, publicly regretted having signed the Whistleblower Protection Act he never signed). Trump also matched Obama's eight-year total of whistleblower prosecutions in just his first two years in office (see *The Intercept's* report at https://www.youtube.com/watch?v=gvDDiKsChsM).

[46] See https://www.cnn.com/2018/08/23/politics/reality-winner-nsa-leaker-sentenced/index.html.

Q: Why has there been so little response from the "immune system"—election administrators, Democrats, the media? You'd think they'd be all over this.

A: Yes, you would. It's always baffling when an entire system with all its disparate players seems to acquiesce in a disaster that you would think any *one* of those players would step up to prevent. But it is hardly unprecedented. There was an array of institutions, for example, that witnessed the rise of the Nazis to power and—each for its own reasons, knowing better—stood passively and silently by.[47] There are fiefdoms (and psyches) to be protected and all else can appear rather abstract and distant to the individual and institutional players faced with a seemingly gradual progress toward what turns out only in retrospect to have been a catastrophe.

---

[47] Although it has been—until very recently, anyway—all but reflexive, when discussing contemporary politics, to eschew all parallels with Hitler or the Nazi era as "offensive" or in bad taste, the lessons of that all-too-real history are there for the taking and should not be ignored for their unpleasantness. Human nature alters and "evolves" less than it would please us to believe and there is much to be gleaned, from close observation of that very dark chapter in human history, about how that nature may play out on the grand political stage today and tomorrow.

It should be noted that a world of rational actors continued to pursue normal relations with the Third Reich for years after it had revealed its unmistakable monstrosity for all to see in its first of many nights of mass public book-burning (May 10, 1933), roaring book-fed bonfires unseen on Earth since the darkest days of the Inquisition.

One need not accuse a contemporary political actor of *being* a Nazi, or even sympathizing with them, to recognize analogous calculations and strategies in contemporary translation—old arsenic in new bottles—and chart to what end a failure to comprehend those calculations and strategies brought our not-so-far-removed predecessors.

The will to absolute power and control—whether sociopathic, psychotic, or merely existential in its genesis—seems to be a recurrent pestilence of civilized humanity, something like a retrovirus in its periodic reemergence. So, it seems, is the public appetite for the simplification and tidiness autocrats so often promise. Yet resistance will inevitably be encountered and will tend to grow in response to the increasingly harsh measures taken to overcome it, until a point of crisis is reached at which, if the "Reich" is to survive, all resistance must be crushed.

It is not unlike a game of all-in poker that can proceed quietly enough only to explode into the highest drama at a critical tactical or strategic moment. Thus are totalitarianisms born and reborn (though not necessarily to the heavy tread of jackboots goose-stepping in torchlight parades) and it would be naïve to think that, fortunate enough to be born into an exemplary democracy but less than a lifespan removed from the Third Reich, we ourselves are utterly immune to one or another variant of such a dynamic, that a *Fourth Reich* is utterly beyond the pale.

Q: OK, but can we look at some specifics? What about the officials who run and certify our elections? If elections are being stolen, isn't it right under their noses?

A: Of the election administrators, Democrats, and the media, the behavior of the election administrators is probably the easiest to explain. Election officials at every level are the front-line guardians of "voter confidence in the outcome of our elections," and they seek first and foremost to avoid controversy. When computers are doing the counting, vote totals magically appear at the end of the pipeline; humans with their potential biases and agendas have (apparently) not been involved; and at the surface everything looks clean and tidy. Election officials get to deal with a known and established vendor rather than with what amounts to an itinerant temporary and motley crew of vote-counters. Human counters need to be trained and supervised; computers need only to be programmed and, in the vast majority of cases, the corporate vendors take care of that.

The terrain is complex but it's not all that different from military contracting: often the official on the local level has little or no choice of which vendor will supply his or her equipment and technical services and, where there is a choice, the winning vendor will generally have done what vendors traditionally do to grease the wheels for the awarding of contracts and the unquestioning allegiance of the decision-making officials. Indeed in the election equipment racket, the wheel-greasing seems to have become rather egregious.[48] The technical demands of programming and testing opscans, BMDs and DREs are generally well beyond the capacities of the local officials who will be deploying them, so they have no real alternative to simply trusting the vendors and their contractors and technicians.[49]

This is all assuming, of course, that the election official is not himself more devoted to a private or partisan agenda than to the public trust. While the vast majority of election officials are almost certainly trying to be, within their

---

[48] See http://www.thestate.com/news/politics-government/article213558729.html; https://www.inquirer.com/politics/election/philly-voting-machines-city-controller-investigation-report-20190925.html; https://fairfight.com/wp-content/uploads/2019/07/Election-Systems-and-Software-ESS-Corruption-07162019.pdf; and https://www.newyorker.com/tech/annals-of-technology/how-voting-machine-lobbyists-undermine-the-democratic-process.

[49] The state of Oklahoma, which generally programs its own equipment, is a rare exception to this arrangement—one that, as we will explore in Chapter V, has bearing on our analysis of the 2016 primaries.

limited technical capacities, decent and fair administrators of their elections, we have also seen outrageous conflicts of interest, where such officials, as lofty as states' chief election administrators, have simultaneously been high-level *campaign* officials—most egregiously Katherine Harris in Florida 2000 and J. Kenneth Blackwell in Ohio 2004, not coincidentally the controversial and decisive states in each of those presidential elections.[50] More recently, as Georgia's secretary of state, in 2018 Brian Kemp was the overseer of his own red-flagged election[51] to the governorship.

The key point to recognize is that *it does not require corrupt, or even conventionally negligent, election administrators to certify a corrupted election.* They simply do not have either the incentive or the chops to dig deep enough to detect the exploits of non-administrative insiders or hackers.

Q: OK, how about the Democrats? They seem very reluctant to challenge or question even the most suspect electoral outcomes and have done little to promote serious reform measures even when they've had the power to do so.

A: A good way to liven up any gathering of understandably morose election transparency activists would be to ask everyone's view on why the Democrats have consistently acquiesced in highly suspect electoral defeats and been so unwilling to look into the role of computerized vote counting in the rightward veer of American politics. You will hear, in six-part harmony, explanations ranging from ignorance to naiveté to denial to intimidation to complicity, and of course stupidity. Frankly, it does boggle the mind. But let me contribute five observations that I hope will be of some help to our understanding:

> **1.** There is enormous pressure on "losing" candidates to concede, move on, and permit the machinery of government to go forward. Consider the plight of Al Gore, who in 2000 was the national popular vote *victor* by over half a million votes (as tabulated), and yet was pilloried for "holding the

---

[50] The specter of administrative bias reared its bipartisan head more recently in the 2016 Democratic primaries—where election officials from New York to Kentucky, Arizona, and California faced well-supported allegations of procedural bias in favor of party-anointed candidate Clinton—and in the administrative component of the successful efforts to thwart the recounting of votes in the election of Trump.

[51] See https://www.nytimes.com/2018/11/16/us/elections/georgia-governor-race-kemp-abrams.html. While egregious voter suppression engineered by Kemp was noted and decried, Kemp's *de facto* control over much of the vote *counting* process itself was all but ignored.

nation hostage" while he challenged the *537-vote* official Bush margin in the state of Florida. If popular vote *winner* Gore could be so effectively painted as a "sore loser," what of other candidates in less sympathetic circumstances?[52] For many such candidates, challenging an election, however suspect the results, can understandably be seen as an act of political suicide—both for themselves and, by association, for their party.

2. As for the Democrats successfully elected and serving in office, it would take a rare politician to challenge, or even support a challenge to, the legitimacy of the very system that brought him or her to power.[53] Anyone who has strolled the marble corridors of Congress should recognize that, recent hyperpartisan politics notwithstanding, it retains much of the feel of an elite club whose members are *all alike* underwritten by the grandeur of high public office and the legitimacy of the electoral process that bestowed it upon them. There is great reluctance to rock the boat at a foundational level or indeed to bite the electoral hand that has fed you.

3. Democrats depend on and are obsessed with *turnout*, particularly among the supposedly marginal voting groups that make up much of their constituency. With good reason. If turnout levels among the rich, the white, the old, the suburban homeowners were equaled among the poor, the non-white, the young, the urban, U.S. politics would scarcely even be competitive; it would be a Democratic rout. But these Democratic constituencies, under the best of circumstances, are reputed to need a lot more prodding to cast a ballot than do their Republican counterparts, and

---

[52] John Kerry, still haunted a decade later by his prompt concession in E2004 (he had accepted $15 million in donations specifically earmarked for legal challenge of suspect electoral results), spoke candidly about these pressures in a remarkable 2015 interview with *New Yorker* editor David Remnick:
http://www.newyorker.com/magazine/2015/12/21/negotiating-the-whirlwind.

[53] I am waiting still for a *victorious* candidate to step to the podium for his or her acceptance speech and say something like the following:

"I am grateful for your votes and the trust you have placed in me today. But if I am to serve you in good conscience I need to *know* that I was in fact your choice, and the secret vote counting system that has given me this apparent victory bestows no such knowledge on you or on me.

Therefore I am requesting that, before this election is certified and before I take office, there be a full public hand count of the ballots [impossible, of course, if DREs were part of the counting system], and I am asking you as citizens and voters to consider this observable counting process to be your right and your duty in every election in our proud democracy."

America's first *sore-winner*: a genuine elevation of the public trust over immediate political self-interest; a "Man Bites Dog" headline and a potent career booster to boot.

Democratic strategists fear that playing up any concerns about the honesty of elections and vote counting will discourage and lose these potential voters, many of whom are already skeptics when it comes to the fairness of "the system." And there is indeed evidence that massive turnout sometimes does overwhelm the rig, which only reinforces Democratic willingness to continue playing on a tilted table what is in the long run bound to be a losing game.

4. In virtually all cases and for obvious reasons, election rigging is *designed* to pass the smell test. Highly competitive elections are targeted, where a shift of just a few percent of the votes can reverse the outcomes. There are generally "benign" explanations for these outcomes—speculations about such factors as the role of money, endorsements, gaffes, and voter turnout (now ironically including *overt* vote suppression via selective purges, diminished access, and restrictive Voter-ID laws). For any given competitive election it is ordinarily possible (and of course psychologically desirable, if not imperative) to find *some* reason, other than computerized manipulation, for disappointing and/or unexpected results.[54] *It is the pervasively one-way pattern into which all these individual elections fall that is inexplicable without reference to rigging.*

Falsely reassured as they have been by the partial electoral victories of 2006; 2008 (which were both the results of bizarre 11th-hour *political* shifts that appeared to overwhelm the rig[55]); 2012 (where credit appears to be due principally to covert intervention by Anonymous[56]); and, on the surface, 2018 (where it is highly doubtful that a GOP hold of the House would have passed even the stuffed-nose smell test in light of Trump's osmium-balloon unpopularity and the huge surge in off-year turnout), the Democrats have consistently ignored or dismissed this *pattern*, and that behavior remains to be explained. It is worth noting, however, that although Democrats could obviously be portrayed as the victims of

---

[54] In fact, even the occasional *noncompetitive* election shocker—e.g., Rawl-Greene in 2010, Cantor-Brat in 2014—can manage to be explained away.

[55] In 2006 the Foley and related GOP September sex scandals; in 2008 the mid-September collapse of Lehman Brothers and the subsequent market crash. Both dramatically altered the electoral dynamics: in 2006, for instance, the Democratic margin in the Cook Generic Congressional Ballot jumped from 9% in the first week of October to 26% the week of the election, a Republican free-fall of epic proportions; a similar fate overcame McCain in the wake of the economy's September 2008 collapse. Manipulations calibrated and deployed prior to these unexpected events would have foundered in the political sea-changes.

[56] This under-reported event is explored in greater detail in Chapter III.

election rigging in America, they are firmly entrenched in the corridors of power and would remain so even as a minority party under Karl Rove's (pre-Trump) projected "40-year dynasty" of Republican rule.

Election rigging, targeting primary as well as general elections and skillfully applied, can transform (and, copious evidence suggests, has already transformed) the American political spectrum, sliding the whole edifice further and further to the right, *without in any way disturbing the two-party system and the power duopoly it bestows on Democrats and Republicans alike*. It is not at all clear that corporate trough-feeding Democrats would care to jeopardize that arrangement, opening the electoral doors to progressives, mavericks, and third parties.[57] *The true victims of election rigging in America are not the Democrats but the uninformed and disenfranchised American people, and ultimately public sovereignty itself.*

5. Finally, there is religion. I don't mean here belief in a deity but rather a secular faith of equal intensity. To illustrate I'd like to recount an experience I had at a national conference on media reform in 2007. At a panel session I publicly asked Cornell Belcher, at the time chief pollster for the Democratic National Committee, a question about poll-votecount disparities and the red shift. Having stated flat-out that the red shift could not be attributable to any problem with vote counting (i.e., election theft), he then added this curious observation, which I give from memory:

> "You know, it's odd but we have the same problem with our own internal polling: in important races, when our polls show our guy [the Democratic candidate] up by 10 percent, we've learned that we need to regard the race as a dead-heat toss-up."

Well. What exactly is to be made of *that*? Such "internal" polls are designed not for political salesmanship but for *maximum accuracy*; they inform the party where support is needed, not needed, or likely to be wasted—where vital campaign dollars should and should not be spent. When such internal polls are consistently "off" in the neighborhood of 10 percent, all sorts of alarm bells should be ringing and ringing loud.

---

[57] Indeed, many continue to accuse the Democratic Party establishment of having employed a variety of hi-jinx to close the electoral doors to the campaign of progressive candidate Bernie Sanders in the 2016 nomination battle.

It takes a religious belief in the sanctity of an entirely unseen process, and everything we so desperately want that process to stand for, to be deaf to those bells. After I pointed this out, Belcher then restated flat-out that the 10 percent disparity between his internal polls and election outcomes could not possibly be caused by election rigging. It felt like something out of *Inherit The Wind* or perhaps *Elmer Gantry*: "Brothers! Sisters! Do ye *believe*?!"[58]

Q: And the media? This is potentially the biggest story of their lives. Isn't the "Fourth Estate" traditionally one of the most important guardians of democracy?

A: Many of us retain a warm spot for the American press still left over from the days of Watergate, when Woodward and Bernstein, *The Washington Post, The New York Times,* and even the networks seemed to be among the big heroes. It wasn't quite that simple in reality, but the impression of both a heroic and a liberal press has been slow to fade, especially with the "liberal" label being flogged mercilessly by the right-wing media machine even as that machine came to dominate both talk radio and newspaper ownership.

Fast forward to 2020: the mainstream media (MSM) is almost entirely a subsidiary of mega-corporations,[59] news budgets are slashed to the bone, opinions (often shouted) have displaced reporting and investigation,

---

[58] *Esquire* blogger Charlie Pierce has spoken brilliantly to this phenomenon, writing:

"[G]iven that there is overwhelming evidence of a national campaign to suppress the potential vote through law, why should we not believe there is a parallel effort to influence votes after they are cast? Why should we believe that the national campaign to rig an election is purely legal, and not technological? The only reason is that *we don't want to believe it*. The will not to believe is the shifting sand beneath the unstable entire architecture of American Exceptionalism.

Because our attachment to the idea is theological, and not empirical, we can look neither at our history nor our politics honestly. Eventually the lies pile up, one atop the other . . . Eventually, the elections become electronic Kabuki. 'Our elections must be honest, not because we make them so, but simply because they are *ours*. It will all work out right in the end because this is America, fk yeah, the shining city on a hill.' Faith eventually undermines reality. We start believing in spirits and incantations. And then we fall, hard." (at http://www.esquire.com/blogs/politics/american-exceptionalism-14056595#ixzz2AdeYV3y2).

[59] As of 2012, 90% of the media in America was under the control of six corporations, with media control becoming only more consolidated since. See http://www.businessinsider.com/these-6-corporations-control-90-of-the-media-in-america-2012-6 .

entertainment is the order of the day, and there are some insidious limits on the stuff that is, as the *Times* continues to put it, "fit to print."

That said, it is still astounding how impervious the MSM has been to this story. We have it, off the record, from several top journalists that their employers have flat-out prohibited them from writing or speaking on the matter of computerized election theft or reviewing any of the evidence that it is occurring.

The MSM has what seems to be a "rule" on this: it's OK to make noise about the potential *vulnerability* of the machines in the run-up to elections (Lou Dobbs, for example, was all over this right up through Election Night in 2006; and we witnessed a virtual repeat in the days preceding E2012 and again in 2016[60]). But *following* the election, when evidence pointing to actual manipulation is made available by forensic analysts, all coverage of such a possibility is *verboten.*

Omerta is the word that comes to mind, an unwritten code of silence. In 2004, when this story was "fresh," Keith Olbermann had the temerity right after the election to start covering what had happened in Ohio, and actually began to dig into things a bit.[61] He wrote to me that he was "very interested" in the statistical evidence that we had gathered. He devoted several powerful, widely-viewed, and very enthusiastically received segments to it and then . . . POOF! He was off on a two-week vacation of which there had been no prior mention. And when he came back . . . not another word, ever. The biggest story, by a factor of ten, of Olbermann's professional career and he walks away mid-sentence?! It should be obvious that there are some powerful forces at work here set on making sure this story never gets legs.

---

[60] See, e.g., Zeynep Tufekci, "The Election Won't Be Rigged. But It Could Be Hacked," NY *Times* 8/12/16; Bryan Clark, "An easy-to-find $15 piece of hardware is all it takes to hack a voting machine," *aol.com* 8/11/16; Ben Wofford, "How to Hack an Election in 7 Minutes," *Politico,* 8/5/16; etc.: all well-written articles; all, by focusing exclusively on outsider hacking and ignoring vulnerability to insider rigging, woefully wide of the mark.

[61] See https://www.youtube.com/watch?v=JkTztPol5_Y for several clips of his "Countdown" show, and http://www.nbcnews.com/id/6442857/ns/msnbc-about_msnbc_tv/t/countdown-keith-olbermann-nov/ and http://www.nbcnews.com/id/6452480/ns/msnbc-about_msnbc_tv/t/countdown-keith-olbermann-nov/#.XcxlzdWIbIU for show transcripts.

And I might as well add that it's not just the MSM. The *progressive* media—ranging from *The Nation* to *Mother Jones* to *The Progressive Populist*—have all taken a virtually complete pass. In their pages they continue to discuss—and bemoan—election dynamics and the "new politics" of first the Tea Party and now the Trump Era, without an iota of attention paid to even the possibility that these bizarre and troublesome results may have something to do with a digital thumb on the electronic counting scale, not so much as a hint that there may be something to question or investigate.

This is perhaps the most mystifying thing of all: watching the progressives of America commit political suicide, as their media buy into a rigged game and seem perpetually to be discussing their own culpability for the latest political setbacks, shocking routs, and disasters—while their entire agenda goes DOA. As far as I can tell, apart from the Wall of Denial itself, the fear in these quarters is *marginalization*, that even mentioning the possibility of actual electronic election rigging will forfeit their hard-earned place at the "serious journalism" table or—in the case of groups such as Common Cause or People For The American Way, the ACLU and even VerifiedVoting—the "serious advocacy" table. If that risk seems exaggerated, simply recall the fate of Dan Rather, a titanic media figure permanently exiled after stepping "out of bounds" regarding George W. Bush's National Guard records. As with the whistle-blowers, even a single such demise sends a powerful and unambiguous message to the rest.

From his place of exile (*Dan Rather Reports* on the little-watched HDNet), Rather himself took on at least some of the story in a program that aired in October 2011.[62] But journalism is classic groupthink and, until you have *more than one* brave soul willing to step concurrently into the breach, the story generally dies on the vine. No one followed Rather's lead. Jon Stewart once questioned the technology in his inimitable way on *The Daily Show*, Garry Trudeau in *Doonesbury*, Scott Adams in *Dilbert*, and I hope they (and/or some of their colleagues) will come back to it. Much more recently, John Oliver devoted a mostly excellent and quite entertaining 19 minutes of *Last Week Tonight* to the vagaries of voting machines, though again steering clear of evidence of actual theft and leaving viewers with the unfortunate misimpression that paper ballots would secure our elections.[63] Lee Camp has

---

[62] Dan Rather: *Das Vote: Digital Democracy in Doubt*, HDNet TV at http://www.huffingtonpost.com/dan-rather/digital-democracy-in-doub_b_774137.html (see link to *iTunes* video download at end of article).

[63] See https://www.youtube.com/watch?v=svEuG_ekNT0.

been a good deal edgier and more persistent on RT's *Redacted Tonight*. Sporadic eyebrow-raising and partial throat-clearing is better than total silence, but it goes only so far and that is not close to far enough given the massive inertias involved.

Ironically, among many in the progressive media, the attitude seems to be, "If there were anything seriously wrong, the *Democrats* would be all over it" (this from the same people who regularly pillory the Democrats as political sellouts!). So, in a classic and deadly illustration of Bystander's Syndrome (action is distasteful or risky and we can each convince ourselves that someone *else* will "call 911"), everyone sort of sits around waiting for someone else to stick out his or her neck. And about the only press willing to do that are web-based sites such as *BradBlog* and *OpEdNews*. They merit high praise indeed for their persistence. But in America if a story doesn't make it to the *Times* or the networks, it's still a tin-hat conspiracy theory, no matter how well presented and documented. Look at how long it took us to take seriously allegations of performance-enhancing drugs in baseball. Look at how long, even after whistleblower Harry Markopolos had stepped forward, Bernie Madoff continued to operate his Ponzi scheme.

With elections the stakes are immensely higher and the fear that *everything will fall apart* if the truth is rigorously pursued is rather paralyzing. To put it slightly differently, investigation would lead to *knowledge* and knowledge would mandate *action*, an inexorable process once begun. But no individual operating within the vast system of American politics can imagine what action he or she might take—both the personal blowback and the national earthquake would be too catastrophic.[64] So the morally compelling but pragmatically daunting "action imperative" itself paradoxically operates to block the road of investigation at its very beginning: "Look at where we might wind up if we went there, so we won't go there."

---

[64] It is perhaps instructive to compare the 544-day saga of "Deflategate," the national crisis that arose regarding the air pressure in Tom Brady's footballs. In America, football *matters*! The pounds-per-square-inch in the footballs used by Brady, and the possible impact of that number's manipulation on performance and wins and losses, was frequently the lead story not just of sports sections but of network *news* programs.

Footballs were impounded (if they had been voting machines or memory cards, the argument that they belonged to the *Patriots* and therefore could not be examined would have prevailed), as were cell phones, emails, etc.; many millions of dollars were spent investigating and litigating.

It was fascinating; it was entertaining; "important" without being "too important," without threatening a 9.6 national earthquake. It was, in short, the perfect story.

To get back to the media, I wrote in 2004 that when the autopsy of American democracy is performed the cause of death will be given as media silence. What I've seen in the 16 years since only strengthens that prediction. To me, in fact, the American media have the most to answer for of all the actors in this tragedy. Those actually doing the rigging—whether it's a Rovean figure playing God or some cadre of domestic true-believers, operatives, or foreign agents— are in a sense "doing their job," just like a lineman "holding" in football to protect the quarterback. The media's job is to *spot the foul*, get at and promulgate the truth. And *they* are the ones who are *not* doing their job. Individually by the hundreds, and collectively as a force, they have served as passive enablers. They appear to be either in deep denial, anaesthetized, or content with a sham democracy, which in many cases would suit their ultimate corporate masters just fine.[65]

I have reached out personally and passionately (and more or less temperately) to a goodly number of media movers and shakers, from top reporters, to well-respected opinion writers, to editors and publishers. Here, for example, is an email I sent in the summer of 2017 to David Remnick, the editor of *The New Yorker*, who and which have been admirably persistent in their opposition to and excoriation of virtually all things Trump. I wrote to him in the wake of the Charlottesville incident, to which he had responded with an anti-Trump column of particular pungency, entitled "The Divider."

Dear David -

Yet another Trumpian outrage (Charlottesville, but does it really matter which one?). Yet another Remnickian outcry ("The Divider," but ditto). "Resist! RESIST!!" you implore. Yes, OK, in every way we can. I assume we're ruling out guns and bombs, so then parades, and petitions, protests, poll responses, and personal acts of decency and fairness and kindness—for whatever that may get us.

And then ... we get to *vote*.

And those votes become strings of 1s and 0s, counted behind an impenetrable curtain in the pitch-dark of cyberspace by the likes of ES&S, Dominion (oh Lord), and Command Central (Yessir!).

---

[65] I suspect also that there is a shared Hamiltonian sneer among some highly educated professional elites who, subconsciously at least, regard public sovereignty *per se*—in an era in which so much of that public finds the NFL, DWTS, or the Kardashians infinitely more absorbing than the facts and nuances underlying policy debates—as not especially worthy of respect, trust, or electoral protection.

Those 1s and 0s "elected" not just Donald Trump but—if you can bring yourself to consider the forensic evidence, the reams of statistical pattern data (relied upon for everything from astronomy to agronomy)—enough right-wingers at both federal and state levels to give the radicalized GOP the majorities it needs to keep enabling him straight over what would be, if our elections were *honest*, the electoral cliff.

So you tell us to "Resist!" but what are you doing to protect our primary—indeed only—effectual means of doing so? On this you have dropped the ball—consistently, disastrously. Indeed you are playing a critical supporting role in this tragedy. All the worse because you have put such superb eloquence and passion into service describing and decrying it.

David, this is not beyond remedy. You'd have to get on the stick though—hard and soon. Start making it a *regular feature* (you know that, in our ADHD nation, once or twice won't do it)—a *running exploration of the rot at the core of the most foundational protocol of our democracy, and a clarion call for the restoration of public, observable vote counting. In time for 2018 and 2020.*

Blame it on the Russians if you must (though insiders have been working this game since HAVA passed in 2002, at least—long before the Russians took an interest). Whatever. Just please recognize that: 1) "Resistance" comes down to elections; 2) Elections come down to the counting of votes; 3) Vote counting in the U.S. is absurdly vulnerable to computerized manipulation and alteration; 4) The political universe is well stocked with ends-justify-the-means true-believers, profiteers, cynics, *and* nihilists more than willing and demonstrably able to exploit that vulnerability; and, most important, 5) This whole damned nightmare could and would end with one stinking honestly and accurately—i.e., publicly and observably—counted election.

Ask the Dutch. Ask the Germans. Ask the Irish. Ask the Canadians. Ask the Norwegians. Is America really that exceptionally stupid as to go it alone in not getting it? Will it be America's fate to succumb to fascism by fraud—because its defenders of democracy could not bear to look seriously and open-mindedly at the evidence of how it was happening?

With appreciation for all your good work. With a shred of hope. With best wishes –
Jonathan

I write many such missives—sometimes as many as a dozen a day, and there have been thousands of days since this barn door was opened and the horses began to head for the hills. I rarely expect answers and my expectations are rarely disappointed. You could overpopulate a small city with bright, thoughtful, patriotic, nonresponding shoulder-shruggers.

To Remnick's and *The New Yorker's* mighty and everlasting credit, staff writer Sue Halpern did ultimately take on the crisis of election (in)security (though generally steering clear of evidence of actual votecount manipulation) in a tenacious and probing series of pieces beginning in 2018 and still ongoing. [66]

I'm not sure how much intimidation is being meted out or even what quarter it may be coming from, but isn't it time more of us found the courage to risk our jobs, or even our lives, in service to the truth? That courage is surely not unprecedented in our nation's history and it is sorely needed now if what the courageous have fought and died for is to survive.

Q: Is it really possible, in a major election, to "count every vote as cast?"

A: In theory, yes; in practice, no. There is going to be a bit of "noise" in any system that attempts to count and aggregate large numbers. So "count every vote as cast" is a quixotic and misleading standard. "Noise" is not the problem and neither are so-called "voter" frauds or genuine "glitches." Computerized election rigging is not about miscounting a vote here and there, nor even about a few people voting twice or in the wrong district. Exploits such as double voting and impersonational voting are open to both parties; are at once low-yield, risky (being punishable as felonies), and labor-intensive; are extremely rare; virtually never alter electoral outcomes; and in the end, over time and space, wind up a wash. *You can't take over and hold onto America by hand.*

Nor will "glitches"—which, with the non-intentionality of a flipped penny, break 50-50, yielding no net advantage—turn that trick (indeed we would *accept* computerized counting if truly inadvertent "glitches" were the only problem). *Only deliberate systemic misrecording of votes and/or deliberate mistabulation at the aggregate level can do it, and only computers and their programmers have that power.*

It is beyond ironic that Republican-controlled state legislatures throughout the country, many of which came to power via the highly suspect 2010 election,

---

[66] See, e.g., https://www.newyorker.com/news/dispatch/election-hacking-lessons-from-the-2018-def-con-hackers-conference. I don't know what part, if any, my urging may have played in this.

have in the past few years enacted restrictive Voter-ID laws, several of which have already been ruled unconstitutionally discriminatory by the courts, to deal with a putative epidemic of "voter fraud" that turns out to be virtually nonexistent.[67] Then President Trump himself, hot on the trail of the "millions of illegal voters" who he imagined crashed the polls and cost him his prized popular-vote victory, set up an "Election Integrity" Commission—co-chaired by Mike Pence and Kris Kobach, the voter suppression-crusading former Kansas secretary of state—to get to the bottom of E2016's massive "voter fraud."[68]

---

[67] The gates were opened to this templated campaign of voter suppression by another in a series of 5-to-4 party-line U.S. Supreme Court decisions. The 2013 holding in *Shelby County v. Holder*, gutting critical Section 4(b) of the Voting Rights Act of 1965, left states that sported a long Jim Crow history (ironically under mostly Democratic state administrations) free to install *new* Jim Crow laws and regulations without federal approval. See generally, Berman A: *Give Us the Ballot: The Modern Struggle for Voting Rights in America*. New York: Farrar, Straus and Giroux (2015); at https://www.amazon.com/dp/1250094720/ref.

[68] The commission was stacked with Republican heavy-hitters and included a few window-dressing Democrats who seemed to have little idea what they were there for, and no success at all in getting briefed by Kobach or the Republican majority. It held a couple of public hearings—including a notable one in New Hampshire at which the vulnerability of computerized counting to fraud was amazingly brought to the attention of the stunned commissioners—and was shortly thereafter disbanded—having issued no report, and of course not having found those lurking hordes of illegal voters, but having first attempted a garishly transparent data grab, requisitioning state voter databases and virtually every bit of information states possessed about their voters (very useful for fine-tuning voter-suppression schemes *and* votecount manipulations).

It would have been interesting to be a fly on the wall when the decision was made to disband. One can imagine the following Trump-Kobach exchange of views:

Trump: "Find me those 5 million illegal voters—or you're fired!"

Kobach: "We sure as hell tried, Mr. President. Just came up a wee bit short."

Trump: "How short?"

Kobach: "Well, about 4,999,995 voters. But here's the thing, sir: if you want to get re-elected so you can continue making America great again, it's going to take a bunch of thumbs (I'll be honest with you, sir: Rasmussen's bogus; you're still at 40%), including of course some serious voter suppression. Now that's the kind of thing you want to do quietly, not shine a big Look-At-Me spotlight on. Fun as it is going after those illegals and collecting all that cool state data, Mike pointed out to me the other day that all this commission is accomplishing right now is drawing unwanted attention and opposition to our schemes (I mean 'patriotic purpose')."

Trump: "So I should shut it down and let you go back to suppressing voters, and whatever else you've got up your sleeve, in peace and quiet?"

Kobach: "Yeah, that's pretty much the 1 and 0 of it—as long as you let me off without having to write a report, sir."

Yet manifestly vulnerable secret vote counting by radically partisan corporations can go merrily on its unchallenged way, pervasive red-shift disparities notwithstanding. There is a real Alice-In-Wonderland feel to it all.

Q: How does America stack up against other long-established democracies when it comes to electoral integrity?

A: Not very well. Indeed, in a joint study conducted by Harvard and the University of Sydney, the U.S. elections of 2012 and 2014 scored *dead last* among the group of 54 long-established democracies.[69] In 2019 the U.S. came in behind *every* European democracy except Turkey (a democracy in name only) and tied with Mexico and Panama. Particularly revealing was each nation's electoral integrity score plotted against per capita GDP.[70] To a significant degree, electoral integrity follows national wealth; in essence, free and fair elections are a commodity that wealthier nations can generally better afford. In the graph of all the world's democracies, the U.S. appears as an egregious outlier far below the wealth/integrity curve: a great deal of wealth *not* being spent here on democracy, at least not on its electoral component. This of course squares with the sadly dilapidated state of America's voting equipment and with the budgetary impracticality of beefing up the invitingly low levels of administrative scrutiny and cyber-security.

A recent foreign example serves to place in context the low standard of fidelity to which the process of counting votes is held in America. The Constitutional Court of Austria held, on July 1, 2016, that the mere possibility of irregularities in the counting process (counting in some places was begun before the prescribed cast of observers was present) was enough to void that nation's presidential election results and necessitate a new election.[71] It was not necessary for the challenger[72] to prove fraud or actual manipulation, merely a

---

[69] See "The Electoral Integrity Project: Why Elections Fail and What We Can Do About It" at https://sites.google.com/site/electoralintegrityproject4/projects/expert-survey-2/the-year-in-elections-2015 (see also https://www.dropbox.com/s/csp1048mkwbrpsu/Electoral%20Integrity%20Worldwide.pdf?dl=0 for the full 2019 Report).

[70] The Electoral Integrity Project 2015 Report (https://www.dropbox.com/s/ziav8ce6c63lx0k/The%20Year%20in%20Elections%202015_pages.compressed.pdf?dl=0), p. 30.

[71] See https://www.washingtonpost.com/15c1c843-368b-44a5-8d99-764fa88c52d8_story.html .

[72] That the challenger, and beneficiary of the Court's ruling, was an extreme right-winger may be food for cynical thought, but we would like to believe that the principles

lapse of full transparency such that outcome-altering manipulation might have occurred unobservably. Quite obviously, if U.S. elections were held to such a standard, our unobservable vote counting process would spawn a continual string of electoral re-dos, until it was replaced with an observable process.

Several nations have now taken that step proactively. Moved in large part by the odors emanating from E2016 in the U.S. and by a rapidly growing recognition of the risks associated with concealed, computerized vote counting, the Netherlands and Norway decided, without much in the way of hand-wringing or equivocating, to count their 2017 national elections manually in public—joining such democracies as Germany, France, Ireland, New Zealand, and Canada as countries that count their national elections at least primarily in public and observably.

Q: Who are these corporations that count our votes? What makes you think they care who wins elections?

A: Democratic elections should by their very nature be a public trust. Instead, virtually the entire vote-counting process in America has been outsourced to a few private corporations and contractors that operate behind a heavy screen of legal and administrative proprietary protections. That's bad enough. The actual history of the shape-shifting electronic voting industry and the cast of characters that has controlled it is still worse.[73]

Republican Senator Chuck Hagel owned a good part of the outfit that counted the votes electing and then returning him to the U.S. Senate in Nebraska. Walden O'Dell, CEO of Diebold and a major Bush supporter and fundraiser, in 2003 penned a letter to potential donors in which he stated that he was "committed to helping Ohio deliver its electoral votes to the president next

---

of electoral integrity and vote counting transparency were upheld by the justices without regard to partisan political impact.

[73] See https://www.verifiedvoting.org/resources/voting-equipment/ for a comprehensive cataloguing of voting equipment vendors and their products. See also http://blackboxvoting.org/reports/voting-system-technical-information/ for an examination of the activities, pedigree, and affiliations of the principal vendors. The cast of characters is highlighted in Victoria Collier's 2012 article "How to Rig an Election" (*Harper's* 10/26/2012, as reprinted at http://readersupportednews.org/opinion2/277-75/14198-focus-how-to-rig-an-election).

More recently, election transparency advocate Jennifer Cohn has detailed the corruption at the core of our voting equipment/election administration complex in a series of well-researched articles: e.g., https://medium.com/@jennycohn1/americas-electronic-voting-system-is-corrupted-to-the-core-1f55f34f346e.

year." O'Dell was seen to be in a unique position to fulfill his commitment, as Diebold was the supplier and programmer of Ohio's voting computers in E2004. Right-winger Bob Urosevich, founder of Election Systems and Software (ES&S), was also the first CEO of Diebold Election Systems (a subsidiary of O'Dell's Diebold, Inc.); his brother, Todd, was Vice-President of ES&S.[74]

As of 2012 the vote-counting corporations had been whittled down to two principals—ES&S and the whimsically named Dominion Voting—that between them controlled the computers that counted the vast majority of the votes in America. When you trace the pedigree of these vendors, every road seems to lead back to the right wing: wealthy Texas oilmen, fanatical Fundamentalists, major Republican donors, and prominent Republican politicians. In fact, Hart Intercivic, a junior partner to ES&S and Dominion, had a board majority controlled by an investment firm known as H.I.G. Capital, which in turn boasted Mitt Romney, his wife, son, and brother as major investors through the closely-held equity fund Solamere.[75] Then there are the satellite corporations that do much of the actual programming, servicing, and deploying of the machines— outfits like Command Central, Triad, LHS, Kennesaw State's Center for Elections Systems, and the late Mike Connell's own SmarTech—secretive to outright impenetrable. Except for Diebold (R.I.P., though a fair amount of its equipment is still in service), virtually all these outfits are privately held and rather small (ES&S has only 450 employees; Command Central was operating out of a Minnesota strip mall; Kennesaw State was essentially a one-man show), and thus not subject to the kinds of regulation and scrutiny that might apply in the case of publicly-traded corporations. It is, all told, one of the shadowiest industries in America.

All the self-promotion and self-congratulation on a sleek website like Dominion's cannot quite obscure the fact that what these Lords of Elections are really saying is, "You may as well trust us. You have no other choice." While the privatization of the vote-counting process gives rise to a situation in which electronic thumbs on the scale could in theory be sold to the highest bidder, the partisanship of the outfits that program, distribute, and service the voting

---

[74] See http://www.sourcewatch.org/index.php/Diebold_Election_Systems. Bob Urosevich turned up again more recently as Managing Director of Scytl, a Barcelona-based firm that has taken control of electronic voter registration databases in a number of states, including several where targeted electronic purges were alleged in the 2016 primaries.

[75] See Ungar C: "Romney-linked Voting Machine Company Will Count Votes in Ohio and Other Crucial Swing States," (10/26/2012) at http://www.salon.com/2012/10/23/romney_linked_voting_machine_company_to_count_votes_in_ohio/ .

equipment is more likely to translate in practice to *politically selective access* or, in the language of criminologists, opportunity and means. The consistently one-sided forensic evidence in the elections of the computerized era supports this assessment. It really *is* the man in the magician's suit with the "Vote For So-And-So" button, if not on his lapel then on the inside of his sleeve, who takes our ballots and disappears behind the curtain.

Q: You state that virtually all the anomalies, disparities, and shifts are in one direction, favoring the right-wing candidates and positions. But what about 2006, 2008, and 2012? Those were Democratic victories! Why would forces on the right rig to lose?

A: They didn't rig to lose, they rigged to win—or, more precisely, *to maximize winnings and minimize losses within bounds of acceptable risk of detection.* With a single very odd exception, to be discussed in the next chapter, *every* post-HAVA biennial election from 2002 forward has exhibited a red shift either nationally or in the key states and districts, or both.[76] The red shifts in 2006 and 2008 were in fact massive but, in both 2006 and 2008, unexpected 11th-hour events (in 2006 the lurid sex scandals and cover-ups enveloping Republican Congressman Mark Foley and several other prominent right-wingers; and in 2008 the September collapse of Lehman Brothers, which ushered in the Great Recession the day after Republican presidential candidate John McCain had proclaimed the economy "strong"), dramatically altered the electoral dynamics.

In 2006, for instance, the Democratic margin in the nonpartisan Cook Generic Congressional Ballot ("On Election Day will you vote for the Republican or Democratic candidate for Congress in your district?") jumped from 9 percent in the first week of October to 26 percent the week of the election, a Republican free-fall of epic proportions; a similar fate overcame McCain in the wake of the economy's nosedive on Bush's watch late in 2008. These leftward political sea changes would have swamped a rightward manipulation that turned out, in light of the unforeseen events, to be under-calibrated; and they came too late to permit rescue via recalibration and redeployment of tainted memory cards and malicious code.

---

[76] In E2002 the red shift could not be measured because the exit polls were withheld from public view. That it *existed* is clear from the fact that the plug was pulled on the exit polls because they were so far "off" that the networks could not come up with a plausible explanation for the magnitude of the red-shift disparities in key races (e.g., Chambliss/Cleland in Georgia, Hagel/Matulka in Nebraska).

The devil is in such details, but these red-shift red flags were ignored, trampled in the 2008 Obama victory parade. It is of course possible for Democrats and left-leaning candidates to win elections and there comes a point where, if the margin is large enough, reversing the outcome through computerized rigging, although technically feasible, would no longer pass the smell test. Nor is it necessary, after a certain point, for every vulnerable contest to be targeted for rigging: in bodies such as the U.S. House and most state legislative chambers, a bare majority will suffice for practical partisan control and "padding" becomes a low-reward gambit. But it should be obvious that, in a delicately balanced nation such as America, it is a long-term, indeed permanent, losing proposition to be required to poll supermajorities of 55 to 60 percent in order to barely eke out electoral victories. Even a relatively light thumb, strategically applied, can effectively wreak havoc with the political scales.

It is now comprehended by strategists across the political spectrum that shifting demographic patterns have handed the Democrats a massive and growing electoral advantage nationwide.[77] The radicalization of the Republican Party should only have heightened that advantage.[78] To win general elections and hold on to power—barring massive scandals and other egregious political fiascoes—Republicans are now obliged to turn to *structural* strategies to offset their demographic and political handicaps.[79] Thus we have witnessed a spate of restrictive Voter-ID laws ostensibly passed to combat a nonexistent "epidemic" of "voter" fraud; ruthless gerrymandering of U.S. House and

---

[77] Indeed the Computerized Vote-Counting Era *began* with reports of "The Emerging Democratic Majority," which was the title of a 2002 book by highly respected political demographers John B. Judis and Ruy Teixeira (see https://www.amazon.com/Emerging-Democratic-Majority-John-Judis/dp/0743254783). There is a whole cottage industry devoted to producing tortured explanations of what became of that emerging Democratic majority. One can certainly imagine the book's role in motivating the emerging Republican minority to take preventive measures, beginning with the Help America Vote Act (HAVA) of 2002.

[78] It is worth recalling what happened to the *Democrats* when they similarly radicalized (Eugene McCarthy, George McGovern) in the Vietnam era when votes were still being *counted* rather than *processed*. They were *crushed* and all-but-marginalized for a generation.

[79] The modern GOP finds itself in an existential predicament remarkably similar to that experienced by southern *Democrats* at the end of Reconstruction (1876). It is hardly surprising, then, to find them resorting to many of the same ugly tactics that post-Reconstruction Democrats fell back on. And—since these tactics tend to be restrained by modern jurisprudence rooted in the Civil Rights Era and not entirely routed by the GOP's efforts to reshape the federal courts—looking to add a *new*, invisible magic arrow to their quiver.

statehouse districts,[80] with lurking proposals to extend the gerrymander's cynical powers to the presidential contest itself;[81] the financial advantage gained through the U.S. Supreme Court's 5-to-4 party-line *Citizens United* and *McCutcheon* decisions[82] and the torrents of corporate campaign cash to which they opened the floodgates; and of course the "Vote Wednesday" flyers and robocalls and related disinformation campaigns, which broke new ground with the Trump campaign and have tendrils being traced far and wide and deep, from Cambridge Analytica[83] to every major social media platform to bot farms and the Kremlin.[84]

---

[80] The gerrymander is of course a tool available as well to Democrats, who have not shied away from its use. Demographics, however, give Republicans a significant advantage here: Democratic constituencies tend to cluster in large urban areas, which can be gerrymandered into near-100% Democratic districts, more effectively "consuming" Democratic voters within a given state than a pro-Democratic gerrymander can consume the less geographically concentrated rural and suburban Republican voters.

E2010 was a critical election at the below-the-radar statehouse level because their key state legislature victories gave Republicans control of the decennial redistricting process, based on the 2010 Census, for the U.S. House and many key statehouses. A subtle beauty of this down-ballot strategy lay in the fact that voters ultimately grow weary of gridlock and, given the at-the-time very dim prospects for wresting the House from GOP control, could ultimately be persuaded to turn to a (Republican) presidential candidate who "would be able to work with Congress." That candidate turned out—with great retrospective irony—to be Donald Trump.

[81] Apportioning presidential Electoral College votes by congressional district rather than the currently prevalent statewide winner-take-all basis has the ring of fairness but would in actual effect subject the presidential election to the gerrymander's tender mercies. The danger of this uber-cynical scheme has been somewhat diminished with erosion of GOP trifecta control, which would be needed to pass such proposals, in several key swing states.

Direct Popular Vote for the presidency (i.e., doing away with the Electoral College) would, unlike the congressional district apportionment scheme, be a genuinely progressive reform, *but only if coupled with the restoration of observable vote counting.* Under the current computerized system, doing away with the Electoral College and simply counting the national popular vote would make it possible for election riggers to shift votes with equal impact *anywhere in the country*, making it even easier to escape the modicum of scrutiny that is currently focused on battleground states.

[82] *Citizens United v. FEC*, 558 U.S. 310 (2010), effectively defined corporate campaign contributions as protected "free speech," gutting much of the framework for regulating or limiting it. *McCutcheon v. FEC*, 572 U.S. 185 (2014), then compounded the damage by striking down aggregate limits to corporate contributions.

[83] See https://www.wired.com/story/what-did-cambridge-analytica-really-do-for-trumps-campaign/.

[84] See http://www.politifact.com/truth-o-meter/article/2017/apr/04/four-things-know-about-russias-2016-misinformation/.

Such tactics have served their purpose if they can bring contests within smell-test distance (in tracking and exit polls), where a computerized mistabulation can be outcome-altering without being *too* shocking, and thus suspicion-arousing, in its magnitude.[85] Restoration of the democracy Americans have been led to believe is their birthright will require removing in turn each of these thumbs from the scale. If we agree that the most covert and direct thumb is the most potent and insidious, we will *begin* with the rescue of the votecount itself out of the partisan, proprietary pitch-dark of cyberspace and into the light of public observation.[86]

Q: If the evidence pointed to a pervasive "blue shift," advantaging the Democrats or progressive candidates, instead of the pervasive "red shift" that you have found, do you think you would still be engaged in this work to the same degree?

A: Very frankly—human nature, or at least my nature, being what it is—I don't think so. But before anyone goes "Aha, I *knew* you were biased!" let me explain why. This is frustrating, depressing, demoralizing, and potentially dangerous work, and there's every incentive to stop banging your head against the spiked wall before you no longer have one to bang. It is common to view vote counting as an abstract, rather academic matter, but it all-too-obviously can be one with very real, concrete, far-reaching, practical and historical consequences. That is a big part of what makes it compelling for me and drives my continuing efforts. Especially now in the Age of Trump, when democracy itself seems to hang in the balance. It could not get much more concrete.

I've always believed that Cassandra's fate—to see the truth and the hidden danger and never to be believed—was the cruelest of all the terrible punishments meted out by the jealous Greek gods. I little thought it would be

---

[85] Harvey Wasserman and Bob Fitrakis have coined the term "strip and flip" to describe this two-pronged strategy, with the "strip" referring to the various overt schemes of suppression and the "flip" to the covert electronic manipulation, both of which appeared to be on display in E2016 (see Fitrakis B & Wasserman H: *The Strip and Flip Selection of 2016: Five Jim Crows & Electronic Election Theft* at https://www.amazon.com/dp/B01GSJLW0I).

[86] Harvard Law Professor Lawrence Lessig, whose 2015 single-issue campaign for the presidency rested entirely on a "clean elections" platform, apparently did not agree—omitting the counting process itself entirely from the set of issues he was willing to address, despite repeated appeals for its inclusion. He told me it just didn't seem "as important" to him. As I wrote to a colleague, "When the fringe treats you like fringe you know you're the fringe."

my lot in life and I don't care for it one bit. If I had uncovered evidence of electronic fraud and it were both sides doing it such that it was a wash, or just the Left doing it so that it was pushing America to the more progressive pole, it would still be a blot on democracy, and I would still have attempted to bring it to the attention of officials, the media, and the public. *Unobservable vote counting is, whomever it benefits, inherently insane.* But, after being ignored or patronized for 18 long years of these efforts, I'm pretty sure I would have been willing to mutter *"c'est la guerre"* and shuffle on to other things. Living in the world of *CODE RED,* and immersing myself in this Alice-In-Wonderland nightmare of the Big Lie, is oppressive. Just not as oppressive as the fascism to which computerized election theft threatens to deliver the democracy I was fortunate enough to be born into and long took too much for granted.

But the "pervasive blue shift" is a rather ridiculous hypothetical because, if it were the *Left* in control of the voting apparatus and the "shocking" results were favoring their cause, it is impossible to imagine that the political strategists and media of the Right would *not* be all over it, demanding investigations and even "observable counting." An odd asymmetry I know, but just look at all the Voter-ID legislation the Right has rammed through in response to a nonexistent epidemic of "voter fraud" with no impact on electoral outcomes.[87] So it's a lead-pipe cinch that they would hardly be supine and acquiescent in the face of evidence of targeted computerized vote counting fraud that was altering the outcome of hundreds of key elections and threatening *them* with permanent minority status. I doubt *my* perseverance would be needed.[88]

I have often been asked how my personal political views impact my capacity to function as a fair and impartial analyst of election forensics. It is a fair question. My answer is that I work to advance the nonpartisan goal of election transparency and accountability, manifest above all in public, observable vote counting. After all the deceptions and outright lies along the campaign trail, after all the perverting infusions of undisclosed corporate cash, even after all the "Vote Wednesday" robocalls and all the other dirty tricks to which the

---

[87] See Minnite L: *The Myth of Voter Fraud,* Cornell University Press 2010, http://www.amazon.com/Myth-Voter-Fraud-Lorraine-Minnite/dp/0801448484; see also Mayer J: "The Voter-Fraud Myth," *The New Yorker* (10/29/2012) at http://www.newyorker.com/reporting/2012/10/29/121029fa_fa_fact_mayer?printable=true.

[88] Though I did question the counting anomalies in the victory of Democrat Doug Jones over Republican Roy Moore in the 2017 U.S. Senate Special Election in Alabama—as detailed, with a twist, in Chapter VI—an effort hardly inspired by partisanship.

desperate make resort, if nothing more than the *counting of the votes* could be trusted, our own particular and rather narrow mission would be fulfilled.

In our quest to restore observable vote counting—which should be a no-brainer on its face but instead seems a quaint and faintly ludicrous notion in the wake of the *fait accompli* blitzkrieg of post-HAVA computerization—we are called upon to document and analyze the red-flag patterns that result from *non-observable* vote counting. *After all, if it ain't broke why fix it?* And in this work, it must be said, there is *nothing random or nonpartisan* about the patterns that keep turning up wherever contests are competitive and carry either direct or indirect national significance. There is hardly ever a "blue shift" anywhere, just a recurring "red shift" election after election[89]—even in the elections where 11th-hour seismic political shifts overcame it and led to (diminished) Democratic victories—and a consequent veering of American politics to the right. This is the *reality*, call it partisan or call it nonpartisan as you choose.

Q: But what if I don't buy that "reality"? What would you say to someone on the other side of the great political divide who believes you've cherry-picked your evidence or that the red shift stems from faulty polls, or who believes that Trump is legitimate but *Obama* stole the White House and it's the *Left* that has found a way to rig American elections?

A: OK, I'm a leftie and you're a rightie. Each of us believes the other side has been rigging elections or would be if given the opportunity. You call the polls "fake news" while I have lost faith in the votecounts. With computerized

---

[89] The shifts that so distort the translation of the public will are by no means restricted to general (i.e., inter-party) elections. As will be detailed in Chapter V, the 2016 Democratic *primaries* produced some of the more egregious red shifts of the computerized era. Narrowing the candidate options available to voters in November has as powerful an impact in altering political direction and thwarting public sovereignty as does rigging November itself.

I should note, however, that not all red shifts are created equal. That is to say that the strength and probative value of this species of evidence varies with factors that may not be immediately apparent to the casual observer. To explain this with an example, in the 2016 presidential general election there were egregious and outcome-reversing red shifts in the Trump table-run battleground states but no such phenomenon in the *national* exit poll. That gave us a baseline for comparison, a very valuable second-order comparative. By contrast we have no such baseline against which to view the sizeable disparities in Joe Biden's favor in the first batch of E2020 Democratic primaries, rendering that data of significantly less probative value. See https://codered2014.com/wp-content/uploads/2020/04/notes-exit-poll-disparities-2020-democratic-primarise-js2rev.pdf for a more detailed discussion.

counting *neither* of us has any reason to trust the other side—particularly in the present political environment, so rich in anger and poor in trust. If you distrust exit polling, ask yourself how unobservable votecounts are any better or more trustworthy. Indeed, electoral legitimacy is now being called furiously into question from all sides. Even veteran observers are asking in all seriousness whether the results of E2020 will be accepted by losing candidates and party.[90]

Under these conditions especially—and to say nothing of the Russians—aren't we BOTH entitled to an observable counting of the votes?

Whether an unobservable computer count leads to actual rigging or not, it has now begun to invite serious, dangerous suspicion, distrust, and unrest. Isn't an observable count, going forward, likely to be the *only* way to restore trust in an electoral system that is breaking down before our very eyes, right *and* left?

Doesn't counting votes publicly and observably just make fundamental sense for our country in the state it's in? Indeed, isn't such transparency suddenly and acutely essential to the well-being, even the survival, of our democracy?

Q: The Blogosphere and Twittersphere are awash in "conspiracy theories," ranging from the truly outlandish to the highly plausible. Where would you place computerized election theft on that spectrum and how do you deal with the reflexive dismissal inherent in the "conspiracy theory" label?

A: It should be obvious that not every conspiracy is a theory. *History* is awash with undisclosed agreements and arrangements to work toward the achievement of some end that would generate opposition and resistance were it openly declared. That is all a conspiracy is.[91]

---

[90] See, e.g., https://slate.com/news-and-politics/2019/09/joshua-geltzer-election-peaceful-transition-of-power-donald-trump.html and https://www.politico.com/story/2019/06/21/trump-election-2020-1374589.

[91] Michael Parenti put it memorably in his 1996 book *Dirty Truths*:

"Those who suffer from conspiracy phobia are fond of saying: 'Do you actually think there's a group of people sitting around in a room plotting things?' For some reason that image is assumed to be so patently absurd as to invite only disclaimers. But where else would people of power get together—on park benches or carousels? Indeed, they meet in rooms: corporate boardrooms, Pentagon command rooms, at the Bohemian Grove, in the choice dining rooms at the best restaurants, resorts, hotels, and estates, in the many conference rooms at the White House, the NSA, the CIA, or wherever. And, yes, they consciously plot—though they call it "planning" and "strategizing"—and they do so in great secrecy, often resisting all efforts at

The real problem with conspiracy theories is separating the wheat from the chaff. It is possible to imagine and allege virtually *anything* when it comes to nefarious or threatening human behavior. Wild allegations and revelations have become a staple of the Information Age and studies have moreover shown that confabulations tend to find far more eyeballs than do honest reporting and analysis. "Fake News" plays twin roles: as both turmoil-inducing genuine disinformation and as an indirect way to bring about dismissal of *bona fide* information that might be damaging to one's cause or brand. Both are terribly dangerous, and both make the evaluation of "conspiracy theories" especially difficult.

Our era calls for heightened wariness of paranoid conspiracy theories, in so many of which is lurking a destructive intent. At the same time it calls for heightened vigilance of "official stories" and opacities that may be tools of subjugation as well as protection. There is no easy escape from this collision of imperatives. As citizens seeking to be informed and to cast informed votes, our job has gotten a lot tougher.

I met a man some years ago who claimed that the U.S. government had, during one or another of his stays at a Veterans Hospital, surgically implanted "chips" in his brain that were being used to wirelessly torment him and send "information" to his consciousness, and claimed moreover that many others had been subject to this same secret manipulation. "Mr. Chips" maintained a calm and rational affect and he discussed other aspects of politics and economics with remarkable acumen. He carried with him a thick folder of MRI films purporting to show the location of the implanted chips.

While politely repressing a reflexive snicker, I found it very disquietingly occurring to me that my own earnest presentation of the red shift and stolen elections likely elicits precisely the same reaction from many auditors. "Mr. Chips" and I are both "conspiracy theorists," each readily dismissed with that damning and clever label. Is there in fact a distinction and, if so, how might it be apprehended? How does one know, without a painstaking review of all the evidence (his MRIs, my tables and graphs) and context, what to take seriously and what does not warrant further investigation?

---

public disclosure. No one confabulates and plans more than political and corporate elites and their hired specialists."

What "Mr. Chips" and election forensics analysts have in common is that the events we are alleging to have taken place are deeply disturbing to the point where the human psyche recoils against acknowledgement.[92] Some concealed behavior is concealed precisely because it would meet with a negative response, ranging from opposition to outrage, were it brought into the open. If Jose Canseco could be dismissed (and ridiculed) for daring to allege that *baseball* was not what it seemed, and that those majestic 500-foot home runs were the derivative of pharmaceutical enhancements rather than wholesome heroics, how much stronger the impulse to dismiss (and ridicule) allegations and evidence that not the national *pastime* but the national *fate* is being systematically subverted—that America is, in effect, a sham democracy?[93]

If we sweep away all alleged conspiracies and all covert activities with a big broom, we get to live in a world of presentable surfaces that seems and feels a lot more hospitable and comfortable. I certainly did not want to "waste my time" exploring the possibility that people are walking around with government-implanted microchips in their brains, and it is exactly such aversion that gives the term "conspiracy theory" such pejorative power and such protective effect for those engaging in covert activities.

So it is up to the auditor to use his or her best judgment, life experience, knowledge of history and basic mathematics, and understanding of human nature in evaluating the evidence presented. That means eschewing the

---

[92] Carl Sagan put it thus: "One of the saddest lessons of history is this: If we've been bamboozled long enough, we tend to reject any evidence of the bamboozle. We're no longer interested in finding out the truth. The bamboozle has captured us. It's simply too painful to acknowledge, even to ourselves, that we've been taken. Once you give a charlatan power over you, you almost never get it back." (*The Demon-Haunted World: Science as a Candle in the Dark,* https://www.amazon.com/gp/product/0345409469/rcf.)

Indeed, recent research has backed up Sagan's observation and established that both individuals and groups can be so maximally averse to the *knowledge* that they have been duped that they often choose to *continue* being duped rather than to be confronted with the evidence that they *have been* duped (see Abby Ellin: "The Drama of Deception," *Psychology Today,* July 2015, at https://www.psychologytoday.com/magazine/archive/2015/07). This phenomenon also seems to shed much light on the bizarre dynamics of the Age of Trump.

[93] It is worth noting that the *vulnerability* of computerized vote counting to fraud—the *risk* of continuing to use it for our elections—can in no sense be considered a conspiracy theory, any more than can the state of disrepair of America's roads and bridges. It is the attempt to present evidence of *actual* fraud and theft that triggers the dismissive "conspiracy theory" label. Yet only suspect elections and suspicions of actual rigging seem to bring major public attention and urgency to the otherwise technical and unsexy topic of vote counting. This is a most unfortunate dilemma.

convenience of easy labels like "conspiracy theory" and conclusory, quasi-religious presumptions like "America is the Beacon of Democracy and therefore such undemocratic things could never happen here."

And it means asking where a given theory is coming from and going to. Is the end goal to stir hatred and division, promote a partisan agenda, or protect a powerful figure by casting aspersions upon his or her opponents or detractors? Or is it instead to support a constructive action such as repair of a vulnerable process like concealed vote counting? Ask what the consequences will be if the theory is proven to be accurate. This "and so" will tell you a great deal about what deserves to be taken seriously.

Q: How do we know for certain, independent of election results, what kind of country America is—how red, how blue?

A: We don't. Even in a very small polity, say a town with 5,000 residents, you can't tell much about a polarizing contest or issue without an actual vote. You may know more people who say they intend to support X, but that says more about the company you keep than about how the rest of the town, let alone the state or the country, plans to vote. This has never been truer than it is today, in a nation tribalized into enclaves and bubbles. One side may have the preponderance of yard signs or radio spots, but that tells us little beyond the relative size of the campaign budgets.[94] Polls might be—and obviously, in the case of major elections, are—taken *ad nauseam*. But polls are highly sensitive to the particular sampling methodology used and usually wind up dancing a fluctuating and conflicting conga when elections are close.[95] Even when polls and predictions are *not* close, in the Age of Trump's post-factual politics they are easily written off as "fake news."[96]

---

[94] In today's post-*Citizens/McCutcheon* "dark money" era, the size of respective campaign war chests is a far better indicator of private than of public favor.

[95] See Chapter VIII, Study V for the additional distorting effect of the votecount-poll feedback loop.

[96] And increasingly ignored when it comes to the making of policy. With the fate of DACA recipients and universal background checks for gun purchasers under debate in Washington, for example, one would never guess that the progressive position on each high-profile issue was polling at or near 90% in favor. Republican office-holders seem strangely comfortable and confident spitting into these gale-force winds—the Age of Trump mantra being "Elections Matter!"—though this new, defiant and seemingly tone-deaf kind of political behavior is exactly what one would expect of office-holders who believed themselves immune to all electoral consequences. Ideally, we don't want our "leaders" always pandering to polls and "following." We want them to take a heartfelt position and then let the public exercise its right of review at election time.

This is what makes voting itself so powerful and, you would think, sacrosanct. Elections are the Official Scorecard—and the *only* Official Scorecard—of American politics. *There is really no other way to know.* As columnist James Graff, having first noted the vagaries of polling, put it most succinctly when speaking of E2012, "The truth won't come until Election Day."[97] What comes on Election Day is a *reality* of elected officials who will govern us, but can anyone say with genuine assurance that they know that this reality equates to the actual *truth* of the votes as they were cast?[98] What if, to put it in Kellyanne Conway lingo, we are placing our faith in "alternative votes?"

Our skepticism of polls and other pulse-takings of our nation is, to an extent, justified. Our blind and absolute faith in the computer-processed votecounts is *not*. What is as irrational as it is deadly is our persisting belief that *all* other measuring sticks *must* be flawed—a belief based squarely on the fact that they all diverge from the votecounts, which *must not* be questioned.

And the "truth" of which Graff spoke is more expansive than the election of Candidate X or Candidate Y. Consider the fortunes of the National Rifle Association, which has held the line against overwhelming public opinion (and passion) because it has become axiomatic that, especially for any Republican politician, to cross the NRA is to sign one's own electoral death warrant. The NRA grew into this 800-ton gorilla because of its virtually perfect track record in defeating—generally in low-scrutiny primary elections—any candidate even hinting at support for even the most tepid gun regulation. A few well-targeted upsets were enough to set in stone the rules of the political game for more than a generation.[99]

But that model presumes the public's right of review is tabulated accurately and honestly.

[97] See *The Week*, 10/19/2012, p.3.

[98] Another, rather more personal, way of framing this question: "How much would you be willing to wager on the accuracy of a given votecount and electoral outcome—say one such as Ohio 2004 or GA-6 in 2017, draped in a forensic red flag—ten bucks, the farm, your life?" If not prepared to bet your life that the official computer count and a full, observable human canvass will produce the same winner, can you say you "*know*?" And, if you were *not* willing to bet your life, why would you be willing to bet your country or the world?

[99] For an excellent account of NRA *modus operandi*, see https://www.newyorker.com/magazine/2018/03/05/the-nra-lobbyist-behind-floridas-pro-gun-policies; note that the NRA's outsized clout with a broad swath of office-holders and candidates rests ultimately on what amounts to a handful of victories in what we might term "demo" elections.

Our biennial elections, far more than the endless parade of opinion polls, *define* America—both in terms of who occupies its seats of power and as the single snapshot that becomes the enduring national self-portrait that Americans of all stripes carry in our mental wallets until at least the next election and often for an era. It is also, needless to say, the portrait we send abroad. False elections bequeath to all Americans—right, left, and center— nothing less sinister than an illusory collective identity and the living of a national lie. Think of altered electoral choices as a testamentary letter that goes out, *over our forged signature*, to the world, to the historians, to our children.

Q: What link, if any, do you see between the opportunity to steal elections and the current hyperpolarization of American politics? Why do you think the GOP itself has veered and continues to veer further and further right? Do you think they all somehow *know* that elections are rigged and that they can win no matter how extreme or politically reckless they get?

A: Logically, a player who knows the fix is in and victory assured will "bet the house." Why not get as much bang as possible for your buck? Or, as the young Bulgarian husband learned in *Casablanca*, when Rick tells you to leave all your chips on 22, you leave all your chips on 22. Translated into contemporary politics, if you believe you can win an election no matter what, there is no incentive to play to the middle. You can ignore how successful "triangulation" was for Bill Clinton or "compassionate conservatism" for G. W. Bush, and indeed ignore all conventional political wisdom that says that you have to dilute your radical agenda, your "true belief," in a bid to capture the moderates and independents in the center of the political spectrum needed to win competitive general elections.[100]

According to the "classical physics" of politics, the extremist behavior of the GOP makes very little political sense and indeed it kept surprising pundits all along the political spectrum, who kept scratching their heads as such behavior

---

[100] Heading into E2020, it is worth noting that cautions against "extreme" politics were still being directed at "far-*left*" Democrats like Elizabeth Warren and Bernie Sanders. No such cautions are delivered to far-right Republicans, even those who have engaged in radical, norm-breaking behavior in support of Trump. It is a challenge to account for this glaring asymmetry without reference to the thumb-on-scale vagaries of the electoral and vote-counting processes.

continued to be rewarded rather than punished electorally.[101] Such would of course be the behavior of politicians who knew the fix was in and it may be driven by chief strategists who are either involved in the rigging of elections or who have deduced that it is going on and adjusted their strategies accordingly.

But it is also possible to understand the Right's new extremism from a behaviorist standpoint as the consequence of electoral experience operating on political strategy. That is, without inferring any *knowledge* of a rigged game, when forays in political extremism are electorally rewarded rather than punished, the conventional wisdom that says you must play to the center is soon enough discarded in favor of a new wisdom that says, "Go ahead, shoot the moon." Each successive "win" further reinforces this new wisdom.[102] As countless behaviorist experiments have shown, it doesn't take much such conditioning to mold new behaviors.[103]

Q: What in your view is the significance of the year 2010?

A: If I had been sitting in a war room with Karl Rove, a map, a timeline, and a blueprint for long-term political domination, I'd have kept zeroing in on 2010 as the year to make it all happen. There is of course much to be gained by capturing the White House but, if one's goal is *enduring political control,* the

---

[101] Of course, since the electoral results are unquestioned *fact*, reasons *must* be found for the strange voter behavior. There is a cottage industry dedicated to "explaining" the electoral results of the computerized era, from Thomas Frank's 2004 bestseller, *What's The Matter with Kansas?* (voters 'distracted' by social issues like guns and abortion) to 2015's *NY Times*/ProPublica piece by Alec MacGillis, "Who Turned My Blue State Red?"

Referring to Maine's far-right then-governor, Paul R. LePage, MacGillis writes, "His [safety-net slashing] crusade has resonated with many in the state, who re-elected him last year." That is, we know and can write that LePage's crusade "resonated" *because* he was re-elected. And we believe that re-election was an accurate gauge of public "resonance" *because* we trust a vulnerable, unobservable, partisan-programmed, computerized vote-counting system. With the election of Donald Trump, this cottage industry had to move into an industrial park.

[102] The Republican leadership in Congress has gone all-in and then some as Trump stomps all over the rule of law. By any rational political calculus, this Thelma & Louise drive over the cliff can't end well for them. Why, then, have they joined hands and hit the gas? It appears to be a rock-solid conviction that, 2018's loss of their House majority somehow notwithstanding, they are immune to all future electoral consequence. Indeed, computerized vote counting has been the GOP's rabbit's foot since 2002. With it swinging from the rear-view mirror, would they not have every reason to believe their car can fly?

[103] Both political omnipotence *and* political impotence have, over time, a disorienting effect on the parties and a corrosive effect on the body politic.

U.S. House of Representatives and key swing-state legislatures and administrative posts become the natural strategic targets—especially in years ending with a "zero," in which the crucial decennial (i.e., census-based) redistricting power is up for grabs.[104]

Taking over the U.S. House and key statehouses in 2010 offered the alluring prospect—via the tactical powers of gerrymandering and administrative control of elections, as well as the enormous advantages of incumbency for both U.S. House members and state legislators—of locking in GOP House and statehouse control virtually irrespective of any but the most extreme adverse trends in either demographics or public opinion.[105] Control of purple (i.e., swing-state) statehouses would permit systematic structural changes (passing restrictive Voter-ID and voter-qualification laws, breaking union power, exercising control of election administration and oversight) with profound impact on the electorate's composition and the electoral process itself.[106] All this was on the platter in 2010.

---

[104] Because U.S. House seats must, by constitutional mandate, be proportioned to population, the decennial U.S. Census generally results in a reapportionment of House seats allocated to different states and provides an opportunity for state legislatures to redraw congressional (and their own) district boundaries—a process known, when undertaken for partisan political advantage, as gerrymandering. There are only very loose restrictions on congressional district geometry and, with the aid of "big data," including house-by-house voter profiles, it has become possible to gerrymander ever more precisely and ruthlessly, to great overall advantage.

The perfect gerrymander would create, from a given population pool, a few districts in which the opposing party would receive 100% of the votes and many districts in which your party would win each election by a small margin. The redistricting undertaken by the GOP after E2010 did not miss that ideal by much. Of course the danger of such an optimization plan is that if adverse political winds should blow too hard, those "small margin" (i.e., too competitive) districts can flip; this may help explain some of the substantial GOP House losses in 2018, when anti-Trump breezes freshened into a gale.

Redistricting also affects state legislative districts, and proposals have been floated by the GOP to apportion *presidential* electoral votes by congressional district, effectively subjecting presidential politics to the gerrymander.

David Daley's 2016 book *RATF**KED: The True Story Behind the Plan to Steal America's Democracy* (https://www.amazon.com/dp/1631491628) examines E2010 as the critical election in a scheme known as REDMAP. Typically, even Daley, who delves deep into the cynicism behind REDMAP, cannot bring himself to question any of the shocking E2010 electoral results essential to its spectacular success.

[105] That is, *ordinary* adverse trends. No one in 2010 would have contemplated among the politically adverse trends the ascension of Donald Trump to the presidency.

[106] See, e.g., Steven Yaccino and Lizette Alvarez, "New G.O.P. Bid to Limit Voting in Swing States," *New York Times*, 3/29/2014, at http://www.nytimes.com/2014/03/30/us/new-gop-bid-to-limit-voting-in-swing-states.html .

Recall as well that U.S. House and state legislative elections are not individually exit-polled and that even pre-election polling for all but a very few of these contests is sparse, so there are virtually no race-by-race baselines for forensic analysts to work from. There are a couple hundred key, but essentially invisible, contests scattered across the country that add up to the *aggregate* partisan victory responsible for cementing the overall political infrastructure of America in place. The *individual components* of the grand outcome receive virtually no media attention (even political junkies would be hard-pressed to keep in focus what is happening in OH-5, OR-4, FL-13, etc., let alone Wisconsin *State Senate-9th*!)[107] and the only forensic red flag is to be found in an anomalous *overall* statistical pattern, which likewise receives no media attention.

With the afterglow of Obama's 2008 triumph further reducing the scope and intensity of election protection efforts, the risk level associated with grand theft of E2010 was negligible, the reward was profound, the reward/risk ratio accordingly off the charts. And indeed E2010 was the election that ensured that Americans would have a choice between gridlock and right-wing hegemony for years to come.[108]

From the very beginning, Election Year 2010 waved a succession of red flags that offered an indication of what was in store for November. The January special election to fill the Senate seat of the late Ted Kennedy in Massachusetts was the first of them. The upset victory of Republican Scott Brown over Democrat Martha Coakley served to put the Tea Party on the map, eliminate the Democrats' 60-vote filibuster-proof Senate majority, and kindle expectations for a big move to the right in November.

Why was this key election suspect? For starters, there was every incentive in the world to rig Coakley-Brown and every opportunity in the world to get away with it. There were no exit polls (itself very strange for a statewide contest with such important implications), no equipment spot checks, no audits, not a single officially-sanctioned handcount to verify any optical scanner tabulation, and not a single optical scanner memory card examined for malicious code (e.g., the +X/-X zero-counter scheme introduced earlier). If in fact the vendor

---

[107] For readers interested in *trying*, I strongly recommend the deeply informative, nonpartisan, and comprehensive www.ballotpedia.com website.

[108] As noted above, the advent of Trump—and the potential impact of his governance and behavior on down-ballot electoral politics—were not on the radar screens of the GOP tacticians of 2010.

corporations, or any insiders or hackers gaining access to the programming or distribution processes, had chosen to serve a private political agenda rather than the public trust, there would be *nothing* in the official processes of voting, vote counting, and election certification to indicate that such a breach had occurred. Thus it was an election that could have been stolen with virtually zero risk to yield an enormous reward.

But was it? We will never *know* because the actual ballots were never excavated (from the bins at the bottom of the optical scanners) to be counted and compared with the machine counts,[109] and all have long since been destroyed.

We were presented with a seismic result with no observable evidence to support it. It could have been legitimate, and it could equally well have been a cheap trick conjured in the darkness of cyberspace. So forensic analysts looked at the only evidence that *was* available—the votes of the 71 Massachusetts jurisdictions that counted their ballots in public by hand.[110] We found that Coakley won in these jurisdictions by a margin of 3 percent, while Brown won by 5 percent where the optical scanners did the counting in secret. The chance of this 8 percent total disparity occurring if the handcounts had been distributed randomly around the state was infinitesimal, one in hundreds of billions. But analysts of course recognized that the handcounts were not randomly distributed and that handcount and optical scanner jurisdictions represented discrete constituencies. Perhaps the handcount communities where Coakley won were more Democratic in voter registration or had a more Democratic voting history, or perhaps they were clustered in a part of the state where Coakley was more popular or perhaps they had seen more Coakley ads.

Analysts looked at each of these "benign" explanations in turn, including such factors as advertising expenditures broken down by media market, and found that none of them held water. The handcount jurisdictions were more

---

[109] An attempt was made at such an excavation, when the organization MassVOTE, using Massachusetts Public Records Law, persuaded a town clerk from the Worcester suburb of Shrewsbury to allow a hand recount of the ballots from a single precinct to take place. The (Democratic) Secretary of State, rather than supporting an extension of the investigation, immediately sent letters to all city and town elections officials strictly forbidding them to follow suit. See http://massvote.org/2010/09/massvote-conducts-first-ever-independent-audit-of-massachusetts-voting-machines/.

[110] See https://codered2014.com/wp-content/uploads/2020/04/believeIt_OrNot_100904_2011rev_.pdf, also included as Study IV in Chapter VIII. Massachusetts, unlike most states, organizes and counts its elections by town rather than county.

Republican by voter registration; they had voted in exact congruence with the optical scanner jurisdictions in the previous *two* U.S. Senate races, which were noncompetitive and thus not targets for rigging; and they had given Coakley a *lower* percentage than the optical scanner jurisdictions in her only previous statewide race. Granted Coakley, thinking she was a shoo-in, ran a very lackluster campaign; granted there was a surge of enthusiasm and a big influx of money from the right, making a tight (and therefore riggable) race out of a blowout. But those factors—which would have had the same impact on voters *regardless of how their votes were tabulated*—do not explain why some 65,000 handcount voters, shown to be to the *right of a random sample*, voted so differently from (i.e., to the *left* of) the voters who voted on optical scanners. That remains entirely without explanation, unless one is willing to consider electronic vote manipulation. Indeed, with every other explanation exhaustively examined and ruled out by analysts, *only the method of vote tabulation appeared to explain what happened in Massachusetts.*

Another red flag waved a few months later over South Carolina. In the Democratic primary for the nomination to oppose incumbent Tea Party favorite Jim DeMint for re-election to the United States Senate, a bona fide candidate (State Circuit Judge Vic Rawl) was the prohibitive favorite (so much so that no one even bothered polling) against a cipher (Alvin Greene) who made no campaign appearances, had no headquarters or website, was facing the prospect of indictment on pornography-related charges, and didn't appear to possess the personal funds needed for the election filing fee, which was paid anonymously on his behalf. The Rawl challenge to DeMint had gathered a good deal of steam, the Democrat's statewide popularity such that, with a fraction of the name-recognition, he had already closed to a threatening seven points in tracking polls against the powerful GOP incumbent in a very red state.

The primary was held in June and the votes were tallied on paperless touchscreen (aka "DRE") computers—the darkest of voting cyberspace. Amazingly, Greene won—*with 59 percent of the vote*. Despite being known to almost literally no one, he officially received *100,362 votes*. In an eyebrow-raising footnote, after losing that November to DeMint by a margin of 34 points, Greene, apparently encouraged by his performance against Rawl, entered another Democratic primary, this time for a seat in the South Carolina House of Representatives. He received 36 votes.[111]

---

[111] For his part, the ultraconservative DeMint, after all that, abruptly left the Senate in 2013, resigning to head The Heritage Foundation, a right-wing think tank.

In response to his baffling defeat, Rawl brought a challenge before the Democratic State Committee, which had original jurisdiction over the conduct of the primary election. Several election integrity experts testified in Rawl's favor, citing, among other glaring anomalies, major disparities between early/absentee votes counted by optical scanner (where the voter-marked ballots would at least theoretically be available for human recount) and the at-poll unrecountable paperless touchscreen tallies. The Committee responded favorably to Rawl's case throughout the hearing, then went into closed session and voted by a margin of 55 to 10 to reject the challenge and close the case without further investigation.[112]

After such appetizers it was not surprising to find a ptomaine-laced main course served up in November 2010. With exit polls thoroughly "discredited"— unless conducted anywhere else on the planet other than in the United States—it did not seem to matter that 16 out of 18 competitive U.S. Senate elections were red-shifted, 11 out of 13 governorship elections were red-shifted, and in the U.S. House elections the total red shift translated to 1.9 million votes, enough potentially to reverse the outcome of dozens of targeted House races. The "Great Tea Party Sweep" was duly reported at face value.

Beyond the dramatic red shifts, though, was an extraordinary vote distribution pattern in the E2010 Republican takeover of the U.S. House. The GOP took comfortable—and, as we shall see, enduring—control of the House by virtue of a massive net gain of 63 seats (or 14.5 percent of the 435-seat chamber), the greatest such pick-up in any midterm election going back to 1970, during which period the average net pick-up was a mere 21 seats (4.8 percent). What was even more remarkable was that the GOP achieved this extraordinary national blowout without any remotely proportional sweep of the total vote. Its aggregate popular vote victory margin for House elections nationwide (as tabulated) was a pedestrian 6.9 percent, yielding an off-the-charts ratio of seat

---

[112] The election and challenge form the core of the 2016 documentary feature film *I Voted?*, directed by Jason Grant Smith and co-produced by Katie Couric; see https://www.ivotedmovie.com; see also http://www.bradblog.com/?p=7902. For an eerily parallel shutdown of U.S. House candidate Clint Curtis's 2006 electoral challenge—a refusal by the (Democratic-led) House Administration Committee to admit or consider evidence in the form of signed voter affidavits indicating that enough Curtis votes had been mistabulated (uncounted or shifted) to alter the election's outcome in his opponent's favor—see http://www.bradblog.com/?p=3947.

gain to vote margin.[113] By contrast, the *larger* Democratic popular vote margin of 8.2 percent in E2006 yielded a pickup of only 31 seats, less than half of the GOP's E2010 haul.[114] And in E2018 the "blue tsunami" resulted in an 8.6 percent popular vote margin but only a 40-seat net gain for the Democrats. Apparently there are routs and there are *routs*, and the pattern throughout the computerized voting era has been chronic, partisan, and asymmetrical. At some point this "result efficiency" stops being a matter of dumb luck: the minimization of losses (E2006 and possibly E2018) and maximization of victories (E2010) *relative to votes received* is exactly what would happen in election years where close races were being targeted for manipulation so that the well-targeted shift of a small percentage of the nation's votes produced a major shift in the overall pattern of wins and losses.

To achieve the coup that was E2010, the GOP had to confound well-set pre-election expectations governing the swath of 111 House elections considered competitive. Specifically, the pre-election consensus identified 40 contests in which Democrats were "expected to win narrowly," 42 contests that were projected as "tossups," and 29 contests in which Republicans were "expected to win narrowly," yielding 11 (40 minus 29) more contests in the Democratic column. What happened was this: the GOP won this overall Democratic-leaning "competitive" swath *by 25 seats*, 68 to 43. They took nine of the 40 contests where the Democrats had the edge, lost *none* of the 29 in their own column, and they took the "tossups" *30 to 12*!

Those are some very uncanny numbers,[115] and they are quite the companion piece to the "Landslide Denied" weirdness we saw in E2006—the previous midterm election, with a far more unpopular sitting president, from which the

---

[113] Note that this disproportionate ratio of electoral wins to aggregate vote margin could not be attributed to the vagaries of gerrymandering, as E2010 *preceded* the decennial redistricting and the majority of in-play districts were still, at the time of the election, gerrymandered to favor *Democrats*.

[114] The numbers look even stranger when one considers the information that Election Defense Alliance received, just prior to Election Day 2010 from a source with ties to the Rove operation, that California, because of the relatively stringent election protection protocols in place, would be "left alone." Sure enough, the E2010 GOP avalanche excluded California entirely: there was *zero* change in the distribution of the state's huge, 53-seat U.S. House delegation. Which of course means that the 63-seat net gain was from an effective pool of only 382 seats rather than 435, a huge chunk of what was in play in a chamber in which the vast majority of seats were recognized as "safe."

[115] The "N" is large enough to make these outcomes highly improbable as a matter of chance: the GOP had a 1% chance of winning 68 or more of the 111 competitive contests and a 0.4% chance of winning 30 or more of the tossups.

Democrats managed to glean so much *less* than expected in the way of representation and governing power. E2010 was quietly seismic at all levels, including the hundreds of *state* legislative races that collectively conferred upon the GOP game-changing decennial redistricting and election administration powers—a gift that, as we have seen, keeps on giving. All we heard was what journalist Bob Koehler once referred to as "the silent scream of numbers."[116]

Q: What about when pre-election polls are accurate? If election rigging on behalf of conservative candidates were happening, wouldn't there *always* be a disparity between the polls and the election results?

A: Yes, there *would* be such a chronic disparity—a "red shift" from the pre-election polls to the election results—if 1) all or most competitive races were being targeted for manipulation, *and* 2) the pollsters were continuing to employ the sampling methodology they used before the computerized voting era. But 1) we recognize that untargeted rigging makes little strategic sense;[117] and 2) in fact pollsters *were* repeatedly embarrassed during the first few years of post-HAVA computerized voting when their polls kept getting key elections *wrong*, consistently predicting outcomes to the left of the official results.

Enter the Likely Voter Cutoff Model (LVCM), a sampling methodology introduced by the prestigious Gallup polling operation.[118] One by one the other pollsters, facing the existential imperative to get elections *right* or go out of business, followed suit and adopted the LVCM.

The LVCM comes in various tweakings but the classic model employed by Gallup uses a series of seven "screening" questions to determine which randomly selected respondents will be included in, and which excluded from, the sample. The questions—which include such factors as stability of residence, political awareness, and prior electoral participation—operate

---

[116] Koehler B: "The Silent Scream of Numbers" (4/14/2005), at http://commonwonders.com/society/the-silent-scream-of-numbers/.

[117] Rigging of noncompetitive contests would have utility in only three circumstances: 1) To "pad" popular vote totals in a presidential election, as may have been attempted in 2004 and 2016; 2) To blur targeting patterns that would be cited by forensic analysts as indicative of deliberate interference; and 3) In rare situations where a full-ballot rig would be technologically easier to implement than one targeting specific races.

[118] Under the direction of the late George H. Gallup III, the evangelically inclined son of the organization's founder; see https://www.nytimes.com/2011/11/23/us/george-gallup-jr-of-polling-family-dies-at-81.html.

disproportionately to screen out students, transients, renters, the impoverished, and less regular voters—in other words, more of the Democratic and left-leaning constituencies.[119]

It is established that these constituencies generally have lower rates of voting than do wealthier, whiter, home-owning constituencies, but their rates of voting *are not zero; in fact, they are a long way from zero*. Assigning such respondents a 0 percent chance of voting by eliminating them from the otherwise random sample, when a significant percentage of these respondents will in fact wind up casting votes, has the effect of skewing the sample sharply to the right. And, because the pollster can choose how *many* "incorrect" answers to the screening questions will disqualify the respondent from inclusion in the poll's sample, *the LVCM operates effectively as a tunable, right-skewing fudge factor*—a mathematically unjustifiable sampling model that mysteriously keeps getting highly competitive and significant elections (which of course are the standard targets for both polling *and* rigging) "right," thereby keeping individual pollsters and the polling industry as a whole in business.

The pollster's job, as pollsters see it, is to do whatever is necessary to generate accurate predictions of election outcomes (fair or foul), not to *question* those outcomes. Thus pre-election polling can, without a trace of malice on the part of the pollsters, become part of a corrupted feedback loop beginning with rigged votecounts, and so become progressively more corroded and less useful as a baseline for verifying electoral outcomes.[120]

---

[119] See Simon J: *The Likely Voter Cutoff Model: What Is So Wrong with Getting It Right?* (Chapter VIII, Study V); see also, with props for being transparent, http://www.gallup.com/poll/143372/Understanding-Gallup-Likely-Voter-Models.aspx for Gallup's explanation of its model, and http://www.huffingtonpost.com/2012/10/09/gallup-poll-likely-voters_n_1950951.html for its potent effect.

[120] Note must be taken here of Scott Rasmussen, one-time pollster for the Bush campaign, whose version of the LVCM is so extreme that he winds up interviewing, with only modest exaggeration, a "roomful of Republicans."

Rasmussen, a consistent outlier well to the right of all other prominent polls (his policy-related as well as election-tracking polls are so far to the right of everyone else's as to have become something of an industry joke), in April 2018 finally gave Trump his first approval rating north of 50%, while other pollsters, even using the ordinary "vanilla" right-boosting LVCM, continued to measure it at 10 points below that.

Trump predictably lost no time crowing about his "popularity," touting Rasmussen's "accuracy" in predicting the results of E2016, and advising all the "inaccurate" other polling firms to "get new pollsters."

The LVCM sometimes "kicks in" a month or two prior to elections (as the likelihood of voting is thought to become more measurable and pollsters alter their methodologies accordingly, switching from "Registered Voters" to "Likely Voters"), at which time Republican and/or mainstream candidates get a "bump" in the polls often mistaken for true momentum. This artificial bump is often seen to alter race dynamics and outcomes, as voters respond positively to the perceived momentum shift. Conversely, many pollsters now use one or another version of the LVCM year-round. The effect of this full-time right-skewed polling via the LVCM has been to paint a false and distorted portrait of the American electorate, such that right-wing electoral triumphs like E2010 and E2014, rather than being shocking and suspect, seem instead to corroborate the poll-established "conservative" mood of the country.[121]

Q: What about the exit polls as a baseline?

A: Exit polls avoid entirely the vexing question of whether the respondents included in the poll results actually wound up casting a vote. We know they voted (though whether that vote was honestly counted is another matter) because they are questioned, for the most part, immediately upon exiting their polling place.[122] The accuracy of exit polls is such that they are relied upon

---

All of which, of course, begs the question of why push-pollster Rasmussen, with his extreme version of an already dubious methodology, managed to be more in line with those votecounts than did all of his competitors.

[121] Ironically, when in the run-up to E2012 certain pollsters moved *away* from the conventional seven-question LVCM screening approach (not in an effort to restore methodological purity but simply because voters would too often hang up on telephone robo-polls that included too many such preliminary questions), causing their polls to edge Democratic, there was an outcry from the pundit chorus on the right about the rash of "left-skewed" polls. Gallup, known along with the more extreme Rasmussen for their consistent lean to the right, set things straight with an LVCM poll that appeared to show, for those unaware of the methodological prestidigitation, a sudden Romney surge of nearly 10% in early October.

Poll-bashing is a favorite pre-election sport of both the Right and the Left (see, e.g., Giokaris J: "Presidential Polls 2012: Skewed Polling and Biased Media Coverage . . ." at http://www.policymic.com/articles/15219/presidential-polls-2012-skewed-polling-and-biased-media-coverage-give-obama-false-advantage-over-romney). The roiling arguments about methodology leave many—right, left, and center—dismissing the polls altogether as chimerical and, again ironically, awaiting the actual election results—unobservable, unverifiable, *more faith-based than the polls*—for the "truth."

[122] With the expansion of early and mail-in voting, some "exit" polling must now be done via telephone, with the screening question being some variation of "Did you cast a vote other than at your polling place in today's election?"

around the world, often with the sanction of the United States government, as one of the principal validators of elections.[123] Exit poll-votecount disparities have, in elections from the Ukraine to Peru, spurred official investigations of electoral fraud and indeed several electoral "re-dos."[124]

Not so in America. In America, final exit polls *always* match the votecounts with what appears to be uncanny precision. Do they do so because America is the very beacon of democracy? Afraid not. They do so because they are *forced* to match the votecounts, "adjusted" (this is the term of art) to virtual congruence with the votecounts on the theory that any disparity between the exit polls and the votecounts *must* stem from the inaccuracy of the exit polls, so "correcting" that "inaccuracy" will make the exit polls more useful for the kind of post-mortem academic analysis that keeps our pundits in such high demand (e.g., "How important was the economy to 35-to-49 year-old males who voted Republican?").[125]

But adjusting the exit polls toward congruence with the votecounts requires (in theory at least) some votecounts to work with. So immediately after the polls close, when there are as yet only a smattering of votecounts available, the first posted exit polls reflect (again in theory) primarily the actual responses of those polled, weighted to the pollsters' best estimate of the demographic composition of the electorate.[126] It is those exit polls—which we refer to as

---

[123] In the U.S., prior to the advent of computerized voting, the problem with the exit polls was that they were accurate enough that networks took to calling even close elections well prior to poll closing times, which often had a negative impact upon turnout (why bother voting when the outcome has already been decided?). A deal was struck to withhold exit poll results until after all the polls had closed in the state in question. There was neither legislation nor regulation involved, merely a 'gentleman's agreement" on the part of the networks, one that appears to be slipping, as pre-poll closing exit poll results have begun to be posted on media websites; see, e.g., https://twitter.com/nytgraphics/status/697246344038256642 for 6:30 pm (pre-closing) posting of NH exit poll crosstabs by NYT[imes] Graphics on Feb. 9, 2016.

[124] For discussion of the claim that U.S. exit polls are so different from those conducted abroad as to be singularly unsuitable as a check on fraudulent vote counting, see note 35 to this chapter.

[125] Lurking behind this explanation for the exit poll adjustment process is a more unsettling concern. In the words of the late Warren Mitofsky, known as the "father" of exit polling: "In a democracy, it's the orderly transfer of power that keeps the democracy accepting the results of elections. If it drags on too long, there's always a suspicion of fraud" (personal email correspondence).

[126] Weighting is necessary because, although we could wish for the mathematical precision of a perfectly random sample, the reality is that there are several non-random factors affecting an exit poll sample: so-called "clustering," which refers to sending interviewers to representative precincts rather than randomly interviewing voters

"unadjusted," though there is growing reason to believe that partial votecounts made available before poll closing are being used to begin the "adjustment" process *prior* to first public posting, thus narrowing any disparities—that give us what is usually our first glimpse of the "red shift," the exit poll-votecount disparity that would be so damning were it to appear anywhere else on Earth other than in our country.[127]

---

throughout the state; access issues, or the comparative difficulties of reaching and polling certain demographic sub-groups; selection bias, the possibility that interviewers will favor certain potential respondents over others; and response bias, the greater or lesser proclivity of certain sets of selected respondents to refuse participation in the poll.

Exit pollsters measure each of these metrics carefully and factor this data into their weighting of responses. If, for example, the response rate of an identifiable group (e.g., a certain race, age group, or gender) is below or above average, the responses from that group will be upweighted or downweighted accordingly.

A great deal of historical data and pattern analysis is brought to bear upon this process. It is not perfect—and critics have, from 2004 on, seized on any imperfection as a fatal flaw—but it has led, in the case of contests where there are *not* grounds for suspecting manipulation (e.g., noncompetitive or unusually well-protected races), to generally good agreement (i.e., within the stated margin of error) between exit poll results and votecounts. Some examples are the Republican presidential primaries of 2016 (see Chapter V) and the Virginia and New Jersey off-off-year elections of 2017 (see Chapter VI).

It was noted in note 35 above but it bears repeating here: Exit polls are to a significant extent dependent on a demographic weighting process that rests in turn on informed advance *estimations* of the particular electorate that will turn out for any given election. For various reasons, such estimates tend to be more precise in some situations (e.g., a general election with stable pre-election dynamics) and more susceptible to error in others (e.g., a primary election with high volatility and late movement, the early Democratic primaries of 2020 being a prime example of such).

Thus the practice of exit poll-based forensics requires an in-depth understanding of a variety of factors that may strengthen or weaken the probative value of any given exit poll or set of exit polls. It is inevitable, I suppose, that some without such understanding, and perhaps in the grip of outcome-driven passions, will scream fraud from the rooftops on the basis of exit poll-votecount disparities that may well be the product of erroneous demographic estimations of the part of pollsters faced with an exceptionally challenging scenario—unfortunately thereby undermining the credibility of exit poll forensics more carefully applied.

[127] Because these "unadjusted" exit poll numbers disappear *forever*, often within *minutes* of appearing on network Election Night websites, analysts must preserve them for forensic use in the form of screenshots. In E2004, when an apparent server glitch allowed the unadjusted numbers to remain up for hours rather than minutes (until after midnight EST), I was able to print out (I didn't yet know how to screen-capture) several hundred pages of unadjusted data (most states and the national exit poll with full crosstabs; it was a slow process that took all evening). I naively assumed that thousands of similar data captures were being made around the country and the globe but, with election integrity activism still in its infancy and as yet no general understanding of the importance of unadjusted exit poll data, I discovered by the early

When the votecounts for competitive and significant elections come out to the right of the exit polls, as they so often do, an explanation of some sort has to be provided. *General* exit poll "inaccuracy" will not suffice, as that would lead to misses in *both* directions, not the unilateral pattern that continues to emerge. And since, because this is America, *the votecounts cannot be questioned*, the "explanation" that has had to be ginned up is that the exit polls chronically and consistently oversample Democrats. This would be comforting—if only it were true. Putting aside for a minute that it would be passing strange for a group of polling experts at the height of their profession— fanatical about pattern analysis and error correction, trying their damnedest to get it right and with a batch of corrective tools at their disposal—to keep making *the same error* in state after state and year after year, the fact is that we have examined exit poll samples from the seven biennial elections 2004-2016 (the E2002 exit polls, the first of the computerized voting era, were so far "off" that they were withheld from the public entirely; E2012 will be examined in the next chapter) and found *zero evidence* of such a left skew.[128] In comparing the first-posted, ostensibly unadjusted exit poll samples to *every other measure of the electorate*, including census and registration data as well as multiple academic surveys,[129] we have found neutral or, more frequently, right-skewed exit poll samples in every case.

We believe a major reason for this is that those valuable first-posted, ostensibly unadjusted exit polls are weighted in large part to demographics drawn from the *adjusted* exit polls of prior elections—because it is the adjusted polls that are deemed "accurate." How were those prior polls adjusted? Almost invariably to the right to match red-shifted votecounts, and when you adjust the exit poll *results* to the right, the exit poll's *demographics* (what the electorate looked like) are carried along for the ride.[130] So a sample that was

---

morning hours that I was in sole possession of this data, which, once released and analyzed, became the initial basis for the questioning of the E2004 votecount.

[128] See, e.g., Simon J, O'Dell B: *Landslide Denied: Exit Polls vs. Vote Count 2006, Demographic Validity of the National Exit Poll and the Corruption of the Official Vote Count* (2007), presented as Study II in Chapter VIII.

[129] See, e.g., American National Election Studies (ANES), affiliated with the University of Michigan, at http://electionstudies.org/index.htm.

[130] The adjustment, or "forced weighting," process involves the imposition of a final weighting factor, keyed to the candidate-preference results (i.e., votecounts), on the existing weighted data.

If, for example, a state's final percentage for candidate Trump were 55% but his weighted exit poll percentage were 50%, the adjustment would upweight Trump's exit

initially 39 percent Democratic to 35 percent Republican, when "adjusted" (i.e., reweighted) to make the "who did you vote for?" numbers match the votecounts, might now become 37 percent Democratic, 37 percent Republican.[131] And that then becomes, in effect, the "truth" about the electorate and the new standard for weighting *future* exit polls (which are then further "adjusted" if even that right-skewed weighting fails to match the votecounts).[132]

---

poll results by 10% (1.10 x .50 = .55). This upweighting factor would be applied not just to the "who did you vote for?" question but to *every* question on the questionnaire of *every* respondent who indicated he/she voted for Trump, including of course all the demographic questions. Thus, if there were 1000 respondents who indicated they had voted for Trump, and 700 of these indicated that they were "Republican" voters, following the adjustment process, that number would become 770 (700 x 1.10), and the percentage of "Republican" voters among the exit poll respondents (and, if we trust the votecount and therefore the adjustment process, among the electorate) would increase accordingly.

This reweighting would also affect such measures as gender, age, race, income, etc.; the strength of the effect would depend on the degree to which the particular measure was correlated with candidate preference (e.g., gender would likely be less correlated than Party-ID). Respondents whose candidates' votecounts came in below their exit poll percentages would of course be correspondingly *down*weighted, along with all the demographic measures on their questionnaires.

[131] This is in fact what occurred in the 2004 Presidential election nationwide (and also in Ohio). A 4% demographic red shift may not look like much but it was enough to provide the "winning" margin for Bush and to give the GOP what amounted to a 4% exit poll handicap in the *next* election, which of course serves from a forensics standpoint to fully negate a would-be 4% red shift and thereby *fully cover* any future manipulation of that magnitude.

[132] It must be noted here that exit polling and pre-election polling are, each in its own way, responsive to official electoral results and hence become part of a feedback loop contaminated when those results are distorted.

In the case of exit polls, the raw response data must be weighted according to the pollster's best estimates of electoral composition (which is to say, oversimplifying a bit, that there should be x% Democrats, y% Republicans, p% whites, q% nonwhites, etc., in a given sample). This weighting of course affects the poll's outcome and it is in turn influenced strongly by the demographic percentages drawn from *previous* elections' exit polls. But the exit polls from the prior election(s) used for this purpose are exit polls that have been *adjusted to congruence with the votecounts in those prior elections* (this is standard practice, on the theory that the votecounts are accurate and so any exit poll that is not congruent with those votecounts must be inaccurate, not only as to its "whom did you vote for?" results but as to its demographics).

Thus (and, again, to oversimplify a bit), if a previous election required a 5% rightward exit poll adjustment in order to match the official votecount, that shift will be reflected in correspondingly shifted exit poll demographics (e.g., %R/%D), and it is those demographics that will find their way into the weighting of the *current* exit poll, pushing the current sample to the right and therefore the exit poll results to the right.

Taking this all into account, when, as is generally the case, the exit polls are "off" such that the votecounts come out to their right, while the exit poll sample is at worst neutral (or, more often, right-skewed), it provides compelling evidence of *vote mistabulation.*

That evidence becomes even stronger when we have the data available to perform *second-order comparisons.* A first-order comparison would consist of measuring the disparity between exit polls (or any other baseline) and votecounts in either a single election or a series of elections. When the disparities are large (near or beyond the margin of error) and in the same direction in a significant proportion of the contests examined, it is possible to calculate some very large numbers representing the odds of the set of such disparities occurring—say "one in 4.24 billion."[133] This certainly *looks* impressive, and the mathematics are correct, but the counter-argument would be that there are difficult-to-quantify factors not impounded in the mathematical margin of error—with exit polls, such factors would be clustering, selection and response biases, along with any significant errors in demographic weightings—that account for much of the disparity pattern.[134] In meeting such arguments, even a very impressive probability number like one in some-odd billion can have limited value. Perhaps the exit pollsters simply screwed up.

Accordingly, a red shift of x% in the previous election should, all else being equal, effectively *cover* a rig of x% in the current election by erasing the votecount vs. exit poll disparity that would otherwise have accrued. That is, if the current election is no more rigged than the previous one, it will appear, using the exit polls as baseline, *not to have been rigged at all.* It is crucial to bear this in mind when discussing the issues that have been raised regarding the E2016 exit polls (see Chapter V, notes 40-41).

[133] The exit polls from the early 2020 Democratic primaries present such a profile and some analysts have, prematurely in my opinion, alleged votecount fraud as the most likely or perhaps only explanation for the pattern; see, e.g., https://tdmsresearch.com/2020/03/08/vermont-2020-democratic-party-primary/.

[134] Analysts attempt to incorporate such semi-quantifiable factors in a measure called Total Survey Error (TSE). While the margin of error (MOE) of a sampling is a purely—and very simply calculated—mathematical measure of the range of proximity within which we can expect the sample (i.e., poll results) to fall relative to the whole (i.e., votecounts) a certain proportion (generally 95%) of the time, the TSE adds other potentially error-producing factors to the calculation. The TSE thus will generally exceed the MOE, though rarely, in well-conducted samplings and absent extraordinary dynamics, will it be more than a third to half again as great as the MOE. The red-flag red shifts of the computerized voting era have generally exceeded the TSEs as well as the MOEs of exit polls.

A second-order analysis finds a related series of contests with which to compare the red-flag series. In a sense we are looking at the disparity of disparities. A classic example presented itself in the presidential primaries of 2016. It is analyzed in greater detail in Chapter V, but the essence of it is that the Democratic primaries exhibited large and unidirectional exit poll-votecount disparities in state after state, while in the Republican primaries the exit polls were essentially spot-on. It becomes much harder to simply dismiss the exit pollsters as incompetent or their methodology as flawed when it performed brilliantly through a whole series of elections in one party's nomination battle but kept over-representing the vote of the same candidate in state after state in the other party's nomination battle. At the very least, such a second-order pattern raises the *question* of whether one set of contests was targeted for manipulation while the other set was left alone.

Again in 2016, this time in November, the national exit poll sample (keyed to the national popular vote for president) was ballpark-accurate, just within the expected error margin, but the exit poll-votecount disparities in key swing states like Wisconsin, Pennsylvania, and North Carolina were far outside the error margins (this pattern will be examined in detail in Chapter V).

Another kind of second-order analysis is the comparison of disparities between votecounts and polls interviewing the *same set of respondents* regarding competitive and noncompetitive contests. The noncompetitive contests, unlikely targets for manipulation, serve as a control and effectively remove any issues of sampling bias.[135] When we find radically different patterns of disparities in a series of competitive versus noncompetitive contests, that is a glaring red flag that can't be explained away by exit poll skeptics.

All that being said, the debate over exit polls as absolute *proof* of votecount fraud is likely to remain inconclusive. Neither side is permitted access to the raw data (held to be the property of the pollster and its major network clients) that might be helpful in resolving the dispute.[136] Nor, in the final analysis, are

---

[135] See, e.g., Simon J, et al: *Fingerprints of Election Theft: Were Competitive Contests Targeted?* (2007), presented as Study III in Chapter VIII.

[136] Two reasons have been given for withholding this data: reluctance to identify exit-polled precincts out of concern that might give rise to an effort to influence voters at those sites; and protection of the confidentiality of respondents, which, it is claimed, could be compromised by a release of the raw data. Neither reason holds any water.

Regarding the first, if the pollsters return to the same set of precincts in successive elections, then any potential "influencers" will know, from simple observation, what precincts to target whether precinct-identifying raw data is released or not. If they

exit polls, or any other form of indirect measurement, the *best evidence* of voter intent and public will.

But can we say that votecounts emerging from the fraud-inviting darkness of cyberspace are *better* evidence? The best evidence, *indeed the only truly reliable evidence,* resides on hand-marked paper ballots (where such exist, and with chain of custody adequately safeguarded), and it is only from an examination of that evidence—i.e., a public and observable count and/or audit of those ballots—that a reliable numerical conclusion can be drawn about what, collectively, the voting public intended.

Q: What about *Citizens United* and the influence of Big Money? Wouldn't that explain the electoral success of the Right?

A: If, having set a goal of "perpetual rule," you are going to rig a lot of elections over an extended period of time, at some point it will become noticeable that the pendulum isn't swinging freely, that not only are *individual* election results "surprising" but far too many of these surprises are in the same direction and the overall *pattern* defies explanation. The pendulum is seen to swing, but oddly and off-center, as if there were a magnet hidden in the wings stage-right. We have at least flirted with that point in our politics: witness a parade of articles in the media straining to explain why, as one put it, "conservatives always win."[137]

This is the hustler's challenge: *figuring out the maximum that can be taken while keeping the mark in the game.* The smartest rigger would of course let the pendulum swing just enough to keep the game going. But the game becomes a whole lot easier if some blanket explanation can be found such that both individual election results and the whole pervasive pattern no longer seem so bizarre. This is where *Citizens United* and the Big Money factor come in: if it can be established as conventional wisdom that Big Money decides

---

change locations from one election to the next, then the post-election release of raw data will not tip anyone off for that or subsequent elections.

Regarding the second, forensic analysts have requested a *very limited* set of raw data: candidate preference responses and the most basic demographics (age, race, gender). There is *zero* risk that, from such a data set, any of the respondents (who fill out exit poll questionnaires anonymously) could be individually identified.

When such specious reasons are given for the withholding of data, it should raise our level of suspicion about the actual reason.

[137] Brewer J: "The REAL Reason Conservatives Always Win," Common Dreams (6/22/2012), at https://www.commondreams.org/view/2012/06/22-12.

elections, the rigger's tracks are effectively covered with the readily available glut of corporate cash that *Citizens United* has swept into the electoral game. It is in fact very difficult to correlate electoral results with expenditures when all other factors are controlled. In some instances, over-saturation of messaging can even antagonize voters and backfire. [138] But it matters not that there is likely a powerful law of diminishing returns such that Big Money ultimately runs out of steam when it comes to buying/influencing voters. All that matters is the established *perception* that Big Money wins elections.

Thus, in the critical Wisconsin Governor's recall election early in 2012—where exit polls revealed a dead heat and also established that *virtually all voters had made their minds up well before the late surge of Big Money into the state*— Republican Scott Walker's "easy" seven-point victory was nonetheless credited by most pundits (David Brooks being a notable exception) to the 8-to-1 ratio of expenditure on Walker's behalf relative to his Democratic opponent. Thus *Citizens United* and the Big Money advantage of the Right can, *even where ineffective in fact*, provide good *cover* for rigged elections—though another explanation will have to be found for routs like E2014 (examined in Chapter IV), where the parties' expenditures were all but equal.

Q: Almost all airtime for hand-wringing has been devoted to the *overt* schemes to win elections—Big Money, voter suppression, gerrymandering, "Vote Wednesday" robocalls, etc. In discussing *Citizens United* just now, you seem to be suggesting that these are just red herrings. Could you clarify?

A: If the minority is going to gain power in a democracy, and then hope to *retain* power in spite of rabidly pursuing policies that operate to the clear detriment of the majority of the governed, that minority is going to have to pull out all the stops.[139] Rove's sought-after "permanent majority" (or even permanent gridlock—holding just enough power to permanently block the

---

[138] For confirmation we might ask former New York City Mayor Mike Bloomberg. The candidate for the 2020 Democratic presidential nomination spent half a billion dollars before bowing out gracefully with 37 pledged delegates (out of 1,991 needed to win). Many criticized the billionaire mayor for trying to "buy" the election, but it should be apparent that no amount of campaign expenditure would have sufficed to achieve that purpose.

[139] Of course the smaller and more extreme the minority, the more suspect its electoral seizure and maintenance of political power. But a nation that counts its votes unobservably, and entrusts that counting process to partisan corporations, should not be surprised to discover that its obituaries for a radical and grossly unpopular splinter such as the Tea Party, a "washed-up" strategist like Karl Rove, or a candidate like Donald Trump were premature.

other side's agenda and vision) requires an *array* of tactical gambits ranging from deceptive messaging to corporate Super-PAC money inundation, to geo-cynical gerrymandering, to voter suppression (through a sub-array of tactics ranging from discriminatory Voter ID laws to selectively scrubbing voter rolls; to closing and consolidating precincts in opponents' territory; to caging[140] and other forms of voter intimidation; to targeted disinformation, both procedural, such as making "Vote Wednesday" robocalls and sending "Vote Wednesday" flyers to likely supporters of the candidate marked for defeat, and substantive, as in falsehoods about candidates' records, scandals, statements).

Each of these tactics takes a heavy toll on what we would recognize as a fair and ethical electoral process and, to the extent that they are practiced primarily by the forces of the minority, all serve to reduce, or indeed reverse, the electoral margin that, in a fair democracy, the majority would otherwise enjoy. I agree that they are all pernicious and they are all ugly. But they are more or less *overt* and also *limited* in their bottom-line effect. When we examine what this new century's election outcomes would have been in the *absence* of the pervasive "red shift" (which, when exit poll-based, reflects the responses of *successful* voters and is therefore is independent of at least the voter-suppression tactics), it tells us that all these overt tactics combined are insufficient to produce the magnetic-pendulum effect we have been experiencing, let alone Rove's "permanent Republican majority."

But what these ugly overt tactics *do* achieve is to narrow the prevailing majority-minority political gap sufficiently that the *covert* tactic of computerized rigging can deliver the electoral *coup de grace* while managing to pass the smell test. So it is almost certainly a case not of either-or but of both-and.[141]

---

[140] Caging involves turning up at the polls with long lists of likely opposing voters and using them to challenge each individual's right to vote. Generally, the result of such challenges, undertaken almost exclusively by right-wing operatives, is to force the voter to submit a "provisional" ballot, and the reality is that many provisional ballots go uncounted. See generally, Palast G: *The Best Democracy Money Can Buy: A Tale of Billionaires & Ballot Bandits;* New York: Seven Stories Press, 2016; https://www.amazon.com/dp/1609807758/ref.

[141] The history and working of these combined "strip and flip" tactics are well-presented in Bob Fitrakis and Harvey Wasserman's *The Strip and Flip Selection of 2016: The Five Jim Crows & Electronic Election Theft*, CICJ Books, 2016, at https://www.amazon.com/dp/B01GSJLW0I.

The overt tactics can also serve as a kind of misdirection, distracting would-be election integrity guardians from the decisive covert game. As a voter, I have been bombarded with literally thousands of institutional emails and letters presenting frenzied alarums about *Citizens United*, voter ID, voter intimidation, gerrymandering, false-info robocalls and flyers, social-media disinformation campaigns, etc. Not one of these alerts and calls to remedial action is willing to contemplate a still darker possibility. None seem to have asked the obvious question: Is there really a bright ethical line between making "Vote Wednesday" robocalls to 10,000 supporters of the candidate targeted for defeat and simply taking the far more *efficient* approach of setting the zero-counters on, say, 50 memory cards to +100/-100, thereby undetectably shifting 10,000 net votes? Once the tactical means are embraced, the sky really is the limit—anything that can pass the stuffed-nose smell test.

And yet the ACLU, People for the American Way, and of course the Democratic Party (to pick on just a few of the many), recognize and decry the robocall and Facebook exploits, while the yet more sinister prospect of computerized rigging is beyond the pale (*here*, though of course *not* in Russia, or Pakistan, or Peru, or Venezuela, or . . .) and hence entirely ignored. Since there is no contesting the manifest vulnerability, as established by experts in study after study and demonstrated at DefCon three years running, it must be the bright ethical line that so reassures these guardians of democracy—that is, *It Could Never Happen Here.* We are watching America fall victim to its own exceptionalism.

Q: What does it take to know that an election has been honest, that the votes have been counted reasonably accurately given the large numbers involved?

A: It takes an open, transparent, and observable process. And it must be "end-to-end." There can't be any point in the counting process where the magician disappears behind the curtain, even for a few seconds, because a few seconds is all it takes to change the outcome of an election inside a computer.

Apologists for the current computerized counting system will point to all the aspects of "openness:" how observers can be present at the polls; how the machines are "certified" and put through a sample ballot test at some point before the election; how, when opscans are used, all the actual ballots can be manually counted if there is any question; how with Barcode BMDs and VVPAT (i.e., "paper-trail") DREs the voter gets to see a summary card or *a receipt*!

What they will conveniently leave out of that reassuring presentation are the crucial concealed passages along the pipeline, and the fact that *a system is only as transparent as its most concealed point*:

- A computer can without difficulty be programmed to pass any pre- or post-election test with flying colors and still shift votes at the time of the actual election.
- "Open source" code can be developed and archived, while alterations and substitutions are made to the code that does the actual ballot reading and counting.
- You can deploy an army of observers at the polling places and central tabulation locations and none of them will be able to see the actual count (or miscount) inside the computers.
- Where opscans are used, the reality is that the actual ballots are virtually *never* examined: mere citizens have no right to do so and candidates, where they might have such a right (and noting that it is generally made prohibitively expensive at precisely the stage at which candidates have emptied their campaign chests), are under enormous pressure not to exercise it, lest they be labeled "sore losers" and so torpedo their political futures.
- Certain states, following Florida's lead, have gone even further and outright banned hand counting to verify the machine counts. "Recounts" consist of running the ballots through the same computers that counted them the first time or hitting the "re-run" switch on a DRE.[142]

---

[142] A prime recent example was the Florida recount of the U.S. Senate and governor's races in 2018. The governor's contest, with a margin of 0.41% favoring the GOP candidate Ron DeSantis, was "recounted" entirely by feeding ballots back through the scanners that generated the initial count (two Florida counties also use paperless DREs). The Senate race margin was smaller, 0.15%, which was below the "mandatory hand count" threshold of 0.25%. So much was made of the fact that the Florida Senate race was being "recounted by hand."

Except that it wasn't. Only "overvotes" and "undervotes" (where the machine recorded either no votes or more than one vote for Senate) were recounted by hand, fewer than 1% of votes cast. The rest, like the ballots for governor, were simply run back through the scanners that had already counted them. The 1% recounted by hand were of course not a random sample of ballots, so could not even serve as an audit. Essentially neither the other 99%+ of the more than 8 million Senate votes nor indeed the accuracy of any of the scanners (and BMDs) that tabulated them were verified by Florida's "recount," though you would have had to search long and hard to find any media report that made this clear (https://www.washingtonpost.com/politics/hand-recount-of-ballots-begins-in-

- Touchscreen (DRE) computers with so-called "paper trails" can easily be programmed to print a vote for "A" on the "receipt" while recording a vote for "B" in the official count, and these often-unreadable receipts for digitally cast votes are even less likely than actual voter-marked ballots to ever see the light of day.
- Where—as recently marketed in Georgia, North Carolina, and a dozen other states—paper ballots are created by ballot-marking devices (BMDs) that generate a barcode (or any other format that the voter cannot easily read and verify) to then be read by a scanner, there is no way to verify either the accuracy or the authenticity of ballots; so while the move to "paper" is ballyhooed, the effect is the opposite of transparency, adding yet another layer of technology and yet another vector for fraud.[143]

An open and observable process would entail visible counting that could be witnessed by representatives of all candidates and the public at every stage. There would be, *as there once was*,[144] a "tabulation tree," with the precinct counts observed directly and publicly posted, and the subsequent aggregations at the town, county, and state levels capable of being reconciled (the process is simple addition) from the lowest level to the highest.

No observation or vigilance will ever ensure a "perfect" count, but the minor inaccuracies, the "noise," in the system will break evenly, only extremely rarely affecting electoral outcomes, and those so close that full recounts would be undertaken as a matter of course. Under an observable counting process there would be no opportunity to, in effect, perpetrate a rolling coup and steal a nation.

---

floridas-broward-county/2018/11/16/f9131ee0-e92f-11e8-bbdb-72fdbf9d4fed_story.html was typical).

[143] See https://medium.com/@jennycohn1/despite-apparent-conflict-of-interest-georgias-safe-commission-is-poised-to-approve-a-new-ba6f683c3727. Intense lobbying by public-interest advocates—including Marilyn Marks with the Coalition for Good Governance, and John Brakey with AUDITUSA—has resulted in a few state- and county-level victories for the election integrity side, most of which have unfortunately and predictably turned out to be temporary. Similar battles are being fought in a number of other states.

[144] It is all too easy to forget that, as a nation, *we have done this before*—indeed, throughout most of our history. The fact that we have grown more populous does not much alter the equation, as the need for and supply of vote counters expand correlatively and *remain proportional*. Vote counting is a scalable enterprise.

Q: What about audits?

A: Post-election audits, for the most part, constitute a well-intentioned effort to make vote counting quasi-observable by requiring a second count of a select portion of the computer-counted ballots for verification of the initial count. If it is well-designed, scrupulously executed, and mandates a hand count rather than simply running ballots through the computer a second time, an audit can expose a computerized fraud and thus can also operate as a powerful fraud deterrent.

The question naturally arises what level of risk a prospective election rigger will tolerate before deciding that stolen electoral victories are not worth the risk of exposure (leaving aside the matter of punishment, exposure would presumably result in reform to a much more secure system; i.e., "TILT—Game Over"). Of course we know of no election riggers who have come forward to discuss their thought processes and calculations, but it is hard to imagine that an enterprise of such pitch and moment is undertaken without a rather fine-tuned rational calculation of risk and reward. Karl Rove has spoken of "perpetual rule" and a reward of that magnitude would seem to be worth a great expenditure of effort and resource as well as a certain amount of risk.

National-grade election riggers, however well-compensated financially or devoted to their belief system, are nonetheless rational actors who can be deterred by high-risk threat of exposure but who also almost certainly have the resources and determination to find and exploit any path left deliberately or inadvertently open.[145] For an audit protocol to be effective as a deterrent, it must set up risk-based roadblocks on all such paths.

Specifically, for an audit protocol to "work":

- It must count enough ballots to have a decent mathematical chance of detecting any outcome-altering mistabulation.
- The selection of such ballots must be random and not telegraphed in advance.

---

[145] Presumably even foreign-state actors such as Russia would greatly prefer not to get caught, as an entirely different set of punitive consequences, ranging from sanctions to war, would be in store. Under the Trump administration, however, it has been far from clear that such punishments would ensue, which has an impact on reward/risk calculus.

- Secure chain of custody of the ballots must be strictly maintained (i.e., they can't be left, as they so often are, stacked up in some unlocked storeroom, warehouse, or garage).
- The audit design must be sensitive enough to pick up deliberate manipulations and at the same time selective enough not to throw red flags at incidental "noise" in the system.
- Failed audits must lead, in a prescribed sequence, to deeper investigation and effective remedial action.

All these requirements are necessary and none of them are trivial. Consider for instance the logistical challenge of selecting the counts to be audited and then immediately proceeding with the audit without allowing any opportunity for the swapping out of ballots in locations now revealed to the riggers to be "hot." In *practice* most of the audits we have thus far seen undertaken have failed on one or more of these counts.[146]

---

[146] Perhaps most egregious was Ohio 2004, where precincts were cherry-picked with the guidance of the equipment vendors, who also provided "cheat sheets" to election administrators to help ensure that the audit counts would square with the official computer counts (see http://www.thelandesreport.com/ConyersReport.htm at p. 81). We have also seen disparities revealed on audit "resolved" by simply retabulating the machine or precinct in question to match the audit numbers. That, of course, undermines the whole purpose of audit sampling (what does the sampled machine or precinct tell us about the others?) as well as the efficacy of the audit as a deterrent.

Recounts have also been plagued with such irregularities and are rife with opportunities to alter or swap ballots to erase evidence of computer mistabulation.

When ballots are counted in a recount, a days-later audit, or even on Election Night at central counting stations that require the ballots to be transported, continual public observation is lost and there is no way to be certain that the ballots being counted are the same ones as were cast. Counting outside the precinct (i.e., central tabulation), delayed audits, and recounts would all require a radical (and expensive) tightening of chain-of-custody protections to qualify as observable counts.

It remains an open question within the ranks of election integrity advocates to what extent a fully hand-marked paper-based system with a mandated and robust audit protocol would provide sufficient public "observation" (albeit indirect) to meet the standard of observable counting. While robust audits, especially risk-limitation audits conscientiously executed, could indeed serve as an effective deterrent to the rigging enterprise, we have seen in practice that audits often have been ineffectual or corrupted. That laxity would have to change dramatically.

It is vital to recognize that if the incentive to manipulate a votecount in order to capture or hold office is x, the incentive to *conceal* that manipulation in the very rare cases where a red flag has been raised and some sort of investigation has been undertaken is $1000x$, orders of magnitude greater. At stake at that point is not merely the office in question but the threat of exposure of the entire fraudulent enterprise and the potential "death penalty" remedy of serious reform of the vote counting system to effectively end the man-behind-the-curtain, faith-based process that currently holds sway.

Three quarters of the states have now adopted audit protocols of widely varying strength and efficacy.[147] Proposed federal audit legislation, most notably a bill introduced in 2007 by Rep. Rush Holt (D-NJ), was assailed for its weakness and in fact bitterly divided election integrity advocates between those who believed "half-a-loaf" incremental progress was the best to be hoped for and those who saw such "progress" as ineffective to stop rigging and falsely reassuring to boot. Sadly, that battle within the ranks is still being fought today.

Some states have begun to experiment with a stronger protocol, known as a risk-limiting audit (RLA);[148] but, with two politically quixotic exceptions,[149] proposed federal legislation has reflected little sense of urgency when it comes to putting teeth into audits—either leaving them optional or setting dates well in the future (e.g., 2024) for their adoption.[150]

---

[147] See National Conference of State Legislatures October 2019 summary "Post-Election Audits" at http://www.ncsl.org/research/elections-and-campaigns/post-election-audits635926066.aspx. To characterize the collection of protocols as hodgepodge would be to grossly understate their non-uniformity. While a few are "risk-limiting," some boil down to little more than spot-checks or even simply checks on whether machine totals were correctly reported.

[148] See, e.g., Colorado: http://thehill.com/policy/cybersecurity/342352-colorado-hires-startup-to-help-audit-digital-election-results.

[149] In the House, the "Secure America's Future Elections" (SAFE) Act, H.R.1562, was introduced by Rep. Mark Pocan (D-WI) in March 2017, (https://www.congress.gov/bill/115th-congress/house-bill/1562/text#toc-HDF8667CF68F64384BF78E8610D057352). In the Senate, the "Protecting American Votes and Elections" Act, S.3049 (https://www.govtrack.us/congress/bills/115/s3049), was introduced by Ron Wyden (D-OR) and several liberal colleagues in 2018 (NB the absence of a single Republican co-sponsor). Notably the prescribed audits would have applied to federal elections beginning with 2018.

With Senate Majority Leader Mitch McConnell (R-KY) refusing to bring any election security/transparency legislation to the Senate floor—all threats, domestic and foreign, be damned—to speak nothing of a Trump veto, the chances of either bill, indeed *any* serious bill, becoming law before the 2020 election are, well, zero.

[150] I should mention here something about "citizen audits," which have been undertaken at various times and with various degrees of sophistication to fill the vacuum left by governmental inaction.

The main problem when private entities offer a "parallel count" of votes, by inviting voters to fill out what amounts to a "copy ballot" to be manually and publicly counted, is that of response bias. Any response rate short of 100% opens the possibility that refusers were predominantly of one or another political persuasion—so no apples-to-apples percentage-vote comparison can carry much weight. On the other hand, a straight numerical comparison might well be of probative value in exposing fraud in the official count, in the case where more voters indicate a vote for "Candidate A" in the

There is little doubt that a well-designed, sufficiently robust, faithfully executed audit protocol, coupled with the use of hand-marked paper ballots,[151] would be a powerful tool for securing our elections. Unfortunately, though, audits have been a kind of non-obligatory afterthought to the computerization of voting and vote counting, as reflected in the patchwork quilt of audits (and non-audits) we find across the country.

Audits can be precinct-based (essentially checking the performance of individual scanners/tabulators selected at random), or aggregate (comparing the audit count to the votecount for an entire contest). They can also be "flat" (a fixed percentage of ballots sampled) or "risk-limiting" (sampling, and expanding the sample, as necessary to produce an agreed-upon level of confidence that the votecount was accurate). The RLA, put forward by several statisticians,[152] is currently in vogue, so I will discuss its pros and cons first. The essence of the RLA is that the extent or magnitude of the audit effectively varies in inverse proportion to the size of the first-count margin of victory in an election—which is to say, closer finishes draw bigger audits.

---

parallel election than were counted by the computers. Unless those voters were lying (and there is no incentive to do so), such evidence is rock solid.

While such "parallel election audits" can consist of simply a table with blank ballots and a collection box outside the polling place, the VeriCount system, a far more sophisticated and comprehensive process, relying on smartphones and blockchain technology, is now in the testing stage (see www.democracycounts.org). It is a promising approach, though its ultimate utility as an election protection protocol remains to be established.

[151] Because most late-model BMDs interpose a programmed function between the voter's intended choices and the barcodes (or QR codes) they create, which are then counted as the votes of record, no less an authority than the inventor of risk-limiting election audits, among others, has concluded that only hand-marked ballots, not those created by BMDs, can be meaningfully audited with that protocol (see Appel, Andrew; DeMillo, Richard; Stark, Philip: "Ballot-Marking Devices Cannot Assure the Will of the Voters" [4/21/19] https://ssrn.com/abstract=3375755).

[152] I give particular credit here to Professor Philip Stark (UC Berkeley), though others have also been involved in the application of risk-limitation principles to the votecount process. For a thorough discussion of auditing principles and pitfalls as well as the operation of various forms of RLA, see https://www.stat.berkeley.edu/~stark/Preprints/RLAwhitepaper12.pdf.

In 2006 my colleague Bruce O'Dell and I proposed an alternative approach, known as Universal Ballot Sampling (UBS), which entailed an observable human count of one of every ten ballots, wherever and however cast, making for a very simple and easily executed protocol and offering a very high level of precision for verifying machine counts (see https://codered2014.com/wp-content/uploads/2020/04/new_UBS_811Update_061707.pdf).

The RLA has much to commend it and, if faithfully executed, is not by any means easy to thwart or evade. The essence of the RLA's rationale is that it is harder to find and catch a tiny fish than a big one *and we don't really care about dead fish of any size.* A "dead fish" is any mistabulation that does *not* alter the outcome of an election. With all respect to the oft-repeated mantra "count every vote as cast," that is not a realistic standard for major elections. Vote counting, like any other operation dealing with large numbers and multiple sub-operations, is *not a perfect process and 99.99 percent of the time does not have to be.* We can and are obliged to tolerate a mistabulated (or misinterpreted) vote here or there; machines and humans will not always see eye to eye on every single ballot.

That is not, however, how elections are stolen. We can't afford to get bogged down in disparities of one or two votes per thousand, unless the election outcome is exceedingly close and those disparities—assuming they were deliberate, cumulative, and unidirectional, and so did *not* cancel each other out—could make the difference.

This is the "mindset" of the RLA. It grows more teeth, or drops more hooks, when the fish is both alive and small because those fish are harder to catch. If, for example, the official margin of a race is 40 points, for any rig to have been *outcome altering* it would have had to shift a net of 20 percent of the votes, or at least one vote out of every five, from the loser to the winner; in other words, a *lot* of votes, a big fish. That magnitude of disparity is quite a sore thumb and easy to catch with even a tiny audit, assuming the precincts to be audited are not telegraphed in advance.[153] Only if the margin is *close* could the theft of relatively *few* votes have altered the *outcome*: and that is when the RLA drops lots of hooks, so that even a small (but successful) rig is likely to be caught.

You don't *need* a big, labor- and capital-intensive audit for the vast majority of election contests; you don't need to waste resources in the name of elevating form over function. One can imagine how huge a selling point that last sentence is to every rational and budget-constrained election administrator out there. And isn't that where we're at now: trying to get effective protocols adopted soon or sooner, before it all becomes academic?

---

[153] RLAs, as noted, can also rely on jurisdiction-wide samples. While this eliminates the danger of telegraphing precincts to be audited, it raises other pragmatic sampling challenges, as will be seen. It should also be noted that when an RLA encounters a reversed-winner election, it will in fact gradually proceed to a full (100%) sample.

The theory of the RLA is sound and, as I have noted above, this audit approach has much to commend it. Nonetheless, I have developed reservations about its performance "in the wild." Election Night, and the days after, present messy, often chaotic rather than laboratory or classroom, conditions. Ballots to be audited may, depending on the specific RLA protocol, have to be drawn from many different "piles" (or, if digital ballot images are used, files). If the audit is the "ballot sampling" species—that is, one that seeks to sample enough ballots for the jurisdiction as a whole to verify the margin of victory for each contest audited—those piles may also include absentee, mailed-in, and provisional ballots.

The basic RLA protocol relies on a kind of "rolling" sample, where the auditors "keep going" until their results verify (or cannot verify) the outcome of a given contest. This means that, in an election with several or many contests to be audited, the sample size for each contest will be unique, as it will be determined by several factors, chief among which will be the machine-count margin of victory for that contest. That's a lot of sampling and— notwithstanding the fact that the basic sampling protocol is rather cookbook— lots of ways to go wrong. Especially when we remind ourselves that the atmosphere for conducting such audits will, in many locations, be highly charged, partisan, and potentially contentious.

With these considerations in mind—and having observed some of the difficulties encountered by states like Colorado and other venues now experimenting with RLAs—I set about developing an alternative protocol, a combination of the Flat and RLA approaches, which I call the "Split-The-Difference Audit" (STDA). My aim is to greatly simplify and routinize the real-world tasks while still retaining the teeth necessary to catch, and therefore deter, outcome-altering fraud.

The STDA is presented more fully as Study VII in Chapter VIII, but its basic feature is a relatively small (1 percent) initial flat sampling of ballots. The all-important "escalation trigger," which determines whether a given contest passes or fails (and is therefore subject to a full manual count), is set in advance at half the margin of victory. Thus, for example, if a given contest resulted in a votecount margin of 60 – 40 percent, an audit result of anything "worse" than 55 – 45 percent would trigger the escalation. Not only is the math remarkably simple with the STDA, but a *single initial sample* will suffice for all elections on the ballot to be audited, down to the state legislative level. The presentation in Chapter VIII includes a variety of examples and explanations that demonstrate how the audit would work and why it would be an effective deterrent without generating confusion or conflict in the difficult real-world setting of Election Night.

Both the RLA and STDA approaches focus specifically on what matters about elections: outcomes that reflect the collective majority/plurality intent of the electorate; i.e., *who won*. The challenge now is to respond to the prospect of a faith-based E2020 with the urgency called for—to incorporate a serious and workable audit protocol, with plenty of teeth and no unnecessary fat, into state and federal legislation *now*, not in 2028 or a "pilot" program in 2024.

Q: I take it that you see Internet Voting as a step in the wrong direction?

A: It should come as no surprise that virtually all election integrity advocates view Internet Voting (I.V.) as an anathema, not merely a step but a giant leap in the wrong direction. It also should come as no surprise that, despite a few notable successes in beating it back, I.V. is spreading, having been adopted in one form or another in a growing number of venues.[154]

I.V.'s seductions are the usual ones of convenience, speed, budgetary savings, and increased turnout (though voters lacking internet access will obviously be put at a serious disadvantage)—all taken one step further. We have already seen how hard it is to say no to that package of goodies and, viewed through the same rose-colored glasses that gave us HAVA and computerized voting in the first place, I.V. presents itself as something of a no-brainer: a logical extension of our technological capacity, making the chores of voting and vote counting still easier and cheaper. Given that the vast majority of us do everything *else* online, you can just about *taste* the inevitability of I.V.

So why fight it? Because I.V. takes the fundamental hazard of *all* computerized voting—that we as citizens and voters haven't a clue about what the programmer is doing with our votes—and not only increases it to an absurdly high level, but also adds to it a gilded invitation to *outside* interference, as it is by now a given that virtually *nothing* that runs on the internet is immune to

---

[154] Internet voting had been adopted for at least some class of voters (e.g., abroad, military) in 31 U.S. states and several territories as of 2019, including four states that allow ballot submission via a web-based portal and one that uses blockchain and a mobile app (see http://www.ncsl.org/research/elections-and-campaigns/internet-voting.aspx; and http://online.wsj.com/articles/pamela-smith-and-bruce-mcconnell-hack-the-vote-the-perils-of-the-online-ballot-box-1401317230?KEYWORDS=Hack+The+Vote).

hacking, manipulation, and surveillance.[155] I.V. drew a major security-based thumbs-down from the National Institute of Standards and Technology (NIST) in 2011[156] and white-hat hackers have had a field day demonstrating the flimsiness and easy penetrability of the security protocols of I.V. systems touted as ready to roll.[157]

Nonetheless I believe that the fight against I.V. is[158] less straightforward than some of my EI colleagues would have it. For one thing it is a delicate matter to oppose I.V. without seeming by inference to defend, or at least be resigned to, the woeful status quo (i.e., the opscans, BMDs and DREs) that I.V. would be replacing. Drawn between I.V. and existing computerized voting, the line of battle slides still further away from our goal of an observable count.

It is also worth thinking about how the ridiculously insecure process of internet voting stacks up against the ridiculously insecure process of good old computerized voting.[159] Two differences jump out at me. The first is that I.V. is a lot like what gangsters refer to as an "open city;" that is, given the ultimate vulnerability of all things internet, I.V. is something of a come-one-come-all cyber-arena, as opposed to the monopolistic fiefdom of a few partisan corporations dealing out discrete memory cards, to the programming of which they alone have access. The second is that, even to the casual observer, I.V.

---

[155] It would be hard to dispute that whatever protection there *is* on the internet these days derives less from impenetrable firewalls and encryptions than from simple "safety-in-numbers." There is so much data to steal and use, only so many sophisticated hackers, and only so much time, so that the odds that *your* little scrap of data will wind up in their clutches *and* that someone will find the time to use it nefariously are tolerably small. But of course this Russian-roulette mode of "protection" does not apply to intrinsically high-value targets such as election results. The hue and cry since 2016 is "The Russians are coming!" but it really could be anyone. Recall that, according to every purveyor of misinformation from Obama to Comey to the DHS, our elections are supposedly safe because the computers are *not* connected to the internet. Even though most of them, directly or indirectly, *are*.

[156] See http://www.nist.gov/itl/vote/upload/NISTIR-7700-feb2011.pdf.

[157] See, e.g., the work of Harri Hursti and Alex Halderman, detailed at notes 4 and 5 to this chapter.

[158] Or *was*—until the advent of COVID-19 and the immediate threat of an online voting fraudfest marketed as salvation for a potentially socially-distanced E2020.

[159] Given the widespread, long-denied but recently admitted, direct and indirect connections of voting computers to the internet, we are in a sense *already* dealing with a disguised form of I.V. (see, e.g., https://fortune.com/2019/08/08/swing-state-voting-systems-connected-internet-vice-report/; https://securityboulevard.com/2019/08/us-voting-machines-internet-connected-despite-denials/; but see, https://www.politico.com/news/2019/10/30/new-voting-machine-rules-061966).

(unlike opscans and even DREs) is obviously and unmistakably *computerized* voting. Much of the public should *get* just what it is being asked to trust and every bigtime online hack headline, every CHANGE YOUR PASSWORD!!! alert, every chilling tale of identity theft, and every new revelation of surveillance-state snooping will chip away at that trust.[160] Embraced at first virtually without reservation, the internet environment and our safety in cyberspace are now objects of a growing queasiness, and there is no sign that full trust is likely to be restored any time soon.

The end result if I.V. is widely adopted? Who knows. But one can easily enough imagine a variety of I.V. meltdowns and disasters—ranging from intrinsic systemic glitches[161] to white-hat hacks ("Mickey Mouse gets 4 billion votes!") to foreign interference—that would sharply focus attention on the vulnerabilities not just of I.V. but of *all* computerized vote counting. I'm thinking here of a principle of judo, where the momentum of an opponent's over-reach is used against him. One can imagine a backlash to the disasters of I.V. carrying us all the way back to an observable counting process. Meanwhile I.V. elections would likely be cyber free-for-alls, more or less equal-opportunity rigging (though perhaps depending on how set up and by whom), and to my eyes even *that* absurdity would be something of an improvement over the current state of affairs, which, as we have seen, has been effectively one-sided.

I don't support internet voting. In fact, given the current and projected state of cyber-security, I am with my EI colleagues in thinking it is *insane*.[162] But I also

---

[160] As an example, I had an experience a couple of years ago that has become all too common: having placed an online order for a subscription to *The New York Times* at $286.00 for a year, I received a receipt notifying me that I would be billed for $286 + tax every *week*, or $16,098.94 for the year (too much, I reasoned, for a paper that wouldn't touch evidence of computerized election theft). It took a fair amount of wrestling with customer service to figure out how to undo this computer "glitch." Of course, had 286 *votes* been magically transformed into 16,099 *votes* (or vice versa), there would have been no collective receipt to put anyone on notice to challenge or even question the results.

[161] E.g., the 2020 Iowa Democratic caucus fiasco, where the use of the internet merely for the transmission of vote totals, not the casting and counting of votes, blew up in the party's face. Fortunately, votes were cast on paper, and were available for recounting, obviously not the case with full-on I.V.

[162] I think the chances are better than even that, in response to the social-distancing imperative triggered by the coronavirus of 2020, there will be calls for greatly expanded I.V. and even concrete plans put forward to vote online in some states in November 2020. I would not be at all surprised to see Trump himself reveal a "great" plan to deal with the problem of voting this year ("Kush, set this thing up, okay?"). Recall that 31 states *already* use I.V. for at least a small subset of their voters, so all it

think that unless arguments made against I.V. nimbly pivot on public recognition of internet-related dangers to call *all* unobservable vote counting similarly into question, we will, even if successful in blocking I.V., have done little more than to perpetuate a *nearly equally insane* status quo.

Q: What are "digital ballot images" and how might they be helpful in the quest to verify election results and deter or detect fraud?

A: Most computerized voting equipment designed within the past few years, whether DRE or Opscan, creates an electronic file (think pdf or jpg) for each cast ballot, which can be read at a later date. These "digital ballot images" (DBIs) contain no indication of the voter's identity but do preserve an image of the ballot cast (in the case of opscans) or a completed template with the voter's choices (in the case of DREs). According to most experts, altering these files or the program that creates them to change the votes cast would require a significantly more sophisticated manipulation than, say, just flipping votes on a scanner or DRE's memory card or off-setting the "zero-counters" to shift votes wholesale. The higher degree of difficulty would constitute, if not a complete roadblock, then at least a rather formidable speed bump. The idea, as is generally the case with election protection protocols, is to confront the would-be meddler with a more challenging task and a less appealing reward/risk ratio.

Thus there are some election transparency advocates who see in DBIs the potential for greatly increasing the transparency of our elections, by effectively crowd-sourcing the verification process. Because the images are digital files, once created they could be downloaded by anyone with a home computer who was interested in checking or auditing the official results for any given precinct or—using the power of crowd-sourcing—for the election as a whole.

---

would take is a scaling up of a structure already in place. The appeal would be obvious: making it possible for more Americans (including the stricken) to vote conveniently without unnecessarily endangering their own health or that of others. Cue the patriotic music.

This prospect is so seductive under prevailing *epidemiological* circumstances, and also so dangerous under prevailing *political* circumstances, that we should martial all our forces to block it before it ushers in an opportunity for an electoral fraud of epic proportions. *This*, we should all realize, is profoundly and emphatically *not* the time for such a dubious experiment, and we should be—as we unfortunately were not with HAVA—ready to expose and pounce on the true motives and masters of those identified as being behind it. Especially if the ties lead to Trump or the GOP—which, remember, has not a gram of genuine zeal for facilitating voting or expanding the electorate.

Somewhat labor-intensive perhaps, but a good deal less onerous than counting the voter-marked ballots—and avoiding the problem that voter-marked ballots are off-limits to public inspection. Intrepid individuals or groups with a bit of tech savvy could create counting programs that would greatly speed up the DBI "audit" process.

If all this is sounding a bit too neat and "mission accomplished" to have a place in this devoutly skeptical book, there are a couple of major catches. Yes, the newer computers are designed to create DBIs—but they are also designed to destroy them, as early as a millisecond after they are created and their votes counted. The computers are in fact equipped with an "On-Off" switch—set it to "On" and the images are preserved; set it to "Off" and they are destroyed. The switches are manned of course not by election transparency advocates but by election administrators under the command of counties and states. Care to guess what switch position the majority of them choose?

Election transparency advocates—led in this particular crusade by John Brakey and Chris Sautter of AUDIT-USA[163]—have brought suit to compel election administrators to preserve the ballot images, on the grounds that they are "election records," which must be maintained under federal law (for federal elections) and the laws of many states.[164] Such a suit succeeded in Alabama court (prior to the Moore-Jones Senate election of December 2017), only to be overturned the morning of the election on appeal by the state to the Alabama Supreme Court. Apparently the court was persuaded that turning the switch to "On" was too burdensome for election administrators. Ohio then-Secretary of State John Husted fought hard to defeat AUDIT-USA's and the Green Party gubernatorial candidate's suit in the Ohio Supreme Court, claiming the secretary of state has no legal authority to require the counties to turn their digital ballot image switches on.[165]

I have made the point several times that the concealment of the vote counting process in the computerized era is a feature not a bug—the system has been

---

[163] Americans United for Democracy, Integrity and Transparency in Elections, at http://www.auditelectionsusa.org/.

[164] See https://www.alternet.org/election-03918/breakthrough-technology-will-count-election-results-never.

[165] See https://whowhatwhy.org/2018/05/07/ohio-goes-to-court-over-ballot-image-preservation/; it is perhaps worth noting that all seven justices of the court were Republicans. For archives of DBI-related news in other venues, see https://www.auditelectionsusa.org/category/news/.

designed for concealment, so it is not surprising that it fights like hell to avoid being *unconcealed*. For digital ballot images to become an effective verification protocol—the equivalent of a public audit—is going to require the cooperation, voluntary or compelled, of the administrative caste. They will have to upgrade to capable equipment, turn the switches to "On," make the files available for download and review, and take seriously reports of disparities in the counts. There is also the potential for a diffuse, or crowd-sourced, approach to wax chaotic or to itself be susceptible to "meddling" by entities seeking to disrupt and undermine the electoral process.[166]

So there are—with digital ballot images, as there are with HCPB and audit protocols—hurdles to be cleared and issues to be addressed. But the potential is there for a significant step toward election protection and a prying open of the black box.

Q: Someone offers the following deal: an observable vote-count *and* photo-ID required to vote. Do you accept?

A: In a cautious heartbeat. Concern about the security and honesty of our upcoming elections may be one of the very few shared agendas bridging the great political divide in America today. In a February 2018 NBCNews-SurveyMonkey poll, 79 percent of those surveyed believed that the country's voting systems are vulnerable to hacking.[167] Couple that with the 69 percent of Trump supporters that, in a Washington Post-ABC News poll before the 2016 election, believed that "voter fraud" occurs "very or somewhat often,"[168] and

---

[166] For an example of the trade-offs involved, consider Chicago, where then-Cook County Director of Elections Noah Praetz officially supported the publication of DBIs—but only after administrators had scrubbed them of all "extraneous marks." The professed rationale for the pre-publication scrubbing was to remove any markings that could tie the ballot to an identified voter and so undermine secret-ballot principles. Fair enough—but such scrubbing also presents administrators with an opportunity to scrub (or alter) as many *votes* as needed to make the digital ballot count agree with the computer count. This possibility is hardly far-fetched in light of what is known about the cheat-sheeting of Ohio recounts in 2004. If the decision of what is a "vote" and what is an "extraneous mark" is to be made in private by an administrator or technician, it merely succeeds in replacing one kind of "trust us" election with another, keeping a crucial step in the verification process concealed from the public.

[167] See https://www.nbcnews.com/politics/politics-news/poll-most-americans-think-russia-will-interfere-again-2018-elections-n845076.

[168] See https://www.washingtonpost.com/news/the-fix/wp/2016/09/15/poll-nearly-half-of-americans-say-voter-fraud-occurs-often/?utm_term=.3c2973235dfb.

you have a major trust problem when it comes to the most basic protocol of our democracy.

Of course, these are two very different worries. The president and his base envision hordes of "illegal" voters crashing the polls to cast their ballots against him and his political affiliates. Many continue to take Trump's word for it that millions of such voters cost him his coveted popular-vote victory in November 2016.[169] On the other hand, at least as many voters worry that it's not illegal *voters* but a vulnerable *counting* process that threatens to undermine our democracy and alter the direction of our nation.

Without revisiting the evidence for and merits of each belief, I am here simply acknowledging that a government that rests on perceived electoral legitimacy now depends on an electoral system that is in serious trouble. I would be the first to propose, and would certainly accept, an approach to this looming crisis that Trump—the artist of the deal—might embrace: a *quid pro quo*. We can move quickly to address *both* bases for burgeoning distrust in our elections.

Why *not* consider an omnibus approach that includes both a requirement for photo-ID at the polls *and* a requirement that ballots be hand-marked on paper and either counted manually or subject to uniform, public audit prior to certification?[170]

Details of course matter and can have powerful partisan impact. So it would, for example, be necessary to ensure that obtaining the required ID be facilitated rather than burdened with bureaucratic and administrative hurdles set up to discriminate against any age, race, or class of voter.[171] And it would

---

[169] See https://www.usatoday.com/story/news/politics/onpolitics/2017/01/23/president-trump-illegal-ballots-popular-vote-hillary-clinton/96976246/; see, also, https://www.npr.org/2018/04/05/599868312/fact-check-trump-repeats-voter-fraud-claim-about-california.

[170] It is clear that Congress would have the power to legislate both ends of the deal for federal elections. Principles of federalism might render its further application to elections for state offices problematic, such that the deal would have to be replicated on a state by state basis—though a national voter-ID card has in fact been proposed and, if federal control of that aspect of state election processes passed muster, it would be hard to argue that the counting aspect was off-limits to federal legislation.

[171] See http://www.newsweek.com/voter-id-laws-discriminatory-disenfranchise-485708. There are also civil-liberties concerns associated with any national ID proposal. Therefore the permissible forms of ID would, like state-issued driver's licenses and non-driver alternatives, have to be narrowly tailored to contain only such information as was needed to establish identity and residence.

likewise be necessary to provide sufficient blueprints and funds for hand-counts to be undertaken or audits conducted without undue compromise of their design.

But the basic idea would be to button up both ends of an electoral process practically everyone now regards as vulnerable to one or another species of fraud. And to do it without further delay, in time for the critical 2020 elections. If each "side" wants its grave concern addressed—even if it thinks the other side's concern is overblown hooey—each should embrace this deal enthusiastically. There is, after all, nothing wrong with an election that turns out to be *too* secure.

Yes, it will cost a bit of money and require some work. We have tried to have our democracy on the cheap (while pouring trillions into wars and occupations to foster "democracy" abroad[172]) and it has come back to haunt us. It is time to pony up a bit for the security of *our* elections—whether one sees Russians, other operatives with access to the cyberspace in which our votes are counted, or undetected illegal or multiple voters as the principal threat to that security.

Q: Given the Snowden revelations about NSA surveillance, along with other signs that American democracy is deteriorating irrespective of which party governs, would an honest vote counting system even matter anymore?

A: There was a brief glimpse during the Occupy movement of what public anger at American Systemic Injustice might come to if it found a way to assemble, to come out of its isolated private homes and apartments and shelters and cubicles into the public squares of the nation. It was a powerful image, and one that so shook America's rulers in their corporate and governmental corridors of power that they soon resorted to a federally-coordinated blitzkrieg to empty those squares and kill Occupy before it multiplied any further and before the Bastille was in any real danger.

One of the most important takeaways from the Occupy experience was the recognition of a previously hidden divide in the American body politic: that of the "99 Percent" and the "1 Percent." Throughout American history our enduring system of representative democracy has thrived on the two-party dialectic. Certainly for living generations, the vision we have of politics is that

---

[172] See http://money.cnn.com/2017/08/21/news/economy/war-costs-afghanistan/index.html.

of the Democratic and Republican parties carrying the ark into battle for their relatively evenly matched constituencies, taking turns holding sway and advancing an agenda as the political pendulum swung.

That is still the image of American politics you'll see in *The New York Times* or on *CNN*: another sporting event really, presenting two venerable teams perennially butting heads somewhere around the 50-yard line, a never-ending political Super Bowl. It is easy enough, if you listen to the play-by-play announcers, not to notice a very important change in the game, a tectonic realignment of which Occupy began to give us a hint and which subsequent developments have confirmed. The battle that is coming to characterize The New American Century is that between the *Elites* (called "the 1 Percent" by Occupy, but more accurately the corporate class that would replace real democracy with its trappings, masking dominion) and *Everyone Else*. And this battle, as the 'treasonous' Edward Snowden brought so dramatically to our attention, is largely about *information*.[173]

Knowledge is indeed power: in the case of the surveillance state, the power to intimidate, the power indeed to blackmail, the power to infiltrate and sabotage any perceived threat, stifle any organized or ultimately individual dissent. And the battle lines are indeed drawn: a ruling elite, corporate and governmental, that is attempting to know as much as possible about you and me while seeing to it that we know as little as possible about them.[174] Of course this is not unprecedented; history offers up its share of J. Edgar Hoovers. But the Information Age has turned a limited and rather selective battle into what amounts to *total war*, whether or not it is yet universally recognized as such.

---

[173] The Digital Age Information War has many fronts, ranging from state surveillance of ordinary citizens and potential dissidents; to the collecting of dirt (referred to by the Russians as "kompromat") to be used in blackmailing or ruining other powerful individuals; to the micro-targeting of information (or disinformation) campaigns based on mining of personal data; to the monetization of such data by such behemoth vacuum cleaners as Facebook for the use of other corporations who just want to sell their products to those who look more likely to buy them. And what would the Information War be without a faceoff between governments trying to get at your information by prevailing upon platforms such as Facebook to give them a back door into your communication and Facebook going to bat for your privacy (if only; see https://www.telegraph.co.uk/technology/2019/10/04/forget-privacy-real-reason-facebook-wants-encryption/)?

[174] The Cambridge Analytica-Facebook scandal has emerged to shed a lurid light on the virtual obliteration of privacy fashioned by the social media behemoths, whose business models have essentially commodified the public. The "battle" thus far has been a rout.

In a very real sense, in this war not over land or even treasure but over knowledge, *The Public* has become *The Enemy*.

The weapon that has been handing the ruling elites one victory after another in this war is *fear*, specifically fear of "terrorism" (though as an American you are currently several thousand times as likely to be killed by an ordinary American with a gun as by a global terrorist), now broadened to fear of immigrants and the "other."[175] With the ghastly and iconic images of planes puncturing towers and bodies leaping from fiery windows—precisely the "new Pearl Harbor" imagined in 1997 by right-wing think tank PNAC[176]—seared into every American's brain, and with Iraq War-incubated ISIS and its various progeny, real and imagined, reanimating those memories on a regular basis, the surrender of privacy on every front became an easy sell. *Whatever it takes* to keep us mythically "safe" in a "war" rather brilliantly conjured to be without end.

Naturally the National Security Agency was not about to let *us* in on its various "legal"[177] spying schemes[178] and, when finally exposed by the treasonous

---

[175] With the onset of COVID-19, or coronavirus, that "other" is in the process of being broadened still further to include the ever-terrifying unseen and the mysterious processes of contagion. While a coordinated response is understood to be in the public interest, the current crisis also provides opportunities to beta test and normalize new protocols of surveillance, movement and assembly restrictions, even martial law. We anticipate as well that internet voting will be among the crisis "solutions" offered "in the public interest," the kind of "helping hand" that is very difficult to reject in the throes of such a crisis.

[176] The Project for the New American Century (PNAC), a non-profit organization founded in 1997 by prominent Republican leaders, called for a transformation of America to exercise military total-spectrum dominance and unchallenged worldwide hegemony. The PNAC program in a nutshell: America's military must rule out even the potential for a serious global or regional challenger anywhere in the world.

PNAC's most important study noted that selling this plan to the American people would likely take *a long time*, "absent some catastrophic catalyzing event like a new Pearl Harbor," (PNAC, *Rebuilding America's Defenses*, 1997, p.51); see also https://en.wikipedia.org/wiki/Project_for_the_New_American_Century.

[177] Apologists from both parties were quick to point out that a special (secret) court, the FISA Court, must approve NSA applications to tap your phone or email. In 2012 there were 1896 such applications, of which the FISA Court approved 1896. And they said DiMaggio's streak would never be broken!

[178] President Obama proudly dubbed the NSA activities "transparent." While Glen Greenwald's publication in *The Guardian* of Edward Snowden's leaked NSA documents was certainly a step in that direction, it is hardly one for which the former president, who had attempted to prosecute Snowden on charges of espionage or treason, could gracefully take credit.

Snowden, took great pains to reassure us that it was "only gathering data" and wouldn't actually read our emails and listen in on our phone calls *unless it really feels it needs to*. For example if you were trying to organize the next Occupy movement, or threatening the "eco-terrorism" of opposing Monsanto, getting serious about a third-party or independent challenge to the D-R power duopoly, or perhaps organizing to "liberate" our ballots from their opscans so that they could be counted observably in public.

This is the *bone structure* of The New American Century, whatever its face and skin may look like. Corporate America has a stranglehold on *both* major parties; the corporate-owned MSM is cheerfully along for the ride; threatening opposition movements like Occupy are infiltrated and, where necessary, obliterated. Where does that leave The People? Where does that leave the 99 Percent on the day they figure out they *are* the 99 Percent?

It leaves them—us—with the electoral process. With the chance—in a fair, observably counted election—to elect to office candidates outside the power duopoly, who have refused to feed at the corporate trough, and who are pledged to bringing genuine change to the system and seriously addressing American Systemic Injustice.[179] And with the chance, it must be said, to remove would-be tyrants and their boosters and apologists from power.

Of course there are other obstacles beside rigged votecounts: money, media, lies, infiltration, assassination. But at least there would be a fighter's chance! Money, as Michael Bloomberg discovered, faces a law of diminishing returns when it is spent in obscene amounts to buy votes and elections; there are means of communicating messages outside the mainstream media; lies can be exposed, infiltration, threats, and even assassination overcome—as we have seen elsewhere around the world and throughout history—when a cause is just and vital and when the forces of greed, repression and control have overplayed their hand. In primaries and in independent challenges, candidates with the courage to oppose the forces of wealth and injustice smothering our democracy could stand for election before an electorate that the ruling elite or a would-be autocrat had finally pushed too far.

---

[179] To see what lies in wait for such a candidate in our current electoral circus, look no farther than Chapter V and the forensic story of the 2016 Democratic primaries.

At that point we had better be counting the votes *in public view*.[180] It is absurdly naive to believe that the same actors who hardly blanch at subverting every *other* mechanism of democracy, would, with a pipeline into the computers counting our votes in secret, go gentle into the good electoral night.

It would be easy to lose sight of this Information Age realignment amidst the many calamities and challenges of the Age of Trump. Certainly, for all Trump's unorthodoxy, American politics right now does look, on the surface at least, something like the old "Super Bowl" model: two teams battling it out in a nation divided, more starkly than ever, red and blue. But that is because Trump, demagogue that he is, presented a big swath of America, for whom politics had ceased to work, with handy enemies, seeming hope, and the illusion of an answer. And because he, his behavior, and his policies are so repulsive to so many and so polarizing that he has personally (with the help of his all-in GOP backers) done what Occupy (cut off at the knees as it was) could not: given birth to a serious, angry, and tenacious resistance. So the two halves of the 99 Percent were split and now face each other, Super-Bowl style, as if their interests were diametrically opposed—a state of affairs always welcome to the 1 Percent, as it cancels or at least forestalls their day of reckoning.

One great irony—and there are many—is that just about the most gilded and contemptuous 1-Percenter imaginable went after, lied to, and won over enough of the 99 Percent to take—with the help of various thumbs on the electoral scales, as we shall soon see—power. Another great irony is that most Trump voters were *already on the winning side* of the political game: they had elected (again with the help of various thumbs) not just Republican but further and further right Republican majorities to Congress and to their state governments. They had the power to keep Merrick Garland off the Supreme Court *before* Trump's ascension. They had the power to beat back any and all threats to "take their guns away." They had the power to legislate, block legislation, cut state taxes and benefits, and turn President Obama into, from the progressive point of view, a political eunuch.[181] Nonetheless they were

---

[180] It goes without saying that in 2016 we were *not* counting the votes in public view.

[181] It is telling that Obama's signature achievement, Obamacare, was rooted in a Republican plan first introduced by Mitt Romney when he was governor of Massachusetts. From 2010 forward, no truly progressive measures or appointments had a chance of emerging from the Republican-controlled Congress. What Obama *did* manage to do, though through no fault of his own, was to shift into high gear the furious backlash that would lead America into the Age of Trump. A progressive colleague recently mentioned in passing that we'd be in far better shape as a country

angry, economically screwed, and felt forgotten, unheard—and they were ripe for a bullshit artist posing as their friend and savior to win them over with the utterly false promise of "draining the swamp," tearing it all down. It seems that our corrupted electoral process had not been responding to *anybody*.

We are suffering from a virulent disease and will need strong medicine. *But let no one yet say it's all so rotten that elections no longer matter—or that politics itself is now so revolting and hopeless that it too no longer matters.* Because after elections and politics all that is left is revolution (or Soviet-style resignation) and, even if we could imagine one here in the Land of Genetically Modified Milk and Honey, such events are not ordinarily festive but chaotic and traumatic. Indeed, it was memories of such traumas that likely gave birth to history's first *elections*. So let us neither mistake the lines of battle nor fail to recognize the crucial part electoral transparency—*beginning with the observable counting of votes*—is destined to play in an age in which the critical lines of battle are all about what can be seen and what cannot.

Q: Would you say that progress has been made in the years you have advocated for election transparency and reform of the vote-counting process?

A: Yes. And no. If you call decline in trust in the electoral process "progress," then we are clearly in a "better" place now than we were 18 years ago when the Help America Vote Act was passed and the fully computerized voting era began, with barely a thought given to the safety and advisability of computerizing the casting and counting of votes. Some of that decline in trust can be attributed to the efforts of electoral transparency advocates and forensic analysts, but much of it has sprung from the evidence-free rantings of Donald Trump and his echo chamber, and much too from a recent fixation on Russian meddling that perversely ignores the mountains of evidence from the decade and a half *before* anyone has suggested the Russians put their hand in.[182] And perhaps some of the decline in trust, some of the concern that we may in fact have a problem, stems simply from general discontent and

---

circa 2020 had John McCain or Mitt Romney won their elections. The more thought I've given it, the more accurate that miserable assessment seems.

[182] While it is certainly not impossible that—the West having brought down the USSR and taken a (relatively dignified) victory lap during Vladimir Putin's formative years— Putin may have cast a vengeful eye on our electoral system (and that of other newly computerized Western nations) as early as 2002, no evidence has been brought forward to suggest concrete steps of sabotage prior to 2016.

suspicion across the political spectrum, itself at least in part a side-effect of the breakdown of the electoral process.

But I do think that awareness of vulnerability to fraud involving computers in general and vote-counting computers in particular has gradually infused the national consciousness. It just has not yet been treated as a national *crisis* demanding full and urgent remedy. This is because—to the political establishment, the media, and most of the populace—the crisis of election theft remains hypothetical, a *possibility*. The evidence of actual manipulation of votecounts has been gathered and analyzed *ad nauseam*, then ignored or dismissed as conspiracy "theory" by the government and media alike. After all, such evidence would undermine voter confidence in the electoral process!

The prevailing national sentiment seems not to be "if it ain't broke, why fix it?" but something closer to "if it ain't smashed to smithereens, why fix it?" Some of the deepest and most damning work in election forensics was done at the *beginning* of the computerized voting era, in the wake of E2004. Much, though not all, of that work was presented in Steve Freeman and Joel Bleifuss' book *Was the 2004 Presidential Election Stolen?* It was based on four very solid evidentiary pedestals: time-stamped, unadjusted exit poll data I had downloaded and printed out; a detailed, comprehensive, but evasive analysis conducted by the Edison-Mitofsky exit-polling firm into its own "errors;"[183] examination of the bizarre events and timeline of Election Night, including the shutdown of the Ohio state election servers and the peripatetic interstate "itinerary" of the votes that produced the Bush victory; and, above all, multiple analyses of numerical patterns that fit no conceivable benign explanation of the glaring anomalies that emerged.[184]

I challenge anyone who picks up and reads that book to write it all off as "conspiracy theory."

---

[183] For a comprehensive point-by-point discussion and rebuttal of Edison/Mitofsky's report ("Evaluation of Edison/Mitofsky Election System 2004"), see https://www.verifiedvoting.org/wp-content/uploads/downloads/Exit_Polls_2004_Edison-Mitofsky.pdf.

[184] See Freeman, Steven F.; Bleifuss, Joel: *Was the 2004 Presidential Election Stolen? Exit Polls, Election Fraud, and the Official Count*, Seven Stories Press 2006, at https://www.amazon.com/Was-2004-Presidential-Election-Stolen/dp/1583226877/ref.

Following E2006 I contributed the first two of a series of analyses,[185] regarding which I issue the same challenge. Many other examinations, ranging from the highly focal to comprehensive meta-analyses, have been undertaken. Together they constitute a data- and evidence-intensive body of work that can leave little doubt that the crisis of election theft In America is *not* hypothetical.

Today—although we are dealing with a cutback to exit polling,[186] a baseline-corrupting partial adjustment of first-posted exit polls, a general skepticism of *all* polling, and the continued withholding of all "hard" evidence like memory cards, code, and voter-marked ballots—we soldier on collecting and analyzing whatever data *is* available for what light it can shed on what is going on in the partisan, proprietary, pitch-dark of cyberspace.

If we take as our measure of progress the growth of awareness, suspicion, and concern that concealed vote-counting is problematic and votecounts cannot be presumed gospel, then things are sort of moving along. If we consider instead the impact of our work on the bottom-line security of the vote counting process, we've gone just about nowhere. There is something of a push for "paper;"[187] there is talk about digital ballot images and audits; there has been

---

[185] See Chapter VIII, Studies II and III: "Landslide Denied: Exit Polls vs. Vote Count 2006, Demographic Validity of the National Exit Poll and the Corruption of the Official Vote Count" (2007) and "Fingerprints of Election Theft: Were Competitive Contests Targeted?" (2007). It should be noted that neither study was grounded on a face-value assumption of exit poll accuracy.

[186] For example, the elimination of 19 states from exit polling in 2012, 22 states in 2016, and the cancellation of the final five crucial exit polls in the 2016 primaries.

[187] Gordon Lightfoot might have been thinking of election transparency activism when he penned the line "feel like I'm winnin' when I'm losin' again," and the current movement from DREs to BMDs serves as a classic example.

The vendors' new bright idea is to replace touchscreen voting machines (DREs) with touchscreen ballot-marking devices (BMDs) and proclaim a major victory for election security and integrity: "We have paper!" But those BMDs, in most cases, are designed to print a *bar code* (or QR code) on that paper, ostensibly representing the voter's choices. A bar code! That code is then read by the optical scanner that counts the votes—but it certainly can *not* be read by the voter who cast the vote. If you are wondering how a humanly unreadable and unverifiable bar code on a piece of paper improves election security and prevents computerized fraud, rest assured you're not crazy.

A few rather obvious questions: How difficult is it to gin up a stack of pre-printed bar-code ballots and feed them into the scanner? How difficult would it be to print a vote for "A" in human-readable language on the "summary card" the voter gets to see and a vote for "B" in the barcode that is read by the scanner? Or a vote for "B" on both when the voter has chosen "A," recognizing that few voters check or can read their summary

money (albeit a relative pittance and with no transparency/security strings attached) appropriated for equipment upgrades; there is something close to consensus that the Russians have come and are coming again; and potential nonacceptance of shocking, or even disappointing, electoral results seems to be in the air—a frightening state of affairs, though apparently an essential precursor to serious reform.

But the current state of election transparency/security advocacy is best described as state- and county-level trench warfare over just what model of fraud-inviting device will be purchased and deployed for E2020. Mostly the choices come down to paperless DREs, RLA-resistant barcode BMDs, and hand-marked paper ballots with grossly inadequate audit and recount provisions, which have been consistently producing most of the red-flagged elections of the computerized voting era. Unfortunately, far too many observers assume we must be making general and widespread progress toward electoral transparency because of the Russian threat, the new stakes of our elections, and our sanity. We're not. And in too many places—Georgia, North Carolina, and Los Angeles County[188] being good examples—we're trending backwards.

We have come a long way down the computerized elections road without even tapping the brakes, let alone executing a stomp and steer. Much damage has been done to our nation and our democracy; authoritarianism is no longer unthinkable here—there are several scenarios and vectors headed in that direction. So if there has been progress, it pales before the task at hand—what needed to be done and what remains to be done.

Q: What *can* be done? Is there any real prospect of observable and honest elections in the United States?

---

cards? Or in "permission to cheat" hybrid BMDs, programming it to alter votes only when the voter has first waived their right to verify their ballot (as most voters do)?

And if the BMD breaks down—as touchscreens and printers are famous for doing—what happens to the voters in line, who now can't vote? There is no such problem when voters hand-mark their ballots, even when counted by opscan—20 or 30 voters can be filling out their ballots at once. Yet these new gizmos are selling like hotcakes to counties and states that have pledged to "upgrade" their election security (see https://twitter.com/jennycohn1/status/991406567097483264 for an account; see also http://bradblog.com/?p=12505). "Sometimes I think it's a sin . . ."

[188] LA County has a population larger than 41 states. Its elections chief, Dean Logan, has dealt with the recent brewing storm over the multifarious flaws of its newly purchased ballot-marking equipment by instructing poll workers not to talk with anyone in the media. So much for transparency.

A: Democracy, contrary to the facile assumptions of those born into it and apt to take both its blessings and its workings for granted, is no sure bet. While political evolution in the modern era had seemed to be inexorably bringing democracy of one sort or another to more and more of the world, the countercurrents—both historical (Hitler, Stalin, Franco, Pinochet, *et al*) and contemporary (Russia, China, Turkey, Brazil, The Philippines, etc.)—are plenty strong and have certainly not ceded the field. Indeed the current trend across much of the globe is a retreat toward what has been euphemistically called "managed democracy," which is to say something that still looks more or less like a democracy (people get to vote) but ain't (challengers to the ruling oligarchy or autocrat have no chance of winning).

Power, always seeking consolidation and control, has a way of finding the chinks, slipping in the explosives and blowing democracies and genuinely representative governance up. Or, more subtly and patiently, slow-dripping its acid onto the scaffolding that holds democracy upright. We've seen in America the early metastasis of the security state; the infiltration of big (and dark) money into politics; the consolidation of the mainstream media under control of a handful of corporations; and finally the ascension to power of a president with authoritarian instincts and little regard for the rule of law, backed to the hilt by a Bund of once-savvy politicians now lining up to gamble it all on an electoral *deus ex machina* miracle. All these developments make America *look* less democratic. The process may not be explosive, like a coup, but it is visibly erosive and many observers have charted it. [189]

Election theft is different in that it allows its perpetrators to keep "democracy" perfectly intact and *looking* like a democracy even after it's been effectively gutted. Election theft is also something that very few Americans of our time ever thought they'd have to worry about, and something that they'd still very much rather not worry about (as it goes against every premise of positive national identity and esteem), especially if they have a seat at or anywhere

---

[189] While there is hope among some, expectation among others, that our democracy will ultimately hold Trump in check, America does seem to be in uncharted territory with the outcome very much on the hazard and very much dependent, the existence of a vibrant resistance notwithstanding, on the outcomes of our next national election. In their 2018 best-seller *How Democracies Die*, Steven Levitsky and Daniel Ziblatt acknowledge how precarious are our democracy's traditional guardrails in the Age of Trump. Yet their entire analysis of how we arrived here and calculus of the means and odds for our survival rests on the conventional assumption that votes have been and will be counted as cast. If that turns out to have been a misdiagnosis, both their prognoses and their prescriptions will likewise be flawed.

near the power table. So we are in a very dark and dangerous place and facing a historic tragedy in the making.

It is not unrealistic to imagine systemic election rigging giving rise to a politics so one-sided or so out of sync with the public will that eventually the inkling that something is very wrong with the whole picture becomes irrepressible.

It is also possible to imagine something ultimately more damning: a carefully titrated rigging strategy that would preserve, perhaps indefinitely, the *illusions* of a freely swinging pendulum and of public sovereignty.

And finally it is not wholly inconceivable that a hidden game of rigging, thwarting, and counter-rigging—a kind of domestic electoral equivalent of the spy-thriller antics of the Cold War—will come to characterize our best-in-class, Made-in-the-USA model of democracy.

Meanwhile, such gaming scenarios have been all-but-supplanted by the more immediate crisis brought on by the anti-democratic putsch of Donald Trump, his backers and his base. After our 2016 election, other countries such as Norway and the Netherlands saw the light; America did not. *They* moved swiftly to public, observable vote counting; *we* remain mired in state- and county-level trench warfare over the niceties of barcode ballot marking devices and *pilot projects* for risk-limiting audits. A slow boat to nowhere.

To meet the existential threat of a Trump autocracy, as well as to restore a sound bedrock protocol on which to re-ground our democracy, we will need a sea change in public attitude and a recasting of the public's Election Night role from passive observer to active participant. We must roll up our sleeves and reclaim the right and the duty of counting our votes and observing that count. After looking deeper into the "why," in Chapter VII we'll get specific about the "how."

E2010 and E2012: A PATTERN EMERGES

Let the lamp affix its beam...

— Wallace Stevens, "The Emperor of Ice Cream"

Tellingly, the reason that Democratic victories dispel concerns about election theft is that the forensic indicators, election after election, are so pervasively one-sided that grounds for suspicion of *leftward* rigging are nonexistent. So a Democratic win, in a competitive election of national significance, would serve to reassure the only partisans with a standing reason to be concerned (until Trump came along, as we shall see), that the game was fair, symmetrical, the pendulum free to swing.

Obama won. Twice. It *must* be safe to go back in the water. The outcome of E2012 proved, if E2008 had left any doubt, that votes are counted honestly and accurately in the United States. Even if electronic rigging is theoretically possible, E2012 provided blanket assurance that it is just not something that anyone—no matter how bent on winning, no matter how in thrall to some agenda, ideology, or worldview—would *do*. Whew! What a relief that we wouldn't have to worry about this anymore or deal with the massive burdens of observable counting or even serious audits! It's all good.

Or was it?

On Election Night 2008, it seemed that all but the most cynical partisans of the left took time out to watch the Obama victory celebration in Grant Square, many to join in. But the election forensics crew stayed glued to their computers, doggedly screencapturing, downloading, and spreadsheeting— focused on the process rather than the outcome. Having seen all the indicators in 2004, 2006, and 2008 (when, Obama's victory notwithstanding, the red shift rivalled that in the prior two elections), we were then not at all surprised by E2010, when the Tea Party swept in, Democrats and Republican moderates were sent packing, and what promised to be an enduring occupation of both federal and key state governments was installed by those same red-shifted votecounts that had somehow escaped general notice two years earlier in 2008—when they weren't red-shifted *enough* to overcome a free-fall brought on by the 11th-hour crash of the economy on Bush's watch and keep Obama out of the White House. Who else, in December 2008, saw E2010 coming? Who, in December 2012, was thinking E2014? Who was paying attention to the emerging pattern, watching the pendulum's weirdly distorted, precessional swing?

Who understood that a corrupted voting system does not equate with every election being successfully rigged?

Obviously, not every election contest is targeted for manipulation: some are relatively unimportant, without sufficient national significance; some are too one-sided to reverse without provoking undue suspicion; some rigs may be under-calibrated in light of subsequent political developments; and still others may be deterred or thwarted in the darkness of cyberspace. There is strong reason to believe that it is this last fate that befell an attempted manipulation of the 2012 presidential race.

Looking at E2012 overall, while the Democrats took what were regarded as the major in-play prizes of the White House and Senate (adding to their narrow majority in the latter), the Republicans maintained a solid grip on the U.S. House (despite Congressional approval ratings hovering in the single digits and despite an overall Democratic victory in the national popular vote for the House[1]), as well as on a sizeable majority of statehouses. In effect, though the election was initially depicted as a pendulum-swinging repudiation of both extreme right-wing politics and the impact of vast corporate and Super-PAC expenditures on voter choice, *little if anything changed in the actual political infrastructure as a result of E2012.*

It is also worth noting that—much as in E2008, when McCain was sunk by the market crash and having Sarah Palin foisted on him as his running-mate—it required a dismal campaign run by a feckless, tone-deaf, and lackluster Mitt Romney trying desperately and all-too-transparently to "Etch-A-Sketch" away an indelible impression of extremism left over from his self-styled "severely

---

[1] It was only the fourth occurrence of this win-the-vote-lose-the-House phenomenon in over 100 years, the others involving outsized Democratic margins in what was then the "solid South."

conservative" primary season—not to mention a series of gaffes by GOP Senate candidates ranging from the seriously injurious to the instantly fatal—to bring about even this tepid electoral result that did little more than maintain the status quo, leaving a leadership class still jarringly out of tune with an American electorate that had *just voted*.

So What Happened?

It does sound like the stuff of spy novels,[2] but there is good reason to believe that a planned manipulation of the presidential vote was blocked in cyberspace on Election Night 2012. The would-be rig that appeared to have been thwarted on Election Night was of the "real-time" variety (i.e., a "man-in-the-middle" attack[3]), but it remains unclear whether or to what extent a pre-set rig (i.e., one programmed into memory cards installed prior to Election Day) may have affected the outcomes of down-ballot (e.g., U.S. House and state-level) elections, critical to the overall political power balance but not exit-polled.

Not Over Till Karl Rove Sings

One of the weirdest indications of submerged 2012 Election Night drama was the infamous public "meltdown" of Karl Rove, star of the Fox News Election Night coverage team, as he stubbornly persisted in challenging *his own network's* call of Ohio and the presidency for Obama, citing a rapidly closing gap between the candidates that did not jibe with *any* publicly reported returns.[4] Of course millions of votes *were* being tabulated on remote networked servers, including many from key swing states such as Ohio. This method of vote "processing" permits votecount manipulation in "real time" calibrated to suit, and a shift of fewer than 170,000 *total* votes among the states of Ohio, Florida, Virginia, and New Hampshire would have reversed the

---

[2] Indeed, there are at least two good ones of recent vintage: *The Lafayette Campaign: A Tale of Deception and Elections*, by Andrew Updegrove, an attorney with thirty years' experience servicing hi-tech clients, at www.amazon.com/dp/0996491910/ref; and *Cassandra, Chanting: An Election Insider's Nightmare*, by a former voting industry insider who chose to remain anonymous, at www.amazon.com/dp/1434353230/ref. A third novel by Hal Malchow, which takes the bizarre 2010 South Carolina Democratic senatorial primary as its historical jumping off point, is in the works.

[3] A man-in-the-middle attack involves the interception and alteration of digitized data in the process of storage or transmission; see, e.g., https://www.rawstory.com/news/2008/Republican_IT_consultant_subpoenaed_in_case_0929.html

[4] See, e.g., https://www.youtube.com/watch?v=rKqQBvWeO6E; see also Pema Levy, "The Real Reason Why Rove Went Into Denial On Election Night," *Newsweek*, 1/21/14, at http://www.newsweek.com/real-reason-why-rove-went-denial-election-night-226695.

Electoral College outcome and put Romney in the White House. It is easy to forget how close the outcome really was.

In disputing his fellow right-wingers on the Fox broadcast, Rove made reference to *server issues*, eerily reminiscent of the parallel scenario in E2004, in which Rove "IT guru" Mike Connell's SmarTech operation took over the official Ohio elections website at about the same late hour of the evening and Bush suddenly surged ahead as the "late" votes came in.[5] So, if in fact he had reason to believe that a repeat performance was on the program and those necessary votes could be ginned up in cyberspace, Rove's insistence was not quite as absurd as it seemed.

Rove—a brilliant, disciplined, and careful calculator, never prone to such humiliations—so clearly and publicly expected a different result, and seemed so clearly and publicly to be counting on something happening that did not happen, that it begs the questions "What?" and "Why didn't it?"

And indeed, the group Anonymous took credit, days after the election, for having disabled Rove's vaunted "ORCA" operation.[6] Billed as a sophisticated GOTV network, ORCA was designed to be capable of accessing votecounts as well as databases. And, sure enough, the servers in Ohio went down on Election Night 2012 exactly one minute earlier than they had gone down on Election Night 2004, when the votes were shunted to Mike Connell's SmarTech servers in Chattanooga for "processing." But, alas, after the untimely 2008 death of Connell, his chief of technical operations, Rove was obliged to rebuild his IT department, and all did not go well in that endeavor. Specifically, as a result of its infiltration of Rove's new IT team, Anonymous reported that ORCA's technicians had been locked out from their own servers by what amounted to a counter-hack. While they feverishly and unsuccessfully keyed in dozens of superseded passwords, Rove continued to wait (and wait . . . and wait) for Romney to surge as Bush had in 2004.[7]

---

[5] In E2012, in addition to SmarTech and its servers operating out of Chattanooga, several other outfits with partisan ties, such as Command Central and Scytl, were also contracted to "process" votes sent through cyberspace to remote servers.

[6] A founding member of the group personally confirmed to me in May 2016 that Anonymous had succeeded in blocking Rove on Election Night 2012 through changing the ORCA passwords and locking out its resident users.

[7] For an illuminating take on the events of Election Night 2012, see Thom Hartmann's "The Big Picture 11/19/2012," viewable at http://www.thomhartmann.com/bigpicture/full-show-111912-did-anonymous-save-election (at 47'23" – 57'56").

As wild as that scenario might seem, it does make sense that, after a decade-long parade of malodorous computerized elections, some countermeasures, some back-channel "immune response," might finally be triggered.[8] It is evident that the crazy-quilt pattern of partial safeguards *intrinsic* to the vote counting process would not have stood in the way of the alternative outcome that seemed plausible only to Rove. Deterrence—a sufficient upping of the risk factor in the reward/risk ratio—or outright rig-thwarting would have had to come from some type of extraordinary *outside* intervention, whether in the form of electronic counter-manipulation, infiltration, or quiet threat of exposure or prosecution. This is a sobering thought and we must ask ourselves as Americans whether we are willing to accept a kind of electoral "Wild West" where elections are won and lost, and our future determined, by "white hats" and "black hats" hacking it out in electoral cyberspace.[9]

Strange Numbers in The House

Looking beyond the presidency, in E2012 America re-elected a Congress of which it overwhelmingly disapproved[10] and we must ask whether the advantages of incumbency, gerrymandering, discriminatory Voter-ID laws, corporate cash, and political dirty tricks—formidable as they are—were enough to explain this jarring incongruence between voter sentiment and electoral result.

Nationally, while the Democrats won the aggregate *vote* for the U.S. House, the Republicans won a comfortable majority of the *seats* (234 – 201), a rare event that echoed the strange outcome in E2010, in which the Republicans achieved a spectacular net gain of 63 seats by virtue of a very pedestrian 6.8 percent aggregate popular vote margin, a seats-to-votes ratio unprecedented in U.S. history.[11] In Pennsylvania, for example, the Democrats won the aggregate House vote but the GOP came away with a *13 to 5* margin of the state's 18 seats. Gerrymandering is reflexively given credit for this

---

[8] Although even then, all the counter-hackers thought, or were able, to save was the presidency, leaving the massive down-ballot ziggurat of American politics unprotected.

[9] Needless to say—given the partisan pedigree of the computerized voting industry, and their consequent "insider" status—advantage black hats. Anonymous itself was cowed by governmental threats into early retirement from its election protection career.

[10] See http://news.gallup.com/poll/1600/congress-public.aspx.

[11] Granting that there is a "first" for everything, when a string of such firsts—patterns and ratios at the outer margins of or beyond the historical record, as we have detected—it bears looking into whether some new causality has been introduced.

disproportionate coup, and its impact was certainly powerful, but what then accounts for the equally bizarre pre-redistricting results of *E2010,* when most of the districts were still drawn to favor *Democratic* candidates?

There was little dispute that a congressional approval rating 35 percentage points below that of the president reflected primarily voter anger over the behavior of *Republicans* in Congress,[12] who consistently used the filibuster to block both legislation and appointments in the Senate and wielded House majority control inflexibly (to put it mildly) against any initiatives that might threaten corporate hegemony, address the gaping New Gilded Age income and wealth inequalities, or attempt to ward off looming environmental catastrophe.[13] It would be difficult indeed, even after giving gerrymandering and incumbency their due, to explain to a visitor from a far-off land why this political intransigence and obstructionism were electorally rewarded rather than punished when voters nationwide finally had the opportunity to weigh in.

How, *in a democracy*, can popularity and power so radically diverge? And how can that radical divergence persist, remain so uncorrectable? What thumbs, visible and invisible, must be on the scale for this to happen?

Pre-set and Real-time Rigging

Based on the body of evidence from the past decade, it appears that attempted electronic election theft on a national level has not confined itself to reliance on a single logistical tactic. Forensic analysis suggests that election rigging evolved into what might best be described as a two-tiered strategy, consisting of pre-set and real-time manipulations.

Of these, pre-set rigging is the more facile. For example, it is quite simple, as we have shown, to set the zero-counters on the memory card deployed in a precinct tabulator to $+X$ for the supported candidate and $-X$ for the candidate whose defeat is desired. At the end of the day, an election administrator will perceive a "clean" election in which the total ballot count matches the poll-book (i.e., sign-in) total of voters, unaware that a net of $2X$ votes has been

---

[12] The abysmal ratings were consistent following a sharp downward plunge dating from the spring of 2011, a few months after the Republicans took control of the U.S. House in the E2010 rout.

[13] The Republican House instead devoted a good part of its energy to the serial passage of bills to repeal all or part of the Affordable Care Act (ironically "Obamacare" was the offspring of the Republican "Romneycare" plan, which had its beta test in Massachusetts under Romney's governorship), reaching an impressive score of 63 such empty gestures by the start of 2016.

successfully shifted per tabulator so tainted. Similar exploits can also be used to rig central tabulators. All that is required is the insertion of a few lines of malicious code among the hundreds of thousands of lines on a given card, and it is possible, for an insider and even for a hacker, to replicate this alteration on hundreds or thousands of such cards. Given the prevailing level and practice of election security, such a rig would be virtually undetectable and need only to pass the numerical smell test.[14]

The difficulty with pre-set rigs programmed into memory cards deployed weeks or months before the election, however, is that of accurate calibration, guessing well in advance the minimum number of votes needed to be shifted to reverse the outcome of a given contest. This is far from a trivial problem: in both E2006 and E2008, late-breaking political developments so changed electoral dynamics that what appeared (from the red-shift numbers) to be robust pre-set rigs were overwhelmed and rendered far less effective, in terms of altering outcomes, than would have been anticipated at time of deployment.[15]

---

[14] Although there is no real technical limit to the magnitude of such a rig, the smell test comes into play at some point because the likelihood of suspicion, investigation, and ultimate exposure of the rigging enterprise increases with the magnitude of the rig (as well as how many contests are targeted). Although there have been a few egregious "outliers," red-shift evidence over the years suggests that the outer limit of electronic rigging is likely in the 7% - 10% range.

The recent forensic contributions of Francois Choquette and James Johnson have relevance here. They have shown, through a precinct-level forensic technique known as Cumulative Vote Share (CVS) analysis, that suspect elections present what could be characterized as a "signature" pattern in which the allegedly benefited candidate's vote share increases with increasing precinct size.

Having controlled for "benign" factors (e.g., urban/rural differences), it appears that the most likely explanation for this recurrent pattern is that larger numbers of votes can be safely shifted in larger precincts without failing the smell test and raising a red flag (compare, for example, 100 votes shifted from a total of 200 votes = 50%, vs. the same 100 votes shifted from a total of 1000 votes = 10%). Larger precincts offer a better reward/risk ratio and would therefore be preferred targets. See Choquette & Johnson: "Republican Primary Election 2012 Results: Amazing Statistical Anomalies" (2012), at http://electiondefensealliance.org/files/PrimaryElectionResultsAmazingStatisticalAnom alies_V2.1.pdf., also the CVS forensic analyses of Elizabeth Clarkson, Chief Statistician at the National Institute for Aviation Research, at http://bethclarkson.com/?cat=4; and Michael Duniho: "Evidence of Vote Counting Fraud," at http://ariwatch.com/Links/EvidenceOfVoteCountingFraud.htm.

[15] In each of these elections, unanticipated events—in 2006 the Foley scandal and in 2008 the collapse of Lehman Brothers and the kickoff of the Great Recession— occurred in mid-September, turning close elections into routs. Recalibration and redeployment of the pre-set rigs would not only have been impractical at that juncture from a technical and logistical standpoint, but would also, in order to be successful in

Real-time rigging, executed as the votes are tabulated on Election Day (or, more often, late on Election Night), avoids this problem. The manipulation can be precisely calibrated to overcome what would be the losing margin and so reverse the outcome. It requires, however, the deployment of infrastructure to intercept and alter votecounts, and thus is bulkier and riskier than a pre-set, memory card-based rig. Unlike the pre-set, memory card-based rig, it also may require some measure of knowing or unknowing cooperation from someone in the chain of election administration. The operation that permitted interference with the Ohio presidential vote in E2004—the SmarTech servers set up under the late Mike Connell's direction in Chattanooga, Tennessee— was eventually detected through its IP footprint, and privately investigated, coming very close to fatal exposure of the entire rigging enterprise.[16] So there is a tradeoff between the upside of real-time control and the downside of risk of detection (or, as we saw with Anonymous in E2012, operational interference).

It is evident that each species of manipulation, pre-set or real-time, is best suited to a specific type of electoral contest. Where the volatility is low and the ultimate outcome can be roughly predicted well in advance, *or where one needs outcome-altering success in only some small fraction of a large set of contests* (e.g., to take majority control of the U.S. House or a state legislature), the pre-set rig is likely to be effective enough.[17] Where the volatility is high, however, and the contest(s) subject to unpredictable shifts in the political wind, or *where the target is a single contest* (e.g., presidency, U.S. Senate seat) rather than a subset of a large group, pre-set rigs are more likely, as in E2006 and E2008, to miss the mark.

Of course there is essentially no *technical* limit on how large a pre-set, memory card-based rig can be deployed, but obviously to take *all* the votes is neither

---

achieving overall Republican victories, have likely had to be of too great a magnitude to pass the smell test.

[16] Had star witness Connell not been the victim of the plane crash that ended his life prior to the completion of his testimony in the *King Lincoln-Bronzeville v. Blackwell* case, such fatal exposure of the rigging enterprise might well have become a reality.

[17] "Effective enough" because, in such a situation, undercalibrating a few contests— letting a few fish off the hook—would not adversely impact the overall goal of attaining an aggregate majority; a decent batting average will suffice. If you needed, for example, to win 30 of 60 competitive contests to take or keep control of the chamber, and targeted 40 of them, shifting dynamics in or undercalibration of as many as 10 would not compromise the overall goal.

necessary nor desirable. Indeed, the *cardinal algorithm* of election rigging is *not* to win every election, but to *maximize significant victories and minimize significant losses within bounds of acceptable risk.* For a given contest—since the risks of suspicion, investigation, and detection increase with the magnitude of the rig—it is advisable, if not imperative, to shift no more votes than are needed to bring about the desired electoral outcome (and, where necessary, avoid either a mandatory or an elective margin-based recount). Rigs of too great magnitude or that cast suspicion on the results of too many contests, such that they do not or might not pass the smell test, are dangerous and inadvisable.

In examining E2012 it is clear enough that the presidential race and the critical U.S. Senate races were of the high-volatility genus. Not only were pre-election polls in fluctuating disagreement about the prospects of these highly competitive contests, but outcomes were further subject to the vagaries of current events such as the recording of Romney's "47 percent" gaffe and the political hay-making opportunities presented by Hurricane Sandy. It would have been extremely difficult to predict with the necessary accuracy even a month in advance what magnitude of vote shift would be necessary to guarantee victories in these top-of-the-ballot battles. Thus real-time manipulation was called for; and Anonymous believed, it would appear correctly, that this was the design of Rove's ORCA operation.

Lower profile down-ballot races for the U.S. House and state legislatures would, on the other hand, be much lower in volatility and far easier to gauge. While it would of course be possible for a given race to turn sharply on a gaffe or a brilliant attack ad, the much greater number of these down-ballot races would, *in the all-important aggregate*, smooth out such one-off bumps. And while it would also in theory be possible to see a repeat of something like the Foley scandal of 2006, which managed to sink a slew of down-ballot Republican boats, the likelihood of such a "perfect storm" event reoccurring and having a comparable impact in 2012 was small.[18]

---

[18] Looking ahead, the problem faced in E2018 was somewhat different: Trump's exceptional unpopularity made it clear in advance that holding the House was something of a lost cause for the GOP. It would have required placing discrete rigs in too many contests and likely failing thereby even the stuffed-nose smell test. There would be little point, and much unnecessary risk, in "saving" too few GOP seats to deny the Democrats a House majority.

It is therefore plausible to posit a two-tiered rigging strategy in which a pre-set rig covering competitive U.S. House and statehouse races would be complemented, where feasible, by a real-time rig targeting the more volatile top-ballot races for president and possibly U.S. Senate.[19]

Older readers who recall playing the popular board game "CLUE" may hear echoes here of "Professor Plum, in the Kitchen, with the Wrench." Given the concealment of the key data (voter-marked ballots, ballot images, memory cards, code, raw exit poll numbers), neither the weapon of choice, nor the site of attack, nor indeed the ID of the perp is our case to make. Perhaps it was Colonel Mustard, in the Conservatory, with the Candlestick. The evidence that *is* available is more than sufficient to establish a *corpus delicti*—a body with enough wounds to spur us to look beyond natural causes. It is not unreasonable to call for an inquest. It goes also without saying that *the whole house is unsafe*, a deadly set-up for our unsuspecting elections.

Our case is that we need as a nation seriously to investigate whether a crime has been or is likely to be committed and, even more importantly, rectify a situation that invites it to be committed over and over again.

E2012, a Democratic win like E2008 before it, set back that cause significantly. But E2012, like E2008 before it and contrary to popular perception, offered no genuine cause for relief or celebration. Part of the rigging enterprise may have been disarmed by what amounted to cyber-vigilantism, but the vote counting system remained concealed, privatized, profoundly insecure, and an open invitation to future manipulation.

Misdirection

American politics shuffles on in a perennial two-step of presidential and midterm election cycles, each with its own electorate, at least until E2018 came along. Given the brightness of the Klieg Lights focused quadrennially on the presidential elections, it is natural to question just what you get, how much political bang for the buck, from stealing off-year and down-ballot elections?

You get what the radicalized GOP got: a guaranteed *minimum* power level of gridlock—an effective and enduring blockade of the opposing agenda— swelling, with control of the White House, to hegemony and the durable prize

---

[19] Recall that reversing the outcome of the 2012 presidential election would have come down to a shift of fewer than 170,000 total votes (about 0.13% of votes cast nationally) in only four states.

of the federal courts (where jurists appointed by the president and confirmed by the Senate serve, barring impeachment, for life). *That Donald Trump has somehow managed to put that all in jeopardy should not blind us to where our politics would currently stand with just about any other Republican in the White House.*

What was achieved in E2010, moreover, had especial strategic value because, along with the shocking U.S. House massacre, the GOP took control of critical statehouses in "purple" swing states throughout America, giving itself command of the decennial redistricting process and immediately using that gerrymandering power to lock in its U.S. House and state legislative majorities—a lock that only the wayward political tornado that is the Trump presidency could begin to rattle. Add in restrictive and discriminatory Voter-ID laws—rammed through by these same legislatures in purported response to a nonexistent "epidemic" of voter-impersonation fraud, but operating in effect as a modern-era poll tax[20]—and a host of other provisions all designed to make the casting of a vote more difficult.[21] Fill in the picture with the now nearly complete displacement of GOP moderates by radicals via primary victories—virtually all of them low-profile, low-scrutiny; many of them, like the 2014 Eric Cantor shocker, [22] suspect—and one can begin to see how it is possible to

---

[20] See Minnite L: *The Myth of Voter Fraud.* Cornell University Press, 2010; at http://www.amazon.com/Myth-Voter-Fraud-Lorraine-Minnite/dp/0801448484/. See also Mayer J: "The Voter-Fraud Myth," *The New Yorker* (10/29/2012), at http://www.newyorker.com/reporting/2012/10/29/121029fa_fa_fact_mayer?printable=true.

[21] See, e.g., Yaccino S, Alvarez, L: "New G.O.P. Bid to Limit Voting in Swing States," *NY Times*, 3/29/2014, at http://www.nytimes.com/2014/03/30/us/new-gop-bid-to-limit-voting-in-swing-states.html.

[22] The defeat of Congressman Eric Cantor, Majority Leader of the U.S. House of Representatives, in the June 10, 2014 Republican primary election in Virginia's 7th CD set a chilling tone. It was an election counted on a combination of DREs (paperless and thus unauditable and unrecountable) and opscans (which, by Virginia law at the time, were recountable only by running the ballots a second time through the same opscans; human inspection was barred). Thus there was literally no way for an electronic rig to be discovered and exposed, and consequently zero risk for any rigging enterprise.

The far-right (though occasionally uncooperative) Cantor—consistently ahead by more than 30 points in both internal and public polls and having outspent his far-far-right Tea Party opponent, David Brat, 20-to-1—lost the election by 12 points, the first Majority Leader *in history* to suffer this fate (another "first"). *The New York Times* echoed virtually every observer of the shocking outcome by terming Brat's feat "unimaginable" ("In G.O.P., Far Right Is Too Moderate;" Times Editorial Board, June 11, 2014; at http://www.nytimes.com/2014/06/12/opinion/in-gop-far-right-is-too-moderate.html).

The entire media and political class, including to my knowledge every *progressive* commentator of note, then proceeded to offer up a smorgasbord of contorted

quietly, massively, and enduringly shift the governmental balance of power in America. E2010 provided the *infrastructure* for nothing less than political hegemony—perpetual rule. In retrospect we can now recognize this jack-in-the-box election as a kind of self-sustaining coup, the gift that keeps on giving—achieved, as are most magician's tricks, with the help of misdirection as audience attention was riveted elsewhere on the "major" battles of presidential years.

With the demographics all trending Democratic and with the radicalized Republicans more and more blithely promoting many unpopular causes and virulently obstructing a host of popular ones—and now group-hugging with the most divisive and reviled president in living memory, if not our nation's history—they may well, nevertheless, remain stuck like a bone in America's throat, until we fire the Man Behind The Curtain and restore public, observable vote counting to our elections.

---

explanations for the "unimaginable," without once entertaining so much as a hint of a question about whether the vote totals—unverified and unverifiable—could possibly be erroneous, whether the secret vote counting process could just possibly have been subject to some species of manipulation or interference. Not one clearing of a throat, not one raising of an eyebrow.

Then all alike moved in quick lock-step into deep and fascinating discussions of the *implications* of this "seismic" political development that none (with the exception of a few of our hallucinating Cassandras) had seen as remotely possible. The implications according to the punditry? No Republican could henceforth dare to ignore or even attempt to finesse the far-far right "base;" the Tea Party, which had been barely on life support, was back with a vengeance; polarization would give way to hyperpolarization, right (if not far-right) become the new center.

Unimaginable result, seismic impact, secret and unverifiable count, child's-play rigging options, zero risk, zero investigation, zero questions asked: welcome to The New American Century!

— IV —

E2014: NOTHING SUCCEEDS LIKE FAILURE

If voting changed anything, they'd make it illegal.

-- Emma Goldman

"They Just Didn't Elect Democrats"

It is one thing to gain power, another thing entirely, having exercised that power badly, to retain it. Representative democracies operate, in effect, by right of review, and the hallmark of a functioning representative democracy is that unpopular representatives and parties must stand for re-election and can be given the boot. "Throw the bums out!" elections are really what stands between public discontent and revolution. Considered in this light, E2014 was nothing less than a failure of democracy. Public discontent, indeed outrage, found no expression in the electoral process.

E2014 was a Republican rout with a mighty strange asterisk. As progressive pundit John Nichols put it, in a column for *The Nation* that was typical of post-mortem analysis:

> "[V]oters who came to the polls on November 4 were sufficiently progressive and populist to support minimum-wage hikes, paid sick leave, crackdowns on corporate abuses of the environment, expansion of healthcare and radical reform of a money-drenched campaign-finance system. *They just didn't elect Democrats.*"

Nichols's explanation for this weird electoral schizophrenia?

> "[P]ersonalities, dark-money interventions *and plenty of other factors* were at play. But the *consistent pattern of progressive policy votes* in combination with Republican [candidate] wins provides the starkest

evidence of the extent to which the Democratic Party was an incoherent force in 2014."[1]

And so a Republican Party whose rule of Congress had earned *single-digit approval ratings*[2] found itself rewarded for its great work with its strongest grip on combined federal and state political power since the days of Herbert Hoover,[3] while the Democrats and progressives could be heard in wailing

---

[1] Nichols J, "Democrats: The Party of Pablum," *The Nation*, Dec. 1 – 8, 2014 (emphases added). A familiar tautology is evident: the Democratic Party *must have been* "an incoherent force" *because they lost*. Or their candidates lost while their ideas were winning. Is that really the way voters work? I combed our electoral history books and could find no comparable prior examples. Needless to say, the possibility of computerized election theft was not among the "plenty of other factors" Nichols chose to explore.

This "the Democrats must be doing something wrong because they keep losing" theme continued to be echoed among the punditry. Nathan Robinson, for example, in his excellent 2017 book *Trump: Anatomy of a Monstrosity*, writes that Trump's shocking moment of victory "was shaped just as much by the collapse of Democratic political fortunes as the ascent of Republican ones." Well yes, the shocking and otherwise inexplicable loss of major elections does suggest a collapse of political fortunes.

[2] Source: Rasmussen Reports at http://www.rasmussenreports.com/public_content/politics/mood_of_america/congressi onal_performance. Rasmussen's measure of congressional approval hovered consistently between 8% and 10% during the months preceding E2014. During pre-election week, just 29% of likely voters Rasmussen surveyed thought their *own* representative was "the best person for the job." This was *the first time in polling history* that at least a plurality failed to approve of their *own* representatives.

[3] Notably, in the most "throw the bums out" political climate yet measured, exactly *two* out of 222 incumbent members of the U.S. House Republican majority seeking re-election lost their seats, *a re-election rate of over 99%.*

When the dust settled, Republicans held a 51 – 49 advantage (two Independents caucused with the Democrats) in the U.S. Senate, a 44-seat margin (237 – 193, with five vacancies) in the U.S. House, a better than two-to-one (33 – 16, with one Independent) proportion of governorships, a better than two-to-one (67 - 32) grip on state legislative chambers, and full control (governorship and both branches of the state legislature) of 26 states to the Democrats' eight (16 remained divided). This power ratio had not been equaled in nearly a century and seemed a strange distortion of contemporary America as measured by any yardstick other than that of its computers tallying elections for public office.

This warped dynamic showed no signs of abatement until Donald Trump actually started governing and queered the pitch (from a Republican standpoint). As described by the analysts at Ballotpedia after E2016: "In 82 of 99 state legislative chambers (82.3%), the Republican Party held more seats in January 2017 than it did in January 2009. Between the time of World War II and the end of the second term of President George W. Bush in January 2009, the political party of an outgoing two-term president or consecutive political party administration lost an average of 450 state legislative seats. During President Obama's two terms in office, Democrats suffered a net loss of

chorus blaming themselves and their campaigns, asking (of course) for more money, and pitching around desperately for yet more new strategies to replace the ones that had apparently just failed so miserably.

It is of course difficult to avoid *looking like,* believing yourself to be, and acting like "an incoherent force" when you've just had your electoral clock cleaned. We all tend to suffer from a cognitive phenomenon known as "results bias." That is, we find it difficult to evaluate strategies, tactics, and circumstantial factors in and of themselves, independent of the results they apparently produce. Another way of putting this is that strategies and tactics tend to look a lot more brilliant, even uncanny, when you "win," and a lot more stupid and inept when you "lose."

Especially viewed through this lens, the "incoherence" of the Democrats took, if anything, a turn for the worse with the E2016 Clinton debacle, and led a host of observers to join Nichols in cataloguing the Democratic Party's increasingly apparent flaws, failures, and necrosis.[4] That raised a fundamental, and I believe yet unanswered, question: Did the Democrats lose their way and then, as a consequence, start losing elections; or did they start mysteriously losing elections and then, as a consequence, lose their way?

In 2014, certainly, everyone was shocked at the sheer magnitude of the beat-down—everyone, that is, except those of us who take seriously the corporate/partisan control of America's electoral apparatus and the perils of unobservable vote counting. To us, E2014 fit rather neatly and symptomatically

---

968 state legislative seats, the largest net loss of state legislative seats in this category since World War II." So much for the "emerging Democratic majority." See https://ballotpedia.org/Changes_in_state_legislative_seats_during_the_Obama_presidency.

Obama's approval rating—which stood at 58% favorable as he left office, never dipped below 40% during his tenure, and hovered around 50% in the run-up to E2014—can hardly be invoked as the probable cause of this more than double the average down-ballot carnage in the least scrutinized of all contests carrying national significance.

[4] A prime example (again) is Nathan Robinson, editor-in-chief of *Current Affairs*, who in *Trump: Anatomy of a Monstrosity* thoroughly excoriates the Clinton campaign, the candidate herself, and the Democratic Party at large for its loving embrace of celebrities and business elites (and their money) and near total loss of touch with actual voters—particularly those of the working class, of all races and ethnicities—that had been the party's base for nearly a century.

Robinson's descriptions ring all too true, but one is left to wonder whether the Democrats, having been stung time and again by shocking defeats *before* they took this turn, were rather driven to it (and to their retreat to blue enclaves) *by* those defeats and by their *perceived* serial failures to compete successfully in vast swaths of the "heartland."

into the pattern we had seen emerging over the previous several election cycles and was, it must be said, eminently predictable.

The Usual Suspects

Let's set aside for the time being any thought that the votecounts behind those ***DECISION 2014*** blinking states and pie charts could possibly have been manipulated, in order to examine the various G-rated explanations that were put forward for the confounding results of E2014: low turnout, voter suppression, dark money, gerrymandering, and skewed polls.

Low Turnout: Low turnout provides a very convenient and rather reflexive explanation for Democratic losses, the assumption being that the "core" of the electorate is made up disproportionately of Republican voters while the Democratic constituencies are more likely to include "fringe" voters. Thus when turnout is low it's a good bet that the Republican voters showed up (because they always do) while the Democratic voters stayed home.[5]

The problem with this analysis is that in most cases there is no reliable direct measurement of which party's voters did in fact show up in greater numbers. The reasoning is instead strictly tautological: The Democrats lost (we know this because the trusty votecounts tell us they did); therefore *their* voters must not have shown up.[6] But we would have no way of knowing if they *did* show up and an outcome-altering share of their votes were "mistabulated" and shifted to their opponents. That would certainly make it *look* like they didn't show up and Republican voters did. But how do we know, except via our faith in the computers and their programmers, that in 2014 it wasn't *Republican* voters who expressed their disgust with a historically unpopular Republican-controlled Congress by staying home?

---

[5] It is interesting that when, in E2018, midterm turnout shot up by an astounding 45% over E2014, it was not, as a corollary, assumed that a vast majority of those 35 million "new" voters were Democrats. Weren't we assuming that in an election like E2014, Republicans, who now self-identify as less than 30% of the electorate, were at or near their turnout ceiling? If low turnout elections explain Republican victories, then surely an off-the-charts ultra-high turnout election would produce a Democratic victory more convincing than E2018, when the GOP held the Senate in the teeth of a supposed "blue tsunami."

[6] Low Democratic turnout was also one of the explanations given for Bush's 2004 victory in Ohio, patently absurd in the face of videographic evidence showing lines, frequently several blocks and hours long, at typically Democratic precincts throughout the state, while voters in Republican precincts could walk in, vote, and head home virtually without breaking stride (see, *No Umbrella*, a documentary by Laura Paglin, at http://www.noumbrella.org/index.htm).

So, while *overall* turnout is measurable and was just marginally lower than in the previous several off-year elections, we really don't know *who* stayed home—or for whom those who came to the polls actually voted. What we do know, from the red-shifted results of the unadjusted exit polls,[7] is that the voters who *did* turn out—i.e., the actual electorate—said that they voted well to the left of how their votes were tabulated. The "low turnout" explanation cannot make this red flag go away. We also know that the actual electorate passed, often by wide margins and often not in blue states, all sorts of progressive ballot measures,[8] and that too does not square with the low (Democratic) turnout theory.

Voter Suppression: Voter suppression encompasses a variety of schemes and tactics cynically aimed at insuring low turnout specifically among the voters likely to support one's political opponents. As practiced by the Republican strategists who in E2010 took control of the legislatures and/or governorships of a swath of key "purple" swing states,[9] voter suppression schemes openly targeted millions of "fringe" voters in the Democratic ranks.[10]

Voter-ID laws, passed on the transparent pretext of countering a factually nonexistent epidemic of voter-impersonation fraud,[11] operated like a

---

[7] "Red shift" refers to a poll vs. votecount disparity in which the votecounts are to the right of the poll results. "Unadjusted" exit poll refers to the initial public posting of the poll's results, before those results are "adjusted" toward congruence with the emerging votecounts. As these unadjusted exit polls are ephemeral and disappear forever shortly after posting, they must be preserved and documented by one form or another of screen capture.

[8] See Study VI in Chapter VIII for specific ballot measures in E2014. See also http://ballotpedia.org/List_of_ballot_measures_by_state.

[9] Vital as well was the E2010 Republican sweep of secretaries of state (17 of 26 states where elections were held for that key position in statewide election administration); see https://ballotpedia.org/Statewide_elections_2010.

[10] The gates were opened in 2013 to a flood of templated voter-suppression laws and regulations by the 5-to-4 party-line Supreme Court decision in *Shelby County v. Holder*, gutting a key section of the Voting Rights Act of 1965 and turning states with a history of voting-related discrimination loose to revive Jim Crow free of federal oversight.

[11] See http://www.washingtonpost.com/politics/election-day-impersonation-an-impetus-for-voter-id-laws-a-rarity-data-show/2012/08/11/7002911e-df20-11e1-a19c-fcfa365396c8_story.html. See also Chapter II, notes 87 and 106. According to the *Washington Post*, 37 states have either enacted or considered tougher Voter-ID laws, including many with stringent photo-ID requirements. All told, an exhaustive Carnegie-

modern-era poll tax by selectively imposing costs and barriers that disproportionately impacted the poor and transient. Ditto the shortening of both poll hours (a serious impediment for working-class voters) and early-voting periods, and the consolidation of precincts to make it more difficult to reach one's polling place without vehicular ownership. Purging of voter lists to remove not just ex-felons but a broad penumbra of non-felons whose names *resembled* those of ex-felons, as well as voters who had changed addresses (renters, transients, college and graduate students, the elderly), stripped even more among the Democratic constituencies of their voting rights. And "caging," or sending operatives to the polls to challenge the rights of targeted voters and thereby relegate them to the casting of (frequently uncounted) "provisional ballots," whittled down the electorate still further. Taken together, these ugly schemes were aimed at disenfranchising over 3 million would-be voters,[12] or about 4 percent of the

Knight investigation into voter fraud found exactly *ten* instances of voter impersonation, the species of fraud that photo-ID would combat, from 2000 to 2012, during which period just short of a *billion* ballots were cast at the polls of America. Specious? Cynical? Intentionally discriminatory? Yes to all, according to a spate of recent federal and state court decisions striking down such laws (see, e.g., https://www.cbsnews.com/news/parts-of-wisconsin-voter-id-law-are-unconstitutional-court-says/; https://www.theatlantic.com/politics/archive/2017/05/north-carolinas-voter-id-law-supreme-court-cert/526713/; http://thehill.com/homenews/state-watch/385107-arkansas-judge-blocks-state-voter-id-law; see generally, https://en.wikipedia.org/wiki/Voter_ID_laws_in_the_United_States). The Supreme Court, however, has signaled more tolerance for discriminatory Voter-ID laws (see https://www.narf.org/cases/nd-voter-id/) and the issue remains unsettled.

[12] See http://www.gregpalast.com/gop-led-purge-threat-to-3-5-million-voters/; and, generally, Palast G, *Billionaires & Ballot Bandits; How to Steal an Election in 9 Easy Steps*. New York: Seven Stories Press, 2012.

The primary coordinated purging program—dubbed Interstate Crosscheck, launched in 2005(!) and now suspended as the result of a legal settlement—was the work of Kris Kobach, erstwhile Republican secretary of state of Kansas, chosen by President Trump to co-chair, with Mike Pence, Trump's short-lived and infamous "Commission on Election Integrity." Kobach was found in contempt of court and fined $1 million by a Bush-appointed federal judge fed up with his refusal to comply with court orders to process voter registrations (see http://www.kansascity.com/news/politics-government/article209268109.html).

Kobach ultimately not only lost his case for requiring Kansans to *prove* rather than attest to citizenship (an onerous burden requiring production of passports or birth certificates) to be eligible to vote, but was ordered by the judge to attend law-school classes on top of ordinary CEU requirements, so slipshod was the AG's (and one-time law professor's) courtroom presentation (see http://www.cjonline.com/news/20180618/judge-sides-with-aclu-in-voter-registration-fight-orders-kobach-to-go-to-school).

Kobach's notorious Crosscheck program, purporting to catch voters who voted under the same name in different states, contained millions of names and was, in Palast's

total electorate, the vast majority of whom were demographically part of the Democratic constituency.

But *none* of these tactics, no form of voter suppression, can account for the red shift. Exit polls included only those voters who could respond that they had actually cast their ballots, and so *excluded* would-be voters who had been purged, were unable to obtain qualifying ID, discouraged or precluded by shrinking of access (hours and/or location), or successfully caged.[13] The effect of the voter suppression schemes and the effect of the tabulation errors reflected in the red shift are *additive*—in the phrase coined by Fitrakis and Wasserman, "Strip and Flip."[14]

Dark Money: If, in the language of the corporate protectorate that was the Roberts Court circa 2014, "money" is translated as "speech," then "dark money" would be the speech of anonymous bag-over-the-head hecklers who wish their words to be heard loud and clear without taking on the risk of being identified as the speaker.[15] After the *Citizens United* decision opened the floodgates to unregulated corporate cash in 2010, the damage was compounded when a Republican Congress failed to enact the source-disclosure requirements that even the Court seemed to expect would bring

---

words, "rife with literally millions of obvious mismatches." These would-be voters, the vast majority of them among the Democratic constituencies, were purged and found themselves disenfranchised.

This sort of naked scheme for suppressing the (Democratic) vote is what passes, with a chuckle, in GOP brainstorming sessions, for "election integrity." Evidence from the 2016 primaries suggests it may have metastasized to *Democratic* brainstorming sessions, though some maintain that what appeared to be the selective purging of would-be Sanders voters was in fact routine voter-list hygiene.

[13] Provisional ballots do present a challenge to the exit pollster. While identifying provisional voters is easy enough, estimating the proportion of provisionals cast that may not be counted, in order to downweight such respondents accordingly, is trickier, though much historical data is now available to inform this estimation.

[14] Fitrakis B, Wasserman H: *The Strip and Flip Disaster of America's Stolen Elections* at https://www.amazon.com/gp/product/1622493915. We might add "and Fool," recognizing the growing reliance on disinformation campaigns to influence elections.

[15] The fear is primarily of consumer boycotts and other forms of populist punishment for perceived corporate attempts to "buy" elections. To return to an earlier observation (p. 101): "[T]he battle lines are indeed drawn: a ruling elite, corporate and governmental, that is attempting to know as much as possible about you and me while seeing to it that we know as little as possible about them."

a necessary element of public accountability to all the "speaking" it had just enabled.[16]

It is not disputed that E2014, like its two post-*Citizens* predecessors, was awash in dark money along with gobs of plain old traceable corporate cash. With the corporate point of view so loudly and expensively presented, many have argued that *Citizens United* was at the root of the rightward electoral veer. But—apart from the fact that, like the turnout numbers and voter suppression, it leaves the red shift unaccounted for—this money-based explanation does not appear to fit the facts we find on even the shallowest of drilldowns. Looking at the aggregate spending for E2014, The Center for Responsive Politics found that the totals for the two sides were all-but-equal: $1.75 billion for the GOP to $1.64 billion for the Democrats[17]—hardly the kind of differential to fuel a rout. More significantly still, major spending advantages were *not* associated with victory in many of the key races.

Clearly money is needed to mount nearly all successful campaigns, whether it goes to establish name recognition, drum in a rudimentary message, get out the vote, or mercilessly pillory one's opponent. Not clear, however, are the levels at which additional spending becomes progressively less effective, ineffective, or even counter-productive. There comes a saturation point, after all, at which beleaguered voters have heard it all and heard enough, such that yet more messaging is as apt to annoy them and turn them off as change their minds or motivate them. There is evidence that money-bath campaigns often cross this line and fail to buy more votes at *any* price.[18] As ugly and inimical to the spirit of democracy as big-donor funded campaigns (and particularly those funded anonymously) seem to

---

[16] Far from applying a corrective, however, the Roberts Court, in yet another 5-4 party-line decision, *McCutcheon v. Federal Election Commission*, 134 S.Ct. 1434 (2014); (see http://www.demos.org/publication/what-mccutcheon-v-fec for a thorough analysis), went *further* and removed all aggregate limits on contributions to national parties and candidate committees, effectively setting out the Billionaire Welcome Mat in front of the door it had blown open with *Citizens United.*

[17] See http://www.opensecrets.org/news/2014/11/money-won-on-tuesday-but-rules-of-the-game-changed/.

[18] In the 2011 Walker recall election in Wisconsin, for example, it was found that most of the lavish spending (eight to one in Walker's favor) occurred after all but a tiny percentage of the voters had made up their minds (see p. 82). In 2020, Michael Bloomberg's half-billion-dollar campaign cost approximately $130 per vote and $18 million per delegate won (see https://www.newsweek.com/michael-bloomberg-campaign-votes-finance-1490372).

be, neither dark money nor the fund-fests enabled by *Citizens United* and *McCutcheon* pass muster as valid explanations for the electoral patterns that have come to characterize the computerized voting age.

Gerrymandering: Gerrymandering, or political redistricting for partisan advantage, can work one of two ways: if you command an aggregate popular majority, you can divide it up among the districts[19] in such a way that your party maintains a slim margin in every one of them,[20] shutting the opposing party out; or, more commonly, you can minimize the opposing party's electoral victories by drawing districts in such a way as to concentrate as many of its voters as possible into as few districts as possible. If this, known as "packing," is done with sufficient ruthlessness and artistry it generally results in a significant incongruity between electoral support (i.e., votes) and representation (i.e., candidates elected to office). In fact, it is often possible for a party with minority status among the electorate to nonetheless hold a majority of the seats within a state.[21]

Gerrymandering takes its name from the Revolutionary Era's Elbridge Gerry, so we can be assured that it has held a place in the arsenal of American political tactics for a very long time. What has changed dramatically, with the advent of the computer age and "big data," is the remarkable, practically house-by-house, precision with which districts can be carved up to include and exclude voters based on their known or

---

[19] Gerrymandering works for both U.S. House and state legislative districts and might be applied as well to the selection of presidential electors in any state that passed a law to apportion electors by congressional district. The U.S. Senate, statewide and thus not subject to gerrymandering, is nonetheless grossly disproportionate as a representative body, with half the U.S. population being represented by just 18 out of 100 senators.

Given this large state-small state imbalance, which correlates fairly strongly with America's blue state-red state division, it is a telling measure of the major parties' respective popularity (at least as measured by the results of top-of-the-ballot, high-profile, exit-polled and high-scrutiny contests) that the Democrats have been more or less able to hold their own in Senate representation even after the collapse of the Solid (Democratic) South.

[20] Naturally, if you cut it *too* slim, there is the danger that shifting political winds or an albatross like Trump in E2018 might cost you such districts, and there is in fact some evidence that this dynamic came into play in 2018.

[21] For example, in 2012 the 18-member U.S. House delegation from Pennsylvania sported 13 Republicans to 5 Democrats, in spite of the fact that the Democratic House candidates had, statewide, received an aggregate *majority* of the vote. The GOP maintained that margin in E2014, also increasing their State Senate margin from 5 to 10 seats and State House margin from 20 to 35 seats, while the Democratic gubernatorial candidate won handily by a 55% - 45% margin.

suspected partisanship.[22] With nearly all the guesswork and blurriness removed, gerrymandering has become an extremely potent political weapon and tool of partisanship.[23,24]

---

[22] See "Redistricting, A Devil's Dictionary" at http://www.propublica.org/article/redistricting-a-devils-dictionary/single. Although gerrymandering for partisan advantage was long of debatable constitutionality, the geographical standards actually applied by the courts were so lax that essentially *any* contiguous shape, however jagged and meandering, would pass muster, allowing ample latitude to divvy up voters for maximum political gain. Justice John Paul Stevens, while on the Court, waged devoted battle against this cynical (in design and effect) distortion of the electoral process, but lost to the bloc led by the late Justice Antonin Scalia.

As federal and state courts began critically to revisit the constitutionality of some of the more egregious redistricting schemes, the U.S. Supreme Court (in yet another party-line 5-4 decision, Gorsuch batting for Garland) in June 2019 abruptly ended the visit of the federal courts, with Chief Justice John Roberts declaring partisan gerrymandering a nonjusticiable "political question" (*Rucho v. Common Cause*, 139 S. Ct. 2484), a ruling and reasoning (essentially leaving the fate of gerrymandering to gerrymandered legislatures) that nicely complements the Roberts Court's existing electoral jurisprudence as manifest in its *Citizens United*, *McCutcheon*, and *Shelby County* decisions, among others.

In Pennsylvania, the State Supreme Court, frustrated by the obvious foot-dragging noncompliance of the Republican legislature, set about having the existing hyper-partisan district map redrawn by an independent expert, resulting in politically highly significant changes (in response, the legislature moved to impeach the Democratic judges on the high court). Most states, however, are highly unlikely to be forced to modify even the most ultra-partisan maps in time for E2020.

[23] Gerrymandering has an understandable appeal to seated members of *both* parties, since it tends to produce "safe" seats and often reinforces the already formidable advantages of incumbency. It is worth noting, however, that Democratic voters, who are more likely to be clustered in dense and enclaved urban communities, present significantly more vulnerable targets for the gerrymanderer's Sharpie. It is a lot easier geometrically and geographically to draw the gerrymanderer's holy-grail 90%+ district of Democratic voters than of their Republican counterparts. California is notable among states for having bestowed the redistricting power on an independent board, the California Citizens Redistricting Commission, ostensibly free of partisan control, though in practice that standard is virtually impossible to achieve.

[24] Although the presidency has thus far been immune to the warpings of the gerrymander, a scheme has been floated to change that.

The American Legislative Exchange Council (ALEC) is a nominally nonpartisan but in fact radically right-wing nonprofit founded in 1973 but relatively quiescent prior to the dawn of the New American Century. Almost entirely corporate-funded, most notably by the billionaire Koch brothers, ALEC templates right-wing legislation, very often procedural in nature (as in Photo-ID bills), for rubber-stamping by GOP-controlled state legislatures—its theater of operations of course greatly expanded by E2010 and E2014 (see generally, http://en.wikipedia.org/wiki/American_Legislative_Exchange_Council).

Among ALEC's more recent brainstorms was a plan to "gerrymander the presidency" by apportioning presidential electors by congressional district in key swing states where

The decennial U.S. Census records population changes and serves as the basis for the major gerrymandering opportunities that present themselves at the beginning of each decade. Under-the-radar state legislative victories in E2010, to which I have previously referred as "the gift that keeps on giving," set the GOP up to seize these opportunities and, predictably, they did so with both fists and all the big data they could feed into their supercomputers.[25] The result was a steep and artificial tilt of the political table, which many have cited as yet another major cause of the E2014 rout.

It would be silly to deny the impact of gerrymandering on the outcome of E2014 and the current political balance of power. The impact is formidable, as the architects of the E2010 rout grasped well before the media, let alone the general public, caught on. It would take a massive GOP political implosion, and/or an observably counted election, to overcome the advantages that gerrymandering has conferred upon GOP candidates for the U.S. House and a broad swath of state legislatures.[26]

Nonetheless, gerrymandering cannot be invoked to account for the rout that was E2014. Gerrymandering has no impact on U.S. Senate and gubernatorial contests, of which dozens were red-shifted, and it has no impact on the red shift in *any* contests, including the aggregate red shift of the U.S. House. It is a heavy thumb on the scale for the U.S. House and state legislatures, but it takes *several* heavy thumbs to produce the kinds

---

Republicans hold trifecta control. This would be a perfectly legal and constitutional, if hyper-cynical, tweak of the presidential election game. States are free to depart from the winner-take-all presidential model (which itself is subject to a pointed fairness-based critique) and replace it with what seems abstractly on the surface to be a fairer and more reasonable one.

The consequence, however, is anything but abstract or fair: by shifting at least half the electoral votes of certain large and ordinarily presidentially blue states to the Republican column (*recall that the congressional districts of these states have already been gerrymandered to the GOP's overwhelming advantage*), it becomes, in the words of one bootless Democratic plea for intervention, "virtually impossible for a Democratic [presidential] candidate to win, even if they win the national popular vote overwhelmingly" (see https://www.dailykos.com/campaigns/1011).

[25] See, Daley D, *RATF**KED: The True Story Behind the Plan to Steal America's Democracy*, 2016, at https://www.amazon.com/dp/1631491628.

[26] The post-E2010 partisan redistricting was designed to confer enduring advantages on GOP candidates for the U.S. House and state legislatures, and was enough to insulate the party against anything short of a massive implosion. It did not, however, anticipate Donald Trump. We will examine the Trumplosion in Chapter VI; but, as of 2014, gerrymandering was working just as planned.

of incongruities that now characterize American politics. Gerrymandering, potent as it may be, is just the set-up for the haymaker.

Skewed Polls: As we have seen, none of the phenomena we have examined—low turnout, voter suppression, dark money, or gerrymandering—has any significant bearing on the red shift, the rightward disparity between exit polls and the votecounts, which we have become accustomed to finding in American elections in the age of computer counting. Since the possibility of votecount manipulation cannot be admitted, it has become axiomatic among the punditry to account for the red shift with a standard line or two about the polls being "off again" because they "oversampled Democrats."

According to this narrative, the Democratic voters then pulled a fast one on the pollsters by not turning out to vote, and we're told to believe this because the Democratic candidates (but strangely not a hefty stack of progressive ballot propositions) *lost* (or did worse than expected), having received a smaller percentage of the vote than the polls indicated. You can see the circularity of this reasoning: the "oversampled Democrats" conclusion rests on a turnout assumption which in turn rests on the presumed accuracy of the votecounts. Everything falls neatly into place *as long as we don't question the presumption of an accurate count.*[27]

The red shift in E2014 was egregious. In the elections for U.S. Senate for which exit poll data was available, the red shift averaged an impressive 4.1 percent, with a half dozen races seeing red shifts of over 7 percent. Out of the 21 Senate elections that were exit polled, 19 were red-shifted. In the exit-polled gubernatorial elections, the average red shift was an even greater 5.0 percent and 20 out of the 21 races were red-shifted.

---

[27] See, e.g., Nate Cohn's 6/27/16 NY *Times* article, "Exit Polls, and Why the Primary Was Not Stolen From Bernie Sanders," at
http://www.nytimes.com/2016/06/28/upshot/exit-polls-and-why-the-primary-was-not-stolen-from-bernie-sanders.html?_r=0. Cohn's analysis is impeccable and his deductions about exit polls, in 2016 and historically, follow with *perfect* logic from his starting point—the unstated premise that all the votecounts tabulated in the computer era have been accurate. It brings to mind the scene from the Harrison Ford movie, *The Fugitive*, in which a reporter raises the question of Dr. Kimble's possible "innocence" to the blowhard spokesman of the Chicago PD, who interrupts to respond, tartly and with great impatience, "He's not innocent. He's guilty. He was convicted in a court of law!" As indeed he was.

In U.S. House elections, which are exit polled with an aggregate national sample,[28] the red shift was 3.7 percent. This is the equivalent of approximately 2.9 million votes which, if taken away from the GOP winners of the closest elections, would have been sufficient to reverse the outcomes of 89 House races such that the Democrats would have emerged from E2014 holding a 120-seat (277 to 157) House *majority*.[29]

Although the thousands of state legislative contests are not exit-polled, it is reasonable to assume that the consistent red-shift numbers that we found in the Senate, House, and gubernatorial contests would map onto these critical (as we have seen) down-ballot elections as well.

So the polls (both exit and pre-election) got it very wrong yet again. But were all these polls "off?" The answer to that question is almost certainly "Yes." But not in the direction commonly supposed.

Approaching E2014—in fact, on the day preceding the election—I published an article, entitled "Vote Counts and Polls: An Insidious Feedback Loop,"[30] detailing the corruption of our forensic baselines as pollsters systematically amended their polling methodologies to remedy the string of embarrassing misses (marked by persistent red shifts) with which they began the computerized voting era. In the article, I addressed two specific methodological changes that together have a potent effect on poll outcomes: the first is the use of the Likely Voter Cutoff Model for selecting the sample, disproportionately eliminating respondents belonging to Democratic constituencies; and the second is the use of demographics (including partisanship) from the *adjusted* exit polls of prior elections to weight the current samples.

---

[28] The sample size of the House poll exceeded 17,000 respondents, yielding a Margin of Error (MOE) of less than 1% and a Total Survey Error (TSE) of less than 2%. The odds of a 3.7% red shift occurring by chance were less than one in a billion. When examined demographically, exit poll samples such as those for E2004 (see Study II in Chapter VIII) were found not to exhibit any leftward partisan skew.

[29] Of course I am not suggesting that vote theft can be targeted with such exquisite and infallible precision. But it would make no sense at all *not* to target vote theft to the closer races and shift enough votes to ensure narrow victories. When one couples the evidence of a nearly 3 million vote disparity with even a modestly successful targeting protocol, the result is easily enough to flip the balance of power in the U.S. House.

[30] http://www.truth-out.org/news/item/27203-vote-counts-and-polls-an-insidious-feedback-loop.

Each of these adaptations is discussed in detail in the aforementioned article and in Study V of Chapter VIII of this book, but the overall effect is to *undersample* Democratic constituencies in both exit and pre-election polling such that, with these methodologies employed, an honestly counted election should produce consistent *blue* shifts (votecounts more Democratic than the polls),[31] or exactly the opposite of what E2014 presented.

I concluded my article with the observation that "on Election Day, *accurate* polls should be seen as a red flag," because a methodological contortion like the Likely Voter Cutoff Model should get election results *right* if and only if those election results are *wrong*. Instead we had wildly *inaccurate* polls, a massive red shift *beyond* that which was, via such contortions, already anticipated by and built into the polls. These "double red flag" results are extremely hard to reconcile with any scenario in which votes were tabulated as cast in thousands of elections across America in E2014.

The Consequences: A Nation Lost in Translation
America prides itself on being the first and best representative democracy, and representative democracies are about the translation—via elections, the casting and counting of votes—of the public will into a representative government, a team of officeholders empowered to set policies and chart direction. A quick review of the post-E2014 scorecard showed the GOP, purged of essentially all of its moderate elements,[32] holding an eight-seat majority (54 − 46[33]) in the U.S. Senate, a 60-seat majority (247 − 187) in the U.S. House, nearly a two-to-one gubernatorial advantage (31 − 18), a better than two-to-one grip on state legislative chambers (68 − 30), and full control (governorship and both branches of the state legislature, now termed the "trifecta") of 23 states to the Democrats' seven. Judging by its array of officeholders, America in the wake of E2014 could only be seen as a very red country.

---

[31] This appears to be precisely what transpired, in an intra-party context, in the 2016 Democratic primary in Oklahoma, a red flag detailed in the next chapter.

[32] It is worth reiterating here that primary elections, and particularly down-ballot primary elections, are the lowest hanging fruit an election rigger can pick. There are almost never any baselines (exit polls or pre-election polls) for forensic analysis, and media/public scrutiny is generally nonexistent. In the exceedingly rare cases where the level of scrutiny spikes and rudimentary baselines *are* available, as in the "unimaginable" (according to the *Times*) primary defeat that unseated House Majority Leader Eric Cantor earlier in 2014, the usual suspects, however perplexing, are trotted out and no investigation of the votecount process is even considered.

[33] Two independent senators caucused with the Democrats.

But a major component of that red-paint reality, a kind of secondary effect of all the shocking and fundamentally inexplicable defeats, goes beyond the array of actual officeholders. Outcomes—winning or losing—are part of an educational feedback loop and when outcomes are distorted it is the political equivalent of receiving a bad education, of being taught that 2 + 2 = 5. Nor is the routed party the only student in the class. The nation itself, in believing its officeholders to be duly elected and thereby representative, develops, through looking into that distorted mirror, a distorted self-portrait: "Well I'll be damned, America *is* a red country!"—it's right there on the blinking Election Night map. It winds its way through every item of political news until it becomes a truth embedded in all our brains and more such outcomes cease to be shocking at all. It takes a long time, many election cycles, however, for another, more ominous recognition to dawn: that *no matter how we all vote, we keep getting a government that most of us don't want*, a government that, divided as we may be on many fronts, we begin to recognize does not truly represent *any* of us, respond to *any* of us, or faithfully translate our collective will into laws, policy, and national direction.

Karl Rove's long-sought *perpetual rule* and *permanent majority* came to near-full fruition. But for Trump, it is not hard to imagine the plan rolling right along. That this was hardly an accurate translation of the public will and the "soul" of America could not matter less to the likes of Rove and his clients, nor to the likes of Roger Stone, Paul Manafort, the Kochs or the Mercers: the permanent majority they engineered is a permanent majority of rulers, not subjects.

But, as the next chapter will explore, it *does* matter to the public itself. Our finally perceived loss of sovereignty—ultimately verging on government without the consent of the governed—began to have a profound impact on the American psyche, and we watched it start to play out in the awful degradation of American politics. This is what the era of computerized vote counting has wrought and, with no pleasure in being such a downer, I suggest that any viable way out begins with facing the full reality of this achievement in all its formidable dimensions.

— V —

E2016: THE CHICKENS COME HOME BIGLY

'What is a Caucus-race?' said Alice, not that she much wanted to know.

— *Lewis Carroll,* Alice's Adventures in Wonderland

The Politics of Disgust

E2014, with approval ratings in the single-digits, was the quintessential throw-the-bums-out election that wasn't, leaving in its wake large swaths of the public, left and right, clenched in political outrage or mired in political despair. That meant a lot—indeed, according to every poll, a super-majority—of frustrated, angry, and disgusted voters ready to go "in a different direction"—populist and, from the corporate point of view, dangerous.

And so we arrived at the year 2016—presidential and perverse. The American electorate wound up being offered a choice between the most despised, distrusted, indeed hated pair of major-party presidential nominees in living memory, if not in history: Hillary Clinton and Donald Trump carried the highest unfavorability ratings ever recorded.[1] This *prix fixe* menu was the product of a primary season featuring a series of highly suspect elections.

Before turning to the evidence gathered in support of that assertion, let's begin by taking note of what the American people came into this critical election year seeming to *want*. It was hard to miss the energy that swirled around two

---

[1] For a snapshot of the numbers, which of course fluctuated but consistently tunneled through the subterranean strata, see, e.g., http://www.gallup.com/poll/193376/trump-leads-clinton-historically-bad-image-ratings.aspx.

An entrepreneurial friend lamented to me that in late October she had—alas, too late!—come up with the idea of selling "Election Sickness" bags, such as the airlines supply in every seat pocket, with a picture of Clinton on one side, Trump on the other, and a set of instructions for use. I have no doubt that had she gone into production in September, she would have made a killing.

candidates, Trump and Senator Bernie Sanders (I-VT[2]), who, from the right and left respectively, were screaming "ENOUGH ALREADY!!" and promising to shake up the status quo in dramatic fashion. This angry, sometimes bordering on nihilistic, energy dwarfed whatever scant enthusiasm greeted the other major candidates—from Clinton down the gamut of then-current and erstwhile Republican office-holders (Marco Rubio, Chris Christie, Jeb Bush, Ted Cruz, John Kasich, et al)—all of whom were perceived, wherever they attempted to position themselves on the political spectrum, as card-carrying members of the establishment.

Let us also notice that, of the two candidates who excited the voting public, the one on the right became the Republican nominee while the one on the left was stopped cold, just short of his party's nomination. And the one on the right was bathed in a constant media spotlight while the one on the left was effectively ignored until it was no longer remotely possible to do so. It does not take an advanced degree in political science to recognize that in the parade of presidential aspirants Sanders was the only one who, from the standpoint of the power elites, was both electable and politically dangerous enough to be seen as real trouble.

The R-Word Comes into Common Usage

By the time of the Democratic Convention, there were millions of hopping mad Sanders supporters, convinced not only that their hero was robbed but also that Hillary Clinton herself was the thief or at least was aware of the heist.[3]

---

[2] Although politically an Independent, Sanders sought the presidential nomination of the Democratic Party. His outsider status did not endear him to the party leadership.

[3] We began in 2016 to witness an unobservable vote counting process give predictable rise to chronic suspicion of fraud, knee-jerk assignment of blame, and a general breakdown in the trust necessary for a legitimate and peaceful electoral and political process.

But, while it is natural enough to assume that the *beneficiary* of a covert manipulation was in fact its *perpetrator*, there are certainly non-candidate bad actors—foreign and of course, though the media seems hell-bent on denying it, domestic—with strong motivation to influence and alter electoral outcomes, such that *the beneficiary of such activities may not only not be their perpetrator but also may be entirely unaware of their existence.*

We must ask, therefore, who besides Clinton herself had a strategic interest in making sure that Clinton and not Sanders was the Republican candidate's opponent in November? It would make sense that any operative, foreign or domestic, charged with producing a Republican victory in November would have begun their work in the Democratic primaries, helping the ultra-vulnerable, FBI-targeted Clinton to the nomination.

What these voters saw had the look of a thoroughly "rigged" game, though it was Trump, not Sanders, who kept resorting to the R-word in reference to the nomination process.[4]

What was it that Sanders voters saw? To begin with, there was the specter of their candidate drawing first large, then huge and wildly enthusiastic crowds—far outstripping those of Clinton—and yet being all-but-ignored by mainstream media. They saw a candidate raise an enormous war chest from millions of individual contributions and entirely without feeding alongside Clinton (and the other candidates) at the corporate trough—a feat with the potential to revolutionize American politics that nevertheless somehow failed to impress the press. Then they saw, often up close and personal, in state after state, obstacles thrown in the path of would-be Sanders voters—sometimes as the result of legitimate, if cynical, regulations governing registration deadlines and qualifications, but often a function of what seemed to be targeted purges of voter databases and suspiciously erroneous instructions given to election administrators and voters. Hundreds of thousands of voters were relegated to the dread "provisional" ballot, with an unknown proportion of those votes going uncounted.[5] And the impact of all these phenomena was all too obviously and disproportionately to Sanders's electoral detriment.[6]

It didn't help when a hacker's and/or insider's leak of emails confirmed that the Democratic National Committee, supposedly an unaligned umpire and facilitator of nomination battles, was surreptitiously promoting Clinton's cause in a variety of ways, and that elements of the mainstream media were also in on the game.[7] And of course there was the thick padding—the 712 "superdelegates" chosen not by the voters but by the Democratic Party establishment, more than 90 percent of whom would vote at the convention for the anointed candidate, Clinton—amounting to a greater than *20 percent*

---

[4] Trump also applied the R-word prospectively to the general election contest, giving rise to concern that results adverse to him might not be accepted as legitimate. It was ironic to contemplate the ark of election integrity being carried into battle by such a champion. Unsettling as well the sudden alarm that our electoral system might be vulnerable to *foreign-state hacking*—the Russians—as if the possibility of *insider rigging* by domestic operatives had never occurred to anyone.

[5] A partial count put the figure at 220,000, with expectations that it would rise (see https://www.huffpost.com/entry/provisional-ballots-not-counted_n_5761bb92e4b0df4d586f15fe).

[6] See, e.g., https://www.huffingtonpost.com/entry/arizona-primary-problems_us_56f41094e4b04c4c376184ca.

[7] See https://en.wikipedia.org/wiki/2016_Democratic_National_Committee_email_leak.

handicap operating against the delegate count of Sanders (or any other "outside" candidate who might have had the temerity to mount an intra-party challenge).[8]

Those were thumbs on the scale that voters *could see*. And because, unlike in a suspect one-day November election such as E2004, the primary season extended for months, the hits kept coming and the distress and eventual outrage kept building, along with ever increasing levels of vigilance and distrust. Questions (and lawsuits) hung over the electoral procedures of many primary (and caucus) states, with egregiously visible fiascoes coming to light in, among others, Arizona, Kentucky, Ohio, New York, and California. This three-ring electoral circus was what the voters *saw*.

What the voters *couldn't see* was what was happening to the votes that had been cast. But the question naturally framed itself: If Clinton had been, as it appeared, the beneficiary of all these *discoverable* thumbs on the electoral scale, how could a vote counting process that was unobservable and so highly vulnerable be blithely presumed to be immune to an *undiscoverable* thumb? And the obvious follow-up: How bright is the ethical line between mass-purging voters to suppress their votes and simply mistabulating their votes? To a multitude of Sanders supporters, at least, not very bright.

Primaries and Caucuses
Taking place in cyberspace, the vote counting process was of course not directly observable; but, as each state weighed in, numerical evidence began to emerge and pause-giving patterns become established. It was hard not to notice, as the Sanders candidacy established itself and the nomination battle heated up, a glaring divergence between the election results in primary versus caucus states. In 14 states, pledged convention delegates were chosen in caucus meetings where the principal method of counting votes was observable and where state totals could be reconciled via a traditional tabulation tree to the counts at each individual caucus—the effect of such relative transparency being to put a major damper on thoughts of rigging. The first caucus, in Iowa, led off the nomination battle and resulted in a razor-thin Clinton victory (49.9 percent to 49.6 percent) amidst various allegations of procedural

---

[8] See https://en.wikipedia.org/wiki/Results_of_the_2016_Democratic_Party_presidential_primaries.

mismanagement.[9] The second caucus, in Nevada, brought forth another narrow Clinton victory (52.6 percent to 47.3 percent) and more allegations.[10]

Following the Nevada caucus and heading into March, it became apparent that the nomination would be a battle and not a coronation. The table below presents the results of the 12 remaining state caucuses:

2016 Democratic Party Caucuses (3/1 - 6/7)			
State (Date)	Sanders %	Clinton %	Sanders Margin
Colorado (3/1)	59.0%	40.3%	18.7%
Minnesota (3/1)	61.6%	38.4%	23.2%
Kansas (3/5)	67.7%	32.3%	35.4%
Nebraska (3/5)	57.1%	42.9%	14.2%
Maine (3/6)	64.3%	35.5%	28.8%
Idaho (3/22)	78.0%	21.2%	56.8%
Utah (3/22)	79.3%	20.3%	59.0%
Alaska (3/26)	86.1%	18.4%	67.7%
Hawaii (3/26)	69.8%	30.0%	39.8%
Washington (3/26)	72.7%	27.1%	45.6%
Wyoming (4/5)	55.7%	44.3%	11.4%
North Dakota (6/7)	64.2%	25.6%	38.6%
Average	68.0%	31.4%	36.6%

As can be seen, *every* caucus was won by Sanders, all by wide margins, ranging from a low of 11.4 percent to a high of 67.7 percent. Sanders's *average* margin of victory was 36.6 percent—and indeed he won a better than two to one aggregate ratio of these caucus voters.

Were the caucus states a discrete and homogeneous swath of America, an identifiable bastion of Sanders support? An argument could be made that, with

[9] Concerns "ranged from the potential for incorrect vote counts due to crowding to confusion over the role of coin tosses to settle some tie results." See http://www.desmoinesregister.com/story/news/politics/2016/07/26/87576058/.

[10] This time the main problem was that many Clinton staffers and supporters were not required to register in order to vote. See http://www.dailykos.com/story/2016/2/26/1491957/-Nevada-and-Iowa-DNC-run-caucuses-full-of-fraud-lies-vote-irregularities-wrong-winner-announced.

the exception of Maine, which could be considered penumbral to Sanders's Vermont, each of these states is located west of the Mississippi; in most of them, voters were more likely to be white (though not young) than in the primary states where Clinton built her narrow margin of pledged delegates. There was, however, substantial political and cultural diversity within the caucus set (Minnesota, Colorado, Washington, and Hawaii hardly mirror Utah, Idaho, Kansas, and Nebraska).

Then there was the divergence of the Dakotas, North and South. In South Dakota, a primary state, Clinton edged Sanders 51.0 percent to 49.0 percent; in North Dakota, a caucus state, Sanders blew out Clinton 64.2 percent to 25.6 percent. The black population of each state is 1 percent. The North Dakota caucus and the South Dakota primary were held on the same date, June 7. Is it unreasonable to wonder what, other than the method of counting votes, might account for such a dramatic difference in outcomes—greater than 40 percent—in these neighboring and demographically similar states? And more generally, *what would account for the entire run of Sanders caucus blowouts?* For there is nothing subtle here in these numbers, nothing that can be reassuringly written off as a figment of race, age, gender, or any other all-encompassing demographic or political explanation.[11]

2016 Exit Polls: A Tale of Two Parties
If there was any remaining doubt that doubt was in order, it was removed by the exit polls. We were treated to yet another revival of the Great Exit Poll Debate, which had its first primetime run in the wake of E2004. In this snarkfest, those questioning the fidelity of the votecounts cite exit poll-votecount (EP/VC) disparities as evidence indicative of votecount mistabulation, while defenders of the faith in turn attack the reliability of exit polls (at least in the U.S.) and often can't resist weaving in an obbligato line of mockery directed at the "conspiracy theorists" who can't seem to understand why we should doubt the exit polls while trusting the votecounts.[12]

---

[11] One explanation attributed much of Sanders's caucus-state strength to the personal and public nature of caucus proceedings—which, it was reasonably argued, played to the strengths of the Sanders campaign—along with the aggressive, at times intimidating, behavior of Sanders partisans at these events. It is, however, hard to imagine that the Clinton campaign, with the muscle of the DNC behind it, would have wilted so completely in the face of such behavior; and Clinton certainly did not have the luxury of writing off these 12 states.

[12] See Karlyn Bowman's comprehensive and relatively balanced survey, "The Trouble With Polling," in *National Affairs*, which cites some of these criticisms and

The problem with the Great Exit Poll Debate is that it is fated to be inconclusive because *neither* side has access to the evidence that could resolve it: neither raw exit poll data (a simple, unweighted tally of individual responses to the exit poll questionnaires) nor voter-marked ballots are publicly accessible; both are held to be proprietary and off-limits. So what we have is in essence a concealed counting system alongside a concealed polling system, *neither of which is self-evidently accurate.* It would be something of a credibility draw, except for the fact that the exit pollsters' business model rests rather heavily on the perceived accuracy of their polls, which translates to an imperative to publish polls[13] that are at least within spitting distance of the electoral results. Major and particularly *serial* departures from those electoral results—no matter what is said by way of disclaimer that exit polls in the U.S. are not "designed" to approximate votecounts[14]—are a serious embarrassment, bad for business.[15] Hence the exit pollsters are ordinarily fanatical about pattern analysis and error correction—they try hard to "get it right" and they have had decades to go about doing that. It is in that context that we must try to comprehend the performance of the exit polls in the E2016 primaries.

In examining the performance of the E2016 primary-season exit polls it would be natural to conclude that each party's primaries had been handled by a *separate* polling outfit, or at least that different methodologies and protocols were employed for the Democratic versus the Republican polls. Of course neither of these things was true: all voters, Democratic and Republican, were polled by the same firm, Edison Research, using the same methodological approach, on the same days, at the same precincts, in the same weather, with the same strict protocols. How then to explain the resulting pattern? Why did the polls perform superbly throughout the run of Republican primaries,[16] while they were such a fiasco in the Democratic primaries that exit polling was

---

examinations, all of which proceed, however, from the presumption of votecount accuracy: https://www.nationalaffairs.com/publications/detail/the-trouble-with-polling.

[13] It is now recognized that, thanks to the work of election forensics analysts, any publicly posted iteration of an exit poll prior to final adjustment to congruence with the votecounts will likely be preserved via screen-capture, thus immortalizing any disparities.

[14] See Chapter II, note 35 for the rebuttal to this claim.

[15] It should of course be noted that voting computer vendors and programmers are under no such scrutiny or pressure, as it is simply *presumed* that such votecount-poll disparities are the fault of erroneous polls.

[16] Time-stamped screen-capture data, necessary for EP/VC comparison, was available for 23 out of the 25 Republican primaries that were exit polled.

abruptly and quietly canceled with the elections in New Jersey, New Mexico, and (critically) California remaining on the schedule?[17]

How stark was the contrast? The mean "error" or exit poll-votecount (EP/VC) disparity for the 23 Republican primaries for which data was available was 0.6 percent.[18] In only *two* of the 23 elections were EP/VC disparities outside the Total Survey Error (TSE),[19] about what we would expect from the rules of probability. Of the individual election disparities greater than 1 percent, 11 favored Donald Trump while 9 favored his opponents, again the kind of balance indicative of both accurate polling and accurate vote tabulation. This level of performance over a long string of elections confirms the competence of the pollsters and the soundness of their protocols and methodology.[20]

It is a competence and a soundness that seem to have vanished when polling Democratic voters. In the 25 Democratic primaries, the mean error or EP/VC disparity was 6.0 percent,[21] *or ten times that in the Republican primaries.* In *10* of the 25 elections the EP/VC disparities exceeded the Total Survey Error; we would normally expect to see *one or two* such failures. And of the individual election disparities greater than 1 percent, *three* favored Bernie Sanders while

---

[17] Other primaries not exit polled took place in Delaware, Kentucky, Montana, South Dakota, Oregon, and Puerto Rico. Although cancellation of the exit polls in 19 states in E2012 was noted by the MSM at the time, a search of *NY Times* and *Washington Post* websites revealed not a single article of any genre regarding the sudden cancellation of the 2016 primary exit polls.

[18] We treated the Republican primaries as a contest of Trump against "the field" of his opponents. We took this approach both because, while Trump was a constant in all of the primaries, the rest of the field varied as candidates dropped out; and because it facilitated an apples-to-apples comparison with the Clinton/Sanders contest. Analysis of the performance of the exit polls in the Republican primaries, although it became somewhat more complex, did not change significantly in result when EP/VC disparities were viewed candidate by candidate.

[19] Total Survey Error, while built on the mathematical Margin of Error (MOE) for a purely random sample, is somewhat larger than the MOE because it takes into account certain non-random factors in the administration of an exit poll. We employed TSE for both Republican and Democratic primaries.

[20] The exit polls for the hotly-contested 2008 Democratic primaries also exhibited an expected level of accuracy.

[21] Although pledged delegates are awarded according to various formulas and not always in strict proportion to voteshares, a shift of this magnitude carried profound implications for the pledged delegate counts of Clinton and Sanders, sufficient to call into question the nomination.

21 favored Hillary Clinton.[22] You can see why Sanders voters began to wonder what might be happening to their votes, questioning the *counting* process along with the registration process and the various thumb-on-the-scale party rules.

The Great Exit Poll Debate Redux focused on this run of disparities and whether it was in any way probative of systemic problems with the vote counting process. On the one side were those who saw in the exit polls *proof* that the Democratic primaries had been rigged. They looked at the math, much as we did in E2004 and other red-shifted elections of the computer-count era, and saw a pattern of disparities that, from a statistical standpoint, was all but impossible. On the other side were those who saw the exit polls as essentially worthless, crude instruments with no probative value at all when it comes to assessing the accuracy of a given votecount or of the entire vote counting process. As in many such polarized disputes, the truth most likely falls somewhere in between.

A key point of contention—given that the Republican polls were essentially spot-on, attesting to the general competence of the exit polling operation and the soundness of its methodology—was whether the Democratic exit polls were distorted by an "enthusiasm gap" between Clinton and Sanders voters. According to the "enthusiasm gap hypothesis"—similar in nature to the (debunked) "reluctant Bush responder" hypothesis of E2004—younger and more enthusiastic Sanders voters were more likely to participate in the exit poll when selected than were older and presumably less enthusiastic Clinton voters.

Of course there is no dispositive evidence either way, since enthusiasm—unlike gender, race, or age—is not a visible trait subject to quantification in those refusing to participate. But we do know that the exit pollsters keep careful count—by gender, race, and approximate age—of refusals to participate, and use this count in weighting their polls. Thus if, as the critics suspect, young voters were more apt to respond to the exit poll when selected, they would be down-weighted accordingly to bring their age cohort in line with its actual proportion of the voting public. And, because enthusiasm and youth were acknowledged to be strongly correlated, the age-based weighting would likely have neutralized most if not all of any enthusiasm gap.

---

[22] For the complete tables, compiled by statistician Theodore Soares, see www.tdmsresearch.com.

It is unfortunately the nature of the Great Exit Poll Debate to come down to skirmishes like "reluctant Bush responder" and "Sanders enthusiasm gap," which most often cannot be decisively settled with the information and data made available.[23] But for those who seek to dispel concerns about the vote counting process, a "tie" is as good as a win. The political timeframe during which elections hang in the balance, such that interest and passions peak, tends to be very short (it often ends with a losing candidate's concession), while the timeframe for in-depth academic debate over the subtleties of data analysis can be measured in weeks, months, even years. Once a debate becomes "academic" in nature, the political "moment" is almost guaranteed to pass and with it, regardless of whether or how the debate resolves, passes all prospect of action. In the case of the 2016 Democratic primaries, concession took place, the Convention following, a time for "healing" and "pulling together." The next battle loomed, the next election, the next exercise in blind faith.

Oklahoma!

Peter Falk's "Columbo" had a famous tagline. Just when the villain seemed to have wriggled out of the net of suspicion with the perfect alibi and a patronizing smirk, Columbo would cock his head slightly to the side, hesitate a beat, and say, "Ah, just one more thing." Then would come the killer question about some little-noticed detail, and the next thing you knew the bad guy was on his way to the slammer.

In that spirit, we direct our attention to Oklahoma. This otherwise uninteresting (to Democrats at least) red state stands out as the contrarian—one of just a few states where Sanders' votecount *exceeded* his exit poll total

---

[23] An unprecedented legal action to obtain the data that might resolve such debates, *Johnson v. Edison Media Research, Inc.*, was filed in federal court in Ohio in July 2016, seeking the release by the exit polling firm of the raw data from the 2016 exit polls. It was dismissed in May 2017 (see https://law.justia.com/cases/federal/district-courts/ohio/ohsdce/2:2016cv00670/195214/8/). Various other recent legal actions to obtain such hard evidence as voter-marked ballots for votecount verification purposes have also failed. The fate of such legal initiatives reflects the thoroughly non-transparent and non-public status of the vote counting process.

It is also very much worth noting that, as of this writing (i.e., more than three years after the 2016 general election), the raw exit poll data ("blurred" to prevent any possible breach of respondent confidentiality) from the 2016 primary and general elections—which exit-pollster Edison traditionally transmits, within several months following a national election, to Cornell University's Roper Institute for archiving and limited-access analysis—had not been received by Roper.

and in fact the *most* Sanders-shifted (6.1 percent) of all the Democratic primaries. This would be unremarkable (every long table has its "least" and "most," most every graph its outlier) except for one factoid, one "little-noticed detail:" *Oklahoma turns out to be the only state on the Democratic primary chart in which the state itself, rather than the vendors or their satellite contractors, plays the principal role in programming the voting computers.*

These are two dots that you don't have to be Columbo to connect: Dot 1) absence of the suspected vector of access to the programming; Dot 2) a reverse EP/VC disparity (i.e., a pattern-defying absence, indeed reversal, of the virtually ubiquitous Clinton-shift). This is quite a correlation.[24] Mere coincidence? Perhaps. But how many such correlations can we brush aside as mere coincidences in the interest of protecting the shield?

Can we also brush aside the stark contrast in exit poll performance for the Democratic and Republican primaries of 2016? Can we brush aside the radically different results in observably-counted caucus states? Can we brush aside the egregious red-shifts of every midterm election from the passage of HAVA in 2002 through 2014? Can we brush aside the glaring disparities between the forensics of competitive and noncompetitive elections? Can we brush aside the 59 percent of the statewide vote won by a cipher candidate in 2010 or the key senatorial election in which the only explanation left standing for the enormous disparity between hand-counted and opscan-counted ballots was the method of counting itself? Can we brush aside the growing data set of Cumulative Vote Share (CVS) graphs that show the telltale upslope of suspect candidates as precincts get larger and votes consequently get easier to shift without risk of detection? Can we brush aside a sudden presidency-

---

[24] We note that the shift in Oklahoma (6.1%) is significant, near the TSE for the poll. If we conclude that the denial of the vendor-programmed access vector led to a "clean" count, then we would expect an *accurate* exit poll result, not a 6.1% shift. All the more so if there was in fact an "enthusiasm gap" in Sanders' favor, as has been hypothesized by critics of exit poll-based forensics.

This suggests something even more ominous. We know that exit pollsters study their own error patterns fanatically, and make whatever tweaks to sampling and weighting they believe necessary to avoid the serial embarrassment of continually getting elections "wrong" in the same direction. Does the glaring exception that is Oklahoma then suggest that *other* states, also being subject to such anticipatory tweaking (which in the case of putatively *not-rigged* Oklahoma seems to have backfired to produce a 6.1% "reverse" shift), displayed mitigated exit poll-votecount disparities significantly *smaller* than they would otherwise have been? If so, then the egregious exit poll-votecount disparities throughout the Democratic primaries would be even larger and screaming even louder that electronic votecount manipulation was endemic.

determining flip in votecounts when a state website "went down" in the early morning hours of November 3, 2004 and the votes were rerouted to a "backup" server set up by none other than Karl Rove's IT guru? How much evidence can we brush aside and continue to sleep at night believing that our democracy is safe and sound?

The Election of Donald Trump

After 15 years of brushing—in the name of ease and convenience, in the name of preserving (at any cost) voter confidence in the electoral process, in the name of elevating the rights of corporations over those of the public— did we finally manage to brush ourselves off the cliff?

Donald J. Trump is, legitimately or illegitimately, in fact our president. And his enablers in Congress and throughout the government are, legitimately or illegitimately, in fact in office. This is, whether by fair play or foul, the Age of Trump. The nation is, to an even greater degree than predicted in earlier editions of this book, riven—its people made enemies and divided into red and blue fortresses, as close to war as they are to meaningful and constructive dialogue.

We have, in this and the preceding chapters, traced many of the steps down this path—the rolling, if not always linear, impact of one suspect computer-age election after another—right up to the cliff's edge. Let us now trace the last big step and tumble, into the 2016 General Election and its still unfolding aftermath.

An election year is made up of innumerable events and constant flux. If we take an alpha-to-omega overview of the 2016 presidential election, the first thing that jumps out from the thousands of event pixels is the fact that America entered 2016 with a near-consensus recognition that something serious needed to be done to deal with runaway economic inequality. The year ended, however, with a president-elect and cabinet carrying water for the 1 percent and wine for the 0.1 percent, portending not merely a step but a giant leap *away* from economic equality and toward outright plutocracy.

The nation that came into the year coalescing around the need to seriously address climate change and the easy availability of guns, exited it in the hands of a climate change denier and new darling of the NRA. A nation that seemed anxious about the relatively mild pay-to-play concerns raised by the Clinton Foundation, wound up with an all-but-branded White House, its chief and ancillary occupants boasting more and deeper conflicts of interest than any in our long history.

In reviewing the year 2016, which culminated shockingly in the Age of Trump, we will want to ask how we wound up, in virtually every dimension, zigging when we meant to zag. How did such a seemingly fundamental reversal of public will (and taste) come to pass? How did the gears of our electoral process mesh (or slip) to lead us here? Are we here—as virtually every pundit, every best-selling "How Did It Happen?" and "Who Are We?" book tells it—because of some strange but ultimately organic conjunction of developments in our body politic? Did a candidate who got trounced in every debate, boasted of his success as a sexual predator, and made dozens of campaign gaffes, any *one* of which would have sunk the candidacy of any of his forerunners, genuinely manage to secure enough votes to put him over the Electoral College top and into the White House? Did the Russians help and, if so, how? Or was it ultimately decided by the trillions of 1s and 0s and the masters (i.e., programmers) of their dance in the dark?

The Road to November
We all experienced the general election campaign of 2016. I have yet to encounter anyone who gave it high marks. For most Americans it was a brutal affair that, even by the low standards of the modern era, broke new ground for mendacity, lack of substance, and, for lack of a better term, personal and political plug-ugliness. Internationally, it was an embarrassment.

While Hillary Clinton generally maintained personal decorum, she rattled around with the cowbells of a festering email investigation and vague suspicions of pay-to-play Clinton Foundation improprieties tied to her tail. In four-and-a-half hours of primetime debates, not once was the question of climate change posed in any meaningful way, while emails and hot-mic tapes and personal threats sucked up the airtime.

For Donald Trump's part, it was literally impossible to keep up with the falsehoods he and his surrogates spouted, quite apart from the media affiliates supporting his campaign. His rallies rang with chants of "Lock her up!" . . . "Drain the swamp!" . . . "Build the wall!" He took on the Muslim parents of a dead American war hero. He gleefully mocked the disabled, including, in the ugliest, crudest, and cruelest display of human behavior I have ever witnessed, physically mimicking a journalist questioning him at a press conference. He gave vent to the kind of misogyny and bigotry that would have been instantly fatal in any previous campaign at any level. He appeared to celebrate and revel in his own boasts of groping women, unwanted sexual advances, and outright assault.[25] It took the media some time to catch on, but even then there seemed little point to pointing out Trump's daily, sometimes hourly, "inconsistencies." For supporters and detractors alike, it seemed to simply become the new normal.[26]

It was a campaign of scandal, incivility, and mendacity, but any equivalence of conduct portrayed here would be a spectacularly false one. The voters emerged from it all mutually disgusted and more horribly hyperpolarized than at any time in living memory. But Clinton, despite FBI Director James Comey's (late) October Surprise,[27] emerged from the muck with a lead in virtually every poll (and there were scores of them), tracking both the national vote and the key states that were the focus of the battle for an Electoral College majority.

On the eve of the election, Nate Silver's FiveThirtyEight.com[28] (which of all handicappers gave Trump his *best* chance) predicted Clinton wins in the swing states of Wisconsin (84 percent probability), Michigan (80 percent), Pennsylvania (77 percent), North Carolina (55 percent), and Florida (55 percent). Trump's likelihood of pulling out victories in *all* these states was on

---

[25] A tangle of civil suits by women alleging such behavior, up to and including rape of an adult woman and a 13-year-old girl, dogged Trump before the was a candidate, when he was a candidate, and as president. Most were settled; one, at least, was refiled. "Hush money" payments also were made to cover candidate Trump's infidelities. See, generally, https://abcnews.go.com/Politics/list-trumps-accusers-allegations-sexual-misconduct/story?id=51956410.

[26] Trump famously boasted that he could "stand in the middle of Fifth Avenue and shoot someone and I wouldn't lose any voters, okay?" (see https://www.realclearpolitics.com/video/2016/01/23/trump_i_could_stand_in_the_middle_of_fifth_avenue_and_shoot_somebody_and_i_wouldnt_lose_any_voters.html). In retrospect, it appears that he might have been quite accurate in that assessment, which of course says as much about Trump voters as about Trump himself (see http://www.newsweek.com/trump-voters-republicans-overall-actually-dont-care-president-shoots-someone-638462).

[27] Comey revealed, a mere 10 days before the election, that the FBI investigation into Clinton's emails, which went on to turn up nothing, had been reopened (see https://www.nytimes.com/2016/11/04/us/fbi-james-comey-hillary-clinton.html).

Comey's explanation, given a year and a half later, for this action, which most analysts believe put Trump in the White House, was that he was concerned that, following what he thought was an all but inevitable Clinton *victory*, it would, if he failed to make the disclosure, appear that he had withheld the information to *protect* her candidacy—and indeed, on the face of it, his position was rock-and-a-hard-place unenviable.

[28] See https://projects.fivethirtyeight.com/2016-election-forecast/.

the order of 1 in 600.[29] Beyond the numbers, expectations were such that, when a Trump victory became apparent, the word "Shocking" was attached to it in headlines across America.

But in retrospect, given that Trump *won*, it all seems to fit. This is how the industry works, how the narrative comes together and the historical novel is written. In something akin to an argument from design, *because* Trump won, he *must* have had the formula for success[30] and, being the psychological savant that he is, must have known the voters would forgive him his boasts, lies, and trespasses—as of course millions did. There is no denying the existence of a "Trump base." The question is: Was it populous enough to elect him in the states that, given the bent math of the Electoral College, mattered?

Screencapture and Shock

Election integrity advocates now approach *every* election with concerns born of the long history of red-flag forensics and suspect results in the era of computerized vote counting. Not just the election integrity crowd, however, but much of America approached Nov. 8, 2016 with concerns about the fidelity of the vote counting process, not the least because Trump himself kept raising the specter of a "rigged" election,[31] going so far as to demur when questioned as to whether he would accept the results of the election should he lose.

There was also substantial media coverage of foreign attempts to "meddle" in the election, including a suspected disinformation campaign and hacking of DNC emails and voter databases. Naturally, this raised the question of whether such meddling could be taken further, even to include interference with the vote counting itself. As Russia or Russian actors were implicated as suspects, and the pro-Trump sympathies of Russian President Vladimir Putin became obvious, the story grew longer legs. Hasty reassurances were provided that, because our voting computers were not hooked up to the internet, vulnerability to Russian or any outside hacking was minimal.[32]

---

[29] If, for whatever reason, that does not seem all that improbable to you, try this little exercise with a partner: have them pick a number between 1 and 600 and try to guess it; ask them to keep picking different numbers for each time you guess; good luck!

[30] In the words of Rep. Peter T. King (R-NY): "[Trump] has a way of getting things done. He had the worst campaign ever. On election night, he was the guy smiling.. (as quoted in *The Washington Post*, 3/3/18, "'Pure madness': Dark days inside the White House as Trump shocks and rages," by Philip Rucker et al).

[31] See http://www.politico.com/story/2016/10/donald-trump-rigged-election-guide-230302.

[32] Thanks to the tenacity of a number of election transparency advocates, including Jennifer Cohn and John Brakey, it subsequently was acknowledged that plenty of

In keeping with the long-standing government/media refusal to acknowledge the possibility of *insider* interference with the vote counting process—that is, by anyone with access to the programming, servicing, or distribution of the equipment—not a word was written or spoken about this corollary concern despite the even greater likelihood that it would present as a vector for manipulation.

Trump's "shocking" victory was sealed before the dishes were done in the Pacific time zone, and its contours subject to analysis by network pundits before bedtime on the East Coast. This is the boon of computerized voting, giving us the media property known as "DECISION 20XX," an extravaganza to rival the Super Bowl. Election forensics analysts forego the entertainment value of Election Night in order to capture the vital data before it disappears.

As explained earlier in this book, the first public posting of exit poll results provides an alternate measure of the intent of the electorate, a baseline against which to attempt to check and verify (one hopes) the reported electoral results, which have been tallied unobservably by privately programmed computers. In other countries, such exit poll data is relied upon routinely to verify the validity of official vote counts.[33]

In America, presumably because here in such an unimpeachable democracy no such check is needed, the exit poll results are "adjusted" to ultimate congruence with the vote tallies, and this process begins from the moment the polls close and the exit poll is first posted (if not sooner in some cases).[34] Any disparities between the unadjusted exit polls and the vote counts are regarded as *exit poll* errors (the vote counts being unquestioned and, by a seemingly universal tacit agreement, unquestionable) that need to be fixed if the exit polls are to become "accurate" and thus useful for demographic and political

---

voting computers were indeed—either directly, or indirectly through other computers used in the programming process—hooked up to the internet and thus vulnerable to remote manipulation.

[33] See https://en.wikipedia.org/wiki/Exit_poll.

[34] It is notable that in elections abroad exit poll results are not, as they are in the U.S., "adjusted" to congruence or near-congruence with the official votecounts. In the most circular, and cynical, of arguments, this adjustment process itself has been cited as a reason U.S. exit polls, unlike their foreign counterparts, are unsuitable tools for verifying election results and detecting possible fraud. As we will see, the work of election forensics in screencapturing unadjusted exit poll results routs that particular argument.

analysis of the electorate. Once the adjustment process begins, no record of the relatively pristine, unadjusted exit poll results is retained—unless those results are screencaptured, which is what forensic analysts do.

The exit polls we screencaptured as each state's polls closed and they were posted, projected a solid Clinton win, a better than 3 million vote popular vote margin and over 300 Electoral College votes (270 being needed for a majority). Experience, however, counseled caution: In the past, red-shift changes have diminished such Democratic exit poll margins and even reversed apparent victories. We witnessed, for example, a 4 percent John Kerry lead over George Bush in Ohio flip at midnight in 2004, and with it the presidential election.[35] And now we began to see signs of such reversals in a *swath* of states, the ones that everyone understood would be decisive in electing our next president.

The polls in all the key states had closed and the work of screencapturing and spreadsheeting the key exit polls was done. Now, the vote tallies rolled in and the picture began to emerge from the darkroom developing tank with ever increasing clarity: Clinton would win the popular vote, the only question being how embarrassingly large for Trump her ultimate margin would turn out to be. But, courtesy of a table-run of victories ranging from narrow to razor-thin in what Nate Silver had termed Clinton's "firewall" states, Trump would capture an Electoral College majority and become our next president.

Red Shift on Steroids
Before sunrise on Nov. 9, I had begun circulating tables documenting the most egregious "red shift" exit poll-to-votecount disparities ever recorded. Even for those accustomed to the mysterious and pervasive rightward shifts between exit poll and votecount results, the results were eye-popping.

Ohio had shifted from an exit poll dead heat to an 8.1 percent Trump win; North Carolina from a 2.1 percent Clinton win to a 3.7 percent Trump win; Pennsylvania from 4.4 percent Clinton to 0.7 percent Trump; Wisconsin from 3.9 percent Clinton to 0.8 percent Trump; Florida from 1.3 percent Clinton to 1.2 percent Trump; and Michigan from a dead heat to 0.3 percent Trump. The table below presents the shift in four key states that essentially decided the election:

---

[35] See https://www.commondreams.org/views06/0601-34.htm.

2016 Presidential Election Exit Poll/Votecount Comparison				
Compiled by Jonathan D. Simon www.CodeRed2020.com				
State (Exit Poll Sample Size and Margin of Error, including 1.45 multiplier for cluster and design effects)	Exit Poll Margin (+ Clinton, - Trump)	Vote Count Margin (+ Clinton, - Trump)	Red Shift (+ indicates shift favoring Trump)*	Electoral College Votes At Stake
National Popular Vote (21753, 1.0%)	3.2%	2.1%	+1.1%	0
NC (3967, 2.3%)	2.1%	-3.7%	+5.8%	15
PA (2613, 2.8%)	4.4%	-0.7%	+5.1%	20
WI (2981, 2.6%)	3.9%	-0.8%	+4.7%	10
FL (3941, 2.3%)	1.3%	-1.2%	+2.5%	29
				Total 74
Official Electoral College Votes As Tabulated	Clinton 232	Trump 306	Trump + 74	President Trump
Electoral College Votes With NC,PA,WI,FL "Flipped"	Clinton 306	Trump 232	Clinton + 74	President Clinton
Exit Poll Source: NEP, as screencaptured at initial public posting (CNN) Votecount Source: USElectionAtlas.org				
A positive percentage in the "Red Shift" column indicates a votecount margin higher for Trump than was his exit poll margin. * A RED number in the "Red Shift" column indicates an exit poll-votecount shift with a 50% or greater likelihood of altering the outcome.				

It must be noted that in Florida and Michigan a small portion of each state extends from the Eastern into the Central time zone. The effect of this was to delay the first public posting of exit poll results until an hour after the polls closed and votecount reporting began in the main part of the state. This, in turn, allowed the adjustment process toward congruence with the votecounts to begin well prior to first public posting of the exit poll results and consequently reduced the exit poll-to-votecount disparity, compromising the utility of the exit polls as a baseline for votecount verification in these states. Indeed, in the era of computerized tabulation and internet-based reporting, so much of the total vote has been counted in these states within that hour that the exit polls, even if initially far out of line with the vote totals, will closely approach congruence with the votecounts by the time they are posted and can be screencaptured. This is in fact what we observed in Michigan and Florida in

2016, although even the substantial adjustment process left modest red shifts in both states. [36]

Not only were the red shifts in Ohio, North Carolina, Pennsylvania, Wisconsin, and even compromised Florida well beyond the error margins for the exit polls, but in the states of North Carolina, Pennsylvania, Wisconsin, and Florida, those shifts clearly resulted in reversals of outcome, such that if the exit polls rather than the votecounts were accurately capturing voter intent, the Electoral College majority would have gone to Clinton and it would not have been close. Ultimately, a mere 77,744 votes out of many millions in the soon-to-be-recounted states of Michigan, Pennsylvania, and Wisconsin determined the outcome of the election. [37]

As noted above in my examination of the 2016 primaries, exit polls in the United States have been subject to devaluation, and often dismissal, based on the assumption that the causes for their chronic (and unidirectional) "inaccuracy" are all intrinsic to the exit polls themselves—errors in design or execution. In the 2016 primaries, the probative value of the exit polls was boosted greatly by the finding that they were highly accurate throughout the Republican primaries. Neither design nor execution seemed to explain why they were wildly inaccurate for the Democratic primaries, even though administered by the same firm, with the same interviewers, on the same days, at the same precincts, using the same protocols.

A similar baseline was available for the general election: Although 22 "safe" states were not exit polled specifically *as states*, depriving us of the kind of "safe state baseline" that was so telling in 2004,[38] a *national sample* was drawn, representative of the electorate throughout the United States.

It was quickly apparent that the red shift for America as a whole—which, of course, included all the safe states where manipulation would have been, from an Electoral College standpoint, pointless—was far smaller than that found in the key swing states cited above. Indeed, once the final votecounts were compiled, swelling Clinton's popular vote victory to just short of 3 million

---

[36] Of interest as well, the fact that in E2018 the exit polls for Michigan and Florida *were* publicly posted immediately after poll closing in the eastern parts of the two states—i.e., without the one-hour delay seen in E2016 and prior elections. It is not clear why this protocol was changed.

[37] See https://ballotpedia.org/Presidential_election_by_state,_2016.

[38] See http://freepress.org/departments/display/19/2004/997.

votes,[39] the disparity between the national exit poll and the national votecount wound up at just 1.1 percent — just about the expected Total Survey Error for a poll of that sample size.[40]

Thus, the same poll that had performed accurately and commendably across the country[41] had apparently broken down spectacularly and unidirectionally

---

[39] The official Clinton-Trump popular vote margin was 2,868,518 (see https://uselectionatlas.org/2016.php).

[40] The official sample size of 21,753 would yield a mathematical margin of error of approximately 0.7% (see www.raosoft.com/samplesize.html), which would translate to a total survey error (including such factors as cluster sampling) of approximately 1%.

When one remembers that any manipulations in putatively targeted swing states, where the statewide exit poll-votecount disparities greatly exceeded the respective total survey errors, would also increase the cumulative disparity in the nationwide poll, it becomes evident that in the noncompetitive "baseline" states as measured in the nationwide poll, the exit poll-votecount disparity was well within the poll's total survey error—the poll performed splendidly.

You simply cannot look at such a pattern, which I call a second-order disparity, without asking *why* the apparent breakdown of the polls so strongly correlates with the states that "mattered." *I cannot state strongly enough how suspect such a pattern is.*

[41] A great deal has been made of the apparently egregious over-representation of college graduates in the national exit poll sample. With an "Aha!" that could be heard on Mars, the poll was declared "garbage" and tossed hastily and permanently in the shredder because 50% of its respondents had declared themselves to be (at least) college grads. The impact of education level on candidate choice was modest (about the equivalent of gender and far below race), but this did not stop the critics from fastening on the 50% figure (which it must be said would not even have been available to fasten on were the exit polls as opaque in their revelations as are the votecounts), which they calculated implied an unrealistic rate of turnout among college grads.

What the scoffing and whewing herd apparently failed to notice was that the exit poll they had just trashed—trashed, it soon became clear, along with every *other* exit poll ever conducted or to be conducted in the United States—was *accurate*! That's right, accurate. As has been noted, the unadjusted national exit poll approximated Clinton's popular vote victory margin within 1.1%. It was accurate enough as to require hardly any adjustment—and, if it hadn't been for the impact on it of the major disparities in the Trump table-run battleground states, would not have required any adjustment at all.

How, then, to read this riddle? How could a poll with such an apparent demographic goof wind up so close to the mark? What no critic apparently understood, or wanted to understand, is something very basic and essential to exit poll methodology: multiple stratification (weighting). Exit pollsters know enough not to *expect* equivalent response rates across race, age, gender, income, education, and partisanship groups. They use data-rich models, as in many other sciences, to weight their samples accordingly. It has been my observation that the aggregate impact of these multiple weightings—because they are grounded at least in part on demographic data derived from prior exit polls that have been adjusted rightward to congruence with red-shifted votecounts—tends to be rightward. These weightings tug against one another—so, for example, the sample

where it counted—in the key swing states that were logically the suspect targets for mistabulation or, as Trump would have had no trouble calling it had the shift gone in Clinton's favor, "rigging."

Nor did polls supply the only quantitative evidence that election thieves had been at work. Anomalies and peculiarities cropped up all over. In Michigan, for example, where Trump's official margin was a razor-thin 10,704 votes, 75,335 ballots turned up with *no vote* for president (these were, moreover, concentrated in traditionally Democratic precincts).[42] DREs "interpret" touches; optical scanners interpret marks geographically: either one can easily be programmed, inadvertently or maliciously, to "miss" votes in targeted precincts for which they have been earmarked. A human recount of such ballots was clearly in order.

Stein Steps Up

Hillary Clinton, being a Democrat and not Donald Trump, lost no time in conceding the election.[43] President Barack Obama dutifully gave Trump the

---

might wind up over-representing the college-educated but under-representing non-white voters. The art and science of exit polling lies in getting those balances right.

It's a complex process and you could say, I suppose, "the secret's in the sauce" (although, again, this sauce is far *less* secret than the votecounts themselves—the numbers are there to inspect and compare, at https://www.cnn.com/election/2016/results/exit-polls/national/president for the adjusted national poll and on my website https://www.CodeRed2020.com for the unadjusted screencaptures, along with a more complete analysis of the polling methodology).

But you can also say "the proof of the pudding's in the tasting." The fact is that the national exit poll—the one torn apart by a posse of critics sorely lacking in understanding of exit poll methodology, many of whom have been hell-bent on discrediting exit polls as a verification tool since 2004—got it *right*, while the exit polls by the same firm, using the same methodological "sauce," in the critical battleground states table-run by Trump were way *off*, *all* in the same direction. That is a damning second-order comparative, and the best evidence we can *get* from a process *designed* for concealment, a system determined to withhold all its "hard" evidence. So far, to my knowledge, no one has established a benign explanation for this or numerous other telling *patterns* of disparity.

[42] See https://www.washingtonpost.com/news/the-fix/wp/2016/12/14/1-7-million-people-in-33-states-and-dc-cast-a-ballot-without-voting-in-the-presidential-race/?utm_term=.ce6f41059f85.

[43] One can imagine how *Trump* would have responded had he found himself in Clinton's position, a "loser," having won the popular vote by nearly 3 million votes and lost three states and the presidency by fractions of a percentage point each, with the exit polls in each case indicating his victory—leaving out of it the "millions of illegal voters" he suspected of lining up to vote (twice) against him. For a glimpse at how it would likely have gone down, see https://www.alternet.org/election-2016/what-would-trump-do-how-we-respond-suspect-election.

White House tour and spoke of a "smooth transition" as shockwaves spread across the country and around the world.

As the post-election days began to pass and the pundits pitched around for reasons "Why,"[44] election integrity advocates and forensics specialists continued to examine the numbers and ask "Whether." We recognized that, as usual, the election circus was pulling up stakes and leaving town, never having verified the unseen and unobservable counting of tens of millions of votes. We also recognized that, worse still, the airwaves were flooded with theories and explanations for the shocking outcome, which had the profound side-effect of quickly *validating* by assumption that which had in no way been *verified* in fact.[45]

---

[44] For a typical such post-mortem, see https://www.pewresearch.org/fact-tank/2016/11/09/why-2016-election-polls-missed-their-mark/.

[45] Given that the election of Trump was a political earthquake all but off the Richter scale, followed by an unending succession of aftershocks as it became clear (to anyone still in doubt) what his presidency would mean, it is not surprising that the pundits and analysts have kept at it and show no signs of letting up: books, papers, podcasts, columns and tweets continue to pile up "explaining" the organic forces behind Trump's election. Clinton's impressive tactical and strategic blunders, the rage of white males, the economic pessimism and anomie of Middle America, the brilliance of Trump's demagoguery, and even the alleged Russian "meddling" continue to compete and combine as factors in Trump's win. Other analysts explain why we can no longer trust polls of any sort. Still others make recommendations for what the Democrats need to do to reverse their fate.

It is a good deal more than a cottage industry. And every book, every chapter, every page, every sentence, every word of this great edifice of scholarship and commentary rests, in its very *raison d'etre*, on the presumed *fact* that enough voters cast their votes for Donald Trump in the states that mattered to secure a legitimate Electoral College victory and the White House. That comes to a megaton of career weight and reputation with a compelling vested interest in making sure that that *fact* remains foundational and unquestioned.

Which is not to say that most of these observations, analyses, and arguments are not fundamentally *true*. There is little doubt, to take one slice from this post-mortem pie as an example, that Clinton ran a tactically-challenged campaign—raising Big Money from fatcats and luminaries while ignoring too many actual voters (when not mocking them as "deplorables") and seemingly avoiding some key swing states like the plague. No appearances in *Wisconsin* of all places looks tactically braindead in retrospect—though, interestingly, Clinton went all-out in Pennsylvania and lost there anyway; and Bush barely set *foot* in Ohio in 2004 but "*won*" there, rescued from paying the ultimate electoral price when Rove's platoons of evangelical phantoms magically flocked to the polls *after dinner* to flip the votecounts and alter the course of history.

But there would be nothing much to analyze, certainly nothing worthy of a best-seller, if, like Bush, Clinton had *won* those razor-thin, pivotal states. The "How Did Trump Win?" Annex to the Library of Congress is mostly well-researched and well-reasoned,

Reports had begun to come in about machine breakdowns, voting problems, large numbers of uncounted provisional ballots, suspiciously high (and low) turnout rates, and big clusters of presidential "undervotes" (where votes are recorded for down-ballot offices but none for president). But what was the import of these glimpses of what appeared to be targeted dysfunction?

It was clear that the openly touted tactics of voter suppression had reaped enormous dividends for Trump and his fellow Republicans. But the reality is that the remedies for any such schemes, even if they were found to be law-breaking rather than simply legislatively or administratively shrewd, would be, as in the past, legal or administrative penalties—wrist-slaps on this or that clerk or official, not any meaningful amendment to the tally of votes or fundamental reform of the voting system. Earlier in the year, Austria's Supreme Court had decreed a "re-vote" when hints of electoral improprieties had surfaced in that nation's presidential election,[46] but that was not about to happen in the United States of Exceptional America.

The question became whether, apart from the general odor of Jim Crow disenfranchisement, there was any evidence of the kind of improprieties that would be *actionable*, leading to remedies that would alter electoral results or expose a nationally unpalatable type and degree of electoral fraud.

It was clear that such evidence—"hard evidence," as we call it to distinguish it from statistical evidence, the probative value of which is discounted to near zero by governmental and media gatekeepers concerned above all about undermining public "confidence" in the electoral process—could emerge only from recounting of all ballots in places where the statistical red flags were flying. This was, after all, the whole point of *having* paper ballots: "If there's any question," the reassuring line always went, "they can always be recounted."

---

fascinating and clever work. But if it were discovered that Trump did not in fact "win" … well it takes only a tiny little factual pin like that to pop a gigantic analytic balloon.

Nor are the "organic" and "artificial" explanations contradictory or mutually exclusive. Trump was so profoundly flawed a candidate that the election should not have been *close*. A number of organic factors did combine to make it close enough for votecount manipulation to have a decisive impact, and, as has been shown, there is independent evidence for that impact in the telltale second-order comparative *pattern* of exit poll-votecount disparities that we ignore at our peril.

[46] See https://www.csmonitor.com/World/Global-News/2016/0702/In-post-Brexit-Europe-why-Austria-s-presidential-re-vote-matters.

Accordingly, Green Party presidential candidate Jill Stein, having considered the recommendations of election forensics analysts who had begun to drill down into unsettling county- and precinct-level data, petitioned for recounts in the three key states of Wisconsin, Michigan, and Pennsylvania.[47]

The motivation for these recounts—to which the Clinton campaign predictably gave no encouragement, playing no public role other than that of an observer—was to address issues of electoral integrity and help shine light on the hidden processes of vote counting in places where less direct evidence pointed to problems. Many hoped, and some feared, that the recount process might result in a reversal of outcome in the three states and, by virtue of that, in the election itself.

For Stein and the electoral integrity community, that reversal could only come about as an incidental byproduct of a far more fundamental and earth-shaking revelation about the validity of our vote counting system.

Recount Not a Real Count

That there was broad-based support for the recount effort was immediately obvious. Stein raised more than $7.3 million from over 161,000 small donors in less than three weeks (contributions were limited by federal law to $2,700 and the average contribution received was $45).[48] It also quickly became clear that there would be ferocious resistance to Stein's quest.

Although Trump had himself raised suspicions that the election could be "rigged," and was claiming that he would have won the *popular vote* if not for the "millions of illegal voters" casting ballots for Clinton, the Trump campaign showed little interest in permitting the recounting of any ballots to substantiate this claim. Indeed, the Trump campaign and/or its surrogates promptly filed suit in each of the three states to block or restrict the recount efforts.[49]

---

[47] As will be seen, the prohibitive expense and tight deadlines associated with recount efforts made it impossible for Stein to undertake recounts in Florida, North Carolina, and Ohio—three *other* states where statistical evidence pointed to questionable results. Clinton, who could have afforded—both financially and in the sense that she held no expectations of a political future that could be torpedoed by the "sore loser" label—to pursue recounts in all of these venues, exhibited no interest in doing so.

[48] See http://www.jill2016.com/fundraising_ends.

[49] See https://www.independent.co.uk/news/people/donald-trump-lawsuit-recount-michigan-stop-a7452651.html.

Given what Trump stood to lose, this behavior was not especially surprising. It was the behavior of the *rest* of officialdom — administrative and judicial — that made a mockery of both electoral integrity and due process.

"Officialdom" comes down to individuals and, certainly in the corridors of power, individuals tend to sort themselves into parties and exhibit strong partisan allegiance. Who were the officials in whose hands the fate of the 2016 recounts rested? This is where the taproot of computerized elections grows long, snaking its way back through midterm and down-ballot elections for 15 years.

In *every* midterm election since the turn of the century—2002, 2006, 2010, 2014—Republican performance had far exceeded consensus expectations, tracking polling, and exit polling. All but 2006 were Republican routs. And 2006, with President George W. Bush's approval rating at a dismal 36 percent,[50] was far less than the expected Democratic landslide. In every other case, pundits scrambled post-election to explain the unanticipated reddening of America. In 2014, no amount of scrambling could make sense of the result: With a congressional job approval rating of 8 percent,[51] Republicans saw 220 out of 222 members of their U.S. House majority re-elected—a better than 99 percent re-election rate on the back of that 8 percent approval rating—and actually gained 13 seats[52] overall!

During President Obama's eight-year tenure, Democratic losses at all down-ballot levels were staggering: nine U.S. Senate seats; 62 U.S. House seats; 12 governor's mansions; control of 15 state upper houses and 14 state lower houses; and a net of 968 state legislative seats lost. [53] The carnage was far worse than under any other president of either party in our history.

You would think that Obama had been a national pariah, his tenure marked by incompetence, misconduct, and catastrophe. But Obama, although an outraged sub-stratum of the voting public may have found him guilty of governing while black, was overall a consistently popular president. He left office with an approval rating of *59 percent* and never in his eight-year tenure

---

[50] See http://www.realclearpolitics.com/epolls/other/president_bush_job_approval-904.html#!.

[51] See https://d25d2506sfb94s.cloudfront.net/cumulus_uploads/document/sulji6cqrq/trackingreport.pdf.

[52] See https://ballotpedia.org/United_States_House_of_Representatives_elections,_2014#Election_results.

[53] See https://www.washingtonpost.com/news/the-fix/wp/2016/11/10/the-decimation-of-the-democratic-party-visualized/?utm_term=.f654c153b319.

had the number fallen below 40 percent.[54] It simply does not add up or follow any previously comprehended political geometry that his years in office were such an unmitigated electoral disaster for Democratic office-holders at every other level of the political ladder.

In the computerized voting era, irrespective of events and the flux of public opinion, the Democrats had progressively surrendered control of the down-ballot political infrastructure of America to Republicans—in fact, to the increasingly radical Republicans who had displaced in primary election battles virtually all moderates in the party ranks. Nowhere was this rolling coup more spectacular than in formerly "blue" states like Wisconsin and Michigan, become bright-red Republican trifectas by E2016.[55] Such power is of great utility in controlling—legislatively, administratively, and judicially—the electoral process, including, as we witnessed in December 2016, recounts.

While Stein was not so naïve as to suppose that her path through Wisconsin, Michigan, and Pennsylvania would be strewn with rose petals, nothing could prepare her, her legal team, or the election integrity specialists providing support, for what ensued. The following list of impediments is, in the interests of space, highly selective:

- Ruling by a Republican Wisconsin judge that—despite her "personal opinions" and while she could recommend hand recounting as the "gold standard"—she would nevertheless permit counties to decide whether to follow that recommendation or just run the ballots back through the same machines that had counted them initially.[56]

- Subsequent refusal to hand count by some of the largest counties in Wisconsin, including counties with the brightest forensic red flags—e.g., Outagamie, Brown, and Rock—where Trump voteshares dramatically exceeded expectations based on past voting patterns. Clerks in these counties "recounted" votes by running the ballots back through the same optical scanners that had produced the suspect first counts. All told, *half* of Wisconsin's ballots escaped manual recount, and that half was chosen not at random but by county

---

[54] See https://www.realclearpolitics.com/epolls/other/president_obama_job_approval-1044.html.

[55] The term of art used to indicate single-party control of the executive branch and both houses of the state legislature.

[56] See https://www.reuters.com/article/us-usa-election-recount/judge-lets-wisconsin-officials-decide-how-to-perform-presidential-vote-recount-idUSKBN13P0FM.

administrators—which is very much like a bank auditor giving the *bank* the choice of which half of its accounts the auditor can inspect. Fred Woodhams, spokesman for Michigan's secretary of state, defended machine recounts in that state, reasoning that "machines are generally agreed to be more accurate than human beings."[57] Of course it was not accuracy, in the conventional sense, that was being questioned—it was deliberately programmed mistabulation, aka fraud.

- Once the Stein campaign had, with surprising rapidity, raised over $6 million to cover the recount expenses in a matter of days, Wisconsin suddenly jacked up its bill from an estimated $1 million[58] to $3.5 million.[59] In 2011, Wisconsin had charged less than $600,000 for a full statewide hand recount,[60] and was now requiring the up-front payment of more than *six* times that amount for a less laborious mixed machine/hand recount of just twice the number of cast ballots. Certain counties, under Republican control, led the way: Racine County, for example, charged more than 50 times as much to count by machine as it had charged for its last county-wide recount, which was done by hand.[61] These ransoms had the effect of draining Stein's recount funds and thus making it harder to meet administrative and judicial fees levied by other recount states, as well as precluding completely any hopes of initiating recounts or contests in other suspect states like Florida, Ohio and North Carolina.[62]

- Suits were filed by the Trump campaign or its surrogates to block recounts in Wisconsin, Pennsylvania, and Michigan. The legal expense

---

[57] See http://www.detroitnews.com/story/news/politics/2016/12/28/stein-audit/95917714/.

[58] See https://www.buzzfeed.com/claudiakoerner/jill-stein-has-raised-more-than-15-million-to-fund-recounts?utm_term=.frv4ePPy51#.beYre44wY6.

[59] See https://www.wpr.org/wisconsin-officials-set-timeline-presidential-recount.

[60] See https://www.bustle.com/articles/197135-how-much-does-a-vote-recount-cost-wisconsin-is-doing-a-second-tally-of-the-election.

[61] See http://elections.wi.gov/node/4448.

[62] That such was the intent was further evidenced when Wisconsin, acknowledging its gross overestimate of the recount's cost in requiring the $3.5 million payment from Stein, subsequently refunded $1.5 million, or over 40% of her payment. Of course by this time all other filing deadlines had passed and the $1.5 million held ransom could no longer be used to "make trouble" in any other state. See http://elections.wi.gov/node/4885, which also offers up a brief, and thoroughly unpersuasive, explanation for the overcharge.

associated with adequately responding to such suits, and appealing lower-court losses, was prohibitive.[63]

- Pennsylvania law was interpreted to require that at least three voters in *every one* of the state's more than 9,000 precincts had to file a petition to proceed with any recount at all.[64]

- Pennsylvania state court required that Stein post a $1 million bond before it would consider her petition for a statewide recount.[65]

- A Michigan court halted the recount in that state on the legal basis that Stein couldn't win even if some votes had been miscounted (there is no such requirement in applicable state law), and that no credible evidence of fraud (which, of course, was precisely what the recount was looking for) had been presented.[66]

- The Michigan Court of Appeals affirmed that decision on a three-to-two straight-party-line vote,[67] ruling that Stein was not "an aggrieved candidate."[68]

- A Bush-appointed federal judge stated in his ruling, effectively ending the recount in Pennsylvania before it started, that it "borders on the irrational" to suspect hacking occurred in that state, where the vast majority of ballots were electronic and unable to be recounted— while ignoring tens of thousands of provisional (paper) ballots, which *could* have been recounted.[69]

The upshot of these and a host of other financial, administrative, operational, and judicial roadblocks was that in one state, Wisconsin, officials chose which ballots to actually recount and which to just run through the computers again (begging the question of the basis on which that choice was made), and in the other two states the recounts were blocked almost entirely. Trump went to the

---

[63] See https://www.nbcchicago.com/news/national-international/Michigan-Trump-Stein-Clinton-Recount-Effort--404258056.html.

[64] See https://www.realclearpolitics.com/video/2016/11/28/fncs_carl_cameron_pennsylvania_laws_make_recount_next_to_impossible.html.

[65] See https://www.nytimes.com/2016/12/03/us/jill-stein-pennsylvania-recount.html.

[66] See https://www.cnn.com/2016/12/08/politics/michigan-election-recount/index.html.

[67] See https://www.nbcnews.com/politics/politics-news/michigan-supreme-court-denies-jill-stein-recount-appeal-n694251.

[68] See https://www.freep.com/story/news/politics/2016/12/06/trump-schuette-michigan-recount-election/95048550/.

[69] See https://www.cnn.com/2016/12/12/politics/pennsylvania-recount-blocked-jill-stein/index.html.

mat to block the recounts; Clinton did not lift a finger to protect them; and, for the most part, partisan judges and administrators were left to make the call on how or whether ballots—where they existed—would be reviewed.

The multi-level, multi-branch full-court-press to keep the recounts from happening does not betoken a high level of confidence in either the electoral outcomes the recounts were attempting to verify or the electoral processes that generated those outcomes. What it makes all too clear, however, is the critical importance of partisan control on the state and local levels, achieved by the steady capture of down-ballot offices in elections for which there were no effective forensic baselines, and which received essentially no scrutiny. The election of Donald Trump in 2016 placed a capstone on the edifice of a "permanent Republican majority,"[70] to borrow a phrase from Karl Rove,[71] that had been built brick by brick, obscure election by obscure election, since the dawn of the computerized voting era. That Trump would be such a heavy and wobbly capstone, putting not only himself but the whole edifice in political peril, was a plot twist yet to be encountered.

Stein, for her troubles, was publicly accused of running a personal-enrichment "scam" on the one hand (which reminded me of the Humphrey Bogart line about having your teeth knocked out and then getting kicked in the stomach for mumbling) and doing Clinton's bidding on the other—neither of which held a grain of truth.[72] The media seemed to breathe a collective sigh of relief when the crippled and farcical recounts ended, having produced no earth-shaking changes in results. Few bothered to note that the "recounts" were shams, and fewer still expressed any concern, let alone outrage, that this should be the case.

---

[70] See http://www.washingtonpost.com/wp-dyn/content/article/2007/08/17/AR2007081701713.html.

[71] See generally, James Moore and Wayne Slater: *The Architect: Karl Rove and the Master Plan for Absolute Power*, at https://www.amazon.com/dp/0307237923.

[72] One persistent line of slander holds Stein responsible, a la Nader, for Clinton's loss of the key swing states and makes her out a "Russian asset"—presenting as "evidence" Stein's presence at a table with Vladimir Putin (and several European officials) at a dinner in Moscow in honor of *RT* network's 10th anniversary, *RT* having done Stein, and other "fringe" candidates resolutely ignored by U.S. media, the service of covering them and their messages.

While there certainly seems enough Kompromat, of one kind or another, to go around in the hallowed halls of U.S. government, being caught in a crowd scene with Putin is not the stuff of which blackmail is made. For anyone interested in sorting it all out for themselves, Stein clarified the reasons for her presence in Moscow in this interview: https://www.jill2016.com/jill_stein_explains_putin_picture_once_for_all_jimmy_dore_show.

Did the Russians Really Come?

While the recount efforts were being beaten back and squelched, the "Russian meddling" story was gathering steam. Various new semi-public investigations got underway, joining others that had been simmering on the secret counterintelligence stove. "RussiaGate" has its own distorted-mirrors Fun House in the Age of Trump Theme Park. Whole books have been written following the allegations, revelations, refutations, implications, and bloviations to date. Some shoes have dropped and some others have doubtless grown wings.[73]

The gist of it is that the intelligence community was prepared to stake its reputation on the charge that various Russians, more likely than not to have been acting at the behest of the Kremlin, went to bat for Donald Trump and against Hillary Clinton in a variety of ways. Indictments eventually came down charging attempts to influence voters through various social media messaging schemes[74]—essentially the most indirect and therefore least pernicious form of meddling (and, of course, something the U.S. has been doing for decades in various nations around the world).[75] There were also investigations into the hacking of DNC servers and various personal email accounts; possible funneling of funds to various pro-Trump organizations such as the NRA; and attempts, some now known to have met with success, to hack into state voter databases.[76] Hanging over all of it, the word "collusion"—the ultimate question of whether Trump and/or his campaign, associates, or family had knowledge of, or took part in, any of this skullduggery.

Shadowy, tantalizing, riveting stuff! Some argued that Trump *acted* so guilty— firing FBI Director James Comey, having to be put into a virtual chokehold to prevent his firing of Special Counsel Robert Mueller, refusing to release his tax returns, screaming "WITCH HUNT!" and "NO COLLUSION!" at every turn—that

---

[73] A December 2019 article by investigative journalist Kim Zetter, "How Close Did Russia Really Come to Hacking the 2016 Election?" testifies to the ongoing nature of the inquiry and how much remains unknown or undisclosed: https://www.politico.com/news/magazine/2019/12/26/did-russia-really-hack-2016-election-088171.

[74] See https://www.usatoday.com/story/news/politics/2018/02/16/read-robert-muellers-indictment-13-russian-nationals-election-meddling/346688002/.

[75] See https://www.nytimes.com/2018/02/17/sunday-review/russia-isnt-the-only-one-meddling-in-elections-we-do-it-too.html.

[76] See https://www.nbcnews.com/politics/elections/russians-penetrated-u-s-voter-systems-says-top-u-s-n845721 and Zetter *op. cit.*

he must be in it up to his eyeballs. Some, on the other hand, saw RussiaGate as a neocon or even "Deep State" plot to revive Russia as a global enemy, make sure Trump was preempted in his signaled embrace of Putin, and gin up "Cold War 2.0." And finally someone thought to ask, "What about E2020?" It appears that what the Russians did (or didn't) meddle with once, they could very well meddle (or not meddle) with again. And what about the North Koreans, the Chinese, the Iranians, Liechtenstein?!

Lost in all this is a fundamental absurdity. However vulnerable E2016 may have been (and E2020 may yet be) to foreign states or outsiders hacking our computerized vote-counting processes, those processes were—and are—even more vulnerable to the "meddling" of insiders with far easier access to the partisan, proprietary, pitch-dark cyberspace in which they take place. And they have *been* this vulnerable to domestic operatives since the dawn of the computerized vote-counting era, long before even the most ardent cold-warrior is alleging the Russians hatched a plan. Yet all attention is focused on the Russians—what they may have done and what they might do—and *none* on those with a short, direct pipeline into the system and the luxury of *programming* in, rather than hacking in, election theft. It is as if, in setting out to guard our electoral house, we are checking the windows for signs of forced entry while ignoring completely the crew of shady characters with keys to the front door. It is a security plan worthy of Inspector Clouseau.

Actually, though, we haven't even been doing much of a job of checking the *windows*. The public has been fed at every turn some version of the "there's no evidence that any votes were actually affected or electoral results changed" line. The Russians may have tried to get into our *heads*, but there was no way they could have gotten into our opscans, DREs, central tabulators, or e-poll books. See, our voting equipment is so decentralized and, what's more, it's not hooked up to the internet—which means that it's not vulnerable to foreign state (or individual) hacking. Whew! Such assurance being given first by none other than then-FBI Director James Comey,[77] one could almost hear the "Praise the Lord!" Of course the Obama administration echoed and re-echoed that blanket reassurance. Voters, be confident!

The only problem was that neither "whew" was true. Eighty percent of the equipment was produced by two outfits, ES&S and Dominion Voting, which

---

[77] See http://www.homelandsecuritynewswire.com/dr20160929-hackers-poking-around-u-s-voter-registration-sites-in-more-than-a-dozen-states-comey.

held the keys to its programming and were potential vectors for manipulation by insiders and outsiders alike. And it turns out that the ES&S DS200 optical scanners, used in Wisconsin and elsewhere, were indeed equipped with a cellular phone signal modem that exposes them and their programming to outsider hacking and is an effective connection to the internet.[78] Further, as IT experts like Andrew Appel have made clear, even individual voting machines that are *not* modem-equipped or directly connected to the internet have to be *programmed*, most often with code uploaded from computers that *are* connected to the internet, providing yet another vector of attack.[79]

Then there are the streams of votecounts from the precinct to the county and state levels, which often pass through an internet transmission pipeline, leaving the data vulnerable to internet-based hacking, commonly known as a man-in-the-middle attack. Central tabulators are particularly vulnerable and, because the internet provides a two-way connection, it is possible for riggers targeting central tabulators to simultaneously alter the upstream data in precinct computers during its upload—thereby making sure that altered aggregate data reconciles with its correspondingly altered precinct-level sources in the (unlikely) event of investigation.

Apart from telling us that the equipment was decentralized and not hooked up to the internet, the Department of Homeland Security took pains repeatedly to assure us that, any vulnerabilities or attempted intrusions notwithstanding, it "had found no evidence that any votes were actually affected, or any election outcomes changed." In somewhat finer print, DHS acknowledged that it had found no such evidence *because it had made a command decision not to look for it.*[80]

That's right, not a single memory card, packet of code, or voter-marked ballot from E2016 was included in whatever investigation DHS may have

---

[78] See https://www.nbcnews.com/tech/security/voting-machine-makers-face-questions-house-lawmakers-more-remain-n1113181 (NB the internet vulnerability of Dominion and Hart equipment along with that of ES&S), https://www.alternet.org/it-doesnt-take-foreign-government-hack-our-flimsy-election-system and https://www.vice.com/en_us/article/3kxzk9/exclusive-critical-us-election-systems-have-been-left-exposed-online-despite-official-denials.

[79] See https://freedom-to-tinker.com/2016/09/20/which-voting-machines-can-be-hacked-through-the-internet/.

[80] See Sam Thielman, "Were Voting Machines Actually Breached? DHS Would Rather Not Know," at https://talkingpointsmemo.com/muckraker/dhs-doesnt-want-to-know-about-vote-hacks.

undertaken—at least not any that DHS was willing to acknowledge having examined. Which is like Deflategate without an air-pressure gauge or indeed the footballs! It strains credulity to think that corporate property rights trumped a *DHS investigation* of a possibly rigged election—making the hard evidence as off-limits to DHS (to the point that they knew better than to even try to obtain it) as it has always been to lesser lights trying to follow the trail of statistical disparities and anomalies. But then, much about the conduct of our elections strains credulity, so it is among the possibilities to be considered.

There is also the possibility that evidence of any such interference, especially if it *had* been found to have compromised the outcome of the election, would meet the fate of the sections of the Warren Commission Report that were sealed away until some future time when the matter of JFK's assassination would be of primarily historical interest.[81] Perhaps the DHS and related investigators really *did* decide not to even peek at any of the hard evidence of what happened in E2016's cyberspace; perhaps it *began* to peek and didn't like what it saw; perhaps it saw enough to sound the alarm but *chose* not to, shrewdly (perhaps) deciding to direct energies to protecting future elections without triggering a national crisis over what it had discovered about this one. The anathema to "undermining voter confidence" in our elections has long been the election rigger's best friend and protector.

When the Dust Settled
It is pretty clear where Election 2016 left America: angry, distrustful, horribly divided, and under the rule of a president without precedent and a Republican majority that, after a certain amount of hemming and hawing, decided rather predictably[82] which side the bread was buttered on. The sprinkling of quasi-non-enablers—Senators Jeff Flake (R-AZ) and Bob Corker (R-TN), the late John McCain (R-AZ), a ragged platoon of moderate House members and state legislators—began exiting the fray and moving on, an exodus that continues. Within the executive branch itself, a steady stream of career civil servants resigned their offices or were forced out, only to be replaced with robotically loyal Trump sycophants or not replaced at all. An unprecedented number of high-level appointees ran afoul of the law, ethical standards, or their Boss' moods, and either resigned or were fired. With a cabinet full of billionaires and corporatists, and with K Street more brazen than ever, the swamp Trump was supposedly elected to drain never showed a dry spot. It has been chaotic,

---

[81] See https://www.usatoday.com/story/news/nation/2013/08/17/jfk-files-still-sealed/2668105/.

[82] Predictably at first, but more and more bizarrely as the events of the Trump presidency have unfolded.

kakistocratic, and, from the standpoint of most Americans, not worthy of even tepid approval.[83]

In the throes of this national fugue state, it is rather disorienting to look back at where the campaign year 2016 started. Bernie Sanders, the "other" populist and bringer of new things, was threatening single-handedly to rewrite the rules of campaign finance—and, indeed, *politics*—by raising an enormous war chest from small, individual contributions, without once stooping to drink at the corporate trough. He was speaking to voters not just in the coastal blue enclaves but across America's heartland, drawing huge crowds, delivering a message that resonated with young and old and across class lines. He represented the first serious threat to corporate hegemony in decades. As such, he had to be stopped; and he was stopped, in a series of primaries so red-shifted that the exit polls had to be canceled entirely for the last several states.

When the primary and then general election dust had settled, Trump, Sanders's far-right pseudo-populist counterpart, was installed—the unorthodox but somehow fitting culmination to the decades-long quest for right-wing hegemony. All this was built, year by year, on the succession of computerized elections that presented opportunity after opportunity to steer America away from a path the voters might otherwise have chosen. Without the hard evidence that even the DHS either could not access or had no stomach for, we cannot know whether the electoral outcomes of the computerized voting era are authentic or a chimera, a figment of manipulated bits and bytes. *But the results and where they have brought us are real enough.* The laws passed and repealed are real. So are the executive orders. Neil Gorsuch, Brett Kavanaugh, litmus-tested lower-court appointees and the decisions these justices and judges hand down are real. Policy and direction are real, actual, historical. History—from melting Arctic ice to separated and caged refugee families to murdered Florida schoolchildren to the fatally slow and feckless response to a pandemic—is being written in ink and does not permit re-dos.

Or, as Trump supporters took to jeering when faced with protests, petitions, parades, and polls: "Elections matter!"

---

[83] Trump, in spite of help from the Likely Voter Cutoff Model (see Chapter VIII, Study V) and the boost given by outlier Rasmussen to polling aggregates, has polled within a few points of 40% approval throughout his presidency. Presidential (dis)approval has, in fact, been one of the least volatile measures of a very volatile time (see https://projects.fivethirtyeight.com/trump-approval-ratings/?ex_cid=rrpromo).

— VI —

TRUTH AND ELECTIONS IN THE AGE OF TRUMP

...Thou shalt remain, in midst of other woe
Than ours, a friend to man, to whom thou say'st,
'Beauty is truth, truth beauty' – that is all
Ye know on earth, and all ye need to know.

-- John Keats, "Ode on a Grecian Urn"

America in the Age of Trump is a nation drowning in lies. From his inauguration through the end of 2019, Donald Trump personally made 16,241 "false or misleading claims" (polite media way of saying "lies"), according to *The Washington Post's* carefully vetted Fact Checker.[1] Examination of that catalog's contents will disabuse anyone of the notion that these presidential statements were primarily minor bendings of the truth about unimportant or peripheral matters. These are, more often than not, *whoppers* concerning critical matters of state, Trump's own behavior and that of others, and key facts and figures. An overall average of 15 every single day. The rate of spew from Trump's lie spigot has, moreover, consistently accelerated: 1,999 in 2017; 5,689 in 2018; and 8,553 in 2019. It shows no sign of slackening. And of course these lies echo and re-echo through the chorus of Trump's supporters, producing a kind of falsity din.

Such a constant barrage of "alternative facts," as presidential advisor Kellyanne Conway once coyly dubbed them, meld into an alternate *reality*, one that comes to compete on essentially equal terms—and then, if a society is not very careful, on superior terms—with what once was regarded as *the* reality. This relativizing of factual reality is a key chapter in the playbook of all dictatorships, communist or fascist, left or right. And the key paragraph in that chapter will tell us that, to be effective, you can't lie selectively; the lies have to be about

---

[1] See https://www.washingtonpost.com/politics/2019/12/16/president-trump-has-made-false-or-misleading-claims-over-days/. WaPo stopped updating its database in January 2020, apparently having thrown in the towel on the increasingly overwhelming and labor-intensive cataloging project.

everything, or enough of *the* reality will stay standing to show up the lies you tell. You have to go all-in, blanket everything, lie then lie about your lies until there is no reality left to hurt you. This is just what Trump has done, and it is why his pace keeps accelerating. To be sure, every president—Federalist, Whig, Democrat, Republican—has lied, just as every *person* has lied. But those have generally been islands in a sea of truth. Now the lies *are* the sea.

It remains to reiterate that a subset of the lies is *numbers*. And that a subset of numbers is *votecounts*. How credulous would we have to be to expect that those particular numbers—the most important of all numbers to Trump and his fellow travelers—would escape the deluge? After all, when you bet everything on an alternate reality, that alternate reality had better *win*. And yet we amazingly approach E2020 as reliant as ever on their presumed accuracy and honesty. We still are being given essentially no choice but to trust the magician behind the curtain. And the clock is ticking—fast.

Tribal America Goes to the Polls
It was T. S. Eliot who wrote "human kind cannot bear very much reality," and Abraham Lincoln who noted that "you can fool some of the people all of the time." These observations seem to have converged in the Age of Trump, in an America crossing swords not merely over competing wish-lists and visions but over fundamental facts and reality itself.

There is little to be said in a positive vein about a country as polarized, tribalized, and locked into rigid political phalanxes as America has become since the 2016 election. One feature of such a predicament, however, is that politics becomes strangely simplified, a steady-state, zero-sum game with very little sloshing around in the middle.[2] Standard political measurements such as approval ratings have largely ossified in the Age of Trump, frozen into narrow ranges with hardly any variation, essentially impervious to the wild volatility of *events*.[3] So it should be easy enough to take the measure of America and translate it into a confident prediction of electoral outcome when the people go to the polls in November 2020.

---

[2] For a fascinating examination of the political implications of this development, see https://www.politico.com/news/magazine/2020/02/06/rachel-bitecofer-profile-election-forecasting-new-theory-108944.

[3] This imperviousness is all the more remarkable in light of the extraordinary events— from military crises, nuclear brinksmanship, and targeted assassinations to scandal, indictment, impeachment, pandemic, and massive economic collapse—that have been in the air.

Of course, nothing of the sort is the case.

Donald Trump has his "base" and the GOP has Donald Trump. Trump has made no serious attempt to reach out—even within his own party, let alone across the aisle—to expand the ranks of his supporters beyond those who would, mystifyingly enough, love him unconditionally even if he should, to take his own hypothetical, shoot someone on Fifth Avenue (or worse).[4] He bears uncanny resemblance, as many have pointed out, to the leader of a cult. And the GOP—those, at least, remaining politically viable—have gone all-in, pitched their lot with this consummate pitchman, damn the electoral torpedoes. Given his approval rating, and his demonstrated three-year inability get it above water, this has the look of a world-class sucker bet. To put it in simple if rather stark terms, Trump has nothing but lovers and haters, and the haters outnumber and should outvote the lovers by a healthy margin.[5]

And yet. Not only are we having a non-ridiculous national conversation about whether Trump will be re-elected (now that the Senate has given him a pass on his high crimes and misdemeanors), but quite a few astute handicappers are actually telling us it's his election to lose. Rational observers of the last three-plus years might be forgiven for asking how this is possible.[6]

The standard answers are the "great" economy[7] and the Electoral College (to which we might add whatever major-event presidential wildcards might happen to drop; and, right on cue, one did). There is, of course, a joker in this deck: how many and how heavy will be the thumbs applied to the electoral

---

[4] Commentators have recently wondered out loud how much of that love Trump would retain were he to "open the economy" by ordering the heartland to mingle with the COVID pandemic still raging and were Americans then to die in droves "for the Dow."

[5] For a graphic illustration of how immutable Trump's numbers have been compared with those of other presidents going back to the end of WW II, see https://projects.fivethirtyeight.com/trump-approval-ratings/ (scroll down).

[6] Because this edition of *CODE RED* goes to press with the pandemic in progress and its outcomes—mortal, economic, and political—still very much up in the air, much of the calculus I am presenting here may have to be recalibrated as this catastrophe unfolds. We will see, in the pages to follow and in Chapter VIIa, how election integrity itself is hardly immune to the impacts of this *biological* virus.

[7] But see https://www.theatlantic.com/ideas/archive/2020/02/great-affordability-crisis-breaking-america/606046/ for an assessment of the pre-pandemic economy as it was actually being experienced by ordinary Americans. The pandemic and shutdowns have shed a lurid light on the rotten underbelly of that "great" economy: how close to the edge of poverty staggering numbers live in this supposedly richest of lands.

scale? How successful will targeted disinformation campaigns, wholesale targeted vote suppression schemes, and votecount manipulation be in deciding the outcome of E2020? We saw evidence of each of these in E2016 and there is every indication that they will be back with a vengeance in E2020. The stakes are manifestly higher, our elections no more secure, and "meddlers" are queuing up to pay their cover charge or pick up their free pass to the show. No one could possibly entertain the slightest doubt now that elections matter—certainly *this* election matters—and yet, unlike the Dutch and the Norwegians, we have taken no steps to ensure that it is an authentic translation of the public will. As in the past, a perceived Democratic "victory" in 2018 has had the Xanax effect.

There are many reasons not to OD on that particular pill. Before getting to them, let's take a look at a few of the elections that have taken place during the Trump presidency, from the special elections of early 2017 through the E2018 midterms themselves and the scattering of elections since. The patterns are anything but reassuring.

The Elections of 2017
For a "non-election" year, 2017 proved worthy of serious attention from both election forensics analysts and election integrity advocates. Virtually every "special election"—and there were a good number of them—was watched intently as a thumbs up or down for Trump, as were the regularly scheduled off-off-year elections in November.

The year began with a string of Republican wins in special elections to fill legislative seats—all in Trump strongholds, so not particularly surprising, but giving early indication that no amount of presidential buffoonery or venality (as Trump was turning out to be at least as bad as anyone who did not vote for him had feared) could shake loose the allegiance of his "base." These culminated in the late-May U.S. House victory of Montana Republican Greg Gianforte, who had been slapped with an election-eve assault charge for body-slamming a reporter whose questions had rubbed him the wrong way. There was a certain amount of speculation that Gianforte's violence had even *helped* him with many voters, as it echoed in deed the stream of belligerence-in-word emanating from the president's mouth and Twitter account. It did not escape notice, however, that these proxy Trump victories were all by considerably narrower margins than Trump's own margins in these districts just a few months before. It was evident that the presidential lead balloon had already begun dragging its passengers groundward.

Explain This Night in Georgia

Then came the first Big One of 2017, the runoff for the special election to replace Republican Rep. Tom Price of Georgia's Sixth Congressional District (GA-6), who had been chosen for Trump's cabinet as Secretary of Health and Human Services, with the challenge to get Obamacare repealed or be fired.[8] Of little pragmatic significance, given the then-unassailable Republican House majority, this election was nonetheless the focus of extraordinary attention and expenditure. More than any of the other 2017 special elections, GA-6 was seen as a proxy for approval or disapproval of the Trump presidency and a harbinger of its fate. Held in a district that had long been solid Republican but that had given Trump the barest 1.5 percent plurality in 2016, the GA-6 Special was also the subject of intense media focus.

The Democratic candidate, 30-year-old Jon Ossoff, a former congressional staffer and first-time office-seeker, faced a crowded field of 17 other candidates in a preliminary contest held in April. Among them was Karen Handel, former Republican Secretary of State of Georgia, along with a host of less serious challengers. If no candidate polled 50 percent of the total vote, the two top finishers would meet in a June runoff. With the wave of Trump disapproval mounting ever higher, Ossoff was seen to be closing on the 50 percent mark going into the April 18 election. On Election Night, as the returns were coming in, Ossoff held steady at just over 50 percent until a supposed "glitch" in Fulton County (the three counties in the Atlanta suburbs that comprise GA-6 are Fulton, Cobb and DeKalb) paused the returns for several hours. When reporting resumed, Ossoff's total had dropped below 50 percent, where it remained through the final count. Ossoff finished at 48.12 percent; Handel finished second with just over 19 percent of the vote and went through to the June runoff against Ossoff.

A "glitch" out of central casting; the fact that all but the mailed-in and "provisional" ballots were cast and counted on DRE computers with no paper record and no capacity for recount, audit, or verification; and the extraordinary security breaches uncovered at the Kennesaw State University Election

---

[8] Which he was. Price, whose conflicts of interest had been subject to repeated inquiry during the course of his legislative career, was forced to resign in disgrace on Sept. 29, 2017, after racking up over $400,000 in expenses for charter flights. This Trump-like behavior did not sit well with a president whose pledge to "drain the swamp" had already been exposed as a mockery. One suspects that if he could have held on for a bit, Price's behavior would have blended right in and his job been safe.

Center,[9] the outfit entrusted with the programming of the computers and the management of voter databases: each of these factors raised red flags of suspicion about what was reported as a "disappointing" Democratic result, as Ossoff fell 1.9 percent short of the magic 50 percent number required for the outright win of the seat (and instant humiliation for Trump and the GOP that was trying to figure out whether to disown or embrace him).

The stage was then set for the June 20 runoff. The perceived proxy significance of this election was mirrored in the funds that poured in for both sides—more than $50 million, an all-time record for a U.S. House seat.[10] The tracking polls averaged to a dead heat.[11] With the exception of a single poll conducted by Trafalgar (a polling firm identified in aggregate poll charts with an "R"[12]—that is, as working exclusively for Republican clients), however, Handel never held a lead in the polls in the six weeks going into the runoff election. Nonetheless, based on my own experience observing and handicapping U.S. elections in the computerized voting era, I publicly predicted[13] (speaking at a conference on June 2) with complete confidence that Ossoff would lose to Handel. Indeed I promised that it was such a lock that, should Ossoff win, I would cease all election integrity activities and concede that I was nothing more than a wild-eyed, tinfoil-hat "conspiracy theorist" after all. Fortunately for my career, Handel came through with flying colors and won by 3.7 percent.

Laughing Their #Ossoff
Presidential Counselor Kellyanne Conway (of "alternative facts" fame[14] and an unpunished serial Hatch Act violator[15]) summed up the reaction among leading

---

[9] See Kim Zetter, "Will the Georgia Special Election Get Hacked?" in *Politico*, at https://www.politico.com/magazine/story/2017/06/14/will-the-georgia-special-election-get-hacked-215255.

[10] See https://www.politico.com/story/2017/05/06/georgia-special-election-spending-record-238054.

[11] See https://www.realclearpolitics.com/epolls/2017/house/ga/georgia_6th_district_runoff_election_handel_vs_ossoff-6202.html. Note that all polls were conducted using the Likely Voter Cutoff Model (see Chapter VIII, Study V) for sampling, a methodology that is recognized to disproportionately eliminate Democratic-leaning constituencies such as renters, students, and less-affluent voters from the sample, thereby advantaging Republican candidates in the poll results.

[12] See https://drive.google.com/file/d/0B4lhKxf9pMitSUE2X2ItLWhoYVU/view.

[13] See https://www.youtube.com/watch?v=i9Ap1IjAsq0&feature=youtu.be.

[14] See https://www.washingtonpost.com/news/the-fix/wp/2017/01/22/how-kellyanne-conway-ushered-in-the-era-of-alternative-facts/?utm_term=.c0431f5cb139.

[15] See https://osc.gov/Resources/Conway%20HA-18-0966%20Final%20Report.pdf.

Republicans when she tweeted "Laughing my #Ossoff."[16] The Democrats, oh-for-five at that point in 2017 special elections and seemingly unable to win *anything* despite Trump's ever-increasing unpopularity, started wailing about new strategies and new leadership. Ossoff's defeat was another serving of the bounteous and bitter fruits respectively of apparent victory and apparent defeat, having profound effect upon political expectations and strategies, and indeed upon all aspects of political behavior, going forward.

Prior to the election, legal action to require that votes be cast on paper (and counted by optical scanner), to provide a durable record for verification purposes, failed when the judge ruled that it would be too burdensome on the state to print ballots for GA-6 and to use its existing optical scanners (which were already being used to count mail-in ballots) to count Election Day ballots.[17] As a result, only mail-in ballots and provisional ballots—approximately 11 percent of total votes—were cast on paper and in any way verifiable. The remaining 89 percent? For that we'd just have to trust Kennesaw State Election Center; its director, Merle King;[18] and their already-breached security protocols.[19]

It is worthy of note that this was a *single-contest election* that *could* easily have been counted *observably, in public, by hand*, within two hours of poll closing, at minimal expense (though plenty of *volunteers* would have poured in). The Dutch, having taken one whiff of our 2016 elections, and aware of the security holes for computerized counting, had changed their protocol after two days of consideration and counted their critical 2017 national election by hand,[20] joining a growing list of other advanced democracies. The Norwegians soon followed. Exceptional America stuck to its computerized guns.

---

[16] See https://twitter.com/KellyannePolls/status/877355893905666048?ref.

[17] See http://www.slate.com/blogs/future_tense/2017/06/13/georgia_judge_throws_out_reque st_to_use_paper_ballots_in_the_upcoming_special.html.

[18] See https://www.washingtonpost.com/news/the-fix/wp/2016/08/31/theres-almost-no-chance-our-elections-can-get-hacked-by-the-russians-heres-why/?utm_term=.be124d0f7cec, which, while presenting the world of election integrity according to King, may additionally serve as an "Exhibit A" of credulous reporting.

[19] See https://arstechnica.com/tech-policy/2017/06/georgias-voting-system-is-uniquely-vulnerable-to-election-tampering-hackers/.

[20] See https://www.theguardian.com/world/2017/feb/02/dutch-will-count-all-election-ballots-by-hand-to-thwart-cyber-hacking. The far-right "populist" Freedom Party was soundly defeated.

Verifiable vs. Unverifiable Counting: An Enormous Disparity

The Georgia Secretary of State Elections website helpfully breaks down vote totals by type of ballot cast.[21] There are four types of voting: Election Day in-person voting, early in-person voting, vote-by-mail, and provisional ballots. The first two were cast and counted on DREs, which permit no meaningful verification, whether by audit or recount. Mail-in and provisional ballots, on the other hand, were cast by hand on paper and counted on opscans, the paper then being retained by federal law for 22 months—which would, at least in theory, permit verification processes to be undertaken, sharply raising the risk factor for manipulation of such votes. Given that nearly 90 percent of the votecount was unverifiable, the incentive to monkey with *any* of the remaining 11 percent would have been all but non-existent.

The results for each type of voting are shown in the table below:

Results in GA-6 June 20 Runoff by Type of Voting/Counting			
Type of Voting	Handel %	Ossoff%	Ossoff Margin
Absentee By Mail (paper)	35.8%	64.2%	28.4%
Provisional (paper)	27.0%	73.0%	46.0%
Advance In Person (DRE)	49.3%	50.7%	1.4%
All Early Voting (Mail + In Person)	46.7%	53.3%	6.6%
Election Day (DRE)	58.2%	41.8%	-16.4%
Total Vote	**51.8%**	**48.2%**	**-3.6%**

Source: Georgia Elections website;
http://results.enr.clarityelections.com/GA/70059/Web02-state/#/cid/30600

We see that, after winning the verifiable mail-in voting by a stunning 28.4 percent margin (and the provisional voting by an even more lop-sided margin of 46.0 percent[22]), Ossoff also polled a narrow win in the unverifiable advance-

---

[21] See http://results.enr.clarityelections.com/GA/70059/Web02-state/#/cid/30600.

[22] It is noteworthy that the provisionals, though a very small slice of the total vote pie, were all cast on Election Day itself. We see at play one aspect of voter suppression whereby Democratic voters are disproportionally relegated to provisional voting (and add to that that this 73%D/27%R split derived entirely from the subset of provisional ballots deemed valid and therefore *counted*). But we also see a result dramatically at odds with the count of ordinary Election Day ballots (58%R/42%D), flying in the face of the claim that Handel won because *Republicans* flocked to the polls in droves on Election Day.

in-person voting (just slightly fewer total votes than were cast on Election Day itself)—only to be blown out by 16.4 percent in an unverifiable Election Day landslide. With the election already under a cloud of known security breaches at Kennesaw State, the larger cloud of known vulnerability to hacking and rigging of unverifiable DREs, and the still larger cloud of more than 15 years of virtually unidirectional vote counting anomalies and red flags in the computerized voting era,[23] this glaring disparity obviously warranted deeper investigation.

The first point to be made—and it is a familiar one—is that neither the Ossoff campaign nor the Democratic Party had any interest in pursuing such an investigation. Nor, for that matter, did *The New York Times*—to which we sent critical data, and with which we engaged in lengthy discussion—nor any other MSM outlets. To be clear, Handel's landslide victory in Election Day voting was *absolutely shocking*. It was not remotely predicted by a single poll, not even the Republican-identified poll by Trafalgar referred to above, which was the *only* poll to show Handel ahead (by 2 percent). Even this outlier poll showed Handel with a mere 1.6 percent lead among likely voters yet to cast their votes a week before Election Day.[24] This begged two obvious questions: 1) Did anything *happen* to swing voters so strongly for Handel or against Ossoff? and 2) Did the huge vote-by-mail Ossoff margin simply reflect that Democratic voters in GA-6 are more prone than are Republican voters to cast mail-in ballots?

The answer to the first question is fairly clear: there was no gaffe or scandal in the week before Election Day. Ossoff did not get crushed in a debate, urinate in public on a statue of Robert E. Lee, or get caught in bed with a farm animal. Handel did not give a speech for the ages or pick up any critical late endorsement. The money and endorsements pouring in from both sides had already done their work—hardly anyone (a scant 3.88 percent of those planning to but yet to cast a vote, according to the Trafalgar poll) remained "undecided" and up for grabs.[25] The Ossoff get-out-the-vote operation, which helped Ossoff to his 6.6 percent overall lead in early voting, did not run out of money, and there was no shortage of volunteers.

---

[23] A pattern that seemed to have its *genesis* in Georgia with the red-flagged shockers that defeated Democrats Roy Barnes (governor) and Max Cleland (U.S. senator) in 2002.

[24] See Trafalgar poll, at https://drive.google.com/file/d/0B4lhKxf9pMitQkVYeExaaV9PczQ/view.

[25] Ibid, p. 3.

The only incident of note was the "baseball practice" shooting in Virginia, in which a Republican congressman as well as several others were seriously wounded a week before the GA-6 election.[26] Although Republicans happened to be targeted by an obviously disturbed individual, the attack was also widely seen as a symptom of a hyper-polarization and breakdown in norms of civility and decency in which Trump's inflammatory rhetoric was regarded by many, including Republicans, to have played a leading role.[27] There was a strong sense as well that, in that hostile "Age of Trump" environment, either side might be the target of such violence. And, of course, the usual fleeting concern about the easy availability of assault weapons, which skews Democratic. I also checked with several colleagues on the ground in GA-6, who responded that there was no sign, based on observed precinct-level turnout, that Election Day voting in GA-6 was swung sharply by either this incident or any other late-breaking news event. Anyone seizing on any such event as a satisfactory (and discussion-ending) explanation for the extraordinary and anomalous apparent late movement in GA-6 really should reflect on whether their reasons include an unhealthy portion of wishful thinking.

The second question required a bit more digging. If it turned out that GA-6 Democrats had displayed a relatively greater historical tendency to mail in their ballots, that would have sufficed to establish a benign explanation for the verifiable/unverifiable disparity. It was a simple enough exercise to download and organize the archived data for the past several GA-6 elections from the Georgia Elections website. As shown on the chart below, it is not Democrats but *Republicans* who consistently prefer to vote by mail in GA-6.

That is, until 2017. In the three preceding elections, from 2012 through 2016, the Republican candidate's margin among Mail-In/Opscan voters exceeded his margin among DRE voters by an average of 11.1 percent. Suddenly—in the Ossoff election—that pattern spun on its heels. Now the Republican candidate (Handel) couldn't seem to *buy* a Mail-In/Opscan vote, *trailing* her DRE showing by 36.0 percent. So it seemed that suddenly and anomalously it was *Democrats* (or, more precisely, voters who selected the Democratic candidate[28]) who flocked to the mailbox to vote.

---

[26] See https://www.cnn.com/2017/06/14/politics/congressional-shooting-victims/index.html.

[27] See https://www.aol.com/article/news/2017/06/15/gop-rep-mark-sanford-trump-partially-blame-rhetoric-scalise-baseball-shooting/22305640/.

[28] The distinction is significant. Analysts were able to obtain the voter registration data necessary to determine what portion of the Ossoff mail-in vote was cross-over by

A Comparison of Vote-By-Mail Patterns For Voters in Georgia Sixth Congressional District 2012 - 2017

ELECTION YEAR	%Total Vote Margin (R win = +)	%DRE[1] Vote Margin	%OPSCAN[2] Vote Margin	%OPSCAN Vote Margin Minus %DRE Vote Margin[3]
2012	29.0%	28.1%	43.1%	15.0%
2014	32.0%	31.9%	38.4%	6.5%
2016	23.4%	22.7%	33.0%	10.3%
2012 - 2016 Aggregate	28.1%	26.9%	38.0%	11.1%
2017 - Runoff	3.8%	7.6%	-28.4%	-36.0%

1. DRE voting includes at-poll and early in-person voting.

2. OPSCAN voting includes only Vote-By-Mail voting.

3. A positive (+) percentage in this column indicates Republican performed better in OPSCAN vote than in DRE vote; i.e., Republican voters were more likely than Democratic voters to use Vote-By-Mail to cast their votes.

Or did they? What if the Ossoff mail-in vote advantage reflected not a flood of Democratic voters suddenly breaking with habit and deciding to vote by mail,[29]

Republicans, a determination of great forensic significance. Using this data, in a drilldown too complex for presentation here, it was shown that no plausible benign scenario existed that could account for the radical disparity in voting patterns between votes cast and counted verifiably (i.e., on opscans) and unverifiably (i.e., on DREs). See https://voterga.files.wordpress.com/2017/10/6th-district-runoff-statistical-analysis.pdf.

[29] Some were led to speculate that the surge of Democratic mail-ins in the June runoff might perhaps have been prompted in part by the Ossoff campaign's encouraging of vote-by-mail as a protection against DRE-based fraud. Having combed the campaign literature for that specific message, what we found was that the *Handel* campaign inserted vote-by-mail applications into at least one of its mailings, while the Ossoff campaign did not. Such "benign" explanations, where remotely plausible, certainly

but instead the verifiability of those paper ballots and their consequent relative resistance to risk-free manipulation? What if the mail-in votes *as cast* were not so wildly divergent from the in-person votes *as cast*? What if, instead, the unverifiable in-person votes were manipulated, *when they needed to be*, with a big Ossoff lead to overcome on Election Day? What if one or more of the numerous known security breaches was exploited to alter the result of the election?

If these questions seem far-fetched, we owe it to ourselves (and to democracy) to ask the "opposite" question: What proof exists that the 90 percent of the vote count conducted on unverifiable and manifestly vulnerable DREs was *not* hacked or maliciously programmed, altered in the pitch-dark of cyberspace?

We might ask Kennesaw State Center for Election Systems Director Merle King or Georgia then-Secretary of State Brian Kemp[30] for that proof, since it was in their possession and easy enough to furnish. And indeed legal action was pursued,[31] in which the server used by the state to tally the votes in the Handel-Ossoff contest—which held the programming for both the April 18 (preliminary) and June 20 (runoff) special elections—was sought in evidence. But—far from providing the sought-after proof—*four days after the filing of that suit,* officials at the Kennesaw State Center for Election Systems destroyed the key piece of hard evidence by completely erasing the server.[32] Ooops.

As justification, it was pointed out that the FBI had been given a copy of the server—but alas it was an *old* copy, given to the FBI in March 2017, prior to the programming of Handel-Ossoff. Then two *other* backup copies—the only ones known to exist with Handel-Ossoff programming—were located by Kennesaw

---

warrant serious investigation and consideration. *But so do the hardware and software that recorded and counted 90 percent of the GA-6 vote in invisible strings of 1s and 0s.*

[30] Kemp is now Georgia's governor, having, as Secretary of State, administered his own election to the state's highest office in 2018. His victory margin over Democrat Stacey Abrams was 1.4% and the election was rife with voter suppression schemes and votecount anomalies (as was the Lt. Governor's contest; see https://www.ajc.com/news/state--regional-govt--politics/lawsuit-alleges-votes-went-missing-georgia-lieutenant-governor-race/waANVVApMPpzkKbNaTZLdI/). Abrams, while acknowledging the reality that Kemp was to be governor, did not concede electoral defeat and has gone on to crusade for voting rights, founding the Fair Fight 2020 campaign against voter suppression in the battleground states. See www.fairfight.com.

[31] See http://bradblog.com/Docs/CURLINGvKEMP(2)-ComplaintWithVerificationAndExhibits_070317.pdf.

[32] See https://www.nbcnews.com/politics/politics-news/georgia-election-server-wiped-after-lawsuit-filed-n814581. The scrubbing of the server occurred on July 7, 2017.

State Center for Election Systems. For good measure, *they* were scrubbed by the Center on August 9, 2017—using a process called "degaussing" that magnetically and permanently destroys all data—the day after the suit was moved to federal court, according to the Georgia attorney general's office.[33]

The ooops defense may work once. Thrice is something else. Even viewed in isolation, such blatant and brazen destruction of evidence fairly screams coverup. When viewed in the context of the election integrity movement's 17-year no-hitter when it comes to access to the hard evidence, living witnesses, or "smoking guns" that are demanded as the ante to even begin a discussion, it screams 10 times louder.[34]

---

[33] For a partial narrative of these maneuvers, see "Georgia Elections Data Destruction Audit," at https://voterga.files.wordpress.com/2018/04/georgia-elections-data-destruction-audit.pdf. See also, https://apnews.com/39dad9d39a7533cfc06c0774615a6d05 and https://coaltionforgoodgovernance.sharefile.com/share/view/s0ef056a62814a43b for sworn testimony that evidence was found, via the FBI's backup copy (obtained in January *2020* after a protracted legal battle) that the server had been tampered with, including deleting of the server's access logs for the period covering the run-up to E2016, the logs being mysteriously restored two days after Trump's election.

The "ooops" defense was also on display in infamous Broward County, Florida, where the paper ballots from the August 2016 Democratic primary—in which challenger Tim Canova took on former DNC Chairwoman Debbie Wasserman Schultz for her U.S. House seat—were "inadvertently" destroyed while the subject of a public-records legal proceeding. The Florida Circuit Court ruled in plaintiff Canova's favor (see http://www.hollerbackfilm.com/blog/canovawinscase) but, alas, the award of damages and attorney's fees won't bring back the ballots. Like the data on the Georgia servers (and like the ballots from 58 Ohio counties in 2004, destroyed while under a standing federal court order), they are gone for good.

[34] Before leaving GA-6, I wish to cite it as an instance of what I have called "electoral resonance"—the impact of elections *beyond* their determination of who is to occupy a given office. Handel-Ossoff—that is, Handel's victory and Ossoff's defeat—found its way into quite a few narratives of the zeitgeist and various trends of the Age of Trump, often quite far afield from mere political handicapping.

One example I came upon was a *New York Times* review by Katha Pollitt of a new book by Cecile Richards, the outgoing president of Planned Parenthood (at https://www.nytimes.com/2018/04/25/books/review/cecile-richards-make-trouble.html?rref). In her review at one point, Pollitt—referring to the 2012 fiasco in which the Susan G. Komen Foundation pulled its funding from Planned Parenthood, only to abruptly reverse course amidst a firestorm of protest—takes Richards gently to task for an omission: "But she [Richards] doesn't say that the woman behind Komen's ill-fated plan, Karen Handler (sic), defeated Jon Ossoff in a much-publicized Georgia congressional race." The "fact" of Handel's victory takes its place in support of Pollitt's larger query: "I would have liked to read why [Richards] thinks the enemies of reproductive rights have been so [politically] successful."

That's a question I would have been happy to take a *forensic* crack at.

E2017 and the LVCM

On November 7, 2017, for the first time in the computerized voting era, the red shift *vanished*. The exit polls were—*mirabile dictu*—accurate.

Indeed we saw—especially in the newly paper-ballot state of Virginia—a "blue shift" from most of the tracking polls (that is, the candidate to the *left* does better in the election than predicted by the polls). This too was essentially unprecedented in the computerized voting era in competitive elections of national significance.

Why would we expect to see that phenomenon in an *honestly* counted election? Because polling and elections constitute a classic feedback loop.[35] As the computerized voting era unfolded, pollsters began to see their predictions going wrong—consistently predicting results to the left of electoral outcomes.[36] They of course assumed that this was because something was wrong with their *polls*, most likely their sampling methodology—even though it had been working fine for pre-computerized voting and a rational analysis would at least have considered the change in *vote-counting* methodology among the causes for the polls' sudden struggles. Instead, the pollsters tweaked their polls. The response by the pollsters—initially from Gallup, but it "worked" so well that it was adopted by the field—was to develop a sampling methodology known as the Likely Voter Cutoff Model (LVCM).[37]

The LVCM operates to disproportionately exclude from polling samples voters from traditional Democratic constituencies (young, low-income, transient/renters/mobile, elderly, marginal). It employs a series of screening questions (e.g., "How long have you lived at your current residence?") designed to "qualify" only the more stable/core/consistent voters—i.e., disproportionately Republicans—as respondents.

That this skewed sampling model "worked" so well was one strong, albeit indirect, piece of evidence that the votecounts it was attempting to mirror had themselves been corrupted. In an *honestly* counted election, the LVCM would

---

[35] See http://www.truth-out.org/news/item/27203-vote-counts-and-polls-an-insidious-feedback-loop.

[36] It is worth reiterating that there is a natural overlap between electoral contests competitive and significant enough to be targets for polling and electoral contests competitive and significant enough to be targets for rigging.

[37] See Study V in Chapter VIII.

fail, predicting results to the right of the votecounts—and that is exactly what we saw in November 2017.

Oh! Susanna

Stephen Foster's "It rained so hard the day I left, the weather it was dry..." might do justice to the twisted tale of the December 2017 Special Election in Alabama to fill the U.S. Senate seat vacated by Jeff Sessions when he became Trump's ill-fated first attorney general. The election was easy to misread, as it inverted pretty much all conventional political calculus. Given the GOP's slender, two-seat Senate majority, the election was significant yet not of critical importance. Even had there been concern among the GOP leadership that a Democratic victory in Alabama coupled with two GOP defections would sink the all-important "tax reform" bill, savvy Senate Majority Leader Mitch McConnell knew that he was under no obligation to seat the Democrat in place of temporary GOP Senator Luther Strange until after the tax war was won.

The Republican candidate was Judge Roy Moore. As if his record and antics— he had twice been removed from the bench for violation of judicial ethics in putting his religious views above the law[38]—were not controversial enough, Moore found himself in the crosshairs of the nascent #MeToo movement when he was accused by multiple women of predatory behavior toward them when they had been teenage girls and he a prosecutor in his 30s. As far back in the rear-view mirror as that may have been, in the emerging national reckoning with the phenomenon of male sexual predation, the roiling scandal transformed what would otherwise likely have been a comfortable Moore win over Democrat Doug Jones into what the polls all indicated to be an exceedingly tight race.

It also put Senate Republicans—and, above all, McConnell—in a very uncomfortable position; so much so that there was serious talk of refusing to seat Moore in the event he won the election, a move that of course would have enraged the Trump base.[39] Even Trump (who was hardly in a position to come down hard on Moore on moral grounds) and the RNC found themselves in a pickle, fancy-dancing and keeping their distance from the toxic candidate before finally going all-in with a hearty "we need him for the taxes" (even though they didn't) endorsement a week before the election. To round out the

---

[38] See https://www.nytimes.com/2017/11/18/us/roy-moore-alabama.html.

[39] *Seating* Moore, on the other hand, would have hung an 800-lb albatross around the GOP's neck heading into E2018, especially after the Democrats cleared their tactical decks by cashiering #MeToo-targeted Minnesota Senator Al Franken.

dramatis personae for this passion play—and to shed some light on the outcome—we must give full screen-credit to none other than Steve Bannon and Karl Rove.

To describe Bannon and Rove as rivals would not begin to do justice to the antipathy the elder operative, once feted as "Bush's brain," harbored for the brash upstart who had displaced him as the right hand of the Right. Bannon had fallen from his White House perch in August but continued to have at least a piece of Trump's ear and to be marshaling his ongoing disruption campaign from his position at the head of *Breitbart News*. Rove, who had slid off the national radar with Trump's rise, nonetheless maintained his reputation and value with the Republican establishment, from the Bushes to McConnell. And his long-time base of operations happened to be Alabama, where he had personally orchestrated the political demise and prosecution of popular Democratic Governor Don Siegelman, finally released from imprisonment in June 2019.[40]

Bannon went all-in and then some on Roy Moore, defending him against all manner of attack and promoting his candidacy with great zeal. Moore was—it was clear to all—*Bannon's guy*. He thus presented a golden opportunity to put a stake through Bannon's political heart. So both Rove—Bannon's mortal enemy—and McConnell (and the GOP establishment more generally) had everything to gain from Moore's *defeat*. This completely reversed the rooting sections and the dynamics for what many erroneously regarded as yet another Trump-proxy contest.

Thus, while many electoral integrity advocates approached the Moore-Jones election with concerns about meddling on Moore's behalf,[41] I refused to

---

[40] See https://www.nytimes.com/2009/04/25/opinion/25sat4.html?searchResultPosition=2.

[41] As has increasingly been the case, this election was the subject of procedural challenge and wrangling—in this instance a pre-election legal attempt to compel the preservation of digital ballot images, which are records of each ballot created by the ballot scanners used to tabulate the votes. This feature of most late-model scanners— including the ES-200 scanners used in Alabama—involves simply turning a switch to either "On," which preserves the images, or "Off," which destroys them.

On December 11, the day prior to the election, an Alabama circuit judge issued an order that the feature be turned on (see http://thehill.com/homenews/campaign/364385-judge-orders-alabama-to-preserve-voting-records-for-senate-special-election). The state made an emergency appeal to the Alabama Supreme Court, which stayed the order, and thereby essentially reversed the lower court, within minutes of the state's filing, early in the morning of December 12, Election Day (see https://techcrunch.com/2017/12/12/alabama-digital-records-vote-roy-moore/).

dismiss the possibility of just the opposite. It certainly appeared that the forces that had produced 15 years of red shift might now find it in their hearts (and their interests) to produce a blue one.

As with virtually every American election, there is not much to go on in assessing whether a votecount has been accurate and honest. We had no access to the voter-marked ballots; we had no digital ballots images, as these were all destroyed (see note 41). We did have exit polls, and indeed there was a "blue shift" of 2.7 percent.[42] And we did screencapture the rolling vote totals.[43]

```
December 12, 2017 - 10:07PM ET
Alabama - 1879 of 2220 Precincts Reporting - 85%
     Name               Party        Votes      Vote %
     Moore, Roy          GOP          511,562    49%
     Jones, Doug         Dem          506,894    49%
     Total Write-Ins     NPD          15,817     2%
December 12, 2017 - 10:10PM ET
Alabama - 1897 of 2220 Precincts Reporting - 85%
     Name               Party        Votes      Vote %
     Moore, Roy          GOP          522,226    50%
     Jones, Doug         Dem          515,187    49%
     Total Write-Ins     NPD          16,422     2%
December 12, 2017 - 10:13PM ET
Alabama - 1897 of 2220 Precincts Reporting - 85%
     Name               Party        Votes      Vote %
     Moore, Roy          GOP          527,231    49%
     Jones, Doug         Dem          527,098    49%
     Total Write-Ins     NPD          16,760     2%
```

We noticed an interesting development shortly after 10 p.m. At 10:10 p.m., with 1897 out of 2220 precincts reporting, Moore is leading by 7,039 votes; at

---

Given that the "burden" on election administrators amounted to the flipping of a switch, it is reasonable to draw the inference that *somebody* well-placed did not want the ballot images to be preserved and possibly made available for verification purposes.

[42] One must ask, if the mantral knock on exit polls is that they "always over-represent the Democratic vote," why *here*—in a contest where for once the lay of the land was such that there were powerful reasons for the *Republican* candidate to be marked for defeat by the *same operatives* who have consistently labored to bring about Republican *victories*—would *those same exit polls* suddenly depart from that etched-in-stone pattern and now instead over-represent the *Republican* vote? Put another way, the direction of the exit poll-votecount disparity appears to be strongly, if not perfectly, correlated with the motive, examined rationally, of right-wing operatives.

[43] The screencaptures were taken from the quasi-official reporting site http://www.al.com/news/index.ssf/page/2017_alabama_us_senate_election_results.html.

10:13 p.m., *still with 1897 precincts reporting*, Moore's lead has been reduced to 133 votes. That is, *without any record of additional precincts reporting*, 11,911 votes were added to Jones' total, while Moore added 5,005 votes, thereby effectively wiping out Moore's 7,000+ vote lead.

It is possible, of course, that the precinct numbers were simply erroneous, a mistake somewhere in the pipeline; though if we accept that to be the case, it is not entirely confidence-inspiring when it comes to the *rest* of the numbers— including, of course, the vote totals.

But there are two other possibilities to consider. One is that a pile of absentee or mail-in ballots, not associated with a particular precinct, was added to the count somewhere between 10:10 and 10:13; this of course raises the specter of batches of ballots floating around or suddenly produced and fed into a central tabulator at the proverbial 11th hour, with no way of tracing them back to precinct-level results and no controls for their authenticity.

The other is electronic fraud—a program or hack that alters running vote totals in real time, in this case carelessly ignoring the "precincts reporting" counter.

We don't know and, in all likelihood, we won't know. Precinct-level drilldowns detected some highly anomalous voting patterns in this election. And the late-shift catch-up-and-pass pattern—specifically featuring the "mystery votes" anomaly here noted—is a fingerprint we've seen before, as early as 2004 for Bush in Ohio.[44] That was a fingerprint associated with the mysterious breakdown and shutdown of the official Ohio state tabulators (under control of Republican Secretary of State *and* honorary Bush campaign chairman J. Kenneth Blackwell) and the porting of the votes to Mike Connell's conveniently-in-place SmarTech "backup" servers in Tennessee—the late Mike Connell, who was known, then and at the time of his untimely death, as Karl Rove's "IT guru." It is curious and perhaps telling to find a clue so similar in the Moore-Jones election 13 years later. That it should accrue to the immediate benefit of a Democrat should not blind us to what, given the peculiar circumstances of this election, appears to be a consistency of both motive and *modus operandi*.

---

[44] And as recently as the April 2017 GA-6 Special Election, in which Democrat Jon Ossoff dropped below the crucial 50% (no runoff) level for the first time, and permanently, after the Fulton County servers were interrupted in their count by a two-hour breakdown.

E2018: A Victory Wrapped in an Enigma

The scattered off-off-year elections of November 2017 gave the first indication that Donald Trump might be an electoral albatross to be reckoned with. Although it might also be argued that local factors were primarily responsible, there did seem to be at least a small message of national import in the E2017 bottle. Democratic candidates succeeded in Virginia,[45] which, in part responding to the ease of hacking exposed at that year's DefCon "Voting Village," had abruptly decertified all its DREs and voted entirely on hand-marked paper; New Jersey; and in a number of previously GOP-run cities and counties around the country, adding a U.S. House seat in Pennsylvania in March 2018.

I found myself fielding a small barrage of calls and emails asking whether I thought these results "proved" that U.S. elections had suddenly been made "secure." A few went so far as to ask whether, all archived evidence notwithstanding, E2017 proved that U.S. elections had *always* been secure. In response I noted that:

1) Virginia elections (see above) *had* actually been made more secure; so there *was* that.

2) The 2017 prizes were droplets in the political bucket, certainly not worth any significant risk. Given the heightened scrutiny of our electoral processes (including growing alarm about the Russians), it would have made little strategic sense to have triggered any red flags in November 2017, thereby putting more urgency into the effort to button up election security before 2020.

3) The major elections for governor in Virginia and New Jersey were won by essentially rig-proof margins.

It made sense that cheaters would save their up-sleeve aces for the big pots. The question then loomed: was E2018 a "big pot?" Was it big enough to risk being caught palming an ace?

E2018 was the nation's first *collective* opportunity to weigh in on the Age of Trump and the direction he was taking America. The gauntlet had certainly

---

[45] See https://www.washingtonpost.com/local/virginia-politics/virginia-scraps-touch-screen-voting-machines-as-election-for-governor-looms/2017/09/08/e266ead6-94fe-11e7-89fa-bb822a46da5b_story.html?utm_term=.b64e40b25979.

been thrown down, and thrown down hard: there was little that was ambiguous about it. Trump's overall approval hovered around 40 percent and, where measured on a 4-point scale, veered sharply to both "strongs," very favorable and very unfavorable.

But Trump, of course, was not on the ballot, so it was anyone's guess how an election that was fought both on traditional grounds of local and economic politics and as a referendum on one of the most polarizing and divisive figures in American history would turn out. Historically, on average, the sitting president's party can expect to lose a net of 25 House and two Senate seats in the first midterm election. When the president's approval rating is below 50 percent, however, those numbers shoot up to 41 House and five Senate seats[46]—well beyond what was needed to shift party control in both chambers.

Two major caveats applied. The historical averages reach back before E2010 ("the gift that keeps on giving"), in the wake of which Republican precision gerrymandering is considered to have stacked the deck against what might otherwise be a "blue wave" sweep in the House, while in the Senate the Democrats were defending three seats for each Republican-held seat—though more significantly seven "battleground" races to five for the Republicans.[47] Then of course there was the inherent unpredictability of politics itself, at its very highest in this careening, reality-TV political moment. Extraordinary events—from military crises and nuclear brinksmanship to Nobel prizes, scandals and indictments—were in the air, and the impact of one or more such bombshells, positive or negative, could not be discounted. Although Trump famously claimed that he could shoot someone on Fifth Avenue and not lose any voters (a boast that events have proven to be not far off the mark), it was not clear, heading into E2018, to what extent his capacity to hyperpolarize was a two-way street—whether, that is, he could win the Nobel Prize, and be knighted for good measure, and not *gain* any voters for his party.

There were plenty of "events" in the weeks leading up to E2018, few of them particularly favorable for Trump or the GOP candidates facing the voters. September began with John McCain's state funeral: his daughter Meghan and ex-Presidents George W. Bush and Barack Obama eulogizing, Trump pointedly not invited and conspicuous by his absence. Then, a few days later, the *Times* ran the scathing opinion piece "I am part of the resistance inside the Trump

---

[46] See https://www.thoughtco.com/historical-midterm-election-results-4087704.

[47] See https://ballotpedia.org/United_States_Senate.

administration," published anonymously by a senior White House official. Then the UN secretary general, Antonio Guterres, called for an urgent climate change conference, saying "climate change [is] moving faster than we are"— Trump's denial of human-caused climate change and withdrawal of the U.S. from the Paris Accords yet again being brought to the fore. That same day, as if to prove a point, Hurricane Florence hit South Carolina, forcing the mandatory evacuation of a million residents; and, although Trump and the GOP caught a break when the deadly Camp and Woolsey fires waited until November 8, two days *after* the election, to get started, the devastating 2018 California wildfire season was already the worst on record while the voters had the chance to consider its implications. The next day Bob Woodward's scorching book *Fear: Trump in the White House* was published. Next, Trump associate Paul Manafort pled guilty to conspiracy charges and agreed to cooperate with investigators, shortly followed by accusations of sexual assault publicly leveled against Trump Supreme Court nominee Brett Kavanaugh. Then China announced $60 billion in new tariffs on U.S. goods in partial retaliation for $200 billion imposed by Trump on Chinese goods, his punishing trade war in full swing. Two days later a mass shooting in a Rite-Aid distribution center in Baltimore reminded America of Trump and the GOP Congress' inaction on gun safety and fealty to the NRA. September was rounded out with a poorly received (to put it mildly) and widely panned address to the UN General Assembly, attacking globalism and Iran in typical Trump fashion, and by Christine Blasey Ford's testimony in the Kavanaugh hearings.

October brought much of the same. It kicked off with journalist/dissident Jamal Khashoggi's disappearance from the Saudi Embassy in Istanbul, which during the course of the month was exposed as a grisly political murder widely suspected to have been orchestrated by the very top-level Saudis with whom Trump was working major weapons deals and whose scandalous behavior he and his party found themselves denying and/or defending to the hilt. The economic news was, unsurprisingly, good, with the Department of Labor reporting an unemployment rate of 3.7 percent, lowest since 1969, and signs of non-trivial wage growth finally beginning to appear—an undeniable political boost, though economies are probably better felt than read about when it comes to political impact. And preliminary agreement on a trade deal to replace NAFTA was announced,[48] but that was about it for pre-election good news.

---

[48] A deal that basically turned out to *be* NAFTA, renamed as USMCA and, ironically improved with some significant worker and environmental protections ultimately

The rest of October was something of a pre-election nightmare. On October 6, Brett Kavanaugh was confirmed—after a transparently pro-forma FBI "investigation"—by a 50-48 Senate vote, an outcome that undoubtedly thrilled Trump's base but one that met with a 10 percent (51-41) margin of disapproval among Americans as a whole and enraged millions, particularly women. On October 9, Trump's popular UN ambassador, Nikki Haley, announced she was resigning her post effective year's end, joining the caravan of departures from the administration. A week later the northbound "caravan" of Central American migrants reached Guatemala and became, to hear Trump tell it, a national crisis, while the Khashoggi revelations continued to roll out and Trump threatened to pull the U.S. out of a decades-old arms-control agreement with Russia. Then came the pipe bombs, sent by a Floridian Trump supporter, first to George Soros then to the Obamas, Clintons, John Brennan, and *CNN*. October 27 saw still another deadly mass shooting, this one a hate crime, as a gunman yelling "All Jews must die!" killed 11 at the Tree of Life Synagogue in Pittsburgh. For tens of millions, the hatred and divisions stoked by Trump were seen reflected in each such new echoing outburst, and indeed both Jewish leaders and Pittsburgh's mayor requested that Trump not attend services for the victims,[49] a shocking rebuff that Trump ignored, though he was uncharacteristically on mute at the cemetery.

Finally, Trump rounded out the month by ordering 5,200 soldiers to the Mexican border to meet some 4,000 straggling and footsore refugees and defend the homeland from their looming "invasion." It played, outside the base, as a strange, unwarranted, and seemingly desperate way to flex military muscle and fashion a politically serviceable crisis out of whatever materials happened to be at hand.

That just about carried us through to the election, though post-election events continued in much the same vein. In fact the pre-election period was not categorically different from the rest of Trump's now three-plus-year reign, though it did have a bit of a madcap feel to it, especially as, while all these events were transpiring, Trump was doubling down on his love affair with his base, holding rally after rally and upping the hostility with each new stop. I have gone into timeline detail to set the scene for a truly remarkable shift in

---

insisted upon in 2019 by the new Democratic House majority using as its leverage Trump's need for a trade "win."

[49] See https://www.npr.org/2018/10/30/662017268/trump-to-visit-pittsburgh-but-not-everyone-will-welcome-him.

electoral dynamics that became apparent even before the dust had settled and the results of E2018 were known.

E2018: Trump's Great GOTV Success

It's no great secret that for a big swath of eligible Americans elections haven't mattered enough to bother to cast a vote. In 2016, for example, Donald Trump was elected by the votes of a mere 26 percent of eligible voters. And that was a *presidential* election—midterms have attracted far fewer voters to the polls. Thus, for example, while 131,689,908 voters, or 55.7 percent of the voting-age population, cast ballots in presidential 2016, in the 2014 midterm the number was 78,812,769, just 36.4 percent of voting-age population.

Voter suppression—the various schemes used to make it more difficult or impossible to vote—accounts for some of the non-participation. And, even with the expansion of early and absentee voting, particularly working-class Americans frequently find themselves faced with a competition between voting and their myriad other responsibilities, a competition that voting often loses. But the vast majority of non-voters is accounted for by those who either don't care at all or don't care enough to make the effort, many of them because they feel that elections don't really matter and that they are not truly represented regardless of who wins them.

From 1962, the first midterm in a 50-state U.S., through 2014, turnout varied only a little as a proportion of the increasing U.S. voting-age population, but barely hit 40 percent in even the best of midterm years. What could change all that in a flash?

Donald J. Trump.

E2018 was a turnout tsunami not because millions of voters suddenly became duty-embracing devotees of democracy or decided that midterm elections were in any *general* sense worth their time, but because Donald Trump had made a point of acting and governing in a way that made die-hard fans of a portion of them while antagonizing, appalling, and frightening an even larger portion. In all, more than 114 million cast votes for the U.S. House, amounting to a net gain of more than 35 million "new" voters who had sat out E2014. Just how radical a departure this was from the norm—six times the historical average—can be seen from the table and chart below.

U.S. Midterm Election Turnout:
Total Votes Cast for House of Representatives 1962 - 2018

Election Year	Total Votes Cast (Turnout)*	Change From Previous Midterm	Percent Change From Previous Midterm	Bar Chart of Election-to-Election Turnout Change
2018	114,016,831	35,204,062	44.7%	44.7
2014	78,812,769	-7,972,188	-9.2%	-9.2
2010	86,784,957	5,809,420	7.2%	7.2
2006	80,975,537	6,268,985	8.4%	8.4
2002	74,706,552	8,101,750	12.2%	12.2
1998	66,604,802	-3,888,846	-5.5%	-5.5
1994	70,493,648	8,138,795	13.1%	13.1
1990	62,354,853	2,596,456	4.3%	4.3
1986	59,758,397	-4,122,447	-6.5%	-6.5
1982	63,880,844	9,296,922	17.0%	17.0
1978	54,583,922	2,270,465	4.3%	4.3
1974	52,313,457	-1,945,428	-3.6%	-3.6
1970	54,258,885	1,356,910	2.6%	2.6
1966	52,901,975	1,659,787	3.2%	3.2
1962	51,242,188	With admission of Hawaii and Alaska, U.S. becomes 50 states.		
Average 1962 - 2014			3.7%	
Abs. Val. Avg. 1962 -2014			7.5%	

*Source: https://history.house.gov/Institution/Election-Statistics/Election-Statistics/

While a turnout surge was anticipated, it wound up exceeding virtually all forecasts. And while many candidates did run "normal" campaigns grounded in policy positions and local or regional issues, many others, particularly Democrats, made it, either forthrightly or subliminally, about Trump, and the record national turnout reflected that theme.

No card-carrying, or freelance, GOP strategist could contemplate such turnout numbers and see anything but a disaster for the party's candidates. The only question would be its magnitude. This was because "core" voters—the ones who vote in every election—have long been understood to be older, whiter, richer, and more Republican in their politics than are "marginal" voters, who vote mainly in presidential elections or for special reasons such as racial identification with a prominent candidate on the ballot. These marginal voters are, of course, younger, darker, poorer, and more Democratic in their politics.

So a flood of 35 million new voters—the vast majority of whom, by virtue of being "new," logically did not come from the electorate's Republican-leaning core—would spell very bad news for Republican candidates. Another way of looking at this is that the more Republican-leaning voters tend to be in the electoral core, voting in every election, the closer the GOP is to its "turnout ceiling." Most of their voters were *already* voting, so not very many were left to leaven the big swell of millions of new marginal voters casting ballots in E2018.

When the counting was done and the dust had settled, the Democrats had picked up a net of 40 House seats and, with them, control of the chamber. But they had actually lost a net of two Senate seats. To complete the picture, Democrats picked up a net of seven governorships and a total of 370 (out of over 7,200) state legislative seats. Let's put these results in perspective.

Lots of Water but No Wave
One of the primary questions analysts ask about an election is whether it qualifies as a "wave" election. Wave elections are defined as being in the top quintile of shift (either way) relative to the historical archives. That is, looking at the Senate, House, governorships, and state legislatures, was the election in the top 20 percent in terms of political movement in each of these four categories?[50] At first blush, the answer for E2018 seems obvious: it was a turnout tsunami, a midterm distinct from all others in our history, and it certainly *felt* like a wave.

But the actual numbers turned out to be underwhelming, closer to a ripple than to a wave, and certainly nothing like the results tsunami one might predict on the basis of the extraordinary turnout numbers. Starting from the top, a wave election would entail a shift of at least seven Senate seats—in E2018 the *GOP* gained two seats, a reverse ripple. Going into the election, the Democrats held 25 of the 34 seats on the ballot, a numerical quirk of the draw that limited Democratic expectations. Of those 34 seats, however, only 12 were remotely competitive (the rest being locks) and, of these, the Democrats were defending seven to the GOP's five. With the Senate line-up being 51R/49D,[51] a Democratic takeover of the Senate hinged on the most competitive contests in this set of

---

[50] For definition and discussion of wave elections in general and E2018 specifically, see https://www.ballotpedia.org/115th_United_States_Congress.

[51] In this and all partisan breakdowns of the Senate in this section, the two Independent senators who caucus with the Democrats are included in the Democratic count.

12 and was certainly in play—especially in a turnout tsunami. The Democratic Win Percentages (the likelihood of a Democratic victory) calculated by FiveThirtyEight.com in the states of Missouri, Florida, and Indiana were 56.8 percent, 70.2 percent, and 72.0 percent respectively. Republicans won in each of these states and, notably, Democrats won in *no* state in which the Republican Win Percentage was greater than 50 percent. Another way of presenting this is to point out that we were looking at a *very* narrow swath of truly competitive contests, in which win percentages were in the 25 percent to 75 percent range—only *five* in all. Democrats were favored in every one of these five contests, yet Republicans won three of them:

E2018 U.S. Senate Highly Competitive Contests				
STATE	CANDIDATES R/D (*Incumbent)	HELD	NEW	D-WIN%
NV	Heller*/Rosen	R	D	56.8%
MO	Hawley/McCaskill*	D	R	56.8%
AZ	McSally/Sinema	R	D	61.9%
FL	Scott/Nelson*	D	R	70.2%
IN	Braun/Donnelly*	D	R	72.0%

We'll return to the dynamics of these races and explanations for their outcomes, but it bears noting that these three races would, if predictions had borne out, have left the U.S. Senate with a precarious 50-50 tie.[52] While there was no real chance, given the ballot lineup in 2018, of a wave election as far as the Senate was concerned, the GOP *gain* was also not in the cards, especially given the remarkable nationwide turnout surge. It worked out unexpectedly

---

[52] The defeat of Democratic incumbent Heidi Heitkamp in North Dakota—whose victory would, with the other projected results noted here, have made it 51D-49R—although not against the pre-race odds, was facilitated by one of the most left-handed voter suppression schemes yet witnessed. The state passed a strict Voter-ID law that required a street address on the ID; much of North Dakota's strongly Democratic-leaning Native American population (perennially undercounted and at 5.3% in 2018) resides in reservation communities with central mail delivery and no street addresses.

"Tough luck," said a Bush-appointed federal judge days before E2018, after SCOTUS had upheld the law itself (see https://www.npr.org/2018/11/02/663417341/judge-rules-native-americans-in-north-dakota-must-comply-with-voter-id-law). So, although Native groups scrambled, many would-be voters remained blocked in a key Senate race decided by 35K votes, with a red shift of 6% from pre-election polling. It was notable that, while turnout in solid R counties increased by only 23.5% over E2014, turnout in the state's two small solid D counties was up by 72.7%, which would at least hint at blue-wave dynamics not reflected in the official results.

well for Trump and for Senate Majority Leader McConnell. In fact, if we include the previously examined and highly dubious E2016 in our field of vision, this time with regard to the red-shift in key *Senate* races, we find strong reason to believe that it would not be Majority Leader but Minority Leader McConnell at the present time. Consider these key Senate contests from 2016:

2016 U.S. Senate Election Exit Poll/Votecount Comparison Compiled by Jonathan D. Simon www.CodeRed2020.com			
State (Exit Poll Sample Size and Margin of Error, including 1.45 multiplier for cluster and design effects)	Exit Poll Margin (+D/-R)	Vote Count Margin (+D/-R)	Red Shift (+ indicates shift favoring R)*
MO (1589, 3.6%)	7.5%	-3.2%	10.7%
PA (2535, 2.8%)	2.9%	-1.7%	4.6%
WI (2970, 2.6%)	3.9%	-3.4%	7.3%
NC (3904, 2.3%)	-0.5%	-5.8%	5.3%
Exit Poll Source: NEP, as screencaptured at initial public posting (CNN) Votecount Source: USElectionAtlas.org			
* A RED number in the "Red Shift" column indicates an exit poll-votecount shift with a 50% or greater likelihood of altering the outcome.			

As with the critical presidential battlegrounds in E2016, we find outcome-reversing red shifts in three of these tight Senate races (and a fourth that shifted from a virtual dead heat to a Republican win). Combining the projected results of E2018 with these projected results from E2016 yields a six-seat (53-to-47) Democratic majority and a quite different Senate from the one that recently voted down witnesses and documents in the impeachment trial of Donald Trump.

The Democrats did, of course, take the House in E2018, gaining a net of 40 seats to turn a 235-193 Republican advantage (there were seven vacant seats) into a 235-200 Democratic edge. Obviously, the shift in control of the lower chamber was of great immediate political import, as we have witnessed it play out—though not necessarily, as of this writing, to the Democrats' long-term advantage. But again the magnitude of the shift fell well short of the threshold for a wave election, which was set at a net shift of 48 House seats.[53]

The state legislative races told much the same story: the Democrats' net pickup of 370 seats fell far short of the 494-seat mark set for a wave election. Only in governorships did the Democratic gain just meet the wave standard of a seven-seat shift. Overall, key victories (e.g., Michigan, Wisconsin) were offset by key losses (e.g., Florida, Georgia). It is worth noting that every one of the E2016 battleground states needed by Trump for his Electoral College victory either remains under full GOP "trifecta" control (Ohio, Florida) or now has a Democratic governor facing off against a double-barreled GOP legislature (Michigan, Wisconsin, Pennsylvania, North Carolina), all of which have taken steps to weaken the powers of the executive.

Ultimately an election that was extraordinary, indeed singular, in turnout proved to be quite ordinary in payout. The forces and pre-election dynamics that drove an amazing 35 million new midterm voters to the polls wound up having little more impact than we would expect in a run-of-the-mill presidential-first-term midterm. Trump was as unpopular at this stage as any occupant of the White House since Herbert Hoover in 1930, a year into the Great Depression. The run-in to the election saw him barred from John McCain's state funeral; Brett Kavanaugh's confirmation rammed through after an FBI show-"investigation;" his UN ambassador resign; his tariff war in full swing; pipe bombs sent by one of his supporters to prominent Democrats, including Trump's presidential predecessor; a spate of mass shootings, culminating in the Pittsburgh "Tree of Life" hate-crime, after which he was pointedly asked to stay away from the memorial service by the city's mayor; and a rush of 5,200 troops to the southern border to deal with a "caravan" of footsore, unarmed, and outnumbered asylum-seeking refugees—hardly the kind of events and developments that foretell electoral success. And yet the Democrats lost three crucial Senate battles they were favored to win, while the GOP lost none in which they were favored, in spite of the conventional wisdom that, recognizing the GOP was closer to its turnout ceiling, told us a turnout tsunami would bring with it at least a Democratic wave.

---

[53] By way of comparison, in the wave election of 2010, the GOP picked up a net of 63 House seats. That gain was not associated with any unusual surge or drop in turnout (see chart on p. 196) and notably occurred *before* decennial redistricting and the implementation of the gerrymandering component of the GOP's "RedMap" strategy.

Third Eye Blind?

Could computerized election theft have played any role in the strange dynamics of E2018? One reason the answer to that question is "We don't know" is that the exit polls we have generally found to be of such value as a measure of voter intent were "tweaked" for E2018 in response to the perceived debacle of inaccuracy in 2016. Recall that the exit polls in E2016 *really* messed things up for their chief clients—the networks and the AP—by leading them to believe that Clinton would win in Florida, North Carolina, Pennsylvania, Michigan, and Wisconsin (and was in a virtual tie in Ohio), giving her not just the popular vote victory but an easy Electoral College win. In the historical computerized-vote-counting-era context of recurring red-shift exit poll-votecount disparities, this was seen as the last straw. The six-member National Election Pool consortium split up, with Fox and the AP breaking ties with Edison Research[54] and turning to a different data source and a different approach that actually didn't use in-field polling at all for 2018.[55]

Post-mortem analysis of the "failure" of the E2016 exit polls fastened on response bias and on the inclusion of too high a proportion of more highly educated respondents in Edison's samples. As explained in note 41 to the previous chapter, the overly high proportion of college graduates included in the *national* sample did *not* result in the kind of egregious red-shift "errors" that bedeviled the critical battleground states where Trump ran the table (see chart presented on page 156). But the accuracy of the exit poll—*except in places where the outcomes were essential to Trump's overall victory*—gave no pause at all to the herd that condemned the poll's methodology and dismissed it as garbage. And so, for those remaining in the shrinking Edison fold for 2018, the sampling methodology was "tweaked." Ostensibly that tweak addressed the way respondents were asked about their education level. But we know the purpose of the change was to lower the proportion of college-educated respondents, so that end was accomplished by *various* means, including simply setting new education-level targets and weighting the raw data accordingly.

The problem is that the education-level and other changes, made to bring the exit polls in line with the red-shifted votecounts in the battleground states of 2016, were applied to a methodology that had been nationally *accurate*, pushing it significantly to the right for E2018. No consideration was given to

---

[54] Edison Research, the successor to "Edison/Mitofsky" as the firm providing exit polling data to the National Election Pool (the media consortium consisting of ABC, CBS, CNN, Fox News, NBC, and the AP) in 2016. See www.edisonresearch.com.

[55] See https://www.politico.com/story/2018/11/01/exit-pollsters-2018-midterms-956511.

the likelihood that the left-skew presumably introduced by the oversampling of more educated voters was actually balancing such right-skew factors as stratifying the sample to the demographics of prior elections' right-adjusted, votecount-conforming exit polls—and that *that* was why the national exit poll in E2016 was accurate. So what was put forward as a *methodological corrective* was actually a *bottom-line conformance*—to votecounts that were *presumed* accurate. No one had questioned why the E2016 poll had exhibited such flaws in the states whose electoral votes Trump needed and *not* in the nation as a whole, and no one had questioned whether it was the *votecounts* in these states, and *not* the exit polls, that needed to be reviewed. At least no one in officialdom or among the polling brain trust.

Though a few red flags were thrown in E2018, the goal of conforming unadjusted exit polls to votecounts by methodological tweaking appears to have been accomplished reasonably well, furthering the trend of reducing their utility as a verification baseline. Forensic analysts felt a bit like a patient in the chair when an optometrist puts blurring lenses in front of her eyes and asks her to read the chart.

F E L O P Z D: Some Familiar-Looking Patterns
We did, however, get past the "E" and at least a few lines down that chart. Let's revisit, for example, the highly competitive U.S. Senate races presented in the table on p. 198, specifically the three in which the Democratic incumbents were favored but which were won by the GOP:

		Votecount Margin R+/D-	EP Margin	Red Shift	Poll Avg. 11/6	Red Shift	Poll Avg. 11/4	Red Shift
State	Candidates R/D *incumbent							
MO	Hawley/McCaskill*	5.8%	-2.4%	8.2%	-1.0%	6.8%	0.4%	5.4%
FL	Scott/Nelson*	0.1%	-1.3%	1.4%	-3.2%	3.3%	-2.1%	2.2%
IN	Braun/Donnelly*	5.9%	3.6%	2.3%	-3.7%	9.6%	-2.6%	8.5%

Key U.S. Senate Contests 2018
Showing Tracking-Poll Aggregate Progression and Exit Poll Comparisons

What this table presents, reading from left to right for each contest, is first the official margin of the Republican's victory followed by the first-post (ostensibly unadjusted) exit poll margin, the running aggregate polling average margin (source: polling aggregator FiveThirtyEight.com) as of early morning on

Election Day (11/6), and finally the running aggregate polling average margin two days before the election (11/4). In each case the Red Shift percentages express the disparity between official results and polling results.

The first thing to note is that every race is red shifted in every poll—that is, the votecounts are to the right of *all* polling results (yielding a positive red-shift percentage) for every race. We note further than the red shifts from the exit polls in Missouri and Florida are outcome-reversing. More subtly if we compare the 11/4 and 11/6 running averages of tracking polls, we see that the late movement in every race was *toward* the Democratic candidate, carrying into Election Day itself and leading to projected Democratic margins of 1.0, 3.2, and 3.7 percent respectively, only to be reversed by the official results.

We don't know what would account for such a pattern, but targeted voter suppression and votecount manipulation should both make the list of causes to be investigated. While the margins in Missouri and Indiana put both of those races safely beyond any mandatory or elective recount thresholds, the razor-thin margin in Florida brought the Senate race, along with the governor's race, squarely into recount range.

As I mentioned in note 142 to Chapter II, the governor's race, with a margin of 0.41 percent, was "recounted" by running the ballots back through the scanners that produced the initial count—obviously useless if the fraud or error is embedded in the code running in those computers. But much was made of the fact that the Senate race—even closer at 0.15 percent and within Florida's 0.25 percent "hand" recount mandate—was to be recounted by hand. That was certainly the impression given by the post-election headlines to anyone keeping score at home.[56] The reality, though, was that the only votes ever recounted by hand were "overvotes" and "undervotes"—ballots in which a "no vote" was entered for the Senate race by the scanners because the ballot had either no mark picked up by the optical device or multiple marks indicating a vote for more than one candidate. All told, these hand-recounted ballots constituted less than 1 percent of ballots cast and, since they were not selected at random, could not even serve as a statistical audit of the Senate race. The remaining 99+ percent of the ballots were, like those from the governor's race,

---

[56] See, e.g., https://apnews.com/797e56eb5f694a0787cbebfcf9370797 ("Florida starts painstaking hand recount in US Senate race") and https://www.cnn.com/2018/11/15/politics/palm-beach-county-recount-deadline-democrats-lawsuit/index.html, ("Florida's Senate race heads to hand recount").

simply run through the scanners again. Shades of Jill Stein's doomed efforts in 2016, these much-ballyhooed efforts were RINOs—recounts in name only.

But the House…

While lingering questions hung over these three critical Senate races, many pointed to the Democrats' capture of the House as clear evidence that E2018 was not rigged, and reasoned further that if it had not been rigged it was because it could not *be* rigged, that our elections are now secure. If they are indeed secure, however, then powerful *unseen* forces must be operating to make them so, because expert consensus remains strong that the vulnerabilities to both outsider and insider fraud have not been addressed and that, if anything, new fraud vectors have been added to the mix.[57]

I have taken pains at various junctures throughout this book and my other writings to point out that Democratic victories do not equate with secure election processes. Obviously, even with the means in hand to win every election, that would be a foolish strategy to pursue, as it would quickly tip off opponents and observers alike that the game was rigged. No one will play with a hustler who sinks every shot or wins every hand. Also obviously, reversing the outcomes of expected *routs* and *waves* is a good way to arouse suspicion and trigger investigation: the all-important reward/risk ratio plummets when such risk skyrockets. From a would-be rigger's standpoint, then, there are multiple factors at play—including access, scrutiny, win-value, and long-view strategic considerations—and it is not always possible to follow the rigger's algorithm to a clear "green/go" or "red/stop" signal. Nor is it possible to know what might be transpiring in the corner offices of RigCorp, where a bad actor might be active one year and sidelined or "on-leave" the next. An operative who made things happen for Bush might take a pass on Trump, or vice-versa.

But there's nonetheless a reflexive urge to say "There! You see, it's all good now!" When Democrats win—whether it's Obama in 2008 and 2012 (the rig-defying mechanisms for which are explained in previous chapters) or the House in 2018—the reflex takeaway for many is that it proves U.S. elections are safe and secure.

---

[57] Chief among these new fraud vectors are the barcode (or QR-code) ballot-marking devices (BMDs) being touted and purchased in many states and counties to replace aging equipment, primarily DREs. See Chapter II, pp. 22-23 and note 187 for more detail.

This is, in large part, because virtually every piece of damning forensic evidence collected over the 18 years of the post-HAVA, computerized vote-counting era points to distortions or manipulations favoring the more right-wing candidate or position.[58] If some champion of the Right is so good at rigging, goes the thinking, and if elections could still *be* rigged, why would they *ever*, in a competitive election, allow the Democrat or left-winger to win? E2018 may offer a strategic answer to that question.

The Oceanographers Get It Right

The GOP came into E2018 with a 235 to 193 advantage in the House (seven seats were vacant) and solid expectations of losing it. FiveThirtyEight.com analyzed polling data, fundraising, and historical voting trends district by district and arrived at a seven-in-eight (87.9 percent) chance that the Democrats would emerge with a House majority; they went further and forecast that Democrats would gain 39 seats, a remarkably accurate prediction.[59] Having examined in turn the data for all House races, the 60 or so in the "competitive" subgroup, and the 28 in the "highly competitive" (margin of victory less than 5 percent) subgroup, I found little that screamed interference. The overall "post-tweak"[60] exit poll/votecount red shift for all House elections in E2018 was a relatively modest, though not entirely insignificant, 1.6 percent. All margin-of-victory distributions were essentially normal: both Democratic and Republican candidates were victorious in close and very close contests; Democrats won virtually all contests in which they were favored and in fact picked off a few Republican-held seats where they were not. If any manipulation of House votecounts occurred, it would have had to have been subtle, not very effective (assuming the goal would have been to keep the House in Republican hands), and overwhelmed by the turnout tsunami. While the GOP's general vulnerability was no mystery to FiveThirtyEight.com, and presumably was therefore no mystery to GOP strategists and operatives, we were of course not privy to their assessments and calculations regarding their race-by-race prospects nor to their strategic thinking regarding the long-term advantages and disadvantages of surrendering control of the House.

The evidence we have points to only two possibilities: either any interference with House races in E2018 was miscalibrated in light of the turnout tsunami, or

---

[58] See https://harpers.org/archive/2012/11/how-to-rig-an-election/7/.

[59] See https://projects.fivethirtyeight.com/2018-midterm-election-forecast/house/.

[60] See explanation of methodological changes at pp. 201-2 above.

the races were left alone. To assess how badly miscalibrated a pre-set rig (likely the only species of rig feasible for a large number of geographically dispersed races[61]) would have had to be to end in such overall failure, we begin by noting that the Democrats wound up with a 235-200 House advantage, a 35-seat majority. We then examine the highly competitive contests and note that the Democrats won 18 of them by a margin of less than 5 percent. What this tells us is that a pre-set rig targeting these races and aimed at maintaining GOP control of the House would have failed in that aim with a marginal miscalibration no greater than 5 percent, which translates to 2.5 percent too few votes flipped. With a 2.5 percent stronger pre-set rig, *all* of these 18 contests would have been won by the Republican candidates, and the GOP would have retained control of the House by the slimmest of margins, 218-217 (any stronger pre-set rig would have expanded that margin accordingly). It also tells us that, if *no* rig was in fact attempted (i.e., the calibration was set at zero), then a relatively modest rig *would*, if well targeted, have kept the House in Republican hands.

The next question to ask is whether the turnout tsunami, with its addition of 35 million voters to the midterm electorate (making it the largest turnout, proportional to voter-age population, since 1966), could have been enough to throw off such a calibration to that extent. A large increase in turnout was of course anticipated. But the extraordinary increase not only exceeded expectations but had a strong directional component: in 2014, votes for House Republicans exceeded votes for House Democrats by 4.6 million; in 2018, the reversed margin was 9.8 million, for a 14.4 million vote swing. In at least 16 states, Democratic House votes in E2018 actually exceeded Democratic House votes in the previous *presidential* election, E2016; this was not true in *any* state for the Republicans. We have no way of knowing how much this bluish turnout wave caught GOP strategists on the hop, but it was certainly far out of the ordinary and of course we can recall here the newsfeed cited above: much of the bad news (for Trump and the GOP) occurring during the run-in to E2018 would have come too late on the calendar to permit widespread recalibration or redeployment of pre-set rigs.

We have no definitive way of determining whether U.S. House elections in E2018 were riddled with pre-set rigs that turned out to be undercalibrated in

---

[61] As noted in the discussion of different species of rig (pp. 116-19), real-time rigs require far more infrastructure and thus are better suited to a few statewide contests (e.g., U.S. Senate, presidential electors) than to dozens of races in widespread locations (e.g., U.S. House).

the face of the turnout tsunami, or whether these races were instead ignored. One can, however, posit quite a few reasons for leaving the House races alone. With the odds of a Democratic takeover so strong (upwards of 85 percent), a Republican hold would have struggled to pass the smell test; and it would have required interference with at least a couple dozen competitive contests spread over many states and voting systems at a time of heightened vigilance related to the on-going disclosure of Russian interference with E2016.

Even more salient, with the strategic focus logically on E2020 and the long game, it was far from clear that Democratic control of the House, and the concomitant pressure to move forward with impeachment, would serve the Democrats' ultimate goal of defeating Trump and the GOP in E2020. And indeed, as events have played out, ceding the Democrats the House in E2018 could be seen as a tactically wise and prescient thing to do. A Republican Senate would continue apace the transformation of the judiciary and would of course block any and all progressive or Trump-restraining legislation emerging from a Democratic House, naturally including election security measures.[62] The Senate, therefore, was a must-win, but how much value would be assigned to holding the House? For a rational actor, or a shrewd strategist bent on long-term control, the reward/risk ratio was hardly compelling, and may in fact have been viewed as not just low but *negative*. Surrendering the House would obviously be an essential precursor to the setting of an "impeachment trap"— if indeed such a trap was set, as some astute observers have come to believe.[63] There is little dispute, based on measures such as presidential approval and E2020 odds of victory, that, at least pre-COVID, it had worked out brilliantly along those lines. E2018 gave us a turnout tsunami but, as was detailed above, did not even qualify as a blue wave. And, for all the "power" it appeared to confer on the Democrats, and all the "drama" it appeared to usher in, the Act One curtain closed on an "emboldened" post-acquittal Trump and seemingly ever-increasing odds for his re-election.

My overarching point here is that, whatever other conclusions we may draw about it, E2018 definitely does *not* stand for the proposition that our elections have somehow magically been made secure. And it does not remotely suggest

---

[62] McConnell's Senate "graveyard" grew to an estimated 250 House-passed bills (90% of them with bipartisan support) by the end of 2019; see https://thehill.com/homenews/senate/475346-democratic-senators-tweet-photos-of-pile-of-house-passed-bills-dead-on-mitch.

[63] See, e.g., https://www.vice.com/en_us/article/zmpmwa/trump-is-setting-an-impeachment-trap-for-democrats.

that E2020 will be a fair election with honest and accurate vote counting. In fact, from an election security and transparency standpoint, we are, as will be seen, in a significantly *worse* position than we were heading into E2016.

Where We Stand

For election integrity advocates, the current reality presents a special challenge. On the one hand, the ranks of the concerned, the ranks of the alarmed, the ranks of the outraged, and the ranks of the committed have all swelled far beyond the small band of probers that first gathered and analyzed data and asked the first troubling questions in the wake of the 2004 election. Not only were there hundreds, even thousands, of individuals crunching numbers and asking questions 12 years later in 2016, there were also tens of millions of Sanders supporters, then Trump supporters, and finally Clinton (and, of course, Stein) supporters who, at various points and for various reasons, began to listen to and echo those questions—who were at least somewhere on the road to "getting it" about the need for a less concealed vote counting process.

They were even joined at times by a media that had previously been all but impervious to coverage of this elephant in the room (though it *remains* impervious to regarding numerical or statistical anomalies, no matter how egregious, as "evidence" of anything). Much of this shift is courtesy of "the Russians," their alleged attempts to "meddle" in E2016, and, if our intelligence services are to be believed, their intention to do so again in E2020. What we couldn't begin to imagine a right-wing true-believer, mercenary, or gamer— say a Karl Rove or Roger Stone or Jeffrey Dean or Mike Connell or Bob or Todd Urosevich—doing or wanting to do, we were perfectly capable of imagining Vladimir Putin doing or wanting to do to our electoral process. Whether this double standard derived from a Deep-State plan to finger the Russians and gin up Cold War 2.0, or simply from an American-Exceptionalist blind spot to home-grown chicanery, remains unclear. But there can be no question that, as RussiaGate grew longer and longer legs, making noise about *potential* (though of course not *actual*) election theft became more and more acceptable in mixed company.

On the other hand, though, prospects for a genuinely secure, public and observable vote counting system anytime soon remain slim to none. Fifteen years ago I first cautioned about a crippling Catch-22 that would one day confront those seeking meaningful electoral reform, stemming from the fact that any electoral reform that would presumably rescue the existing electoral and political systems would be dependent for its adoption on the realities and dynamics *of* those existing electoral and political systems.

Put bluntly: How is it possible to force reform upon a majority (even assuming there were full cooperation from the minority, which, of course, there is not) that had achieved that majority status via the *very system* we would be urging them to replace with something "fairer?" For a majority that has, by whatever means, managed to achieve what it perceives as virtual electoral immunity—exemplified by a 99 percent-plus reelection rate with an 8 percent approval rating—it would seem that no amount of public pressure within the bounds of ordinary politics would suffice to move the needle, let alone the mountain. Why, in other words, should Mitch McConnell and the GOP kill the computerized goose that has been laying their electoral golden eggs when building a wildlife preserve to *protect* that goose likely gives them their best, if not only, chance of holding onto power? Without a credible threat at the ballot box—which itself would depend on a secure, accurate, honest electoral process—how can serious reform of that very process stand a chance?

This is not an abstract dilemma. There has been no positive action whatsoever from Congress on the election integrity front in the 18 years since the Help America Vote Act brought us near-universal computerized counting in 2002.[64] Meanwhile, the Republican-majority Supreme Court has, with its twin *Citizens United*[65] and *McCutcheon*[66] decisions, opened the floodgates to unlimited dark

---

[64] The naïve might label as "positive action" by Congress the $380 million appropriated—as part of the $1.3 trillion 2018 omnibus spending bill—for election equipment upgrades and security. Aside from the woefully inadequate sum itself (a mere left-over tenth of the funds initially allocated by HAVA to computerize in 2002 and equivalent to about *one day* of spending in Iraq and Afghanistan, or one-sixtieth of Trump's Wall), the money comes with no actual security mandates or directions for use. Congress, in effect, made available to the states a left-over spool of thread so that they can sew some pleats into the cybercurtain behind which our votes are counted.

Another $250 million was OKd by Congress in 2019, again without any security-related strings (see https://www.nytimes.com/2019/09/25/us/mitch-mcconnell-election-security-bill-.html). Meanwhile Mitch McConnell cheerfully continues to block all legislation addressing security or transparency issues, including mail-in voting for a 2020 general election that is likely to be conducted in the midst of a pandemic. Congress instead seems bent on HAVA-redux—throwing another $4 billion in federal funds to the states (and vendors) with no security mandates. Where have all the flowers gone, long time passing?

[65] See http://www.scotusblog.com/case-files/cases/citizens-united-v-federal-election-commission/ for decision and analysis.

[66] See http://www.scotusblog.com/case-files/cases/mccutcheon-v-federal-election-commission/ for decision and analysis.

money (i.e., undisclosed campaign contributions) in our elections; in *Shelby County v. Holder*[67] gutted the key "pre-clearance" provision of the Voting Rights Act of 1965 that had been instrumental in holding back the new wave of voter suppression in the very states with a sordid history of Jim Crow disenfranchisement; and, for good measure—five to four, Gorsuch batting for Garland[68]—in 2019's long-anticipated *Rucho* decision,[69] greenlighted partisan gerrymandering no matter how ruthless its impact.

At the state level, the trend in virtually *all* the red (and some purple) states has been *backwards*: more efficient gerrymandering; more restrictions on voting (rationalized as the need to combat a phantom chimera of individual "voter fraud"); fewer neighborhood polling places (making voting problematic for those without vehicular ownership); diminished voting hours; longer voting lines; and less transparency (e.g., voter-marked ballots removed from public record status; digital ballot images destroyed a split second after creation). Thumb after thumb after thumb on the electoral scales. It is no wonder that the Harvard-based Electoral Integrity Project in 2016 ranked American elections *last* among those of all Western democracies.[70]

The post-E2016 political "coup" in swing-state North Carolina, with the GOP-led legislature stripping the newly elected Democratic governor of powers and effectively seizing control of the state's election administration,[71] served as fair warning about the greeting election integrity reformers might expect for their legislative initiatives. Researchers at the Electoral Integrity Project scored North Carolina 58/100 for its handling of the 2016 election,[72] in line

---

[67] See http://www.scotusblog.com/case-files/cases/shelby-county-v-holder/ for decision and analysis.

[68] The blocking of President Obama's nomination of centrist Merrick Garland to the Supreme Court—in fact, the denial of even a hearing on his nomination—was proclaimed by Senate Majority Leader McConnell to be one of the "proudest moments" in his Senate career (see https://www.washingtonpost.com/news/powerpost/wp/2016/08/16/the-forgotten-nominee-merrick-garlands-fate-rests-on-forces-beyond-his-control/?utm_term=.a3387c2b0ea0; see also https://www.snopes.com/mitch-mcconnell-one-of-my-proudest-moments/).

[69] *Rucho v. Common Cause*, 139 S. Ct. 2484 (2019).

[70] See https://www.electoralintegrityproject.com/eip-blogs/2017/1/7/its-even-worse-than-the-news-about-north-carolina-american-elections-rank-last-among-all-western-democracies.

[71] See https://www.washingtonpost.com/blogs/plum-line/wp/2016/12/16/the-gop-coup-in-north-carolina-previews-what-were-going-to-see-everywhere/?utm_term=.2d928d34dc7a.

[72] See https://www.electoralintegrityproject.com/eip-blogs/2016/12/22/was-there-fraud-in-us-elections.

with Florida, Cuba, Indonesia, and Sierra Leone. Meanwhile, the state's legislative redistricting plan—i.e., gerrymandering—scored 7/100, the worst not only in the United States, but in the world,[73] the Supreme Court's *Rucho* shrug notwithstanding.

The Odd Ray of Light?
Lest it be objected that I have my telescope focused here on the dark side of the Moon, I am obliged to point to a few bright spots detected over the past couple of years—a bit of pushback, as it were, in the midst of this rout. Courts in several states—including North Carolina, Wisconsin, and Pennsylvania—before being shown the error of their ways by our Supreme Court (see *Rucho* decision above), did find a few of the more egregious GOP-drawn gerrymanders to violate one or another standard (which, for lack of a more definitive bar, seem for the most part to come down to camouflaging the racial component and exercising overall good taste in disguising the quest to assure maximum partisan advantage).

Virginia moved in 2017 to scrap its paperless DREs and vote on hand-marked paper ballots. This action, taken by the state's Election Commission ahead of the high-profile gubernatorial election in November 2017, was spurred by both the national spike in concern over hacking vulnerabilities and, more specifically, the demonstrations, in the "Voting Machine Hacking Village" at the annual DefCon hackers' convention that July, of just how vulnerable that particular computerized voting equipment was. If nothing else, Virginia's action, fully accomplished in the August-to-October timeframe, illustrated just how quickly significant election reform and equipment replacement *can* come when sufficiently motivated. Notably, however, the action did not require approval by Virginia's then-Republican legislature—which, in 2014, had cut from the budget the funds requested by Democratic Governor Terry McAuliffe to upgrade the state's antiquated equipment.

E2018 ballot measures in Michigan and Florida proposed significant reforms and passed by wide margins. In Florida, the voters approved the restoration of voting rights to ex-felons who had fully served their time; and in Michigan, sweeping reform measures made it easier to register, vote, and prompt an audit of election results, as well as providing for the establishment of a nonpartisan Redistricting Commission.[74]

---

[73] See www.newsobserver.com/opinion/op-ed/article122593759.html.
[74] See https://www.mlive.com/news/2018/11/hold_michigan_proposal_3s_elec.html.

But the story, as we tour the country, is on the whole anything but encouraging. In Georgia, the Republicans tried to sell as "reform" their plan to "upgrade" from DREs to BMDs (ballot-marking devices) that turn votes into barcodes or QR codes read by opscans—replacing one level of computerization with another one and leaving the voting process as impervious to verification and vulnerable to manipulation as ever.

As in Georgia, so too in North Carolina, Pennsylvania, Texas, Tennessee, Kentucky, Michigan, Wisconsin, et al, where either the state itself or counties within it have opted for BMDs, generally over the fierce but futile objections of election integrity experts and advocates. The community of disabled voters has, as with HAVA, unfortunately once again been mobilized to demand the expansion of mandatory BMD use to *all* voters, on the specious theory that accommodating disabled voters with such devices, as originally intended, singles them out, somehow discriminates, and jeopardizes the secrecy of their ballots. These battles are on-going at present and—despite the valiant and tenacious efforts of such advocates as Jennifer Cohn, Marilyn Marks, Lynn Bernstein, and John Brakey—not going well. The arguments can get complicated and technical but the upshot is that ballots created by BMDs are effectively unauditable and unverifiable as to voter intent.[75] The barcode or QR code becomes the official vote of record and, created by computer, is readable only by another computer, as graphically illustrated in this example drawn from the work of Jennifer Cohn:[76]

Is This Joe Biden or Donald Trump?

Although not every Democratic official has been immune to the sales pitch and lobbying of the BMD vendors (primarily ES&S and Dominion), the GOP in state

[75] See https://voterga.files.wordpress.com/2019/01/expertslettertosafecommission_ga_bmds_010719.pdf.

[76] Links to Cohn's many valuable articles and investigations may be found at https://medium.com/@jennycohn1/jennifer-cohn-links-to-articles-podcasts-talks-and-interviews-8e7916bdfc77.

after state has fought tooth and nail to rush through their purchase, ignoring security-based objections and expert testimony. Although many have attributed this to the vendors' lobbying in pursuit of their business interests, the fierce determination on the part of GOP officials to have the BMDs in place for E2020 seems far out of proportion to the vendors' wheel-greasing. The determination instead seems to be to have manifestly insecure technology— BMD's with "Rig Me" Post-Its stuck to them—both creating and counting the votes in our next election.[77]

In Arizona, the Republican-led Senate launched a stealth attack on the state's bipartisan districting commission, aiming to wrest away its powers and reclaim them for the legislative majority. The Utah GOP-controlled legislature is gearing up to scotch that state's voter-approved districting commission. In Pennsylvania, the Republican-led state legislature went beyond merely filing an appeal to the U.S. Supreme Court, also threatening the Pennsylvania Supreme Court justices—who had the temerity to throw out one of the most contorted (and effective) gerrymandering plans in the nation—with *impeachment*.[78]

In Michigan, the state GOP promptly brought suit to prevent the establishment of the nonpartisan redistricting commission approved by voters, in the E2018 ballot measure cited above, by a two-to-one margin. Although a federal judge denied the Republicans seeking to retain their legislative control over gerrymandering a temporary stay,[79] the GOP has not withdrawn their suit and decision on the merits is pending. In Kentucky, the GOP legislature is attempting to put new limits on the power of the governor—now that Democrat Andy Beshear has been surprisingly elected to that office—and ram through a Photo-ID law, despite literally zero evidence of voter impersonation,

---

[77] A move to electronic poll books and registration databases has added a whole new level of electoral insecurity. The fraud vector here is electronic ballot box stuffing—the creation and counting of large numbers of fake ballots. That vector can be effectively exploited *only* where ballot creation is itself a computerized mass-production enterprise—i.e., where BMDs are is use. The simultaneous computerizations of the voter qualification *and* ballot creation processes dovetail so well, from the riggers' standpoint, that it is reasonable to question whether they are merely coincidental developments.

[78] See https://www.courthousenews.com/experts-balk-at-judicial-impeachment-moves-in-pennsylvania/.

[79] See https://www.bridgemi.com/michigan-government/judge-rejects-gop-bid-delay-michigan-redistricting-commission.

in time for November and Mitch McConnell's potentially competitive reelection bid.[80]

In Florida, the GOP-trifecta state government lost no time in ramming through a law that conditioned the re-enfranchisement of the approximately 1.4 million ex-felons—whose voting rights had just been restored by a two-to-one margin of Florida's E2018 electorate—on the payment of fines and restitution, thereby re-disenfranchising most of them pending payments that most could not afford. The pre-24th Amendment (1964) poll tax had nothing on this ingenious suppression scheme cooked up by the modern GOP.[81]

And so it goes: it would be hard to mistake this nation-spanning partisan fight-to-the-procedural-death for anything remotely high-minded. Which is why the deck is stacked mightily against anything bipartisan or serious finding its way out of Washington or all but a few statehouses—Colorado[82] and Virginia[83] being two exceptions that prove the rule—anytime soon.

Things as They Are

I have found no solid ground for optimism that either the legislative or the judicial process will step up with the urgency and bravery required to steer our electoral ship off the shoals where it is foundering in time for our critical upcoming election in 2020.

There is nothing in my observation and understanding of human nature, modern American politics, or the specific behavior of those now in control of the federal and key state governments that leads to any real hope of imminent legislative reform to a secure, accountable, and above all observable, vote counting process for America. [84] An encryption algorithm here, a machine audit

---

[80] See https://www.msn.com/en-us/news/politics/kentucky-house-committee-passes-voter-id-bill/ar-BB10cYlT.

[81] A three-judge federal panel very recently reached the same conclusion, blocking the legislation, pending SCOTUS appeal, and thus re-restoring the voting rights for now.

[82] See https://www.npr.org/2017/11/22/566039611/colorado-launches-first-in-the-nation-post-election-audits.

[83] See https://www.washingtonpost.com/local/virginia-politics/virginia-scraps-touch-screen-voting-machines-as-election-for-governor-looms/2017/09/08/e266ead6-94fe-11e7-89fa-bb822a46da5b_story.html?utm_term=.b64e40b25979.

[84] Some have attributed my depiction of this whole situation to "cynicism." Aside from the fact that it would be tough to be a card-carrying cynic and continue for 18-odd years quixotically to advocate for election integrity in America, there is a world of difference between cynicism and a realistic appraisal of the cynicism of others.

or bar-coded paper trail there: these *a la carte* tweaks, and accompanying lip-service, should not be confused with meaningful reform leading to an observable process that warrants public trust.

Our electoral process was *designed* to be concealed. That concealment is fortified with a host of ancillary provisions designed to impede and ultimately thwart efforts—like the 2016 and 2018 "recounts" or the post-election suit in GA-6—to un-conceal it. The office-holders (of either party) it has elected have no compelling incentive to change that—and the GOP has a compelling incentive *not* to.

They are very unlikely to be moved by ringing appeals to "fairness" or "democracy," by letters or petitions or protests. As for "lobbying"—or, we might say, *buying* a little electoral integrity—well the EI forces have yet to tap into quite the cash reserves of Big Oil, Big Pharma, or Big Finance.

Beyond that, what we have recently witnessed in the Senate trial of Donald Trump should disabuse us of any and all notions that America will be fine with the electoral process as it is now because we've pretty much always been fine. In explaining his sole Republican vote to convict, Utah Senator Mitt Romney memorably said from the Senate floor: *"Corrupting an election to keep oneself in office is perhaps the most abusive and destructive violation of one's oath of office that I can imagine."* In voting to acquit—and offering up a stewpot of excuses, obfuscations, and justifications for that violation—*every one* of the 52 other Republican senators (not to mention the 200 Republican House members who voted unanimously against Trump's impeachment) very publicly indicated they saw no fundamental problem with such actions, of one form or another, taken to "[corrupt] an election to keep oneself [or one's party] in office."

If that is the *public* stance of the latter-day, Trump-era GOP, one can only imagine what standard of permissibility these office-holders and their party strategists would apply to the corruption of our elections in *private*.

The question we should all be asking, as we approach an election that few see as anything but absolutely critical for the fate of our nation (at least), is what, if anything, we can do about the situation we are in. As I argue in proposing action steps in the next chapter, it is critical that we take stock of things as they are, not as we would wish them to be, so that we can begin to plan realistically, organize effectively, and do what needs to be done.

— VII —

THE WAY FORWARD

Those who make peaceful revolution impossible make violent revolution inevitable.

-- John F. Kennedy

I guess by now you've seen enough—more than enough, I hope—to be saying something like, "My God, this is serious. What can we, what can *I*, do about it?" The answer is *a lot*. Let's begin with what we are, and what we're not, asking for.

You'd have to search long and hard to find a subject more important and less sexy than election forensics. Dependent as it is on charts full of numbers, indirect measurements, statistics, probabilities, baselines, margins of error, and meta-analyses, even our best work has serious eye-glazing potential. And yet the reality is that only in the immediate forensic aftermath of shocking elections does election integrity seem to *come alive*, hit home, and become a focal interest to more than a handful of full-time advocates. The rest of the time, after the shockwaves and suspicious odors have dissipated, our vital subject customarily recedes into obscurity and seeming irrelevance. Separated from the drama of suspect and bizarre electoral outcomes and the transient outrage they may engender, vote counting again becomes a "process" issue, rather abstract, something to discuss politely—or, better yet, let other people discuss politely—but hardly a top-priority, urgent, storm-the-Bastille matter.

Nonetheless it is on that seemingly unspectacular process issue—the simple question of whether votes counted unobservably can ever be the trusted basis for the electoral translation process at the core of democracy—that I believe we must ultimately make our stand. If you took all the analyses in this book—every calculation of the red shift, every flipped vote, every suspect result, all evidence of fraud, and the whole big picture of political veer and incongruence—and tossed them in the trashcan, if you said it was all a conspiracy theorist's mirage, *what we'd still have sitting on the table in front of us is an unobservable vote counting process.* Without a public and observable count or audit, elections are fatally compromised as the legitimate foundation of democracy, *and this basic truth requires no forensics, direct or indirect, to establish.*

There is essentially no way of knowing what the collective intent of the public, as expressed in the votes cast in thousands of elections in the computerized voting era, really has been. Successfully rigged, unsuccessfully rigged, partially rigged, pristine; legitimate or illegitimate: *the count is unobservable so there is simply no way to know.* That is one hell of a stupid risk and *that is the real problem*, though it very unfortunately seems to come into focus only when specific outcomes are such that major-league fraud is suspected.

Indeed, there are some who long demanded a "re-vote" of E2016[1]—with good reason, perhaps, though no real hope. *But we neither expect, nor indeed seek, to remedy past fraud, to re-do elections, to unseat even the most suspiciously elected officeholders.* We can't go back to E2014, let alone E2010 or E2004; even actionable investigation into 2016's putrescent election has long exceeded its sell-by date and become academic, the Russians notwithstanding. There *is* no going back. That is all water under the bridge and, even if we suspect it is filthy and polluted water, there is nothing in the real world to be done about it.

The only remedy we seek is prospective—that we *begin*, in our communities and as a nation, to count our votes once again in public and not in the partisan, proprietary, pitch-dark of cyberspace. That is the very most—or, to put it another way for those fearful of upheaval or instability, the very "worst"—that can come of all our efforts to have the matter of vote counting in America taken seriously.

An observable count of votes will not immediately undo the anti-democratic damage that has been inflicted upon our electoral and political systems during the era of computerized voting. Districts will remain gerrymandered; voter suppression schemes will still be on the books; *Citizens United* will remain the law of the land and floods of corporate cash will not be readily diverted; the federal courts will stay stacked. The Age of Trump may have arrived by fraud

---

[1] See, e.g., https://twitter.com/mikefarb1?lang=en; see also
https://www.cnn.com/2017/09/18/politics/hillary-clinton-2016-trump/index.html.

but arrive it did and it's our working reality. It is a very, very deep hole America has dug. *But without observable vote counting, Americans will have not even a shovel with which to try to dig our nation out.*

With foreign-state threats looming; with a prominent constitutional scholar having asserted on the floor of the Senate that electoral interference by the president—or, by extension, any office-holder—is *not* abuse of power if it is commissioned in the belief that his own re-election is *in the public interest*;[2] with 11-year-olds able to hack into the voting equipment with ease, as demonstrated the past two years at the annual DefCon hackers' convention's Voting Village;[3] and with serious doubts already being raised about whether the apparent losers next November will accept defeat:[4] is it not time as a nation to think this through afresh and get beyond our feckless tinkering with one form or another of concealed, computerized vote counting?

Rights and Duties

The great task that confronts us is that of changing a process passively accepted as a *fait accompli* and currently possessing the vast weight of legal, bureaucratic, and habitual inertias.

This simple but fundamental change, to an observable counting system, will require a reawakening in the American citizenry of a compelling sense of both its collective rights in, and concomitant duties to, our democracy. For can we not agree that the majestic *right* to honest elections and an observable votecount carries with it the comparatively trivial *duty* once in each of our lifetimes to be a participant in that counting process? If we nevertheless insist on outsourcing that collective duty to others, indeed to a few unvetted corporations operating behind a proprietary curtain of secrecy, have we not thereby acquiesced in the compromise of the treasured right? If we place convenience, expediency, or our own ease and entertainment first, ahead of

---

[2] See
https://www.realclearpolitics.com/video/2020/01/29/dershowitz_not_impeachable_if_presid
ent_does_something_he_believes_will_help_him_get_elected_in_the_public_interest.html.
While many pushed back against Professor Alan Dershowitz's bizarre exculpatory
logic, which boiled down to greenlighting election rigging because all politicians
believe their own election or re-election to be in "the public interest," it is worth noting
that the entire GOP Senate majority, with the sole exception of Mitt Romney (R-UT),
voted in agreement that that very behavior was just peachy.

[3] See https://www.usatoday.com/story/tech/nation-now/2018/08/13/11-year-old-hacks-
replica-florida-election-site-changes-results/975121002/.

[4] See https://www.wbur.org/cognoscenti/2019/07/30/2020-partisan-divide-austin-sarat.

this basic duty to our democracy, can we really be judged to *deserve* that democracy as our right?

So three fundamental questions must be addressed in the name of election integrity:

1) Are the citizens of America willing to stand up for the right to an observable count as intrinsic to the right to vote?

2) Are the citizens of America willing to fight secret vote counting with the same energy that they would fight mass discrimination and disenfranchisement or pursue passionate policy goals such as gun control, environmental stewardship, economic justice, or peace?

3) Are the citizens of America willing to assume the modest burden of direct participation that an observable count or audit would impose on them?

Progress on each front will require powerful initiatives of education and outreach, encompassing all age-groups[5] and political creeds, employing all available media, including a major reliance on bottom-up social media to compensate for the sluggishness, stubborn indifference, and deliberate gatekeeping and stonewalling of established top-down media. And "opinion leaders" *outside* of politics—writers, athletes, students, entertainers with Facebook and Twitter audiences that guarantee that your thoughts and messages will be heard collectively by millions—*please take special note*: this is your era; your influence can be profound; you are indeed "followed."

Fortunately, the ground is fertile for this campaign: when voters were asked in a national poll taken in October 2012, "Would you be willing to work as a volunteer vote counter for 4 hours at some time during your lifetime as part of a national effort to make vote counting in our elections public and observable?" a solid majority of 57 percent responded "Yes" (to 23 percent

---

[5] Recent developments following the Parkland school shootings demonstrate the energy and determination of America's young. The Parkland students have led and inspired millions across America to insist upon change and a legislative response to their demands. These young voters and voters-to-be quickly came to recognize and articulate that electoral change would be essential to their ultimate success. They are but one small step away from embracing with equal fervor the necessity of protecting those elections upon which their hopes hang.

"No").[6] That represents at least 80 million Americans willing to put in the hours necessary to have a fully public, unpaid, vote-counting "labor force" for American elections.[7] In 2020, in an America where elections suddenly appear to "matter" more than they have in living memory, that number would likely be still higher.

It is now our job not only to impress this reality upon reflexively nay-saying election administrators and politicians, but to let the American people know what we may not yet know about ourselves: that we are ready and willing to work for and serve our democracy, that we are more genuinely patriotic than anyone would have guessed.

Mother of All Monkey Wrenches

I think this may be the moment to formally rub noses with the newborn but gargantuan elephant in the election integrity room known as COVID-19. I neither wrote nor revised this book with the potentially profound effects of the pandemic in mind. They are too new and still too uncertain to know what impact they will have on Election 2020—either the horse race or the modes of voting and counting—and beyond. Possibilities range from not much at all, to massively reduced turnout, to wide adoption of mail-in voting, to expansion of internet voting, to postponement or cancellation of the election, to an entirely legal scheme whereby GOP-led legislatures in states controlling 294 Electoral College votes (a majority) could bypass popular voting altogether and simply appoint electors pledged to vote for Donald Trump.[8] And that's all apart from

---

[6] Positive response was found among majorities of both Democratic and Republican voters, across all age groups, among both white and minority voters, and in all geographic regions. In response to a companion question, fully 60% of voters expressed either some or a great deal of "worry" that "insiders or hackers could change the results of important elections by manipulating the Electronic Vote Counting Systems that count the votes here in America," a majority again maintained across the political spectrum—and of course years prior to any thoughts of Russian meddling (poll conducted by Zogby Analytics 10/28 – 10/30/2012; Margin of Error +/- 3.4%; polling in advance of an election provides a better picture of public concern regarding election integrity than do post-election polls, in which doubts are expressed disproportionately by the losers).

[7] In a typical protocol that has been proposed, citizens would be vetted, as they are for jury duty, and would work in teams of three counters selected from pools representing each major party and minor party/independent voters, so both major parties and the growing remainder of the electorate would be represented in each counting team and at least three sets of eyes would be on every ballot counted or audited.

[8] See https://slate.com/news-and-politics/2020/03/trump-cancel-election-day-constitution-state-electors-coronavirus.html.

how the pandemic itself, how it is handled, and how that handling is spun might affect the horse race and the betting odds for races up and down the ballot.

There are too many variables and too many wildcards to know where we will be half a year from now as an electoral process, a political system, a nation, a world. But I think there are three things at least that we can count on. The first is that any reform that depends on humans sitting down together to count ballots and observe the count has gone in a stroke from a difficult sell to an "Are you nuts?!" The second is that, extrapolating conservatively from the behavior we have witnessed over the past few years, we cannot expect Trump, McConnell, and the GOP to miss a trick when it comes to exploiting the exigencies of this crisis to advance their political agenda and maintain their increasingly tenuous hold on power—and at least some of those tricks will directly involve the electoral process, how we vote and how we count votes. And finally, the third is that there *will* be post-COVID politics of one sort of another and, going forward, elections unencumbered by the dictates of social distancing—and that the battle for (and against) election integrity and transparency will pick up once again, though perhaps not quite where it left off.

So my intention now is to proceed as planned with what amounts to a pre- and post-COVID roadmap for reform—what we must ultimately do to make our elections worthy of our trust—and address the more immediate COVID-engendered imperatives, as they may impact our work on E2020, in a brief supplemental chapter. I invite you to read what follows here as subject to the temporary disruptions caused by a deadly virus, but enduring and evergreen in its relevance to the ultimate survival of our democracy.

WeCountNow!

At this point in pre-E2016 editions I proposed steps like counting or auditing mock elections as training for the real thing and to show it could be done.[9] We're past that now. We're in the Age of Trump, the Age of Lies, a fractured nation living on the edge, and the time is short. If we are going to allow a dictator or a plutocratic oligarchy to rule our country, we really don't have to *bother* with elections. But if we're *going* to bother with elections, we'd damned

---

[9] Having participated in a pilot for such an undertaking, I am happy to report that even the counting of mock ballots in what we all knew was a mock election brought out a real *esprit de corps* in every one of the two dozen or so counters. Two hours flew by and, although the election was "mock," the feeling of civic pride in the room was genuine and palpable.

well better restore their integrity before fatal damage is done, and done in our name. It could not be more clear: *a sea change is needed. Now.*[10]

So I have forged a "WeCountNow" campaign to recruit a public counting force for our elections, collaborating with established good-government and civil-liberties organizations and using our growing understanding of social media to spread the word far and wide and fast. The Dutch took a whiff of our 2016 election and then took one weekend to decide to count their 2017 national election by hand in public; the Norwegians not much longer. They joined a growing roster of democracies—including Germany, Ireland, Canada, and New Zealand—that have all recognized the high price paid for the speed and convenience of computerized elections and so ask humans to count all or most of the ballots in public.[11]

Some are quick to point out that these are all *parliamentary* democracies where national elections have short ballots, often just one or two offices. In the U.S., a November ballot can have *dozens* of offices and propositions, making the counting job far more onerous and time-consuming. This is of course true. But the U.S. is also a *federal* republic, where the power to determine national direction devolves upon the federal government, and increasingly upon the executive. While all elections are important in one way or another, our federal elections—for president, Senate, and House—are *critical*, perhaps now more than at any time in living memory (at least). They are certainly the highest-value targets for both foreign and domestic interference.

There are a maximum of *three* federal races on any ballot.[12] So if we non-riggable humans were to count just these two or three critical contests observably in public, it would not differ much from what they do in Norway, the Netherlands, Germany, New Zealand, et al. Yes, some results might come

---

[10] Whether "now" can be E2020 will depend on the course of the pandemic. Much now exists in a state of suspended animation. If assembly remains unwise or impossible by November, then "now" will have to mean "later" and "asap."

[11] With cyberspace the latest front on the geopolitical battlefield (see https://modernciso.com/2019/04/16/why-you-should-care-about-cyber-geopolitics/), it may be worth observing the uncanny resistance of each of these hand-count countries to the kind of far-right "populist" electoral veer experienced by computer-count countries such as Hungary, Brazil, and the United States.

[12] In presidential years, each ballot will have a choice for president and U.S. House, and in about two-thirds of the states a choice for Senate. In midterm elections, just subtract the presidency.

as late as the following *morning*; we might go to bed not knowing who our president would be on Inauguration Day 10 weeks hence.[13] The networks would certainly grumble. So we must ask a national question: *Is having our president (or possibly even Senate or House majorities) known half a day earlier—primarily for our viewing pleasure and to fit the profit-driven demands of the news cycle—worth the risk of stolen elections or even roiling uncertainty about that president's or government's legitimacy?*

Up till now, at least, the answer to that question in the United States has been "You betcha!" Any and all proposals for public, observable counting have been reflexively written off not only as a Luddite retreat (who needs humans to do anything when you have all these computers booted up and ready to go?) but also as impractical and unduly burdensome to administrators and citizenry alike. We have to work? We have to wait? Ugh, who wants that!

We have been, as a public, effectively hypnotized into assuming an Election Night role of passive spectator, and a blinded one at that. WeCountNow aims to turn spectators into participants and a passive public into an active one— one that embraces both the right and duty to secure our electoral process by counting the votes observably in public.

"But where are we ever going to dig up folks willing to stay late and count?" is the first question election administrators generally ask.

It is up to us as a public to *show* them where, to present state and county Election Boards with rosters full of signees, each testifying that he or she is volunteering for the job and prepared to be called upon as a counter on Election Night. "We are not demanding that our country do something for *us*," our WeCountNow campaign, echoing JFK, lets it be known to all. "We are demanding that we be permitted to do this for our country." The crucial first

---

[13] Even this problem could be alleviated by delegating a preliminary, unofficial count to the computers (scanning hand-marked paper ballots), a count the media could use in real-time with the proviso that it had no official weight. Indeed, the counts computers *currently* produce on Election Night also have no official weight—that weight does not come until days or weeks later with the official certification process.

Our new system would mandate that such certification be based on completed public, observable hand-counts of the federal contests. It could take a day, two days, a week— only where the computer counts were so wrong that *outcomes flipped* would the public even notice a hiccup. And, since public, observable counting would serve as a massive *deterrent* to such exploits, such instances would be extremely rare bordering on non-existent.

step is to bring visibly and dramatically to national attention that the *capacity* for public, observable counting does in fact exist and that a *sea change* in public attitude is underway. Our democracy, our votes, our count.

And yes, it is *doable*. One county does it now and has been doing it for 10 years. In Columbia County, New York, the Elections Board opens their opscans at the close of voting, bipartisanly returns the voter-marked ballots to the board, and the next day proceeds to count all the races, conducting in many cases (and especially upon request) a full 100 percent canvass as a check against the computers. The two Co-Commissioners of Elections who established the practice, Democrat Virginia Martin and Republican Jason Nastke, recognized the vulnerability of the computers to error and manipulation and resolved that they would not be signing their names to and certifying election results embodying that risk. They fine-tuned and streamlined their process over several election cycles. No bad actor, of course, would think of pulling a routinely discoverable stunt like off-setting the zero-counters. And Columbia County became a shining example of civic engagement. Perhaps some of the other 3,143 counties in our country will take notice, give now former Commissioner Martin[14] (who will be pleased to offer guidance) a call, and ask her how it's done. It is time to ask, ourselves and each other: "Why not?"

The website www.WeCountNow.org presents more detailed information, including draft informational flyers, sign-up sheets, and election administrator contact information. This is what a sign-up sheet, with its participation pledge, looks like:

---

[14] For reasons that remain mysterious, Martin was not reappointed to her commission at the beginning of 2020 (see https://imby.com/hillsdale/article/the-loss-of-virginia-martin-the-case-against-the-ex-commissioner-crumbles/ and https://imby.com/hudson/article/my-view-setting-the-record-straight/); nor was Nastke. Martin remains an advocate for election security in general and Columbia County's robust hand count in particular, and she welcomes inquiries; contact me (see Author Bio) and I will be happy to put you in touch.

Over and over—in person at events, on Twitter, and by readers of previous editions of this book—I am asked the same question: "I know we're in trouble. Please tell us, what can we do? What can we *do*?"

Millions of voters want to step up, to act. WeCountNow will give us all that opportunity.

One can imagine an Election Night as congregational and celebratory as New Year's Eve—Americans of all stripes at work together in our democracy's service.[15] This vision, this *revival* can be ours—our answer to the troubling tribalism of the Age of Trump, and our new reality for the New American Century. Why not, indeed?! It is, ultimately, up to us.

---

[15] Many different studies have shown that one of the best ways to bridge the divisions between factions or "tribes" is to engage members of both sides in cooperative work on a common task, especially one that benefits or symbolizes the whole. Voting, as much as it can separate us in the fury of a campaign, ultimately unites us as stakeholders in the democracy we sustain. And vote counting is the fundamental work of that sustenance—a most precious opportunity for rejoining and pulling together, once it again becomes safe to do so.

Linking Arms, Metaphorically and Physically

Looking forward then, our plan of action is first and foremost to raise consciousness about the critical importance of observable vote counting for the health, well-being, and ultimate survival of our democracy; about the public duties inherent in this process; and about its demonstrable practicality. We believe the American people are prepared for this revisiting of the meaning of participatory democracy and will respond with enthusiasm and determination to a well-framed, well-presented, and well-publicized call to action.

We need to understand though that scattered and inchoate demands for observable vote counting will not be enough. This is no "niche" issue. Its implications could not be broader or deeper—yet it has wandered the streets like an orphan in rags. One can only imagine where we would be today if just a few of those groups whose agendas and visions rest so heavily on the outcomes of American elections had devoted even a tithing of their energies to electoral integrity and reclaiming the vote counting process from behind the cyber-curtain.

Instead, here we are, our political discourse plunging lower than most of us would have ever thought possible and promising to descend lower still, our nation fractured and sinking in the quicksand of political disgust and mistrust, the short road to fascism and authoritarianism paved with our own hubris. Now, at this late hour, I call again upon *all* activists—all advocates for all the specific embodiments of peace, justice, fairness, humanity, ecological sanity, and democracy itself—to grasp the big picture and recognize that the strife of the New American Century, now manifest in the surreal Age of Trump, is not simply a scattered bunch of isolated skirmishes and battles. It is, sadly, a war.

The forces of control and domination understand this and are pursuing an integrated strategy to drive us off common ground and destroy democracy at its roots. Failure to comprehend that and respond accordingly will lead the defenders of democracy and advocates for its many blessings to a general and catastrophic defeat. The immediate threat may be Donald Trump's willingness to use any and all means to remain in office and expand his power. But the fundamental corruption of electoral process holds in store a nightmarish saga of which the Trump presidency is only one chapter. As my colleagues Victoria Collier and Ben Ptashnik—in calling for all advocates of progressive, ecological, human-rights, and pro-democracy causes to recognize the critical salience of honest elections and observable vote counting to the fate of their own individual agendas—wrote in 2014:

> We cannot continue struggling separately for myriad causes, while social progress is reversed piecemeal and democracy itself dismantled. Unless we organize *to preserve the ability of the people to shape public policy (i.e., to have their votes counted honestly and accurately)*, it is crystal clear that there will be no justice, no peace, no ecological sustainability, no amelioration of climate change and no end to poverty and economic oppression. Now is the time to link our formidable strengths as organizers and activists.[16]

It is a great mistake to believe that Donald Trump has done this work for us simply by provoking an impassioned opposition. Sure, there is a raging "resistance," and every day you can read dozens of erudite condemnations of this or that revolting policy or behavior and thousands of tweets and comments conveying varying degrees of revulsion.

What does it all add up to? Pending E2020, just about *nothing*.

I have made this point several times in earlier chapters, but it bears repeating now. Elections remain the official scorecard, and the *only* official scorecard, of American politics. When we ask what is fake and what is real, what is truth and what is lie; what is good for our country or the planet, what is very bad; who is the friend of the people and who is the enemy: the polls and our eyes and ears tell us that none of these questions have consensus answers, however strong our own feelings may be. We await the *election*, when the nation is permitted to exercise its collective right of review, when the official scorecard is filled out in ink, when democracy enjoys what should be its finest moment. Everything in the meantime—every disclosure, every argument, every momentary "touché!" triumph—waits upon that day of judgment. And never has it been more truly said that he who laughs last, laughs best.

And yet, if we fail to galvanize, we will, in that election, be sending our votes into the partisan, proprietary, pitch-dark of cyberspace—to face the tender mercies of those with the know-how and the access to make the 1s and 0s dance—with nothing more than our "thoughts and prayers" to protect them. In this climate why should *whoever* loses accept that outcome? Chaos beckons.

---

[16] See "A National Call to Link Arms for Democracy," *Truthout* (5/31/2014); http://www.truth-out.org/opinion/item/24033-a-national-call-to-link-arms-for-democracy.

Consider, then, the Parkland students, who had enough of thoughts and prayers. What began as a cry of anguish and a plea for remedial action soon morphed into an electoral exhortation. The students organized, marched, petitioned—what they were asking for was sane and reasonable, a basic protection, not to have to go to school in mortal fear, not to keep seeing happen to others their age, in the schools and in the streets, what had happened to their classmates and friends—but they quickly realized that there would be no action, no redress, nothing but thoughts and prayers and lip service, without a seismic change in the political lineup in Washington and in the states. So they began to talk about voting and look to our elections as the key to the realization of their goals. One group began a movement called "Parents Promise to Kids,"[17] centered on a contract consisting of a single sentence:

"I/We [parent name(s)] promise to [child name(s)] that I/We will vote for legislative leaders who support our children's safety over guns."

They established a Twitter presence and produced candidate ratings for E2018. Parkland student David Hogg, as of this writing, has a million Twitter followers (180,000 more than the NRA); his fellow student Emma Gonzalez has more than half again that many.

The students rolled up their sleeves, started speaking their minds and hearts, and truth and sense to power, used the gifts of the Information Age, and became a political force to be reckoned with virtually overnight. They, along with millions of others across America, will be old enough to cast a presidential vote for the first time this year. They will go to the polls—and they will urge their friends, families, followers to go to the polls—to make a difference, to bring a vital change to our country.

The Parkland students are smart and they are well educated. They certainly know about some of the obstacles in their path (aside from the personal mud flung at them by petrified right-wing critics): gerrymandering, Big $$, voter suppression, the legendary muscle of the NRA. They seem to believe these can all be overcome. But they, along with many advocates for other good and vital causes in our country, are less likely to take account of computerized election theft. One can imagine what an inexplicable (to them) electoral defeat would

---

[17] See https://www.parentspromisetokids.org/.

do to their zeal for participatory democracy, their sense that they have a voice. Will the young—momentarily inspired—then join the ranks of the other disillusioned and self-disenfranchised constituencies whose "low turnout" is said to be responsible for the political lay of the American land, why things are as they are? Such disillusionment defeats democracy as surely as do dictators rolling tanks.[18]

But what if the Parkland students and their host of followers went one step farther? They quickly recognized that *marching* wasn't enough, that it would take *voting*. What if they grasped that *voting* wasn't enough, that it would take ensuring the honest and accurate *counting* of those votes? And what if they took it even one step *farther* and said, "That's a job we can do!" and then produced *another* contract, also consisting of a single, simple sentence:

> "I [name of student/parent/teacher] promise that I will be available to serve as a volunteer counter or auditor of votes in one primary or general election in my county this year."

The "WeCountNow" concept. A great group of students to help bring it to life and show us all the way. How powerful would that be! How "Ask not what your country can do for you . . .!"

Perhaps it will come to pass, just so. But the rest of us should not be proud of waiting for the students to come to our rescue. Some 137,125,484 of us (officially) voted for president in 2016; millions more were frustrated in the attempt by various, often discriminatory, hurdles; and millions too have given up, either in political disillusionment or in the conviction that their votes have no impact or are outright not counted.

---

[18] As Adam Serwer recently wrote in *The Atlantic*:

> People may think of authoritarian nations in Cold War terms, as states with bombastic leaders who grant themselves extravagant titles and weigh their chests down with meaningless medals. These are nations without legislatures, without courts, with populations cowed by armies of secret police.

> This is not how many authoritarian nations work today. Most have elections, legislatures, courts; they possess all the trappings of democracy. In fact, most deny that they are authoritarian at all...

> Similarly, the typical image of an authoritarian nation involves violently suppressing dissent and assassinating or imprisoning political opponents and journalists. But violent suppression has tremendous risks and costs, and so authoritarians have developed more subtle methods... The frequent worries that *it can happen here* are arrogant in one respect: It already has happened here.

See https://www.theatlantic.com/ideas/archive/2020/02/trump-regime/606682/.

Like the Parkland students, we all have causes, we all have passions (especially now), and we all have a stake. One way or another, we will have to come together and work together in our demand for observable vote counting. And we will have to *focus* that demand and apply it like a welder's torch to the joints of the electoral system—from the local administrators who are responsible for many of the decisions impacting the conduct of our elections, to the state and federal governments that could provide comprehensive reform with the stroke of a pen.[19]

We will also have to be prepared to back up our demand for observable vote counting with civil action and, to the extent that all more cooperative tactics have been exhausted, with civil disobedience.

Why such a drastic call to action? Why not just start, or continue, writing letters to the editors and our representatives? Why not just keep gathering data, doing analyses, comparing exit polls and votecounts, making alarming statements about this or that aspect of this process that has long been a rock of national faith, quite likely the very first thing that comes into your mind when you think of the great achievements of America?

Because the system has proven itself terminally unresponsive. And because it has been designed, or re-designed, to withhold its best evidence, to tease us with exit polls and baselines, anomalies and upslopes, while keeping concealed the only data that could definitively answer the critical questions of whether the vote counting was honest and accurate, and who actually won each and every election.

And because the national crisis that is the Age of Trump has changed the game and drastically shortened what was already an urgent timeframe. Our concealed electoral process, like a maliciously programmed self-driving car, has carried America off-road to the edge of a cliff. We have, measured in political time, a split second to take the wheel and start steering again. The "gains" that have been made through the "inside game" of conventional

---

[19] In the short term—given the manifest vulnerability of E2020 and given that, in many if not most states, recounts are effectively unobtainable—an immediate push must be made for legislation opening the door (and removing the insurmountable hurdles, both financial and administrative) to recounts when reasonable questions arise regarding the computer counts in contests this November. See https://www.opednews.com/articles/US-Elections-Under-Attack-by-Allegra-Dengler-Elections-And-Campaigns_Elections_Candidates_Funding_Hackers-180426-397.html.

lobbying for change—some DREs ditched in one state, equipment "modernized" in some others, a dreadful bill blocked here, a slightly less dreadful one passed there, a paltry and grossly inadequate sum appropriated for upgrades with provision to vote on paper with computer-generated barcodes, and a few experiments with audits—fall so far short of what is needed that, with full respect for the efforts invested in this approach, it is like bringing a cup of water to put out a wildfire.

What is needed is the restoration of a public, observable vote counting process—achieved either through the manual counting of hand-marked paper ballots or, failing that, through a uniform, public, and statistically sufficient manual auditing process. Nothing less will serve to protect our electoral process from both foreign and domestic subversion. And nothing less will provide a basis for the restoration of public trust in the legitimacy of our electoral results.

With conventional approaches having shown their inadequacy to this purpose—the reform being far too little and far too slow, if not outright running in reverse—and with the voting process itself so likely compromised and the power of the vote itself thereby effectively negated, where can we as a public turn? What can we do if our WeCountNow offer to serve is waved off with yet more excuses and laments? Put very bluntly, what are our remaining weapons in this fight?

We're Not Buying
If you are a voter, the odds are that you are also a worker and/or a taxpayer, and you are almost certainly a consumer. Your power as a voter may be compromised by voter suppression schemes, gerrymandering, the Electoral College, and of course votecount manipulation. But your powers as a worker, taxpayer, and consumer remain very much intact. General strikes and tax revolts have served throughout both ancient and modern history as instruments for conveying the public will when the electoral process or democracy itself has broken down.[20] They are blunt instruments, certainly not to be taken up lightly, and they are risky in terms of the welfare of both the participants and those adversely affected by the interruption in commerce or services.

---

[20] Aristophanes, in *Lysistrata* (411 BC), conjures a general strike of sorts, in which the women of Greece band together to withhold sex from their men until they end the Peloponnesian War and make peace. The women of Greece, of course, were not voters.

I submit, however, that it is our power as *consumers* that holds the greatest promise and leverage. It has grown immense, while carrying by far the least risk of collateral damage. America, for better or worse, is the epitome of consumer capitalism—its economic engine runs on a fuel in which consumer demand is the most essential ingredient. Put simply, "[p]ersonal expenditure by U.S. consumers accounts for two-thirds of all spending in the United States and is the primary driver of economic growth."[21] And of course, by decree, "growth" is essential, so consumers must do their patriotic duty by finding more and more not-really-necessary products to buy. And corporations, like sharks, must swim (that is, grow) or die. The vast majority of corporations are exquisitely sensitive to even the most modest declines in revenue. A 2 percent drop is a sure bet to send a boardroom into panic mode.

If I were an American CEO with a religious bent, I think that I would kneel by my bed every night and pray that when I awoke American consumers would still be oblivious to the power they wielded over me and, through me, over their unresponsive elected representatives.[22] Imagine yet another Parkland contract, even simpler:

"We're not buying till kids stop dying."

That's right, nothing but what is truly needed, the essentials. No new flat screens, no iPhone XVIII (won't the XVII do?), no Netflix, no to that new SUV, no to jewelry, no to designer jeans, no to that Instapot upgrade, no to the latest "smart" appliance. Or at least a lot *less* of such stuff.

Of course the power to stop buying nonessentials depends on what portion of one's wealth and income goes to the purchase of *essentials*. Income and wealth inequalities in America are such that, for too many millions, virtually every purchase is an essential.[23] But everyone with disposable income knows what they need and what they don't, what they buy to keep up with the Joneses or because it's bright and shiny and feels good to buy. Everyone can

---

[21] See https://247wallst.com/special-report/2017/12/22/what-americans-spent-in-2017/.

[22] This frustration crosses the aisle. In a 2018 Rasmussen poll of Republican voters (Rasmussen's LVCM methodology is, ironically, more reliable when sampling this partisan subset), a mere 24% believed their own GOP representatives have done a good job representing their party's values; 62% said their representatives had lost touch (see http://www.rasmussenreports.com/public_content/politics/general_politics/april_2018/voters_think_both_parties_have_lost_touch).

[23] A situation all but guaranteed not to change absent a change in how we count votes.

reckon honestly with themselves whether there is something they can do without—and, collectively, we can do without quite literally trillions of dollars in bright and shining stuff every year.[24] That is one hell of a dent in the corporate bottom line.

This is a sleeping giant, an enormous power yet untapped. *The goal, of course, is not to bring down the American economy.*[25] Rather it is to compel legislative and administrative action in the face of a broken and corrupted electoral process—essentially an alternate way of speaking clearly when a corrupted counting process has garbled the speech of votes. We witnessed the force of economics in action when, to take one fairly recent example, North Carolina passed the execrable "bathroom bill" that illogically compelled genders to use the bathroom dictated by their birth certificates, regardless of their life choices, actual nature, and appearance. Businesses, institutions, and

---

[24] See https://www.bea.gov/iTable/iTable.cfm?ReqID=19&step=2#reqid=19&step=3&isuri=1&1921=underlying&1903=2017; total U.S. personal consumption expenditures for 2017 topped $53 trillion; televisions alone accounted for over $160 billion.

If these numbers seem absurdly high, it is because money *circulates*, so the same dollar will find itself in the hands of many consumers and subject to many individual spending choices in the course of a year—which is part of what lends consumer choice such staggering potential political force.

[25] I am all too aware of the irony of this section. A deadly pandemic has done in short order something akin to that which I advocate here as a last-ditch means to a vital end. But the virus, our overdue and so far still incomplete public-health response of social distancing, and the inevitable accompanying economic shutdown have struck blindly and bluntly and with a potency for which our nation, perhaps more than most, was unprepared.

In so doing it has exposed the fragility and vulnerability of the vast economic engine we have taken entirely for granted in the modern era. The loss, even "on paper," of so much investment value and wealth has and will continue to reverberate through our core economic, social and political structures, and we will be fortunate indeed if a market collapse does not usher in a general economic collapse as in the Great Depression. Politicians scramble; Donald Trump desperately floats a rapid "re-opening" of the economy that critics equate with calling upon Americans to "die for the Dow."

That is a book unto itself and the time for writing it will come. My observation here is just that concerted economic action—*voluntary* withholding of a portion of our participation as consumers—need not be the wrecking ball that is COVID-19 to have a persuasive impact upon our recalcitrant non-representatives. We have seen how sensitive late-stage consumer capitalism is—a little dab will do it, if, after what has befallen us, we have the stomach for it. The potency of economic action has, in an unanticipated and shockingly catastrophic way, been *affirmed*.

individuals reacted by pulling out of the state in various ways and, in short order, the politicians reconsidered and passed a new, less draconian bill.[26]

Take any state. Let's choose, for example, Wisconsin—following Trump confidant Roger Stone's remarkable assertion that multiple elections in the state have been electronically rigged.[27] What would a Parkland-style pledge look like in Wisconsin?

> "We the voters and consumers of Wisconsin pledge to refrain from purchasing all luxury items and other nonessential consumer goods until such time as the state government drafts and passes legislation restoring public, observable vote counting to all elections within the state's jurisdiction."

I can't speak for all, but I personally would find the passing up of the latest 67" plasma TV in service to such a vital cause to be relatively painless. It would most likely feel *good* to save some money *and* come to our democracy's rescue. On the other end, how long would it take before the *corporate* prelates and poobahs met with the *political* prelates and poobahs to implore them to draft and pass that legislation? I doubt they'd hold out for a month. So Wisconsin—and, by replication, the nation—could have hand-counted paper ballots (certainly a *federal* hand-count) and/or a solid audit process[28] in place in no time flat.

Invitation to an Opscan Party

Such economic actions are by nature *mass* actions, requiring broad participation—or buy-in, if you will—to be successful. There is also a more focal approach, specific to the conduct of the election itself, that may be undertaken to good effect on the local level and yet achieve national impact. It relates back to the design-for-concealment of the computerized voting system, the withholding of its best evidence. *That evidence is the voter-marked ballot.* With the slow turn away from DREs, the paper ballot is once again becoming increasingly prevalent, and may even soon be mandatory. Yet it remains, for

---

[26] See https://www.reuters.com/article/us-north-carolina-lgbt/seeking-end-to-boycott-north-carolina-rescinds-transgender-bathroom-law-idUSKBN1711V4.

[27] See http://thehill.com/blogs/pundits-blog/presidential-campaign/291534-can-the-2016-election-be-rigged-you-bet.

[28] See Chapter VIII, Study VII for my draft proposal for such an audit protocol.

all practical purposes, entirely concealed, imprisoned in the catch-bins of the opscans that count the lion's share of our votes throughout the land.[29]

When the Civil Rights movement sought a breakthrough in overcoming the deeply ingrained prejudices and practices of oppression, its leaders knew that letters and speeches, and even great marches, were not enough. The torch had to be applied to the joint—the school bus, the lunch counter, the college steps—the situs for the denial of rights. When the anti-nuclear movement sought to stop the proliferation of weapons and power plants, the situs was the missile silo and the power plant gate. When the earliest, Civil War-era suffragettes sought the vote for women, the situs was the voting booth, where they went to cast a vote and be arrested for having done so.[30]

The situs for an observable vote count is where the ballots *are*. On Election Night.

Secret vs. observable vote counting comes down to the question "Whose ballots are they? To whom do they belong?" I think the answer could not be clearer: those are *our* ballots; they should belong to the voters, the people, with the state as custodian. But, right now, not only don't they belong to us, we can't even *borrow* them, can't even *look* at them, let alone *count* them. They've been handed over, uncounted, to the state, which has outsourced them to a few private corporations, and all powers agree that that is the last

---

[29] Unfortunately, in many states and counties, that "paper ballot" is now being generated by a computer known as a Ballot Marking Device (BMD) with the voters' choices made electronically on touchscreens and represented on the ballot by barcodes or QR codes, which become the official votes of record. This movement to barcode BMDs (see pp. 22 - 23) has introduced a new layer of fraud-inviting opacity into the process by which we cast and count votes. Such ballots are impossible to hand count and, even when accompanied by a plain-English summary card that *should* mirror the barcodes or QR codes on the ballot, present major obstacles to verification of voter intent.

Like the BMD wars, the battle over digital ballot images—their creation and destruction—is being fought state by state. While these images could bring a measure of transparency and verifiability to elections, the resistance to their preservation among election administrators, especially in states and counties that have been host to some of the most suspect elections of the computerized voting era, has been formidable (see https://www.electiondefense.org/digital-ballot-images/).

The efforts of election integrity advocates Jennifer Cohn, Marilyn Marks, Lynn Bernstein, John Brakey and Chris Sautter in the BMD and ballot-images battles have been tenacious and heroic. Their *successes* have been sporadic at best.

[30] See Jill Lepore, "The Woman Card," *The New Yorker* (6/27/2016), p.23.

the voters will ever see of them.[31] They are off-limits, along with the hardware and software used to turn them into 1s and 0s and combine and process and transport those bits and bytes behind a proprietary cyber-curtain where none of us can see.

The Boston Tea Party, which took place in 1773, was an on-site protest against the "taxation without representation" to which the American colonists were subjected. It was instrumental in the process that gave birth to our nation—though it was essentially about money and involved the destruction of property, the 342 chests of tea dumped into Boston Harbor.

Now, nearly two and a half centuries of national history later, we find *ourselves* in the shoes of patriots aggrieved by a loss of sovereignty. We have written the letters, gathered the data, performed the analyses, offered the evidence, begged and pleaded and protested—to no avail. Elections remain outsourced, secret, suspect; our politics ever more poisonous. Can we act? Can we gather and link arms for an Opscan Party?

Our latter-day act of nation-saving disobedience, an Opscan Party involves neither money nor the destruction of property. It is a peaceful and amazingly simple reclamation and demonstration of the right to a public and observable counting of our votes. To participate, you would simply pull together a group of about a dozen voters from your precinct; remain there at the close of voting; form a circle around the optical scanner; link arms[32] and request that the scanner be opened, the ballots removed, a public and observable human count of at least one major contest initiated, the numbers compared with the tally from the opscan, and the ballots then returned to the precinct for storage. You would remain in a circle around the opscan until that request was honored or until you were removed. When asked what right you are asserting, you could answer, "The people's right to an observable vote count. Those are our ballots." You would record the proceedings for public posting and sharing. It would surely go viral.

---

[31] Needless to say, in the case of barcode BMDs, the voter *never* has meaningful custody of his or her own votes of record (unless, that is, someone teaches us humans to read barcodes and QR codes). While mail-in ballots (or the broader category of ballots voted on at home, which might be mailed in or dropped off) pose certain security challenges of their own, they at least, where permitted, afford the voter an opportunity to create a *hand-marked* paper ballot, which stands as a human-readable record of their intent.

[32] Looking ahead to the time when the health risks of such physical contact recede.

An Opscan Party is a powerful and appropriate action in a number of ways. It is neither labor- nor capital-intensive. It is quintessentially local yet would carry profound national impact. It is neither destructive nor dependent on force. It meets the problem exactly where the problem *is*, where and when our ballots are captured and taken away from us. And perhaps most important, it is unmistakably *just*, and can hardly be perceived or fairly portrayed as anything but.[33]

Imagine an Election Night with a hundred (or more) Opscan Parties organized across our nation. In some localities, where poll workers or administrators were cooperative, opscans would be opened and public counts undertaken. Perhaps disparities will be revealed, perhaps not; the breakthrough act of public counting is enough. In other places, the request would be denied and the "partiers" removed. Perhaps among them will be a few who are widely known, opinion leaders, celebrities: their removal would, by the handbook of modern media practice, *have* to be covered. And social media would spread the videos showing the encounters, whether cooperative or confrontational, at the place and at the time of greatest relevance and impact—*our* lunch counter, *our* school bus, *our* college gate.

Any of the above outcomes would be, in its own way, a game-changer. All have in common the recognition that the public is no longer on the outside trying in vain to look in through windows that have been painted black. This is not academic. This is not statistical. This is a very simple and direct question about a very precious kind of information. To whom does it belong? "Those are our ballots and we are here to assume the duty of counting them!"

For those made queasy by the prospect of "civil disobedience," confrontation, arrest, I can only point to the fact that freedom of assembly is a crucial right

---

[33] A crucial distinction must here be drawn between an Opscan Party, which is nonviolent and focuses on process, and the kind of violent and results-focused reaction that many now fear from Donald Trump's followers should he lose his bid for re-election. I understand both the wish that our elections continue to be greeted with calm acceptance and the fear that any other response, no matter how benign in intent and nonviolent in execution, will play directly into the hands of those, like Trump, who would exploit and augment any turmoil or disruption to justify the seizure of authoritarian powers in the "public interest."

The fact is that we have reached a point in the breakdown of societal and political norms at which such scenarios are likely in store *irrespective* of our efforts to assert the right to a public, observable count of votes. We must, in any event, not be cowed by such anxieties into passive and resigned acceptance of the very corrupted process that has brought us to this pass. That course will only hold worse in store for us.

with roots in the deepest strata of our political and cultural heritage, and ask that we do more than pay mere lip service to it as a useless relic. We are being told to be good little passive citizens, cast a vote (or not) then go home and sit back and enjoy the show. *We are better than that.* And we are stronger, if we only knew. If we want our democracy, if we are to deserve it, we have the right *and* the duty to do more.

I ask what has become of the courage that founded this country, that steered it through shoals of prejudice, inequity, and oppression to the America The Almost Beautiful into which most of us were born? Have we not the energies of our forebears—the Suffragettes, the Freedom Riders, Joe Hill, Rosa Parks, Dorothy Cotton, Medgar Evers, Martin Luther King Jr., Heather Heyer, the Standing Rock Water Protectors, the countless protesters against injustice? We would not be what and where we are as a people and a nation without their energies, their often-lonely bravery.

Can we bring a fraction of such energy and such bravery to bear on the test of *our* times, the reclamation of this most fundamental right of all, an honest election, the bedrock protocol of any democracy? Are we content instead to stand futilely by as the concealment of the vote counting process enables a distortion of the public will that results in a loss of public sovereignty and an all-too-visible breakdown of the political process? That loss of sovereignty and that breakdown lead ultimately either to destructive revolution or to torpid resignation—America The Ugly. There is just too much at stake to stand by.

Final Word
It all begins with communication. The most important single action you and I can take—it is my charge to all who have read this book—is to *communicate*: to write, or text, or email, or simply *talk* to others about this issue, about CODE RED, about what we are facing, about what we can do. Organization builds on communication. And meaningful action will spring from organization.[34]

My goal in writing this book has been to bring the issue of vote counting, and the perils it presents in the New American Century, into the public discourse. I hope also that reading CODE RED will help those who have been keeping to themselves their suspicions, concerns, or outrage about our faith-based, man-

---

[34] If the pandemic—for all its disruption and horror and all that it destroys—bequeaths us something of potentially great value, it is the greater opportunity for many of us to communicate, to take stock with each other, and converse about where we are and what we must do. Like it or not, millions of us have the time now—will we use it?

behind-the-curtain electoral system to recognize that they are neither crazy nor alone.

There are genuinely difficult problems facing us as a nation and as a species in the years to come: climate change, over-population, food and resource distribution, weapons control, the security-versus-privacy dilemma, and all manner of public-health and bio-ethical challenges, just to name a few. Difficult problems to solve and hard choices to make. Religious or secular, we have long approached our planet from a standpoint of dominion and are just now learning—with great reluctance and resistance from some quarters—to assume a ministerial rather than magisterial role on Earth.

Compared to these challenges, the basic counting of votes—in an observable way that ensures the legitimacy of our elections and vouchsafes the public an undistorted voice in the making of all these hard choices—is an easy assignment. We need only to break a spell that has been cast on us—a spell of convenience, passivity, helplessness. We need only remember that democracy is not something that we watch; it is something that we do.

— VIIa —

CODA: WHAT *NOW*?
E2020 UP CLOSE AND AT A DISTANCE

"So what can you do in a case like that, what can you do except sit on your hat...?"

— Burl Ives, *"The Whale"*

Voting and Counting in a Plague Year

The reality narrated and analyzed in this book is painful enough without the sudden entrance of a biblical plague to further darken its pages and pull the ground out from under its proffered solutions and calls to action. While the fundamental challenge of restoring public, observable vote counting to our elections will almost surely remain relevant post-COVID19 and whatever shapes and forms of devastation it may leave in its wake, the game for the year to come and for E2020 has changed significantly, and there is no point in ignoring or denying that.

Whatever one believes or ultimately finds out about the genesis of the pandemic; how it was handled; how, by whom, and for what purposes it may have been exploited, the upshot of immediate relevance here is that we cannot assume that E2020 will be conducted as other elections have been conducted. We're not yet sure what the new temporary (or permanent) normal will be, but we are obliged to prepare for an election impacted in various critical ways by the imperative of social distancing.

This in turn translates to a situation where coming together physically to count votes may well be a non-starter—discouraged or indeed forbidden. It also translates to a situation where the in-person casting of votes may be seen as hazardous for many voters—driving down turnout if alternate modes of casting their ballots are not made available to them.

With so much unknown and unpredictable, and with so much needing to be settled on months in advance, the contours of E2020 have already begun being reshaped—and, as might be expected, reshaped with a latent and sometimes blatant focus on partisan advantage. [35]

We have seen the election integrity battlefront shift rather dramatically and, from the standpoint of the kinds of reforms we were pursuing, unfavorably. I think it fair to say that if widespread hand-counting—and our best-laid plans to recruit volunteers to do that work—was gaining traction pre-corona, it is now, for the present anyway, effectively DOA. While I have been presented a proposal for counters using webcams such that they can observe each other and be observed (a key part of any hand-counting protocol) from a social distance, I see that as adding a whole new span to a bridge that already stretched fairly far.

Instead the newly recognized challenge we're facing is that of *casting* votes in a safe and convenient way. If COVID19 is still with us in November (and because these plans have to be laid months in advance, we can't afford to wait very long to find that out), at-poll voting—especially on the touchscreen ballot-marking devices (BMDs) we've seen proliferate of late—will be viewed as hazardous by many, driving down turnout, perhaps massively. Such an impact traditionally suits the GOP, though those most affected would likely be older voters, so the pragmatic calculations may be quite subtle and granular.

Mailing It In?
A universal no-excuse vote-by-mail (VBM) option was proposed in March by Senate Democrats, with mail-in ballots being guaranteed for every registered voter.[36] Senate Majority Leader Mitch McConnell (R-KY), running true to

---

[35] See Steven Rosenfeld, "New Voting Rights Battles Erupting In Key Swing States" (4/19/20), at https://www.nationalmemo.com/new-voting-rights-battles-erupting-in-key-swing-states.

[36] Senators Ron Wyden (D-OR) and Amy Klobuchar (D-MN) outlined the purposes and provisions of the legislation, known as the Natural Disaster and Emergency Ballot Act of 2020, in an op-ed appearing in *The Washington Post*: https://www.washingtonpost.com/opinions/2020/03/16/heres-how-guarantee-coronavirus-wont-disrupt-our-elections/. See also http://electionquality.com/ for an astute analysis.
It should be acknowledged that there are subtle but important differences among the various remote-voting options. Remote voting can be mandatory (e.g., Washington, Colorado) or optional (e.g., California); via mail or drop-off (the term "vote-at-home" [VAH] impounds both options); by voter request or automatic (every voter mailed a ballot). Significantly, among several other common-sense provisions, the Wyden-Klobuchar legislation would ban federal money from being used to expand *internet* voting.

form,[37] made sure the proposal was excluded from all of the massive relief bills passed through the end of March. It remains to be seen whether it can be shoehorned into a future bill, but I wouldn't count on it. So the VBM battle will most likely devolve to the states. Here is the current lay of the land with respect to VBM (as can be seen, a swath of red states lags far behind):

There is fierce debate among election integrity advocates whether VBM is, generally speaking, a good idea. Without getting too deep into that thicket, I will venture to say that, *in the context of the current crisis*, on the whole I think it is, and that seems to be the majority position.[38] It does open up a few additional fraud vectors, but the experience of Oregon, Washington, and more recently Utah and Colorado, all of which have universal VBM, has been forensically encouraging.[39] It should be noted as well that VBM is hardly a novelty or a boutique experiment: a *majority* of states currently provide no-excuse mail-in voting as an *option* for their voters. There will be, if sound security measures are not mandated and enforced, opportunities for ballot

---

[37] For an instructive contemporary profile of McConnell, see Jane Mayer, "How Mitch McConnell Became Trump's Enabler-In-Chief," *The New Yorker* (4/20/20) at https://www.newyorker.com/magazine/2020/04/20/how-mitch-mcconnell-became-trumps-enabler-in-chief.

[38] A large majority (72%) of Americans (79%D/65%R), as measured by a Reuters/Ipsos poll published 4/7/20, favor VBM if COVID is still a factor in November (see https://www.reuters.com/article/us-usa-election-poll-idUSKBN21P3G0). Many critics of VBM seem to have taken the Churchillian view that, given what we're up against, VBM is the worst possible solution—except for all the others.

[39] Only very rarely have complaints surfaced in the universal VBM states, and these states have consistently been among the cleanest in terms of forensic red flags and red shift. Of course vote buyers and sellers or coercers would not voluntarily make their activities public, but we'd expect to see at least a *tip* if there were an iceberg.

trashing[40] and ballot-box stuffing; so, *as with other aspects of the voting process*, much will depend on the specific design and execution of the security protocols.

That said, I very much doubt there is a security silver bullet here. Secure drop boxes would help a lot. So would what used to be called "certified, return receipt requested," but in this situation applicable to all mailed or box-dropped ballots and sent not by the USPS but by the local election administration. These would confirm receipt and "check-in" of each ballot, though it would be more difficult to account for the subsequent treatment and whereabouts of the ballot—for example, by numbering the ballot and receipt to allow the voter to check whether her ballot is in the counting pile immediately before and after the count is to be performed[41]—without making some concessions regarding ballot secrecy. But, as mail-in voting *already* compromises ballot secrecy (opening a door to vote-buying and coercion) to some degree and in certain circumstances, it appears that line has already been crossed nationwide with no sign yet of the sky having fallen.

The other good VBM news is that fraud on a scale necessary for national significance[42] would be difficult to commit and even more difficult to hide. A centralized national-grade operative/rigger is not likely to have a widely deployable stealth army of ground troops, and throwing out (or stuffing) enough ballots in enough places to do national damage, while remaining undetected, would be a mighty challenge, especially if there is heightened vigilance.

As noted above, McConnell and the GOP Senate are blocking all federal VBM provisions.[43] But, where states pass VBM or if Democrats somehow manage to

---

[40] Partisanship by zip code is well-established. If your zip is 80D/20R and either the carrier or some man-in-the-middle "loses" 1000 ballots sent from that zip, odds are overwhelming that that would achieve a roughly 600-vote net shift to R, without seeing or knowing the votes on any particular ballots.

[41] Bear in mind that the voter doesn't actually have to do this, just *be able* to do it, for it to have powerful fraud-deterrent impact.

[42] The more feasible targets for VBM fraud would likely be local races, even perhaps the odd U.S. House seat, as we saw in North Carolina's 9th CD in 2018. If such exploits were widespread or aimed at altering the national power balance, the risk of exposure, as in NC-9, would mount accordingly and become unacceptable to the putative rigger. Unfortunately, we do not have the luxury, under the present circumstances, of "count every vote as cast" idealism.

[43] Ever ready to blurt the truth, the president was happy to provide the reason. Referring to the Wyden-Klobuchar VBM proposal in the stimulus package, Trump said: "The

leverage it in at the federal level, the accompanying security protocols, perhaps enhanced by a few higher-tech ideas, will matter a great deal.[44]

Finishing Democracy Off?

Remember the climactic scene in Hitchcock's *North by Northwest* where Cary Grant is clinging to a Mount Rushmore cliff edge by his fingertips (and Eva Marie Saint is hanging from his ankle) crying for help and Martin Landau walks over and, smirking as only arch-villains can smirk, steps on Grant's fingers and grinds them into the rock? Reviewing that scene might be good preparation for what may happen next in the climactic scene for American democracy, hanging as it is by its fingertips from the cliff. There are three potentially catastrophic possibilities to worry about and be prepared to battle.

One is the indefinite postponement (or outright cancellation) of the election. We're seeing precedent for that in the primaries, and we suspect that Donald Trump would have little hesitation in exploiting even the thinnest pretext to postpone or cancel an election he was told he was likely to lose. It's an extraordinary move, but these are extraordinary times and we've seen quite a few such firsts being normalized.[45]

---

things they [the Democrats] had in there were crazy. They had levels of voting, that if you ever agreed to it *you'd never have a Republican elected in this country again*" (emphasis added; see https://www.rawstory.com/2020/03/watch-trump-admits-if-democrats-make-voting-easier-youd-never-have-a-republican-elected-in-this-country-again).

And Trump has already begun ramping up his campaign against VBM with false claims (which, following the playbook, he will keep repeating until, for many, they start to have the ring of truth) of rampant fraud enabled by the mail-in process (see https://www.nbcnews.com/politics/donald-trump/trump-pushes-false-claims-about-mail-vote-fraud-here-are-n1180566?cid=eml_nbn_20200410).

And a final tactic, if all else fails, will simply be letting the U.S. Postal Service run out of funds and shut down sometime between now and November. VBM, incredible as it may seem, faces a steep uphill battle.

[44] For a comprehensive VBM/VAH how-to guide, see http://voteathome.org/VAH-scale.

[45] Columnist Kurt Bardella, writing in *USA TODAY*, gives a bracing account of the collaborative norm-shattering (see "Oversight erased, Supreme Court hijacked: Trump turns the presidency into a dictatorship," at https://news.yahoo.com/oversight-erased-supreme-court-hijacked-071510076.html?soc_src=community&soc_trk=ma. Ominously, he closes:

> At this point, the only recourse we will have left to save our democracy, repair the institutions of government, and restore accountability to the American people, is to *vote in November* to save "the soul of this nation." That is, assuming Trump, the Republicans and the Supreme Court let us. (emphasis added)

Technically, constitutionally, Trump *must* leave office on the January date the new president would have been inaugurated—and, should there be no new president, the

But why cancel or put off an election when you can steal it? So option two is the plan, brought out in a recent *Slate* article,[46] by which Republican legislative majorities currently in control of 294 electoral votes (270 needed to win) would vote to simply appoint their states' electors for Trump, bypassing popular elections entirely. There are a few incidental complexities having to do with the obligation of electors to vote as directed, currently in SCOTUS litigation, but it's actually a pretty straightforward and entirely legal and constitutional theft. It's also a great way to start a civil war, but that may not necessarily be a deal-breaker for Trump and the GOP.

Third is a *deus ex machina* proposal for *online voting*. Thirty-one states already have internet voting for small select groups (overseas military, e.g.), so full-on internet voting (I.V.) could be sold as a mere scale-up expansion. *The seductive appeal is overwhelming:* vote easily, conveniently from the comfort of home, no health risks to voters or counters or poll workers!

I can't begin to do justice to how catastrophic this would be in the current circumstances. Why? Because the invitation to fraud is also overwhelming.

Experts are *unanimous*: internet voting cannot, at least with current or near-future technology, be made end-to-end secure. It will be—and it will make any election of which it is a significant part—impossible to audit, impossible to verify, and wide open to outcome-altering shifts in the counts. And at precisely the moment in our national trajectory at which, given the stakes and the ethics of the *dramatis personae*, we are maximally vulnerable to such! This is taking blind faith to a whole new level. *We might as well make our democracy take a bath with a plugged-in toaster.*

McConnell's blocking of the sensible VBM option may be, apart from any fine-grain calculations that VBM cuts against GOP interests, intended to create a solutions vacuum into which Online Voting can charge to save the day for Election 2020 (and beyond). It certainly seems that I.V. would make it easier for most Americans, and especially young Americans, to vote and thereby would both expand the franchise *and* skew the electorate Democratic. We also know that such franchise expansion, to say nothing of a younger electorate, is

---

Speaker of the House would assume the presidency. History, however, instructs us to be wary of relying on such assumptions during times of crisis, real or trumped up.

[46] See https://apple.news/AvnYfvCiESkOtyZapFEiPSw.

anathema to McConnell and the GOP. So, as should have been the case with HAVA long ago, the very first question to ask is *"What's in it for them?"*

Based on literally every behavioral observation and data point collected in the Age of Trump, we can rest assured that, when the GOP promotes or endorses any such proposals,[47] they are doing it for the most cynical and malicious reasons imaginable: they will have concluded that their enhanced capacity to rig the counts will neutralize the adverse (to their candidates) impact of the expanded (and younger) electorate *and then some*. That is, it will enable them to 'win' the 2020 election(s). So, thinking like a Republican, electoral integrity advocates (and Democrats) must be prepared to beat back the seductive "salvation" seemingly offered by online voting with everything they've got.

And, crucially and ironically, there's one *other* gambit for which those looking out for the integrity of E2020 must be prepared: *bogus* challenges to electoral defeat. Many of us have long worked to expose votecount inaccuracies that bear the marks of fraud, with virtually all of the evidence we've produced being dismissed or ignored. Now we are facing what, given the concealed design of our vote counting system, may be an even greater challenge: establishing that the voting process and votecounts behind the E2020 results are *accurate*, authentic and fraud-free, in the face of any such bogus challenges. Donald Trump famously would not commit in advance to accepting the results of E2016 if he lost,[48] and even as a *winner* has not left off levying absurd charges of massive "voter fraud" as the reason he failed to win the popular vote. It would be beyond naïve to assume that Trump, and his enablers and backers, would accept defeat in E2020, given *any* pretext, however absurd, that could be ginned up to challenge it—especially when we consider that post-election chaos itself would play straight into the hands of aspiring authoritarians.

Emily Levy, founder of the new organization Scrutineers, has addressed this concern and proposed prophylactic steps to be taken in the months

---

[47] Online voting has already been floated by both parties to "rescue" some of the remaining primaries (see https://www.salon.com/2020/03/24/will-congress-pass-a-rare-bipartisan-bill-to-allow-online-voting-in-light-of-coronavirus_partner/), and mission creep to November is in the cards. The HAVA history lesson tells us to expect the GOP to get behind online voting for November 2020 *when and only when* GOP strategists are reasonably confident they can author ("Hey Kush, go set this thing up, OK?") or control it. *"Plus ça change, plus c'est la même chose."*

[48] See https://www.alternet.org/election-2016/what-would-trump-do-how-we-respond-suspect-election for a hypothetical enactment of steps Trump would likely have taken had he found himself in Clinton's position.

remaining.[49] She emphasizes the importance of working *with* election administrators both to improve the verifiability of election processes and results and to help prepare them to respond to post-election challenges, whether bona fide or bogus. Our work has, in a sense, come full circle.

"The Future is a Serious Matter..."

There are way too many wild cards to chart just how this crucial year will play out.[50] The one thing I strongly suspect we can take to the bank, though, is that Trump, McConnell, and the latter-day GOP will be seeking to exploit for their political gain, and perhaps survival, *every* opportunity offered by the instability and flux now upon us—and no pretext will be too flimsy to serve as a basis for strategic offensives ranging from online voting to bogus electoral challenges to martial law.

In closing, it is my personal conviction that, if social distancing remains in force this November, we should nonetheless move heaven and earth to count *this election of all elections* observably in public.

If that means setting up webcams to allow opposing parties to observe each other's counters at work from a suitably safe distance, then that's what we should do. If it means taking two days to perform handcounts of the federal races, then that's what we should do. If it means taking six *weeks* to get the final results, having counted the votes observably in public, then that's what we should do.

Look at *all* we've done and will do for our health, for the health of our neighbors—look at all we've borne and how we've stepped up, changed, adapted. Now it's the health of our two-and-a-half-century-old *nation* that needs looking after. *What are two days, what are six weeks, to a nation and a democracy quite literally fighting for its life?*

I am under no illusions, however, that our nation as a whole will heed this call— a call to which it's been all but deaf for nearly 20 years—no illusions that its leaders, its media, its people will take such a bold stand.

---

[49] See https://www.scrutineerscommunity.org.

[50] For a retrospective (and one can only *hope* fictional) *guess*, see George Saunders's brilliant and chilling story "Love Letter" at https://www.newyorker.com/magazine/2020/04/06/love-letter. Rarely has a writer put a finger more squarely on the trouble of his time, or issued a more pointed warning.

So our work will go on. Should we somehow survive this year's maelstrom with our democratic faculties intact, and *whenever* the next opportunity for a good old-fashioned *normal* election arises, the need for public, observable vote counting will remain as urgent as ever, along with the viability of such initiatives as WeCountNow. You will find that *CODE RED* keeps well in the fridge and will retain its potency and pungency for however long it takes to put it to use.

— VIII —

EVIDENCE AND ANALYSIS[1]

"The devil is in the details."

— Anonymous

STUDY I.

The 2004 Presidential Election: Who Won the Popular Vote?

An Examination of the Comparative Validity of Exit Poll and Vote Count Data

January 2, 2005

Jonathan D. Simon, J.D.

Ron P. Baiman, Ph.D.
Institute of Government and Public Affairs
University of Illinois at Chicago

Published by the Free Press (http://freepress.org)

The views expressed are the authors' own and are not necessarily representative of the views of their respective institutions. Comments or questions directed to the authors are welcome.

---

[1] The studies in this chapter are presented as initially published. Certain references and links available at the time of publication may no longer be accessible.

Executive Summary

> There is a substantial disparity—well outside the margin of error and outcome-determinative—between the national exit poll and the popular votecount.

> The possible causes of the disparity would be random error, a skewed exit poll, or breakdown in the fairness of the voting process and accuracy of the votecount.

> Analysis shows that the disparity cannot reasonably be accounted for by chance or random error.

> Evidence does not support hypotheses that the disparity was produced by problems with the exit poll.

> Widespread breakdown in the fairness of the voting process and accuracy of the votecount are the most likely explanations for the disparity.

> In an accurate count of a free and fair election, the strong likelihood is that Kerry would have been the winner of the popular vote.

The Significance of a Popular Vote Victory

Although it is the Electoral College and not the popular vote that legally elects the president, winning the popular vote does have considerable psychological and practical significance. It is fair to say, to take a recent example, that had Al Gore not enjoyed a popular vote margin in 2000, he would not have had standing in the court of public opinion to maintain his post-election challenge for more than a month up until its ultimate foreclosure by the Supreme Court.

In the 2004 election now under scrutiny, the popular vote again has played a critical role. George Bush's apparent margin of 3.3 million votes clearly influenced the timing of John Kerry's concession. Although the election was once again close enough that yet-to-be-counted votes offered at least the mathematical possibility of a Kerry electoral college victory—and although, once again, concerns about vote counting were beginning to emerge from early post-election reports and analyses—Kerry apparently believed that, unlike popular vote-winner Gore, he did not have effective standing to prolong the race.

As ongoing inquiries continue to raise serious vote counting issues, Bush's apparent popular vote margin has loomed large as a rationale for minimizing these issues, at least as far as their impact on the outcome of the race. While much concern has been expressed about "counting every vote," even the Kerry camp has issued disclaimers to the effect that their candidate does not expect that so doing will alter the outcome.

With the results in Ohio currently subject to both recount proceedings and legal contest, dramatic developments compelling a reversal of the Ohio result cannot be ruled out at this time. Yet to overturn the Ohio result, giving Kerry an electoral college victory (or even to disqualify the Ohio electors via challenge in Congress, which would deprive Bush of an electoral college majority and throw the election to the House of Representatives), would likely be regarded as unjust and insupportable by a populace convinced that Bush was, by some 3.3 million votes, the people's choice.

Thus, although the popular vote does not legally determine the presidency, its significance is such that we must give due consideration to any evidence that puts the popular vote count itself at issue.

Sources of the Exit Poll and Votecount Numbers
As the analysis we undertake below is based upon the conflict between two sets of numbers, one generated by the exit polls for the presidential race and the other generated by the vote counting equipment, it is necessary to review the nature of the two sources of results. Exit polling, since its invention several decades ago, has performed reliably in the projection of thousands of races, both here at home and, more recently, abroad.[2] The record of exit polling from the 1970s through the 1990s was essentially free of controversy, except for the complaint that publication of exit poll results prior to poll closings dampened voter turnout by discouraging late-in-day voters from bothering to vote, the race having already been "called."[3] Voters could be so influenced because they had come, indeed, to regard exit poll projections as all but infallible. Significant exit polling problems began to appear along with the development and spread of computerized vote counting equipment, since which time exit polls have had a notably poorer track record in spite of improvements in polling methodology.

Compared to standard pre-election polling, exit polling has certain advantages and disadvantages. On the plus side, exit polls sample actual rather than just "likely" voters and do not fail to include voters who are not attached to a

---

[2] See *Polling and Presidential Election Coverage*, Lavrakas, Paul J, and Holley, Jack K., eds., Newbury Park, CA: Sage; pp. 83-99.

[3] This problem was theoretically resolved by a gentlemen's agreement to withhold release of exit poll calls until the polls had closed.

conventional phone line or who screen their calls.[4] This results in significantly greater accuracy. On the minus side, exit polls employ a cluster sampling technique, grouping respondents by precinct, rather than a fully homogenized random sample of the target venue. This results in somewhat less accuracy. On the whole, the advantages in accuracy an exit poll enjoys over a pre-election poll of the same sample size tend to outweigh the disadvantages.

The exit polling in Election 2004 was performed by the combined firms of Mitofsky International and Edison Media Research, under exclusive contract as "official provider" of exit poll data to six major media organizations (CBS, NBC, ABC, CNN, Fox News Channel, and the Associated Press), which collectively formed the National Election Pool.[5] Exit polling operations were under the principal direction of Warren Mitofsky, credited as the inventor of exit polling and recognized throughout the world as the leading expert in the field. With over 35 years of exit polling experience, encompassing nearly 3,000 electoral contests in the United States and abroad, Mitofsky has achieved consistent success in the field and has continued throughout his career to refine and improve the methodologies and protocols of exit polling.[6] In 1999 Mitofsky received the Award for Lifetime Achievement from the American Association for Public Opinion Research.

Election 2004 presented a particular challenge and opportunity for Mr. Mitofsky, whose exit polling operation was hampered in 2002 by a massive computer breakdown.[7] It has been reported that preparations for Election 2004 were especially thorough, entailing increased staff numbers and training, upgraded computer hardware and software, expanded surveys of absentee and early voters, and dry runs beginning in July to prepare analysts for the full spectrum of possible election night scenarios.[8] It may fairly be said that the exit

---

[4] Because only actual voters are included, these might more accurately be referred to as "exit samples" rather than "exit polls."

[5] As described in the National Election Pool Edison Media Research/Mitofsky International homepage: www.exit-poll.net/index.html.

[6] Exit polling has been relied upon as a check mechanism for the vote counting processes in numerous foreign elections. Indeed, Mitofsky himself received public commendation from Mexican President Carlos Salinas for his contribution to the credibility of that nation's 1994 election. Most recently, exit polling has been instrumental in the overturning of election results and the ordering of a new election in the Ukraine.

[7] As a result, exit polls were not employed in the projection of election outcomes in 2002.

[8] Newark *Star-Ledger*, 10/28/2004, page 1, "Networks Will Look to Somerville on Tuesday." See also, Bauder, D., "TV Networks to Test New Exit Polling System," The

polling for Election 2004 was a more advanced, sophisticated, and meticulous operation than any previously undertaken.

In contrast to the uniform methodology of the exit polls, a variety of methods are employed to record votes on election day, including optical scan devices, direct electronic recording (DREs or "touchscreens"), punch cards, paper ballots, lever machines, and data-point devices, in that order of prevalence. An additional variety of methods are then employed to transmit these votes to central locations and tally them at the county and state levels. Ownership and operation of this mosaic of machinery is fully privatized and is concentrated predominantly in the hands of four corporations: Diebold, ES&S, Sequoia, and Hart Intercivic. The partisan proclivities and activities of each of these corporations are a matter of public record.[9]

Because of the proprietary nature of the election system throughout the United States, these vendors of the voting equipment design, program, operate, maintain, and repair it at every level, most often without outside or public scrutiny, and with at best a minimal process of testing and certification.[10] Boards of Election and state level authorities over election protocols have often accepted financial support from the equipment vendors[11] and have also been seen at times to act under the influence of partisanship, appearing to elevate outcomes over fairness of process.[12] Such systemic conflicts of interest do little to enhance the integrity or credibility of the vote counting system.

Associated Press, Oct. 13, 2004, reprinted at
http://aolsvc.news.aol.com/elections/article.adp?/id=20041013122209990005&_ccc=6&cid=946. The specific methodologies and protocols employed are detailed on the websites for Mitofsky International (www.mitofskyinternational.com), Edison Media Research (www.edisonresearch.com), and the National Election Pool (www.exit-poll.net).

[9] See, e.g., Smyth, J., *Cleveland Plain Dealer*, August 28, 2003, reprinted at: http://www.commondreams.org/headlines03/0828-08.htm; see also http://blogs.salon.com/0002255/.

[10] See Zeller, T., "Ready or Not, Electronic Voting Goes National," *The New York Times*, Sept. 19, 2004 (reprinted at http://aolsvc.news.aol.com/elections/article.adp?id=20040918145609990001&cid=842).

[11] See "On the Voting Machine Makers' Tab," *The New York Times*, Sept. 12, 2004, Editorial Page.

[12] See, e.g., Welsh-Huggins, A. "The Next Katherine Harris?" Associated Press Report Oct. 27, 2004, reprinted at http://aolsvc.news.aol.com/news/article.adp?id=20041027161309990012 (detailing actions taken by Ohio Secretary of State J. Kenneth Blackwell).

Computer experts have documented the susceptibility of both the recording and tabulating equipment to undetected errors, hacking, and deliberate fraud.[13] A substantial component of the system (DREs, which are responsible for recording approximately 30% of the vote) generates no paper record and is effectively immune to meaningful recount. Central tabulators responsible for compiling over 50% of the vote employ an operating system that has been demonstrated to be vulnerable to entry and manipulation through a standard laptop PC.[14] In spite of these vulnerabilities of the counting system, few if any questions about the accuracy of the numbers it produced were raised on election night.[15]

Election Night 2004: The Exit Poll/Votecount Differential

On Election Night 2004, the exit polls and the vote counting equipment generated results that differed significantly. In the early morning of November 3, 2004, a CNN.com website screenshot entitled "U.S. PRESIDENT/NATIONAL/EXIT POLL" posted national exit poll results updated to 12:23 A.M., broken down by gender as well as a variety of other categories.[16] The time of the update indicates that these results comprised substantially the full set of respondents polled on Election Day, but were free

---

[13] See, e.g., Rubin, A., "An Insider's View of Vote Vulnerability," *Baltimore Sun,* March 10, 2004 (reprinted at www.commondreams.org/views04/0310-02.htm); Levy, S., "Black Box Voting Blues," *Newsweek,* Nov. 3, 2004 (reprinted at http://msnbc.msn.com/id/3339650/)

[14] The GEMS system, employed by Diebold in central tabulators serving about half the venues, is particularly susceptible to entry and manipulation (hacking or preprogramming) as was dramatically demonstrated on national television (CNBC: "Topic A with Tina Brown") when critic Bev Harris led Howard Dean through the necessary steps in less than two minutes (see Hartmann, T., "Evidence Mounts That the Vote May Have Been Hacked," at http://www.commondreams.org/headlines04/1106-30.htm).

[15] Such unquestioning acceptance may be portrayed in a positive light. As Warren Mitofsky himself has said: "In a democracy, it's the orderly transfer of power that keeps the democracy accepting the results of elections. If it drags on too long, there's always a suspicion of fraud." The perils of unquestioning acceptance of what may, given the vulnerabilities of our vote counting system, be falsified results should, however, be self-evident.

[16] The time-stamped screenshot was printed out by Simon at 1:29 A.M. on Nov. 3, 2004, and is attached for reference as Appendix A. The posting time of 1:25 A.M. may be seen faintly on the top banner. The data derived from the CNN screenshots printed by Simon for the individual states may also be referenced at http://www.scoop.co.nz/mason/stories/HL0411/S00142.htm.

from the effects of a subsequent input of tabulated data used to bring about ultimate congruence between the exit poll and votecount results.[17]

The CNN posting indicates the number of respondents (13,047), the gender breakdown of the sample (male 46%, female 54%), and the candidate preferences by gender (males: 52% Bush, 47% Kerry; females: 45% Bush, 54% Kerry). For the national exit poll taken as a whole, therefore, the result was 48.2% Bush, 50.8% Kerry.[18] The vote counting equipment produced a markedly different result: 50.9% Bush, 48.1% Kerry.[19] The differential between the two counts, which were virtually mirror images of each other, was 5.4% overall (see Chart 1).

Chart 1: Exit Poll vs. Popular Vote Comparison (National)

	Bush %	Kerry %	Bush Margin%
National Exit	48.2%	50.8%	-2.6%
Popular Vote Count	50.9%	48.1%	2.8%
Difference	2.7%	-2.7%	5.4%

The reaction of Election Night analysts interpreting this differential was immediately to query what had "gone wrong" with the exit polls. This was a curious approach both in light of standard accounting practice, which compels independent examination of *both* sets of numbers that are found to be in conflict, and in light of much-voiced pre-election concerns about the accuracy and security of the computerized vote counting systems. We offer an alternate

---

[17] This practice is referenced in "Methods Statement: National Election Pool Exit Polls Nov. 2, 2004," at http://www.exit-poll.net.

[18] The totals for the full sample are computed by combining the candidate preferences of male and female respondents: Bush = [(males)46% x 52%] + [(females)54% x 45%] = 48.2%; Kerry = [(males)46% x 47%] + [(females)54% x 54%] = 50.8%.
Alternatively, if Kerry's exit poll share is minimized by assuming maximum female and minimal male shares subject to rounding (to zero decimals), whole integer numbers of voters, minimal Nader votes, and minimal gender vote shares subject to rounding, Kerry would get at least 50.22% of the vote. The reported actual Kerry vote of 48.1% is still far outside of the 95% confidence interval of + 1.1% and has just a one in 10,256 chance of occurrence (see analogous calculations for a Kerry exit poll result of 50.8% in text). Full-sample totals can also be checked by cross-multiplying any crosstab.

[19] Approximately 1% of the total vote went to minor candidates. Therefore, a vote percentage of 49.54% rather than 50.0% constitutes a winning margin for either Bush or Kerry. It is important to bear this in mind in reading the analysis below.

approach to the conflicting data, based on fundamental statistical and accounting principles.

Statistical Analysis of Exit Poll Results

Steven F. Freeman of the University of Pennsylvania has analyzed Election 2004 exit poll results for battleground states,[20] and has drawn certain conclusions regarding the significant disparities between exit poll results and votecounts for several critical states. In particular, the odds against the disparities in Ohio, Florida, and Pennsylvania occurring together are computed at 662,000-to-one, or a virtual statistical impossibility that they could have been due to chance or random error. Receiving somewhat less emphasis is the overall pattern of disparity in the state polls—again with the votecounts turning in Bush's favor, though less dramatically in the non-battleground states, as will be discussed below. The national popular vote is not addressed in that paper, but the same statistical principles are applicable, and will be employed in this analysis.

While the individual state samples totaled 73,678 reported respondents,[21] a national sub-sampling was undertaken by Edison/Mitofsky, which comprised 13,047 reported respondents, chosen as a representative random sample of the nation as a whole. This sample was drawn from 250 targeted polling places and from 500 individual telephone interviews with absentee and early voters.[22]

What is remarkable about this national sample of 13,047 is its size. When compared with more familiar pre-election poll samples of about 2000 - 2200 respondents, it is approximately six times as large. Such augmentation of sample size reduces a poll's margin of error (MOE) from the ±3% to which we have become accustomed, down to ±1.1%.[23]

---

[20] Freeman, S., "Was the 2004 Presidential Election Honest? An Examination of Uncorrected Exit Poll Data," Working Paper #04-10, rev. Nov. 23, 2004; http://www.buzzflash.com/alerts/04/11/Expldiscrpv00oPt1.pdf.

[21] For the 47 states and District of Columbia for which data was captured by Simon, see: http://www.scoop.co.nz/mason/stories/HL0411/S00142.htm.

[22] See "Methods Statement: National Election Pool Exit Polls: National/Regional Exit Poll," available from the National Election Pool in .pdf format at www.exit-poll.net/index.html.

[23] *Ibid*, p. 2, Table. Calculation of the margin of error may be checked as follows:

Calculate the standard error of a random sample using the formula $\sqrt{\dfrac{p(1-p)}{N}}$ = 0.00437, where p = Kerry percentage of the vote (0.481) and N = the sample size

The ±1.1% MOE tells us that, barring specific flaws in the design or administration of the poll and in the absence of significant mistabulation of the votecount itself, the exit poll result for the selected candidate will fall within ±1.1% of his votecount 95% of the time. In this case it tells us that we can be 95% certain that Kerry's popular vote percentage would fall in the range 49.7% to 51.9%; that is, it would fall outside that range only once in 20 times. Kerry's reported votecount of 48.1% falls dramatically outside this range.[24]

To carry our analysis further, we can employ a normal distribution curve (see Figure 1) to determine—again assuming proper poll methodology and an accurate and honest popular vote count—that the probability that Kerry would have received his reported popular vote total of 48.1%, or less is one in 959,000—a virtual statistical impossibility.[25]

The Popular Vote Winner

We can proceed one helpful step further and calculate the likelihood, based on the exit poll results, that Kerry would receive more popular votes than Bush. The break-even point would be 59,024,629 votes, or 49.54% of the total.[26] This percentage lies, significantly, outside the MOE of the national exit poll and in fact we find that Kerry would receive fewer votes than Bush only 1.3% of the time. Put another way—given the exit poll results, proper poll methodology, and

---

(13,047). The fact that an exit poll is a cluster sample, grouping respondents by precinct, rather than a fully homogenized random sample of the target venue, increases the standard error by 30% to 0.00568 (see Merkle, D. and Edelman, M. "A Review of the 1996 Voter News Service Exit Polls from a Total Survey Error Perspective," in *Election Polls, the News Media and Democracy*, ed. P.J. Lavrakas, M.W. Traugott, New York: Chatham House, pp. 68 - 72). Ninety-five percent of the time, a result predicted on the basis of a random sample will be within 1.96 standard errors, or ±0.011 (1.1%) for a sample of this size.

[24] It is dramatic because a 2.7% "miss" at these levels of precision is extremely unlikely to occur. The statistician's measure of such likelihood is known as a "standard deviation." A result which is off, as in this case, by 4.7 standard deviations is without question "dramatic:" the odds against its occurrence are 959,336 to one (see text below).

[25] Probability of a 48.1% vote share assuming an exit poll vote share of 50.8%: P(0.481) = 1 - NORMDIST(0.481, 0.508, 0.005686, True) = 0.0000010424 (where NORMDIST is an Excel spreadsheet function that gives the probability of obtaining 0.481 for a normal distribution with a mean of 0.508 and a standard deviation of 0.005686). 1/0.0000010424 = 959,336.

[26] Based on final election numbers from the *Washington Post*, Nov. 24, 2004.

an accurate and fair voting process—Kerry would be the popular vote winner of Election 2004 98.7% of the time.

Is Something Wrong with the Exit Poll Results?

The clear implication of our analysis is that neither chance nor random error is responsible for the significant incongruence of exit poll and tabulated vote results, and that we must look either to significant failings in the exit poll design and/or administration or to equally significant failings in the accuracy and/or fairness of the voting process itself to explain the results. Given the dramatic implications of our analysis, we of course must consider carefully any argument that has been put forward suggesting that the exit polls failed as an accurate measure of voter intent. We examine the two least implausible hypotheses that have been put forward.

The first deals with the proportion of respondents by gender. The composition of the national sample by gender was 46% male, 54% female, which prompted a claim that females were over-represented, skewing the results towards Kerry. While it is not proven that this is in fact the case, if it is taken as stipulated and the sample is reweighted to reflect a "normal" gender breakdown of 52% female, 48% male, the effect is to increase Bush's exit poll percentage by 0.2% to 48.4% and decrease Kerry's to 50.6%. The effect on the bottom line is minimal: Kerry would be the popular vote victor 96.9% of the time.[27]

The second hypothesis put forward is the "reluctant Bush responder" hypothesis. It suggests that Bush voters were for some reason less willing to fill out an exit poll questionnaire, and therefore were undercounted in the poll results. If such a phenomenon could be proven, it would be a source of significant skewing and effectively invalidate the polls. The proponents of this hypothesis, however, have yet to offer any supportive evidence for their theory.[28] The hypothesis also does not explain the nonuniformity of the pattern

---

[27] For reference, even a clearly "male-skewed" 50% male, 50% female sample would have resulted in a Kerry victory 93.5% of the time.

[27] There is some intriguing evidence to the contrary, drawn from an analysis performed by William Kaminsky, a graduate student at MIT. Kaminsky finds that in 22 of 23 states that break down their voter registrations by Party ID the ratio of registered Republicans to registered Democrats in the final, adjusted exit poll was larger than the ratio of registered Republicans to registered Democrats on the official registration rolls. In other words, the adjustments performed on the exit polls in order to get them to agree with the official tallies would, if valid, require Republicans to have won the get-out-the-vote battle *in essentially every state.*

We find this requirement implausible, and indeed observational evidence pointed to just the opposite: massive new voter turnout, which virtually always cuts in favor of the

of state-by-state disparities.[29] In fact, one could equally well imagine that a "reluctant Kerry responder" phenomenon was at work, and that the exit polls systematically underrepresented Kerry's vote.[30]

Conclusion

In light of the history of exit polling and the particular care that was taken to achieve an unprecedented degree of accuracy in the exit polls for Election 2004, there is little to suggest significant flaws in the design or administration of the official exit polls. Until supportive evidence can be presented for any hypothesis to the contrary, it must be concluded that the exit polls, including the national mega-sample with its ±1.1% margin of error, present us with an accurate measure of the intent of the voters in the presidential election of 2004.

According to this measure, an honest and fair voting process would have been more likely than not—at least 95% likely, in fact—to have determined John Kerry to be the national popular vote winner of Election 2004.[31] Should ongoing

---

challenger; huge lines in Democratic precincts; unadjusted exit poll data showing *greater* Democratic turnout; etc. Exit polls appropriately stratified to official Party ID percentages, which would effectively neutralize any suspected "reluctant Bush responder" phenomenon by including the expected proportions of Republican and Democratic voters, would on the basis of Kaminsky's analysis have yielded results at least as favorable to Kerry as those upon which we have relied in our calculations.

[29] A complete analysis of all 45 states and the District of Columbia for which comparable exit poll data is available shows that four out of the 11 battleground states had exit poll/vote count disparities that were outside of a standard 5% (one-tail) margin of error, whereas this was the case for only *one* of the 35 non-battleground states. Moreover, all of these statistically significant disparities were in favor of Bush. This data is at odds with claims of "systemic" pro-Kerry exit poll skew. See Baiman, R. Dec. 19, 2004 at: http://www.freepress.org/departments/display/19/2004/997 (some figures have been updated by the author to reflect more recent data). It is of course more than a little implausible that Bush voters would be reluctant to respond only in purple (i.e., swing) states (the logical targets for manipulation) but not in either red or blue states.

[30] It is by no means self-evident that either candidate's supporters were systemically more likely to be intimidating or more easily intimidated. While it might be more reasonably argued that voters finding themselves in a dwarfed minority in their communities might have been less willing to be exit poll respondents, in light of the even division of the national electorate, any such tendencies would have resulted in a wash, with no net effect on the validity of the national exit poll. We would of course welcome the release by Edison/Mitofsky and/or the National Election Pool of the data that would facilitate further analysis of these and other factors.

[31] It should be clear that more is at stake than the presidency itself. Use of computerized vote counting will only increase, as mandated by law. Vote counting is the bedrock protocol of a democracy and meaningful reform of a broken counting system is

or new investigations continue to produce evidence that, to an extent determinative of the electoral college outcome, votes have not been counted accurately and honestly, the re-examined popular vote outcome may well be deemed relevant to the question of what remedies are warranted.

Figure 1:

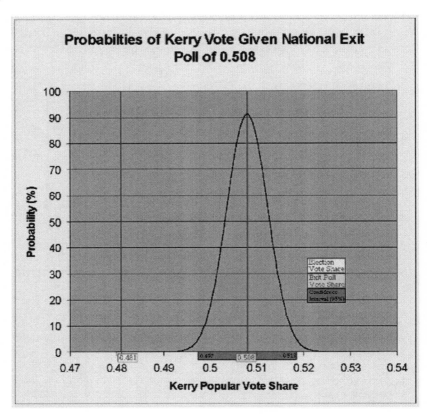

---

dependent on an expression of public will ultimately exercised *at the ballot box* and fairly, accurately, and honestly tabulated. If the system has broken down and is no longer counting accurately and honestly, there is no effective democratic mechanism to bring pressure upon a governing majority to reform a vote counting *status quo* that is seen to work in its favor. This is, as may be seen, a potentially crippling catch-22 for a democracy.

Appendix A: Printout of typical exit poll cross-tabs page (#28 of 354)

CNN.com ELECTION RESULTS

AMERICA VOTES 2004

Posted 1:23 a.m. ET, November 3
CNN projects the Republican party will retain control of the U.S. Senate.

BREAKING NEWS

U.S. PRESIDENT / NATIONAL / EXIT POLL

SEARCH FOR EXIT POLLS

President: Pick state: Senate: Pick state: Other: Pick Others:

- How to read exit polls
- Party key

13,047 Respondents

Updated: 12:23 a.m.

VOTE BY GENDER

	BUSH		KERRY		NADER	
TOTAL	2004	2000	2004		2004	
Male (46%)	52%	n/a	47%		1%	
Female (54%)	45%	n/a	54%		1%	

VOTE BY RACE AND GENDER

	BUSH		KERRY		NADER	
TOTAL	2004	2000	2004		2004	
White Men (36%)	58%	n/a	40%		1%	
White Women (41%)	51%	n/a	47%		1%	
Non-White Men (11%)	28%	n/a	68%		2%	
Non-White Women (13%)	22%	n/a	77%		1%	

VOTE BY RACE

	BUSH		KERRY		NADER	
TOTAL	2004	2000	2004		2004	
White (77%)	55%	+1	44%		1%	
African-American (11%)	10%	+1	90%		1%	
Latino (8%)	41%	+6	56%		3%	
Asian (2%)	39%	-2	61%		*	
Other (2%)	38%	n/a	56%		2%	

VOTE BY AGE

	BUSH		KERRY		NADER	
TOTAL	2004	2000	2004		2004	
18-29 (17%)	42%	-4	56%		1%	
30-44 (29%)	49%	+0	48%		2%	
45-59 (30%)	47%	-2	51%		1%	
60 and Older (24%)	51%	+4	48%		0%	

VOTE BY AGE

	BUSH		KERRY		NADER	
TOTAL	2004	2000	2004		2004	
18-64 (84%)	48%	+0	51%		1%	
65 and Older (16%)	50%	+0	50%		0%	

VOTE BY INCOME

	BUSH		KERRY		NADER	
TOTAL	2004	2000	2004		2004	
Under $15,000 (8%)	34%	n/a	65%		1%	
$15-30,000 (15%)	36%	n/a	60%		1%	
$30-50,000 (22%)	46%	n/a	53%		1%	
$50-75,000 (23%)	53%	n/a	46%		1%	
$75-100,000 (14%)	51%	n/a	48%		0%	
$100-150,000 (11%)	53%	n/a	44%		2%	
$150-200,000 (4%)	55%	n/a	45%		*	
$200,000 or More (3%)	59%	n/a	39%		2%	

VOTE BY INCOME

	BUSH		KERRY		NADER	
TOTAL	2004	2000	2004		2004	
Less Than $50,000 (45%)	41%	n/a	58%		1%	
$50,000 or More (55%)	53%	n/a	46%		1%	

VOTE BY INCOME

	BUSH		KERRY		NADER	
TOTAL	2004	2000	2004		2004	
Less Than $100,000 (82%)	46%	n/a	53%		1%	
$100,000 or More (18%)	55%	n/a	43%		2%	

STUDY II.

Landslide Denied:
Exit Polls vs. Vote Count 2006
Demographic Validity of the National Exit Poll and the Corruption of the Official Vote Count

Jonathan Simon, JD, and Bruce O'Dell[1]
Election Defense Alliance

Pre-Election Concern, Election Day Relief, Alarming Reality

There was an unprecedented level of concern approaching the 2006 Election ("E2006") about the vulnerability of the vote counting process to manipulation. With questions about the integrity of the 2000, 2002 and 2004 elections remaining unresolved, with e-voting having proliferated nationwide, and with incidents occurring with regularity through 2005 and 2006, the alarm spread from computer experts to the media and the public at large. It would be fair to say that America approached E2006 with held breath.

For many observers, the results on Election Day permitted a great sigh of relief—not because control of Congress shifted from Republicans to Democrats, but because it appeared that the public will had been translated more or less accurately into electoral results, not thwarted as some had feared. There was a relieved rush to conclude that the vote counting process had been fair and the concerns of election integrity proponents overblown.

Unfortunately, the evidence forces us to a very different and disturbing conclusion: there was gross votecount manipulation and it had a great impact on

---

[1] Jonathan Simon, JD (http://www.electiondefensealliance.org/jonathan_simon) is Co-founder of Election Defense Alliance.

Bruce O'Dell (http://www.electiondefensealliance.org/bruce_odell) is EDA Data Analysis Coordinator.

the results of E2006, significantly decreasing the magnitude of what would have been, accurately tabulated, a landslide of epic proportions. Because much of this manipulation appears to have been computer-based, and therefore invisible to the legions of at-the-poll observers, the public was informed of the usual "isolated incidents and glitches" but remains unaware of the far greater story: The electoral machinery and vote counting systems of the United States did not honestly and accurately translate the public will and certainly cannot be counted on to do so in the future.

The Evidentiary Basis

Our analysis of the distortions introduced into the E2006 votecount relies heavily on the official exit polls once again undertaken by Edison Media Research and Mitofsky International ("Edison/Mitofsky")[2] on behalf of a consortium of major media outlets known as the National Election Pool (NEP). In presenting exit poll-based evidence of votecount corruption, we are all too aware of the campaign that has been waged to discredit the reliability of exit polls as a measure of voter intent.

Our analysis is not, however, based on a broad assumption of exit poll reliability. **Rather we maintain that the national exit poll for E2006 contains within it specific questions that serve as intrinsic and objective yardsticks by which the representative validity of the poll's sample can be established, from which our conclusions flow directly.**

For the purposes of this analysis our primary attention is directed to the exit poll in which respondents were asked for whom they cast their vote for the House of Representatives.[3] Although only four House races (in single-district states) were polled as individual races, an additional nationwide sample of more than 10,000 voters was drawn,[4] the results representing the aggregate vote for the House in

---

[2] Warren Mitofsky, the inventor of exit polling, died suddenly on September 1, 2006, of an apparent aneurysm, while fine tuning the exit polling system to be used by the National Election Pool in E2006. His successors at Edison/Mitofsky were, if anything, less cooperative in sharing information about their operation.

[3] Edison/Mitofsky exit polls for the Senate races also present alarming disparities and will be treated in a separate paper. The special significance of the House vote is that, unlike the Senate vote, it offers a nationwide aggregate view.

[4] The sample size was roughly equal to that used to measure the national popular vote in presidential elections. At-precinct interviews were supplemented by phone interviews where needed to sample early and absentee voters.

E2006. The sample was weighted according to a variety of demographics prior to public posting, and had a margin of error of +/- 1%.[5]

When we compare the results of this national exit poll with the total votecount for all House races we find that once again, as in the 2004 Election ("E2004"), there is a very significant exit poll-votecount disparity. **The exit poll indicates a Democratic victory margin nearly 4%,** *or 3 million votes,* **greater than the margin recorded by the vote counting machinery.** This is far outside the margin of error of the poll and has less than a one in 10,000 likelihood of occurring as a matter of chance.

The Exit Polls and The Votecount

In E2004 the only nontrivial argument against the validity of the exit polls—other than the mere assumption that the votecounts *must* be correct—turned out to be the hypothesis, never supported by evidence, that Republicans had been more reluctant to respond and that therefore Democrats were "oversampled." And now, in E2006, the claim has once again been made that the Exit Polls were "off" because Democrats were oversampled.[6] Indeed this claim of sampling *bias* is by now accepted with something of a "so what else is new?" shrug. The 2006 Exit Poll, however, contains *intrinsic yardsticks* that

---

[5] We note with interest and raised brows that the NEP is now giving the MOE for their national sample as +/-3% (http://www.exit-poll.net/faq.html#a15). This is rather curious, as their published Methods Statement in 2004 assigns to a sample of the same size and mode of sampling the expected MOE of +/-1% (see Appendix 2 for both NEP Statements). Perhaps the NEP intends its new methodology statement to apply to its anticipated effort in 2008 and is planning to reduce the national sample size by 75% for that election; we hope not. It of course makes no sense, as applied to E2004 or E2006, that state polls in the 2000-respondent range should yield an MOE of +/-4%, as stated, while a national poll of more than *five times* that sample size should come in at +/-3%. It would certainly be useful in quelling any controversy that has arisen or might arise from exit poll-votecount disparities far outside the poll's MOE, but it is, to our knowledge, not the way that statistics and mathematics work.

[6] See for example David Bauder, AP, in a November 8 article at http://www.washingtonpost.com/wp-dyn/content/article/2006/11/08/AR2006110800403.html. Oddly enough, "oversampling" of Democrats has become a chronic ailment of exit polls since the proliferation of e-voting, no matter how diligently the nonpartisan collection of experts at the peak of their profession strives to prevent it. Of course the weighting process itself is undertaken to bring the sample into close conformity with the known and estimated characteristics of the electorate, including partisanship; so the fact that more of a given party's adherents were actually sampled, while it would be reflected in the unpublished raw data, would not in fact bias or affect the validity of the published *weighted* poll. *That is the whole point of weighting,* in light of which the hand-wringing about Democratic oversampling strikes us as misunderstanding at best, and quite possibly intended misdirection.

directly refute this familiar and convenient claim. But before turning to the yardstick questions themselves, we need to clarify certain aspects of exit polling data presentation that have often proven confusing.

Any informed discussion of exit polling must distinguish among three separate categories of data:

1) **"Raw" data**, which comprises the actual responses to the questionnaires simply tallied up; this data is never publicly released and, in any case, makes no claim to accurately represent the electorate and cannot be usefully compared with votecounts.

2) **"Weighted" data**, in which the raw data has been weighted or stratified on the basis of numerous demographic and voting pattern variables to reflect with great accuracy the composition and characteristics of the electorate.

3) **"Forced"** or **"Adjusted"** data, in which the pollster *overrides* previous weighting in order to make the "Who did you vote for?" result in a given race match the votecount for that race, however it distorts the demographics of the sample (that's why they call it "forcing").

Because the NEP envisions the post-election purpose of its exit polls as being limited to facilitating academic dissection of the election's dynamics and demographics (e.g., "How did the 18-25 age group vote?" or "How did voters especially concerned with the economy vote?"), the NEP methodology calls for "correcting" or "adjusting" its exit polls to congruence with the actual vote percentages after the polls close and actual returns become available. *Exit polls are "corrected" on the ironclad assumption that the votecounts are valid.* This becomes the supreme truth, relative to which all else is measured, and therefore it is assumed that polls that match these votecounts will present the most accurate information about the demographics and voting patterns of the electorate. A *distorted* electorate in the adjusted poll is therefore a powerful indicator of an invalid votecount.

We examined both "weighted" and "adjusted" exit polls of nationwide vote for the House of Representatives published by the NEP. On Election Night, November 7, 2006 at 7:07 p.m., CNN.com posted a national exit poll that was demographically weighted but not yet adjusted to congruence with the votecounts.[7] We call this the **Weighted National Poll**. At various intervals over

---

[7] The 7:07 p.m. poll reported a 10,207 sample size and, in accordance with NEP methodology, the raw data had been weighted to closely match the demographics of the electorate.

the next 18 hours, as polls closed and official tabulations became available, the results presented in the Weighted National Poll were progressively "corrected" to match the official vote totals, culminating in a fully adjusted national exit poll posted on CNN.com at 1 p.m. November 8, 2006. We call this the **Adjusted National Poll**. We will make reference to both polls in the analysis that follows.

The 2006 national vote for the House, as captured by the Weighted National Poll, was 55.0% Democratic and 43.5% Republican—an 11.5% Democratic margin. By 1:00 p.m. on November 8, the Adjusted National Poll reported the overall vote for the House as 52.6% Democratic and 45.0% Republican, just a 7.6% margin.[8] This 7.6% Democratic margin of course matched the tabulated votecount but was 3.9% smaller than that recorded by the Weighted National Poll the night before. *This was a net difference of 3 million votes fewer for the Democrats.*

Did the 2006 Exit Poll Oversample Democrats? Cross-tabs Answer this Question

The national exit poll administered by Edison/Mitofsky for the NEP is not, as some may imagine, a simple "Who did you vote for?" questionnaire. It poses some 40 to 50 additional questions pertaining to demographic, political preference, and state-of-mind variables. Voters are asked, for example, about such characteristics as race, gender, income, age, and also about such things as church attendance, party identification, ideology, approval of various public figures, importance of various issues to their vote, and when they made up their minds about whom to vote for.

When the poll is posted, these characteristics are presented in a format, known as "cross-tabs," in which the voting choice of respondents in each subgroup is shown. For example, respondents were asked whether they thought the United States "is going in the right direction." In the Weighted National Poll, the cross-tab for this characteristic (see below) shows us that 40% said Yes and 56% said

---

[8] Analysts noticing the substantial increase in "respondents" between the Weighted (10,207) and Adjusted (13,251) National Polls may understandably but erroneously conclude that the shift between the two polls is the result of a late influx of Republican-leaning respondents. This is not the way it works. Since these are both weighted polls, each is in effect "tuned" to a profile of the electorate assumed to be valid—the Weighted National Poll to a set of established demographic variables and the Adjusted National Poll to the vote count once it is tabulated. The published number of respondents is *irrelevant* to this process and has significance only as a guide to the poll's margin of error. 10,000+ respondents is a *huge* sample (cf. the 500 – 1500 range of most tracking polls), and obviously an ample basis on which to perform the demographic weighting manifest in the Weighted National Poll.

No; and further that, of the 40% subgroup who said Yes, 21% voted Democrat and 78% voted Republican for House of Representatives, while, of the 56% who said No, 80% voted Democrat and 18% voted Republican. We also see that this question is quite highly correlated with voting preference, with fully four-fifths of the "pessimists" voting Democratic.

IS U.S. GOING IN RIGHT DIRECTION?

TOTAL	Democrat	Republican
Yes (40%)	21%	78%
No (56%)	80%	18%

Cross-tabs vary greatly in the degree to which the characteristic is correlated with voting preference. The more strongly correlated, the more important the cross-tab becomes in assessing the poll's validity as an indicator of the vote.

Prior to public posting the exit poll data is weighted according to a *variety* of demographics, in such a way that the resulting cross-tabs closely mirror the expected, independently measurable characteristics of the electorate as a whole. The cross-tabs, in turn, tell us about the sample, giving us detailed information about its composition and representativeness. This information is of critical importance to our analysis because among the many questions asked of respondents there are several that enable us to tell whether the sample is valid or *politically biased* in one direction or another. These are the "intrinsic yardsticks" to which we have made reference.

Among the most salient yardstick questions were the following:

- Job Approval of President Bush
- Job Approval of Congress
- Vote for President in 2004

With respect to each of these yardsticks the composition of the sample can be compared to measures taken of the voting population as a whole, giving us a very good indication of the validity of the sample. Examining these cross-tabs for the Weighted National Poll—the 7:07 p.m. poll that was written off by the media as a "typical oversampling of Democrats"—this is what we found:

- Approval of President Bush: 42%
- Approval of Congress: 36%
- Vote for President in 2004: Bush 47%, Kerry 45%

When we compare these numbers with what we know about the electorate as a whole going into E2006, we can see at once that the poll that told us that the Democratic margin was 3 million votes greater than the computers toted up was not by any stretch of the imagination an oversampling of Democrats. Let's take each yardstick in turn.

Presidential Approval Rating

We can compare the 42% approval of President Bush in the Weighted National Poll with any or all of the host of tracking polls measuring this critical political variable in the weeks and days leading up to the election. It is important when comparing approval ratings to make sure that we compare apples with apples, since the question can be posed in different ways leading to predictably different results. The principal formats of the approval measure are either simply "Do you approve or disapprove. . .?" or "Do you strongly approve, somewhat approve, somewhat disapprove, or strongly disapprove. . .?" We can call these the *two-point* and *four-point* formats respectively. By repeatedly posing the question in both formats on the same days, it has been determined that the four-point format consistently yields an approval rating 3-4% higher than the two-point format.[9]

Bearing this in mind and comparing the Weighted National Poll respondents' approval of President Bush with that registered by the electorate going into the election, we find very close parity. PollingReport.com catalogues 33 national polls of Presidential approval taken between October 1 and Election Day using the two-point format, with an average (mean) approval rating of 37.6%.[10] This translates to a 41% approval rating in the four-point format used for the Weighted National Poll. A direct comparison is also possible with the Rasmussen tracking poll, which unlike the other tracking polls uses the four-point format. The Rasmussen approval rating for October 2006 is also 41%, with 57% disapproving.[11] Thus, the 42% approval of President Bush in the Weighted National Poll matches the figure established for the electorate as a whole going

---

[9] See http://www.rasmussenreports.com/public_content/politics/polling_methodology_job_approval_ratings. As Rasmussen notes, the 3-4% upwards adjustment in the four-point format impounds the virtual elimination of the "Not Sure" response obtained with greater frequency in the two-point format.

[10] See http://www.pollingreport.com/BushJob.htm. Typical of the national polls included are Gallup, AP-Ipsos, Newsweek, Fox/Opinion Dynamics, CBS/New York Times, NBC/Wall Street Journal, and ABC/Washington Post. The median approval rating is 37.4%, indistinguishable from the mean, and there is no discernible trend up or down over the Oct. 1 – Nov. 7 period.

[11] See http://www.rasmussenreports.com/public_content/politics/political_updates/president_bush_job_approval. The rating combines "strong" and "somewhat" approve and is the average of Rasmussen's daily tracking polls conducted throughout the month.

into the election; in fact, it is 1% "over par." As Bush approval correlates very strongly with voting preference (see below), an oversampling of Democrats would unavoidably have been reflected in a lower rating. The rating at or above the established level thus provides the first confirmation of the validity of the Weighted National Poll.

HOW GEORGE W. BUSH IS HANDLING HIS JOB

TOTAL	Democrat	Republican
Approve (42%)	15%	84%
Disapprove (58%)	83%	15%

Congressional Approval Rating

As with the Presidential approval yardstick, comparison between the 36% of the Weighted National Poll sample that approved of how Congress was handling its job and the value established for the electorate in numerous tracking polls corroborates the Weighted National Poll's validity. The mean of the 17 national polls catalogued by the PollingReport.com measuring approval of Congress between October 1 and Election Day (all employing the two-point format) was 27.5% approval.[12] Translating to the four-point format used for the exit poll yields a comparable approval rating of 31%, a full 5% *below* the Congressional approval given by the Weighted National Poll respondents. As with the Presidential rating, approval of what was at that point a Republican Congress correlates strongly with voting preference (see below). We would have expected an oversampling of Democrats to give a *lower* approval rating to Congress than did the electorate it was supposedly misrepresenting. Instead the Weighted National Poll yielded a significantly *higher* Congressional approval rating— indicative, if anything, of an oversampling of Republicans.

HOW CONGRESS IS HANDLING ITS JOB

TOTAL	Democrat	Republican
Strongly Approve (5%)	29%	70%
Somewhat Approve (31%)	25%	73%
Somewhat Disapprove (32%)	62%	37%
Strongly Disapprove (30%)	81%	16%

Vote for President in 2004

---

[12] See http://www.pollingreport.com/CongJob.htm.

Edison/Mitofsky asked all respondents how they had voted in the 2004 Presidential election. The Weighted National Poll sample included 45% who said they had voted for Kerry and 47% who said they had voted for Bush (8% indicating they had not voted or voted for another candidate). This Bush margin of +2% closely approximates the +2.8% margin that Bush enjoyed in the official popular vote count for E2004.

VOTE FOR PRESIDENT IN 2004

TOTAL	Democrat	Republican
Kerry (45%)	93%	6%
Bush (47%)	17%	82%

While poll respondents have often shown some tendency to indicate they voted for the sitting president when questioned at the time of the next presidential election (i.e., four years out), Bush's historically low approval rating, coupled with his high relevance to this off-year election, and the shorter time span since the vote in question, make such a generic "winner's shift" singularly unlikely in E2006.

And while we present the reported 2.8% Bush margin in 2004 at face value, it will not escape notice that the distortions in vote tabulation that we establish in the current paper were also alleged in 2004, were evidenced by the 2004 exit polls, and were demonstrably achievable given the electronic voting systems deployed at that time. We note that, if upon retrospective evaluation the unadjusted 2004 exit polls prove as accurate as the 2006 exit polls appear to be, and their 2.5% margin for *Kerry* in 2004 is taken as the appropriate baseline, a correctly weighted sample in 2006 would have included even more Kerry voters and even fewer Bush voters than Edison/Mitofsky's Weighted National Poll, with a substantial consequent up-tick in the Democratic margin beyond the 3 million votes thus far unaccounted for.

These critical comparisons between measures taken of the Weighted National Poll sample and established benchmarks are presented together in the chart immediately below:

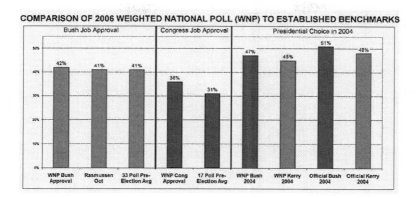

COMPARISON OF 2006 WEIGHTED NATIONAL POLL (WNP) TO ESTABLISHED BENCHMARKS

There should be little question that the three yardsticks presented above conclusively refute the glib canard that the National Exit Poll disparity was due to an oversampling of Democrats. Two additional cross-tabs are, however, worthy of note in this regard: Vote by Race and Vote by Party ID.

Vote by Race

The Weighted National Poll sample, as can be seen below, is 80% White, 10% African-American, and 8% Latino in composition, with Whites splitting their vote evenly between the parties while Latinos and particularly Blacks voted overwhelmingly Democratic.

VOTE BY RACE

TOTAL	Democrat	Republican
White (80%)	49%	49%
African-American (10%)	88%	12%
Latino (8%)	72%	26%
Asian (1%)	65%	35%
Other (2%)	59%	36%

We can compare these demographics with an established measure of the electorate published by the University of Michigan Center for Political Studies. The ANES Guide to Public Opinion and Electoral Behavior is a longitudinal study of many aspects of the American electorate, including racial composition.[13] The chart below presents the ANES results for the past six biennial national elections.[14]

	'94	'96	'98	'00	'02	'04
White :	78	72	74	74	75	70
Black :	12	14	12	13	12	16
Asian :	2	2	1	3	2	3
Native American:	3	5	3	3	2	4
Hispanic :	6	8	9	7	8	8
Other :	-	-	-	-	2	-

As can be seen by comparing the charts above, in *none* of the past six elections was the White participation as high or the Black participation as low as represented in the Weighted National Poll.[15] The average White proportion of the electorate was 74%, 6% below the exit poll's representation of Whites, while the average Black proportion was 13%, 3% above the exit poll's representation of Blacks. The relative under-representation of every strong Democratic constituency in this cross-tab, in favor of the least Democratic voting bloc, hardly jibes with the "Invalid: Oversampled Democrats" label cheerfully pasted on the Weighted National Poll.

Vote by Party ID

Though Vote by Party ID generally fluctuates relatively modestly from one election to the next, it is, not surprisingly, nonetheless sensitive to the dynamics of atypical turnout battles. While we will address the E2006 turnout dynamics more fully in a later section, for the present we will simply note that a

---

[13] The American National Election Studies; see www.electionstudies.org. Produced and distributed by the University of Michigan, Center for Political Studies; based on work supported by the National Science Foundation and a number of other sponsors.

[14] The full chart, dating to 1948, may be referenced at
http://www.electionstudies.org/nesguide/toptable/tab1a_3.htm.

[15] Asian and Native American voters, also strong Democratic constituencies, likewise seem to be significantly under-represented in the Weighted National Poll. The ANES results for 2006 are due to be published later this year. In *E2004* the Weighted National Poll was 77% White and 11% Black, as opposed to the ANES proportions of 70% and 16% respectively. It was this disproportionately White sample—supposedly short on "reluctant" Bush responders, but in reality overstocked with White voters who favored Bush by a margin of 11% and under-stocked with Black voters who favored Kerry by a margin of 80%! —that gave Kerry a 2.5% *victory* in the nationwide popular vote.

Democratic turnout romp was generally acknowledged in 2006, Republican voters having a number of late-breaking reasons for staying home.

In the Weighted National Poll, Democratic voters comprised 39% of the sample to 35% for the Republicans, as shown below.

VOTE BY PARTY ID

TOTAL	Democrat	Republican
Democrat (39%)	93%	6%
Republican (35%)	9%	90%
Independent (26%)	58%	38%

Only 20 states register their voters by party so there is no direct comparison to be made to actual registration figures. But the ANES Guide once again proves useful. The chart below records party identification amongst the electorate as a whole on a seven-point scale, but the comparison is convincing.[16]

	'94	'96	'98	'00	'02	'04
Strong Democrat :	15	18	19	19	17	17
Weak Democrat :	19	19	18	15	17	16
Independent Democrat :	13	14	14	15	15	17
Independent Independent :	11	9	11	12	8	10
Independent Republican :	12	12	11	13	13	12
Weak Republican :	15	15	16	12	16	12
Strong Republican :	15	12	10	12	14	16
Apolitical :	1	1	2	1	1	0

In each of the past six biennial national elections through 2004, self-identified Democrats have outnumbered Republicans. The margins for 1994, 1996, 1998, 2000, 2002, and 2004 have been +4%, +10%, +11%, +10%, +4%, and +5% respectively. If Independent leaners are included, the Democratic margin increases every year, to +5%, +12%, +14%, +12%, +6%, and +10% respectively. These are very consistent numbers confirming a consistent plurality of self-identified Democratic voters from election to election.[17] The 4%

---

[16] The full chart, dating to 1952, may be referenced at http://www.electionstudies.org/nesguide/toptable/tab2a_1.htm.

[17] It is worth noting that among the most suspicious demographic distortions of the Adjusted National Poll in *E2004* was the Party ID cross-tab, which indicated an electorate *evenly* divided between self-identified Democrats and Republicans at 37% apiece. Not only was this supposed parity unprecedented, but it flew in the face of near-universal observational indications of a major Democratic turnout victory in 2004: not only in Ohio but nationwide, long lines and hours-long waits were recorded at inner-city and traditionally Democratic precincts, while literally no such lines were observed

Democratic plurality in the Weighted National Poll sample is seen to be at the extreme *low* end of the margins recorded since 1994, matching only the 4% Democratic margins recorded in the major *Republican* victories of 1994 and 2002. But E2006 was a major *Democratic* victory and, as will be seen, a likely *turnout landslide*.

While it would probably insult the intelligence of the media analysts who proclaimed that the E2006 Weighted National Poll was "off" because it had oversampled Democrats to even suggest the possibility that one or more of them took the 39% - 35% Democratic ID margin in the poll to be indicative of Democratic oversampling—such misinterpretation quickly spreading among, and taking on the full authority of, the Election Night punditry—it is very difficult to comprehend by what *other* measure the Election Night analysts, and all who followed their lead, might have reached that manifestly erroneous, though obviously comforting, conclusion.

In short, there is no measure anywhere in the Weighted National Poll—in which the Democratic margin nationwide was some 3 million votes greater than tabulated by the machines—that indicates an oversampling of Democrats. Any departures from norms, trends, and expectations indicate just the opposite: a poll that likely undersampled Democratic voters and so, at 11.5%, *understated* the Democratic victory margin.

The Adjusted National Poll: Making the Vote-Count Match

In the wake of our primary analysis of the validity of the Weighted National Poll, consideration of the Adjusted National Poll is something of an afterthought, though it does serve to further reinforce our conclusions.

As we described earlier, in the "adjusted" or "corrected" poll the pollster overrides all previous weighting to make the "Who did you vote for?" result in a given race (or set of races) match the votecount for that race, however it distorts the demographics of the sample. In the Adjusted National Poll, which appeared the day after the election and remains posted (with a few further updates not affecting this analysis) on the CNN.com website, Edison/Mitofsky was faced with the task of matching the tabulated aggregate results for the set of House races nationwide. This translated to reducing the Democratic margin from 11.5% to 7.6% by giving less weight to the respondents who said they had voted for a Democratic candidate and more weight to the respondents who said

---

and no such complaints recorded in traditionally Republican voting areas (see EIRS data at https://voteprotect.org/index.php?display=EIRMapNation&tab=ED04).

they had voted Republican. Of course this process, referred to as "forcing," also affects the response to every question on the questionnaire, including the demographic and political preference questions we have been considering.

The most significant effect was upon "Vote for President in 2004." In order to match the results of the official tally, the Adjusted National Poll was forced to depict an electorate that voted for Bush over Kerry *by a 6% margin* in 2004, more than twice the "actual" margin of 2.8%, taken charitably at face value for the purposes of this analysis.

VOTE FOR PRESIDENT IN 2004		
TOTAL	Democrat	Republican
Kerry (43%)	92%	7%
Bush (49%)	15%	83%

As might be expected, other yardsticks were also affected: Bush approval increases to 43%; Congressional approval to 37%; and Party ID shifts to an implausible 38% Democratic, 36% Republican.

There were, as we identified earlier, indications that the Weighted National Poll itself may have undersampled voters who cast their votes for the Democratic House candidates.[18] The Adjusted National Poll compounds such distortions in order to present an electorate cut to fit the official vote totals. If such an adjusted poll yields inaccurate and distorted information about the demographics and voting patterns of the electorate, then very basic logic tells us that the votecount it was forced to match is itself invalid. This of course corroborates the story told by the Weighted National Poll, as well as by the pre-election polls, as shown in the graph below.[19]

---

[18] To the extent that weighting is based on prior turnout patterns, a significant shift in the turnout dynamic, as was apparent in E2006, would be one cause for this undersampling. A second and more disturbing cause: "actual" results from recent elections, which themselves have been vulnerable to and distorted by electronic mistabulation, fed into the weighting algorithms.

[19] The 11.5% Democratic margin in the Weighted National Poll was strictly congruent with the 11.5% average margin of the seven major national public opinion polls conducted immediately prior to the election. Indeed, this 11.5% pre-election margin was drawn down substantially by the appearance of three election-week "outlier" polls, which strangely came in at 7%, 6%, and 4% respectively. To put this in perspective, excluding these three polls, 30 of the 31 other major national polls published from the beginning of October up to the election showed the Democratic margin to be in double-digits, and the single exception came in at 9%. See http://www.realclearpolitics.com/epolls/2006/house/us/generic_congressional_ballot-22.html.

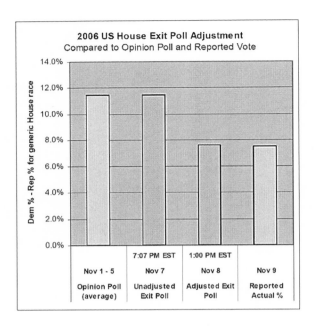

2006 US House Exit Poll Adjustment
Compared to Opinion Poll and Reported Vote

See Appendix 1 for detailed tabular presentation of the above data.

It is also worth noting that most pre-election polls shift, in the month before the election, to a "likely-voter cutoff model" (LCVM) that excludes *entirely* any voters not highly likely (on the basis of a battery of screening questions) to cast ballots; that is, it excludes *entirely* voters with a 25% or even 50% likelihood of voting. Since these are disproportionately transients and first-time voters, the less educated and affluent, it is also a correspondingly Democratic constituency that is disproportionately excluded.

Ideally these voters should be down-weighted to their estimated probability of voting, *but that probability is not 0%.* By excluding them entirely, these pre-election polls build in a pro-Republican bias of about 2-5%, which *anomalously* in 2006 appears to have been offset by the significantly greater enthusiasm for voting on the part of the Democrats, reflected in an elevated LCVM failure rate among Republicans responding negatively or ambivalently to the battery question about their intention to vote in E2006. Dr. Steven Freeman, visiting professor at the University of Pennsylvania's Center for Organizational Dynamics, has examined this phenomenon in great detail.

Of course, one of the reasons for the recent shift to the LVCM—a methodology that pollsters will generally admit is distorted but which they maintain nonetheless "gets it right"—is that pollsters are *not* paid for methodological purity, *they are paid to get it right.* From the pollster's standpoint, getting it right is the measure of their success whether the election is honest or the fix is in. The reality is that distorted vote counts and a distorted but "successful" pre-election polling methodology wind up corroborating and validating each other, *with only the exit polls (drawn from actual voters) seeming out of step.*

Plausible Explanations?

Since, as we have seen, the Weighted National Poll's inclusion of Democratic voters (or, better put, voters with characteristics making them likely to vote Democratic) either jibes with or falls somewhat short of established benchmarks for the electorate, there are only two possible explanations for the dramatic disparity between it and the official votecount: either Republicans unexpectedly turned out in droves and routed the Democrats in the E2006 turnout battle, or the official votecount is dramatically "off."

To our knowledge no one has contended the former. With good reason: there are a plethora of measures, including individual precinct tallies and additional polling data that we will examine in the next section, that confirm the obvious—the Democrats were the runaway winners of the 2006 Get-Out-The-Vote battle. Indeed, it is generally acknowledged that Republican voters stayed home in droves, dismayed and turned-off by the late-breaking run of scandals, bad news, and missteps.[20]

Hence it must be the reported nationwide vote tally which is inaccurate. Although this is, to put it mildly, an unwelcome finding, it is unfortunately consonant with the many specific incidents of vote-switching and mistabulation reported in 2006, with an apparent competitive-contest targeting pattern,[21] and with a host of other evidence and analysis that has emerged about electronic voting technology as deployed in the United States.

So Why Did the Republicans *Lose*?

It will no doubt be objected that if such substantial manipulation of the votecounts is possible, why would it stop short of bringing about a general electoral *victory*? While we would naturally like to credit the heightened scrutiny engendered by the untiring efforts of election integrity groups, an awakening media, and a more informed and vigilant public; an alternative, more chilling, explanation has emerged—simply that the mechanics of manipulation (software modules, primarily; see Appendix 3) had to be deployed before late-

---

[20] Indeed, once on-going analysis fully quantifies the extent of the Democrats' turnout victory, it will be time to recalculate upward the magnitude of the vote miscount in 2006.

[21] Our paper on competitive contest targeting is scheduled for publication in August 2007.

breaking pre-election developments[22] greatly expanded the gap that such manipulation would have been calibrated to cover.

To quantify the extraordinary effect of the various "October surprises," we reference below the Cook Political Report National Tracking Poll's Generic Congressional Ballot, ordinarily a rather *stable* measure:[23]

GENERIC CONGRESSIONAL BALLOT (Most Likely Voters)

Date	This Poll	
Sample Size/MoE	807/3.5%	

MLV	Dem	Rep
Oct. 26-29	**61**	**35**
Oct. 19-22	57	35
Oct. 5-8	**50**	**41**
Sept. 27-30	51	35
Sept. 21-24	49	41

Thus the Democratic margin among most likely voters increased from 9% (50% - 41%) to 26% (61% - 35%) during the month of October, an enormous 17% jump occurring *after* the vote-shifting mechanisms were, *or could be*, deployed.

It should be noted that among the various tracking polls, there were some that did not pick up the dramatic trend reflected in the Cook poll. Indeed, Cook's own parallel tracking poll of all *registered* voters (not screened for likelihood of turnout) found only a modest gain of 2% in the Democratic margin over the

---

[22] The powerful impact of the succession of lurid scandals (Foley, Haggard, Sherwood, et al) is clear from the Weighted National Poll responses in which voters were asked about the importance of "corruption/ethics:" 41% responded "extremely important" and another 33% "very important," *the highest response of all the "importance" questions*, outstripping even the importance of "terrorism." Iraq, another source of late-breaking negatives for the GOP, also scored high on the importance scale (36% extremely, with this category breaking for the Democrats 61% -38%).

[23] See http://www.cookpolitical.com/poll/ballot.php.

same period. This is indicative of the phenomenon to which we have already made reference: what most boosted the Democrats during the month of October was an extraordinary gain in the relative *motivation and likelihood of turning out* among their voters. It supports our belief that it was primarily the exceptional turnout differential, understandably missed by exit polls calibrated to historical turnout patterns, that would have given the Democrats an even greater victory than the 11.5% reflected by the Weighted National Poll, in an honestly and accurately counted election.

Implications

The 2006 Election gave the Democrats control of both houses of Congress, by margins of 31 seats (233 – 202) in the House and two seats (51 – 49) in the Senate. The Democrats won 20 House races and four Senate races by margins of 6% of the vote or less.[24] The odds are very good that the outcomes of most if not all of these races would have been reversed a month earlier, post-deployment of vote shifting mechanisms but pre-October surprises, before the resulting dramatic movement to the Democrats as reflected in the 17% Generic Ballot jump. The ballpark *sans*-October Surprise numbers: 222R – 213D in the House and 53R – 47D in the Senate.

Absent a very Blue October, *which came too late to be countered by deployment of additional vote-shifting mechanisms*, we can conclude that, with the assistance of the vote-shifting mechanisms *already* deployed, the Republicans would almost certainly have maintained control of both houses of Congress.

This should be a rather sobering observation for Democrats looking ahead to their electoral future and assessing to what extent the system is broken as they contemplate the various legislative proposals for reform.[25]

---

[24] In the House: four races by 1%, four races by 2%, one race by 3%, five races by 4%, one race by 5%, five races by 6%, one race by 7%, five races by 8%, two races by 9%; in the Senate: two races by 1%, one race by 3%, one race by 6%, one race by 8%.

[25] If we are correct in our assessment that the limitations on vote shifting were more temporal than spatial—that is, had more to do with timing of deployment than with the potential size of the shift—then only extraordinary and unanticipated eleventh-hour pre-election surges *a la* E2006 will suffice to overcome future foul play. However, whatever quantitative limits may apply to electronic vote shifting, *it should obviously not be necessary to enjoy super-majority support in order to eke out electoral victories.*

Conclusion

There is a remarkable degree of consensus among computer scientists,[26] security professionals,[27] government agencies,[28] and independent analysts[29] that U.S. electronic vote tallying technology is vulnerable both to unintentional programming errors[30] and to deliberate manipulation—certainly by foul-play-minded insiders at voting equipment vendors, but also by other individuals with access to voting equipment hardware or software.[31]

We have arrived at a system of "faith-based" voting where we are simply asked to trust the integrity of the count produced by the secret-software machines that tally our votes, without effective check mechanisms. In the context of yet another election replete with reported problems with vote tallying,[32] the continuing mismatch between the preferences expressed by voters as captured in national exit polls and the official vote tally as reported to the public is beyond disturbing. It is a bright red flag that no one who values a democratic America can in good conscience ignore.

False elections bequeath to all Americans—right, left, and center—nothing less sinister than an illusory identity and the living of a national lie. Our biennial elections, far more than the endless parade of opinion polls, *define* America—both in terms of who occupies its seats of power and as the single snapshot that becomes the enduring national self-portrait that all Americans carry in their mental wallets for at least the biennium and more often for an era. It is also, needless to say, the portrait we send abroad.

While the reported results of the 2006 election were certainly well-received by the Democratic Party and were ballpark-consistent with public expectations of a Democratic victory, the unadjusted 2006 exit poll data indicates that what has been cast as a typical midterm setback for a struggling president in his second

---

[26] For instance, http://www.acm.org/usacm/weblog/index.php?cat=6.

[27] See the credentials of the interdisciplinary Brennan Center Task Force membership at http://brennancenter.org/programs/downloads/About%20the%20Task%20Force.pdf.

[28] See http://www.gao.gov/new.items/d05956.pdf.

[29] See http://www.blackboxvoting.org/BBVtsxstudy.pdf, http://www.blackboxvoting.org/BBVtsxstudy-supp.pdf, and http://www.blackboxvoting.org/BBVreport.pdf.

[30] Credible reports of voting equipment malfunctions are all too common; one good starting point is http://www.votersunite.org/info/messupsbyvendor.asp.

[31] For example, http://brennancenter.org/programs/downloads/SecurityFull7-3Reduced.pdf.

[32] Election 2006 incidents at http://www.votersunite.org/electionproblems.asp.

term was something rather more remarkable – a landslide repudiation of historic proportions.

We believe that the demographic validity of the Weighted National Poll in 2006 is the clearest possible warning that the ever-growing catalog of reported vulnerabilities in America's electronic vote counting systems are not only *possible* to exploit, *they are actually being exploited.* To those who would rush to find "innocent" explanations on an *ad hoc* basis for the cascade of mathematical evidence that continues to emerge, we ask what purpose is served and what comfort is given by relying on a series of implausible alibis to dispel concerns and head off effective reform?

The vulnerability is manifest; the stakes are enormous; the incentive is obvious; the evidence is strong and persistent. Any system so clearly at risk of interference and gross manipulation cannot and must not be trusted to tally the votes in any future elections.

Appendix 1 – U.S. House Exit Poll Data

1. National Generic U.S. House Exit Poll summary

US House Exit Poll 2006	Opinion Poll (average) Nov 1 - 5	Unadjusted Exit Poll Nov 7 7:07 PM EST	Adjusted Exit Poll Nov 8 1:00 PM EST	Reported Actual % Nov 9	Reported Actual Vote Nov 9
	7 polls**	Sample size 10,207	Sample size 13,251		
Total Democrat vote for US House*	55.0%	55.0%	52.6%	52.7%	40,323,525
Total Republican vote for US House	43.5%	43.5%	45.0%	45.1%	34,565,872
Total Other Parties vote for US House		1.5%	2.4%	2.2%	1,694,392
Total US House					76,583,789
*CBSnews.com, 11/9/06 + additional sources for unopposed candidates					
Democrat - Republican spread (%)	11.5%	11.5%	7.6%	7.6%	
Variance: Exit Poll - Actual [%]	3.9%	3.9%	0.0%		
Democrat - Republican spread (count)		8,807,136	5,820,368	5,820,368	
Variance: Exit Poll - Actual (count)		2,986,768	0		
Variance from actual					
Democrat	2.3%	2.3%	-0.1%		
Republican	-1.6%	-1.6%	-0.1%		
Other	-2.2%	-0.7%	0.2%		

**Fox News, CNN, USA Today/Gallup, ABC News/Wash Post, Pew Research, Newsweek, Time as reported on RealClearPolitics.com

2. Exit Poll Screen Captures

Exit poll screen capture files will be posted at http://www.electiondefensealliance.org/ExitPollData after the release of this report.

3. **U.S. House – preliminary reported tallies by state as-of 11/09/2006, CBSNews.com**

State	U.S. House – D	U.S. House – R	U.S. House - Other	Dem %	Rep %	Other %
AL	224,350	351,650	3,396	38.7%	60.7%	0.6%
AK	81,408	115,062	6,236	40.2%	56.8%	3.1%
AZ	478,573	576,061	72,435	42.5%	51.1%	6.4%
AR	448,058	299,496	0	59.9%	40.1%	0.0%
CA	3,549,128	2,478,884	207,821	56.9%	39.8%	3.3%
CO	727,914	571,699	70,877	53.1%	41.7%	5.2%
CT	652,025	420,995	6,087	60.4%	39.0%	0.6%
DE	196,700	291,052	20,674	38.7%	57.2%	4.1%
FL	1,496,686	2,162,353	68,197	40.2%	58.0%	1.8%
GA	798,809	1,117,086	0	41.7%	58.3%	0.0%
HI	219,588	118,075	0	65.0%	35.0%	0.0%
ID	172,530	243,062	19,401	39.7%	55.9%	4.5%
IL	1,732,380	1,381,232	13,602	55.4%	44.2%	0.4%
IN	802,751	820,569	22,128	48.8%	49.9%	1.3%
IA	489,508	519,796	17,629	47.7%	50.6%	1.7%
KS	360,356	449,548	16,213	43.6%	54.4%	2.0%
KY	596,402	608,771	39,362	47.9%	48.9%	3.2%
LA	294,100	579,514	27,028	32.7%	64.3%	3.0%
ME	344,870	161,335	22,689	65.2%	30.5%	4.3%
MD	827,674	475,065	41,292	61.6%	35.3%	3.1%
MA	792,619	197,722	76,951	74.3%	18.5%	7.2%
MI	1,793,200	1,626,459	97,334	51.0%	46.2%	2.8%
MN	1,153,624	925,500	99,493	53.0%	42.5%	4.6%
MS	251,027	295,184	35,077	43.2%	50.8%	6.0%
MO	965,390	1,031,489	54,436	47.1%	50.3%	2.7%
MT	314,998	476,062	15,494	39.1%	59.0%	1.9%
NE	257,214	329,003	0	43.9%	56.1%	0.0%
NV	286,761	259,237	26,535	50.1%	45.3%	4.6%
NH	209,424	188,774	3,777	52.1%	47.0%	0.9%
NJ	948,740	885,007	25,070	51.0%	47.6%	1.3%
NM	304,058	241,202	0	55.8%	44.2%	0.0%
NY	2,285,026	1,268,408	8,251	64.2%	35.6%	0.2%
NC	935,490	907,236	0	50.8%	49.2%	0.0%
ND	284,242	148,728	0	65.6%	34.4%	0.0%
OH	1,970,118	1,784,993	8,052	52.4%	47.4%	0.2%

State	U.S. House – D	U.S. House – R	U.S. House - Other	Dem %	Rep %	Other %
OK	372,822	517,948	14,278	41.2%	57.2%	1.6%
OR	713,441	522,846	28,446	56.4%	41.3%	2.2%
PA	2,060,969	1,705,435	48,949	54.0%	44.7%	1.3%
RI	264,101	41,753	66,176	71.0%	11.2%	17.8%
SC	466,473	592,639	13,252	43.5%	55.3%	1.2%
SD	460,946	195,736	10,470	69.1%	29.3%	1.6%
TN	860,025	797,431	54,970	50.2%	46.6%	3.2%
TX	1,783,304	2,069,491	142,391	44.6%	51.8%	3.6%
UT	234,024	282,554	31,583	42.7%	51.5%	5.8%
VT	279,170	234,442	11,110	53.2%	44.7%	2.1%
VA	810,365	1,220,073	117,870	37.7%	56.8%	5.5%
WA	802,873	498,872	6,584	61.4%	38.1%	0.5%
WV	258,438	187,895	0	57.9%	42.1%	0.0%
WI	1,001,254	836,054	15,311	54.0%	45.1%	0.8%
WY	184,454	186,394	7,465	48.8%	49.3%	2.0%
Sub-total	37,798,400	34,195,872	1,694,392	51.3%	46.4%	2.3%
Total	73,688,664					

4. **Estimation of votes in uncontested U.S. House races**

Near complete election results were published shortly after November 7th for contested U.S. House races. Most media outlets do not publish the number of votes in uncontested House races, which can be substantial. Public opinion and exit pollsters may sample voters in districts with uncontested candidates. In order to have an accurate baseline for any measurements based on the actual U.S. House vote, it was necessary to estimate the total number of votes cast for unopposed candidates.

To estimate the number of votes in U.S. House races with unopposed candidates:

> We identified jurisdictions, such as Florida, where uncontested candidates do not appear on the ballot at all. These races were excluded from the national aggregate U.S. House votecount.

> For every other uncontested race we looked at historical data on ballots cast for uncontested candidates for a midterm election in exactly the same district. In most cases, the same districts were uncontested in 2002.

> In a few cases, districts with uncontested races in 2006 were not uncontested in recent elections. For those districts, we used the winning margin of the candidate of the same party in a recent midterm election.

> Our overall estimate of votes in uncontested elections – 2,525,125 votes cast nationwide for unopposed Democrats and 370,000 nationwide cast for unopposed Republicans – produces an estimated national grand total that matches quite closely the grand total vote that appears to have been used to calibrate the adjusted U.S. House exit poll on November 8.

Appendix 2 – NEP Methodology 2004 and 2007

METHODS STATEMENT

NATIONAL ELECTION POOL EXIT POLLS
November 2, 2004

NATIONAL/REGIONAL EXIT POLL

Edison Media Research and Mitofsky International conducted exit polls in each state and nationally for the **National Election Pool** (ABC, AP, CBS, CNN, FOX, NBC). The polls should be referred to as a **National Election Pool** (or NEP) **Exit Poll,** conducted by **Edison/Mitofsky. All questionnaires were prepared by NEP.**

The National exit poll was conducted at a sample of 250 polling places among 11,719 Election Day voters representative of the United States.

In addition, 500 absentee and/or early voters in 13 states were interviewed in a pre-election telephone poll. Absentee or early voters were asked the same questions asked at the polling place on Election Day. The absentee results were combined in approximately the correct proportion with voters interviewed at the polling places. The states where absentee/early voters were interviewed for the National exit poll are: Arizona, California, Colorado, Florida, Iowa, Michigan, Nevada, New Mexico, North

Carolina, Oregon, Tennessee, Texas and Washington state. Absentee voters in these states made up 13% of the total national vote in the 2000 presidential election. Another 3% of the 2000 total vote was cast absentee in other states in 2000 and where there is no absentee/early voter telephone poll.

The polling places were selected as a stratified probability sample of each state. A subsample of the state samples was selected at the proper proportions for the National exit poll. Within each polling place an interviewer approached every n^{th} voter as he or she exited the polling place. Approximately 100 voters completed a questionnaire at each polling place. The exact number depends on voter turnout and their cooperation.

For the national tabulations used to analyze an election, respondents are weighted based upon two factors. They are: (1) the probability of selection of the precinct and the respondent within the precinct; (2) by the size and distribution of the best estimate of the vote within geographic sub-regions of the nation. The second step produces consistent estimates *at the time of the tabulation* whether from the tabulations or an estimating model used to make an estimate of the national popular vote. At other times, the estimated national popular vote may differ somewhat from the national tabulations.

All samples are approximations. A measure of the approximation is called the sampling error. Sampling error is affected by the design of the sample, the characteristic being measured and the number of people who have the characteristic. If a characteristic is found in roughly the same proportions in all precincts the sampling error will be lower. If the characteristic is concentrated in a few precincts the sampling error will be larger. Gender would be a good example of a characteristic with a lower sampling error. Characteristics for minority racial groups will have larger sampling errors.

The table below lists typical sampling errors for given size subgroups for a 95% confidence interval. The values in the table should be added and subtracted from the characteristic's percentage in order to construct an interval. 95% of the intervals created this way will contain the value that would be obtained if all voters were interviewed using the same procedures. Other non-sampling factors, including nonresponse, are likely to increase the total error.

% Error Due to Sampling (+/-) for 95% Confidence Interval							
Number of Voters in Base of Percentage							
% Voters with Characteristic	100	101-200	201-500	501-950	951-2350	2351-5250	5251-8000	8001-15000*
5% or 95%	6	5	3	2	2	1	1	1
15% or 85%	11	7	5	4	3	2	1	1
25% or 75%	13	9	6	5	3	2	2	1
50%	15	10	7	5	4	3	2	1

* chart bolding ours

From National Election Pool FAQs 2007

What is the Margin of Error for an exit poll?
Every number estimated from a sample may depart from the official votecount. The difference between a sample result and the number one would get if everyone who cast a vote was interviewed in exactly the same way is called the sampling error. That does not mean the sample result is wrong. Instead, it refers to the potential error due to sampling. **The margin of error for a 95% confidence interval is about +/- 3% for a typical characteristic from the national exit poll and +/-4% for a typical state exit poll.*** Characteristics that are more concentrated in a few polling places, such as race, have larger sampling errors. Other non-sampling factors may increase the total error.

* bolding ours.

Appendix 3 – Mechanics of Vote Manipulation

Practical Constraints on any Nationwide Covert Vote Manipulation Capability
Some critics of the initial draft of this paper released in November 2006 questioned whether it was possible that a systematic tabulation bias could ever be deployed to electronic voting equipment on a nationwide scale without being detected. Others claimed that if that capability truly existed, it should guarantee that one party would remain in permanent control.

The technical and logistical challenges inherent in any attempt to secretly corrupt vote tabulation on a nationwide basis are of course hardly trivial, but expert consensus is that there are multiple credible methods. We believe that the potential methods that could feasibly be used to implement widespread electronic vote manipulation on a national scale with a high probability of remaining undetected are such that a significant lead time would be required prior to the election. There is therefore a risk that any unexpected late-breaking pre-election developments could overcome a pre-programmed bias.

Voting systems risk assessment

Modern American electronic voting systems are geographically dispersed, distributed computer systems that are used intensively but infrequently. The end-to-end voting systems contain thousands of central tabulators and hundreds of thousands of in-precinct voting devices, all of which are purchased, maintained, upgraded, programmed, tested and used in actual elections in over 170,000 precincts across the United States on irregular schedules.

Through hands-on access, individual voting machines can be compromised one at a time through a variety of well-documented exploits.[33] But the sheer number of devices in use makes hands-on vote manipulation on a national scale a massively labor-intensive enterprise. The more individuals that are involved, the greater the likelihood of disclosure. The very ability successfully to orchestrate the collective behavior of tens of thousands of devices to achieve a desired outcome—election after election, without being detected—would depend on minimizing the number of people involved and so would require a significant degree of sophistication.

Undetected widespread votecount corruption would certainly be not only the greatest computer security exploit of all time, it would be the greatest—and, in terms of the ultimate stakes, most lucrative—undetected crime in history. One must presume that any individuals capable of successfully pulling off such an exploit are clever, ruthless, and utterly determined to cover their tracks. We would not expect them to display naiveté nor simplicity, but rather to act at every step to preserve total secrecy of their presence and activities.

Voting system attacks that minimize the number of people involved

The June 2006 Brennan Center report described in great detail precisely how software patches, ballot definition files, and memory cards could be used to

---

[33] See footnotes 26 – 32 above.

enable just one individual to alter the outcome of an election conducted either on touchscreen DREs[34] or on optical scan equipment.[35]

As the Brennan Center report notes:

> . . . [I]n a close statewide election . . . "retail" attacks, or attacks on individual polling places, would not likely affect enough votes to change the outcome. By contrast, the less difficult attacks are centralized attacks: these would occur against the entire voting system and allow an attacker to target many votes with few informed participants.
>
> Least difficult among these less difficult attacks would be attacks that use Software Attack Programs. The reason is relatively straightforward: a software attack allows a single knowledgeable person (or, in some cases, small group of people) to reach hundreds or thousands of machines. For instance, software updates and patches are often sent to jurisdictions throughout a state. Similarly, replaceable media such as memory cards and ballot definition files are generally programmed at the county level (or at the vendor) and sent to every polling place in the county.
>
> These attacks have other benefits: unlike retail denial-of-service attacks, or manual shut off of machine functions, they could provide an attacker's favored candidate with a relatively certain benefit (i.e., addition of x number of votes per machine attacked). And if installed in a clever way, these attacks have a good chance of eluding the standard inspection and testing regimens currently in place.[36]

Long-term evasion of detection

Since it is clear that the motivation exists to take covert control of electronic voting in the United States and that there are credible mechanisms for a small number of malicious insiders at voting equipment vendors to do so, long-term success boils down to evading detection—and so maintaining this power over time. One critical element of maintaining long-term secrecy would be the tradeoff of carefully calibrating the degree of vote manipulation to avoid attracting suspicion, while also ensuring the desired political outcome.

---

[34] Brennan Center June 2006 Report: "The Machinery of Democracy: Protecting Elections in an Electronic World," pp. 34 – 40.

[35] Ibid, p. 78.

[36] Ibid, p. 48.

An individual in the position to introduce a covert vote manipulation software component into the operating system, firmware, device driver, or voting application itself would want to minimize risk of future detection and maximize the ease of changing the outcome of future contests. Ideally covert vote manipulation logic itself should be built into the machine as close to the factory as possible, rather than requiring redistribution of malicious program logic every election cycle; any change to the logic of a complex system could introduce new errors into the behavior of "benign" tabulation logic. And since political circumstances change, not all contests, elections and machines would be subject to the same type and degree of vote manipulation in every election, or the existence of the "Trojan Horse" itself would become all too evident.

Perhaps the easiest method to achieve both goals—long-term secrecy and long-term flexibility—is to introduce a general-purpose vote manipulation component that remains hidden within in the voting equipment for a long period of time, and that can be activated on demand by receipt of an external trigger. The trigger would not only activate the malicious software, but would also contain a parameter defining the size of the manipulation to implement. This is far from science fiction; parameterization is a basic computer software technique in use since the dawn of computing, and parameterization of voting equipment exploits is a powerful attack that is certainly technically feasible.[37]

Although of course we cannot know for certain in the absence of a proper investigation whether this was actually done in 2006, there is strong support for a hypothesis that the logistics of introducing malicious programming on a targeted nationwide basis is both technically feasible and would likely require a substantial lead time, necessitating deployment prior to this past October's "perfect storm."

---

[37] Ibid, p. 38.

STUDY III.

Fingerprints of Election Theft:
Were Competitive Contests Targeted?

Comparison Between Exit Poll and Votecount Disparities in Competitive vs. Noncompetitive Contests in Election 2006

Jonathan Simon, JD, Bruce O'Dell,
Dale Tavris, PhD, Josh Mitteldorf, PhD[1]
Election Defense Alliance

Abstract

In this report, we describe results from a telephone poll conducted the night of the national election of November 2006. The poll methodology was explicitly designed to detect partisan manipulation of the votecount, and to separate evidence for manipulation from poll sampling bias. Our premise was that politically motivated tampering would target races that were projected to be competitive, while the perpetrators would be less motivated to interfere in races that were not projected to be close. Designing our poll to be maximally sensitive to such a pattern, we selected 16 counties around the country where, of the three most prominent races (Governor, Senator or U.S. House), there was at least one competitive contest and one noncompetitive contest. In our study, the responses of the same group of respondents were compared to official election results for pairs of races, one competitive and one noncompetitive. We used paired data analysis to compare disparities between poll and official count for these matched pairs. Our results revealed much larger disparities in competitive than in noncompetitive races ($p<0.007$), suggesting manipulation that consistently favored Republican candidates. We also found a linear relationship between the

---

[1] Jonathan Simon, JD, is Co-founder of Election Defense Alliance (EDA); Bruce O'Dell and Dale Tavris are EDA Data Analysis Co-coordinators; Josh Mitteldorf is a statistician, evolutionary biologist, and election integrity advocate.

---

size of the pro-Republican disparity and the tightness of the election (p<0.000022). These results corroborate analyses published elsewhere, also suggesting significant vote manipulation in favor of Republican candidates in the 2006 general election.

Background

Recent American elections have been tabulated by computerized voting equipment that has been proven through independent investigation by qualified security experts to be wide open to systematic insider manipulation.[2] This fact has been acknowledged in the mainstream American press, and indeed in government reports.[3] Nevertheless, those who, taking the next logical step, gather and present evidence to suggest that at least some recent elections may have *actually been* compromised continue to be met with skepticism and indifference.

In light of this skepticism, election forensics experts have endeavored to take the measure of recent elections from several complementary perspectives. Several methods by which systemic election theft can be perpetrated electronically and invisibly—and with high confidence of evading immediate detection—have been documented.[4] With vote-counting software and hardware both ruled 'proprietary' and off-limits to inspection—and with limited access to, and the scheduled destruction of, paper election records, where they exist— *direct* proof of an electronically-altered election outcome may well be impossible.[5] Yet although systematic electronic vote manipulation may well go undetected both during and after an election, it can still leave behind rather glaring mathematical 'fingerprints'. And when multiple analytic methods find mathematical 'fingerprints' that are all consistent with the same pattern of apparent mistabulation, the case becomes very strong—at least for anyone

---

[2] See, e.g., http://brennancenter.org/dynamic/subpages/download_file_39288.pdf, http://itpolicy.princeton.edu/voting/ts-paper.pdf, http://www.sos.ca.gov/elections/elections_vsr.htm, http://www.blackboxvoting.org/BBVtsxstudy.pdf, or http://www.blackboxvoting.org/BBVreport.pdf.

[3] See, e.g., Government Accountability Office, Oct. 2005, at http://www.gao.gov/new.items/d05956.pdf.

[4] See note 2.

[5] To these difficulties we may add the simple-enough employment of self-deleting tabulation code, which would leave no trace of foul play even in the unlikely event inspection were permitted.

willing to contemplate the evidence, even though the implications are profoundly disturbing.

In *Landslide Denied: Exit Polls vs. Vote Count 2006*,[6] a study published shortly after the 2006 election ('E2006'), authors Simon and O'Dell analyzed the nationwide disparity between official votecounts and the E2006 exit polls. They concluded that mistabulation of votes reduced the Democratic margin in total votes cast for the House of Representatives by a minimum of 4%, or *3 million votes*. Based on the official margins of House races, the authors further concluded that, accurately tabulated, E2006 would have been an epic landslide, netting the Democrats a very substantial number of additional seats in Congress.

By examining in detail the 2006 U.S. House exit poll data's underlying demographic and voter-preference questions, the authors were able to confirm both the validity of the exit poll sample and the size of the official mistabulation.

Past comparisons between exit polls and official results have been questioned on the grounds that sampling bias may have played a role. By comparing the national sample's responses to a variety of established demographic and voter-preference benchmarks, *Landslide Denied* established that the national exit poll certainly did *not* 'oversample Democrats'.[7] *Landslide Denied* also argued that the Republicans might have succeeded in holding on to the House and the Senate, but for the fact that the manipulation that apparently benefited them was calibrated and engineered based on pre-October polling numbers, which subsequently shifted dramatically further toward the Democrats in the final weeks before the election. If the election had been held a month earlier, the vote-shift evidenced by the exit poll disparity would have sufficed to keep the Republicans in power.

This analysis has not been rebutted or challenged, although its evidence and conclusions are clearly presented and quite straightforward. On the other hand, it has gone almost completely unreported.[8]

---

[6] See https://codered2014.com/wp-content/uploads/2020/04/landslideDenied_v.9_071507.pdf.

[7] The national sample that had allegedly 'oversampled Democrats' gave President Bush approval numbers at or above established benchmarks. Several other key indicators (such as racial composition, Party ID, vote for President in 2004, and Congressional approval) all corroborated the fact that the sample leaned, if anything, to the right.

[8] *Landslide Denied* was posted on the Election Defense Alliance website on 11/17/06, and simultaneously distributed through U.S. Newswire to hundreds of media outlets. It was picked up by *one*, a passing reference in a small publication in North Dakota. *Landslide Denied* was also submitted for inclusion in the record of Senate Rules Committee hearings on election fraud and security. It was not accepted and no explanation was offered for its rejection.

In the 2006 elections, the national House exit poll could provide, at most, an indication of aggregate mistabulation on a nationwide basis. Even so, in planning and preparing for forensic analysis of the 2006 elections, it was fair to assume that any damning evidence exit polls might provide would once again face skepticism in the press (as in 'as usual, the exit polls oversampled Democrats and cannot be relied upon'), and among official voices of both political parties. Therefore, Election Defense Alliance sought to capture data from the 2006 election from a different and, we hoped, complementary angle.

Our Approach and Methodology

In order to counter the anticipated dismissal of 2006 national exit poll evidence on the basis of sample bias, we turned to an approach that would effectively remove sampling bias as a factor by measuring how *the same sample of voters responded with respect to different electoral contests.* Our study was based on the premise that vote theft would be targeted to races that were within striking distance of a shift. We hypothesized that races that appeared close in the pre-election polls would be targeted for theft, while races that were projected to be landslides would not be corrupted. We designed a study to compare pairs of competitive and non-competitive races in such a way that responses from the same polling respondents would be used for both.

Therefore, we selected counties in which we anticipated, based on pre-election polling, that there would be at least one competitive contest and at least one noncompetitive contest among the races for U.S. House, U.S. Senate, and the governorship of the state.[9] For the purpose of paired (t-test) analysis, we viewed contests decided by a margin smaller than 10% as 'competitive' and contests decided by a margin of 10% or greater as 'noncompetitive.'[10]

---

[9] Although hundreds of counties nationwide would have met these basic criteria, our selection was further constrained by budgetary considerations: with approximately $36,000 available for this project, the counties chosen had to be sufficiently small that the cost of obtaining the voter lists would not be prohibitive, and that enough counties could be surveyed to generate a statistically meaningful number of data points for analysis. Altogether 19 counties were surveyed for this project, of which 16 turned out to meet the criterion of having at least one competitive and one noncompetitive contest. These 16 counties form the basis of our primary analysis.

[10] Our 'paired' analysis of course necessitates a categorical line of demarcation. While 10% is a common-sense choice, others might be imagined. As will be seen below, the actual race margins tended to a bi-modal distribution (mean margin for competitive races = 3.2%, mean margin for noncompetitive races = 20.5%), generally distant enough from the 10% line to remove any concern about its arbitrariness. In fact, the divider could have been placed at 9% or 8% without having any impact on our paired analysis.

All contests in each selected county were sampled by a *single* Election Night survey of actual voters (whether at-precinct, early, or absentee) conducted by telephone on our behalf by the polling firm Survey U.S.A. As a result, the *same set of respondents* was asked to indicate how they had voted in each of the contests within each selected county. This 'apples-to-apples' comparison, rather than any presumed freedom from bias in the samples themselves,[11] provided the basis for our analysis.

Hypothesis

Our hypothesis was that, although there would of course be disparities between survey results and votecounts in most (if not all) contests, in the absence of vote shifting foul play *selectively targeted to competitive races* there would be no statistically significant pattern of disparities by which competitive and noncompetitive contests could be distinguished.

Results

Table 1 on the following page presents our core data for the 16 counties which had both competitive and noncompetitive contests. An expanded table— showing the actual winning margins of these contests, as well as the actual votecount and exit poll percentages within the sampled counties—is presented as Appendix 1.

Reading from left to right, Table 1 presents the county surveyed, the office contested, whether that contest proved to be competitive or noncompetitive, the disparity between votecount and survey results in competitive and noncompetitive races respectively, and the difference within each county between the disparities found in competitive and noncompetitive races (using the mean disparity when there were two competitive or noncompetitive races within a county).

'Red shift' and 'blue shift' defined

---

[11] In this type of survey, calls are placed on Election Night to all voters on the county registration lists, but only those respondents who indicate they actually cast a vote are included in the survey results. Response rates are typically quite low and there is no attempt to eliminate self-select response bias (e.g., if Republicans or Democrats have a greater tendency to respond and are therefore over-represented) via stratification techniques. Such efforts are not necessary for our purposes because response bias does not adversely affect our *comparison* between competitive and noncompetitive races drawn from the same set of respondents.

We designate an official votecount more Republican than the survey results to be a 'red shift,' and an official votecount more Democratic than the survey results to be a 'blue shift.'

TABLE 1

Comparison Between Survey and Votecount Disparities in Competitive vs. Noncompetitive Contests in Election 2006
(All Contests in Each County Sampled by A Single Election Night Survey of Actual Voters)

County, State	Contest	Competitive?*	Within-County Exit Poll - Vote Count Disparity Competitive Contests (R-/D-)	Within-County Exit Poll - Vote Count Disparity NonCompetitive Contests (R-/D-)	Within-County Difference Between Avg. Competitive and NonCompetitive Disparities***
Hardee, FL	Governor	C	7.5%		11.25%
	Senator	NC		-3.5%	
	House: FL-13	C	8.0%		
Okeechobee, FL	Governor	C	5.5%		12.50%
	Senator	NC		-9.5%	
	House: FL-16	C**	0.5%		
Emanuel, GA	Governor	NC		-1.0%	4.00%
	House: GA-12	C	3.0%		
Jefferson, GA	Governor	NC		0.0%	0.00%
	House: GA-12	C	0.0%		
Jefferson, IA	Governor	NC		0.5%	11.00%
	House: IA-2	C	11.5%		
Van Buren, IA	Governor	NC		8.0%	10.50%
	House: IA-2	C	18.5%		
Mower, MN	Senator	NC		-2.5%	6.00%
	House: MN-1	C	3.5%		
Pipestone, MN	Senator	NC		-1.5%	1.00%
	House: MN-1	C	-0.5%		
Cedar, MO	Senator	C	-1.5%		12.50%
	House: MO-4	NC		-14.0%	
Henry, MO	Senator	C	-1.5%		16.50%
	House: MO-4	NC		-18.0%	
Humboldt, NV	Governor	C	5.0%		-2.25%
	Senator	NC		5.0%	
	House: NV-2	C	0.5%		
Adams, OH	Governor	NC		-2.5%	8.75%
	Senator	NC		-1.0%	
	House: OH-2	C	7.0%		
Bradford, PA	Governor	NC		6.0%	-6.75%
	Senator	NC		7.5%	
	House: PA-10	C	0.0%		
Wyoming, PA	Governor	NC		-3.0%	-1.50%
	Senator	NC		-1.0%	
	House: PA-10	C	-3.5%		
Haywood, TN	Governor	NC		-2.0%	8.00%
	Senator	C	5.0%		
	House: TN-8	NC		-4.0%	
Lancaster, VA	Senator	C	-1.0%		-4.00%
	House: VA-1	NC		3.0%	
AVERAGE			3.6%	-1.7%	5.47%

* Contests decided by a 9% or smaller margin are designated competitive; 10% or larger noncompetitive.
** Contest for seat vacated by Mark Foley; shifted from noncompetitive to competitive status during October 2006.
*** Number is positive (+) where net shift is to Republican in competitive vs. noncompetitive contests.
All surveys conducted via telephone on Election Night 2006 by Survey USA.

The right-hand column conveys the overall picture. A positive percentage in the right-hand column indicates that there was more of a red shift (or less of a blue shift) in competitive than in noncompetitive contests in that county. That is, a positive percentage indicates a net shift toward the Republican candidate in the competitive versus noncompetitive contest(s) within a given county.

An Individual County Example

To take Hardee County, Florida, as an example: the competitive contests were for Governor and U.S. House and the noncompetitive contest was for the U.S. Senate. The competitive contests exhibited a red shift of 7.5% and 8.0% respectively: meaning the official votecounts in Hardee in those races were 7.5% and 8.0% more Republican than the survey results, an average of 7.75%.

In the noncompetitive contest for U.S. Senate we see a blue shift of 3.5%, meaning the official votecount was 3.5% more Democratic than the survey results.

Overall, therefore, in Hardee County - *as measured by the survey responses of precisely the same group of voters* - the official votecounts in competitive contests were shifted by a net of 11.25% (that is, by 7.75% + 3.5%) to the Republican candidates, relative to the official votecount in the noncompetitive contest.

Sixteen-county analysis

We find that relative red shift toward the Republican candidate in competitive contests occurred in 11 of the 16 counties. Only four counties exhibited a relative blue shift away from the Republican candidate in competitive contests.[12] One county exhibited no net shift, red or blue.

More significantly, we found that for the 19 competitive contests, the average survey vs. votecount disparity was a red shift of 3.6%, and for the 20 noncompetitive races the average disparity was a blue shift of 1.7%. *Competitive*

---

[12] Interestingly, two of the four 'net blue shift' counties are located in Pennsylvania, a state which stood out in E2006 for bucking the red shift pattern in statewide U.S. Senate races. While a total of 21 Senate races exhibited red shifts (mean = 4.2%), Pennsylvania, a state under Democratic administrative control, was one of only five states to exhibit a blue shift (2%) in its Senate race. At this point we can do little more than speculate about the possible effects of partisan administrative control upon both aggregate mistabulation and targeting patterns. (See also http://kdka.com/topstories/local_story_311194635.html)

contests were therefore relatively more red-shifted by an average of 5.3% per contest.[13]

Statistical significance of competitive race 'red shift'

Employing the paired t-test (two-tailed) to evaluate the statistical significance of this result, we find it to be statistically significant at the $p<0.007$ level, meaning that that much of a difference between disparities in competitive and noncompetitive contests would be expected by chance only *seven in 1000 times.*[14]

According to our hypothesis, the string of positive percentages in the right-hand column should not occur unless systematic election mistabulation is occurring—selectively, in competitive contests, and favoring Republican candidates. In the absence of targeted mistabulation, the mean value at the bottom of the right-hand column would be at or very close to zero.

Discussion

We have already discussed the evidence for an *aggregate* mistabulation of votes in E2006 of a magnitude sufficient to alter the outcome of dozens of federal and statewide elections.[15] The aggregate evidence is based on the quasi-official exit polls conducted by Edison Research and Mitofsky International ('Edison/Mitofsky') for the media consortium known as the National Election Pool ('NEP').

In *Landslide Denied* it is shown not only that the NEP sample of the national electorate (i.e., the aggregate vote for all House races) was of a size that makes it a virtual impossibility that the 4% poll-vote disparity could occur as a result

---

[13] Because of the above-mentioned averaging within counties, the 16-county mean difference between disparities in competitive and noncompetitive contests was a slightly higher 5.47%.

[14] A one-tailed t-test, justifiably employed if we are testing only for the likelihood of an overall competitive contest *red* shift, would yield a p value of 0.003, a 3/1000th prospect of chance occurrence. It should also be noted that a regression analysis of magnitude/direction of shift relative to magnitude of contest margin yields an F value of 21.9, corresponding to a p value of $p<0.000022$ and strongly corroborating our finding of strong correlation using the paired testing approach. Such an analysis also dispenses with what some might consider an arbitrary dividing line between competitive and noncompetitive contests at a margin of 10%, necessary for the paired-test approach. The shift-margin correlation is powerful using either approach. Please see Appendix 2 for this analysis.

[15] In *Landslide Denied*, the authors established a net shift to the Republican candidates for U.S. House of Representatives of at least 3 million votes nationwide.

of chance or sampling *error* but also, more significantly, that the alleged political *bias* of the sample towards the Democrats *did not exist*, as proven by the demographics of the exit poll sample itself.

Yet whenever a direct comparison between poll results (whether pre-election, exit, or post-election) and official votecounts is made and a disparity is noted, it is, inexplicably, always the *polls* that the media chorus hastens to discount and dismiss. Demonstrating the lax standards of computer security and the inadequate procedural safeguards universally applied to our electronic voting systems seems to make no impression. The present study was undertaken because we anticipated—correctly, as it turned out—that direct poll-vote comparisons, if they appeared to indicate outcome-determinative mistabulation, would likely face hasty dismissal, predictably on the grounds of sample bias. We therefore sought a methodology that would serve to eliminate *any* effect of sampling bias from the equation.[16]

How our study neutralizes the impact of sample bias
In the vast majority of federal and state political contests, it is possible to ascertain well in advance of Election Day the degree to which the race will be competitive. It is therefore possible to target competitive contests for fraudulent manipulation in a timeframe that allows the necessary mechanisms to be selectively deployed[17] (for example, tainted memory cards,[18] or malicious code

---

[16] Much of the analysis in E2004 focused on the astounding individual exit poll-votecount disparities that turned up in certain states and in the national popular vote. But some attention was also given to the telling *distribution* of disparities between states that were considered 'battlegrounds' on the one hand and 'safe' states on the other. It emerged that, of the 11 battleground states, 10 were red-shifted. It further emerged that, relative to their respective average MOEs (the battleground states were more heavily sampled than the safe states, which makes a shift of the same magnitude less likely to occur in a battleground state), the battleground states as a group were nearly three times as red shifted as the safe states.

So in a sense, in E2004, there was already a rough but glaring comparative analysis of competitive and noncompetitive states, pointing strongly to targeted vote-shifting. The question raised was, if the exit poll-votecount disparity was caused by 'reluctant Bush responders', why did this very convenient phenomenon (for which no evidence was ever presented) occur so disproportionately in competitive states; that is, why were Bush voters reluctant in Ohio and Florida (where it counted) but not in, say, Utah or Idaho (where it did not)? No cogent answer was ever given.

[17] See http://brennancenter.org/dynamic/subpages/download_file_39288.pdf pages 37-39 for parameterized attacks on voting systems.

[18] See http://itpolicy.princeton.edu/voting/ts-paper.pdf for attacks on voting systems via centrally-programmed memory cards.

or code parameters installed under the guise of a legitimate software distribution).

We found that we could identify such targeting patterns using poll-vote comparisons from which sampling bias had been eliminated as a factor. In the 16 counties we studied, *in the absence of fraud targeted to competitive contests*, we would expect no particular correlation between poll-vote disparities and the competitiveness of the contests. Disparities would of course be expected, both as predicted by the statistical margin of error ('MOE') of each poll and as a result of any sampling *bias* independent of such pure statistical considerations.[19]

But, since we are not relying upon a direct poll-votecount comparison, but rather upon comparison between disparities, we are not concerned with the impact of either sampling error or sampling bias on the poll-votecount disparities that constitute our data set. Indeed, sampling bias in any given county survey could be very substantial *without affecting the validity of our competitive-noncompetitive comparison*, because the *same* putatively biased set of respondents would be our benchmark for both competitive and noncompetitive contest votecounts.

Take, as an example, Van Buren County, Iowa. In this county the noncompetitive Governor's race votecount margin was shifted 8% towards the Republican relative to the poll, a result on which it might be suggested that sampling bias (oversampling of Democrats) might have had an impact. But in the same county, *and with the same set of respondents*, the competitive House race votecount margin was shifted *18.5%* towards the Republican relative to the poll. We can see that sampling bias, whether or not it was in fact present, *drops out of the equation entirely*, because it would be *equally* present in both races

---

[19] It is important to understand the distinction between sampling *error* and sampling *bias*. Sampling error, generally reflected in a poll's stated MOE, derives from the statistical chance that a fairly drawn sample (i.e., one drawn at random and without bias) will misrepresent the whole to some quantifiable, and usually very small, degree.

Sampling bias, on the other hand, extends beyond any such purely statistical limitations to impound any intentional or inadvertent biases in the sampling process that yield further misrepresentation. A classic example would be interviewers who ignore random selection instructions by choosing respondents whom they know or who look more 'like them'; another would be a differential response rate based on categorical receptivity to being interviewed or ownership of the technology (e.g., telephone, computer) used for the poll.

Effects of sampling bias can be virtually eliminated by a thorough demographic weighting process such as that employed by the NEP prior to publication of their poll results. Such a process was not, however, necessary to the design of the current study, as explained in fn. 11.

(using the same set of respondents) and could not account for the 10.5% difference between the two shifts.

Thus, in the absence of a competitive contest targeting pattern, disparities would be just about equally likely to occur, and equally likely to be in the "red" or "blue" direction, in competitive and noncompetitive contests alike.[20]

This is not what we found. *We found a strong correlation between the competitiveness of a contest and the poll-vote disparity for the county we surveyed.* Competitive contest votecounts, taken as a group, were strongly red-shifted, with an official votecount more Republican than poll result, as compared to noncompetitive contest votecounts.

The goal of our study was not to identify particular contests, counties, or districts as having been targeted for rigging, but rather to determine whether there existed an overall *pattern* indicative of a targeting process, an indelible fingerprint of electoral manipulation.

In this we succeeded, to a high level of statistical significance.

Methodological limitations

No discussion would be complete without a frank acknowledgement of our study's limitations. We were compelled by budgetary considerations to select a small set of relatively small counties for our study. We could not afford to test any of the larger counties, where the cost of registration lists and survey completions would have been prohibitive.

In applying our approach to future elections, in particular to 2008, we hope to significantly expand the number and scope of counties surveyed. Should E2008 be as much a victim of targeted rigging as E2006 appears to have been, the expanded study we expect to undertake will expose and quantify the pattern to a 'DNA-level' of statistical certainty.

Or, put another way, it would appear that in light of political circumstances any effort to seize national control through manipulation of the vote counting in 2008 will have to be either of an aggregate magnitude that is truly shocking and so carries a high risk of exposure, or so well-targeted that the targeting pattern itself sticks out like a sore thumb.

---

[20] "Just about equally" because the MOE decreases very slightly between a 50%-50% contest and a 75%-25% contest (most competitive and least competitive ends of our spectrum of contests). At the 200 – 300 sample sizes we are primarily working with, the MOE decrease is about 1%. This minor variation had no quantitative impact on our analysis.

To deter or expose massive electoral subversion, both modes of attack must be anticipated and monitored.

Conclusion

Our study was modest in scope because of financial constraints, but it was tightly-focused in its design. The result shines a powerful triple beam into the dark corner of secret electronic vote-counting in American elections.

> First, it detects a clear pattern indicating a wholesale shift in tallied votes. This is consistent with our study of aggregate vote shifting presented in *Landslide Denied*.

> Second, it identifies the overall direction of the shift: in favor of Republican candidates, once again corroborating our aggregate findings in *Landslide Denied*.

> Third, it confirms the common-sense notion that any group with the will and ability to secretly manipulate vote tabulation would likely focus their efforts on changing the outcomes of close contests, where the power of electronic vote-shifting would be maximized through selective targeting, while at the same time minimizing the size of the aggregate shift—and the corresponding risk of discovery.

We found evidence, in *Landslide Denied*, of an aggregate net shift of 3 million votes nationwide from Democratic to Republican candidates for the U.S. House. If one imagines those shifted votes distributed randomly and evenly across the 435 contests, it would amount to a net shift of just under 7000 votes per contest. If we apply this model by taking 3500 putatively shifted votes from each Republican candidate and transferring them back to the Democratic candidate (for a net shift of 7000 votes), it would reverse the outcome of 15 House contests in 2006. This is not an inconsiderable effect, as it would have given the Democrats a 30-seat greater margin (248 – 187). If, however, we target and apply those same 3 million shifted votes to the most competitive Republican victories, we find it would instead reverse the outcome of 112 contests, giving the Democrats an overwhelming 345 – 90 majority in the House.

We naturally do not suggest that vote-shifting in 2006 was, or could be, targeted with such hindsight-aided precision. Our point is rather that targeting, even at the modest level of precision obtainable months in advance (from historical voting patterns and pre-election polling) can vastly increase the bottom-line effect of the covert shift of a given total number of votes or—conversely and more ominously—can enable a political control-shifting electoral manipulation that leaves only the smallest and all-but-undetectable fingerprint of *aggregate* mistabulation.[21]

In E2006, the explosive movement toward the Democrats in the month of October[22] would have overwhelmed a rational targeting plan finalized during the pre-October period, after which the logistics of further deployment or recalibration of vote-shifting mechanisms would most likely have been prohibitively problematic.[23] Such an extraordinary pre-election dynamic certainly cannot be counted on again to defeat attempts to seize political control via electoral manipulation. We submit that our findings regarding targeting in the present study, coupled with our earlier findings in *Landslide Denied*, sound an alarm for democracy, *and make a compelling case for expanded monitoring of future elections.*

We restate here the concluding sentences of *Landslide Denied*, as these latest findings only serve to increase the urgency of our warning:

> 'The vulnerability is manifest; the stakes are enormous; the incentive is obvious; the evidence is strong and persistent. Any system so clearly at risk of interference and gross manipulation cannot and must not be trusted to tally the votes in any future elections.'

---

[21] This is especially ominous in light of the fact that, in the absence of any effective system of *intrinsic* electoral audits, the only check mechanism of sufficient sensitivity and statistical power to effectively challenge the official numbers spit out by the computers is the demographically validated national exit poll (assuming that 'unadjusted' exit poll results are made available in 2008). But this check mechanism detects only an aggregate disparity. Targeted rigging allows the theft of both the Presidency and Congress with a footfall light enough to avoid setting off this sole remaining burglar alarm.

[22] See *Landslide Denied* pp. 13 – 15.

[23] See *Landslide Denied*, Appendix 2. Although the vulnerabilities of vote-counting computers make it possible to shift (or delete or fabricate) virtually unlimited numbers of votes, the size of the footprint and the likelihood of detection of course increases accordingly. The logical vote-shifting algorithm therefore remains 'take no more than you need'. A possible exception is the Presidential race, in which there is a rather compelling advantage to shifting enough votes nationwide to ensure a popular-vote victory, even though an Electoral College victory might be secured with a well-targeted fraction of those votes. A popular vote victory–as reflected in the contrasting behavior of the Democratic candidates in 2000 and 2004—plays a major role in granting or denying a Presidential candidate the standing, in the media and in the court of public opinion, to challenge even quite egregious anomalies in decisive battleground states.

**Comparison Between Exit Poll and Vote Count Disparities
In Competitive vs. Noncompetitive Contests In Election 2006**
(All Contests In Each County Sampled By A Single Election Night Survey Of Actual Voters In That County)

County, State	Contest	Contest Margin / Statewide or CD-wide	Competitive/NonCompetitive* / C/NC	Within-County Exit Poll		Within-County Vote Count		Within-County Exit Poll - Vote Count Disparity Competitive Contests (R+/D-)	Within-County Exit Poll - Vote Count Disparity NonCompetitive Contests (R+/D-)	Within-County Difference Between Avg. Competitive and NonCompetitive Disparities***
				R	D	R	D			
Hardee, FL	Governor	7% [R]	C	49%	45%	57%	38%	7.5%		11.25%
	Senator	22% [D]	NC	50%	46%	48%	51%		-3.5%	
	House: FL-13	<1% [R]	C	51%	45%	61%	39%	8.0%		
Okeechobee, FL	Governor	7% [R]	C	45%	51%	51%	46%	5.5%		12.50%
	Senator	22% [D]	NC	44%	54%	35%	64%		-9.5%	
	House: FL-16	1% [D]	C**	45%	52%	45%	51%	0.5%		
Emanuel, GA	Governor	20% [R]	NC	59%	35%	60%	38%		-1.0%	4.00%
	House: GA-12	<1% [R]	C	56%	38%	63%	37%	3.0%		
Jefferson, GA	Governor	20% [R]	NC	50%	49%	50%	49%		0.0%	0.00%
	House: GA-12	<1% [D]	C	46%	52%	47%	53%	0.0%		
Jefferson, IA	Governor	10% [D]	NC	38%	56%	39%	56%		0.5%	11.00%
	House: IA-2	2% [D]	C	43%	54%	55%	45%	11.5%		
Van Buren, IA	Governor	10% [D]	NC	43%	56%	50%	47%		8.0%	10.50%
	House: IA-2	2% [D]	C	45%	54%	64%	36%	18.5%		
Mower, MN	Senator	20% [D]	NC	33%	62%	31%	65%		-2.5%	6.00%
	House: MN-1	6% [D]	C	33%	64%	38%	62%	3.5%		
Pipestone, MN	Senator	20% [D]	NC	55%	44%	52%	44%		-1.5%	1.00%
	House: MN-1	6% [D]	C	56%	43%	56%	44%	-0.5%		
Cedar, MO	Senator	3% [D]	C	59%	38%	56%	38%	-1.5%		12.50%
	House: MO-4	39% [D]	NC	56%	37%	43%	52%		-14.0%	
Henry, MO	Senator	3% [D]	C	46%	50%	44%	51%	-1.5%		16.50%
	House: MO-4	39% [D]	NC	40%	57%	22%	75%		-18.0%	
Humboldt, NV	Governor	4% [R]	C	65%	28%	69%	22%	5.0%		-2.25%
	Senator	14% [R]	NC	65%	30%	70%	25%		5.0%	
	House: NV-2	6% [R]	C	59%	34%	60%	34%	0.5%		
Adams, OH	Governor	23% [D]	NC	45%	52%	43%	55%		-2.5%	8.75%
	Senator	12% [D]	NC	46%	52%	46%	54%		-1.0%	
	House: OH-2	2% [R]	C	47%	51%	55%	45%	7.0%		
Bradford, PA	Governor	20% [D]	NC	48%	48%	58%	44%		6.0%	-6.75%
	Senator	18% [D]	NC	48%	49%	57%	43%		7.5%	
	House: PA-10	6% [D]	C	51%	45%	53%	47%	0.0%		
Wyoming, PA	Governor	20% [D]	NC	47%	49%	46%	54%		-3.0%	-1.50%
	Senator	18% [D]	NC	54%	42%	55%	45%		-1.0%	
	House: PA-10	6% [D]	C	59%	38%	58%	42%	-3.5%		
Haywood, TN	Governor	29% [D]	NC	20%	77%	19%	80%		-2.0%	8.00%
	Senator	3% [R]	C	30%	68%	36%	64%	5.0%		
	House: TN-8	46% [D]	NC	19%	77%	17%	83%		-4.0%	
Lancaster, VA	Senator	1% [D]	C	57%	40%	57%	42%	-1.0%		-4.00%
	House: VA-1	26% [R]	NC	60%	37%	64%	35%		3.0%	
Average								3.6%	-1.7%	5.47%

* Contests decided by a 3% or smaller margin are designated competitive; 10% or larger noncompetitive.
** Contest for seat vacated by Mark Foley; shifted from noncompetitive to competitive status during October 2006.
*** Number is positive (+) where net shift is to Republican in competitive vs. noncompetitive contests.
All surveys conducted via telephone on Election Night 2006 by Survey USA. (Hyperlinks show survey details including MOEs)

Appendix 2 – Regression Analysis

The purpose of regression analysis was to look at the correlation between vote margin and within-county exit poll-votecount disparity. We included in this analysis as a separate data point each of the 39 races in each of the 16 counties that served as the basis for our paired t-test analysis. This analysis represents a way of looking at the same data as we looked at in our paired t-test analysis, but from a different angle, with two advantages over the paired t-test analysis and two disadvantages.

The disadvantages were:

1. The regression analysis doesn't completely eliminate bias (though it eliminates the great majority of potential bias) as an explanation for our results, since some counties contributed data points to a non-competitive race without being matched by a competitive race, or vice versa. Therefore, the exact same population was not used for competitive and non-competitive races in this analysis. However, the two populations were very similar, and whereas a *potential* for a small amount of bias exists in this analysis, we see no reason to suspect that it does exist.

2. The rationale for using the paired t-test was that competitive races were characterized by the potential for fraud, whereas there would be no reason for committing fraud in non-competitive races. With that assumption, the *vote margins* would be unimportant, as long as the races could be characterized as competitive or non-competitive. If this assumption was accurate, then an analysis that included the *vote margins* of the race would include meaningless data, which could weaken the ability to detect meaningful differences between competitive and non-competitive races.

The advantages were:

1. When analyzing continuous variables (which vote margins are), regression analysis generally provides more power to detect meaningful differences than t-tests, which do not make use of the continuous nature of the variable, but dichotomize it instead.

2. To the extent that it might have been difficult to ascertain whether a race was competitive vs. non-competitive prior to the election, it would be reasonable to assume that the more competitive a race was the more likely that it would be subject to fraud. And, it is reasonable to suspect that the closer a race was presumed to be, the more susceptible it would be to fraud.

The regression analysis provided an F value of 21.85, corresponding to a p value of p<0.000022. That means that the correlation between vote margin and within-county exit poll-votecount disparity was so strong that it would have occurred only about one out of 50,000 times on the basis of chance alone (see graph below).

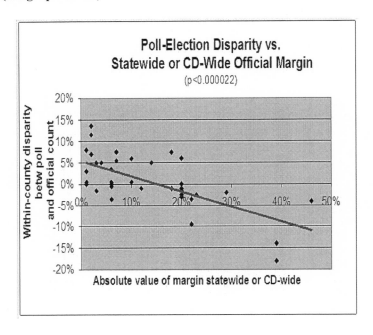

Appendix 3 – SurveyUSA Data Links

State	County	Link
MO	Henry	http://www.voterrollcall.com/client/PollReport.aspx?q=a6e072a1-a39e-4f6c-95e4-af1a0150bcac
MO	Cedar	http://www.voterrollcall.com/client/PollReport.aspx?q=cfd957af-bc6d-406e-b05e-23f025dd91a3
TN	Haywood	http://www.voterrollcall.com/client/PollReport.aspx?q=f5256fb4-48be-434f-a8ac-1e6c9c768e00
FL	Hardee	http://www.voterrollcall.com/client/PollReport.aspx?q=7bf59ee4-894f-43fd-9113-23bc4a8a21a8
FL	Okeechobee	http://www.voterrollcall.com/client/PollReport.aspx?q=aae0d44f-8fd7-426b-9186-cdd8d2222292
PA	Bradford	http://www.voterrollcall.com/client/PollReport.aspx?q=d3b628f5-5da3-42c7-96b9-350bc4fd11d2
PA	Wyoming	http://www.voterrollcall.com/client/PollReport.aspx?q=f04c2158-acee-4a6e-912f-14eef91303f0

MN	Mower	http://www.voterrollcall.com/client/PollReport.aspx?g=f065fa14-3452-4321-99dc-42fa8c48ee53
MN	Pipestone	http://www.voterrollcall.com/client/PollReport.aspx?g=6889cbbc-ade1-400e-a49e-c629be32bce0
OH	Adams	http://www.voterrollcall.com/client/PollReport.aspx?g=42f186df-1fdc-4f41-b5d6-b9b30026106d
GA	Jefferson	http://www.voterrollcall.com/client/PollReport.aspx?g=b962e036-0513-423b-9a5b-5d29892bf0c3
GA	Emanuel	http://www.voterrollcall.com/client/PollReport.aspx?g=dd565bbb-8dfc-4143-bd8c-016ac197203b
IA	Van Buren	http://www.voterrollcall.com/client/PollReport.aspx?g=b19fd14c-f493-406f-a18c-cf62dc1e1df6
IA	Jefferson	http://www.voterrollcall.com/client/PollReport.aspx?g=2b03ce9c-121a-45f4-a3d5-5453d177465d
NV	Humboldt	http://www.voterrollcall.com/client/PollReport.aspx?g=a36dfabf-2b31-4513-bc83-5b416056f84d
VA	Lancaster	http://www.voterrollcall.com/client/PollReport.aspx?g=70c3610b-c22e-49ed-b5a1-e102cf6ad4cf

STUDY IV.

Believe It (Or Not):
The 2010 Massachusetts
Special Election for U.S. Senate

Jonathan D. Simon
August 27, 2010[1]

Background

On January 19, 2010, the Commonwealth of Massachusetts held a Special Election to fill the Senate seat left open by the death of Senator Edward Kennedy. It would be difficult to overstate the political implications of this election. Because the seat was the 60th for the Democrats, it carried with it the effective balance of power in the Senate: without it, in a dramatically polarized and decidedly uncooperative political environment, the Democrats would not be able to override a GOP filibuster. As the media let Americans know, everything from the shape of healthcare policy to financial regulation, from energy and environmental policy to critical judicial appointments hung in the balance.

Just as significantly, the victory by Republican Scott Brown over supposed shoo-in Martha Coakley was taken and trumpeted as a "sign:" the political calculus for the upcoming general elections in 2010 and 2012 was instantly rewritten, with the anger and unrest that apparently produced Brown's victory establishing expectations of catastrophic losses for the Democrats in November and beyond. All in all, the political impact of this single, under-the-radar state election was seismic, very nearly "presidential."

---

[1] Revised October 28, 2011.

The Electoral System

With stakes that high, citizens not only of Massachusetts but of the rest of the United States would hope to find firm basis for *knowledge*, as opposed to mere *faith*, that the votes were accurately counted as cast and that the seating of the certified winner, along with the massive implications alluded to above, at least reflected the will and intent of the voting constituency. Instead, this is what a citizen seeking such knowledge about the Massachusetts Special Election would find:

- 97% of the ballots cast were counted unobservably by optical scan equipment ("opscan"), scanning voter-marked paper ballots; 3% of the ballots cast were publicly hand-counted.[2]

- The opscan devices were programmable computers manufactured by two corporations, Diebold/Premier Election Solutions ("Diebold/Premier") and Elections Systems and Software ("ES&S"), which together supply 80% of such equipment nationwide,[3] and 100% in Massachusetts.[4]

- The vast majority[5] of the opscan devices were programmed, distributed and serviced by the highly secretive LHS Corporation, located in Methuen, Massachusetts.

- No systematic audit of the count was performed.

- No spot-checks of the count were performed.

- There was no recount of any ballots.

- There were no exit polls performed.

---

[2] Vote counting protocols identified by Massachusetts City and Town Directory at http://www.sec.state.ma.us/ele/eleclk/clkidx.htm; election returns at http://www.boston.com/news/special/politics/2010/senate/results.html.

[3] Source information at http://www.verifiedvoting.org/verifier/.

[4] Of the 280 opscan communities in Massachusetts, 223 use the Diebold/Premier AccuVote-OS scanner; 56 use the Optech Eagle scanner, originally manufactured by ES&S but whose distribution was split between ES&S and the smaller vendor Sequoia Voting Systems as a result of a court order in an antitrust action; and one employs the ES&S M100 scanner. Diebold/Premier was recently sold to ES&S for the brow-raising underprice of $5 million (about the value of *a single* large-county voting equipment *contract*), and indeed the sale was nixed by the U.S. Department of Justice, Antitrust Division, as it would have given ES&S a virtually complete vote counting monopoly in the United States. In the absence of Diebold/Premier or any other substantial competitors, however, ES&S continues to enjoy near-monopolistic market domination.

[5] 79.6%, or 223 of the 280 opscan communities, were serviced by LHS.

- No actual ballots stored within the opscan equipment were examined or are permitted to be examined.

- No memory cards, which internally direct each opscan's counting process and store the results, were examined or, as proprietary information belonging to their corporate programmer, are permitted to be examined.

- No computer code directing the recording and counting of ballots or the display of results was examined or, as proprietary information belonging to the programmer, is permitted to be examined.

The inquiring citizen or, for that matter, *public official* or *candidate* would unfortunately discover **no information** about the 97% of ballots counted by opscan equipment, other than the vote totals as displayed by that equipment after the last ballot had been scanned. That is, he or she would be reduced to 100% pure, unadulterated, blind faith that the totals displayed were accurate—fact and not fiction.

If, in fact, the vendor corporations, or any insider(s) with access to the programming and distribution processes, had chosen to serve a private political agenda rather than the public trust, *there would be nothing in the official processes of voting, vote-counting, and election certification to indicate that such a breach had occurred.* If, for example, certain memory cards had been programmed to tally any ballot bearing a stray mark as a vote for Candidate X, this single exploit might result in an outcome-determinative shift of votes, and no one except the programmer would ever know. Or if certain memory cards had been programmed to shift every n^{th} vote for Candidate A to Candidate B, who but the programmer would know? Or again, if the "zero counters"[6] on an opscan are set to +X for the candidate whose victory is sought and –X for the candidate marked for defeat, at the end of the day the total votes recorded by the opscans will match the number of voters who have signed the poll book and the election administrator will be satisfied that the opscan has counted accurately and there has been a "clean" election, while 2X net votes have been stolen per machine so rigged.

---

[6] The "zero counter" refers to the number assigned to the first vote recorded for a given candidate or proposition. Logically that number is "1" but a single line of code can be inserted into the 500,000+ lines already on the memory card to alter that to *any* number, positive or negative. There are no technical limitations to this manipulation, the only limiting concern being whether the rigged vote totals will pass the "smell test."

Such vulnerability to fraud has by now been well researched and documented.[7] Unfortunately it tends to be regarded in the abstract, a technical possibility rather than an actual menace. The thinking appears to be that, *because this is America*, such things simply do not happen. Let us now set aside this comforting *a priori* conclusion and biopsy the Massachusetts Special Election with such tools as are available.

Our Analysis

We turn, in the absence of any direct validation of the opscan votecount, to the only ballots *not* counted invisibly. Just over 65,000 ballots, in 71 communities,[8] were counted by hand under public observation. Had these ballots been distributed randomly throughout the Commonwealth, we would expect the handcount results to fall within 1.0% of the opscan results with better than 99.9999% confidence.[9] Since the handcounts derive from discrete communities, however, and since Massachusetts is not politically homogeneous, an attempt must be made to quantitatively characterize and relate the two "meta-jurisdictions" which we shall call "Handcountville" (consisting of the 71 handcount communities) and "Opscanshire" (consisting of the remaining 280 opscan communities) respectively.

The first and most obvious way to relate Handcountville and Opscanshire would be by party registration. Such data is available from the Massachusetts Secretary of State, updated to October 2008.[10] It is given in Table 1.[11]

TABLE 1

Two-Party Registration - Massachusetts 2008			
Comparative Totals	**GOP Reg**	**Dem Reg**	**Dem Margin**
Handcount %	31.8%	68.2%	**36.4%**
Opscan %	23.7%	76.3%	**52.6%**
Differential	**-8.1%**	**8.1%**	**16.2%**

---

[7] See http://sites.google.com/site/remediaetc/home/documents/Scientific_Studies_7-20-08.pdf for a collection of such studies.

[8] See fn. 2.

[9] See http://www.raosoft.com/samplesize.html.

[10] See http://www.sec.state.ma.us/ele/elepdf/st_county_town_enroll_breakdown_08.pdf.

[11] Full data presented in the Appendix.

The two-party registration numbers paint Handcountville as significantly more Republican territory than is Opscanshire. Two-party registration is, however, a limited indicator in Massachusetts because just over half the voters in the Commonwealth (50.75%) are registered as "unenrolled" in either major party.[12] Without knowing more about the unenrolled voters in each meta-jurisdiction, reaching beyond this impression to a conclusive quantitative characterization is not feasible.

Fortunately, there exist indicators other than party registration that illuminate the political characteristics of voting constituencies. Massachusetts held contests for United States Senator in each of the two past biennial elections. The results, as broken down by meta-jurisdiction, are given in Table 2.

TABLE 2

Comparative Totals	U.S. Senate - 2008			U.S. Senate - 2006		
	Beatty-R	Kerry-D	Kerry Margin	Chase-R	Kennedy-D	Kennedy Margin
Handcount %	31.5%	68.5%	37.0%	31.1%	68.9%	37.8%
Opscan %	32.0%	68.0%	36.0%	30.5%	69.5%	39.0%
Handcount-Opscan Disparity	0.5%	-0.5%	1.0%	-0.6%	0.6%	-1.2%

In each of these statewide senatorial elections, Handcountville and Opscanshire exhibited virtual political congruence, much as we would expect if indeed Handcountville votes were a random sample of the state as a whole, establishing baseline expectations for the political divisions of the two meta-jurisdictions in similar contests such as the 2010 Massachusetts Special Election. In fact, when we combine the vote totals for the previous two Senate elections (2006 and 2008), we find *exact* congruence between the voters of Handcountville and Opscanshire, as shown in Table 3.

---

[12] See http://www.sec.state.ma.us/ele/elepdf/st_county_town_enroll_breakdown_08.pdf.

TABLE 3

Combined Vote for U.S. Senate 2006 and 2008			
Comparative Totals	GOP	Dem	**Dem Margin**
Handcount %	31.3%	68.7%	**37.4%**
Opscan %	31.3%	68.7%	**37.4%**
Handcount-Opscan Disparity	**0.0%**	**0.0%**	**0.0%**

When we turn to the 2010 Special Election, however, we find a radically different comparative outcome. The results of the Brown-Coakley contest, as broken down by meta-jurisdiction, are given in Table 4.[13]

TABLE 4

U.S. Senate - 2010 (Special)			
Comparative Totals	Brown-R	Coakley-D	**Brown Margin**
Handcount %	48.6%	51.4%	**-2.8%**
Opscan %	52.6%	47.4%	**5.2%**
Handcount-Opscan Disparity	**4.0%**	**-4.0%**	**8.0%**

Where votes were observably counted by hand, the Democrat Martha Coakley defeated the Republican Scott Brown by a margin of 2.8%; where votes were counted unobservably and secretly by machine, Brown defeated Coakley by a margin of 5.2%.

There is no evidence that this whopping marginal disparity of 8.0% is attributable to divergent political leanings of the two meta-jurisdictions. In fact,

---

[13] The percentages exclude, for clarity, the Libertarian Party candidate, who received less than 1% of the vote, and whose inclusion does not appreciably affect the results. For a complete, town-by-town breakdown of the Brown-Coakley vote, the vote in prior Senate elections serving as baselines, and voter registration data, please see the Appendix published with the original paper, available at http://electiondefensealliance.org/files/BelieveIt_OrNot_100904.pdf.

there is strong evidence to the contrary: as the previous two Senate contests and what we can glean from party registration indicate, Handcountville is no more Democratic, and likely less so, than Opscanshire. Nor is there reason to suspect a demographic bias as cause: Handcountville consists primarily of small rural communities; Coakley, born and raised in the northwestern part of Massachusetts, had spent the past 30 years since graduation from Boston University Law School as a Boston-based, big-city attorney and prosecutor, serving from 1999 to 2007 as high-profile District Attorney of Middlesex County, home to 54 communities of which only four are in Handcountville.

Nonetheless it is incumbent upon our analysis to consider what would be the last-standing "benign" explanation for the handcount-opscan disparity and Coakley's Handcountville victory: that Handcountville impounds relatively more western towns near Coakley's old "home base," and that her Handcountville victory therefore reflects nothing more insidious than a "favorite daughter" phenomenon at work. Fortunately for our analysis, Coakley ran statewide for Attorney General in 2006, allowing us to assess whether Coakley enjoys "favorite daughter" status in Handcountville. The contest, against a Cambridge-based opponent, was, like the senatorial elections of 2006 and 2008, not sufficiently competitive to be a rational target for manipulation. The results are given below in Table 5:[14]

TABLE 5

Massachusetts Attorney General - 2006			
Comparative Totals	Coakley-D	Frisoli-R	Coakley Margin
Handcount %	72.6%	27.4%	45.2%
Opscan %	73.0%	27.0%	46.0%
Handcount-Opscan Disparity	0.4%	-0.4%	0.8%

We observe that in 2006, her only other statewide election, Martha Coakley performed just as well in Opscanshire as she did in Handcountville; in fact, she ran slightly better in the opscan communities. There was no "favorite daughter"

[14] Full returns at http://www.boston.com/news/special/politics/2006_elections/general_results/attorney_general.html, as referenced by Kathy Dopp of ElectionMathematics.org.

phenomenon, no regional effect, and no Coakley advantage in the handcount jurisdictions. There was also, given the 45% margin, no incentive to manipulate and nothing at all to be gained from a "small" shift of votes on the order of the 5% shift sufficient to reverse the outcome of the 2010 Special Election.

The handcount vs. opscan disparity in the 2010 Special Election for Senate in Massachusetts stands as an unexplained anomaly of dramatic numerical proportions. We stated at the outset of our analysis that if the hand-counted ballots had been distributed randomly throughout the Commonwealth, we would expect the handcount results to fall within 1.0% of the opscan results with better than 99.9999% confidence. The odds of an *8.0%* marginal disparity would be *beyond astronomical*. We have now further established that the handcount "sample" is, for comparison purposes, "better" than random: that is, based on demographics and voting patterns, the handcount voters would be more likely than the opscan voters to vote for Brown. The odds therefore of an 8.0 marginal disparity *in the other direction* would be, and there is no better way to say this, *beyond beyond astronomical*. Statisticians never say "impossible" but that is, for all earthly intents and purposes, what it is.

It remains to be noted that, as with the prior Coakley statewide race, neither the 2006 nor the 2008 Senate election that preceded it—and that we have presented as baseline contests—was competitive enough to invite manipulation: the risk entailed in shifting a net of 36% of the votes statewide is prohibitive;[15] and a shift in, say, the 5 – 10% range would not alter the outcome and would therefore garner no reward. *Such was not the case with the Brown-Coakley contest, where the risk-reward ratio was extremely favorable: a net shift of a mere 5% of the machine-counted votes would be sufficient to reverse the outcome.* As seismic as the Brown victory was, it was numerically plausible enough to pass the smell test, rendering the risk minimal. The reward, as noted at the beginning, was politically astronomical.

Not A Fluke

Should it be objected that this election somehow constitutes an isolated instance perhaps influenced by unperceived but legitimate factors peculiar to its particular terrain and moment in time, we may expand our inquiry to a neighboring time and a neighboring venue where, fortunately, both opscan and hand counting also continue to coexist. The state of New Hampshire also uses

---

[15] While such a massive shift of votes is technically feasible, the election result would not begin to pass the smell test, opening computerized electoral manipulation to intense scrutiny and undermining the entire enterprise nationwide.

computerized voting equipment manufactured by Diebold/Premier, and is also serviced exclusively by LHS Corporation. In the 2008 general election we find Obama running significantly better in Handcountville, NH than in Opscanshire, NH—a disparity that increases to alarming proportions when party registration data is used to normalize the two meta-jurisdictions, as presented in Table 6.[16]

TABLE 6

NH Vote for President 2008 Relative to Party Registration

New Hampshire Statewide E2008	Dem	Rep	Total
Opscan Presidential Vote	54.51%	45.49%	100.00%
Opscan Registered Voters	50.00%	50.00%	100.00%
Opscan vs. Party-Registration Differential	4.51	-4.51	0
Handcount Presidential Vote	56.51%	43.49%	100.00%
Handcount Registered Voters	46.69%	53.31%	100.00%
Handcount vs. Party-Registration Differential	9.82	-9.82	0
Handcount vs. Opscan Relative To Party Registration	5.31	-5.31	10.62

We see that Obama ran 4.51% ahead of (and McCain a corresponding 4.51% behind) two-party registration numbers in opscan jurisdictions but 9.82% ahead of two-party registration numbers in handcount jurisdictions. The normalized net disparity is 10.62%, comparable in eye-popping magnitude to the 8.0% disparity observed in the Massachusetts Special election.

Furthermore, in New Hampshire as in Massachusetts, we were fortunate to have a noncompetitive contest which can, as do the 2006 and 2008 Senate and the 2006 Attorney General contests in Massachusetts, function as a baseline for comparison. The results for the 2008 New Hampshire gubernatorial contest are presented in Table 7:

---

[16] Full data for New Hampshire is too extensive for inclusion in the Appendix; it is compiled from the NH Secretary of State website, at http://www.sos.nh.gov/general2008/index.htm.

TABLE 7

New Hampshire Statewide Vote for Governor 2008			
	Lynch-D	Kenney-R	Lynch Margin
Handcount %	71.76%	28.24%	43.52%
Opscan %	71.76%	28.24%	43.52%
Handcount-Opscan Disparity	0.00	0.00	0.00

Once again we find that, in a noncompetitive contest, the handcount and opscan jurisdictions exhibit political congruence (in this case, exact congruence to the second percentage decimal place), where in a presumptively competitive contest (the Presidential race), we find a glaring disparity.

Conclusion

It may fairly be objected that none of this numerical or "circumstantial" evidence, however strong, *proves* that computerized fraud has taken place or that the Massachusetts Special Election was "stolen," and we readily agree. To furnish such proof, beyond not just a reasonable doubt but any shred of doubt, we would need access to either memory cards, the code that actually ran in the opscans on Election Day, and/or the actual voter-marked ballots (chain of custody of course preserved), *all of which are conveniently off-limits to inquiry*. For anyone wondering, though, how much trust to place in privatized, concealed, and computerized vote counting—past, present and future—we suggest that the MA Special numbers scream for themselves.

And as numbers as implausible as these continue to rear their heads in high-stakes elections throughout the United States—invariably revealing a shift of votes *in the same direction*, whether measured against exit polls, pre-election polls, or observable votecounts[17]—we ask how the prevailing and irrational

---

[17] See generally, Charnin R, *Proving Election Fraud*. Bloomington, IN: AuthorHouse, 2010; Miller MC Ed., *Loser Take All: Election Fraud and the Subversion of Democracy 2000-2008*. Brooklyn, NY: Ig Publishing, 2008; Freeman S, Bleifuss J, *Was The 2004 Presidential Election Stolen?* New York: Seven Stories Press, 2006; Simon J, O'Dell B, *Landslide Denied: Exit Polls vs. Vote Count* (2006); Simon J, O'Dell B, Tavris D, Mitteldorf J, *Fingerprints of Election Theft: Were Competitive Contests Targeted?* (2007).

Note particularly the rightward or "red" shift measured in the presidential election of 2008, which—though it was, as a result of the Republican free-fall following the late-level of trust in invisible, unobservable vote counting can be maintained? We further ask how we can continue to employ a system that keeps software, code, memory cards, and all key aspects of the vote counting process secret, and relegates anyone seeking evidence of electoral validity to such an *indirect* quest for comparisons and baselines and numerical fingerprints as we have been obliged to undertake?

We return to the Massachusetts Special Election, which has not only dramatically altered the balance of power in Washington but has indeed ushered in a dramatically altered set of political expectations going forward into the critical elections of 2010 and 2012, as the hyper-polarization of American politics continues.[18] We cannot say with 100% certainty that the 97% of votes counted on optical scanners were subject to manipulation. But we can fairly ask: *"What evidence exists that they were not?"*

We have found *none*—no checks, audits, ballot inspections, hand tallies, exit polls, memory card or computer code examinations. Not a thing beyond pure *faith* that the corporations (and we have, for the purposes of this analysis, ignored their documented and self-proclaimed partisan proclivities) and insiders charged with the secret, unobservable counting of 97% of the votes in Massachusetts, have decided to honor the public trust at the expense of any other

---

September crash of the markets and the general economy, insufficient to alter the outcome—was in fact of a magnitude even greater than that measured in 2004. The election of Barack Obama, contrary to the general impression, was thus anything but an "all clear" with respect to computerized electoral manipulation.

It must further be noted, however, that exit polls and tracking polls alike are now weighted according to demographics drawn largely if not exclusively from *prior election* exit polls that were distorted rightward when "adjusted" to match official vote tallies. Thus, because votecounts *were* treated as sacrosanct, and all currently employed demographic baselines "tuned" to those red-shifted numbers, prior electoral manipulation clears the path for ongoing and future electoral manipulation by red-shifting the baselines against which such manipulation might be measured.

With pre-election polls and exit polls so corrupted to oversample to the right, the telltale disparities between these previously reliable baselines and the votecounts shrink or disappear (making manipulated elections appear to be more in line with expectations), and comparison between computer and hand counts may survive as the sole reliable resource for numerical forensic investigation.

[18] It is easy enough to see how capacity to manipulate would lead to hyper-polarization: as victory becomes a given, the player is incentivized to make that victory *mean more* by moving further and further from the center; this appears to be what is occurring on a systemic level, and accounts at least in part for the bizarre politics of the computerized voting era. To wit, with rigged elections, it is not necessary to "move to the center" to win; but this newfound "freedom to be radical" is, alas, *one-sided*, and that is precisely the political dynamic we are witnessing unfold.

personal, economic, or political agenda of their own *or of anyone who would seek to influence them.* In an age of steroids and hGH, credit default swaps, Ponzi schemes, and massive institutional frauds coupled with hyper-partisan, true-believer politics, such "faith" amounts to little more than rank denial.

Nor, in the final analysis, is it evident to us that *additional* layers of technology would ultimately suffice to thwart a determined electoral manipulator—and, given the massive stakes in a politically polarized 21ˢᵗ Century America, we must anticipate the highest level of determination to bring about desired outcomes by any and all means. We have seen exit polls discredited, audits (Ohio 2004, e.g.) gamed, chains of ballot custody observed in the breach. Perhaps most critically, as long as it takes an expert to implement, or indeed to comprehend, a security protocol, every non-expert citizen is left on the outside looking in, never receiving knowledge, as opposed to mere *assurance*, that the bedrock protocol of his or her democracy has not been corrupted. Only transparency, *visible and observable counting by humans or non-programmable devices[19] at every step*—which is just as feasible today as it was a mere generation ago[20]—can bestow that knowledge.

Computers can help us in many ways and will continue to play a major role in our lives—periodic glitches, hacks, and meltdowns notwithstanding. But to blindly and needlessly entrust our nation's *elections*—particularly its federal elections, which so directly determine our national direction—to private, corporate and, it must be said, partisan enterprises operating and calculating in secret beyond our capacity to observe and validate, is, to put it with the bluntness this emergency demands, collective insanity.

---

[19] E.g., lever machines, in which each aspect of counting can be monitored.

[20] Using a parametric tool developed by Dave Berman, it has been shown that hand counting all contests for federal office (the maximum number of such races on any ballot is three) would require citizen participation averaging *one hour per voter lifetime* (one four-hour shift for which each citizen would have a one in four chance of being selected during his or her life), a civic obligation far less onerous than jury duty.

STUDY V.

The Likely Voter Cutoff Model:
What Is So *Wrong* with Getting It *Right*?

Jonathan D. Simon[1]
March 17, 2011

Logic tells us, and experience confirms, that political pollsters stay in business and prosper by predicting election outcomes accurately. Pollsters are now publicly ranked by various scorekeepers[2] according to how brilliantly close or embarrassingly far off they turn out to be when the returns come in. A "Certificate of Methodological Purity" may make a nice wall ornament, but matters not a whit when it comes to success within the highly competitive polling profession.

If election returns in competitive races were being systematically manipulated in one direction over a period of several biennial elections, we would expect pollsters to make methodological adjustments necessary to match those returns. Indeed, it would be nothing short of professional suicide not to make those adjustments, and turn whatever methodological handsprings were required to continue "getting elections right."

In the computerized election era—where virtually every aspect of the vote counting process is privatized and concealed; where study after study, from Princeton to the GAO, has concluded that the vote counting computers are extremely vulnerable to manipulation; and where statistical analyses pointing to such manipulation have been reflexively dismissed, no matter how compelling—it may be that the methodological contortions required for pollsters to "get elections right" constitute the most powerful evidence that computer-based election fraud and theft are systemic and rampant.

---

[1] Jonathan D. Simon, JD, is Executive Director of Election Defense Alliance.

[2] See, e.g., the Fordham University 2008 ranking:
http://www.fordham.edu/campus_resources/enewsroom/archives/archive_1453.asp.

Enter the Likely Voter Cutoff Model, or LVCM for short. Introduced by Gallup about 10 years ago (after Gallup came under the control of a right-wing Christianist heir), the LVCM has gathered adherents until it is now all-but-universally employed, albeit with certain fine-tuning variations. The LVCM uses a series of screening questions—about past voting history, residential stability, intention of voting, and the like—to qualify and disqualify respondents from the sample. The problem with surveying the population at large or even registered voters, *without* screening for likelihood of voting, is obvious: you wind up surveying a significant number of voters whose responses register on the survey but who then *don't vote*. If this didn't-vote constituency has a partisan slant it throws off the poll relative to the election results—generally to the left, since as you move to the right on the political spectrum the likelihood of voting appears to rise.

But the problem with the LVCM as a corrective is that it far overshoots the mark: that is, *it eliminates many individuals from the sample who will in fact cast a vote*, and the respondents/voters so eliminated, as a group, are acknowledged by all to be to the left of those who remain in the sample, skewing the sample to the right (a sound methodology, employed for a time by the NY Times/CBS poll, would solve the participation problem by down-weighting, *but not eliminating*, the responses of interviewees less likely to vote). So the LVCM—which disproportionately eliminates members of the Democratic constituency, including many who will in fact go on to cast a vote, by falsely assigning them a *zero percent* chance of voting—*should get honestly tabulated elections consistently wrong*. It should over-predict the Republican/Right vote and under-predict the Democratic/Left vote, most often by an outcome-determinative 5-8% in competitive elections.

Instead it performs brilliantly and has therefore been universally adopted by pollsters, no questions asked, not just in the run-up to elections as in the past, but now all year round, setting expectations not just for electoral outcomes but for broad political trends, contributing to perceptions of political mojo and driving political dynamics—rightward, of course. In fact, the most "successful" LVCM models are now the ones that are *strictest* in limiting participation, including those that eliminate all respondents who cannot attest that they have voted in the three preceding biennial elections, cutting off a slew of young, poor, and transient voters. The impact of this exclusion in 2008 should have been particularly devastating, given the millions of new voters turned out by the Democrats. Instead the LVCM got 2008 just about right.[3] Pollster Scott

---

[3] We note in passing that an extraordinary, 11th-hour Republican free-fall, triggered by the collapse of Lehman Bros. and the subsequent economic crash, produced an Obama

| C O D E   R E D

Rasmussen, formerly a paid consultant to the 2004 Bush campaign, employs the LVCM most stringently to winnow the sample, eliminating more would-be Democratic voters than do most if not all of his professional colleagues. A quick survey of his polls at www.rasmussenreports.com shows a nation unrecognizably canted to the right, and yet Rasmussen Reports was ranked "the most accurate national polling firm in the 2008 election" and close to the top in 2004 and 2006.

There is something *very* wrong with this picture and very basic logic tells us that the methodological contortion known as the LVCM can get election results so consistently right *only if those election results are consistently wrong*—that is, shifted to the right in the darkness of cyberspace.

A moment to let that sink in, before adding that, if the LVCM shift is not enough to distort the picture and catch up with the "red-shifted" votecounts, polling (and exit polling) samples are also generally weighted by partisanship or Party ID. The problem with this is that these Party ID numbers are generally drawn from prior elections' final exit polls—exit polls that were "adjusted" in virtually every case *rightward* to conform to votecounts that were to the right of the *actual* exit polls, the unshakable assumption being that the votecounts are gospel and the exit polls therefore wrong. In the process of "adjustment," also known as "forcing," the demographics (including Party ID, age, race, etc.) are dragged along for the ride and shift to the right. These then become the new benchmarks and baselines for *current* polling, shifting the samples to the right *and enabling prior election manipulations to mask forensic/statistical evidence of current and future election manipulations*.

To sum up, we have a right-shifting tunable fudge factor in the LVCM, now universally employed with great success to predict electoral outcomes, particularly when tuned to its highest degree of distortion. And we have the incorporation of past election manipulations into current polling samples, again pushing the results to the right. These methodological contortions and distortions could not be successful—in fact, they would put the pollsters quickly out of business—absent a consistent concomitant distortion in the *votecounts* in competitive races.[4]

Since polls and election outcomes are, after some shaky years following the advent of computerized vote counting, now in close agreement (though still not

---

victory in the face of a "red shift"—votecounts more Republican and less Democratic than the exit polls—even greater than that measured in 2004.

[4] *Noncompetitive* races tend neither to be polled (no horserace interest) nor rigged (an outcome reversal wouldn't pass the smell test).

exit polls, which are weighted to false demographics but of course do *not* employ the LVCM, and therefore still come in consistently to the left of votecounts until they are "adjusted" rightward to conformity), everything looks just fine. But it is a consistency brought about by the polling profession's imperative to find a way to mirror/predict votecounts (imagine, if you will, the professional fate of a pollster stubbornly employing *undistorted* methodology, who insisted that his/her polls were right and both the official votecounts *and* all the other pollsters wrong!). It is a consistency, achieved without malice on the part of the pollsters, that almost certainly conceals the most horrific crime, with the most devastating consequences, of our lifetimes.

STUDY VI.

E2014: A Basic Forensic Analysis

Jonathan D. Simon

Any comparative forensic analysis is only as "good" as its baselines. In *Landslide Denied*[1]—our archetypal post-election comparative forensics study, in which the "red shift" (the rightward disparity between exit poll and votecount results) was identified and measured—a critical component of the analysis was to establish that the exit poll respondents accurately represented the electorate. We employed a meta-analysis of multiple measures of the demographics and political leanings of the electorate to demonstrate that the exit polls in question had not "oversampled" or over-represented Democratic or left-leaning voters (in fact any inaccuracy turned out to be in the opposite direction), and therefore that those polls constituted a valid baseline against which to measure the red-shifted votecounts.

In *Fingerprints of Election Theft*,[2] we went further and removed all issues of sample bias from the equation by conducting a separate poll in which we asked *the same set of respondents* how they had voted in at least one competitive and one noncompetitive contest on their ballot. The noncompetitive contests, being presumptively unsuitable targets for rigging, thus served as the baselines for the competitive contests, and the relative disparities could be compared without concern about any net partisan tendencies of the respondent group.

More recently we have commented on the feedback loop that develops between election results and polling/sampling methodologies, such that consistently and unidirectionally shifted votecounts trigger, in both pre-election and exit polls, methodological adaptations that mirror those shifts.[3] Approaching E2014, we observed that the near-universal use of the Likely Voter Cutoff Model (LVCM) in pre-election polling, and stratification to demographic and partisanship quanta derived from (rightward) adjusted prior-election exit polls in all polling,

---

[1] See Study II.

[2] See Study III.

[3] See Study V; see also http://truth-out.org/news/item/27203-vote-counts-and-polls-an-insidious-feedback-loop.

were methodological distortions that pushed both exit polls and pre-election polls significantly to the right, corroding our baselines and making forensic analysis much less likely to detect rightward shifts in the votecounts.

Indeed, given the rightward distortions of the adaptive polling methodologies, we noted that *accurate* polls in E2014 would serve as a red-flag signal of rightward manipulation of the votecounts. In effect, the LVCM and the adjusted-exit-poll-derived weightings constituted a rightward "pre-adjustment" of the polls, such that any rightward votecount manipulations of comparable magnitude would be "covered."

It is against this backdrop that we present the E2014 polling and votecount data, recognizing that the adaptive polling methodologies that right-skewed our baselines would combine to reduce the magnitude of any red shift we measured and significantly mitigate the footprint of votecount manipulation in this election.

The tables that follow compare polling and votecount results, where polling data was available, for U.S. Senate, gubernatorial, and U.S. House elections. The exit polling numbers represent the first publicly posted values, prior to completion of the "adjustment" process, in the course of which the poll results are forced to congruity with the votecounts.[4] The "red shift" represents the disparity between the votecount and exit poll margins. For this purpose, a margin is positive when the Democratic candidate's total exceeds that of the Republican candidate. To calculate the red shift, we subtract the votecount margin from the exit poll margin, so a positive red shift number represents a "red," or rightward, shift between the exit poll and votecount results.

---

[4] Because these "unadjusted" exit polls, which have not yet been tainted by the forcing process, are permanently removed from public websites often within minutes of poll closings, they must be captured as screenshots or in free-standing html format prior to their disappearance. At Election Defense Alliance we archive these captures as part of our forensic operations.

Table 1

	E2014 U.S. SENATE EXIT POLL-VOTECOUNT DISPARITY ("RED SHIFT")						
STATE	**EXIT POLL %**		**Margin**	**VOTECOUNT %**		**Margin**	**RED SHIFT**
	D	**R**	**(D - R)**	**D**	**R**	**(D - R)**	
KY	45.0%	52.0%	-7.0%	40.7%	56.2%	-15.5%	8.5%
SC(1)	41.6%	50.6%	-9.0%	36.8%	54.3%	-17.5%	8.5%
GA	48.8%	48.2%	0.6%	45.2%	52.9%	-7.7%	8.3%
WV	38.9%	58.6%	-19.7%	34.5%	62.1%	-27.6%	7.9%
ME	35.7%	64.4%	-28.7%	31.7%	68.3%	-36.6%	7.9%
KS(I)[5]	45.6%	49.4%	-3.8%	42.5%	53.3%	-10.8%	7.0%
SD	33.2%	47.8%	-14.6%	29.5%	50.4%	-20.9%	6.3%
LA	44.7%	38.4%	6.3%	42.1%	41.0%	1.1%	5.2%
NC	49.0%	45.6%	3.4%	47.3%	48.8%	-1.5%	4.9%
MN	56.6%	41.4%	15.2%	53.2%	42.9%	10.3%	4.9%
AR	42.1%	54.4%	-12.3%	39.4%	56.5%	-17.1%	4.8%
IA	46.7%	50.8%	-4.1%	43.8%	52.1%	-8.3%	4.2%
SC(2)	39.6%	59.4%	-19.8%	37.1%	61.1%	-24.0%	4.2%
IL	54.4%	42.1%	12.3%	53.1%	43.1%	10.0%	2.3%
OR	58.5%	38.1%	20.4%	55.7%	36.9%	18.8%	1.6%
VA	49.6%	47.4%	2.2%	49.2%	48.3%	0.9%	1.3%
NH	52.1%	47.9%	4.2%	51.5%	48.2%	3.3%	0.9%
TX	35.2%	61.8%	-26.6%	34.4%	61.6%	-27.2%	0.6%
MI	56.1%	42.4%	13.7%	54.6%	41.3%	13.3%	0.4%
AK	46.4%	49.1%	-2.7%	45.8%	48.0%	-2.2%	-0.5%
CO	45.8%	49.8%	-4.0%	46.3%	48.2%	-1.9%	-2.1%
AVERAGE RED SHIFT							**4.1%**

---

[5] In the Kansas race the Republican was opposed by an Independent candidate.

Table 2

E2014 GUBERNATORIAL EXIT POLL-VOTECOUNT DISPARITY ("RED SHIFT")							
STATE	EXIT POLL %		Margin	VOTE COUNT %		Margin	RED SHIFT
	D	R	(D - R)	D	R	(D - R)	
OH	40.4%	56.1%	-15.7%	32.9%	63.8%	-30.9%	15.2%
SD	31.7%	62.9%	-31.2%	25.4%	70.5%	-45.1%	13.9%
CA	62.5%	37.5%	25.0%	58.9%	41.1%	17.8%	7.2%
NY	56.8%	36.8%	20.0%	54.0%	40.6%	13.4%	6.6%
GA	47.3%	48.7%	-1.4%	44.9%	52.7%	-7.8%	6.4%
OR	55.0%	43.1%	11.9%	49.9%	44.1%	5.8%	6.1%
WI	49.7%	49.4%	0.3%	46.6%	52.3%	-5.7%	6.0%
ME	45.7%	44.7%	1.0%	43.4%	48.2%	-4.8%	5.8%
MN	54.2%	42.9%	11.3%	50.1%	44.5%	5.6%	5.7%
SC	44.2%	53.8%	-9.6%	41.4%	55.9%	-14.5%	4.9%
PA	57.0%	42.5%	14.5%	54.9%	45.1%	9.8%	4.7%
KS	48.6%	47.9%	0.7%	46.1%	50.0%	-3.9%	4.6%
IA	39.6%	57.4%	-17.8%	37.3%	59.0%	-21.7%	3.9%
MI	49.2%	49.8%	-0.6%	46.9%	50.9%	-4.0%	3.4%
IL	48.0%	48.5%	-0.5%	46.4%	50.3%	-3.9%	3.4%
AR	43.2%	53.8%	-10.6%	41.5%	55.4%	-13.9%	3.3%
TX	40.8%	58.2%	-17.4%	38.9%	59.3%	-20.4%	3.0%
FL	47.0%	47.0%	0.0%	47.1%	48.1%	-1.0%	1.0%
AK(I)[6]	49.5%	46.6%	2.9%	48.1%	45.9%	2.2%	0.7%
NH	52.7%	47.4%	5.3%	52.5%	47.3%	5.2%	0.1%
CO	49.2%	47.2%	2.0%	49.2%	46.1%	3.1%	-1.1%
AVERAGE RED SHIFT							5.0%

---

[6] In the Alaska race the Republican candidate was opposed by an Independent.

Table 3

2014 U.S. HOUSE EXIT POLL - VOTECOUNT DISPARITY ("RED SHIFT")			
	D %	**R %**	**Margin**
GENERIC CONGRESSIONAL BALLOT	43.2%	45.4%	-2.2%
U.S. HOUSE NATIONAL EXIT POLL	48.1%	49.9%	-1.8%
U.S. HOUSE NATIONAL VOTECOUNT	45.2%	50.7%	-5.5%
RED SHIFT			**3.7%**
Total Votes Counted			77,564,577
Net Votes Red Shifted			2,897,414
Maximum Contests Reversed			89

To summarize the data presented in Tables 1 – 3:

- The U.S. Senate red shift averaged 4.1% with a half dozen races presenting red shifts of over 7%. Of the 21 Senate elections that were exit polled, 19 were red-shifted.

- The gubernatorial red shift averaged 5.0% and 20 out of the 21 races were red-shifted.

- In U.S. House elections, which are exit polled with an aggregate national sample,[7] the red shift was 3.7%. This is the equivalent of approximately 2.9 million votes which, if taken away from the GOP winners of the closest elections, would have been sufficient to reverse the outcomes of 89 House races such that the Democrats would now hold a 120-seat (277 – 157) House majority.[8]

- Although the thousands of state legislative contests are not exit-polled, it is fair to assume that the consistent red shift numbers that we found

---

[7] The sample size of the House poll exceeded 17,000 respondents, yielding a Margin of Error (MOE) of less than 1%.

[8] Of course I am not suggesting that vote theft can be targeted with such infallible precision. But it would make no sense at all *not* to target vote theft to the closest races and shift enough votes to ensure narrow victories. When one couples the evidence of a nearly 3 million vote disparity with even a modestly successful targeting protocol, the result is easily sufficient to flip the balance of power in the U.S. House.

in the Senate, House, and gubernatorial contests would map onto these critical (as we have seen) down-ballot elections as well.

These red shift numbers, well outside applicable margins of sampling error, are egregious even by the dubious historical standards of the elections of the computerized voting era in America. Although it is an *indirect* measure of mistabulation, the red shift has been, with very few exceptions, pervasive throughout that era, and it is not reflective of the impact of any of the overt tactics of gerrymandering, voter suppression, or big money. It represents a very telling incongruity between how voters indicate that they voted and the official tabulation of those votes. While it is not "smoking gun" proof of targeted mistabulation, it is, in the magnitude and persistence we have witnessed over the past half-dozen biennial election cycles, just about impossible to explain without reference to such fraud. It is simply too much smoke for there not to be a fire.

We relied as well on pre-election polling averages as a corroborative baseline,[9] and found that the red shifts from these predictions were comparable, though somewhat smaller than the exit poll-votecount red shifts (3.3% vs. 4.1% for the U.S. Senate races; 3.5% vs. 5.0% for the gubernatorial races; and 3.3% for the Generic Congressional Ballot[10] vs. 3.7% for the U.S. House Aggregate Exit Poll). We suspect that these differences can be accounted for by the impact of the Likely Voter Cutoff Model in pre-election polling, which pushes samples even further right than does the use of prior elections' adjusted exit poll demographics to weight the current exit poll sample, thereby further reducing the poll-votecount disparity.

The standard arguments have of course been put forward that all these exit polls (and pre-election polls) were "off," that essentially every pollster in the business (and there are many), including the exit pollsters, overestimated the turnout of Democratic voters, which was "known" to be historically low because the official votecounts and a slew of unexpected Democratic defeats tell us it was. In response to this entirely tautological argument, there are two non-jibing realities to be considered.

---

[9] The pre-election polling numbers represent an average of all polls available from the two-months prior to Election Day (Source: RealClearPolitics at http://www.realclearpolitics.com/epolls/latest_polls/elections/. See also www.ballotpedia.com, a very flexible and useful resource).

[10] The Generic Congressional Ballot is a tracking poll that asks a national sample of respondents whether they intend to vote for the Democratic or Republican candidate for U.S. House in their district.

The first is that the sampling methodologies of the polls were *already* distorted to impound the anticipated low turnout rate of Democratic voters in off-year elections, a model that has been grounded on the official votecounts of this century's three previous suspect computerized midterm elections, E2002, E2006, and E2010.

The second is what would have to be termed the apparent schizoid behavior of the E2014 electorate, in which—from county-level referenda in Wisconsin backing expanded access to healthcare and an end to corporate personhood, to state-level ballot proposals to raise the minimum wage across America (see Table 4)—voters approved, by wide margins, the very same progressive proposals that the Republican candidates they apparently elected had violently opposed.

Table 4

E2014 - Ballot Propositions	Margin of Passage	Status
AK Minimum Wage Increase	38.7%	Pass
AK Legalized Marijuana	6.4%	Pass
AK Protects Salmon vs. Mining	31.8%	Pass
AR Campaign Finance Reform (Lobbyist Regulation)	4.8%	Pass
AR Minimum Wage Increase	31.8%	Pass
FL Water and Land Conservation	50.0%	Pass
FL Medical Marijuana (60% required)	15.2%	Pass
IL Right to Vote (anti-VOTERID)	45.4%	Pass
IL Minimum Wage Increase	32.8%	Pass
IL Birth Control Inclusion in Prescription Drug Insurance.	31.8%	Pass
IL Millionaire Tax Increase for Education	27.2%	Pass
NE Minimum Wage Increase	19.0%	Pass
NJ Funds for Open Space and Historic Preservation	29.2%	Pass
NM Student Included on Board of Regents	29.4%	Pass
NM Public Library Bond	25.9%	Pass
NM Education Bond	19.6%	Pass
OR ERA	28.4%	Pass
OR Legalized Marijuana	12.0%	Pass
RI Clean Water, Open Space, Healthy Communities Bonds	41.8%	Pass
SD Minimum Wage Increase	10.1%	Pass
SD Health Provider Inclusion (anti insurance corps)	23.6%	Pass
SD Minimum Wage Increase	10.1%	Pass
WA Universal Background Checks for Gun Purchases	18.6%	Pass
Average Margin of Passage	**25.4%**	
CO "Personhood" (Anti-Abortion)	-29.6%	Fail
ND Life Begins at Conception	-28.2%	Fail
WA Gun Rights (pro gun owner)	-10.6%	Fail
Average Margin of Failure	**-22.8%**	

The wide margins are significant because they tell us that, unlike the key contests for public office, these ballot propositions were well outside of smell-test rigging distance. Thus, even had defeating them been an ancillary component of a strategy that appears riveted on seizing full governmental power rather than scoring points on isolated issue battlefields, these ballot propositions would have failed any reasonable risk-reward test that might have been applied, and thus were left alone.[11]

Table 5

CONGRESSIONAL APPROVAL RATING		
Approve	Disapprove	Margin
8%	89%	**-81%**
OBAMA APPROVAL RATING		
Approve	Disapprove	Margin
47%	52%	**-5%**
OWN REPRESENTATIVE DESERVE REELECTION?		
Yes	No	Margin
29%	41%	**-12%**
HAS CONGRESS PASSED ANY LEGISLATION THAT WILL IMPROVE LIFE IN AMERICA?		
Yes	No	Margin
11%	69%	**-58%**

Source: Rasmussen Reports (Week Preceding E2014)

With so much not making sense about E2014 it seems hardly necessary to add that it makes no sense at all for an historically unpopular Congress to be shown such electoral love by the voters that exactly TWO (out of 222) incumbent members of the Republican House majority lost their seats on November 4, 2014, while the GOP *strengthened* its grip on the House by adding 12 seats to

---

[11] As was the state of California, the one place in America where Democrats actually made U.S. House *gains* in E2014. This perpetuates a pattern we have noted in several previous elections that may speak to the deterrence value of a well-designed audit protocol and a higher level of scrutiny from the (Democratic) Secretary of State's office than is found in the vast majority of other states.

its overall majority, and of course took control of the U.S. Senate, 31 governorships, and 68 out of 100 state legislative bodies.

It would seem to require magicianship of the highest (or lowest) order to pull these results from a hat known to contain a Congressional Approval rating in the single digits (See Table 5). In handing over vote counting to computers, neither the processes nor the programming of which we are permitted to observe, we have chosen to *trust the magician*, and we should not be at all surprised if for his next trick he makes our sovereignty disappear.

STUDY VII.

Split The Difference Audit: An Election Audit that Can Work 'In the Wild'

A Protocol Combining the Best Features of 'Flat' and 'Risk-Limiting' Audits

Jonathan D. Simon

Abstract

With audits increasingly coming into focus as a necessary tool for securing and restoring trust in the U.S. vote counting process, developing a template for an audit process that is both conceptually sound and capable of readily being understood and executed in the field is a critical priority for electoral reformers.

Risk-Limiting Audits (RLA) – which peg the size of the audit to a contest's margin of victory -- have received much positive consideration, and have now been adopted by several states.[1] A number of other states continue to employ "flat" audits, sampling a fixed percentage of ballots or precincts.[2] Many states, however, continue to run elections that are either unaudited or ineffectually audited.[3]

The Split-The-Difference-Audit proposal presented here combines the relative simplicity of a flat audit with the precision and labor-saving features of the RLA.[4] *It achieves this by sampling a fixed percentage (generally 1 percent) of the ballots and pegging the accuracy threshold of the audit---that is, the pass/fail percentage disparity between votecount and audit margins of victory—*

---

[1] See, for example, Colorado, at https://www.denverpost.com/2017/11/22/colorado-election-audit-complete/.

[2] See, for example, Massachusetts, at https://www.sec.state.ma.us/ele/elepostelection/postelectionidx.htm.

[3] Thirty-three states have no audit or inadequate audit provisions, according to the Center for American Progress (https://www.americanprogress.org/issues/democracy/reports/2018/02/12/446336/election-security-50-states/).

[4] For a detailed explication of the RLA protocol, see https://www.eac.gov/assets/1/28/Risk-Limiting%20Audit%20Report%20-%20Final%20CO.pdf and https://www.stat.berkeley.edu/~stark/Preprints/gentle12.pdf.

directly to the votecount margin of victory. This concept would allow a flexible and effective standard to be written into audit legislation and executed simply and straightforwardly—without increasing reliance on yet more computerization or experts—in the often messy real-world that confronts election administrators.

Why audits are "in"

There is a clear parallel between the lessons we are learning about computerized voting and the lessons we are learning about living more generally in a "cyber-world." In each case the "gift" seemed to be "free," ours for the taking—convenience, speed, ease, expansion of possibilities. In each case we are learning, in relatively short order (though even the brief delay may well have tragic consequences), the substantial hidden costs: in the case of life in the cyber-world, the great costs associated with theft of information and identity; in the case of computerized voting, the concealed counting of votes in the pitch-dark of a privatized cyberspace, the great costs to democracy associated with theft of elections. Protecting identity and protecting elections are major problems with different potential solutions—but neither one is likely to be doable "on the cheap." And both will require a significant adjustment of behavior and expectations.

Several other nations—including Germany, Ireland, The Netherlands, and most recently Norway[5]—have, in response to concerns about security and fraud, returned to public, observable vote counting in the form of hand-counted paper ballots (HCPB).

Because, however, the United States is not a parliamentary system and because its elections therefore typically involve much longer ballots with more contests to count than in these other nations, HCPB have been viewed by virtually all U.S. election administrators as impractical. The public has long been sold on convenience, speed, and entertainment ("DECISION 20XX" as a kind of media extravaganza—a Super Bowl of American politics—dependent upon having results by bedtime in every U.S. mainland time zone), and there are massive inertias impeding such a fundamental change in the Election Night ethos as HCPB would entail.

The question thus arises whether any counting and verification processes short of HCPB might be relied upon to secure and protect U.S. elections and restore both public sovereignty and public trust. The first and most obvious step would

---

[5] See https://thebarentsobserver.com/en/life-and-public/2017/09/norwegian-votes-be-counted-manually-fear-election-hacking.

be eliminating counting processes that are not subject to any form of verification—essentially the Direct Recording Electronic (DRE) method that involves no paper at all.[6] Such votes, which still represent nearly a quarter of all votes in the U.S., are cast on "touchscreen" computers and can neither be audited nor recounted by any method other than asking the computer to "have another go" and spit out the exact results it presented the first time. DREs are regarded by virtually every cybersecurity analyst as an open invitation to undetectable manipulation and fraud.[7]

Ditching the DREs is obviously necessary but, perhaps less obviously, insufficient. Many have been lulled into the belief that simply having "paper"—capable of being manually audited, or recounted if necessary—is an adequate safeguard. There are two major reasons, however, that this is a false security.

First, recounts are a poor approach to verifying and protecting elections: they are expensive—often beyond what candidates in the financially-depleted post-election period can afford—and burdensome. Beyond these impediments are the chain-of-custody issues that arise when a second count takes place days or weeks after the first count. It is very difficult to secure all ballots and prevent ballot substitution, as several recent recounts featuring torn, unsealed, and misnumbered ballot bags have illustrated. Finally, where either mandatory or elective recounts are pegged to a "close" election within a certain margin of victory—often as low as 0.25%; in California, an absurd 0.015% is the threshold for state-funded recounts[8]—it stands as an invitation to manipulators to simply shift enough votes to exceed that margin.

Second, experience has shown that audits are too often weak and toothless, and too often set up with the specific intention of "checking the consistency of the machines" (that is, do they spit out the same result twice?) rather than verifying election outcomes. The absence of a well-designed audit protocol that can be uniformly applied and made subject to public observation and review is an egregious flaw in our current electoral process and one that must be addressed in any proposals for reform. Without an effective audit process, the "good news"

---

[6] Add to that computerized Ballot-Marking Devices (BMD), that convert voter choices into barcodes that are then read and counted by a scanner. Currently being hawked by several established vendors, such as ES&S, such BMDs somewhat sarcastically produce a "paper ballot," but of course one that no voter will be able to verify as having recorded his or her vote (for the defeat of one such bill, see http://gwmac.com/barcode-voting/).

[7] See https://www.csoonline.com/article/3099165/security/a-hackable-election-5-things-you-need-to-know-about-e-voting-machines.html.

[8] See http://www.sos.ca.gov/elections/statewide-recounts/statewide-recounts-faq/.

that an election is to be conducted "with paper" is really a form of "fake news": it is rather useless for an election to be *auditable* if it is not in fact effectively *audited*.

What an effective audit does and does not have to do

Before turning to the specifics of this Simplified Audit proposal, it will be useful to set forth guidelines for *any* form of successful election audit. Each of the following is a requirement for an effective, trustworthy electoral audit process:

1. All votes in the venue (state, CD, etc.) must be on paper ballots available for human review. The votes to be audited can *not* be embodied in barcodes or QR codes.

2. All aspects of the audit—including ballot selection, counting, computation, and posting of results—must be performed observably, in public view.

3. Selection of ballots to be audited must be made by random process.

4. If the audit is designed to sample by *precinct*—that is, to employ a full count of ballots at a certain percentage of a venue's precincts—then the random selection of precincts must be made at the close of voting, with no prior "telegraphing" of sites to be audited.

5. The audit must be completed within a short period of time once all votes have been cast—within days, not weeks or months, of Election Night—with rigorous chain of custody protocols followed to protect against ballot alteration or substitution.

6. The audit must be conducted by local election administrators and open to observation by, at minimum, one designated representative of each major party and one representative of voters not affiliated with either major party.

7. The audit must be *sensitive* enough to detect outcome-affecting mistabulation of votes and *selective* enough to distinguish between such actionable fraud or error and the minor, non-outcome-affecting counting errors, or "noise," inevitable in any large-scale counting process.

8. The audit must *specify* an "escalation" process, whereby, if the results of the initial audit disclose votecount-audit disparities exceeding established accuracy parameters, provision is made for expanding the audit, up to and including a full manual count of the ballots.

It should be apparent that the burdens of time and effort are significant, both for those conducting and for those observing the audit process. With the alternatives to the audit approach being either a full hand-counting process or an unverified counting process taking place in the pitch-dark of cyberspace, a fundamental choice must be made about the value of secure and verified elections.

For those who despair that "in the wild"—in the messy, at times chaotic world of real-world elections—audits will too often fall short of the standard of perfection seemingly set out in the eight points above, there is a bit of good news. Electoral audits are designed to detect significant and impactful mistabulations—those that jeopardize the "who won?" outcome of elections. But an audit will also have done its job—and done it well—if it manages to *deter* bad actors from interfering with the vote counting process with the aim of altering outcomes.

For this purpose, audits need not be perfect. They need to be strong enough and sound enough to pose a serious and significant *threat* of exposure of any deliberate manipulation of the vote counting process with potential to alter electoral outcomes. Once such an interference is exposed numerically by the audit, it is then up to the investigatory process to pinpoint and prosecute its source. If the audit is basically sound and cannot be readily gamed, this is a risk rational would-be election thieves would not be inclined to take.

By making it part of the risk/reward calculation of any such bad actor, the audit would have served its fundamental purpose of protecting each election from interference and theft—whether by outsiders hacking into the computerized process or by insiders programming mistabulation into the process "at the factory." So, while an audit can't be so slipshod in design or execution as to be subject to compromise by the very same forces that would seek to subvert the democratic process through the mistabulation of votes, if it is designed and conducted in good faith and in adherence to the basic requirements set forth above, it will work as a powerful tool to secure our elections from meddling.

Issues with each of the main audit approaches: RLA and Flat

Election audits can be divided into two major categories: 1) sampling ballots, and 2) sampling precincts.

The ballot sampling approach treats all ballots for a given contest (e.g., statewide, congressional district, state assembly district, etc.), however and wherever cast, as if they were collected in one big bucket, from which a representative (i.e., random) sample is drawn and counted. The results of that count (i.e., the percentages for each candidate in a contest, or Yes/No on a proposition) are then compared with the computed votecounts for that contest and a determination made whether the election "passes."

The precinct sampling approach, instead of treating all ballots as collected in one bucket, considers them as discrete batches (precincts) and chooses a certain percentage of those batches (precincts) at random for auditing. In most cases, when a precinct audit is performed, it functions something like a *spot check*, which is to say that the comparison made is between the computer count and the hand count of all the ballots *in that precinct*.

Although it is possible to treat the random selection of precincts as representative of the jurisdiction (e.g., state, CD) as a whole, and thus compare the aggregate audit tally with the votecount for the entire contest, this approach introduces certain complexities into the sampling process, such as the fact that precinct size must be taken into account in order to generate a precinct sample that is representative of the jurisdiction as a whole. Because a given precinct will often have strong partisan character, a small sampling of precincts, even if random, risks a significant partisan skew.

Audits can further be categorized as "flat" or "risk limiting." In the flat audit a pre-set percentage of either ballots or precincts is sampled; in the risk-limiting audit (RLA), that percentage varies and is determined by the margin of victory in the contest being audited (note that for the purposes of this presentation, only binary elections between two candidates [or yes/no on a proposition] are being considered—with suitable modification, the principles can be applied to multi-candidate contests). With RLAs, the larger the margin of victory, the smaller the sample generally needed to confirm it—and this holds true whether sampling ballots or precincts.

Although the precinct sample—or "spot check"—approach is obviously the more convenient, its efficacy has often been called into question. In theory, what amounts to pulling the ballots out of a scanner storage bin, manually counting them, and comparing that count with the machine tally, should provide a check against machine counting error whether that error is the product of a "glitch" or of fraud. In practice, there are several problems that may compromise the capacity of the audit to detect fraud. The first involves the selection of precincts, in particular the "cherry-picking" of precincts known to be fraud-free for auditing (e.g., Ohio 2004, where "cheat sheets" were provided to ensure that audit and votecount numbers matched[9]). The second involves the problem of timing—the interval between the selection of precincts and the performance of

---

[9] See https://www.motherjones.com/media/2005/11/recounting-ohio/.

the audit is a time during which ballot substitution and/or scanner recalibration can be performed. The third involves the fact that precinct spot checks do nothing to verify the aggregation process above the precinct level, so that if the fraud is in the central tabulators it will likely go undetected. As a result, the ballot-sampling approach has come to be favored in the design of RLAs.

While there is no question that contest-wide ballot sampling is the stronger and less fallible approach, its logistical challenges should not be underestimated. It is by no means undoable. But it behooves us to be realistic about what it entails—especially if mandated to complete the audit within a short period after the close of voting (a choice also has to be made about whether to audit the whole ballot or more selectively—this will make a major difference in the overall burden[10]). Whatever the sampling rate, this approach necessitates having both sampler/counters and observers deployed to every place where ballots are gathered (precincts, mailbags, etc.). It will of course be more convenient if ballots are transported to a central location (e.g., county elections department), with chain of custody protections maintained. It should also be noted here that, where the scanners produce "digital ballot images," it may provide an opportunity for off-site auditing, which would greatly facilitate the process, though some have expressed concern about the digital chain-of-custody issues raised by reliance on such ballot images). That's a lot of peoplepower in the real world and a lot to organize and worry about—and also a lot of potential for dispute and conflict, particularly if any unnecessary complexities are introduced into the protocol.

How the new Split-The-Difference Audit works

The Split-The-Difference Audit (STDA) presented here was developed with the aim of simplifying the protocol, reducing confusion and potential conflict in the execution of a ballot-sampling audit, without sacrificing either its sensitivity to fraud or selectivity regarding noise.

It turns out that for the vast majority of contests bearing national significance (statewide, congressional, and even most state legislative races), the *size* for a flat, random sample of ballots is one of the *less* important choices. In fact, for statewide and congressional contests, a 1 percent sample will generally suffice. State legislative contests—depending on the size of the district—may ultimately

---

[10] At this stage, we are recommending that federal and statewide contests be given priority for the audit proposed here (the STDA). All elections warrant protection; in the crisis that has overtaken U.S. elections and our political process, however, elections of direct national significance should come first.

require a larger sample, but we will see that this "escalation" process is built into the STDA design.

Of far greater importance than sample size is the selectivity/sensitivity issue— or knowing when an audit result is a red flag that requires an escalated sample, full recount, or some such investigation. This is where bringing in the "risk-limiting" concept works. To conduct an RLA (as proposed by Berkeley Professor Philip Stark and others) generally requires a recursive algorithm to determine the percentage of ballots to be sampled. In essence, you keep going until the count of sampled ballots guarantees accuracy of the initial (computer) count to within an acceptable and pre-determined level of confidence.[11] As a result, the percentage of ballots to be counted will vary and a separate sampling be necessary for each contest on the ballot, leading to complexities and potential problems in execution. It is fair, based on observation and experience, to say that election administrators and workers want *routines*—the less variation, the better.

The STDA developed from the insight that you can conduct a flat audit and build the risk-limiting concept into the escalation provision. *The way to do this is to peg the "accuracy threshold" of the audit—that is, the acceptable percentage disparity between votecount and audit margins of victory—to the votecount margin of victory (VMOV).*

The audit legislation can provide, for example, that if the audit margin of victory (AMOV) is *less than half* the VMOV, that will trigger escalation. Note that we do not care about *any* situations in which the AMOV is *greater* than the VMOV—we're concerned here (in simple binary elections) strictly about who won, not by how much.

I cannot emphasize this point too strongly. With apologies to any "purists" in the room, pragmatism must prevail in this enterprise. Given the demands, the delays, the administrative, institutional and cultural resistance—in short, all the inertias, rational or otherwise, that have thus far locked in a manifestly vulnerable computerized vote counting process—the whole quest for reliable audits is inevitably going to be seen (especially by those upon whom the demands are being made) as a bridge too far. It is imperative not to make it an inch longer than it absolutely has to be.

Probably the best way to show the STDA at work is through two sets of basic examples.

---

[11] See note 4.

Our first set will audit a run-of-the-mill noncompetitive election. The vast majority of binary (two-candidate or yes/no proposition) races are not close. While reversing the outcome of such elections might risk failing the smell test, it is not beyond the pale from a technological standpoint. All elections deserve quantitative protection, but if the huge swath of noncompetitive ones can be handled simply and quickly, the audit process as a whole will be seen to be far more practical.

For our noncompetitive example, let's posit a votecount of 70 percent for "A" and 30 percent for "B," a VMOV of 40. We assume that the "one-half VMOV" standard (VMOV/2) has been written into the audit legislation; in this case VMOV/2 = 20. Let's now look at a few possible audit outcomes:

1) If the audit result is 66%A - 34%B, the AMOV = 32; 32 > 20, so do nothing further; the election PASSES.

2) If the audit result is 95%A - 5%B, the AMOV = 90; 90 > 20, so do nothing further; the election PASSES. Note that in this example, the audit is "way off," but not in the direction that would suggest any possibility of an outcome reversal; as a general rule, whenever AMOV > VMOV, the election passes.

3) If the audit result is 58%A-42%B, the AMOV = 16; 16 < 20; the election FAILS, so *ESCALATE*; this would be a red flag if, as we began by assuming, the legislation sets the "one-half VMOV" standard. Note that most contests will be the 70%-30% species (i.e., noncompetitive) and in these contests the STDA will virtually *never* have to escalate unless either something has gone seriously blooey or some election thief has gone seriously crazy.

It gets more interesting in the instances when contests are close. For our second set, let us take a *competitive* election in which the votecount is 52 percent for "A" and 48 percent for "B," a VMOV of 4. We again assume that the "one-half VMOV" standard has been written into the legislation; in this case, VMOV/2 = 2. Again, let's look at a few possible audit outcomes:

1) If the audit result is 55%A - 45%B, the AMOV = 10; 10 > 2, so do nothing further, the election PASSES (remember, *whatever* the VMOV is, if AMOV > VMOV, the election passes).

2) If the audit result is 49%A - 51%B, the AMOV = -2 (negative because it is now A's margin of *loss*); -2 < 2; the election FAILS, so *ESCALATE*; it can be seen that the impact of our simple formula for escalation is that *whenever* the audit produces a different victor from

the votecount, AMOV will perforce be less than VMOV/2, and it will be a red flag triggering escalation by provision of the legislation.

3) If the audit result is 51.2%A - 48.8%B, the AMOV = 2.4; 2.4 > 2, so do nothing further; the election PASSES.

4) If the audit result is 50.8%A - 49.2%B, the AMOV = 1.6; 1.6 < 2; the election FAILS, so *ESCALATE*.

I hope those examples make clear how this audit and pre-set standard would work in practice. It is based on a simple "flat" sampling of a fixed and pre-determined percentage of the cast votes for a given race. This means that, unlike with the standard RLA protocol, ballots don't have to be re-sampled at different rates for each race to be audited. *A single sampling of the ballots will enable auditing of all races subject to audit.*

Note also that the escalation decision was in all cases *independent* of the statistical margin of error (MOE) of the audit. The MOE is a gauge of the likely accuracy of a sampling, with smaller MOEs indicating a more "powerful" sample. Logically the MOE decreases with increasing sample size—but, perhaps counterintuitively, it is virtually independent of the size of the pot being sampled, once that pot reaches about 20,000 in number, as is the case with virtually every election bearing national significance. For illustrative purposes, a random sampling of 1,500 ballots from such a large pot will yield a result within 3 percent of the full votecount 95 percent of the time; a 3,000-ballot random sample will come out within 2 percent; and a 10,000-ballot random sample within 1 percent.

In our STDA, however, assuming the sample of ballots is of a reasonable size—which would be provided in nearly all cases by a 1 percent level of sampling—the MOE can effectively be (purists, cover your eyes) *disregarded*. This is because the MOE doesn't really come into play in *noncompetitive* elections—the audit results can be well outside the MOE without triggering the "one-half VMOV" standard, and will work just fine. And in very *close* elections, we will want to escalate if the one-half VMOV standard is triggered, *even if the results are within the audit's statistical MOE.*

Note that, for the purposes of illustration, we assumed a one-half VMOV (VMOV/2) standard for escalation—and that one-half standard gives the new audit its name, Split-the-Difference Audit. That standard could, however, be legislatively established to be higher or lower: for example, a "one-quarter VMOV" standard, which would make escalation less likely and "weaken" the audit; or a "three-quarters VMOV" standard, which would make escalation more likely and "strengthen" the audit. I propose the one-half VMOV standard as being just about right in balancing selectivity and sensitivity.

And, of course, a more *complex* standard could be concocted, incorporating the MOE as a second trigger and essentially hybridizing the standard. But I don't see much value in that. That hands it all back over to the computers and the experts without an appreciable gain in auditing power, selectivity, or sensitivity. The closer to KISS this can be, without sacrificing detective or deterrent power, the better.

Sheep may safely graze

It may be of value, for anyone yet unclear about how the STDA is designed, to consider a pictorial/schematic representation of the audit at work. Picture a meadow with sheep grazing that ends in a cliff. There are sheep all over the meadow, some closer to the cliff's edge, some farther away. Each represents a computerized vote-count of one of the contests on a ballot. Then the sheep begin to move. Some move closer to the cliff, some move further away. Their new positions represent the results for each contest given by the STDA. The cliff, of course, is the 50-50 line, the place at which there would be a different winner.

We don't have to worry about any sheep that move further away from the cliff (statistically, that will be half the audit results); they're safe. And we don't have to worry about any sheep that move towards the cliff but don't get halfway there (while you don't get a statistical guarantee, the likelihood that the audit is signaling a miscount severe enough to fall off the cliff and change the winner is very low).

But any sheep that moves *more* than halfway to the cliff is in danger of falling off—a red flag, so you escalate to a full manual count (or an expanded count). There will be, unless fraud is rampant and bold, very few, if any, of those. Very close races will, of course, be more likely to escalate—which is how it should be, and just what is provided for in the RLA approach.

The STDA protocol is basically measuring via audit how close either riggers or errors have come to the cliff's edge of altering the winner. And it does that with a minimum of sampling/counting sweat, complexity, and opportunity for confusion and error—and no nontransparent calculations whatsoever.

Conclusion

The Split-The-Difference Audit combines the best features of the flat and risk-limiting species. The "flat" (pre-determined sampling percentage) aspect allows for simplicity of execution, a single sampling for multiple contests, and the development of a routine that is replicable from one venue and one election to the next. The RLA aspect bestows greater efficiency and calls for more labor *only where such labor is truly need*ed *to verify winners and losers of elections.*

The STDA is appropriately sensitive to potentially outcome-changing fraud or error, while sufficiently selective to make quick work of elections that are not in such jeopardy. It provides powerful anti-fraud deterrence while keeping Election Night complexity, confusion, conflict, and exhaustion to acceptable minimums. It should thus commend itself to election administrators concerned that the implementation of a serious audit protocol (particularly one of the RLA type) will trigger such issues in their real world—"in the wild," as it were. It also should gain the approval of election integrity advocates seeking an executable audit with built-in escalation provisions—in short, an audit with sharp teeth and very little fat.

Although the political and administrative inertias, even in "good" places, remain formidable, one can sense, in these politically-fraught and security-challenged times, a certain reweighting of concerns and desiderata—and, with that, the growing prospect of rescuing our elections from cyberspace and the black box in which they have become trapped.

STUDY VIII.

Timeline of Events and Anomalies in the Computerized Voting Era: 2000 - 2020[1]

Jonathan D. Simon

> 2000 | The "hanging chads" debacle in Florida not only is center-ring in the circus that leads to the election of George W. Bush to the presidency, but also conveniently sets the stage for the push to rapidly and fully computerize vote counting in the U.S.

> 2002 | Computerized voting gains a foothold in the wake of the Help America Vote Act, Mitch McConnell's brainchild, fronted by the soon-to-be-incarcerated Rep. Bob Ney (R-OH) and passed with the support of Democrats won over by the promise of increased turnout. The VNS (network) exit polls are withheld from the public (ostensibly because of a system glitch), masking glaring disparities in at least several key contests, including the Georgia Senate (Cleland—13% swing from tracking polls) and Governor (Barnes), where unverifiable paperless DREs (touchscreens) had just been deployed, and where software "patches" were inserted by Diebold shortly before the election in 22,000 DREs.[2]

> 2003 | Death of Raymond Lemme, official of Florida Inspector General's Office charged with investigating the election rigging allegations made by Clint Curtis, in Georgia motel room ruled a suicide; Lemme's body photographed with bruising and slash wounds consistent with battery; investigation shut down.[3]

> 2004 | Computerized voting achieves predominance, with DREs and Optical Scanner (Opscan) equipment counting more than 80% of the votes nationally. Ohio votes "processed" in Tennessee on the SmarTech "back-up" servers set up

---

[1] For an excellent "expanded" timeline of events, see Fitrakis R, Wasserman H: *The Strip & Flip Selection of 2016*, pp. 54 – 101, at https://www.amazon.com/dp/B01GSJLW0I/ref.

[2] See "Diebold and Max Cleland's 'Loss' in Georgia," by Robert F. Kennedy Jr., in Miller MC, Ed., *Loser Take All: Election Fraud and the Subversion of Democracy, 2000-2008*. Brooklyn, NY: ig Publishing, 2008.

[3] See http://www.democraticunderground.com/discuss/duboard.php?az=show_mesg&forum=104&topic_id=5567680&mesg_id=5567680.

prior to the election by Karl Rove's IT chief, Mike Connell, after the state servers operating under Republican Secretary of State J. Kenneth Blackwell (Honorary Chairman of the Bush campaign) "went down" just after midnight. Exit polls showed Kerry the victor in Ohio. Following the SmarTech takeover, margin flipped as Bush "surged" ahead. Exit polls are "adjusted" accordingly.

Votecounts are red-shifted, relative to exit polls, in 11 of the 12 "battleground" states. The networks and pollsters hasten to discredit their own polls, though they had been accurate enough for decades pre-HAVA to permit early calls of even the tightest contests. It is put forward that Bush voters were more reluctant to respond to the exit polls, though careful analysis revealed that the *highest* level of exit poll response was in Bush *strongholds* and the hypothesis doesn't fit the data. There is no evidence of "reluctant Bush responder" dynamics in noncompetitive states. And the pollsters, in offering the "reluctant Bush responder" excuse, ignore the fact that they had in any case weighted their polls to Party ID in such a way as to neutralize any such response biases. Keith Olbermann briefly covers the uproar in several successive programs, then departs on a long unannounced vacation and drops it cold.[4]

Death of Athan Gibbs Sr., Microsoft-backed inventor of Tru-Vote system to allow voter verification of ballots cast on computerized voting equipment. Gibbs, who was actively marketing his system, is killed when the car he is driving suddenly jumps lanes in front of an 18-wheel trailer.

> **2005** | Ohio election reform ballot proposition, leading by 28% in *Cleveland Plain Dealer* tracking poll on the eve of the election, is defeated by 25% when the votes are counted, an overnight net swing of 53% *statewide*; in the three other ballot propositions, the *Plain Dealer* poll is spot-on.

Death of Reverend Bill Moss, the lead plaintiff in the Ohio election challenge lawsuit *Moss v. Bush*, following an apparent stroke or aneurysm.

> **2006** | The capacity to manipulate proliferates while forensic tools grow more refined. The result is a measure of covert manipulation that was, or should have been, alarming.[5] There is a national red shift in the elections for the House of a total of 3 million votes relative to exit polls (there is a comparable red shift relative to tracking polls and a comparable red shift in competitive Senate

---

[4] See Freeman S, Bleifuss J: *Was the 2004 Presidential Election Stolen? Exit polls, election fraud, and the official count.* New York: Seven Stories Press, 2006.

[5] See Study II in this chapter; also reprinted in *Loser Take All*.

races).[6] Of critical importance, this analysis cannot be debunked on the basis of alleged exit poll sampling bias, because the sample is shown to be to the *right*, not the left, of the actual electorate.[7] The analysis is not challenged nor is an attempt made to refute it; it is simply ignored. Additional analysis reveals a "targeting" pattern, in which the more competitive a contest the more likely it was to be red shifted, a pattern pathognomonic of targeted rigging.[8]

President Bush, at the urging of Karl Rove and via Attorney General Alberto Gonzales, fires (Republican) U.S. Attorney David Iglesias and eight other U.S. attorneys for various politically-motivated reasons, including refusal to pursue dubious and fictional "voter fraud" cases, a political agenda of the Bush administration.

Death of Warren Mitofsky—"father" of exit polling and head of Edison/Mitofsky, official exit polling provider for U.S. elections—of apparent aneurysm.

> **2008** | E2008 is an Obama victory and Democratic sweep. Many ask why the suspected manipulators would rig to lose? Again there is a massive red shift, in fact greater than in 2004 and 2006.[9] But, in both the 2006 and 2008 elections, unexpected 11th-hour events (in 2006 the Foley and related GOP sex scandals, in 2008 the collapse of Lehman Brothers and the subsequent economic crash) dramatically altered the electoral dynamics (in 2006, for instance, the Democratic margin in the Cook Generic Congressional Ballot jumped from 9% in the first week of October to 26% the week of the election, a Republican free-fall of epic proportions; a similar fate overcame McCain in the wake of the economy's collapse). These political sea changes swamp a red shift that turned out in retrospect to be under-calibrated, and they come too late to permit recalibration and redeployment of tainted memory cards and malicious code.[10] These red flags are again ignored, trampled in the Obama victory parade.

---

[6] This exit poll-votecount red shift of course does not account for the additional impact of voter suppression tactics, as voters who stay at home or are turned away from the voting booth are not exit polled.

[7] See "Landslide Denied," cited in note 5.

[8] See Study III, this chapter.

[9] See Charnin R., *Proving Election Fraud: Phantom Voters, Uncounted Votes, and the National Exit Poll.* Bloomington IN: AuthorHouse, 2010.

[10] Any attempt at such recalibration and redeployment on a scale large enough to be effective would have been a rather visible and highly suspect undertaking.

Death of U.S. Representative Stephanie Tubbs Jones (OH-11), a Democrat who had formally challenged the seating of the Ohio Bush electors following E2004, at age 58 of apparent aneurysm while driving.

Death of Mike Connell, Karl Rove's IT "guru," in December crash of plane he was piloting. Connell had been compelled in November to give a sealed deposition in the *King Lincoln-Bronzeville v. Blackwell* case, challenging the votecount of the 2004 Ohio presidential election in federal court, and was expected to return to complete his testimony in January. Connell's widow, combing the crash site, finds the earpiece to his Blackberry device, known to contain extensive email correspondence with Rove, but the device itself is never located.[11]

> **2010** | Republican Scott Brown's victory in the Coakley-Brown special election in Massachusetts puts the Tea Party on the map, takes away the Democrats' filibuster-proof Senate majority, and set expectations for a major move to the right in November. There are no exit polls, no spot checks, no audits, not a single opscan's memory card examined for malicious code: the result is 100% faith-based, a *critical election that could have been stolen with virtually zero risk.* In the 71 jurisdictions where ballots are hand-counted, Coakley wins.[12] Statewide, there is an 8% disparity from hand-count to computer-count jurisdictions, a red shift in line with that measured in 2004, 2006, and 2008, and enough to reverse the outcome and avoid a recount. Analysts ask were those hand-count jurisdictions more Democratic? They weren't; they were more Republican. Were they in Coakley's part of the state? They weren't; in fact, in her only other statewide race, a noncompetitive race, she did *better* in the opscan than in the handcount jurisdictions. Ultimately analysts examine and rule out every benign explanation for the outcome-determinative disparity.[13]

The Massachusetts special election is followed by a Democratic primary in South Carolina that pits a known and respected candidate (Judge Vic Rawl) against a cipher (Alvin Greene) who makes no campaign appearances, has no website, is threatened with indictment on pornography-related charges, and lacks the personal funds for the election filing fee, which is paid anonymously on his behalf. The contest is for the nomination for U.S. Senate, and a November match-up with incumbent Republican and Tea Party favorite Jim DeMint,

---

[11] See Worrall S: *Cybergate: Was The White House Stolen by Cyberfraud?* Amazon Digital Services, 2012, https://www.amazon.com/dp/B0074NQ5UK/ref.

[12] See Study IV, this chapter.

[13] Ibid.

against whom Rawl had already closed to a threatening 7% in tracking polls. The votes are tallied on paperless DREs and Greene wins *with 59% of the vote*. Rawl brings a challenge before the Democratic State Committee. Several election integrity experts testify, citing, among other gross anomalies, large disparities between early/absentee votes counted by opscan (where the ballots would at least in theory be available for comparison with the computer counts) and the DRE tallies. Greene does not appear. The Committee reacts favorably to Rawl's challenge throughout the hearing, then goes into closed session and votes by an overwhelming margin to reject the challenge and close the matter.[14]

The November election is a great sweep for the Tea Party and the Right, with seismic implications for the nation. It appears that the professionals at Edison/Mitofsky and the National Election Pool (NEP) still cannot figure out how to get exit polls right because, once again, the red shift turns up everywhere: in the Senate elections (16 out of 18 competitive races red shifted); the Governorship elections (11 out of 13 races red shifted); and in the House (a total red shift of 1.9 million votes). In a telling comparison with 2006—when an election-eve Democratic margin of 26% in the Generic Congressional Ballot ("Whom do you intend to vote for in the election for U.S. House in your district?") translated into a net gain of a mere 31 House seats by the Democrats—a Republican Generic Congressional Ballot margin of 9%, and an even smaller tabulated national popular vote margin of 6.8%, in E2010 translates into a net gain of *63* seats, a completely unprecedented "efficiency" ratio, and the "epic sweep" the media duly reports at face value.

The infrastructure needed for computerized election theft has become progressively more sophisticated and efficient. The off-site "processing" that is believed to have been pioneered in Ohio in 2004, has now been deployed in other key states. This mechanism allows *real-time targeting and calibration of manipulations*, which was not possible with pre-set, memory card-based rigs. Using the off-site processing scheme, aka "man in the middle attack," votecounts can be altered surgically and elections stolen with a tidy numerical footprint. Election theft thus becomes increasingly difficult to detect—barring serious investigation of the off-site IP networks now processing many of the votes.

Compounding the forensic difficulties, forensic baselines—all except the surviving smattering of handcounts—are part of a feedback loop and are themselves being distorted to the right. The pollsters—under the imperative to *get elections right* or go out of business—have turned to a tunable fudge factor

---

[14] See http://www.bradblog.com/?p=7902.

known as the Likely Voter Cutoff Model (LVCM), which skews their samples about 5% to 8% to the right by disproportionately eliminating from the sample members of left-leaning constituencies such as young, transient, poor, and non-white respondents.[15] Both exit polls and pre-election polls are now also weighted using demographic baselines, such as party identification, drawn from the "adjusted" exit polls of prior elections. Since these adjustments are virtually always to the right, to bring the exit polls to conformity with the votecounts, and because they carry the demographics along to the right in the process, *current exit polls and pre-election polls are further skewed to the right.* The unadjusted exit polls—themselves red-shifted by this weighting process but lacking the LVCM to complete the distortion—remain somewhat to the left of the votecounts, but the pre-election polls, with the combined distortions of false-stratification and the LVCM pushing them well to the right, manage to accurately predict the electoral outcomes in competitive races. Logically, such methodologically contorted polls can get election results consistently *right* only if those election results are consistently *wrong*.

The U.S. Supreme Court's party-line 5-to-4 decision in *Citizens United v. FEC*, 558 U.S. 310 (2010), defines corporate campaign contributions as protected "free speech," gutting much of the framework for regulating or limiting such spending and opening the floodgates to a deluge of "dark money" when Congress fails to pass expected disclosure requirements.

> **2011** | In the Wisconsin Supreme Court election, another "proxy" election (cf. Coakley-Brown in Massachusetts the year before) with outsized national political implications, out-of-state funding pours in as Karl Rove emphasizes the significance that the Republican's victory would have. In spite of the election's national significance, no exit polls are conducted. Many votes are tabulated on servers run by the storefront outfit Command Central, located across the state line in a Minnesota strip mall. Apart from the 7583 votes (just enough votes to dodge a mandatory recount) "discovered" for the Republican candidate (found by a former employee of that candidate) the day *after* the election, there are major red-flag anomalies in returns, concentrated most strongly in Democratic Milwaukee and Dane counties, relative to established voting patterns, recent prior elections, and other races on the ballot.[16] The recount, demanded by the losing Democratic candidate, appears to be as corrupted as the election itself: bags of ballots are found by monitors to be improperly sealed and frequently ripped open in the very jurisdictions where the

---

[15] See Study V, this chapter.

[16] For details of the forensic analysis, see https://codered2014.com/wp-content/uploads/2020/04/memorandumToLegalTeamRe.Milwaukee-final.pdf.

electoral anomalies had been identified. In the face of this widespread evidence that ballots had been swapped out to match machine totals, objection after objection is lodged, duly recorded, and then ignored. The Democratic candidate ultimately bows to pressures to concede, rather than pursue a grueling litigation before a partisan and adverse state Supreme Court.[17]

There follow the State Senate recall elections in Wisconsin, and again strong anomalies emerge, this time complemented by a red shift in citizen-conducted exit polls that are admittedly of uncertain probative value. When it falls to citizen exit polls to provide the only check on secret votecounts on partisan-controlled computers, it is not surprising that the Carter Center, which monitors elections around the world, had determined that U.S. elections don't meet the minimum standards required for such monitoring. The Republicans win exactly the number of recalls needed to keep control of the Wisconsin state senate by one seat.

Having gained control of key state legislatures and governorships in the 2010 rout, Republican lawmakers and administrators, guided by the American Legislative Exchange Council (ALEC), waste little time in responding to the 2010 Census by gerrymandering the states under their control; passing restrictive and discriminatory Voter-ID laws; and adding a variety of other discriminatory burdens to the registration and voting processes.

> **2012** | The recall election for Republican Governor Scott Walker of Wisconsin is dubbed "the second most important election" of this presidential election year. Corporate cash and partisan luminaries flood into the state and all stops are pulled, particularly on behalf of the embattled, union-busting Republican Governor, who enjoyed an eight-to-one spending advantage over his Democratic opponent.

When the dust settles, Walker has won a surprisingly easy 7% victory, which is ascribed by the punditry to his massive *Citizens United*-enabled funding advantage and to the right-trending mood of the country.

What the media fails even to *footnote* is that the NEP exit poll had the race at 50%-50% (an exit poll weighted, we should not forget, to right-shifted Party ID demographics drawn from the right-adjusted exit polls of recent prior elections). This exit poll is as "official" as any conducted on November 6th for the general election: same outfit (Edison/Mitofsky), same methodology, same large sample. What is curious is that, if you had looked for it on Election Night, you would

---

[17] See https://codered2014.com/wp-content/uploads/2020/04/irregularitiesinWISupremeCourtElectionandRecount.pdf.

have found it in only one place: online briefly (before it was adjusted to match Walker's 7% margin) at the Milwaukee *Journal-Sentinel's* website. You would not have found it posted on any network, though the networks certainly were looking at that poll because they all came out talking about a "deadlock" and "a long night ahead." Until *about 15 minutes later* it suddenly morphs into "an easy Walker win ... yet another triumph for the politically born-again Karl Rove" and "a grim prospect for the Democrats." The networks commission and pay for that exit poll and then decide, one and all, to withhold it from public view (the Milwaukee *Journal-Sentinel* either did not get the message or brazenly decides to ignore it). Because it is impossibly far "off"—at least relative to the votecount, which must be "on," else this is not *America*.

While the public battle rages over Voter ID and "voter" fraud, no media attention is accorded to continuing, indeed intensifying, evidence of covert electronic fraud. An egregious but typical omission is an analysis, covered by the press in the U.K. but predictably ignored in the U.S., by Michael Duniho (retired National Security Agency analyst), Francois Choquette, and James Johnson, who examined election returns from the 2012 Republican presidential primaries. The authors find a consistent pattern: after controlling for all other factors, such as urban/rural differences, Mitt Romney's share of the vote increases, and his opponents' shares decrease, as the *size* of the precinct where the votes were being counted increases.[18]

This pattern, disclosed by Cumulative Vote Share analysis ("CVS"), is not "naturally occurring;" that is, it is not found in "ordinary" elections that would not be targets for rigging. In *those* races, when voteshare is plotted against cumulative votes cast by increasing precinct size, the slope is a flat line; there is *no correlation* between voteshare and precinct size.

The authors can find *nothing* to account for the Romney "upslope" pattern other than the selection by a rigger of larger precincts as safer places to shift votes without arousing suspicion (100 votes shifted in a precinct of 1000 total votes cast will pass the smell test; the same 100 votes stolen in a precinct of 250 total votes will not). In primary after primary throughout the bruising Romney run to the nomination the analysts find the same pattern. They then extend their analysis to suspect races as far back as 2008 and pick up essentially the same red-flag pattern for these elections, including an overall shift of up to 10% from Democratic to Republican in key contests such as the Coakley-Brown race in Massachusetts.

---

[18] See http://www.themoneyparty.org/main/wp-content/uploads/2012/10/Republican-Primary-Election-Results-Amazing-Statistical-Anomalies_V2.0.pdf.

Obama's "reassuring" re-election victory is likely a result of covert intervention by the group Anonymous, which, having infiltrated Rove's ORCA operation, locks his operatives out of their own servers. Ohio's own official servers "go down" at 11:13 pm (cf. E2004) while Rove, in a bizarre on-air "meltdown," disputes the call of Ohio and the election for Obama by his own employer, Fox News. In addition to the actions of Anonymous, a lawsuit filed the day before the election, challenging the placement of "experimental" software patches in 44 Ohio counties and on the state's election website, is credited by some with thwarting the planned manipulation of E2012.

> **2013** | The U.S. Supreme Court—by a party-line 5-to-4 decision in *Shelby County v. Holder*, 570 U.S. 2 (2013)—guts the mechanism for enforcing the restraints imposed by The Voting Rights Act of 1965, freeing nine states with a Jim Crow history of franchise discrimination to change their election laws without federal review. As in the wake of *Citizens United* (2010), Republican legislatures and administrations in these states waste no time in passing a swath of discriminatory procedural laws and regulations targeting minorities and other Democratic constituencies. Many of these provisions face legal challenge and are ruled unconstitutional by the courts.

> **2014** | Carrying a single-digit approval rating, *the lowest in history*, the Republican-led Congress *gains* seats in E2014. Of 222 Republican House incumbents who stand for re-election, *two* are defeated, a re-election rate of better than 99%; Republicans take control of the Senate and gain 13 House seats overall. This astounding result is reflexively attributed by pundits to "low turnout" among Democratic and progressive voters. Yet, across a wide swath of states, progressive ballot propositions, strongly opposed by these same Republican candidates, are passed by wide (i.e., rig-proof) margins. The question of how these results square with the "low turnout" hypothesis is never answered. Nor is a pervasive red shift deemed at all remarkable.

The U.S. Supreme Court—by yet another party-line 5-to-4 decision in *McCutcheon v. FEC*, 134 S.Ct. 1434 (2014)—removes all restrictions on aggregate corporate campaign contributions. The Court is aware, by the time of *McCutcheon*, that Congress had failed and would fail to pass any disclosure requirements that the Court had supposedly anticipated in the wake of its *Citizens United* decision. Thus the Scalia bloc decides *McCutcheon* fully aware that it is ushering in an era in American politics not just of dark (i.e., undisclosed) money, but of *unlimited* dark money.

> **2015** | The Harvard Electoral Integrity Project ranks the United State 45th among fully developed democracies in election integrity. The "Beacon of Democracy" places immediately between Mexico and Colombia.

> 2016 | Political anger, distrust, disgust, and nihilism are the hallmarks of the E2016 campaign. The word "rigged" is brought into common usage (and misusage) by Donald Trump, and that impression of the electoral process is bolstered by a variety of visible tactics appearing to place thumbs of significant weight on the scales in favor of certain candidates. The perception of unfairness is particularly strong among supporters of Vermont Senator Bernie Sanders's candidacy, a nearly successful bid astoundingly funded almost entirely by individual as opposed to corporate donors. But it is Trump's warnings of a rigged November that reflect most ominously what happens when vote counting is unobservable and trust in the process has broken down.

Although Trump prevails in what appears to be a fair Republican nomination battle, the Democratic battle is riddled with uncanny numbers and patterns that accrue to the benefit of Clinton. Among those patterns: the radically divergent performance of the candidates in caucuses (where vote counting is observable and Sanders routs Clinton) vs. primaries (where vote counting is computerized and unobservable and Clinton bests Sanders); the radically divergent performance of the exit polls in the Republican primaries (where they are within expected error levels) vs. the Democratic primaries (where they are far outside expected error levels and virtually unilateral in their shift); and the odd reverse-shift of Oklahoma, the only primary state where the voting computers are programmed mainly by the *state itself* instead of the *vendors*.

Trump's alarms about "rigging," echoing those of Sanders supporters and election integrity advocates, are therefore, while undeniably both scatter-shot and self-serving, neither as irrational as portrayed by the media nor indeed lacking in evidentiary basis.[19] Trump does break new ground in responding to the question whether he would accept the legitimacy of the election if he lost it. He demurs, raising the prospect of post-election chaos. A few other candidates had prepared in advance for trouble, most notably John Kerry, who in 2004 had raised a fund of $15 million for post-election legal challenges, of which he then

---

[19] Others echoed the hue and cry. Most eye-opening was an article by the inimitable Roger Stone, one-time Trump advisor, veteran of Republican campaigns dating to the Nixon years, convicted felon awaiting presidential pardon, and NY *Times* best-selling author: "Can the 2016 election be rigged? You bet," at http://thehill.com/blogs/pundits-blog/presidential-campaign/291534-can-the-2016-election-be-rigged-you-bet. Stone writes:

> Both parties have engaged in voting machine manipulation. Nowhere in the country has this been more true than Wisconsin, where there are strong indications that Scott Walker and the Reince Priebus machine rigged as many as five elections including the defeat of a Walker recall election. . . The computerized voting machines can be hacked and rigged and after the experience of Bernie Sanders there is no reason to believe they won't be.

chose not to spend (or return) a penny. But there is not much doubt that Trump would not follow suit and graciously accept results about which he had any reason, evidence-based or otherwise, to be suspicious.

This scenario does not materialize and Clinton loses no time conceding, in spite of Trump's improbable table-run of virtually every battleground state, most by a whisker, while losing the popular vote by nearly 3 million votes; and in spite of reports from the field of targeted voter suppression, computer breakdowns, a red-flag (i.e., focal) pattern of red-shift exit poll disparities, and concerns about vulnerabilities to foreign interference (which at that point had not been publicly presented).

It is left to Green Party presidential candidate Jill Stein, a recipient of just over 1 percent of the popular vote, to pursue recounts in three battleground states—Wisconsin, Michigan, and Pennsylvania—in which Trump's combined victory margin is a mere 77,744 votes, or about one half of one percent of the votes cast in those states. Stein, facing a series of deadlines, as well as inflated charges threatening to derail her efforts, succeeds in raising over $7 million, in individual contributions averaging $45, in less than a week's time. Her campaign is thus able to file for recounts in Wisconsin, Michigan, and Pennsylvania, though the high fees demanded by these states (a good part of which are ultimately refunded to the Stein campaign as unnecessary) make it impossible to pursue recounts in Florida and North Carolina, two other Trump razor-thin table-run states flying forensic red flags.

Various other barriers are relied upon and tactics employed to effectively thwart each of the three recounts. In Pennsylvania, where most of the votes were cast on unrecountable DREs, recounts, where possible, are impeded by a requirement for three petition filings from *every one* of the state's 9,000+ election districts; in litigation brought by Stein, a Bush-appointed federal judge rules that it "border[s] on the irrational" to suspect hacking of the unauditable, unrecountable computers might have affected the election outcome. In Michigan, ballot bags found torn or tampered with are ruled ineligible for recounting, and the courts ultimately halt the recount on the grounds that Stein has no chance to win, even if votes had been miscounted. In Wisconsin, a Republican judge leaves it to each county to choose whether to recount manually or just run the ballots through the same machines that provided the initial count; Stein is charged a fee more than five times that charged for a fully manual statewide recount in 2011; over 40% of Stein's payment is ultimately refunded, too late for meeting the recount deadlines of other states or funding appeals of rulings blocking the counts. Stein is pilloried in much of the media for undertaking the recounts as a for-profit scam. The results of the partial, selective, and thwarted recounts are taken as proof that no potentially outcome-altering miscounts had occurred.

> **2017** | Trump's campaign pursued legal action to block each attempted recount but the candidate himself, as president-elect, immediately levels charges of fraud: "voter fraud." Seemingly unable to accept or tolerate his nearly 3 million vote loss nationwide, Trump alleges that it was caused by "millions of illegal voters" voting against him—either noncitizens voting illegally or legal voters illegally voting multiple times. Repeated investigations have found no evidence of this "voter fraud" phenomenon, but Trump hastily assembles an "Election Integrity" commission to get to the bottom of it all—chaired by Vice President Mike Pence and Kansas Secretary of State Kris Kobach, the voter-suppression czar whose "CrossCheck" operation uses a data-matching algorithm patently aimed at the purging from the voter rolls of millions of *legal* voters. The commission, stacked with Republican heavyweights (including none other than Ohio's own J. Kenneth Blackwell), predictably finds nothing, is sued for its utter lack of transparency, and is quietly disbanded by Trump—without issuing a report, but not before making a controversial gambit to obtain confidential voter-registration and personal data from every state—nearly all of which refuse to comply.

From the beginning of his presidency, Trump's approval ratings sit at record lead-balloon lows, reflecting both the extreme polarization fostered by his campaign and the failure of that campaign or of his post-election activities to win support outside his hardened "base." His inauguration, and the lies he insists on telling about its sparse attendance, set the tone for the steady spew of lies and the virtually ceaseless tumult that mark the Age of Trump. Truth, ordinarily a casualty of war, is now a casualty of a psychological war—waged on the American media, governmental institutions, law, body politic, and the public itself by a man who appears capable of sacrificing the world to be a "winner" and avoid the scourge of deep-embedded shame. Although "politics" becomes too "dangerous" for discussion over dinner, little by little, scandal by scandal, sacking by sacking, blurt by blurt, tweet by tweet, depravity by depravity, and lie by lie, the desperate longing for rescue from this nightmare among an extraordinary swath of the population becomes palpable. There are petitions, protests, parades, and of course the polls—but, with the GOP leadership showing no sign of moving against a president who they finally grasped was a plutocrat (i.e., one of them) masquerading as a populist—the focus turns inevitably to E2018. Trump opponents—from environmentalists to immigrants, from #MeTooers to the Marchers for Life, from those who value knowledge and science to those who simply value basic honesty, from those distressed by corruption to those disgusted by bullying, from those terrified by an impulsive and transactional foreign policy to those still waiting for the buck to stop within a thousand miles of a leader constitutionally incapable of taking responsibility for any failure or shortcoming—begin to look to the midterms almost literally for salvation.

Naturally then, every electoral tea leaf is scrutinized for any hint of what awaits when the public is permitted its first Age-of-Trump national right of review. What the verdict will be is far less clear than the story told by the polls—which is that Trump even at his "peak" is historically unpopular and, because sentiments are running historically high, indeed historically reviled. But polls can be "off"—though the chances for that when all polls but one or two acknowledged outliers like Rasmussen are in general agreement are very small—and things may, of course, change.

The year 2017 starts out with a run of (narrow) Republican wins in special elections for vacant seats, culminating in the most expensive U.S. House election in history, in which $50 million is poured into Georgia's 6th congressional district (GA-6) race. Bright forensic red flags fly as, first in the GA-6 preliminary election and then in the run-off, highly suspicious events and anomalies combine to, by the narrowest of margins, keep the seat in Republican control. The extraordinarily high expense level reflects not the contest's strategic importance (a Democratic win would have put only the smallest of dents in the Republican House majority) but its symbolic importance as a proxy for the impact of the first half year of Trump's presidency on national politics. Because the district had been solid congressional red territory, a win by the Democratic candidate, Jon Ossoff, would have been a result of utmost embarrassment to Trump and a black omen for the president and the GOP going forward.

In the preliminary round in April, a server shutdown and reporting hiatus reminiscent of Ohio 2004 is implicated in bringing Ossoff just below the 50% of the total vote level necessary for outright victory and putting him into a runoff with the top Republican finisher, who receives 19%. Then in the run-off between the two in June, Ossoff wins the verifiable mail-in vote by a margin of 28% but is defeated in Election Day voting (which is counted by unverifiable paperless touchscreens) by 16%, losing overall by 3.6%.

This pattern is so improbably bizarre that forensics analysts search for a "benign" explanation for the anomaly (e.g., do GA-6 Democrats tend more than Republicans to vote by mail?), but are able to find nothing. The Ossoff campaign shows no interest in challenging but, as part of a lawsuit filed by election integrity advocates seeking to decertify the paperless computers going forward, production and examination is sought of the servers programmed by the

Kennesaw State University Elections Center to record and count the votes. It is subsequently discovered that, three days after the suit's filing (in fact over the July 4th weekend), the server was scrubbed (using a high-gauss "industrial" magnet) by the Elections Center, deleting all code and data and destroying the only available "hard" evidence capable of shedding light on the counting process and egregious anomalies. Two back-up servers meet the same fate.

The Ossoff loss appears to mark a turning point, after which Democratic fortunes improve. They begin chalking up wins in the scattered down-ballot special elections and roll to decisive wins in the off-off-year general election in November. They take the governorships of Virginia (where the state had decided to ditch its paperless DREs and replace them with paper ballots counted by opscan) and New Jersey (where outgoing Governor Chris Christie's great unpopularity ensured that the Democratic margin of victory would not be riggably close). In both cases, the ubiquitous "red shift" disappears, as exit polls (which "always" overcount Democrats) suddenly stop overcounting Democrats.

Many interpret the Democratic wins not only as the footstep of doom for Trump and the GOP in E2018, but as a clear indication that election theft is either a fantasy or a thing of the past. There are compelling strategic reasons, however, for refraining from manipulating this set of elections for the benefit of Republican candidates.[20] These strategic considerations make it highly likely that all these "drop in the bucket" elections, up through the victory of Democrat Conor Lamb over Trump-supported Republican Rick Saccone (PA-18) in March 2018, were left alone.

The U.S. Senate special election in Alabama, pitting the controversial and scandal-plagued far-right Republican Roy Moore against Democrat Doug Jones is *sui generis*. Jones' victory in December 2017 is taken by many at face value as a triumph of #MeToo and more trouble for Trump and the Republicans in E2018. Some, having noted several strange anomalies accruing to the benefit of Jones, suggest that the Democrats have finally learned the art of computerized election theft. Given, however, the equipment used and the administrative control exercised by Republicans in this state, the opportunity for Democrats to manipulate votecounts is slim to none. Returning to the caveat that the beneficiary of meddling may well not be its perpetrator (see, e.g., Clinton in the 2016 primaries), a few analysts read Alabama very differently. To begin with, there is a substantial exit poll-votecount *blue* shift, putting the lie to the standard

---

[20] See Simon, J: "What an Honestly Counted US Election Might Look Like," at
https://www.mintpressnews.com/election-2017-what-an-honestly-counted-us-election-might-look-like/234586/.

rationale for discrediting exit polls, which is that they "always overcount Democratic voters." Then, screencapture of the rolling vote totals reveals a late-evening "glitch" in which, without any increase in the number of precincts reporting, vote totals increase such as to reduce Moore's margin from 7,039 to 133 votes. This anomaly so closely resembles the pattern seen in the Ohio count in E2004 (where major shifts in vote totals accompanied a late-evening "glitch") that it suggests a "fingerprint match." And indeed, when taking into account the factors that effectively reverse the rooting sections for this particular election (Moore, a certain E2018 albatross, is the last man McConnell and the GOP leadership want to see in the Senate; he is, moreover, "Bannon's guy," and Bannon has made himself Rove and McConnell's mortal enemy), it is no stretch to see that, for once in a way, it is the *Democratic* candidate who would be the expected beneficiary of the meddling suggested by the anomaly noted above as well as by anomalous precinct-level patterns found on deeper drilldown.

> 2018 | The density of events and developments in the years 2018, 2019, and into 2020 having direct or indirect bearing on election integrity and electoral politics is such that any synopsis short of book-length is certain to be riddled with gloss-overs and omissions. I try here to do month-by-month justice to the slide toward authoritarianism that I believe chroniclers will recognize in this extraordinary passage in our history, as well as to the rising stakes and developing "total war" aspect of our electoral politics.

> January Trump boasts that *his* nuclear button is "much bigger" and "more powerful" than North Korea's Kim Jong-un's. Trump, in a meeting with lawmakers on immigration, reportedly asks: "Why are we having all these people from shithole countries come here?" Democrat Patty Schachtner wins the special election for Wisconsin's 10th Senate District, the same district Trump won by 17 points in 2016. Trump's short-lived Presidential Advisory Commission on Election Integrity disbands after most states balk at the commission's demands that they turn over comprehensive voter data; commission finds no evidence of "voter fraud," blamed by Trump for his nearly 3-million-vote popular-vote loss in E2016. **Published**: David Cay Johnston: *It's Even Worse Than You Think: What the Trump Administration Is Doing to America*; Michael Wolff: *Fire and Fury: Inside the Trump White House*; David Frum: *Trumpocracy: The Corruption of the American Republic*.

> February Mass shooting at Marjory Stoneman Douglas High School in Parkland, Florida kills 17, spurs March For Our Lives and ongoing political action by surviving students and fellow students and their families nationwide. Special Counsel Robert Mueller announces that 13 Russians have been charged with interfering in the 2016 Presidential election. Former Trump Deputy

Campaign Manager Rick Gates pleads guilty to federal charges; former Trump Campaign Chairman Paul Manafort indicted on federal charges including money laundering. Immediate impact of Parkland shooting and outrage, as a number of major corporations—including Hertz, Avis, Met Life, Delta, United, and Symantec—sever ties with the NRA.

> **March** Trump imposes 25% steel and 10% aluminum tariffs. Gary Cohn, Trump's top economic adviser, resigns, replaced by Larry Kudlow. Secretary of State Rex Tillerson is fired, replaced by CIA Director Mike Pompeo. Democrat Conor Lamb wins special election for Pennsylvania 18th CD, previously considered a safe Republican seat. FBI Deputy Director Andrew McCabe dismissed by Trump days before his scheduled retirement date, depriving him of his pension; DOJ will open an investigation into McCabe that extends into 2020. Facebook suspends Cambridge Analytica, a data analysis firm that it will be revealed mined user profiles in order to benefit Trump politically. British TV airs a documentary about Cambridge Analytica: undercover reporters, talking to executives from the firm, discover the use of bribes, honey traps, fake-news campaigns and operations with ex-spies to swing election contests around the world. Trump adds $60 billion in tariffs on Chinese goods. He replaces National Security Advisor H. R. McMaster with John Bolton. Twelve states reported to sue the Trump administration over planned "citizenship question" in U.S. Census. Trump dismisses Secretary of Veterans Affairs David Shulkin via tweet; nominates his personal physician, Ronny Jackson, to be his replacement; withdraws Jackson nomination amidst allegations of mismanagement and misconduct while at White House post. **Published:** Michael Isikoff, David Corn: *Russian Roulette: The Inside Story of Putin's War on America and the Election of Donald Trump*; Yascha Mounk: *The People vs. Democracy: Why Our Freedom is in Danger and How to Save It*; Jerome R. Corsi: *Killing the Deep State: The Fight to Save President Trump*.

> **April** China retaliates with politically targeted 25% tariffs. It's revealed that 87 million Americans had their private information accessed by Cambridge Analytica through their Facebook accounts. FBI raids home and hotel room of Trump's long-time lawyer, Michael Cohen. House Speaker Paul Ryan (R-WI) announces he will not seek reelection. Mass shooting in Nashville Waffle House kills four. **Published:** James Comey: *A Higher Loyalty: Truth, Lies, and Leadership*; Madeleine Albright: *Fascism: A Warning*; Sarah Kendzior: *The View From Flyover Country: Dispatches from the Forgotten America*.

> **May** The national unemployment rate, as calculated by the Department of Labor, is 3.9%, lowest level since 2000; many question the measurement's meaning in the new "gig" economy; some question its veracity. California

officially becomes the world's fifth largest economy. The Senate Intelligence Committee releases an unclassified version of its investigation into Russian cyberattacks in 2016, concluding: "Russian-affiliated cyber actors were able to gain access to restricted elements of election infrastructure... In a small number of states, these cyber actors were in a position to, at a minimum, alter or delete voter registration data; however, they did not appear to be in a position to manipulate individual votes or aggregate vote totals." Trump announces intention to withdraw U.S. from Iran Nuclear Agreement. Trump cancels NASA's Carbon Monitoring System. School shooting at Santa Fe High School in Texas kills eight students and two teachers. SCOTUS (Gorsuch batting for Garland) 5 – 4 decision upholds law banning employee class-action suits over pay and hours. It is reported that Trump's personal lawyer, Michael Cohen, received a secret payment of at least $400,000 to fix talks between Trump and the Ukrainian president. Roseanne Barr's show canceled after her tweet likening Obama adviser Valerie Jarrett to an ape. Missouri Republican Governor Eric Greitens resigns amidst sex scandal. Trump extends steel and aluminum tariffs to Mexico, Canada, and EU, effectively immediately. **Published:** James R. Clapper: *Facts and Fears: Hard Truths from a Life in Intelligence*; Jonathan Simon: *CODE RED: Computerized Elections and the War on American Democracy* (Election 2018 Edition); Laurence Tribe, Joshua Matz: *To End a Presidency: The Power of Impeachment*; Jon Meacham: *The Soul of America: The Battle for Our Better Angels*; Michael V. Hayden: *The Assault on Intelligence: American National Security in an Age of Lies*; Theodore Roosevelt Malloch, Roger Stone: *The Plot to Destroy Trump: How the Deep State Fabricated the Russian Dossier to Subvert the President.*

> **June** At G7 Summit, Trump pushes for a G8 to include a readmitted Russia; also proposes the elimination of tariffs and refuses to sign the summit's joint communique. Trump meets, historically, with Kim Jong-un. Paul Manafort's bail canceled and he is ordered jailed for witness tampering. U.S. announces its withdrawal from UN's Human Rights Council. SCOTUS (Gorsuch batting for Garland) approves Trump's travel ban 5 – 4. Also in *Janus v. AFSCME* overturns long-standing case protecting unions 5 - 4. Justice Anthony Kennedy announces his retirement effective July 31; McConnell vows to fill seat by fall. Deadly 2018 North American heat wave begins. Mass arrest of 575 women protesting in D.C. against ICE policies. Mass shooting at Maryland newspaper kills five. Hundreds of thousands demonstrate nationwide against Trump's child-separation policies. **Published:** Malcolm Nance: *The Plot to Destroy Democracy: How Putin and His Spies Are Undermining America and Dismantling the West.*

> **July** Scott Pruitt resigns as EPA administrator under a corruption cloud; Trump replaces him with coal industry lobbyist, and critic of all limits on greenhouse gas emissions, Andrew Wheeler. Trade war with China escalates as $34 billion in U.S. tariffs take effect, Trump threatens increases up to $550 billion, and China retaliates. Trump nominates Brett Kavanaugh for Kennedy's vacated SCOTUS seat. Trump attends NATO Summit, blasts Germany and EU. Advisors, fearing a repeat of Trump's disruptive G7 behavior, secure key agreements prior to Trump's attendance. Trump's visit to U.K. met with mass protests. Mueller charges 12 Russian intelligence officers with hacking in 2016 election. Trump meets with Putin in Helsinki for private talks, lavishes praise on Putin and Russia and laughs off their interference in E2016 in post-talks press conference, which Senator John McCain (R-AZ) describes as "one of the most disgraceful performances by an American president in memory." Two days later, in *CBS News* interview, Trump, in apparent damage-control mode, reverses course and holds Putin personally responsible for the election interference. Trump administration proposes cutback on habitat protections for endangered species. Northern California wildfires continue to rage.

> **August** Trump demands immediate end to Russia investigation, calls on AG Jeff Sessions to halt it and accuses Special Counsel Robert Mueller of being "totally conflicted." Trump admits to his son Donald Trump Jr's participation in Trump Tower dirt-collection meeting, says he himself "did not know about it!" and it's "done all the time in politics." U.S., having withdrawn from the nuclear deal, reimposes sanctions on Iran. Missouri voters reject union-busting "right-to-work" law by two-to-one margin. The DNC drops its ban on contributions from fossil-fuel industry. Trump revokes former CIA Director John Brennan's security clearance, a relatively early move in what was to become a pattern of retribution against Trump's critics. Michael Cohen, Trump's lawyer for the past twelve years, pleads guilty to eight federal charges. Paul Manafort, former Trump campaign chairman and deal-maker in Russia and Ukraine, convicted on eight charges of bank and tax fraud. Federal intelligence contractor Reality Winner, who brought Russian penetration of voter databases in E2016 to public attention, accepts plea deal and is sentenced to five years and three months in federal prison. Arizona Republican Senator John McCain dies from brain cancer; Trump is not invited to his funeral, at which former presidents George W. Bush and Barack Obama deliver eulogies. **Published:** Craig Unger: *House of Trump House of Putin: The Untold Story of Donald Trump and the Russian Mafia*; Omarosa Manigault Newman: *Unhinged: An Insider's Account of the Trump White House*.

> **September** Op-Ed in *Times* outlines, anonymously, the work of an internal resistance within the Trump administration. Hurricane Florence hits North

Carolina, causing evacuation warnings to be issued for more than a million residents. Christine Blasey Ford alleges sexual assault by SCOTUS nominee Brett Kavanaugh when both were teens; a week later a second woman makes a similar allegation against Trump's nominee; three days later, a third woman comes forward. Ford testifies in a tense, emotional session before the Senate Judiciary Committee reviewing Kavanaugh's nomination. **Published**: Bob Woodward: *Fear: Trump in the White House*; Jason Stanley: *How Fascism Works: The Politics of US and Them*.

> **October** *Washington Post* journalist Jamal Khashoggi murdered inside Saudi Consulate in Istanbul. Nikki Haley, the U.S. ambassador to the UN, resigns unexpectedly. Trump announces termination of Intermediate-Range Nuclear Forces Treaty with Russia, in place since 1987. Discovery of unexploded bombs mailed by Trump supporter to George Soros, Barack Obama, and Hillary Clinton. Packages containing explosives or suspicious powder are subsequently found to be addressed to former Attorney General Eric Holder, U.S. Rep. Maxine Waters (D-CA), former CIA Director John Brennan, former Vice President Joe Biden, Senator Corey Booker (D-NJ), former Director of National Intelligence James Clapper, and the actor Robert DeNiro (all potential victims are political opponents or vocal critics of Trump). Mass shooting at Tree of Life Synagogue in Pittsburgh results in 11 deaths and is investigated as hate crime. Trump is requested by mayor of Pittsburgh and leaders of the Jewish community there not to attend the memorial. Trump sends first 800 of 5,000 U.S. troops to the Mexican border as part of "Operation Faithful Patriot" to defend the border against "caravans" of Central American migrants and refugees. The Boston Red Sox defeat the LA Dodgers four games to one to win World Series (following the exposure of the video sign-stealing scandal by 2017 World Series-winner Houston Astros, the Red Sox victory is currently under investigation by Major League Baseball). **Published:** Michael Lewis: *The Fifth Risk*.

> **November** E2018: Democrats gain 40 House seats, and seven governorships, lose two Senate seats. Several states see passage of various electoral-reform ballot measures, affecting gerrymandering and voting rights. Trump forces Attorney General Jeff Sessions to resign. Mass shooting at LA-area bar and grill kills 13. White House shares apparently doctored footage posted by InfoWars, a conspiracy-theory website, showing Jim Acosta making contact with a Trump aide, in a bid to justify its suspension of the CNN reporter's press pass. Raging Woolsey and Camp wildfires in California result in at least 88 deaths and the destruction of 20,000 buildings. Although the fires are officially attributed to electrical transmission resulting from inadequate protections taken by corporate electricity/gas giant PG&E, Trump says Californians could stop the fires by "spending a lot of time raking and cleaning" the forest floor. Trump's former

lawyer Michael Cohen pleads guilty to lying to Congress in the Russia election-interference inquiry. Former President George H. W. Bush dies at 94: Trump attends funeral but does not eulogize the ex-president. **Published:** Seth Abramson: *Proof of Collusion: How Trump Betrayed America*; Bernard L. Fraga: *The Turnout Gap: Race, Ethnicity, and Political Inequality in a Diversifying America*; Michelle Obama: *Becoming*.

> **December** Michael Cohen receives three-year jail term. Senate votes 56 – 41 to end U.S. military assistance to Saudi Arabia in Yemen and, separately, to hold Trump-family familiar, Saudi Crown Prince Mohammed bin Salman, personally responsible for the killing of Jamal Khashoggi. The Donald J. Trump Foundation is shut down amid allegations that Trump and others illegally misused its funds. Defense Secretary Jim Mattis resigns the day after Trump suddenly decides to withdraw all U.S. troops from Syria; U.S. Envoy Brett McGurk also resigns; Trump ultimately reverses this decision. The Dow has its worst week since 2008, closing at 22,445.37. Soon after, the Fed begins pumping money into markets via the repo market—a new, quiet form of "quantitative easing," previously reserved for recessionary periods.

> **Generally, with regard to election security:** The working narrative is that the Russians "meddled" in the 2016 election. Who the Russians are and what they did (specifically) are less clear. But the working hypothesis is that whatever they did in 2016 they plan to do again (at least) in 2020. There appears to be genuine uncertainty, bordering on anxiety, about the vulnerability of E2020 (and even E2018)—that is, whether it will be meddled with and, if so, how. This state of affairs is progress (of sorts) in the quest for election integrity.

"Meddling" is generally sorted into three categories of interference, ranging from the least to the most direct. The first "tier" consists of efforts aimed at altering voter behavior—whether changing voters' preferences or causing would-be voters to stay home or would-be nonvoters to vote. It is not clear that spreading disinformation per se is illegal (campaigns get away with it all the time). Ordinarily a certain degree of *caveat auditor* and "consider the source" applies to such messaging but, in the "Information Age," sources can be as easy to disguise as news is to fake. In any case, there is a bad odor when foreigners are found to influence our election outcomes even in this most indirect of ways. Thirteen Russian nationals are accordingly indicted, though they are effectively beyond the reach of the Special Counsel investigating the Russian interference in E2016 and possible involvement (i.e., collusion) of the Trump campaign in such activities. The mining—by Mercer-funded Cambridge Analytica—of the personal data of tens of millions of Facebook users, at least in part to target political messaging on behalf of the Trump campaign, raises the specter of a different sub-species of Tier-1 meddling.

The second tier involves interference with the vast voter eligibility infrastructure. It was reported that more than 20 state voter databases had been targets for Russian hackers and that they had been successful in at least three states. What "successful" meant, what impact the hackers may have had in suppressing the vote was, again, not made clear by federal or state investigators. But with voter registration databases and poll books becoming ever more computerized, the risks are growing for legal voters to find themselves targeted and turned away or relegated to provisional ballots on Election Day. Electronic poll books along with the growing trend of mail-in voting also enable electronic ballot-box stuffing—the mass creation and casting of fake ballots corresponding to fake voters or non-voters. Subverting the registration and eligibility processes can potentially wreak havoc on the voting process and/or serve as a targeted weapon of voter suppression and disenfranchisement or outright rigging.

The third tier—the most direct vector for meddling—is of course interference with the vote counting process itself. While the Department of Homeland Security hastened to assure (and reassure) the public that it found no evidence that E2016 votecounts or electoral outcomes were affected by the various attempts at meddling (you have to dig a bit to discover that they acknowledge that they found no such evidence because they made a decision not to look for any), there is an undispelled ground fog of concern socking in E2018 and E2020 when it comes to what might go bump behind the cybercurtain. Might the Russians come again? Might they bring their big cyberguns and hit our opscans, DREs, or central tabulators? How would we know if they did? How can we stop them? Or do we just punish them afterwards with some sanctions, which seemed to be enough to fit the 2016 crime, whatever it was?

These questions are apparently enough to spur a bit of congressional interest, in the form of a $380 million appropriation to "upgrade" America's voting equipment, though neither paper ballots nor audits are mandated, and the funds (less than 10% of the original HAVA funds) are grossly inadequate to secure E2018 (and E2020) against foreign hackers, let alone malicious domestic operatives and insiders.

It becomes clear that the legislative process, in Washington and the key states, will not deliver necessary protection to the electoral process. The Supreme Court (Gorsuch batting for Garland) reluctantly reconsiders partisan gerrymandering—arguing over the proper care and feeding of a horse that left the barn years ago and is romping somewhere in the next county.

> **2019** | This year brings yet another uptick in the rates of presidential tweeting and lying; the presentation of the long-awaited Mueller Report; Trump's impeachment on charges of abuse of power and obstruction of Congress; and a major expansion of the Senate Graveyard to which House-passed legislation, including all serious provisions for electoral security, goes to die. It does not bring anything but intensification to the national divide, as the GOP places all its chips on Trump and, in the process, seems to go all-in on a frankly authoritarian vision for America, to be set before the voters in November 2020.

> **January** Government shutdown over Trump's border wall lasts 35 days, by far the longest in U.S. history; 800,000 government employees are unpaid; although a petulant Trump says the shutdown could last "months, maybe even years," it ends when airports begin shutting down for lack of air-traffic control staff and Trump's hand is forced. Trump associate Roger Stone charged by Special Counsel on seven federal counts, including obstruction of justice and witness tampering. Chinese tech firm Huawei charged with fraud by DOJ, heightening U.S.-China tensions. Teachers in Denver strike for higher pay. Extreme polar vortex hits much of U.S. Sandusky, Ohio becomes first city in U.S. to make Election Day a paid holiday. **Published:** Steven Levitsky, Daniel Ziblatt: *How Democracies Die*; Cliff Sims: *Team of Vipers: My 500 Extraordinary Days in the Trump White House.*

> **February** Mass shooting kills five in Aurora, Illinois. Trump declares "national emergency" to free up funds for his border wall. U.S. Coast Guard Lieutenant Christopher Paul Hasson, an avowed white-nationalist, is arrested for planning a domestic terrorism attack targeting left-wing politicians and journalists. Trump and North Korea's Kim Jong-un meet in Hanoi for a summit that ends early and is recognized as a diplomatic failure and embarrassment. **Published:** Rick Wilson: *Everything Trump Touches Dies: A Republican Strategist Gets Real About the Worst President Ever*; Andrew McCabe: *The Threat: How the FBI Protects America in the Age of Terror and Trump.*

> **March** College admissions bribery scandal becomes public. Trump vetoes bipartisan Senate resolution to end his national emergency declaration to build a border wall; public opinion continues to run strongly against the wall. Students walk out and rally to demand action on climate change in over 1600 cities globally, including at the U.S. Capitol. Washington state Senate passes legislation requiring release of five years of tax returns by all presidential candidates in order to appear on primary and general election ballots. Special Counsel Robert Mueller turns in his Report to DOJ; Attorney General William Barr "summarizes" Mueller's report in a distorting and controversial four-page

letter to Congress. Trump issues new permit for controversial Keystone Pipeline. **Published:** Bandy X. Lee, et al: *The Dangerous Case of Donald Trump*; Victor Davis Hanson; *The Case for Trump*.

> **April** Lori Lightfoot becomes Chicago's first openly gay and first Black woman mayor. House Ways and Means Committee sends letter to IRS requesting Trump's tax returns; House Judiciary Committee subpoenas full Mueller Report. Trump vetoes bipartisan legislation ending U.S. military assistance to Saudi Arabia in Yemen. U.S. designates Iran's Islamic Revolutionary Guard Corps as a terrorist group. Ohio becomes sixth state to ban abortion at six weeks, effectively challenging *Roe v. Wade*. AG William Barr releases heavily redacted version of Mueller Report. School shooting at UNC Charlotte leaves two dead. **Published:** Timothy Snyder: *The Road to Unfreedom: Russia, Europe, America*; The Washington Post: *The Mueller Report*; Rick Reilly: *Commander in Cheat: How Golf Explains Trump*.

> **May** After Facebook bans Infowars, Milo Yiannopoulos, and several other far-right and white-nationalist influencers from its platform, Trump tweets against such "targeted censorship" against "conservatives" on social media. Department of Labor puts unemployment rate at 3.6%, lowest in 49 years. Trump tweets his displeasure with the disqualification of apparent Kentucky Derby winner. Trump reaches 46% approval in Gallup poll, his highest Gallup rating. New York Times publishes tax information showing Trump's huge ($1.17 billion) business losses from 1985-94, the largest by any taxpayer in U.S. history. Trump's 25% tariff hike on $200 billion worth of Chinese imports takes effect. Mass shooting at Virginia Beach municipal center kills 12.

> **June** Journalist and advice columnist E. Jean Carroll accuses Trump of having sexually assaulted her in a Bergdorf Goodman department store dressing room in the mid-1990s. In *Rucho v. Common Cause* and *Benisek v. Lamone*, SCOTUS issues partisan 5 – 4 rulings essentially greenlighting partisan gerrymandering. Trump promises Chinese President Xi Jinping that U.S. will not speak out on suppression of pro-democracy protests in Hong Kong while U.S. and China continue trade talks. **Published:** Joy-Ann Reid: *The Man Who Sold America: Trump and the Unraveling of the American Story*; Benjamin Carter Hett: *The Death of Democracy: Hitler's Rise to Power and the Downfall of the Weimar Republic*; Michael Wolff: *Siege: Trump Under Fire*.

> **July** Trump breaks from a seven-decade tradition to address a crowd on the National Mall on Independence Day in an event featuring a military parade inspired by one Trump attended on Bastille Day in France. Billionaire financier and suspected career sexual blackmailer Jeffrey Epstein arrested on sex-trafficking charges. Labor Secretary Alex Acosta resigns a week later, following

revelations of sweetheart plea deal he engineered as prosecutor in 2007 sex-crimes case against Epstein. Facebook fined a record $5 billion in settlement with FTC over the social media giant's data privacy violations. Self-described Antifa member attacks an ICE detention center in Washington state. Trump tweets that four progressive Democratic congresswomen, nicknamed "The Squad," should "go back and help fix the totally broken and crime infested places from which they came. Then come back and show us how it is done" (three of the four congresswomen were in fact born in the U.S. and the fourth became a naturalized citizen in her youth). After passage of a House resolution condemning his racist comments, Trump persists in his attack at a rally the following day, saying "If [they] don't like it, let 'em leave, let 'em leave. ... I think in some cases they hate our country," while the crowd chants "Send her back! Send her back!" Attorney General William Barr announces reinstatement of federal death penalty. Senate Majority Leader Mitch McConnell blocks legislation to improve election security less than 24 hours after Special Counsel Robert Mueller warns of the continued threat of interference in American elections. Mass shooting at Garlic Festival in Gilroy, CA, kills four. Fed cuts interest rates for the first time since 2008; ordinarily a tactic to counter a weakening economy, the move comes days after the Dow hits 27,000 for first time in history. Leslie McCrae Dowless faces new charges of electoral fraud in North Carolina; Dowless, a Republican operative, was arrested in 2017 and charged with trying to rig the election in North Carolina's 9th CD in favor of Mark Harris, the Republican candidate. **Published:** Tim Alberta: *American Carnage: On the Front Lines of the Republican Civil War and the Rise of President Trump.*

> **August** U.S. formally withdraws from 1987 Intermediate-Range Nuclear Forces Treaty with Russia. Mass shooting in El Paso Walmart, targeting Latino immigrants, kills 22; the following day, mass shooting in Dayton, Ohio kills 10; thoughts and prayers abound. Largest immigration raids in more than a decade result in 680 arrests in Mississippi. North Dakota Supreme Court upholds state law that disenfranchises at least 10 percent of the state's Native Americans for living on reservations and lacking a street address. Jeffrey Epstein dies in a New York jail while awaiting trial; although the death is ruled a suicide, questions swirl: Epstein is found on autopsy to have a fractured hyoid bone rarely if ever found in short-drop hangings as would have been possible in his cell, and a "perfect storm" of supposed negligence and missing video evidence leave many skeptical of the official story. Within hours of Epstein's death, DOJ/FBI SWAT teams raid both his New York City and Caribbean residences in a rush to seize "evidence," which was suspected to include an extensive collection of "dirt" (i.e., blackmail material) on major figures ranging from Bill Clinton to Britain's

Prince Andrew to Donald Trump and many former and current politicians and business leaders. Trump administration issues new rules that reject applicants for temporary or permanent visas for failing to meet income standards or for receiving public assistance such as welfare, food stamps, public housing, or Medicaid. Department of Interior weakens its enforcement of Endangered Species Act of 1973. ICE employee drives his truck through crowd of protesters, injuring several. Denmark rejects Trump attempt to purchase Greenland; Trump calls off Danish state visit in response. Anti-gun rallies are held in over 100 cities in all 50 states. NASCAR bans advertisements of "assault-style rifles/sniper rifles." A federal judge in Georgia rules that the state must replace all of its voting machines or use paper ballots in time for the March 24, 2020 presidential primary election. Several faulty voting machines are reported during the Mississippi gubernatorial primary on August 27. Mass shooting near Midland, Texas kills seven and wounds 21. **Published:** Angela Denker: *Red State Christians: Understanding the Voters Who Elected Donald Trump.*

> **September** Retailers like Walmart and Kroger adopt more restrictive policies on sales of weapons most often used in mass shootings. Trump reveals plan for, then cancels, Camp David peace talks with Taliban after Kabul bombing kills a U.S. soldier. House Intelligence Committee notified by intelligence inspector general about an urgent and credible whistleblower complaint regarding July 25 Trump phone call with Ukrainian President Volodymyr Zelensky, in which U.S. aid appeared to be conditioned on Ukrainian investigation of potential presidential opponent Joe Biden and his son; White House denies any wrongdoing and refuses to release the complaint. The following day, National Security Advisor John Bolton is dismissed by Trump. UAW goes on strike at General Motors. Trump revokes California's authority to set auto emission standards for vehicles registered in the state. Massive student demonstrations against climate change inaction, led globally by 16-year-old activist Greta Thunberg. Saudi oil refineries attacked; Trump sends Patriot missiles and other military hardware to Saudi Arabia and UAE. Tropical Storm Imelda dumps 40 inches of rain in 72 hours on Southeast Texas; five deaths reported. Vice President Mike Pence ignores 100-year prohibition of automobiles on Mackinac Island, Michigan, sending an eight-car motorcade to a Republican meeting. House Speaker Nancy Pelosi announces opening of formal impeachment inquiry against Trump; White House releases summary of Trump-Zelensky phone call, establishing publicly that Trump asked for investigation of Bidens in a transactional context. Trump administration announces target of 18,000 refugees allowed to enter U.S. in FY2020, lowest level since the modern program began in 1980. *Times* reports that NRA head Wayne LaPierre offers Trump financial support for his defense if he will back off any support for action

on gun violence. Kurt Volker, U.S. special envoy to Ukraine, resigns. Rep. Chris Collins (R-NY), the first member of Congress to endorse Trump's presidential bid, resigns, then pleads guilty to insider trading and lying to the FBI. Teenage climate activist Greta Thunberg address UN Climate Summit, famously asks assembled dignitaries "How dare you?" **Published:** Seth Abramson: *Proof of Conspiracy: How Trump's International Collusion is Threatening American Democracy.*

> **October** Florida DOE announces go-ahead to some teachers carrying guns in classrooms. CNN refuses to run Trump campaign add that it says includes false claims against former Vice President Joe Biden; Fox rejects Biden campaign's request not to run the ad. Trump publicly calls on both Ukraine and China to investigate the Bidens. *The Washington Post* reports an IRS employee filed a whistleblower complaint alleging that an unnamed political appointee at the U.S. Dept. of Treasury tried to interfere with the tax audits for Trump and Vice President Pence. Microsoft says a group called "Phosphorus," which is linked to the Iranian government, has attempted to hack accounts belonging to American journalists, former government officials, and the 2020 U.S. presidential election. A federal judge orders Trump to turn over eight years of tax returns, saying he cannot endorse a "categorical and limitless assertion of presidential immunity from judicial process;" an appeals court grants a temporary stay of the order. Lev Parnas and Igor Fruman, associates of Rudy Giuliani in Ukraine dealings on behalf of Trump, arrested on campaign finance charges. Kevin McAleenan, Trump's *fourth* homeland security advisor, resigns. Former U.S. Ambassador to Ukraine Marie Yovanovitch defies State Department order and testifies to Congress in Trump impeachment inquiry. U.S. sends additional troops and weapons to Saudi Arabia. Students at Georgia Southern University burn books written by a Cuban-American author who had been invited to the school to discuss white privilege. State Department wraps up Hillary Clinton email investigation, finding various minor violations by employees but no wrongdoing on Clinton's part. Refugee flights to U.S. canceled, as U.S. reaches cap for year (18,000). Thirty Republican House members, led by Matt Gaetz (R-FL), storm a secure hearing room and violate security precautions, demanding they be allowed to participate in the impeachment inquiry despite not being members of the committees that are investigating the president; they falsely claim that Republican members of those committees have been excluded. Journalist Max Blumenthal ("The Grayzone") is arrested and charged with assault in a case related to a May 7 incident at the Venezuelan Embassy in Washington. Trump announces death of ISIL leader Abu Bakr al-Baghdadi in U.S. raid; he gloats that al-Baghdadi went to his death (detonating a suicide vest) "whimpering and crying and screaming," an evident

fabrication. Wildfires in California lead governor to declare a state of emergency there. North Carolina court enjoins 2020 primary elections there on account of partisan gerrymandering. Trump makes first visit to Chicago, calling the city "embarrassing to us as a nation." Speaking there, he also calls for "a surge" and militarization of the nation's police forces. Keystone Pipeline rupture spills thousands of barrels. Independent review by one of the world's leading forensic pathologists finds Jeffrey Epstein's injuries more consistent with murder than with suicide. Fed makes third interest rate cut in four months; also continues funneling cash to banks and brokerage houses in a quiet form of quantitative easing previously reserved for recessionary periods; combined result is soaring U.S. stock indices and the "great" economy on which Trump stakes his hold on office. U.S. national debt surpasses $23 trillion for first time in history, an increase of 16% since Trump took office. Mass shooting kills four in Orinda, California. **Published:** Steven Hassan: *The Cult of Trump: A Leading Cult Expert Explains How the President Uses Mind Control*; Rachel Maddow: *Blowout: Corrupted Democracy, Rogue State Russia, and the Richest, Most Destructive Industry on Earth*; Sebastian Gorka: *The War for America's Soul: Donald Trump, the Left's Assault on America, and How We Take Back Our Country.*

> **November** Trump's Border Wall reported easily breached using cheap and easily obtained electric saws. Trump threatens wildfire federal aid cutoff to California. Democrats take control of both houses of Virginia legislature in E2019. Supposed Ukraine whistleblower's name publicly revealed by several prominent Republicans, including Donald Trump Jr. Multiple witnesses— including Gordon Sondland, Kurt Volker and Alexander Vindman—testify behind closed doors in impeachment inquiry re. "quid pro quo." Trump lawyer and confidante Rudy Giuliani hires three defense attorneys. White House aide Stephen Miller accused in Southern Poverty Law Center report of promoting white nationalism; 80 Democratic members of Congress call on Miller to resign. Trump begins spate of controversial pardons, including of military officers convicted of war crimes. Mass shooting kills four, wounds six at Fresno, California party. In public testimony at impeachment hearing, EU Ambassador Gordon Sondland states there *was* a *quid pro quo* in Ukraine scandal, ordered by Trump through Giuliani. Roger Stone found guilty on all seven counts of lying to Congress and witness tampering. Trump orders Defense Secretary Mark Esper to fire Navy Secretary Richard Spencer after the latter removes Trump-pardoned war criminal Eddie Gallagher from SEAL Team 7; Trump goes on to feature Gallagher at subsequent campaign rally. Federal judge rules that former White House Counsel Don McGahn must testify at impeachment hearing, a ruling White House says it will appeal. National Center for Medical Intelligence

(NCMI) produces report warning that an epidemic was sweeping through Wuhan region of China and concluding that it could develop into "a cataclysmic event;" the NCMI report was briefed "multiple times" according to a source, to both Pentagon and White House (National Security Council); a detailed explanation of the threat appeared in the President's Daily Brief of intelligence matters in early January. **Published:** Neal Katyal: *Impeach: The Case Against Donald Trump*; Anonymous (a senior Trump administration official): *A Warning*; Doug Wead: *Inside Trump's White House: The Real Story of His Presidency*; Donald Trump Jr.: *Triggered: How the Left Thrives on Hate and Wants to Silence Us*.

> **December** White House announces Trump will not participate in impeachment hearings. Energy Secretary Rick Perry resigns. Rep. Duncan Hunter (R-CA) pleads guilty to corruption charges and resigns from Congress. House Intelligence Committee issues report accusing Trump of using his office to further his personal interests. Mass shooting by Saudi aviation student on Florida military base kills four. Department of Labor reports unemployment rate of 3.5%, lowest in 50 years. House passes bill to restore parts of the Voting Rights Act of 1965 (in long-delayed response to SCOTUS's *Shelby* decision gutting the act's enforcement provisions); Trump threatens veto should House measure pass Senate. DOJ Inspector General issues report concluding that FBI's investigation into the 2016 Trump campaign was legally justified and without political bias. Formal impeachment charges announced: abuse of power and obstruction of Congress. Mass shooting in kosher grocery store in New Jersey, classified as domestic terrorism. U.S. blocks appointment of all new World Trade Organization members, leaving the body unable to intervene in any trade disputes. Defeated and outgoing Republican governor of Kentucky, Matt Bevin, controversially pardons or commutes sentences for 428 convicts, including child rapists and murderers; one commutation was for the brother of a family that raised $21,500 to pay off Bevin's campaign debt. *Time* magazine names Greta Thunberg its Person of the Year for 2019; Trump falsely claims he rejected *Time's* invitation. Trump impeached by U.S. House (December 18), with all Republicans voting No on both articles; Trump is third president in U.S. history to face a Senate impeachment trial. The GAO raises ethics questions about a federal contract awarded by the Dept. of Transportation to Boone County, KY that appears to be designed to help the reelection campaign of Senate Majority Leader Mitch McConnell; DOT is headed by McConnell's wife, Elaine Chao. Trump administration proposes drastic cuts to SNAP, the federal food-stamp program, potentially cutting off millions of recipients. Judge temporarily blocks North Carolina voter-ID law. **Published:** *The Impeachment Report: The House*

Intelligence Committee's Report on its Investigation into Donald Trump and Ukraine.

> **2020 | "We appear yet again headed for a disquieting November and a disquieting electoral future." The last time I wrote this, we landed in the Age of Trump, the shocking culmination, to this point, of the computerized vote counting era. It is hard to fathom how our nation could have gotten there without thumbs, overt and covert, on the electoral scales. If we harbored any doubts, we now know that elections, honest or rigged, *matter*. Unobservable vote counting has reached a predictable crisis of confidence and our entire political system has reached a predictable and parallel crisis of confidence after just 18 years of computerized elections. The window for reform is narrow. We are a nation traumatized and on the brink, as close to civil war as to civil discourse. Our democracy, resilient as it may seem, is mortal. May this new year yet surprise us, and we it, in some good way.**

> **January** Trump approves "targeted killing" (aka assassination) of top Iranian military leader Qasem Suleimani and paramilitary leader Abu Mahdi al-Muhandis via missile strike in Baghdad, Iraq; Trump did not seek congressional approval and revealed his plans only to select Republican members of Congress; move is met with international condemnation and fears of war in the Middle East. Iran makes an essentially token response, hitting certain Iraqi military bases hosting U.S. troops, which Trump reports resulted (improbably) in no casualties (Iran forewarned the bases), though it turns out that over a hundred U.S. soldiers suffered traumatic brain injuries; VFW demands an apology from Trump for knowingly downplaying the extent of the injuries. House passes non-binding War Powers Resolution to limit Trump's ability to pursue military action against Iran without congressional consent. DOJ's two-year investigation into Hillary Clinton's business dealings wraps up having found "nothing of consequence." Trump and Chinese vice premier sign U.S.-China Phase One trade deal. U.S. officials alerted to initial outbreak of novel coronavirus (1/3). Senate impeachment trial of Trump begins (1/16). HHS Secretary Alex Azar (whose phone calls Trump had not taken for nearly two weeks) finally reaches Trump by phone to warn him of looming COVID-19 pandemic; Trump interrupts to ask about renewed marketing of vaping products (1/18). First case of COVID-19 coronavirus confirmed in U.S. (1/20). Senate votes 51-49 against calling witnesses or subpoenaing documents in Trump impeachment trial. Trump adds six new countries to his travel ban. Trump says of coronavirus (1/22): "We have it totally under control. It's one person coming in from China." And "We do have a plan and we think it's gonna be handled very well, we've already handled it very well." The White House Chief of Staff Mick Mulvaney and other aides try to persuade Trump that COVID-19 poses a danger that he

must take seriously (1/27); Trump ignores them and continues to downplay the threat in all his public addresses. Top Trump trade adviser Peter Navarro sends (1/29) memo to National Security Council warning that the novel coronavirus may cause up to 543,000 U.S. deaths and $5.7 trillion in losses. Trump imposes restrictions on travel to the U.S. by non-citizens who have traveled to China within past two weeks (1/31); although Trump later refers to his only early action in response to the pandemic as a "travel ban," it actually applied to relatively small subgroup of travelers from China; it was also not "early," in light of the alarm sounded in intelligence briefings throughout the month of January. **Published:** Philip Rucker, Carol Leonnig: *A Very Stable Genius: Donald J. Trump's Testing of America.*

> **February** A day after yet again bragging about his "great economy," Trump cites "serious economic conditions" in submitting his budget proposal to cut pay raises for federal workers. Trump says of coronavirus (2/2): "We pretty much shut it down coming in from China. It's going to be fine." Iowa Democratic caucus fiasco as new and unvetted internet vote reporting system fails; GOP operatives also acknowledge deliberate jamming of back-up reporting phone banks. At his third State of the Union address, Trump (still awaiting Senate verdict on impeachment charges), highlights various guests-of-color ostensibly helped by his programs but awards the Presidential Medal of Freedom to Rush Limbaugh; House Speaker Nancy Pelosi (D-CA) publicly and pointedly rips up the lie-filled draft of Trump's speech; Rep. Matt Gaetz (R-FL) files ethics complaint against Pelosi. Trump acquitted on both impeachment charges, all Democrats voting for conviction and all Republicans for acquittal, except for Sen. Mitt Romney (R-UT), who votes for conviction on first article (abuse of power) and so becomes the first senator in U.S. history to vote for conviction of a president of his own party; many Republicans call, on this basis, for Romney's expulsion from the Republican Party. Two days later, Trump fires impeachment witnesses EU Ambassador Gordon Sondland and NSC staffer Lt. Colonel Alexander Vindman (along with his twin brother, an NSC attorney; both being "escorted" from their work premises); other patently retaliatory firings and demotions follow. The South Korean film *Parasite* wins the Best-Picture Oscar; Trump voices his displeasure at a rally: "What the hell was that all about? We got enough problems with South Korea with trade. On top of it, they give them the best movie of the year? Was it good? I don't know." He adds "Can we get *Gone With The Wind* back please?" Convicted Trump associate Roger Stone is sentenced to 40 months in prison after intervention by Attorney General William Barr reduces the DOJ's recommended sentence; four career DOJ prosecutors resign from case in protest of Barr's action. Trump's controversial pardons extend to high-profile fraudsters Michael Milken, Rod Blagojevich and

(Giuliani friend) Bernard Kerik; Blagojevich claims he was a "political prisoner." Nevada's Republican caucuses are canceled, giving Trump the delegates by default; a number of states similarly cancel GOP primaries and caucuses. New electronic voting machines apparently fail in Dominican Republic municipal elections, causing Election Commission to end voting and postpone the elections and triggering massive on-going protests in the DR and in U.S. cities with Dominican populations, as decades of electoral and political corruption come to a head. Trump confirms existence of blacklists of "disloyal" officials to purge and replace with Trump loyalists; the lists—assembled by right-wing activists, including the wife of Supreme Court Justice Clarence Thomas—identify "snakes" and "bad people" throughout the administration but especially among "deep state" intelligence officials; Trump says he wants "people who are good for the country, loyal to the country." Johnny McEntee, Trump's former bodyguard and current personnel director, asks federal officials to out anti-Trump colleagues for staff purges he said were likely after the 2020 election. Trump sacks Acting Director of National Intelligence Joseph McGuire (whose deputy had the previous day briefed a congressional committee on Russian efforts to influence E2020 in Trump's favor), replacing him with Richard Grenell, ultra-Trump loyalist and highly frictional U.S. ambassador to Germany. Trump then re-nominates Rep. John Ratcliffe (R-TX) for the permanent DNI post, despite having withdrawn his nomination a year previously over Ratcliffe's inflated CV claims. Trade Adviser Peter Navarro sends second memo (2/23), directly to Trump, warning of a COVID-19 worst-case scenario of 2 million dead in U.S. Trump tweets regarding COVID-19 (2/24): "The Coronavirus is very much under control in the USA... Stock Market starting to look very good to me!" Director of the CDC's National Center for Immunization and Respiratory Diseases Nancy Messonnier warns (2/25) spread of COVID-19 in the U.S. is "not a question of if, but when." Trump tweets (2/25): "CDC and my Administration are doing a GREAT job of handling Coronavirus... No matter how well we do, however, the Democrats [sic] talking point is that we are doing badly... So far, by the way, we have not had one death. Let's keep it that way!" Trump states (2/25): "I think that's a problem that's going to go away. But we lost almost 1,000 points yesterday on the market, and that's something. You know, things like that happen where — and you have it in your business all the time — it had nothing to do with you; it's an outside source that nobody would have ever predicted. If you go back six months or three months ago, nobody would have ever predicted." Rush Limbaugh likens COVID-19 to "a common cold," joins other Trump backers and the president himself in accusing the Democrats of "another hoax;" Donald Trump Jr. says Democrats "seemingly hope" the coronavirus "kills millions so that they could end Donald Trump's streak of winning." Trump appoints Vice President Mike Pence to head up federal efforts to combat COVID-19. U.S. and Taliban sign conditional peace agreement, highly favorable to Taliban and violated by Taliban within the week. First COVID-19 death in U.S. reported in Washington State. Wall Street has worst week since 2008 crash, with the S&P broad market index losing over 13% of its value. Trump states (2/26): "We're going very substantially down [in COVID-19 cases], not up." And "Because of all we've done, the risk to the American people remains very low... When you have 15 people, and the 15 within a couple of days is going to be down to close to zero. That's a pretty good job we've done." Trump states (2/27): "One day it's like a miracle, it will disappear." Trump tells reporters on White House lawn (2/28): "We're ordering a lot of supplies. We're ordering a lot of elements that frankly we wouldn't be ordering unless it was something like this. But we're ordering a lot of different elements of medical." Later, at South Carolina rally, Trump says (2/28): "Now the Democrats are politicizing the coronavirus... This is their new hoax." And "My administration has taken the most aggressive acts in history to prevent the spread in the United States... So far, we've lost nobody to coronavirus." And "The Democrat policy of open borders is a direct threat to the health and wellbeing of all Americans." Joe Biden's landslide victory over Bernie Sanders and remaining rivals in South Carolina Democratic primary revives Biden's campaign and deals heavy blow to Sanders. Significant shift in Biden's favor from unadjusted exit polls to votecounts (from ballots generated by BMDs) prompts some to suspect fraud in the count; but the difficulty of demographic weighting of the polls, already substantial in party primaries, is augmented by a very fluid and volatile political dynamic; thus, the disparity may be caused by such nonquantifiable factors rather than vote mistabulation or fraud. **Published:** David Enrich: *Dark Towers: Deutsche Bank, Donald Trump, and an Epic Trail of Destruction*; The Congressional Record: *The Impeachment Trial of President Donald J. Trump.*

> **March** Trump asks (3/2): "You take a solid flu vaccine, you don't think that could have an impact, or much of an impact, on corona?" Trump says (3/2): "A lot of things are happening, a lot of very exciting things are happening and they're happening very rapidly." In "Super Tuesday" Democratic primaries (3/3), Joe Biden takes a commanding delegate lead; exit poll-votecount disparities are again cited by some as evidence of fraud against Bernie Sanders, but several key factors shed doubt upon that conclusion. California Governor Gavin Newsom declares (3/4) state of emergency. Trump says (3/4): "If we have thousands of people that get better just by, you know, sitting around and even going to work—some of them go to work, but they get better." After this comment causes major controversy, and universal condemnation by health

professionals, Trump clarifies on Twitter (3/5): "I never said people that are feeling sick should go to work. This is just more Fake News and disinformation put out by the Democrats, in particular MSDNC [sic]. Comcast covers the CoronaVirus situation horribly, only looking to do harm to the incredible & successful effort being made!" Aid package of $8.3B becomes law (3/5). Trump, touring the CDC in Atlanta, says (3/6): "We were going to hit 30,000 on the Dow like it was clockwork. Right? It was all going—it was right up, and then all of a sudden, this *came out*" (emphasis added). Also from the CDC tour (3/6): "Anybody right now, and yesterday, anybody that wants a test gets a test [this was, and continued to be, false]. And the tests are beautiful. They are perfect just like the letter was perfect. The transcription [of Zelensky phone call] was perfect. Right?" More from the CDC tour (3/6): "I like this stuff. I really get it. People are surprised that I understand it. Every one of these doctors said, 'How do you know so much about this?' Maybe I have a natural ability. Maybe I should have done that instead of running for president." And for a CDC encore (3/6): "I like the numbers [of COVID-19 cases on U.S. soil] being where they are. I don't need to have the numbers double because of one ship [permitting the ship's passengers to be brought ashore]." South By Southwest Festival canceled (3/6). Sports leagues cancel spring and, in some cases summer seasons. Masters Golf Tournament canceled. Mick Mulvaney is fired as acting White House chief of staff (3/6). Trump tweets (3/9): "The Fake News media & their partner, the Democrat [sic] Party, is [sic] doing everything within its semi-considerable power (it used to be greater!) to inflame the Coronavirus situation, far beyond what the facts would warrant. Surgeon General, 'The risk is low to the average American.'" And "So last year 37,000 Americans died from the common Flu. It averages between 27,000 and 70,000 per year. Nothing is shut down, life & the economy go on. At this moment there are 546 confirmed cases of CoronaVirus, with 22 deaths. Think about that!" Dow plunges over 2,000 points (3/9). COVID-19 cases in U.S. exhibit exponential growth. Speaking to reporters, Trump says (3/10): "Well this was unexpected. This was something that came out of China... And we're prepared, and we're doing a great job with it. And it will go away. Just stay calm. It will go away." Trump addresses nation from Oval Office (3/11); states [erroneously], "we will be suspending all travel from Europe to the United States for the next 30 days [the ban did not apply to Americans currently in Europe, and the UK and Ireland, for reasons never explained, were not added for five days]." Dow loses nearly 10% of its value (3/12). Trump (3/13) declares a National Emergency. He also states, in Rose Garden press conference (3/13): "We have forty people right now. Forty. Compare that with other countries that have many, many times that amount. And one of the reasons we have forty and others have — and, again, that number is going up, just so you understand. And a number of cases, which are very small, relatively speaking — it's going up. But we've done a great job because we acted quickly. We acted early." Trump states (3/15): "This is a very contagious virus. It's incredible. But it's something that we have tremendous control over." Fed cuts target interest rate to 0 to 0.25 percent (3/15). Dow falls by nearly 3,000 points, greatest daily percentage drop in its history, greater than in 1929 (3/16). With confirmed COVID-19 cases in the U.S. at 6,400, Trump (3/16) finally announces social distancing "guidelines." A clear division develops among governors, with primarily blue-state governors issuing social-distancing and stay-at-home orders while most red-state governors keep their states "open for business" and mingling. Marked contrasts develop between large blue states like California and New York on the one hand and large red states like Texas and Florida on the other. Trump states (3/16): "If you're talking about the virus, no, that's not under control for any place in the world." Trump states (3/18): "I always treated the Chinese Virus [he alters his speaking notes by crossing out 'corona' and writing in 'CHINESE'] very seriously, and have done a very good job from the beginning." And "No, I've always viewed it as serious, there was no difference yesterday from days before. I feel the tone is similar but some people said it wasn't." Dow tumbles again (3/18), erasing nearly all of Trump-era gains. Democratic-sponsored Families First Coronavirus Response Act signed into law (3/18), providing paid-sick leave, funding for COVID-19 testing, and other benefits. Senator Rand Paul (R-KY) tests positive for COVID-19 (3/22). Trump, reacting to Wall Street plunges, tweets (3/23): "WE CANNOT LET THE CURE BE WORSE THAN THE PROBLEM ITSELF. AT THE END OF THE 15 DAY PERIOD [3/30, when federal social distancing guidelines were due to expire], WE WILL MAKE A DECISION AS TO WHICH WAY WE WANT TO GO!" Nevada Governor Steve Sisolak (3/24) bans the use of anti-malarial drugs chloroquine and hydroxychloroquine, unproven but repeatedly touted by Trump in his briefings, in COVID-19 treatment. Dow jumps (3/24) over 2100 points, largest one-day percentage gain since 1933. Gallup poll (3/24) measures Trump approval at 49%, a record high for that poll. With U.S. confirmed cases [a significant undercount because of the shortage of tests] at 65,800, Trump states, at a Fox News Town Hall (3/24): "I would love to have the country opened up and just raring to go by Easter [4/12]... I think Easter Sunday you'll have packed churches all over our country." U.S. deaths attributed to COVID-19 top 1,000 (3/25). U.S. reported COVID-19 cases exceed 80,000 (3/26), more than any other country. DOL reports (3/26) 3.28 million filed for unemployment in past week; previous record was 695,000. CARES Act—a $2 trillion stimulus package that includes $500 billion corporate "slush fund" to be administered, with limited oversight, by Treasury Secretary Steve Mnuchin—signed into law (3/27); Trump issues "signing statement" asserting his right to reinterpret the law and not forward information to Congress about the corporate bailout fund. COVID-19 death toll in U.S. reaches 3,000; 75% of U.S. population under county- or state-ordered lockdown (3/31).

> **April** COVID-19 death toll reaches 4,000 (4/1); Trump tells reporters: "Did you know I was No. 1 on Facebook [fact check: he isn't]? I just found out I was No. 1 on Facebook. I thought that was very nice for whatever it means." Trump minister plenipotentiary, reputed head of a "shadow" corona task force, and son-in-law, Jared Kushner, in White House Briefing Room address, declares (4/2): "The notion of the federal stockpile was it's supposed to be our [the federal government's?] stockpile. It's not supposed to be the states' stockpile that they then use… [in the wake of Kushner's address, HHS changed its website within hours to comport with his assertion, which contradicted the website's previous content]." And: "Don't ask us [the Trump administration] for things when you don't know what you have in your own state, just because you're scared… What a lot of the voters are seeing now is that when you elect somebody to be a mayor or governor or president, you're trying to think about who will be a competent manager during the time of crisis. This is a time of crisis and you're seeing certain people are better managers than others." Trump fires (4/3) Michael Atkinson, the watchdog for the intelligence community who helped set off impeachment proceedings by forwarding an anonymous [whistleblower] complaint about Trump to Congress. Centers for Disease Control recommends (4/3) that Americans wear cloth or fabric face coverings when in public; Trump, in briefing, tells American public that he himself doesn't plan to follow this recommendation. With 273,880 confirmed U.S. cases and over 7,000 COVID-attributed deaths, Trump states at a White House briefing (4/3): "I said it was going away—and it is going away." U.S. COVID-19 death toll tops 10,000 (4/6). Wisconsin primary held as scheduled (4/7) when GOP-controlled state legislature refuses to postpone—GOP strategists having calculated that a reduced electorate cuts in the party's favor, especially with regard to a high-profile and important election for a seat on the State Supreme Court—and State Supreme Court invalidates Democratic Governor Tony Evers's executive order postponing it. SCOTUS further strikes down provision to allow voters seven additional days to post absentee ballots, effectively forcing them to either not vote or to vote in person on 4/7. Because of the severe shortage of poll workers, many polling sites are closed, others crowded (there is a standing state stay-at-home order in effect); Milwaukee's 180 polling places have been reduced to five; lines at some polling places stretch more than half a mile; Trump, asked about the lines in Wisconsin at his daily press briefing, says: "I don't know

anything about their lines. I don't know anything about their voting. I love the state. I won the state." Trump (4/7) removes highly regarded Glenn Fine from his position as DOD acting inspector general, making Fine ineligible to oversee the distribution of the $2 trillion CARES Act stimulus package; Fine was the consensus choice of a committee of inspectors general for the critical watchdog position. Trump (4/8) threatens to pull U.S. funding from the World Health Organization (WHO), declaring that WHO "receives vast amounts of money from the United States" and that the organization "called it wrong... They could have called it [the virus] months earlier." Trump, who voted by mail in 2020 Florida primary, tweets (4/8): "Republicans should fight very hard when it comes to state wide mail-in voting. Democrats are clamoring for it. Tremendous potential for voter fraud, and for whatever reason, doesn't work out well for Republicans." Trump tweets (4/8): "Once we OPEN UP OUR GREAT COUNTRY, and it will be sooner rather than later, the horror of the Invisible Enemy, except for those that sadly lost a family member or friend, must be quickly forgotten. Our Economy will BOOM, perhaps like never before!!!"

GLOSSARY OF TERMS

Election Integrity (or EI) – Refers to the degree to which elections earn and warrant, as opposed to simply assume or demand, the trust of the public. Also refers to the movement, or collective efforts, to bring security and transparency to the electoral process, specifically to its vote-counting component. Because the term "election integrity" has also been used by the far right and white supremacists to promote targeted disenfranchisement and a racially restricted electorate, Election Transparency is preferred by some to describe the advocacy of public, observable vote counting and similar reforms.

Election Forensics – Refers to examination (primarily) of data patterns for anomalies and disparities that may be indicative of votecount mistabulation, whether resulting from error or fraud. More broadly, refers to the general study of the conduct of an election to assess whether it has been free and fair and a more or less accurate translation of the public will into electoral results. Because "hard" evidence—such as memory cards, code, machine hardware, and voter-marked ballots—are almost never available for examination, forensic investigation of election results almost always depends on statistical analysis and inference. Analytic approaches may differ markedly in probative value.

Red Shift – Refers to the disparity between computerized votecounts and other measures of voter intent, such as exit polls, tracking polls, or hand-counts. The shift is "red" when the votecount disparity favors the more right-wing candidate (or position). If, for example, the unadjusted exit poll result for an election was 52%D/45%R (D+7) and the official votecount was 49%D/50%R (R+1), the red shift would be +8%. A "blue shift," which has occurred extremely rarely, would refer to a disparity in the opposite direction. Note that red (or blue) shifts may or may not change the winner.

Margin of Error – MOE refers to the expected variance of any sample of a larger whole regarding a particular characteristic. In polling, that characteristic is often voting preference, though it might be approval/disapproval or some other opinion. It is important to understand that MOE is a strictly *mathematical* calculation that presumes perfect randomness of the sample in question (e.g., white and black marbles picked at random out of a box that has been thoroughly shaken). It is expressed as a range in which we expect the sample to fall, generally (though not necessarily) 95 percent of the time. It does *not* consider aspects of sampling design or execution that introduce non-random factors.

Total Survey Error – TSE is an expansion of MOE that considers aspects of sampling design or execution that introduce non-random factors. Such factors might be the "cluster" sampling that is typical in exit polling (discrete precincts are sampled rather than a random selection of voters from an entire jurisdiction), as well as anticipated or measured selection and/or response biases. As these factors can be difficult to quantify, TSE is generally a somewhat less precise parameter than is MOE. MOE *never* exceeds TSE.

Tracking Poll – Refers to candidate-preference polls taken prior to an election, as well as such things as job-approval ratings. Polling aggregators such as FiveThiryEight.com combine, weight, and average tracking polls to present a less noisy, more reliable indicator of voter preference and opinion.

Likely Voter Cutoff Model – Refers to a tracking poll sampling methodology modification, introduced by pollsters several years after the start of the computerized vote counting era, that screens out all but likely voters from polling samples. Since even the less likely voters, who get excluded, sometimes wind up casting a vote, the LVCM is a significant sampling distortion. Since the screening questions cover such factors as stability of residence and prior frequency of voting, the LVCM disproportionately eliminates more left-leaning respondents (students, transients, renters, young voters, urban voters) from the sample, and thus skews it right. The LVCM should *fail* if votes were counted as cast—it has generally succeeded.

Exit Poll – Refers to surveys taken of voters as they leave polling places after voting. In addition to "Who did you vote for today?" questions, a substantial amount of demographic information is generally gathered. Voters fill out questionnaires anonymously. Because much voting now takes place prior to Election Day and by mail, exit polling now also surveys voters remotely. The exit poll sample will generally have several non-random aspects; the pollster (primarily Edison Research in the U.S.) uses data-rich models to weight samples to reflect the demographic composition of the electorate. Although exit polls in the U.S. tend to be controversial when used as baselines for votecount verification, they often provide virtually the only data indicative of "problems" with the official count. They are used routinely for verification and fraud-detection purposes in the elections of countries other than the United States.

Exit Poll Adjustment – Refers to the process by which exit poll percentages are brought into virtual congruence with votecount percentages as votecounts become available on Election Night. Although the process is complex, it essentially consists of a forced reweighting of the exit poll responses with the "Who did you vote for?" question overriding all others. Thus, if the unadjusted exit poll underrepresented votes for Candidate A (relative to the official votecount) by 5 percent, every question on every response indicating a vote for "A" will be upweighted accordingly; that is, if a respondent who indicated a vote for "A" also indicated she identifies as a Republican, she will now count as 1.05 of a Republican voter and the apparent proportion of "Republicans" in the sample will increase proportionally.

Unadjusted Exit Poll – Refers to a weighted exit poll in which the votecounts for the election being polled do not factor into the weighting. That is, the poll results are not "contaminated" by votecount data and provide our best (if imperfect) forensic baseline for votecount validation. Election forensics analysts generally regard the first publicly posted exit poll results—often within a minute or so of poll closing in a state (though it can be an hour later in "double time zone" states)—as "unadjusted," though we would not know for sure if any adjustment (always toward congruity with votecount percentages) had occurred prior to first public posting.

Pre-Set Rigging – Refers to votecount manipulations deployed into equipment code (memory cards, e.g.) some time (often more than a month) in advance of the equipment's use in an election. Such rigs, although comparatively easy to install, must accordingly be calibrated in advance and are susceptible to late movement in electoral dynamics, which may cause them to fail in their purpose.

Real-Time Rigging – Refers to manipulation of votecounts during the voting or counting phase of an election. Most frequently a "man-in-the-middle" exploit, such rigs require the deployment of significantly more infrastructure than the pre-set variety, but are more flexible, allowing real-time calibration of the magnitude and distribution of the interference. Online voting would be particularly susceptible to this type of manipulation.

Second-Order Comparative – Refers to a statistical forensics analysis that relies on a secondary baseline to assess the potential causes of red-flag anomalies or disparities. Best explained by example: looking at the disparities between votecounts and exit poll in a single election or general set of elections would be a first-order comparative; comparing two discrete subsets of votecount-exit poll disparities, one consisting of non-competitive contests and the other consisting of competitive contests, would be a second-order comparative. Other comparisons might be, swing states versus national, one party versus another party's primaries, hand-count vs. computer-count jurisdictions; contests counted by one type or brand or equipment versus a different type or brand, etc. The probative value of second-order comparatives, where a "disparity of disparities" is found, is often much greater than that of first-order comparatives.

Baseline – Refers to any data set that serves as a control or norm against which a particular data set can be measured. The baseline can be contemporaneous (a national poll might serve as a baseline against which battleground-state polls, and their disparities, can be measured) or temporal (for example, a sequence of previous contests from which the contest to be analyzed departs in some significant way). Baselines are critical to the work of statistical forensics analysts.

CVS Analysis – Cumulative Vote Share Analysis refers to a statistical forensics approach that sorts and orders precincts or counties within a large jurisdiction by size and looks for unexpected patterns of candidate voteshare. The Law of Large Numbers predicts cumulative voteshare curves that flatten to near-flat lines as precinct/county size increases. When we instead find sloping lines, it raises the question of why voteshare correlates with precinct/county size. While there may be benign explanations for such correlation, one red-flag explanation to consider is that votecount manipulators have targeted larger precincts/counties where the shift of a given number of votes will be less noticeable.

Fraction Magic – A term coined by Bev Harris and Bennie Smith to refer to the fractionalization of votes, which are encoded as decimal (e.g., 0.54) rather than integral (e.g., 1, 5, 84) values. An unknown percentage of voting equipment currently in use is fraction-capable. Although only *very* rarely needed (e.g., elections in which votes are proportioned to acres of land owned), fraction-capability can greatly facilitate votecount manipulation and make precision-calibrated real-time rigging feasible without elaborate infrastructure.

Help America Vote Act – HAVA was national legislation passed in 2002 that greatly accelerated the full computerization of U.S. elections. It used carrots (funding) and sticks (mandates) to push states particularly into touchscreen voting (DREs) and was entirely lacking in cyber-security provisions to protect the increasingly concealed process it promoted. Authored by leading Republicans, including Mitch McConnell, HAVA was sold to naïve Democrats as a means of increasing turnout—a red flag, as the GOP had long been on a mission to *reduce* turnout to its advantage.

HCPB – Acronym for Hand Counted Paper Ballots, ballots cast on paper and counted in public by humans (counting teams to generally include representatives of each major party and a non-party-affiliated member).

HMPB – Acronym for Hand Marked Paper Ballots, ballots marked by the voter's hand rather than by a mechanized or computerized device. The distinction is crucial, as ballot-marking devices (BMDs) introduce new and powerful fraud vectors, and the call for "paper" or "paper ballots" has frequently come to dress up in faux integrity a shift from pure touchscreens (DREs) to barcode or QR-code BMDs, which are equally inviting to digital fraud.

Equipment Vendors – The manufacturers, distributors, and often programmers of the equipment used for voting, vote-counting, and votecount-reporting. Principals are currently Election Systems and Software (ES&S), Dominion Voting, Hart Intercivic, and Scytl. At one time Diebold, which became Premier, had a major share of the equipment market. Major subcontractors—such as Triad, VR Systems, Command Central, LHS, and Kennesaw State University's Election Center—program, distribute, and service the equipment. Most of these manufacturers and vendors have close ties to the political right.

DRE – Direct Recording Electronic voting machine, also known as a "touchscreen." DREs can be paperless or fitted with a "paper trail" printout, generally similar to a gas-station receipt roll. The voter can, in theory, check his or her vote, though the programmer can easily code the DRE to print a vote for "A" while recording a vote for "B". Recounting or auditing the paper trail, where available, tends to be difficult if not impossible, as the roll frequently jams, causing incomplete recording, and is in any event hard to read.

BMD – Ballot Marking Device refers to programmable equipment that takes the place of the voter's hand in creating or marking his or her ballot. Originally designed to assist disabled voters, BMDs have been adopted in some states and counties for general use. The voter usually indicates each choice on a touchscreen, with the program transforming that choice into a machine-marked paper ballot.

Barcode BMD (or QR-Code BMD) – Refers to a BMD that, rather than printing checks or Xs onto an ordinary ballot template, instead encodes the voter's choices (and possibly other information) in a bar code or QR code readable only by a scanner (often only a proprietary scanner). As the voter cannot read the barcode, which is the official ballot of record, a "summary card" is sometimes provided to the voter indicating his or her choices. Such summaries have been problematic as they are difficult to read and, when tested, voters only rarely catch errors and omissions. Risk-Limiting Audits are not capable of auditing or verifying the process by which the BMD translates voter intent into an official vote.

Permission To Cheat – A term coined to describe a species of BMD that gives voters the option to waive verification of whether their ballot summary card accurately reflect their intent *before* the ballot makes its final pass under the print heads, thereby allowing the programmer to alter, risk-free, only the subset of votes that the computer "knows" will not be verified. In effect, the computer makes the voter "play first," so it can cheat with impunity.

Risk-Limiting Audit – Refers to a kind of audit that, instead of drawing a flat (e.g., 2 percent) sample of ballots, instead samples each audited contest in a progressive manner until a set level of confidence is reached that the correct winner has been identified by the initial count of votes. Can result in a full (100%) audit if that level of confidence is not achieved, which would be because of computerized counting error or fraud sufficient to alter the apparent winner.

Digital Ballot Image – DBI refers to images of cast ballots created by certain ballot scanners enabled with such capacity. Each ballot becomes, in essence, a discrete file (e.g., pdf or jpg) that is stored and can be reviewed for audit or recount purposes. This feature is generally *optional*: an on/off switch on the computer, set by election administrators, determines when the created DBI is preserved or instead destroyed within milliseconds of creation. Certain DREs can also create a voted-on digitized template that is in many respects the equivalent of a DBI.

Modem-Equipped – Refers to whether a given piece of voting equipment is networkable; that is, equipped with a modem and capable of outputting and inputting data or programming code via the internet. Such equipment, of which much more exists than was long acknowledged, is of course more vulnerable to interference by hackers.

Internet Voting – Also known as online voting, refers to remote voting via the internet. It is already an option in 31 states for a small sub-group of absentee voters, primarily military, but experts have warned that it cannot be made secure with current or foreseeable technologies. It is effectively unauditable, unrecountable, and unverifiable—open to both hacking and malicious programming. It is a seductive but, from an election transparency standpoint, catastrophic solution to the problems posed by COVID-19 for holding the 2020 elections.

Vote By Mail – VBM is a species of at-home voting (VAH), which refers to the casting of hand-marked paper ballots via U.S. mail or drop-off. No-excuse mail-in voting is an option in the majority of states, and the *only* option in four, where forensics have generally been favorable and voters pleased. Ballot trashing and stuffing are potential problems to be considered, along with weakening of secret-ballot protections. Urged by Democrats in light of social distancing's potential impact on in-person voting in E2020, VBM has been opposed at national and most state levels by Republicans leery of expanding the electorate.

Voter (or Vote) Suppression – Refers to tactics and strategies, whether public or private, aimed at making the casting and counting of a vote more difficult or impossible. These tactics and strategies—which might include such measures as requiring a difficult-to-obtain Voter-ID, shortening early voting periods, closing local polling places, deploying machines that inherently cause bottlenecks and long lines or are prone to breaking down, purging voting rolls of legitimate voters, and at-poll challenging of individual voters' right to vote and forcing them onto provisional ballots—generally target specific groups of voters identified by the suppressors as likely opponents.

Voter Fraud – As distinct from "election theft" or "vote counting fraud," refers to fraud allegedly committed by individual voters, such as voting illegally, voting more than once, or impersonating another voter. Studies have shown it is exceedingly rare—if nothing else because it is a felony and the reward/risk ratio is abysmal—but that has not prevented it from being invoked by GOP lawmakers as a pretext for the passage of discriminatory and suppressive Photo-ID laws.

Voter-ID Laws – Refers primarily to laws requiring voters to have photo ID to be able to cast a ballot. These laws—passed mainly in red states, and originally templated by right-wing organization ALEC—have been justified as necessary to counter a supposed epidemic of "voter fraud," for the existence of which no evidence has been presented. The laws generally impose logistical burdens that strongly impact constituencies (e.g., urban, poor, minorities, non-drivers) identified by Republican strategists as adverse.

Provisional Ballot – Refers to a type of ballot, created initially under the Help America Vote Act (2002), that voters experiencing problems with registration, identification, or location are permitted to cast. Provisionals are generally the last ballots to be counted (they require a validation process), are frequently rejected as invalid, or not counted at all when it appears that they can't alter the outcome of a given election.

Dark Money – Refers to campaign funding, often from corporations, that does not require sourcing to the donor. A series of primarily 5-to-4 party-line SCOTUS decisions over the past two decades found unlimited campaign expenditures with no sourcing to be constitutional, opening the flood gates to unknown amounts of "dark money" pouring into U.S. election campaigns.

Gerrymandering – Refers to drawing of jurisdictional boundaries for partisan advantage. Practiced throughout U.S. political history, gerrymandering has become an even more powerful political tool with the availability of "big data," enabling more precise and electorally-effective boundary drawing. One result has been U.S. House delegations—such as those in Pennsylvania, Ohio, and North Carolina—in which, while the majority of votes statewide have been for Democratic candidates, the lion's share of the states' delegations have gone to GOP representatives. Gerrymandered state legislatures have also distorted representation at the state level, and have had recursive impact on the setting of laws and procedures governing the administration of elections. SCOTUS (5-to-4, party-line) in 2019 effectively gave a constitutional green light to gerrymandering for partisan advantage per se. Gerrymandering is often cited for individual and collective results favorable to one or another party, most often the GOP.

FOR FURTHER REFERENCE

These are the days of miracle and wonder and don't cry, baby, don't cry, don't cry, don't cry.

-- Paul Simon, "The Boy in The Bubble"

Books:

Collier, James M.; Collier, Kenneth F.: *Votescam: The Stealing of America,* Victoria House Press 1992, ISBN 0963416308, http://www.amazon.com/dp/0963416308

Conyers, John; Miller, Anita; Vidal, Gore: *What Went Wrong in Ohio: The Conyers Report on the 2004 Presidential Election,* Academy Chicago Publishers 2005, ISBN 089733535X https://www.amazon.com/dp/089733535X/ref

DeLozier, Abbe W.; Karp, Vickie (eds): *Hacked! High Tech Election Theft in America,* Truth Enterprises Publishing 2006, ISBN 9780615132556 https://www.amazon.com/dp/0615132553/ref

Douglas, Lawrence: *Will He Go? Trump and the Looming Election Meltdown in 2020, Twelve 2020* https://www.amazon.com/dp/1538751887/ref

Fitrakis, Robert J.; Rosenfeld, Steven; Wasserman, Harvey: *What Happened in Ohio? A Documentary Record of Theft and Fraud in the 2004 Election,* The New Press 2006, ISBN 1595580697 http://www.amazon.com/dp/B005HKT4JQ/ref

Fitrakis, Robert J.; Rosenfeld, Steven; Wasserman, Harvey (eds): *Did George W. Bush Steal America's 2004 Election? Essential Documents,* CICJ Books 2005, ISBN 0971043892 https://www.amazon.com/dp/B01GSJLW0I/ref

Fitrakis, Robert J.; Wasserman, Harvey: *The Strip & Flip Disaster of America's Stolen Elections,* Biblio 2017, ISBN 1622493915
https://www.amazon.com/dp/1622493915/ref

Freeman, Steven F.; Bleifuss, Joel: *Was the 2004 Presidential Election Stolen? Exit Polls, Election Fraud, and the Official Count,* Seven Stories Press 2006, ISBN 1583226877
https://www.amazon.com/dp/1583226877/ref

Harris, Bev: *Black Box Voting; Ballot Tampering in the 21st Century,* Talion Publishing 2004, ISBN 1890916900
https://www.amazon.com/dp/1890916900/ref

Hartmann, Thom: *The Hidden History of the War on Voting: Who Stole Your Vote and How to Get It Back,* Berrett-Koehler 2020, ISBN 1523087781
https://www.amazon.com/dp/1523087781/ref

Kreig, Andrew: *Presidential Puppetry: Obama, Romney, and Their Masters,* Eagle View 2012
https://www.amazon.com/dp/0988672812/ref

Miller, Mark C.: *Fooled Again: How the Right Stole the 2004 Election,* Basic Books 2005, ISBN 0465045790
https://www.amazon.com/dp/0465045790/ref

Miller, Mark C. (ed): *Loser Take All; Election Fraud and the Subversion of Democracy, 2000-2008,* Ig Publishing 2008, ISBN 9780978843144
https://www.amazon.com/dp/0978843142/ref

Palast, Greg: *The Best Democracy Money Can Buy: A Tale of Billionaires & Ballot Bandits,* Seven Stories Press 2016, ISBN 1609807758
https://www.amazon.com/dp/1609807758/ref

Parks, Sheila: *WHILE WE STILL HAVE TIME: The Perils of Electronic Voting Machines and Democracy's Solution: Publicly Observed, Secure Hand-Counted Paper Ballot (HCPB) Elections.*
http://www.amazon.com/dp/1479156531/ref

Pepper, David: *The Voter File*, G.P. Putnam's Sons 2020, ISBN 9780593083932
https://www.amazon.com/dp/B07YRTR3ZM/ref

Raymond, Allen: *How to RIG an Election: Confessions of a Republican Operative,* Simon & Schuster 2008, ISBN 9781416552239
https://www.amazon.com/dp/1416552235/ref

Rosenfeld, Steven: *Count My Vote: A Citizen's Guide to Voting,* Alternet Books 2008, ISBN 9780975272459
https://www.amazon.com/dp/0975272454/ref

Shimer, David: *Rigged: America, Russia, and One Hundred Years of Covert Electoral Interference*, Alfred A. Knopf 2020, ISBN 9780525659006
https://www.amazon.com/dp/0525659005/ref

Siegelman, Don: *Stealing Our Democracy: How the Political Assassination of a Governor Threatens Our Nation*, NewSouth Books 2020, ISBN 9781588384294
https://www.amazon.com/dp/1588384292/ref

Steele, Marta: *Grassroots, Geeks, Pros and Pols: The Election Integrity Movement's Rise and Nonstop Battle to Win Back the People's Vote, 2000-2008*, The Free Press 2012
https://www.amazon.com/dp/1622490266/ref

Tavris, Dale: *Democracy Undone*, Bitingduck Press 2012, ASIN B009KR7MCI.
https://www.amazon.com/dp/B009KR7MCI/ref

Ventura, Jesse (with Russell, Dick): *American Conspiracies*, Skyhorse Publishing 2011, ISBN 1616082143
https://www.amazon.com/dp/1616082143/ref

With, Barbara: *Steal This Book Not My Vote,* 2012
http://barbarawith.com/stealthisbook.html

Worrall, Simon: *Cybergate: Was the White House Stolen by Cyberfraud?*
Amazon Digital Services, 2012
https://www.amazon.com/dp/B0074NQ5UK/ref

Selected Evidentiary and Analytical Studies:

Blaze, Matt: Testimony to U.S. House Committee on Oversight and Government Reform, Subcommittee Hearing on Cybersecurity of Voting Machines (11/29/2017) https://oversight.house.gov/wp-content/uploads/2017/11/Blaze-UPenn-Statement-Voting-Machines-11-29.pdf

Choquette, Francois; Johnson, James: *Republican Primary Election 2012 Results: Amazing Statistical Anomalies* (2012) https://codered2014.com/wp-content/uploads/2020/04/primaryElectionResultsAmazingStatisticalAnomalies_V2.1.pdf

Clarkson, Elizabeth: *How trustworthy are electronic voting systems in the U.S.?* (June 2015) https://www.significancemagazine.com/politics/265-how-trustworthy-are-electronic-voting-systems-in-the-us

Common Cause, Rutgers School of Law, Verified Voting Foundation: *Counting Votes 2012: A State by State Look at Election Preparedness*, (August 2012) http://countingvotes.org/sites/default/files/CountingVotes2012_Final_August2012.pdf

Dopp, Kathy; Mitteldorf, Josh; et al: *US Count Votes' National Election Data Archive Project: Analysis of the 2004 Presidential Election Exit Poll Discrepancies* https://www.verifiedvoting.org/wp-content/uploads/downloads/Exit_Polls_2004_Edison-Mitofsky.pdf

Favorito, Garland: *Georgia 6th District Runoff Statistical Analysis* (10/16/2017) https://voterga.files.wordpress.com/2017/10/6th-district-runoff-statistical-analysis.pdf.

Friesdat, Lulu; Sampietro, Anselmo; (in collaboration with) Scheuren, Fritz: *An Electoral System in Crisis*, (July 2016) http://www.hollerbackfilm.com/electoral-system-in-crisis/

Simon, Jonathan; Baiman, Ron: *The 2004 Presidential Election: Who Won the Popular Vote? An Examination of the Comparative Validity of Exit Poll and Vote Count Data* (2004) http://freepress.org/images/departments/PopularVotePaper181_1.pdf

Simon, Jonathan; O'Dell, Bruce: *Landslide Denied: Exit Polls vs. Vote Count 2006, Demographic Validity of the National Exit Poll and the Corruption of the Official Vote Count* (2007) https://codered2014.com/wp-content/uploads/2020/04/landslideDenied_v.9_071507.pdf

Simon, Jonathan; O'Dell, Bruce; Tavris, Dale; Mitteldorf, Josh: *Fingerprints of Election Theft: Were Competitive Contests Targeted?* (2007) https://codered2014.com/wp-content/uploads/2020/04/fingerprintsOfElectionTheft_2011rev_.pdf

Simon, Jonathan: *Believe it (Or Not): The Massachusetts Special Election for U.S. Senate* https://codered2014.com/wp-content/uploads/2020/04/believeIt_OrNot_100904_2011rev_.pdf

Simon, Jonathan: *The Likely Voter Cutoff Model: What Is So Wrong with Getting It Right?* https://codered2014.com/wp-content/uploads/2020/04/theLVCM_0.pdf

Simon, Jonathan; O'Dell, Bruce: *UBS: Universal Ballot Sampling to Validate Computerized Vote Counts in Federal and Statewide Elections* https://codered2014.com/wp-content/uploads/2020/04/new_UBS_811Update_061707.pdf

Various Authors: *Compendium of Studies of Electronic Voting Prepared for New York Litigation (2008).* http://sites.google.com/site/remediaetc/home/documents/Scientific_Studies_7-20-08.pdf

Related Published Papers and Articles:

Ananda, Rady: "Fatally Flawed Systems Await Voters," (9/1/2008) http://www.opednews.com/articles/Fatally-Flawed-Systems-Awa-by-Rady-Ananda-080909-59.html

Anderson, Pokey: "Peering Through Chinks in the Armor of High-Tech Elections" (2007) http://www.votersunite.org/info/PeeringThruChinks.pdf

Associated Press: "Recounts or No, US Elections Are Still Vulnerable to Hacking" (12/26/2016) https://www.newsmax.com/Newsfront/Election-Hacking-US-Vulnerable/2016/12/26/id/765581/

Bernstein, Jessica: "How Progressive Media Won't Let Us Talk About Election Fraud," *HIGHBINDER* (7/19/2016) http://highbinder.org/progressive-media-election-fraud/

Cohn, Jennifer: "How New Voting Machines Could Hack Our Democracy," *The New York Review of Books* (12/17/2019) https://www.nybooks.com/daily/2019/12/17/how-new-voting-machines-could-hack-our-democracy/

Cohn, Jennifer: Links to Articles and Podcasts https://medium.com/@jennycohn1/jennifer-cohn-links-to-articles-podcasts-talks-and-interviews-8e7916bdfc77

Collier, Victoria: "How to Rig an Election," *Harper's Magazine* (10/26/2012)
https://archive.harpers.org/2012/11/pdf/HarpersMagazine-2012-11-0084140.pdf

Collier, Victoria: "The 'Shocking' Truth About Election Rigging in the United States," *Truthout* (9/6/2016); http://www.truth-out.org/op-ed/item/37486-the-shocking-truth-about-election-rigging-in-america

Collier, Victoria; Ptashnik, Ben: "A National Call to Link Arms for Democracy," *Truthout* (5/31/2014); http://www.truth-out.org/opinion/item/24033-a-national-call-to-link-arms-for-democracy

Friedman, Brad: "Diebold Voting Machines Can Be Hacked by Remote Control," *Salon* (9/27/2011) http://www.salon.com/2011/09/27/votinghack/

Halpern, Sue: "Voting in the Time of the Coronavirus," *The New Yorker* (3/20/2020) https://www.newyorker.com/news/campaign-chronicles/voting-in-the-time-of-coronavirus-social-distancing

Halpern, Sue: "The Iowa Caucuses and the Menace of Untested, Privately Owned Election Technology," *The New Yorker* (2/5/2020) https://www.newyorker.com/news/our-columnists/the-lesson-american-voters-can-learn-from-iowa

Halpern, Sue: "Mitch McConnell is Making the 2020 Election Open Season for Hackers," *The New Yorker* (6/12/2019) https://www.newyorker.com/tech/annals-of-technology/mitch-mcconnell-is-making-the-2020-election-open-season-for-hackers

Halpern, Sue: "How Voting-Machine Lobbyists Undermine the Democratic Process," *The New Yorker* (1/22/2019) https://www.newyorker.com/tech/annals-of-technology/how-voting-machine-lobbyists-undermine-the-democratic-process

Halpern, Sue: "The Campaign for Mobile-Phone Voting Is Getting a Midterm Test," *The New Yorker* (10/22/2018) https://www.newyorker.com/tech/annals-of-technology/the-campaign-for-mobile-phone-voting-is-getting-a-midterm-test

Halpern, Sue: "Election-Hacking Lessons from the 2018 Def Con Hackers Conference," *The New Yorker* (8/23/2018) https://www.newyorker.com/news/dispatch/election-hacking-lessons-from-the-2018-def-con-hackers-conference

Halpern, Sue: "How Voting-Machine Errors Reflect a Wider Crisis for American Democracy," *The New Yorker* (10/31/2018) https://www.newyorker.com/news/news-desk/how-voting-machine-errors-reflect-a-wider-crisis-for-american-democracy

Halpern, Sue: "Trump, Election Hacking, and the Georgia Governor's Race," *The New Yorker* (7/24/2018) https://www.newyorker.com/news/news-desk/trump-election-hacking-and-the-georgia-governors-race

Halpern, Sue: "America Continues to Ignore the Risks of Election Hacking," *The New Yorker* (4/18/2018) https://www.newyorker.com/news/news-desk/america-continues-to-ignore-the-risks-of-election-hacking

Hommel, Teresa: "Democracy or Trump: Our Choices Now," *Sinister Wisdom*, Issue 110, Fall 2018, reprinted at https://codered2014.com/democracy-or-trump/

Hommel, Teresa: "Does Touchscreen Voting Violate The 5th Principle?" (6/27/2009) http://www.wheresthepaper.org/DREsViolate5thPrinciple090627.pdf

Kennedy, Robert F. Jr.: "Was The 2004 Election Stolen?" *Rolling Stone* (6/1/2006) as reprinted at http://www.commondreams.org/views06/0601-34.htm

Perlman, Diane: "The Silence of the Scams," *OpEdNews* (4/21/2005) as reprinted at http://www.truthisall.net/Diane_Perlman/diane_perlman.html

Pynchon, Susan: "Election Dirty Tricks: Business as Usual or Treason at the Ballot Box?" (5/1/2006) http://votetrustusa.org/index2.php?option=com_content&do_pdf=1&id=1249

Rosenfeld, Steven: "New Voting Rights Battles Erupting In Key Swing States," *Voting Booth* (4/19/20) https://www.nationalmemo.com/new-voting-rights-battles-erupting-in-key-swing-states

Simon, Jonathan: "Computerized Vote Counting: The Hole in United States' Political Bucket," *Buzzflash* (3/5/2015) http://buzzflash.com/commentary/computerized-vote-counting-the-hole-in-united-states-political-bucket

Simon, Jonathan: "What Would Trump Do? How We Respond to a Suspect Election," *Alternet* (11/26/2016) https://www.alternet.org/election-2016/what-would-trump-do-how-we-respond-suspect-election

Simon, Jonathan: "Recounts Are Only as Good as They Are Allowed to Be," *WhoWhatWhy* (12/15/2016) https://whowhatwhy.org/2016/12/15/recounts-good-allowed/

Simon, Jonathan: "What an Honestly Counted US Election Might Look Like," MintPress News (11/20/2017) https://www.mintpressnews.com/election-2017-what-an-honestly-counted-us-election-might-look-like/234586/

Simon, Jonathan: "Notes on Disparities in 2020 Democratic Primaries" https://codered2014.com/wp-content/uploads/2020/04/notes-exit-poll-disparities-2020-democratic-primarise-js2rev.pdf

Seals, Tara: "Leaked NSA Doc: Election Hacks Far More Widespread Than Originally Thought" (6/7/2017) https://www.infosecurity-magazine.com/news/nsa-election-hacks-more-widespread/

Thiesen, Ellen: *Vendors are Undermining the Structure of U.S. Elections* (2008) http://www.votersunite.org/info/ReclaimElectionsSumm.asp

Ungar, Rick: "Romney Family Ties to Voting Machine Company That Could Decide the Election Causing Concern," *Forbes* (10/20/2012)

https://www.forbes.com/sites/rickungar/2012/10/20/romney-family-investment-ties-to-voting-machine-company-that-could-decide-the-election-causes-concern/3/#7d03065075d8

Zetter, Kim: "The Crisis of Election Security," *The New York Times Magazine* (9/26/2018) https://www.nytimes.com/2018/09/26/magazine/election-security-crisis-midterms.html

Zetter, Kim: "How Close Did Russia Really Come to Hacking the 2016 Election?" *Politico* (12/26/2019) https://www.politico.com/news/magazine/2019/12/26/did-russia-really-hack-2016-election-088171

Zetter, Kim: "Will the Georgia Special Election Get Hacked?" *Politico* (6/14/2017) https://www.politico.com/magazine/story/2017/06/14/will-the-georgia-special-election-get-hacked-215255

Compendium: "ELECTION FRAUD Beginner's Guide: A Broken Democracy Crash Course" http://www.organikrecords.com/corporatenewslies/beginner_v2.htm

Videos and DVDs:

Stealing America: Vote by Vote, Dorothy Fadiman, director; http://www.stealingamericathemovie.org/

Uncounted – The New Math of American Elections, David Earnhardt, director; http://uncountedthemovie.com/

KILL CHAIN: The Cyber War on American Elections, Simon Ardizzone, Russ Michaels and Sarah Teal, directors (*HBO*); https://www.youtube.com/watch?v=3c8LMZ8UGd8

Atticus v. The Architect: The Political Assassination of Don Siegelman, Steve Wimberly, director, (2017); https://www.amazon.com/dp/B078SKNXZ4/ref

Murder, Spies & Voting Lies: The Clint Curtis Story, Patty Sharaf, director; http://votinglies.com/

I Voted? Jason G. Smith, director; http://www.ivotedmovie.com/

The Best Democracy Money Can Buy, David Ambrose and Greg Palast, directors; https://www.amazon.com/dp/B078SHBQLB/ref

Dan Rather: *Das Vote, "Digital Democracy in Doubt,"* HDNetTV http://www.huffingtonpost.com/dan-rather/digital-democracy-in-doub_b_774137.html (see link to iTunes video download at end of article)

Electile Dysfunction, Penny Little, director; http://www.electile-dysfunction.com/

No Umbrella, Laura Paglin, director; www.noumbrella.org

Hacking Democracy, Simon Ardizzone, director; https://www.amazon.com/dp/B01LX1WH9E/ref

Stephen Spoonamore, cybersecurity expert, interview; http://www.velvetrevolution.us/electionstrikeforce/2008/08/worlds_leading_computer_securi.html

Princeton hack demonstrated; http://www.youtube.com/watch?v=OJOyz7_sk8I

Selected Author Interviews and Presentations:

Webinar: Will The 2020 Election Be Stolen? **(with Jennifer Cohn and Former Senator Tim Wirth), August 2020**
https://www.youtube.com/watch?v=4Gah0vqEyUI&feature=youtu.be

No Lies Radio, **with Kevin Barrett, July 2020**
https://archive.org/details/kb-tj-2020-0803-simon-web

Politics Done Right, **with Egberto Willies, July 2020**
https://politicsdoneright.com/2020/07/jonathan-simon-talks-about-the-dangers-of-computerized-elections/

Red State Radio, **with Mark Faulk, May 2019**
https://www.toginet.com/podcasts/redstateradio/RedStateRadioLIVE_2019-05-16.mp3?type=podpage

National Press Club, **April 2019**
https://vimeo.com/333860874

Radio New Zealand, **October 2018**
https://www.radionz.co.nz/national/programmes/saturday/audio/2018668605/jonathan-simon-fraud-fears-in-us-mid-terms

The Shift, **with Doug McKenty, April 2018**
https://www.youtube.com/watch?v=esfHLMRleaA&t=2s

Red State Radio, **with Mark Faulk, March 2018**
https://www.toginet.com/podcasts/redstateradio/RedStateRadioLIVE_2018-03-29.mp3?type=podpage

KPFK *Solartopia*, with Harvey Wasserman, March 2018
http://greenpowerwellnessshow.podbean.com/e/solartopia-green-power-and-wellness-hour-032218/

Left Forum Panel, June 2017
https://www.youtube.com/watch?v=qyEKNuwlkeE

***Living Well*, with Donna Descoteaux, December 2016**
https://beta.prx.org/stories/191624 (Pt. 1), https://beta.prx.org/stories/191622 (Pt. 2)

***Guns + Butter*, with Bonnie Faulkner, November 2016**
https://soundcloud.com/guns-and-butter-1/fingerprints-of-election-theft-jonathan-simon-354

KPFK *Solartopia*, with Harvey Wasserman, November 2016
http://greenpowerwellnessshow.podbean.com/e/solartopia-green-power-and-wellness-hour-110316/

Alliance for Democracy, with David Delk, June 2015
https://www.youtube.com/watch?v=JZR9NOp4YSA&t=703s

***KBOO* Radio, with Ethan Scarl, June 2015**
https://archive.org/details/codered-interview-kboo

***Voice of the People*, with Tony Trupiano, May 2015**
https://archive.org/details/jonathan-simon-voice-of-the-people

***KGO* Radio, with Pat Thurston, January 2015**
https://archive.org/details/january-31-7pm-kgo

***Coast To Coast*, with George Noory, January 2015**
http://www.coasttocoastam.com/show/2015/01/22

***Corporations and Democracy*, with Steve Scalmanini, December 2014**
https://archive.org/details/candd2014-12-09

***Guns + Butter*, with Bonnie Faulkner, November 2014**
https://archive.org/details/guns-and-butter

***Corporations and Democracy,* with Steve Scalmanini, October 2014**
https://archive.org/details/codered-interview-14

National Democracy Conference, August 2013
https://www.youtube.com/watch?v=i2Kaaxv_djY

***Soapbox*, with Cindy Sheehan, August 2013**
http://www.radio4all.net/index.php/program/70646

Left Forum Panel, March 2011
https://www.youtube.com/watch?v=WoqDoW6AWqU (Pt. 1)
https://www.youtube.com/watch?v=7wGoatRapcY (Pt. 2)

National Conference on Media Reform, January 2007
https://www.youtube.com/watch?v=Q40EOvo6jaE

Websites:

www.CodeRed2020.com

www.Scrutineers.org

www.ProtectOurVotes.com

www.ProtectTheResults.com

www.DemocracyCounts.org

www.smartelections.us

www.democracymovement.us

www.auditelectionsusa.org

www.CoalitionForGoodGovernance.org

www.FairFight.com

www.voteathome.org

www.Votescam.org

www.BlackBoxVoting.org

www.TrustVote.org

www.Bradblog.com

www.OpEdNews.com

www.VotersUnite.org

www.electiondefense.org

www.michiganelectionreformalliance.org

www.electionquality.com

www.WheresThePaper.org

www.HandCountedPaperBallots.org

www.thealliancefordemocracy.org

www.FreePress.org

www.solarbus.org/election

www.VerifiedVoting.org

www.VoterGA.org

www.WeCountNow.org

ACKNOWLEDGEMENTS

I want to begin by gratefully acknowledging every individual who has ever made even a single phone call or written even a single email or letter or Post-It note, or spoken even once to a friend, partner, co-worker, or stranger on a train on behalf of election integrity. You have been willing to be bothered, to bother others, in many cases to take some measure of risk. Thank you for doing the daily work of citizenship and patriotism: it is on you that a happy ending will ultimately depend.

Thank you to all my colleagues in the Election Integrity movement who, having been barred from the endzone, nevertheless line up for play after play, even if it's just a bruising three yards and a cloud of dust.

With especial appreciation for the collaborative forensic work of Josh Mitteldorf, Steve Freeman, Dale Tavris, Bruce O'Dell, Kathy Dopp, Beth Clarkson, Francois Choquette, Alex Halderman, Dave Griscom, Richard Hayes Phillips, J.Q. Jacobs, Howard Stanislevic, and Ron Baiman.

For the tireless efforts and eloquent voices of Dorothy Fadiman, *Bradblog's* Brad Friedman, *OpEdNews's* Rob Kall and Joan Brunwasser, AUDIT-USA's John Brakey, Governor Don Siegelman, Bev Harris, *The New Yorker's* Sue Halpern, Jenny Cohn, Mimi Kennedy, Bob Fitrakis, Harvey Wasserman, Cliff Arnebeck, Jim Soper, Garland Favorito, Marilyn Marks, Joel Simpson, Lulu Friesdat, Emily Levy, Mark Crispin Miller, Greg Palast, Stacey Abrams, Kim Zetter, and the late Jeannie Dean.

For Election Defense Alliance co-founders Dan Ashby and Sally Castleman, and for Sally's devoted and continuous collaboration, friendship, and support over the past dozen years in the trenches.

For my former spouse and always friend Julie, who endured and understood.

And for the generous support of The Threshold Foundation, The Silicon Valley Community Foundation, Victoria Ward, and EDA's many other individual donors, who have made possible much of our forensic work and election integrity advocacy.

Thank you to Mark Adams, Perry Adler, Judy Alter, Rady Ananda, Pokey Anderson, Andrew Appel, Simon Ardizzone, Barbara Arnwine, Patricia

Arquette, Cindy Ashy, Dick Atlee, Marc Baber, Russ Baker, Jane Bark, Ray Beckerman, Jan BenDor, Jessica Bernstein, Lynn Bernstein, Matt Blaze, John Bonifaz, Harvie Branscomb, Ellen Brodsky, Jennifer Brunner, Bill Bucolo, Lee Camp, Kathleen Campbell, Ernest Canning, Tim Canova, Henry Carey, Leonard Carpenter, Renee Carpenter, Stephen Caruso, Lora Chamberlain, Richard Charnin, Lucius Chiaraviglio, Barbara Clancy, Jenny Clark, Victoria Collier, Michael Collins, Peter B. Collins, Rev. Judy Conoyer, Marge Creech, Elliot Crown, David Delk, Abbe Delozier, Greg Dinger, Desi Doyen, Mickey Duniho, Ron Earnhardt, Bernie Ellis, Dan Engelke, Jeremy Epstein, John Ervin, Annie Esposito, Jack Evans, Jim Fadiman, Mark Faulk, Bonnie Faulkner, Michael Feinstein, Ed Felten, Mike Ferriter, Lowell Finley, Bob Fleischer, David Frenkel, Chandra Friese, Laure Gaussen, Paul George, Jessica Gimeno, Jordan Glogau, Mike Goldfarb, Jack Gordon, Jeffrey Gottesman, Lori Grace, Michael B. Green, Avi Green, Chris Gruener, Spencer Gundert, Alex Halderman, Ken S. Hantman, Angela Harden, Sherry Healy, James Heddle, Frank Henry, Mike Hicks, Jim Hogue, Teresa Hommel, Chris Hood, Mickey Huff, Harri Hursti, Phyllis Huster, Jacqueline Janecke, Richard Jefferson, Pete Johnson, Hon. Hank Johnson, Dennis Karius, Vicki Karp, Kim Kaufman, Brett Kimberlin, Mary Howe Kiraly, George Klees, Bob Koehler, Andrew Kreig, Hon. Dennis Kucinich, Kat L'Estrange, Lynn Landes, Susan Lazar, Arlene Leaf, Pat Leahan, Paul Lehto, Dave Lewit, Pippa Leys, Joe Libertelli, Roy Libscomb, Warren Linney, Ralph Lopez, Victoria Lovegren, Lianda Ludwig, Joanne Lukacher, Ray Lutz, John Maa, Mary Magnuson, Hal Malchow, Ben Manski, Jim March-Simpson, Klaus Marre, Nancy Matela, Joyce McCloy, Doug McKenty, Karen McKim, Hon. Cynthia McKinney, Rebecca Mercuri, Sherona Merel, Russ Michaels, Andrea Miller, Jen Miller, Arlene Montemarano, David Moore, Sandy Morganstein, Jim Mueller, Michelle Mulder, Lee Munson, Catherine Musinsky, YahNe Ndgo, Shyla Nelson, Sierra Nolan, Pippa Norris, Andrea Novick, Laura Paglin, Sheila Parks, Suzanne Patzer, Peter Peckarsky, Grant Petty, Linda Pinti, Hon. Mark Pocan, Michael Polsinelli, Laura Pressley, Nancy Price, Ben Ptashnik, Susan Pynchon, Larry Quick, Casey Reed, Karen Renick, Francesca Rheannon, John Paul Rice, Michael B. Richards, George Ripley, Bill Risner, Ron Rivest, Carl Romanelli, Steve Rosenfeld, Ginny Ross, Avi Rubin, Dick Russell, Anselmo Sampietro, Chris Sautter, Steve Scalmanini, Ethan Scarl, Fritz Scheuren, Jake Schlachter, Kate Scott, Toni Serafini, Cindy Sheehan, Kevin Shelley, David Shimer, Alex Shvartzman, Barbara Simons, Bill Simpich, Jill Simpson, Stephanie Singer, Bennie Smith, Ted Soares, Philip Stark, Marta Steele, Sean Steinberg, Lois Steinberg, Donna Sumner, David Swanson, Richard Tamm, Jim Tarbell, Heleni Thayer, Diane Thodos, Maggie Thomas, Keith Thomson, Nancy Tobi, Bruce Underhill, Craig Unger, Andrew Updegrove, Paul Velleman, Jesse Ventura, A.J. Vicens, Dan Wallach, Julie Weiner, Nancy White, Tim White, Laura Wigod, Rob Williams, Egberto Willies, Bob Wilson, Daniel Wolf, Gail Work, Simon Worrall, Kevin Zeese, John

Zogby, and the late Rev. Bill Moss, Raymond Lemme, Andy Stephenson, Tom Courbat, Athan Gibbs, Beverly Campbell, Harold Lecar, Hon. John Conyers, Hon. Stephanie Tubbs Jones, and John Gideon. *More* than a village and all have worked selflessly and given greatly of themselves to defend our democracy.

Especially meaningful have been the work and voices of Paul Craig Roberts, Chuck Herrin, Stephen Spoonamore, Clint Curtis, and the late John Washburn. Each set aside his political partisanship to honor the truth and pursue the evidence wherever it might lead.

And I salute the courage and integrity of Virginia Martin and Jason Nastke, former Co-commissioners of Elections, Columbia County (NY); Ion Sancho, former Supervisor of Elections, Leon County (FL); and former California Secretary of State, Debra Bowen; whose care and responsibility have gone far beyond the surface appearance of things. And the tenacity of Senator Ron Wyden, who has not rested a day from this often lonely quest.

Thank you, Jill Stein, for trying and paying the price.

With appreciation for the efforts of Keith Olbermann, Dan Rather, Robert Kennedy, Jr., and Thom Hartmann, who have anteed up powerfully at the Election Integrity table. This is one hand that, however bad, deserves to be played to the last card, all-in.

For the late Jim and Ken Collier, who saw this coming before any of us, who did go all-in, and who never got up from the table.

To all the journalists, pundits, politicians, opinion leaders, and institutions in the Bystanders' Brigade, who have responded to our entreaties to join us in speaking out about computerized election theft by wishing us good luck in our work: thank you for the encouragement. I hope one day you will simultaneously find the "bandwidth" (as one of you put it) and the courage to leave the Bystanders' Brigade and actually do something to rightfully earn both a more genuine appreciation and your place in history.

With great appreciation for the able (and infinitely patient) assistance of Carin Handsun (iwebresults.com) with *CODE RED*'s cover, website, and all things PR.

Finally, may I stuff the ballot box of gratitude for my partner Carla, who, besides her own election integrity efforts and editorial contributions to this book, has been in my corner all the way, keeping us both in tolerably good cheer on this trip down the rabbit hole and on through Wonderland.

ABOUT THE AUTHOR

Jonathan Simon served for ten years as executive director of Election Defense Alliance, a nonprofit organization founded in 2006 to restore observable vote counting and electoral integrity as the basis of American democracy.

As a result of his prior experience as a political survey research analyst in Washington, Dr. Simon became an early advocate for an exit poll-based electoral "burglar alarm" system, independent of media and corporate control, to detect computerized vote shifting in Election 2004.

In the absence of such a system, he was nevertheless able to capture and analyze official exit poll data briefly posted on the web prior to its Election-Night disappearance, realizing as the following day dawned that he was in fact the only person in the world in possession of this critical data, which went on to serve as the initial basis for questioning the validity of the 2004 presidential election.

Dr. Simon has gone on to author, both individually and in collaboration, numerous papers and articles related to various aspects of election integrity. He has worked in cooperation with many election integrity organizations; appeared in several election integrity-related films, including *Stealing America: Vote by Vote* and *Uncounted: The New Math of American Elections,* and as an interviewee on dozens of live broadcasts. He tweets @JonathanSimon14 and invites all interested in corresponding to connect with him through LinkedIn, the *CODE RED* website www.CodeRed2020.com, or by email at verifiedvote2004@aol.com.

Dr. Simon is a graduate of Harvard College and New York University School of Law. He is admitted to the Bar of Massachusetts.